iChat	www.ichat.(
International Personnel Management Association	www.ipma-|
Internet Business Network	www.interb
JobStar California	www.jobsm
Kansmen Corporation	www.charred.com
Kelrsey Temperament Sorter	www.davideck.com /links/k-disc.html
LaborNet	www.labor.org.au/about_unions/why_join
Law Enforcement Technologic Resources	www.letr.com
Law Journal Extra	www.lawnewsnetwork.com /practice /employmentlaw
Learn2.com	www.learn2.com
Liszt Mailing List Directory	www.liszt.com
Los Alamos National Laboratory Performance Forms	http://hrntserver1.lanl.gov/Performance /forms
Martindale-Hubbell Law Directory	www.lawyers.com
Minority Career Network	www.minoritycareernet.com /op-board.shtml
Monster.com	www.monster.com
NABET-CWA Local 57	http://habet57.com
National Ad Search	www.nationaladsearch.com
National Committee for Quality Assurance	www.ncqa.org
National Credit Information Network	www.instant-info.com
National Labor Management Association	www.nlma.org /wpl-viol.htm
National Writers Union	www.nwu.org /grv/grvdiv.htm#grvhow
Net Grocer	www.net-grocer.com
Nike	www.nikebiz.com /jobs/jobs_nj.html
Occupational Outlook Handbook	http://stats.bls.gov/ocohome.htm
Occupational Safety and Health Administration	www.osha.gov
Ohio Department of Administrative Services	www.state.oh.us
1ClickCharge	www.chabang.com
Panorama Business Views	www.pbviews.com
PAQ Services, Inc.	www.paq.com
Peapod	www.peapod.com
Pension Benefit Guaranty Corporation	www.pbgc.gov
Pension Plan Information	www.pensionconsultant.com /library.htm
Performance Benchmarking Service	www.iti.org /pbs
PlaceWare Web Conferencing	www.placeware.com
Presidentís Committee on Employment of People with Disabilities	www.jan.wvu.edu
qualitycoach.net	www.qualitycoach.net /links.htm
RealNetworks	www.realaudio.com
Recruiters Online Network	www.recruitersonline.com
Reid System	www.reidsystems.com /jobsnow1.htm
Robert Charles Lesser & Co.	www.rclco.com
Salary Negotiations Information	http://members.aol.com /payraises
Securities and Exchange Commission	www.sec.gov/edgarhp.htm
Social Security Administration	www.ssa.gov
Society for Human Resource Management	www.shrm.org
Teknekron Infoswitch	www.teknekron.com
Tennessee Criminal Law Information	www.tncrimlaw.com /foia_indx.html
Testing Materials Resource Book Online	www.psychtest.com
Union Resource Network	www.unions.org
University of Arizona Human Resources	www.hr.arizona.edu /ratingfactors.html
University of Memphis Human Resources	www.people.memphis.edu /,hresources /employ-pa/pahome.htm
William M. Mercer	www.wmmercer.com
Willow Cybercenter Networks	www.willowcsn.com
Working Wounded	www.workingwounded.com /1main.html
Workscience Corporation	www.workscience.com

Human Resource Management

Human Resource Management

A Practical Approach

Second Edition

Michael Harris
University of Missouri–St. Louis

The Dryden Press
A Division of Harcourt College Publishers

Fort Worth   Philadelphia   San Diego   New York   Orlando   Austin
San Antonio   Toronto   London   Montreal   Sydney   Tokyo

Publisher	Michael Roche
Acquisitions Editor	John Weimeister
Developmental Editor	Bobbie Bochenko
Project Editor	Rebecca Dodson
Production Manager	Lois West
Art Director	Biatriz Chapa
Picture and Literary Rights Editor	Linda Blundell

ISBN: 0-03-025972-X

Library of Congress Catalog Card Number: 99-74022

Address for Domestic Orders
The Dryden Press, 6277 Sea Harbor Drive, Orlando, FL 32887-6777
800-782-4479

Address for International Orders
International Customer Service
The Dryden Press, 6277 Sea Harbor Drive, Orlando, FL 32887-6777
407-345-3800
(fax) 407-345-4060
(e-mail) hbintl@harcourtbrace.com

Address for Editorial Correspondence
The Dryden Press, 301 Commerce Street, Suite 3700, Fort Worth, TX 76102

Web Site Address
http://www.hbcollege.com

THE DRYDEN PRESS, DRYDEN, and the DP LOGO are registered trademarks of Harcourt Brace & Company.

Printed in the United States of America

9 0 1 2 3 4 5 6 7 8   039   9 8 7 6 5 4 3 2

The Dryden Press
Harcourt Brace College Publishers

To my wife,
Pat

Anthony, Perrewé, and Kacmar
Strategic Human Resource Management
Third Edition

Bereman, Lengnick-Hall, and Mark
*Compensation Decision Making:
A Computer-Based Approach*
Second Edition

Bergmann, Scarpello, and Hills
Compensation Decision Making
Third Edition

Boone and Kurtz
Contemporary Business
Ninth Edition

Bourgeois
*Strategic Management:
A Management Perspective*
Second Edition

Bracker, Montanari, and Morgan
Cases in Strategic Management

Brechner
*Contemporary Mathematics for
Business and Consumers*

Calvasina and Barton
*Chopstick Company: A Business
Simulation*

Carrell, Elbest, and Hatfield
*Human Resource Management:
Strategies for Managing a Diverse
and Global Workforce*
Sixth Edition

Costin
Readings in Total Quality Management

Costin
*Managing in the Global Economy:
The European Union*

Costin
Economic Reform in Latin America

Costin
*Management Development and
Training: A TQM Approach*

Costin
*Readings in Strategy and Strategic
Management*

Costin
Strategies for Quality Improvement
Second Edition

Czinkota, Ronkainen, and Moffett
International Business
Fourth Edition

Czinkota, Ronkainen, Moffett, and Moynihan
Global Business
Second Edition

Daft
Leadership

Daft
Management
Fifth Edition

Daft and Marcic
Understanding Management
Second Edition

DeSimone and Harris
Human Resource Development
Second Edition

Dilworth
Operations Management
Third Edition

Foegen
Business Plan Guidebook
Revised Edition

Gatewood and Feild
Human Resource Selection
Fourth Edition

Gold
*Exploring Organizational Behavior:
Readings, Cases, Experiences*

Greenhaus and Callanan
Career Management
Second Edition

Harris
*Human Resource Management:
A Practical Approach*
Second Edition

Higgins and Vincze
Strategic Management: Text and Cases
Fifth Edition

Hodgetts
Modern Human Relations at Work
Seventh Edition

Hodgetts and Kroeck
*Personnel and Human Resource
Management*

Hodgetts and Kuratko
Effective Small Business Management
Sixth Edition

Holley and Jennings
The Labor Relations Process
Sixth Edition

Holt
*International Management: Text and
Cases*

Jauch and Coltrin
*The Managerial Experience: Cases and
Exercises*
Sixth Edition

Kindler and Ginsburg
Strategic & Interpersonal Skill Building

Kirkpatrick and Lewis
*Effective Supervision: Preparing for the
21st Century*

Kuratko and Hodgetts
*Entrepreneurship: A Contemporary
Approach*
Fourth Edition

Kuratko and Welsch
Entrepreneurial Strategy: Text and Cases

Lengnick-Hall, Cynthia, and Hartman
Experiencing Quality

Lesser
Business Public Policy and Society

Lewis
Io Enterprises Simulation

Long and Arnold
*The Power of Environmental
Partnerships*

Morgan
Managing for Success

Oddou and Derr
Managing Internationally:
A Personal Journey

Ryan, Eckert, and Ray
Small Business: An Entrepreneur's Plan
Fifth Edition

Sandburg
Career Design Software

Vecchio
Organizational Behavior
Fourth Edition

Walton
Corporate Encounters: Law, Ethics, and
the Business Environment

Weiss
Business Ethics: A Stakeholder and Issues
Management Approach
Second Edition

Zikmund
Business Research Methods
Sixth Edition

Michael Harris is Professor of Management at the School of Business Administration, University of Missouri–St. Louis. His area of interest is human resource management and he has conducted research on a variety of related topics, including interviewing, performance management, and compensation. His work has been published in such journals as the *Journal of Applied Psychology*, *Personnel Psychology*, and the *Journal of Management*. He has served on several editorial boards, including the *Journal of Applied Psychology* and the *International Journal of Organizational Analysis*, and is co-editor of the *Employment Interview Handbook* (Sage Publications).

Professor Harris is also the columnist for "Practice Network," which appears in *The Industrial-Organizational Psychologist (TIP)*, the official newsletter of the Society for Industrial and Organizational Psychology (SIOP). His columns have covered such topics as the use of the Internet and executive coaching. He regularly conducts workshops for supervisors, line managers, and human resource managers on employee staffing, diversity awareness, sexual harassment, and general management topics. Dr. Harris has served as an expert witness in a number of legal cases involving the Civil Rights Acts of 1866, 1964, 1991, the Americans with Disabilities Act, and the Age Discrimination in Employment Act.

Most of us spend a major portion of our lives at work. Whether you are a job applicant searching for your first full-time job or you are currently employed, human resource management practices affect you in a variety of ways. The premise of this book is that you, the reader, will want to know how human resource management affects your career. Consequently, each topic will be examined from a variety of perspectives. While the book focuses on the implications of human resource management issues for employees and job applicants, close attention is also paid to the managerial and supervisory perspective. Thus, regardless of your career stage or job responsibilities, this book will be of value to you. The nature of our jobs, the way in which we are paid, the type of benefits we receive, as well as many other aspects of our employment, have important implications for the quality of our lives and our personal happiness. This book addresses the features and conditions of work that are typically regarded as human resource management concerns, such as recruitment, employee selection, career management, compensation, benefits, training and development, health and safety, as well as others. To help you understand and learn more about human resource management, you will find useful Web sites throughout this book.

This textbook is written for students taking an overview course in Human Resource Management, either as an elective or as a required credit. Below you will find a detailed outline of what this textbook offers, how it is organized, what support materials are available, and the features that make this book different and distinct from the others.

Most introductory HRM textbooks are written with a managerial focus. They assume that the reader is or will be hiring, supervising, rewarding, and terminating other employees. This book takes a slightly different approach, one that shares the focus of the managerial perspective with that of the employee perspective. The first reason for this shared vision is that the majority of students are more motivated to read and understand a textbook when they see its *immediate* application. Many students are not managers or supervisors; therefore, they may have a better understanding of the material by seeing the application and relevance of material that assumes they are employees/applicants. Second, supervisors and managers are also employees of the organization, and are consumers as well as managers of human resources. Although they may supervise employees, they are also applicants for jobs, affected by benefits, responsible for their own career management, and so on. This textbook allows for managers and employees alike to see the visible personal and professional relevance.

Addressing the Essential Issues

The Reality of Business Today

Today's managers are faced with a different workplace and workforce than that of 20, 10, even 5 years ago. Human resource managers especially feel the impact of organizational decisions that affect the workforce. Succeeding in business today requires skills above and beyond insurance benefits, employee evaluations, and staffing issues. HR managers and general managers alike must be able to address these and other important issues.

- Chapter 5, "The Selection Process," addresses the uses of job analysis, the factors used in choosing selection procedures, and the advantages and disadvantages of the different selection procedures. Particular emphasis is given to structured interviewing.
- Chapter 6, "Career Management," talks about organizational layoffs, downsizing, and right-sizing in today's organizational climate. It also addresses the changing nature of work and of organizations.
- Chapter 7 is devoted to the subject of Performance Management and discusses how to handle and conduct performance reviews, how to give and receive constructive feedback, and performance management and the law.

Realistic Emphasis on Participative Management

The traditional way of managing people is a thing of the past. Managers are now required and many professors are being asked to teach students the "soft skills," such as managing a diverse workforce, how to team-build and utilize work teams, and how to develop employees' potential, both personally and professionally.

Today's business world needs participative managers to address these growing issues.

- Chapter 11 is devoted to Employee Training and Development and covers how to maintain competitiveness and improve productivity by using training and development techniques.
- Chapter 12, "Work Redesign for Productivity and Quality Improvement," includes such topics as quality circles, total quality management, the work team, employee empowerment, and reengineering.

Driving Forces that Impact the Complexities of HRM

Issues such as management and labor relations, current career patterns, and providing a safe, healthy working environment are the driving forces that affect the complexities of HRM. Learning how to balance the need for the company's success with the need for the employees' success is a skill that is in demand. We live and work in a complex world that needs managers equipped to solve these complexities in a positive, effective way.

- The Family and Medical Leave Act of 1993 is covered in Chapter 10, "Employee Benefits."
- Chapter 13, "Safety and Health," covers current topics such as repetitive stress injuries, drug/alcohol use, stress, and indoor air pollution, as well as OSHA regulations, employee assistance programs, maintaining a safe and healthful workplace by empowering, rewarding, training, and testing employees.
- Two chapters concentrate on unions: Chapter 14 discusses the organizing process, while Chapter 15 covers negotiating and administering an agreement.
- Genetic discrimination is discussed in Chapter 2.

Social and Cultural Contexts

No HRM textbook would be complete today without addressing the issues of the social and cultural contexts in which we work. The workplace is now leaner and more efficient, more diverse, and more open to societal changes and challenges than ever before. These social and cultural contexts are the threads interwoven throughout our organization and our workforces.

- The virtual organization is discussed in detail in Chapter 12.
- Alternative work arrangements such as flextime, shift work, the compressed work week, and telecommuting are discussed in Chapter 16, "Employee Rights."
- Affirmative action, race discrimination, and other discrimination laws are discussed in Chapter 2, "Employment Discrimination Laws," as well as women and the glass ceiling and sexual harassment in the workplace.
- The issue of workplace romance is covered in Chapter 16, "Employee Rights."
- Cultural diversity is integrated into every chapter.

Organization

The book is organized into five parts. Part 1 explores the context of human resources by addressing what human resource management is, the major discrimination laws that play a critical role at work, and issues and events that affect careers. Chapter 1 introduces the student to the functions of HRM, evaluating the external and internal environments, determining the HRM department mission, the roles of the HRM professional, and the different careers available to the HRM student. Chapter 2 details the employment discrimination laws and the effects of each on the workforce, the facts an HRM manager needs to know about proving a discrimination case, and other topical issues such as sexual harassment and the glass ceiling. Extensive coverage is given to the Americans with Disabilities Act. Chapter 3 addresses the issue of planning for HR managers. Why is planning important? What are a company's capabilities and needs? The chapter places particular emphasis on an organization's mission and vision as a guide to making HR plans.

Part 2 covers staffing, and examines recruitment, selection, and career management. Chapter 4 discusses recruitment practices, who to recruit, internal and external recruitment sources, and also includes appendices on the job search and how to write a cover letter and resume. Particular attention is given to using the Internet for finding applicants and locating jobs. Chapter 5 details the selection process, job analysis, typical selection steps, and miscellaneous selection devices. Special emphasis is given to interviewing, particularly structured interviewing. Chapter 6 covers career management for the HRM professional. Issues such as why career patterns have changed, the different career stages, and organizational advancement systems are addressed. Methods of obtaining global work experience are described.

Part 3 addresses the subject of evaluation and compensation. Chapter 7 discusses performance management and measures, performance appraisal problems and solutions, performance feedback, performance reviews, and performance management and the law. Special attention is given to 360-degree feedback. Chapter 8 covers compensation administration, compensation laws, maintaining equity among employees, conducting a job evaluation, and alternatives to traditional pay structures. Chapter 9 details the pay-for-performance plans and why companies use them, the kinds of and alternatives to PFP plans, and the different kinds of incentive plans. Chapter 10 discusses benefits, and covers legally required benefits, pension and health insurance programs, the different kinds of health insurance programs, miscellaneous employee benefits, and paid time off benefits. The latest approach, the cash balance plan, is discussed.

Part 4 concentrates on improving the workplace. Chapter 11 employee training and development discusses what training and development is and why it's important, current trends and practices, training techniques and principles, on-the-job and off-the-job training techniques, and evaluating the success of training programs. The use of computer based technology, including the Internet, is described. Chapter 12 looks at work redesign for productivity improvement and alternatives to the classical work design model such as quality circles, work teams, TQM, reengineering, and the virtual organization. A special section addresses the question, "Is work redesign the answer?" Chapter 13 covers safety and health in the workplace. The laws concerning these issues are presented, as well as discussions about reducing workplace accidents, current safety and health issues in the workplace, and workplace violence.

Part 5 concerns maintaining effective employee-employer relationships. Chapter 14 on unions discusses the organizing process. A brief history of unions is presented, as well as tactics to gain more members, managers' attitudes toward unions, and how companies become unionized. Chapter 15 covers negotiating and administering agreements with unions. Information on negotiating and administering the union contract, current trends in contract negotiations, and developing harmonious relationships between labor and management is provided. Chapter 16 details employee rights by looking at terminations, contracts, personnel files, privacy rights, workplace romance, employee disciplinary procedures, termination meetings, and alternative work hours. The latest information on the privacy of your e-mails is provided.

Human Resource Management: A Practical Approach covers all aspects of HRM, focuses on the **practical approach** and emphasizes how human resource issues are relevant to everyone within an organization. Written in a **simple, conversational tone,** the text emphasizes the relevance of the material to employees, job applicants, managers and supervisors, not just future human resource managers, allowing students to answer the important question: **"How is this material relevant to me?"**

This textbook is **shorter** and more succinct. **Sixteen chapters** focus exclusively on the basics of HRM without distracting information from other disciplines such as economics, finance, or marketing. The textbook covers what an HRM professional needs to know, as well as information the consumer of HRM can apply to his or her own experience. **Web sites** that provide further information are provided throughout the text.

Chapter 1 immediately involves students in **real-life human resources situations** with its coverage of current topics and challenges. The historical information has been placed in an appendix for professors to cover in class or assign as outside reading. **Core concepts** are also identified at the beginning of each chapter, with a series of questions and then revisited at the end of each chapter for use as class discussions or individual team exercises.

The book covers a number of pedagogical techniques that help the reader to understand and apply the information. Each chapter begins with a **brief case** that provides a context for the core concepts and raises relevant questions. An **experiential exercise** is provided at the end of each chapter to enable readers to apply the concepts they have learned and to develop their critical thinking skills. Many of these experiential exercises are based on actual situations or composites of actual situations that have occurred. Thus, students will be able to apply basic concepts and research to "real world" issues and problems.

In addition to an opening chapter case and an end-of-chapter exercise, each chapter contains **numerous in-text examples** of how human resources are managed in different companies and by different individuals. Each chapter also includes:

- "Tales from the Trenches" boxes that present actual stories from the work world of human resources and management in general, as well as focus on intercultural and diversity concerns.
- "Webbing Around" is a new feature that provides relevant Web sites for each chapter, with some commentary about what is contained in each of the sites. Appropriate Web sites are also provided throughout the chapters to provide additional information.

Instructor's Manual / Test Bank / Transparency Masters

Revised by Cheryl Wyrick of California State Polytechnic University Pomona, the Instructor's Manual includes detailed lecture outlines, answers to the questions for discussion, suggestions for teaching concepts, research project suggestions, and detailed teaching notes for the experiential exercises written by the author herself. In addition, transparency masters of a majority of the figures and tables from the textbook are included.

The Test Bank, by Satish Deshpande of Western Michigan University, contains approximately 50 questions per chapter, including true/false, multiple-choice, short-answer, and essay questions. A computerized test bank is available in IBM 3.5, Mac, and Windows versions. Special functions allow an instructor to add, delete, edit or scramble questions (to create up to 99 versions of the same test). A phone-in testing service for creating test masters is also available with a 48-hour turnaround period.

NEW TO THIS EDITION: The PowerPoint CD-ROM, also by Satish Deshpande of Western Michigan University, brings Human Resource Management to life in classroom lectures and presentations. This extremely instructor friendly multimedia tool is organized by chapter and enables instructors to custom design their own presentations, using figures, tables and other important material from the text, along with important material from outside sources.

Visit The Dryden Press Web site at *www.hbcollege.com* for numerous resources associated with Human Resource Management and Contemporary Business.

The video program in Human Resource Management demonstrates the breadth of the video program. Eight videos are now available for classroom viewing and each video contains several class-tested questions by Amit Shah of Frostburg State University to encourage discussion and thought. Companies spotlighted include:

University National Bank   A very innovative financial institution, University National Bank follows progressive human resource policies and has a compensation policy, organizational structure, and employee benefits to enable employees to provide excellent service. (10 minutes)

Wainwright Industries, Inc.   This video shows how a company transformed itself to win the coveted Malcolm Baldrige National Quality Award in 1994. (10 minutes)

Valassis Communication, Inc.   This video focuses on Valassis' application of teams through the organization, its strict JIT system, and communications within and among teams. (10 minutes)

Harley-Davidson   Labor and management come to the realization that they have to work together and this video shows how they made the transition to a cooperative management/labor climate. (10 minutes)

Fighting for the Rights of Workers with Disabilities   How an AFMSME employee who is legally blind copes with her workday and counsels others with disabilities. She also talks about issues of managing those with special needs. (18 minutes)

ADA . . . The Time to Understand   An AFSCME (Association of Federal, State, County, and Municipal Workers) profile of one compelling case in North Dakota of a mentally disabled county employee tormented by his co-workers and supervisor. (18 minutes)

Southwest Airlines People Department   Southwest has a different management style, including a manager who calls his style "Management by Fooling Around." He feels it is better to rule by love than by fear and instills confidence in his employees by treating them as people instead of as employees. (10 minutes)

La Madeleine French Bakery   The story of how La Madeleine treats its employees and the community like family and supports both in tangible and intangible ways. The owner extends his open arms philosophy of managing people to his community by weekly trips to Dallas to feed the homeless fresh-made French onion soup and croissants. (10 minutes)

Acknowledgments

I would like to acknowledge the help of many individuals in this project. In terms of The Dryden Press staff, I would like to thank John Weimeister, acquisitions editor, who helped oversee the entire process, and Bobbie Bochenko, developmental editor, who deserves much credit for her advice, encouragement, support, and most importantly, for her listening ear. I would also like to thank the people who worked so hard on the production side of this book, namely Rebecca Dodson, project editor; Lois West, production manager; Biatriz Chapa, art director; and

Linda Blundell, picture and literary rights editor. Without their support and expertise, this book would not have become a reality.

I would also like to recognize the following reviewers and survey respondents for their help in making both editions of *Human Resource Management: A Practical Approach* a success:

Reviewers:
Maha Alul, *Maryville University*
Edwin Arnold, *Auburn University*
Charles Beem, *Bucks County Community College*
Curtiss K. Behrens, *Northern Illinois University*
Ralph Braithwaite, *University of Hartford*
Win Chesney, *St Louis Community College–Meramec*
Elizabeth Cooper, *University of Rhode Island*
Satish Deshpande, *Western Michigan University*
Jean Forray, *University of Massachusetts*
Thomas Lloyd, *Westmoreland County Community College*
David Murphy, *Madisonville Community College*
James L. Nimnicht, *Central Washington University*
John Pappalardo, *Keene State College*
Robert J. Paul, *Kansas State University*
Pamela Pommerenke, *Michigan State University*
Robert H. Schappe, *University of Michigan–Dearborn*

Survey Participants:
Ellen J. Frank, *Southern Connecticut State University*
Gary C. Raffaele, *University of Texas at San Antonio*
Alan Cabelly, *Portland State University*
Sandy J. Wayne, *University of Illinois at Chicago*
Jon Monat, *CSU Long Beach*
Jerry B. Madkins, *Tarleton State University*
Yohannan T. Abraham, *Southwest Missouri State University*
Jeff Mello, *Golden Gate University*
Walter E. Greene, *University of Texas–Pan American*
Edwin C. Leonard, Jr., *Indiana University/Purdue University at Fort Wayne*
Lynn Hoffman, *University of Northern Colorado*
Charles J. Capps III, *Sam Houston State University*
Vicki Kaman, *Colorado State University*
Marcus Sandver, *Ohio State University*

Acknowledgments are also due to my teachers, students, colleagues, and friends who encouraged me during the writing of both editions of this book. While I cannot list all of these individuals by name due to space limitations, I would like to single out two persons in particular: Rabbi Jeffery Bienenfeld and Rabbi Chona Muser. Both of these individuals have been the source of much direction, encouragement, and advice in all of my life endeavors and I owe them a great deal.

I also wish to thank my children, David, Anne, and Yoni, and my stepchildren, Nosson and Rochel, for their companionship and love. Thanks also to my parents, Monford and Rivkah Harris, who remain a continuing source of love, advice, and encouragement. Finally, I wish to thank my wife, Pat, to whom this edition is dedicated. She is truly a "woman of valor."

Brief Contents

Contents

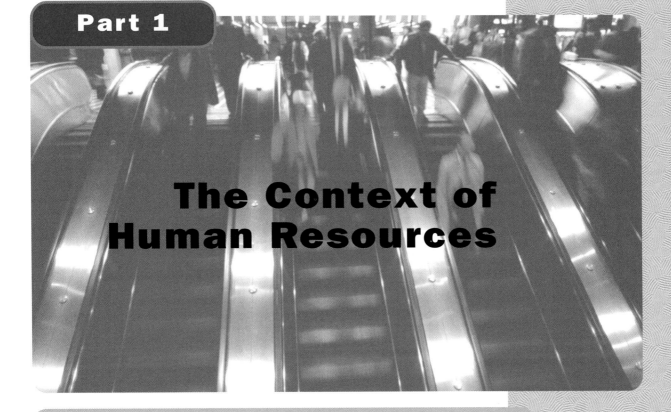

Part 1

The Context of Human Resources

Chapter 1
An Introduction to Human Resource Management

Chapter 2
Employment Discrimination Laws

Chapter 3
Human Resource Planning

Chapter 1

An Introduction to Human Resource Management

1. Identifying the major human resource management processes.
2. Understanding the factors that affect human resource management processes.
3. Identifying major human resource management outcomes and their determinants.
4. Explaining what a human resource management job entails.

Opening Case

Consider the following situation: Sandy Sanazaro is being interviewed for a financial analyst job. After the interviewer introduces herself to Sandy, she asks her the following question: "Tell me about a time when you were under a great deal of stress. How did you handle the situation? What did you learn from it?" Following several similar questions, she asks Sandy whether she is married, single, divorced, or engaged. After about an hour of questioning, she says to Sandy, "I have one last question: What starting salary do you expect?" How would you answer these questions? Are all of these questions legal?

Now consider this situation: Douglas Weir is supervising an employee, Phil Stone, who has been working for the company for one month. So far, Phil has made numerous errors, such as billing the wrong client, erasing an important file, and turning in a report late. For the first few weeks, Douglas assumed Phil needed time to catch on. Now he is beginning to realize that experience alone may not improve Phil's performance. Douglas has decided that he must meet with Phil to discuss these problems and to try to improve Phil's performance. How should Douglas go about giving Phil the feedback? If Phil's performance does not improve, can Douglas discipline him? Can he fire Phil? Are there restrictions on Douglas' ability to discipline or terminate him?

Now consider this situation: Tonya Powell has been given the responsibility of teaching new employees how to use a computerized cutting machine. The last employee to use this machine ended up breaking it, and the repair work was quite expensive. How should Tonya instruct the new employees? Do some training techniques work better than others?

Finally, place yourself in the following situation. You have been with your company for about one month. Three days after you began working, the area manager approached you and said, "Hey, how about a drink after work?" You politely answered, "No, thanks, I'm busy tonight." The invitation for a drink after work was repeated each day, until yesterday, when the area manager became more persistent, and said, "If you want to keep your job, I'm going to insist you go out for a drink with me so that we can get to know each other better—know what I mean?" You wonder whether this is considered sexual harassment under the law; if so, what do you need to do to stop the area manager's behavior?

All of these situations describe common human resource management (HRM) problems faced by managers, supervisors, employees, and job applicants. These, and other issues, are obviously important for both employees and organizations. What did you think was the best strategy in each situation? You will learn more about these situations throughout the book

The remainder of this chapter is divided into three sections. First, we will more precisely define HRM. After that, we will present a model of HRM, which will provide an overview of different HRM processes, key HRM goals, and factors that affect HRM processes and goals. You will learn more about the HRM mission, and you will read about careers in human resource management. We begin first with a definition of human resource management.

What Is Human Resource Management?

Human resource management (HRM) may be defined as programs, policies, and practices for managing an organization's workforce.[1] Consider, for example, a company that manufactures electronic devices, such as VCRs, televisions, and radios. The company must hire employees and train them in specific areas where they lack expertise. Production workers, for example, may need instruction in how to use various tools and machines in the manufacturing processes. In return for their employment, the workers must receive an appropriate wage. The company must also provide certain required benefits to the employees, such as workers' compensation (in case they are injured as a result of the job) and unemployment compensation (if they are terminated). The company may also offer additional benefits, such as health insurance. During the course of employment, workers are likely to receive feedback on their performance, particularly if their performance is below expectations. At some point in time, top management may introduce a productivity improvement program, which changes the way in which the work is performed. For example, rather than each worker performing one simple task (for example, packing the product as it comes off the production line), the productivity improvement program may make workers responsible for a complete order (for example, taking the order, setting up the machinery, packing the product, and so forth). Some employees eventually may be promoted to shift supervisor, and from there to a managerial job. Other employees may be dismissed by the organization for poor performance. Certain employees and job applicants may believe they were discriminated against, and file a complaint with the Equal Employment Opportunity Commission (EEOC). The Occupational Safety and Health Agency (OSHA) may conduct an inspection of the facilities and issue citations charging violations of safety conditions, which the company will need to address.

All of the above processes describe what this book calls human resource management, or in previous years, personnel management. While most medium-sized and large organizations have a specific department responsible for human resources, many small organizations may not. The company just described, for example, may employ one or two individuals to address general administrative issues, including human resource management.

At this point you may be thinking, "My major is marketing (or finance, management information systems, accounting, management science, or even liberal arts), and I certainly don't plan to be an HRM manager!" If that is what you are thinking, you are probably right—most companies have only one HRM employee for every 100 or so employees. But HRM staff are not the only people responsible for HRM programs, policies, practices, and decisions. Consider, for a moment, your current job or a job you have had in the past. Who was responsible for hiring, pay raises, performance management, and training? In most cases, the supervisor or manager was responsible—not an HRM staff person. Supervisors and managers, then, play an extremely important role in HRM. Even if you are not an HRM manager, you are likely to be responsible for HRM processes. Supervisors and managers who have a good grasp of HRM programs and practices make better HRM decisions, which in turn makes them more effective in their jobs. Box 1.1 addresses the ethical implications of global-level HRM decisions and practices.

Now you might say to yourself, "I don't plan to be a supervisor or manager of any kind. I'd rather not be responsible for any subordinates. So, how does a book on HRM pertain to me?" The answer to this question goes back to the situations presented in

INTERCULTURAL ISSUES IN HUMAN RESOURCES

Box 1.1

The Ethics of International Human Resource Management

Although U.S. workers may suffer when companies manufacture products in other countries, U.S. consumers are pleased when lower production costs in places such as Mexico, China, and India make products less expensive to purchase. But lower costs are often attained in an ethically questionable way, because laws that protect workers in the United States are often nonexistent in other countries of the world. Consider, for example, a plant in Mexico, where the workers (all of whom were women) worked with vats containing PCBs, the poisonous environmental pollutants. Their only protection from the chemicals were rubber gloves, which did little

to protect their arms and faces from being splashed with the liquids. The children born to these workers often had birth defects, including Down's syndrome, webbed feet, and deformed hands. In many other countries, children are often employed in jobs requiring heavy physical labor.

Some U.S. businesses are beginning to take action. Reebok, the athletic shoe company, recently stopped using a Pakistani contractor that had been employing workers younger than fourteen years old. The U.S. government is encouraging companies to voluntarily adopt guidelines for foreign companies in regard to HRM practices.

Some consumer groups are taking notice as well. One such group is urging Asian rug makers to use a stamp to identify products that are not made by children; another group is urging Starbucks (a coffee company) to improve worker conditions in Guatemala.

Would you pay more for products if they were produced under humane conditions? Would you boycott a firm that does business with a plant in another country that mistreats its workers even if you paid 10 percent less for the goods? What if the goods were 25 percent cheaper?

Source: Adapted from G. P. Zachary, "The Outlook: Multinationals Can Aid Some Foreign Workers," *Wall Street Journal*, April 24, 1995, A1; and M. Butler and M. Teagarden, "Strategic Management of Worker Health and Safety Issues in Mexico's Maquiladora Industry," in *Readings and Cases in International Human Resource Management*, ed. M. Mendenhall and G. Oddou (Cincinnati: South-Western, 1995), pp. 418–32.

the beginning of this chapter. Remember that the first situation involved interview questions. The fourth situation described a potential sexual harassment incident. Even employees without any supervisory responsibility face these situations. In such ways HRM affects all of us, regardless of whether we are HRM managers, line supervisors or managers, or employees. Regardless of what job you have, HRM affects you.

Let us take this definition of HRM and learn more about the different areas of HRM, as well as the issues that affect HRM processes and HRM goals. As you can see in Figure 1.1, HRM processes may be divided into the following categories:

1. Planning
2. Staffing
3. Evaluating and Compensating
4. Improving the organization
5. Maintaining effective employer–employee relationships

The term *processes* reflects that these are on-going, interconnected activities. The way in which an organization designs the staffing processes, for example, is likely to affect the way in which that organization evaluates its employees.

Let us examine each of these five processes in greater detail.

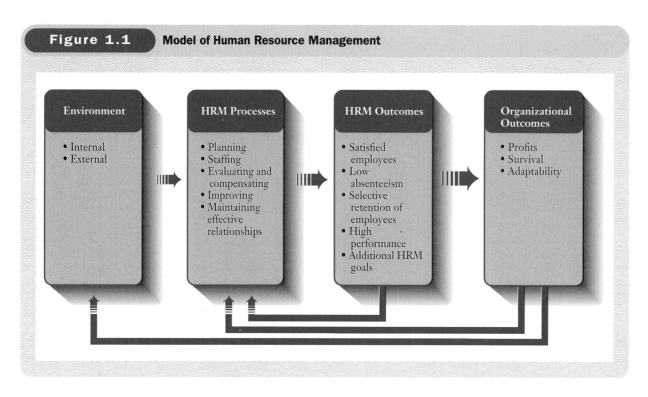

Figure 1.1   **Model of Human Resource Management**

Human Resource Processes

Planning

One aspect in today's business world you can count on is constant change (or, as a colleague of the author says it, "The only certainty is uncertainty"). Constant change, in turn, necessitates careful HRM planning.

The electric utility industry provides a good example of why HRM planning may be critical for an organization. This industry is changing rapidly due to deregulation and extensive consolidation and merger activity. As a result, electrical utility companies are facing greater pressures to reduce their costs and become more efficient. But electrical utility companies rely heavily on what are referred to in the industry as "linemen," workers who are responsible for repairing faulty high-voltage power lines. One issue here is that such workers require expensive, frequent training and some experts worry that pressure to cut costs will lead to reduced training for the linemen. A second issue is that demand for linemen fluctuates dramatically. Many electric utility companies have reduced the number of linemen they employ, as a way of reducing costs. But, as Pacific Gas & Electric discovered when strong winds cut power to some 1 million customers, times arise when having a surplus of workers comes in handy. Other electric utility companies are "outsourcing," subcontracting line work to handle peak demand for service repairs. Some experts, however, believe that outside contractors are less well trained and perform lower quality work than full-time, regular employees. A few utilities have decreased the frequency of maintenance work they perform; other utilities are changing the nature of the technology used to provide power, which in turn requires a different set of worker skills. HRM planning for this industry, then, will help ensure that enough properly trained, qualified linemen can handle emergen-

Box 1.2

Supplying Mickey Mouse with Helpers:
Human Resource Management at Walt Disney World

The human resource division at Walt Disney World, located near Orlando, Florida, plays a major role in the operation of this giant facility. After all, Walt Disney World houses three major businesses, Magic Kingdom, Epcot Center, and Disney-MGM Studios, which together employ fifty thousand employees, the biggest single site employer in the country. To run effectively, Walt Disney World must hire one hundred new employees each day. The human resource department has five hundred professionals, who must manage ten different collective bargaining agreements, in addition to a myriad of other HR responsibilities.

As you probably know, Walt Dis-ney World maintains a unique culture, which it reinforces at every stage of the HRM function. The instillation of the Disney culture begins with the application process. Candidates who pass the initial telephone screening process are usually invited for a face-to-face interview at the "Casting Center," the largest interviewing facility in the country. The walkway to this building is decorated with Disney pictures and memorabilia. Candidates are asked to arrive at least one hour early to complete applications and to see a film that describes the history of Disney and provides information about compensation, work scheduling, transportation, and personal appearance.

In addition, applicants receive a pamphlet describing the appearance standards, which are strictly enforced. Women, for example, must wear only natural-looking makeup and fingernail polish; only one ring per hand is allowed. Men are prohibited from having facial hair and may not wear earrings. Neither men nor women may wear necklaces or bracelets. On what basis does Disney justify its conservative dress code? What do you think? Disney argues that anything unusual or eye catching will distract visitors from the attractions and therefore is disruptive. Do you agree?

cies when needed. Too many linemen, however, would prove to be an unnecessary expense.[2]

Finally, HRM planning is not something that only organizations do. You, as an employee, must plan for the future to ensure that you have the necessary abilities and experiences to succeed as your job and industry change. In today's world, no employee can sit by passively; you must do your own HRM planning. Box 1.2 shows one view of what the hiring experience can be for both employers and employees of a major business.

Staffing

Staffing includes recruiting, hiring, promotions, and dismissal processes. If you have ever been hired for a job, you probably completed an application, responded to interview questions (perhaps some that were used in the first situation described in the beginning of this chapter), and maybe even took a drug test. Although you may have been completely unaware of it, the company that hired you may have also contacted some of your previous supervisors. Do you recall any other steps in the hiring process, such as taking a paper-and-pencil or computer-administered test? Consider the U.S. Army, which has hundreds of thousands of applicants for jobs each year, and must make hundreds of hiring decisions each day. Moreover, the army must decide for what job each qualified candidate is best suited. Not surprisingly, then, the army uses an objective, computer-based test to facilitate these decisions.

The army is a large organization, but small organizations must be even more careful about their staffing procedures. Whereas one poorly qualified employee will have a relatively small effect on an organization as large as the U.S. Army, the same poorly qualified employee might have a much larger impact on an organization that has only ten employees.

As you will see in subsequent chapters, there are a variety of resources for generating job applicants and selection methods for choosing the most qualified candidate. Regardless of whether you are a job applicant or the hiring manager, it will be helpful for you to know the advantages and disadvantages of different recruiting sources and the strengths and weaknesses of various selection devices.

Promotions and terminations are increasingly important HRM issues as we begin the twenty-first century. Compared to previous years, promotions are increasingly rare. Companies are attempting to refocus employees' attention away from advancement and toward other rewards, such as interesting work and learning new skills. At the same time, given frequent mergers, changes in business conditions, and various other issues, companies often end up reducing the size of their workforces. Losing a job is a far more common experience today than it was twenty years ago. Whether you are a supervisor or manager in charge of making promotion or firing decisions, or an employee who will be affected by those decisions, it is in your interest to learn more about those aspects of the staffing process as well.

Like all HRM decisions, staffing decisions have legal ramifications. If applicants or employees believe they have been discriminated against in recruiting, hiring, promotions, layoffs, or any other staffing decisions, they have the right to file a complaint and pursue a lawsuit. For this reason, companies have become extremely cautious whenever they make a staffing decision. You will read about the basic HRM discrimination laws in Chapter 2.

Compensating and Evaluating

Organizations evaluate their employees for several different reasons, including determining pay raises, giving feedback, and assessing training programs. Organizations compensate employees through wages and salaries, bonuses, and benefits, such as health insurance, vacation time, and pension programs. These processes are important for achieving HRM goals. Without evaluations, for example, employees have a difficult time knowing how they are performing compared to company expectations, or where they can make improvements. Recall the second situation described in the beginning of this chapter. How would you have given performance feedback to Phil? If you have had to give performance feedback to a poorly performing employee, you know that it can be a stressful and difficult experience. Have you ever been given performance feedback by your supervisor? How did you act during the feedback session? Many employees are uncomfortable receiving feedback, too. Chapter 7 provides some suggestions for how you can both effectively give feedback to others and receive helpful performance feedback.

Everyone has heard of lottery ticket winners who became instant millionaires and yet said they would continue working in the same job. Although a significant number of employees at Microsoft are millionaires as a result of stock options, they continue to work. There is more to working than just the pay, but for those of us who are not millionaires, our compensation is extremely important. Chapter 8 describes how companies determine your base pay and offers some suggestions for how you as an employee might negotiate your salary. Chapter 9 discusses some of the programs companies use to link some pay to the employee's performance. As you will see in that chapter, some of these programs are rewarding to both the employees and the organization. Finally, Chapter 10 discusses issues related to nonmonetary compensation, namely, employee benefits. The benefits your company provides can be extremely valuable to you, even if they are not in the form of direct cash.

Improving the Organization

In today's world, organizations are constantly on the lookout for ways to improve the organization, including employee training, implementing work redesign programs, and enhancing safety and health in the workplace. Organizations must constantly improve themselves for several reasons. First, technology is always changing, which in turn requires that employees receive training for these new procedures and equipment. Second, new ideas regarding organizational productivity are constantly emerging. Third, competition from other organizations forces companies to continually improve.

Recall the third situation described in the beginning of this chapter. How would you recommend that Tonya train workers? If you have ever been responsible for a company training program, you know that there are many different approaches to this subject. More and more companies are now moving to computer-based (for example, CD-ROM) and distance learning (for example, Internet-based) techniques, which is changing the way that training is being conducted. Today, many organizations are implementing productivity improvement programs, often with major implications for jobs and workers. Finally, many organizations now pay closer attention to safety and health matters, as the costs associated with injured and ill workers have steadily increased over the years.

Maintaining Effective
Employer–Employee Relationships

Maintaining effective employer–employee relationships is important to companies for two reasons. First, dissatisfied employees are more likely to quit. Dissatisfied employees who are not unionized may seek out a union to represent them, a move that most organizations will oppose. If they are already unionized, the employees may file many grievances and in some cases even go on strike. In short, poor employer–employee relationships can create many problems for the organization. Second, dozens of laws pertain to the employer–employee relationship. For example, can your employer listen in on your phone calls? Does your supervisor have the right to monitor the Internet sites that you surf at work? Can your employer terminate you because you are having a romantic relationship at work? Do you have the right to examine your personnel file?

If your department or company is unionized, additional regulations exist with which the organization must comply. For these reasons, maintaining effective employer–employee relationships is an important aspect of HRM. In the fourth situation described in the beginning of this chapter, the manager threatened to terminate an employee who refused to go out for drinks after work. As you will see in subsequent chapters, such behavior can lead to much trouble for both the manager and the organization.

In sum, human resource management covers a wide range of processes. Regardless of whether you are an employee, supervisor, or manager, it behooves you to become knowledgeable in this area. We now turn to an overview of some of the environmental factors that affect an organization's HRM processes.

Environmental Factors

As shown in Figure 1.1, environmental factors may be divided into internal and external categories. The external environment refers to conditions that are outside of the organization, including business conditions, workforce characteristics, laws, and unions. The internal environment refers to those factors that are within the organization and under its control, such as the work structure, business strategy, and technology. Although in Chapter 3 we discuss in greater detail many external and internal factors, let us examine some preliminary comments as follow.

External Environment

HRM processes are strongly affected by the external environment. One of the primary factors affecting HRM processes is business conditions. You probably have heard the term *globalization of business* many times. Indeed, the international nature of the workplace has many implications for HRM. For example, consider the experience of Gillette Company, which recently introduced a worldwide stock plan for its employees. Much to its surprise, the company discovered that what works in the United States may not work in other countries. Employees in Belgium were prevented from participating because of national wage controls. Workers in China and Brazil were barred from the program because of laws prohibiting the purchase of stocks listed on the New York Stock Exchange. Mexican employees rejected the plan because stocks are viewed as risky, and cash is favored over investments.[3]

Workforce characteristics is another external factor that affects HRM processes. As shown in Figure 1.2, profound changes are occurring in the composition of the U.S. workforce in terms of race, gender, unionization, and age.[4] In turn, these changes have many implications for HRM processes. As an example, what would you conclude if a subordinate to whom you were giving feedback kept staring down at the ground? You kept trying to make eye contact with him, but he continued to look at the ground. Would you conclude that he was embarrassed or that he was hiding something? In most Western countries, failure to make eye contact is viewed as a sign of insincerity or embarrassment. In other cultures, particularly the Asian culture, people are taught to lower their eyes when talking with a superior; it would be considered disrespectful to make eye contact with one's supervisor.[5]

Laws comprise another external factor that has a major effect on HRM practices. As you will see, we have laws to protect employees from discrimination, laws to protect employees from potential abuses of work conditions (such as wages that are too low), laws that provide employees with the right to unionize, and laws that protect employees from health and safety hazards on the job. Undoubtedly, these laws have a significant impact on HRM processes.

Unions also have a major effect on HRM processes. The possibility of a union has a significant effect on an organization's HRM practices; for example, the nonunionized organization may maintain relatively high wages and benefits so that workers are not tempted to seek out a collective bargaining agreement. A company that has a union (a

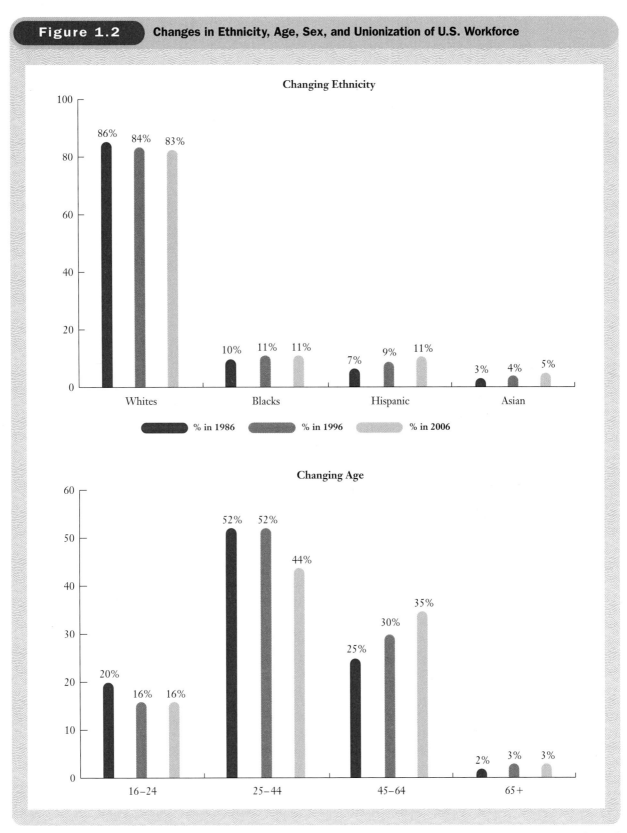

(continued)

Figure 1.2   (*continued*)

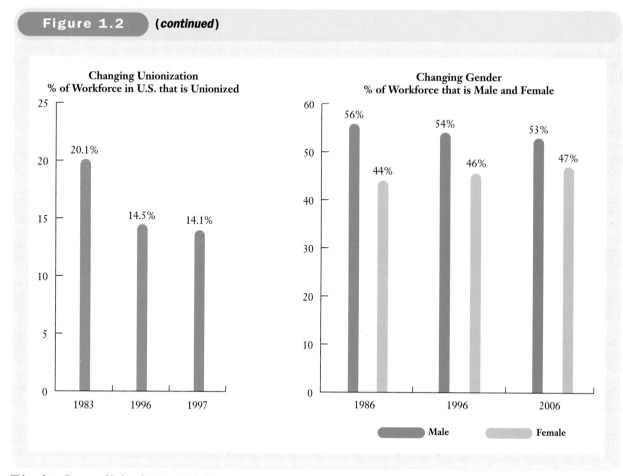

Taken from Bureau of Labor Statistics Web Site.

characteristic of the internal environment) often must use an approach to HRM issues much different from that of a nonunionized company. For example, most unionized organizations base HRM decisions far more on seniority than do organizations that are not unionized.

Workforce characteristics, laws, and unions become even more complex when an organization develops a global presence. Consider, for example, an organization that is deciding where to build a new plant. In making this decision, the nature of the workforce, the relevant laws, and the presence of unions will be important factors to consider. China, on the one hand, has an estimated workforce of more than five hundred million people, but the literacy rate is only modest (81 percent). Compare this to Hong Kong, where the workforce is only about three million people, but the literacy rate is over 92 percent. Countries also differ in terms of the salary premium payable to expatriates (citizens of one country who go to work in a different country). China, for example, would command a salary premium of 15–25 percent for a U.S. citizen who goes to work in that country, while Hong Kong would command no salary premium.

Employment laws are another important responsibility of HRM professionals. These laws can have a major impact on managing employees. For example, workers in Mexico must be paid twice their wages for overtime; if they work more than nine hours overtime in a given week, they must be paid three times their wages. In the Social Republic of Vietnam, international firms must pay the income taxes for their employees. Union laws differ widely from country to country; for example, unions in Brazil are well positioned to negotiate high wages and good benefits for their employees. But one of the biggest challenges for HRM in the global arena is the task of hiring a qualified local professional. Bill Fontana, for example, was trying to hire a local top level manager for the Citibank office in Indonesia. After one year of searching, he made an offer of $150,000, which was promptly rejected by the candidate, who was offered more money by the Bank of Bali.[6]

Internal Environment

One of the biggest issues in the workplace today is the changed nature of jobs. According to one expert, in the next decade or so, only about 35 percent of employees will be full-time, permanent employees. The remaining employees will be contingent employees (25 percent), employees from an outsource business (25 percent), and contract specialists (15 percent). An interesting implication of this, of course, is that the HRM department may spend more time formulating and implementing processes for nonpermanent employees than for permanent ones.[7] Other experts predict that the nature of jobs, for the most part, will remain the same: most, but not all, employees will continue to be full-time, regular workers on the organization's site, with traditional supervisors and managers. Regardless, there *is* consensus that the workforce will increasingly be divided between the "haves" and the "have-nots." That is, highly skilled employees will be increasingly in demand as compared to employees with fewer skills, and the salary difference between highly skilled employees and less-skilled employees will continue to grow.[8] Human resource managers must pay close attention to these differences to ensure that one segment of the organization's workforce does not perceive that it is mistreated compared to another segment of the workforce.

A second trend in business today is changes in thinking about organizational structure. Every business has at least contemplated eliminating the familiar department-based hierarchical structure and replacing it with something quite different. The move away from the traditional organizational structure has many implications for HRM processes. As one example, when much of the hierarchy is removed, thereby eliminating many opportunities for promotion, how will workers continue to find motivation? As a second example, consider the responsibilities of the HRM department. If the organization no longer has a separate department for human resources, how might this change the HRM manager's job? These are just two of the many issues that must be addressed when organizational structures change.[9]

An organization's business strategy also has major implications for HRM processes. Consider Cable & Wireless Communications, a company that sells long-distance telephone service to other businesses. For a variety of reasons, the company cannot compete on price, so it emphasizes customer service. As part of that business strategy, all sales personnel have the authority to determine the price at which they will sell, as well as control over budget decisions for advertising and trade shows. This enables sales staff to give personal attention to customers and to make the best decisions about pricing. Successful performance depends heavily on how well employees handle customers, how successfully they maintain interpersonal relationships, and how effective salespeople are in meeting the unique needs of the customers. Compare this to a different company, Price/Costco, a nationwide chain of warehouse club stores. The company has a highly centralized purchasing department that carefully chooses one brand in each product category. Individual stores have little discretion over pricing. Pricing decisions are made at the corporate office, because the company is competing over price. Successful employee performance at Price/Costco involves following directives, keeping costs down, and improving efficiency. Clearly the employee behaviors that are rewarded are going to be very different depending on the company, which in turn affects staffing, compensation, and training. Can you think of some ways in which HRM processes would differ in the two companies? [10]

Technology, or the way in which the work is organized, is another factor that affects HRM processes. We live in a world of increasing highly sophisticated technology, which can be both a blessing and a curse.

Consider, for example, Abigail Roitman, an electronic stock trader and mother of a seventeen-month-old daughter. Roitman, thirty-five, earns a six-figure salary. She struggles to balance her work and home life, because they sometimes conflict. Roitman tries to reduce the conflict by having a computer at home, with mixed results. On the negative side, one evening, Roitman put her daughter to bed and continued working until 12:30 A.M. studying the stock market and monitoring Japan's stocks. She then woke up at 5:30 A.M. to check the latest news. On the positive side, having a computer enabled her to work more at home, such as when she was ill during her pregnancy. The ability to work at home can make it difficult for employees to separate work demands from home needs. How do you think this kind of technology will affect HRM processes? [11]

In sum, an organization's internal and external environments have major effects on HRM processes. We now turn to consideration of HRM goals and objectives. As shown in Figure 1.1, HRM has a number of goals. Let us discuss these goals in greater detail.

HRM Goals

Satisfied Employees

Some organizations view employee satisfaction as an important HRM goal. For example, Celestial Seasonings, a tea company based in Boulder, Colorado, states as one of its beliefs that the organization "allows our employees the opportunity to have authorship and personal satisfaction in their accomplishments, as well as sharing in the financial rewards of their individual and team efforts." But other organizations view employee satisfaction as important only because it can affect other factors, such as turnover and unionization interest.

Although some experts believe that employee satisfaction affects other important outcomes, such as customer satisfaction, the evidence is really quite mixed. Before we can discuss job satisfaction, however, we need to define it. Job satisfaction refers to how pleased an employee is with his or her job and organization. What percentage of U.S. workers do you think rate themselves as being "very satisfied" with their employment? If you answered about one-third, you are correct. Interestingly, the smaller the business, the more likely employees are to rate themselves very satisfied. Although only 28 percent of employees in large businesses are extremely satisfied, almost half (44 percent) of employees in small companies are extremely satisfied. Can you guess what percentage of workers indicated that they were extremely dissatisfied? If you said 4 percent, you were right. Surprised? The typical U.S. worker appears to be more satisfied than many experts would think.

Job satisfaction can vary, depending on the particular aspect of the job under consideration. For example, when asked if they have been compensated fairly for their work, almost one-third (30 percent) said no. But when asked if they had been given the opportunity to learn and grow, 84 percent of employees asserted that they had.[12] Have you ever completed a job satisfaction survey at work? Some organizations use formal satisfaction surveys in order to detect issues of concern for employees before they become problems.

Managing Absenteeism

Workers who miss work without prior arrangement are considered absent. Absenteeism poses a major problem for many organizations. To understand why, think about a time when one or two of your coworkers were absent from work. What were some of the problems you experienced? One of the biggest problems was that you probably had a heavier workload. You may also have had to work overtime, when you would rather have gone home. The company also is likely to be negatively affected—productivity may be lower and, in some cases, the company may still have to pay the absent employee. If the absenteeism becomes more frequent, the supervisor or manager may have to take time from work to counsel the employee. On the other hand, absenteeism sometimes serves legitimate personal needs and may help reduce job-related stress and tension. Employees sometimes arrange to miss work to extend a weekend, take a longer vacation, or because their children are on vacation from school. Anticipated absences can even have rewards both for companies and for remaining employees: When your coworker is away, you may be forced to perform that person's job, which helps develop your skills. Your organization may save money, since some workers will not be paid when they are absent. Finally, have you ever been absent from work to extend your weekend, take a longer vacation, or do some other pleasurable thing? Have you ever missed work because your children were on vacation from school? In general, however, absenteeism creates more problems than it solves for organizations.[13]

Why are employees absent from work? Two basic factors determine whether an employee will have an unplanned absence:[14]

1. Motivation to attend work
2. Ability to attend work

Motivation, or willingness, to attend work is determined by several factors. Certain individuals and organizations have a strong set of norms regarding absenteeism. Some such norms eschew absenteeism, others may encourage high absenteeism. Other factors that contribute to motivation to attend work include organizational policies about absenteeism (companies that enforce penalties have lower absenteeism) and job satisfaction (satisfied employees are more likely to show up for work).

In general, three major influences on ability to attend work are illness, family responsibilities (such as a sick child), and transportation problems (for example, a car that won't operate). A recent survey indicated that the most common reason for absenteeism was family responsibilities (26 percent), followed by illness (22 percent). Large businesses lose an estimated $757 annually per employee in direct costs from absenteeism. The cost for small businesses is even higher ($1,044 per employee).[15]

In order to reduce absenteeism, organizations resort to different approaches. To increase workers' motivation to attend work, some organizations have introduced rewards, including participation in company lotteries, for workers with excellent attendance records. They seek to improve workers' attendance by implementing wellness programs, on-site day care centers with facilities for sick children, and special transportation arrangements (for example, van pools). The most effective way to reduce absenteeism, however, is to implement a flexible scheduling program.[16]

Selective Retention

How might your organization react if you decided to quit and go to work for another company? Do you think your supervisor would beg you to stay and offer you a large salary increase? Or would your supervisor shake your hand and wish you good luck? Your answers to these questions probably depend on various considerations. Table 1.1 lists some circumstances under which your company would be disappointed if you left, as well as some circumstances under which your employer might be pleased with your departure.[17]

Turnover rates vary widely from company to company. A recent survey found that 53 percent of workers planned to change their jobs within five years.[18]

What about from your perspective as an employee? Might changing jobs be good or bad for you? Table 1.2 provides some thoughts about the positive and negative aspects of changing jobs.

Have you ever thought about changing jobs? If you had a job offer from another company, what factors did you consider in deciding whether to change jobs? Employees generally consider three basic factors when deciding to change jobs:

1. Job satisfaction of current job
2. Expected job satisfaction of alternative employment
3. Investments

The first consideration is how satisfied you are with your work. The more satisfied you are with your current job, the less likely you are to change jobs. Expected job satisfaction with alternative employment refers to how content you predict you will be with the other job opportunity; in other words, how satisfied do you think you will

Table 1.1	Circumstances under Which Turnover Is Good versus Bad for the Organization
Turnover Is Good When	**Turnover Is Bad When**
1. Poor performer leaves.	1. Company must spend money hiring replacements.
2. New employees with innovative ideas can be hired.	2. Company must spend time and money training replacements.
3. New employees can be hired at lower wages and benefits.	3. Remaining employees become demoralized.
4. Remaining employees have new promotion opportunities.	4. Former employee takes business away from company.

Source: Adapted from P. Hom and R. Griffeth, *Employee Turnover* (Cincinnati: South-Western, 1995).

Table 1.2	Positive and Negative Effects for Employees Who Change Jobs	

Positive Effects	Negative Effects
1. Relocate to better community.	1. Forfeit seniority.
2. Obtain better job (for example, higher pay, more interesting work).	2. May reduce value of pension.
	3. Relocation costs.
3. Improve spouse's job.	4. Transition stress.
4. Change may be energizing.	5. New job may not meet one's expectations.

Source: Adapted from P. Hom and R. Griffeth, *Employee Turnover* (Cincinnati: South-Western, 1995).

be with the new job. The less satisfied you believe you will be, the less likely you are to change jobs.

Investments refer to various aspects of your job that are not sources of satisfaction but are factors that commit you to staying, such as seniority rights and pension plan considerations. A major investment may occur over time because, psychologically, many people become reluctant to change jobs simply because they prefer a known quantity (their present job) to an unknown quantity (the alternative job). Unfortunately, then, people sometimes stay in a job with which they are dissatisfied simply because they feel safer remaining rather than trying something new.

As noted above, organizations can have quite different turnover rates, particularly depending on their industry. The fast-food business has one of the highest turnover rates—140 percent annually. The software industry also has a high turnover rate—almost 19 percent of the professionals in this field change their jobs each year. Companies in these industries can reduce their costs if they cut their turnover rates even slightly. Box 1.3 offers a case example of how one small business reduced a turnover problem.[19]

Organizations that wish to reduce turnover must be sure that they are appropriately rewarding their employees. If, for example, other organizations are paying more money, the company must either increase the salaries offered or provide other rewards of value to job applicants. A company may also need to consider how to increase employees' investments in the organization through pension plans and by promoting more from within the organization. Of course, some turnover is inevitable and may be beneficial for the organization. From both an employee's and a company's perspective, then, turnover is sometimes good and sometimes bad.

High Performance

High employee performance is obviously one of the most important HRM goals, both from the organization's and the employee's viewpoint. Performance is a multifaceted concept. That is, performance refers not only to the *amount* of work produced (for example, number of sales made or dishes washed), but to other aspects as well. For example, the *quality* of work is important for many jobs. In fact, many organizations emphasize "quality" in their mission statements. Although quality has been defined many different ways, including excellence, value, and meeting customer expectations, probably the best definition of quality is the degree to which a product or service conforms to the required specifications. For workers on an automobile production line,

Tales from the Trenches

Box 1.3
How One Small Business Reduced a Turnover Problem

IHS HelpDesk Service is a small business ($21 million in sales) that specializes in supplying contract employees for technical services to large businesses. After several years, the owners realized that they had greater demand for their service than they could provide. When they examined why the demand outweighed their ability to supply services, they discovered that turnover was a major reason. In fact, 30 percent of newly hired employees quit within three months; annual turnover was reaching a whopping 300 percent. Even more astonishing, the average employee stayed on the job for only 3.5 months. The owners of the firm, Sean Durham and Eric Rabinowitz, first calculated that it cost $3,000 to recruit a new employee. But as they considered the problem more, they realized that there were other less tangible costs, such as decreased productivity (such as time costs to train new employees to perform at the highest level), and poor customer satisfaction. Based on their

analyses, they estimated that by increasing the average stay for employees to 18 months, they would save $2.9 million each year.

Durham and Rabinowitz looked for problems related to the high turnover rate. First, they discovered that employees were often unaware of the many benefits offered by the company. For example, many employees were unaware that the company offered a stock ownership plan. Employees had little information about career possibilities within the firm; many viewed their job at IHS as temporary. Many employees felt that communication was quite poor. The owners also discovered that a major reason many employees left within three months was frustration, as they were given little training in the many problems that they encountered in their job.

To address these problems, the organization expanded its orientation for new employees and included information on the types of frustration that they would likely encounter in the be-

ginning. In addition, Durham and Rabinowitz spoke with their customers and explained the need to be patient with new employees. Durham and Rabinowitz also found that their policy of laying off people who were in between contract assignments for more than a few weeks often led to the loss of good employees. They therefore continued to pay employees to update themselves on the latest technology. Finally, the owners created a daily newsletter for the organization to help increase communication.

Since implementing all of these changes, IHS turnover has dropped to 25 percent annually, billing is up, and customer satisfaction has moved from an average of 2.75 (on a five-point scale) to 3.3. The cost of change hasn't been cheap. The owners estimate that IHS has laid out $600,000 for consulting charges, training costs, and travel expenses. Is it worth it? The owners say it is. They have gone so far as to use the low turnover rate in their marketing materials.

Adapted from C. Caggiano, "How're You Gonna Keep 'Em Down on the Firm?" *Inc.*, January 1998, 20, 70–1, 73–4, 76, 79, 81.

quality work would mean that the components they are responsible for attaching and fixing on the cars are placed according to the prescribed engineering standards.[20]

Another aspect of performance, related to quality, is customer satisfaction. Measuring customer satisfaction is particularly important when no tangible product is produced (for example, entertainment). Many organizations today take careful surveys of customer satisfaction with their product or service, because ultimately, if customers are not happy with the product or service, they will take their business elsewhere.[21]

A final facet of performance, referred to as either contextual or prosocial organizational citizenship behavior, involves employee behavior that supports the broader social and psychological goals of the organization. Contextual performance would include such behaviors as volunteering to perform tasks beyond the official job duties, helping other employees, and actively supporting organizational and departmental decisions and rules.[22]

Now that you have a more complete understanding of what performance is, let us consider the factors that determine performance in any given job. The three primary determinants of employee performance are shown in Figure 1.3. We will discuss each of these in greater detail.

Competencies. Competencies are the underlying bodies of knowledge, abilities, experiences, and other requirements necessary to successfully perform the job. For example, to be effective, an algebra instructor would need to understand algebra. Similarly, to be effective, a lawyer would need to understand basic legal principles; a brain surgeon must have a thorough understanding of various anatomical and physiological reactions.[23]

Of course, knowledge is rarely the only competency necessary to employee success. Most jobs require various abilities or mental aptitudes for making decisions, communicating, reading, and interacting effectively with other people. To return to our example of the algebra instructor, a successful algebra teacher probably needs to be effective in oral communication. An outstanding algebra teacher will probably also be effective in explaining the information in a way students can understand. The ability to learn new things may be one of the most important competencies today. And, some

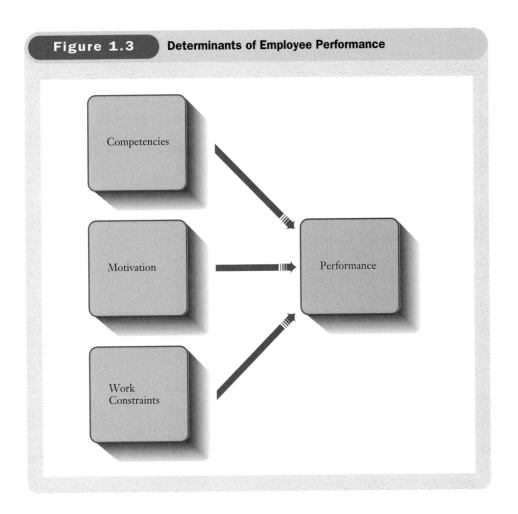

Figure 1.3   **Determinants of Employee Performance**

aptitudes are of a more psychomotor nature, such as eye-hand coordination, physical agility, and manual dexterity. A dentist generally needs good eye-hand coordination and manual dexterity to perform that job. Finally, recent evidence suggests that conscientiousness, a major aspect of one's personality, is a competency that varies from person to person and plays an important role in job performance.[24]

From an HRM perspective, the two most important processes to ensure that employees have the necessary competencies are effective staffing systems and training and development programs, topics that will be examined in much greater detail in subsequent chapters. What can you, as an employee, do in this regard? First, be sure that you choose a career and job that provides a good match with your competencies. Second, be sure that you seek out training and development programs that will benefit your career. We now consider the second determinant of job performance—employee motivation.

Motivation. Even people with the necessary competencies will be poor performers unless they are motivated, or willing, to devote time and effort to their work. Table 1.3 lists different rewards that might motivate an employee to achieve higher performance. Which of the aspects listed in Table 1.3 might motivate you to be a productive worker? Have your jobs provided those rewards? Have companies you've worked for provided other rewards? The importance of motivation has made developing effective employee reward programs a major HRM activity.[25]

Although many HRM programs focus on *extrinsic* (that is, financial) rewards to motivate employees, organizations are increasingly recognizing the importance of *intrinsic* rewards (such as the nature of the work itself) as a motivating factor. To understand the importance of intrinsic rewards, think about a college course you have had that involved many interesting and fun assignments. Were you motivated to perform well? Now think about a course that involved dull and uninteresting assignments. Did you find it more difficult to do the work? In sum, both intrinsic and extrinsic rewards are useful motivators. Effective organizations use both intrinsic and extrinsic means to motivate their employees to successful performance, and effective supervisors know

---

> **Table 1.3**   **Some Factors That Motivate Job Performance**

1. Pay increases
2. Bonuses and related financial incentives (for example, company stock)
3. Extra vacation time
4. Verbal compliments from supervisor
5. Promotion to a better job
6. Free tickets to sports events
7. More interesting work
8. Special projects
9. Better office (for example, one with a window)
10. Employee-of-the-month award
11. Your name in the company newsletter
12. All-expenses-paid vacation
13. Free movie tickets
14. Better job title

What other factors motivate you to increase your job performance?

how to reward their employees in meaningful ways. For example, a single parent may value work schedule flexibility much more than a season's ticket to the ballpark. From your perspective as an employee, it is critical that you choose a job involving work you enjoy.

Work Constraints. Work constraints are those features of the work environment that negatively affect job performance.[26] Table 1.4 lists some of the more common work constraints that employees experience. As you can see from Table 1.4, these include insufficient information and inappropriate tools and equipment. Total quality management (TQM) programs often address these concerns and develop solutions to them.[27]

Although TQM will be discussed in much greater detail in Chapter 12, a brief description is appropriate here. TQM is a program that focuses on continuous improvement of the organization's product or service quality. A key emphasis in TQM is enhancement of customer satisfaction. Toward that end, TQM programs assign teams of employees to search for ways to eliminate barriers to quality and improve work processes.[28]

Now that you understand the factors that determine job performance, you will read about three additional HRM outcomes, namely, cost containment, meeting legal requirements, and counterproductivity.

Additional HRM Goals

Cost Containment. Especially in today's competitive business environment, cost containment—keeping expenses down—is a critical HRM goal. As you will see in subsequent chapters, compensation and benefit costs can be extremely high. This is particularly true in labor-intensive organizations, such as educational institutions, consulting firms, and service businesses.

Legal Requirements. Meeting legal requirements is one of the most important HRM goals. As mentioned previously, virtually every HRM decision—including hiring, promoting, firing, starting pay and pay raises—has legal ramifications. Many

Table 1.4	Common Work Constraints That Affect Productivity

1. Insufficient information
2. Inappropriate tools and equipment
3. Missing materials or supplies
4. Limited budget
5. Insufficient support from others
6. Insufficient task preparation
7. Limited time
8. Poor physical conditions
9. Poor scheduling

Source: Adapted from L. Peters, E. J. O'Connor, and J. Eulberg, "Situational Constraints: Sources, Consequences, and Future Considerations," in *Research in Personnel and Human Resources Management*, vol. 3, ed. K. Rowland and G. Ferris (Greenwich, CT: JAI Press, 1985).

additional regulations must also be met, such as safety and health rules. Because supervisors and managers make many HRM decisions, it is also critical that they have a
basic understanding of these laws. And, as an employee, knowing your legal rights will
help you deal with problem situations.

Violations of legal requirements can be costly to an organization. Aside from
lawyers' fees and employee time and energy spent handling legal complaints, an organization may be required to pay various fines and to implement special training programs. An organization that neglects to stay abreast of legal developments may,
therefore, pay dearly.

Counterproductivity. Counterproductive behaviors can be best understood if you
think of them as forming a continuum from serious to relatively minor. At one end of
the spectrum, murder and violent assault are extremely serious counterproductive behaviors. Behaviors such as theft of company property fall in the middle of this continuum. Toward the relatively minor end of the spectrum, counterproductive behaviors
may include starting and encouraging malicious rumors, claiming credit for others'
work, and attempting to derail others' careers.[29]

Counterproductive behavior costs businesses and organizations estimated billions
of dollars annually.[30] Certain industries, such as retail, are particularly susceptible to
employee theft. Crime against employees is also a growing problem, some of it caused
by coworkers and some of it caused by customers and others. It is estimated that about
a half million workers each year must take time off from work because of injuries they
received from crime. The National Safe Workplace Institute calculates that companies
lost more than four billion dollars as a consequence.[31]

Why do employees engage in counterproductive behavior? Although we have no
simple answer to this question, employees are likely to engage in counterproductive
behavior when they feel that they have received an unfair outcome (for example, a low
raise; loss of a job). However, it is not enough for an employee to feel he or she has received an unfair outcome; the employee generally must also believe that the organization used unfair *procedures* to make the decision.[32] Finally, people react differently to
the same unfair situation because of personality traits. Self-control is one personality
trait that affects the likelihood an employee will react in an aggressive, irresponsible
way. People low in self-control tend to be impulsive, restless, and adventurous. On the
other hand, people high in self-control can be overly controlling and therefore may
overreact to unfair situations. People who have moderate self-control are likely to be
the best at responding to unfair situations.[33]

From an HRM perspective, several actions can reduce counterproductive behavior, including careful selection of employees, surveillance of the workplace, and thorough investigations of possible employee misconduct. As you will see, however, these
processes are fraught with legal restrictions, and therefore organizations must operate
carefully here.

Reexamine Figure 1.1. Note that HRM goals and outcomes will affect organizational goals and outcomes, such as profitability, survival, and adaptability. Most businesses today recognize that they must establish and achieve HRM goals in order for
the organization as a whole to succeed.[34] A recent survey of small businesses found that
their biggest challenge was finding and training new employees.[35]

Figure 1.1 includes arrows that point from organizational outcomes to HRM processes and the environment; similarly, HRM outcomes have arrows that point back to
HRM processes and the environment. These arrows show that organizational outcomes and HRM outcomes also affect HRM processes and the environment to some

degree. For example, a highly profitable organization will have different HRM programs and policies than an organization that is struggling to survive. An organization that has a high absenteeism rate may change its disciplinary procedures. Thus, much interplay goes on between the environment, HRM processes, HRM goals, and organizational outcomes.

We now turn to a discussion of the HRM mission and the roles HRM staff play in performing their jobs.

HRM Mission

The nature of the HRM mission varies from company to company. One can view the mission of the HRM department, and the way in which success is measured, on a continuum from basic to highly sophisticated. (See Figure 1.4.) At the most basic level—particularly common in a small, relatively new organization—the mission of the HRM department is to provide basic services, such as distribution of paychecks and collecting resumes in response to job openings. To prove its success in this mission, the HRM department will have to demonstrate that tasks are completed adequately (for example, there are few, if any, complaints about the delivery of paychecks).

At the next level, the mission of the HRM department is to provide *optimal* delivery of human resource processes; in other words, HRM processes must be delivered in a cost-effective way. For example, rather than simply distributing paychecks, the HRM department must demonstrate that it uses the most effective procedure (for example, electronic distribution, perhaps). This level represents the mission of many HRM departments, particularly in small to medium organizations.

At the third level, the HRM department's mission is to build competitive advantage for the organization through human resources. Success here is measured by demand for HRM services. For example, at this level, the HRM department must convince managers that it provides the best service compared with an outsource alternative. Many large companies' HRM mission is probably at this level in the 1990s.

At the fourth level, the HRM function is viewed as a full-fledged partner with top management. The mission of the HRM department at this level is to help shape organizational success by sharing in the development of business strategy. The HRM department is measured by its impact on business strategy. For example, HRM may suggest the outsourcing of the manufacturing function, which in turn may save the company considerable amounts of money and lead to higher quality products.

At the most sophisticated level, which only a few companies maintain at any given time, the HRM mission is the creation, preservation, and utilization of intellectual capital. At this level, HRM success is measured by the nature, quality, and preservation of the organization's intellectual capital and the enhancement of organizational reputation. As an example, the HRM department may be instrumental in attracting and retaining the best software development experts, enabling the organization to capture the market share in sales.[36]

Organizational reputation is increasing in importance in attracting and retaining top employees. Many magazines, such as *Fortune*, have drawn attention to organizational reputation by compiling rankings of the best workplaces (see www.pathfinder.com/fortune/1998/980112/int.html). *Computerworld* has initiated a list of the thousand best companies for information systems workers (see www2.computerworld.com/inc/programs/bestplaces) and *Working Mother* has a similar list of best companies for working mothers. There is evidence that job seekers use these lists to

Figure 1.4	Five Different HRM Missions

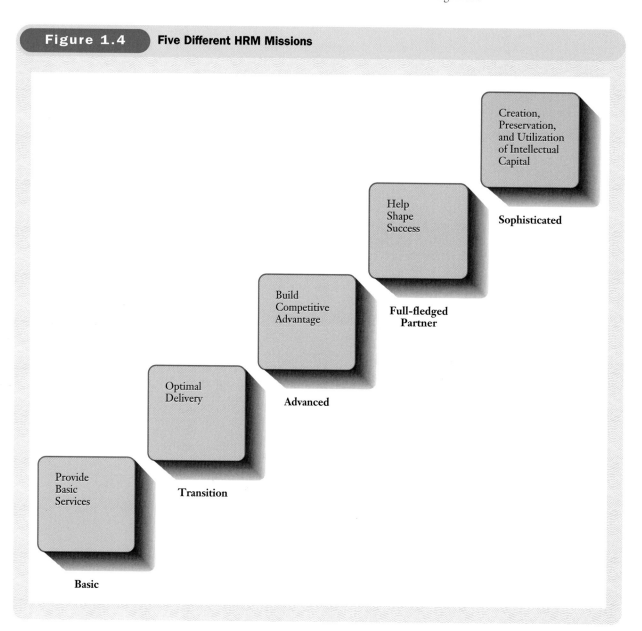

choose among different employment offers. After reading a list of best places to work, Ms. Koc noted that SAS Institute, a software company located in Cary, North Carolina, was rated among the best. She was able to talk her husband into quitting his job in New York and moving to Cary, even though she was not aware of any job openings at SAS. She applied for several jobs (all of which involved a pay cut) and subsequently landed a job. Cinergy, another company that has ranked well on such lists, says that such recognition helps it attract job seekers from large cities to its offices, which are located in small- to medium-size cities. Finally, more financial analysts are beginning to take note of companies' reputations as an important factor in determining the value of the company stock.[37]

Table 1.5	**Typical HRM Staff Tasks**

1. Answer employee questions about the benefits program.
2. Contract with health providers to provide medical service.
3. Provide orientation programs for new employees.
4. Conduct employee attitude surveys.
5. Give advice to line managers on problem employees.
6. Respond to EEOC investigations.
7. Create job openings on the Internet.
8. Screen resumes responding to job openings.
9. Approve salary raise recommendations made by managers and supervisors.
10. Create a sexual harassment policy.
11. Conduct sexual harassment investigations.
12. Conduct preretirement workshops.
13. Implement an affirmative action program.
14. Maintain records on employee hours and pay.
15. Develop a human resource information system.
16. Review company policies and procedures.
17. Write rejection letters to applicants who were not hired.
18. Interview job candidates.

Table 1.5 lists some basic HRM tasks. As the HRM mission becomes increasingly more sophisticated, HRM staff must assume more varied roles, including the following:[38]

1. **Business Expert.** All too often the human resource specialist has only a limited understanding of the organization's business. Not only will this hurt his or her credibility with others, but it may limit his or her ability to make sound HR decisions. HRM staff members may improve their understanding of the business in many ways, including taking courses in finance, marketing, and strategic planning; participating in business task forces; and rotating into line management positions.

2. **Change Facilitator.** This is a new critical role for human resource managers and, indeed, all managers and supervisors. As discussed previously in this chapter, many organizations are changing the way they are structured and designed. As the change facilitator, HRM staff will affect how to change, assist in facilitating the change, and monitor reactions to change. To prepare for this role, HRM employees should take workshops and seminars in organizational change, read books on the change process, and talk with other professionals about such programs.

3. **Strategy Consultant.** Human resource experts are more frequently being called upon to participate in making major, long-term decisions regarding the organization's business direction, plans for opening new facilities or closing existing facilities, and so forth. Toward that end, HRM staff will play a more active role as strategy consultant to managers and executives. To prepare for this role, HRM employees should learn more about the business through conversations with a variety of people from different functions of the organization, reading books and magazine articles about business strategy, and taking seminars in the area of strategic human resources.

Box 1.4
The Use of Technology in Human Resources

With the growth of high-tech communication devices, such as e-mail and videoconferencing, and the increasing popularity of virtual organizations, more and more human resource systems are relying on these tools. Take for example VeriFone, a small virtual firm (only 7 percent of its employees are based at the headquarters). When it came time to hire a new director of information systems, the senior vice president decided to create a committee of five people to complete this task. In addition, ten other top managers agreed to help conduct the interviewing. Because most of the people involved in this hiring effort worked in different locations, the committee relied heavily on e-mail, telephones, and videoconferencing. To facilitate matters, initial interviews with job finalists took place by conference call so that all committee members could participate. For later interviews, the company made sure that at least one committee member was physically present, while other committee members participated over the telephone or via videoconferencing.

Although interviewing the candidate in this fashion may have seemed awkward, the senior vice president asserted that this method provided a picture of a candidate's ability to successfully use high-tech communication devices, a necessary skill in a virtual firm such as VeriFone. The task, however, did not end with the hiring of a new director of information systems. In order to facilitate the transition, the senior vice-president asked committee members to maintain contact, via telephone and e-mail, with the new employee and provide information about the organization and job. The end result was a successful new employee.

Source: Adapted from W. Pape, "Hiring Blind," *Inc.*, November 1998, 18.

In all of these roles, success in HRM depends in part on your ability to adapt your skills to the technologies in use at your company. Box 1.4 provides an example of how some companies use technology as part of their hiring methods to screen for competent employees and, later, to help integrate and train new employees.

In sum, regardless of whether you are a full-time HRM employee or have several responsibilities, including HRM, you will need to fulfill an increasingly diverse set of roles. Your ability to serve effectively in each of those roles will greatly affect your career. We now turn to the last section of this chapter, a brief discussion of careers in HRM.

Careers in Human Resource Management

Many different types of HRM jobs are available, ranging from interview specialist to training manager and including generalist positions such as manager of human resources. Most medium and large companies have a vice president or director of human resources as well. As you read through this book, think about whether certain areas seem particularly interesting to you. For example, the chapter on safety and health issues may intrigue you; if so, consider a career in that area. If you want further information about careers in HRM, contact the Society for Human Resource Management (1-800-283-SHRM or their Web site at www.shrm.org). In addition to providing career information, this organization sponsors student groups on many college and university campuses. Check with the student organizations office at your campus to see if a chapter has been organized.

Pursuing an HRM Career: Tips for Students

If you are interested in a career in HRM, here are some suggestions for you.[39]

1. **Work Experience Is as Important as Education.** In order to enter the human resource field, it is extremely important to have some work experience. This is especially true if you plan to obtain a master's degree. Accrue some work experience first. A good internship program may suffice.
2. **Obtain a Well-Rounded Educational Background.** A basic understanding of business (marketing, finance, and so forth) will be important to success in the human resource field. If you are an undergraduate business major, there will be considerable overlap with course work you receive in an MBA program, unless you enter a more specialized master's program in human resources or organizational development.
3. **The "Soft" Skills Will Become Increasingly Important.** Although traditional areas of HRM, such as compensation and benefits, remain important, changes in both the internal and external environment have increased the importance of communication, conflict resolution, and interpersonal abilities. Consider other means of obtaining these abilities, including workshops and seminars, if these areas are not covered in your school. Your local chamber of commerce, community college, or management consulting firm may have additional information on such programs.
4. **Experience in Leadership Roles Will Be Helpful.** Serving in leadership positions in your school, your community, and volunteer organizations provides evidence that you are capable of managing and leading people in a variety of situations. More companies view such experiences as important for HRM positions.
5. **Exposure to International Issues and Cultural Diversity.** HRM issues increasingly must be addressed at a global level, and more HR positions will appear in countries other than the United States. In addition, the United States is becoming more culturally diverse. Knowledge of a foreign language, such as Spanish, Japanese, or Chinese, will be invaluable. Does your school provide an opportunity for you to go overseas for a semester or a year? Does your school provide any international business courses? Participation in these activities will be helpful for those seeking a career in HRM.
6. **Become Technically Proficient.** HRM will increasingly require knowledge of computers and computer-based technologies. For example, Internet-based training programs, computerized resume databases, and Enterprise Resource Planning tools will become increasingly important HRM tools.

Careers in HRM: Becoming an Independent Consultant

Have you thought of going into business on your own as a human resource consultant? Because many companies have begun outsourcing their human resources function, many new opportunities are arising in this area. Before you become an independent consultant, however, here are some suggestions you should consider.[40]

1. **Most HRM Consultants Have Extensive Previous Work Experience.** Prior experience is important for two reasons. First, it gives you credibility with potential clients; second, former employers may be an initial source of business. You are best off working in the HRM department of several companies before you start your own consulting business.

2. **A Diverse Set of Skills Is Essential.** If you are a private consultant, you need to have more than just knowledge of HRM. You will need to manage your time well, have considerable patience, and enjoy working alone. Marketing ability is most essential. Experts recommend that consultants spend at least 30 percent of their time engaged in marketing activities, such as making presentations, developing materials, and so forth. New consultants may need to spend as much as 80 percent of their time marketing their business.

3. **Acquire the Proper Materials.** In addition to business cards, you will probably need a fax machine, a computer, and a separate telephone line and answering machine. You should also develop a business plan and obtain information on how to set up your business.

4. **Obtain Information.** Numerous books and articles provide guidelines on how to establish and run a consulting business. Some of the recommended ones are the following:

   Flawless Consulting, Peter Block (University Associates, San Diego, CA).

   Do-It-Yourself Publicity, David Ramacitti (AMACOM Books, American Management Association, New York).

   Become an Outside Consultant, American Society for Training and Development, March 1994, Issue 9403, Alexandria, VA.

5. **Talk with People.** Meet other successful consultants, and learn what they do. Talk with potential customers and explore their needs. See what niche you could fill as a consultant.

We end this chapter with Box 1.5, which tells the story of how strong leadership skills combined with effective human resource management helped revitalize a troubled business, and with Box 1.6, which includes some World Wide Web resources to help inform and inspire you.

❖ Conclusion

Human resource management is a complex area, with many environmental factors that must be taken into account. Among the processes included in HRM are planning, staffing, evaluating and rewarding, improving the organization, and maintaining effective employer–employee relationships. The major goals of HRM include low absenteeism, selective retention of employees, and high job performance; additional goals include compliance with legal requirements and reduction of counterproductive employee behavior. It is not surprising that the role of the HRM staff has become much more complex over the years. Today's business environment demands that HRM play more than just an administrative and advisory role; the human resource manager must serve as a business expert, change facilitator, and strategy consultant as well. Students

Box 1.5

How Human Resources Helped Turn Around a Troubled Airline

In 1994, Continental Airlines was heading toward bankruptcy for the third time in a decade. Continental was considered to have one of the worst labor–management relationships and to be one of the least successful in the airline industry. Chief executive officer (CEO) Gordon Bethune (the tenth CEO in ten years) and chief operating officer (COO) Greg Brenneman were determined to radically change and rebuild Continental. Toward that end, Bethune and Brenneman decided on four major goals: (1) return to profitability; (2) reduce debt; (3) improve flying service; and (4) create a positive work environment for employees. The HR function was responsible for playing a lead role in achieving the latter two objectives. To achieve those goals, Continental made numerous changes in its training and reward systems. Perhaps the most significant change made by the company was the decision to pay each employee a $65 bonus for each month that the airline was in the top half of Department of Transportation (DOT) rankings for on-time performance (for the last few years, Continental had been last on all DOT indices). Although this program was expensive (the company spent an additional $22.5 million annually), Continental was on the top half of on-time performance rankings in 1995 and 1996. The program was then changed to a $65 bonus for each month the company ranked second or third—and a $100 bonus if the company ranked first.

The HR department viewed the objective of creating a positive work environment as being particularly difficult in light of employees' lack of trust. A number of highly symbolic actions were therefore taken to dramatize top management's new attitude. First, thirty-six vice presidents were dismissed and replaced with twenty-one new vice presidents who had been highly successful elsewhere. Second, the company staged an event where the 800-page employee manual was burned. Third, the company initiated a monthly meeting open to all employees and led by Bethune and Brenneman, as well as the vice president of human resources. Any inquiries or suggestions by employees would be responded to within twenty-four hours of that meeting. Fourth, once or twice a year, all executive and corporate employees went to Continental's major hubs to work shoulder to shoulder with the employees who were responsible for customer service (for example, boarding passengers). These, as well as other changes, led to significant improvements in the work environment, as measured by reductions in absenteeism, turnover, and employee satisfaction.

Source: Adapted from K. Carrig, "Reshaping Human Resources for the Next Century—Lessons From a High-Flying Airline," *Human Resource Management* 36 (Summer 1998): 277–89.

planning a career in HRM must plan wisely and take a diversity of college courses, supplemented by additional experiences such as work, international exposure, and volunteer positions.

❖ Applying Core Concepts

1. How do you think the Internet will change the way in which human resource processes, such as hiring, training, compensating, evaluating, and benefits, are performed?
2. How can the Internet be of help to you as an employee?
3. What do you think are the most important HRM outcomes at the organization you work for (for example, selective retention of employees, high performance)? How about at the school you attend?
4. What kinds of HRM processes have you participated in or do you expect to participate in soon?

Webbing Around

Box 1.6

Here are some good, general, HRM-related Web sites for you to use. Some of them are for serious work; others are for fun.

www.shrm.org This is the Web site for the Society of Human Resource Management, the largest and most well-known professional association for human resource managers. You will find a variety of information, including articles, dis-

cussion forums, and other useful resources.

www.ipma-hr.org This is the Web site for the International Personnel Management Association, the largest professional association for public sector human resource managers. You will find a variety of useful information, articles, and discussion forums here.

www.workingwounded.com/ 1main.html What bothers people at work? How can you find advice on dealing with work-related problems? That is what this site is all about—a Web-based "gripe" session.

www.hardatwork.com Feeling as if you work too hard? Here is an opportunity to share your complaints with others. Enjoy and learn about the work world!

5. What do you consider the most interesting aspect of human resource management?
6. Contact a human resource professional (there is probably a human resource department at the college or university you attend) and interview that person about his or her job. Be sure to ask (a) what he or she does on a typical workday, (b) what he or she enjoys most about the job, (c) what he or she enjoys least, and (d) how he or she expects the field to change in the next five years.
7. Examine HR department Web sites from different organizations. Two sample ones are *www.hitachi.com.my/human-resources.htm* and *www.hsc.colorado.edu/uh/human/index.htm*. In what ways do these different Web sites differ? What are some things that most of them have? Was there any information that surprised you?

❖ CHAPTER 1 *Experiential Exercise*

Making Changes at Electrik, Inc.

Introduction. Electrik, Inc., is a highly sophisticated electronics manufacturer. Given the increasing competition, it is in the process of making many changes. One major change is the new chief executive officer (CEO), who comes from a much more progressive company. Given the apparent low morale among employees, high turnover, and concerns about a possible buyout by another company, the new CEO asked you to conduct an employee survey. Based on the survey results, described below, the top executives have brainstormed a brief list of possible changes. Assume for the case that

all changes will take the same amount of time and cost. You must recommend only two of the possible changes. You should be prepared to:

1. Discuss which two changes you would recommend. Explain why these two. Explain why you did not choose the other five changes.
2. Explain what problems you anticipate in implementing those two changes, and what you will do to successfully implement them. Discuss the role the HR department should play in this situation.

Electrik, Inc., Corporate Structure. Electrik has a traditional hierarchical structure. Reporting to the CEO are five executives. Reporting to the executives are thirty managers. About fifty supervisors report to these managers. The company employs approximately five hundred clerical, professional, technical, and production employees. In the past, a formal reporting structure has been used, with most decisions made by the executives.

Electrik, Inc., Business Conditions. When the company was founded twenty years ago, it experienced rapid growth. However, recent trends have begun to reduce profits. There are several reasons for the changing business conditions. First, more companies are shifting their work to production facilities in Asia. Second, there has been a significant increase in the amount of automation in this industry (so far, Electrik has had relatively little automation). Third, Electrik has spent relatively little money on research and development (R&D), compared to its competitors, who tend to be much larger and can afford more R&D. Fourth, Electrik has always been an extremely high-quality producer (even though the company's products are slightly more expensive than the competitors); however, other competitors have begun to improve their quality, and thus have become more competitive on that dimension as well, while not raising their prices.

Results of the Employee Survey

Pay and Benefits. A frequent employee complaint was low pay. A major problem seemed to be a sense of internal unfairness (for example, some people in the company were being paid more than other employees thought they were worth). Clerical and production employees, in particular, believed they were underpaid relative to managers and professional employees. On a positive note, employees like their basic benefits package (for example, retirement and health insurance).

Management Style. Many complaints were leveled at the management style exhibited by managers and supervisors. In general, managers and supervisors were perceived as "heavy-handed," indifferent to employee feelings, and often tactless. On the positive side, the existing grievance system seemed well regarded, and the "open door" policy of the new CEO appeared to be working well.

Promotions. Despite Electrik's heavy emphasis on internal promotions, many complaints were leveled against the promotion procedures. First, employees cited far too little guidance and advice regarding career development. This was particularly true among technical employees. Second, employees complained that they often were not informed when a position became open. Third, employees felt completely unaware of how promotion decisions were made and what criteria were used, and they wondered why they were not promoted. In some cases, employees suspected discrimination.

Training and Development. The company had occasionally offered training seminars on such topics as computer use, safety, and communications, but had no systematic employee development plan. A generous tuition reimbursement program was available to employees, but only about 15 percent had participated in it.

Performance Evaluations. Although performance appraisals were supposed to be conducted once a year for each employee, several employees indicated they had never received any performance appraisal. Most employees believed that the performance appraisals provided no useful feedback and were simply "another piece of paper to fill out." A significant portion of employees related the lack of career development and limited information about pay raises and such to the lack of an effective performance appraisal system.

Employee Input. Without exception, employees believed that they had far too little input on important issues relevant to their jobs and the company. Even on minor decisions (such as where to have the annual company party), employee input was considered nonexistent. Everyone desired to have more "say," particularly given the changes in business conditions.

Quality of Work Life. Despite the problems with supervisors noted above, employees were fairly positive about work conditions. The work sites were perceived to be clean, safe, and pleasant. The company's flextime schedule was well-liked by the people who used it, although so far only 50 percent of the employees had made use of it.

Human Resources Department. To date, the HR department has played a minor role in the company. The HRM manager has three assistants, including an interviewer, a compensation and benefits specialist, and a secretary. So far, the HR department has primarily been responsible for hiring production workers, making sure everyone is paid on time, and ensuring compliance with basic laws.

Possible Changes

1. Devise and implement a new (mandatory) performance appraisal system that is more specific and formalized, and focuses on career development.
2. Conduct a systematic review of the pay system to address any potential inequities.
3. Implement supervisory training programs.

4. Create and implement an employee committee to address specific issues and problems.
5. Develop and implement a subordinate appraisal of boss program that will provide feedback to all supervisors and managers.
6. Develop and implement a computer-based job posting system for company job openings.
7. Institute a company-wide profit-sharing program to cover all employees. The profit-sharing plan would give employees a yearly share of the company's profits (the company must make a profit for employees to get a share). As currently conceived, the profit-sharing could produce as much as a 15 percent bonus for the employees.

❖ Chapter 1 References

1. M. Beer, B. Spector, P. Lawrence, D. Q. Mills, and R. Walton, *Managing Human Assets* (New York: Free Press, 1984).
2. P. Mario, "Jobs on the Line," *Wall Street Journal*, 14 September 1998, R16.
3. T. Parker-Pope, "Culture Clash," *Wall Street Journal*, 12 April 1995, R7.
4. P. Harris and R. Moran, *Managing Cultural Differences* (Houston: Gulf Publishing, 1991).
5. J. Segal, "Stop Making Plaintiffs' Lawyers Rich," *HRMagazine*, April 1995, 31–6.
6. C. Solomon, "Don't Get Burned by Hot New Markets," *Global Workforce* (Supplement to *Workforce*) 3 (January 1998): 12–22.
7. F. Kemske, "Will HR Go Free-Lance by 2008?" *Workforce*, January 1998, 56.
8. M. Minehan, "SHRM Futurist Task Force," *HRMagazine* 43 (special issue 1998): 77–8, 80, 82, 84, 188–90, 192.
9. T. Stewart, "Welcome to the Revolution," *Fortune*, 13 December 1993, 66–80.
10. M. Treacy and F. Wiersema, "How Market Leaders Keep Their Edge," *Fortune*, 6 February 1995, 88–98.
11. S. Shellenbarger, "Work and Family," *Wall Street Journal*, 9 September 1998, B1.
12. M. Hopkins and J. Seglin, "Americans @Work," *Inc.*, May 1997, 77–85.
13. S. Rhodes and R. Steers, *Managing Employee Absenteeism* (Reading, MA: Addison-Wesley, 1990).
14. Ibid.
15. S. Ross, "Personal/Family Reasons Are No. 1 Cause of Absenteeism," *St. Louis Post-Dispatch*, 19 October 1998, BP4.
16. Ibid.
17. P. Hom and R. Griffeth, *Employee Turnover* (Cincinnati: South-Western, 1995).
18. Hopkins and Seglin, "Americans @Work."
19. M. Hofman, "Staying Power," *Inc.*, 20 January 1998, 74.
20. C. Reeves and D. Bednar, "Defining Quality: Alternatives and Implications," *Academy of Management Review* 19 (1994): 419–45.
21. J. Dean and D. Bowen, "Management Theory and Total Quality: Improving Research and Practice Through Theory Development," *Academy of Management Review* 19 (1994): 392–418.
22. S. Motowidlo and J. VanScotter, "Evidence that Task Performance Should be Distinguished From Contextual Performance," *Journal of Applied Psychology* 79 (1994): 475–80.

23. J. Campbell, "Modeling the Performance Prediction Problem in Industrial and Organizational Psychology," in *Handbook of Industrial/Organizational Psychology*, vol. 1, ed. M. Dunnette and L. Hough (Palo Alto, CA: Consulting Psychologists Press, 1990).

24. M. Barrick and M. Mount, "The Big Five Personality Dimensions and Job Performance: A Meta-Analysis," *Personnel Psychology* 44 (1991): 1–26.

25. R. Kanfer, "Motivation Theory and Industrial and Organizational Psychology," in *Handbook of Industrial and Organizational Psychology*, vol. 1, ed. M. Dunnette and L. Hough (Palo Alto, CA: Consulting Psychologists Press, 1990).

26. L. Peters, E. J. O'Connor, and J. Eulberg, "Situational Constraints: Sources, Consequences, and Future Considerations," in *Research in Personnel and Human Resources Management*, vol. 3, ed. K. Rowland and G. Ferris (Greenwich, CT: JAI Press, 1985).

27. G. Dobbins, R. Cardy, and K. Carson, "Examining Fundamental Assumptions: A Contrast of Person and System Approaches to Human Resource Management," in *Research in Personnel and Human Resources Management*, vol. 9, ed. G. Ferris and K. Rowland (Greenwich, CT: JAI Press, 1991).

28. H. Costin, *Management Development and Training: A TQM Approach* (Fort Worth, TX: Dryden, 1996).

29. J. Collins and R. Griffin, "The Psychology of Counterproductive Job Performance," in *Dysfunctional Behavior in Organizations: Non-Violent Dysfunctional Behavior*, ed. R. Griffin, A. O'Leary-Kelly, and J. Collins (Greenwich, CT: JAI Press, 1998).

30. P. Sackett and M. Harris, "Honesty Testing for Personnel Selection: A Review and Critique," in *Personality Assessment in Organizations*, ed. H. J. Bernardin and D. Bownas (New York: Praeger, 1985).

31. J. Greenberg and B. Alge, "Aggressive Reactions to Workplace Injustice," in *Dysfunctional Behavior in Organizations: Non-Violent Dysfunctional Behavior*, ed. R. Griffin, A. O'Leary-Kelly, and J. Collins (Greenwich, CT: JAI Press, 1998).

32. Ibid.

33. Collins and Griffin, "The Psychology of Counterproductive Job Performance."

34. N. Napier, "Strategy, Human Resources Management, and Organizational Outcomes: Coming Out from Between the Cracks," in *Human Resources Management: Perspectives and Issues*, ed. G. Ferris and K. Rowland (Boston: Allyn & Bacon, 1988).

35. "The Challenge of Recruiting," *Inc.*, March 1997, vol. 19, 102.

36. R. Wintermantel and K. Mattimore, "In the Changing World of Human Resources: Matching Measures to Mission," *Human Resource Management*, 36 Fall 1997, 337–342.

37. S. Shellenbarger, "Work and Family," *Wall Street Journal*, 26 August 1998, B1.

38. R. S. Schuler, "Repositioning the Human Resource Function: Transformation or Demise?" *Academy of Management Executive* 4 (1990): 49–60.

39. B. Kaufman, "What Companies Are Looking for in Graduates of University HR Programs," *Labor Law Journal* 45 (1994): 503–10.

40. N. C. Tompkins, "How to Become a Human Resources Consultant," *HRMagazine*, August 1994, 94–98.

Employment Discrimination Laws

Core Concepts After reading this chapter, you should be capable of:

1. Specifying the major laws pertaining to discrimination in the workplace.
2. Explaining three ways for an employee or job applicant to prove discrimination and for the organization to defend a discrimination charge.
3. Understanding the circumstances under which affirmative action programs may be used in an organization.
4. Identifying current discrimination issues being actively discussed in the popular media.

Opening Case

Yesterday, when you went out to lunch with Maria Martinez, both of you took turns complaining about your jobs. But after about twenty minutes of complaining about unpleasant customers, low pay, and difficult deadlines, Maria lowered her voice and said, "I think I'm being mistreated because I'm young and female. For example, three other employees, who were hired the same week I was, have long since been promoted—and all three were men older than me. But the worst of my problems is my boss, Pat. About twice a day, I catch him staring at me. A couple of times he has said to me that he really likes the shirt or dress I'm wearing. And yesterday he asked me to go out for a drink with him after work at Down Under, the bar across the street from the office. When I hesitated, he said something about discussing ways I might advance in the company. I really don't like it when he stares at me, and I'm uncomfortable with the comments he makes. Frankly, I have no interest in any romantic relationship or even friendship after work. I'm afraid if I say something, though, he will be angry and will hinder my attempts for a promotion. What do you think I should do?"

Now that you have thought about what Maria said, you are wondering what you should recommend she do. Certainly the fact that other people are being promoted while she stays in the same job seems unfair, but isn't it possible that her performance hasn't been as good as theirs? What her boss, Pat, is doing certainly seems unethical, but is it illegal? If it is illegal, what laws would Pat's actions violate? And what should Maria do next?

The purpose of this chapter is to discuss employment discrimination laws. As you will see, employment discrimination laws apply to virtually all employment decisions, including hiring, firing, promotions, and transfers. Even behavior on the job, such as Pat's activities, may be prohibited by employment discrimination laws. You will learn who is covered by these laws, what you would have to prove, how you would show you were discriminated against, and how companies defend themselves in a lawsuit. You will also read about affirmative action, as well as several current issues in the discrimination area. We begin first with an overview of the discrimination laws.

Discrimination Laws: An Introduction

Laws prohibiting racial discrimination in the United States go back to the 1860s, just after the Civil War.[1] However, Congress did not pass a comprehensive law banning workplace discrimination, the Civil Rights Act of 1964, for another 100 years. One of the major forces behind this law was the increasingly recognized disparity in the economic health of blacks and whites. In the early 1960s, black unemployment was about twice as high as white unemployment; the average black family's income was about half that of the average white family. The civil rights movement of the 1960s brought the plight of African Americans to public attention and helped generate national support for a comprehensive federal law that would, among other things, ban race discrimination in the workplace. The result was the passage of the Civil Rights Act of 1964.[2]

It may surprise you to learn that the Civil Rights Act of 1964 was a controversial law that produced a great deal of debate and discussion within Congress. The debate within the Senate lasted more than five hundred hours before the bill passed by a vote of 76 to 18. It passed the House by a vote of 289 to 126. After President Lyndon B.

Johnson signed the bill into law, a number of additional laws providing coverage against such acts as age discrimination were passed.[3]

Major Discrimination Laws

The major federal fair employment laws, along with the types of discrimination banned and the organizations covered by each law, are summarized in Table 2.1. You should also be aware that many states have laws that provide additional protection to employees. Because these laws are quite numerous and often change, they will only be mentioned briefly in subsequent sections. The readers should also note that the question of "what is an employer?" is more complicated today than it was in the past, due to the more complicated nature of business today. For example, consider a temporary employee officially employed by a temporary agency but assigned to various organizations, which may differ from day to day. Although in a sense employed by the temporary agency, the employee might be considered to have two employers, because they both control his or her work. Under current thinking, if discrimination had occurred, such an employee could sue both the temporary agency and the employer to whom he or she was assigned. The same is true for employee-leasing arrangements.

Finally, a company that contracts with another firm to provide a service may be responsible for a discriminatory act caused by the firm. For example, if your company contracts with a health benefits firm to provide health insurance for employees, both your company and the health benefits firm might be liable if the policy discriminates against people with a disability.[4]

Table 2.1	Summary of Key Federal Employment Discrimination Laws	
Law	**What Is Covered**	**Employers Covered**
CRA 1866	Race discrimination	Private companies, unions, employment agencies
CRA 1871	Anyone deprived of equal rights under state law	State and local governments
CRA 1964, CRA 1991	Race, color, religion, sex, national origin	Private companies with 15 or more employees, government unions, employment agencies
Rehabilitation Act of 1973	Physical and mental disabilities	Federal contractor, federal government
Americans with Disabilities Act of 1990	Physical and mental disabilities	Employers with 15+ employees
Executive Order 11141	Age discrimination	Federal contractors and subcontractors
Age Discrimination in Employment Act (ADEA) of 1967	Age discrimination	Private companies with 20 or more employees, unions, employment agencies

Source: Adapted from J. Ledvinka and V. Scarpello, *Federal Regulation of Personnel and Human Resource Management* (Boston: PWS-Kent, 1991).

Some laws and cases pertain specifically to compensation; they will be addressed in Chapter 8. The key points of the laws summarized in Table 2.1 are discussed in greater detail next, followed by some additional topics, such as genetic discrimination and retaliation.

Discrimination on the Basis of Race, Color, Religion, Sex, and National Origin

Although the Civil Rights Act of 1866 passed almost one hundred years earlier, not until the Civil Rights Act of 1964 did employment discrimination laws have much impact. The Civil Rights Act of 1991 clarified a number of subsequent issues that arose. Why wasn't the Civil Rights Act of 1866 more helpful in combating employment discrimination? Examination of the Civil Rights Act of 1866 may provide some clues. The law states that "All persons within the jurisdiction of the United States shall have the same right in every State and Territory to make and enforce contracts . . . as is enjoyed by white citizens." What exactly does that statement cover? For many years this law was interpreted very narrowly by the courts. For example, it was initially understood to apply only to cases involving a governmental organization discriminating against someone, but not to a private company (for example, General Motors). A person charging discrimination by a private-sector company therefore could not win under this law. In addition, the **Civil Rights Act of 1866** prohibits only racial discrimination, not other forms of discrimination.[5]

The **Civil Rights Act of 1964** was, therefore, the first comprehensive, broad federal law banning employment discrimination in the United States. This law has many different parts. The section of the Civil Rights Act of 1964 that is most applicable to the employment area is known as Title VII. The highlights of Title VII are as follows:

1. Prohibits discrimination on the basis of race, color, religion, sex, or national origin (it doesn't matter what race, color, religion, sex, or national origin you are);

2. Provides for an agency, the **Equal Employment Opportunity Commission** (or, as it is usually referred to, the **EEOC**), to process discrimination charges and write regulations pertinent to congressional laws. One of the best-known set of regulations is called the Uniform Guidelines on Employee Selection Procedures, which outlines technical requirements for defending employment tests in a discrimination charge. In addition to these responsibilities, the EEOC is responsible for receiving EEO-1 reports, filed annually by companies with one hundred or more workers, which report the number of women and minorities employed at the organization. Other organizations, such as employment agencies, apprenticeship programs, and labor unions, must file similar reports.

Amendments and changes have been applied to the Civil Rights Act of 1964 over the years. One of these amendments is the **Pregnancy Discrimination Act of 1978,** which Congress passed to overturn a related Supreme Court decision. Under this law, an employer

1. Cannot require a maternity leave of a particular length, unless specifically related to ability to perform the job.

2. Must provide the same terms and conditions for a leave of absence for childbirth as is provided for other medical conditions.

Civil Rights Act of 1866
The first of many laws banning race discrimination in private companies, unions, and employment agencies, passed in 1866.

Civil Rights Act of 1964
A comprehensive law banning workplace discrimination (which covers race, color, religion, sex, and national origin) passed in 1964.

Equal Employment Opportunity Commission (EEOC)
Created by Title VII of the Civil Rights Act of 1964, the agency that processes discrimination charges and writes regulations pertinent to congressional laws.

Pregnancy Discrimination Act of 1978
An amendment to the Civil Rights Act of 1964 which states that an employer cannot require maternity leave of a particular length; must provide the same terms and conditions for a leave of absence for childbirth as is provided for other medical conditions; and must offer those returning from medical leave the same or an equivalent job and employment conditions.

3. Must offer those returning from medical leave the same or equivalent job and employment conditions.[6]

The impetus behind the **Civil Rights Act of 1991** derived from controversial Supreme Court decisions during the late 1980s. Key changes resulting from the Civil Rights Act of 1991 include:[7]

1. Making it somewhat easier for employees and job applicants to win lawsuits (unlike some Supreme Court decisions that had made this more difficult).
2. Prohibiting the use of different norms, based on race or sex, for scoring tests (which in some cases had become commonly used).
3. Permitting use of jury trials (which was not allowed under the Civil Rights Act of 1964).
4. Expanding coverage of discrimination laws to U.S. citizens working for U.S. companies based in other countries (who previously were not covered in that case).
5. Allowing employees and job applicants to win punitive damages in certain circumstances (this was not allowed under the Civil Rights Act of 1964).
6. Prohibiting individuals who had notice of a proposed consent decree (i.e., *affirmative action* program) and an opportunity to object to this program from later suing on the grounds that they were discriminated against under this program.

In addition to the Civil Rights Acts of 1866, 1964, and 1991, other laws prohibit discrimination on the basis of national origin. The **Immigration Reform and Control Act (IRCA),** for example, provides additional protection against discrimination on the basis of national origin and even protects certain noncitizens of the United States, such as permanent residents of the United States or those who have declared an intention to gain citizenship in the United States.[8]

Discrimination on the Basis of Disabilities

Not until the early 1970s did a law, the **Rehabilitation Act of 1973,** pass that prohibited discrimination against disabled individuals. Even so, as you can see in Table 2.1, this law was relatively limited in coverage, as it applies only to government employers or businesses having contracts with the federal government. It took almost 20 more years to pass the **Americans with Disabilities Act (ADA) of 1990** to prohibit most other employers from discriminating against the disabled. That it took so long for a comprehensive law of this nature is surprising, given that it has been estimated that 8.6 percent of Americans between the ages of sixteen and sixty-four have some form of disability, and almost one-third of these either work or are actively seeking work.[9]

Given the widespread coverage of ADA, most of what you will read here pertains to this law. Keep in mind, however, that for the most part, the Rehabilitation Act of 1973 is similar in scope and application.

Defining *Disability*

Simply put, according to the ADA, an organization cannot discriminate against an individual with a disability who is otherwise qualified to perform the job. Each of the key terms here needs to be clearly understood. First, what is a disability? If you examine Table 2.2, you will observe that the employee or applicant need not have an *actual* dis-

---

Civil Rights Act of 1991
A further delineation of civil rights, resulting from several controversial Supreme Court decisions during the late 1980s. Some key changes include making it easier for employees and job applicants to win lawsuits; prohibiting the use of different norms, based on race or sex, for scoring tests; permitting use of jury trials; expanding coverage of discrimination laws to U.S. citizens working for U.S. companies based in other countries; and allowing employees and job applicants to win punitive damages.

Immigration Reform and Control Act
Provides additional protection against discrimination on the basis of national origin, and even protects certain noncitizens of the United States, such as individuals who are permanent residents of the United States or who have declared an intention to gain citizenship in the United States.

Rehabilitation Act of 1973
Prohibits discrimination against disabled individuals; applies only to government employees or businesses having contracts with the federal government.

Americans with Disabilities Act of 1990
Prohibits most other employers from discriminating against the disabled. Addresses the definition of disability and requires that employers offer reasonable accommodations.

ability. Even if the individual once had the disability or is *assumed* by the manager to have a disability, he or she may be protected from discrimination by this law. Now, consider more closely the first type of individual covered by this law: An individual with a physical or mental *impairment* that substantially limits one or more *major life activities*. According to the EEOC, an impairment could affect neurological, respiratory, skin, digestive, or other body systems. A major life activity includes walking, seeing, caring for one's self, hearing, speaking, or even learning.[10]

Now that you know how an actual disability is defined, how do you think the courts would consider someone who is HIV-positive? Remember that HIV is the virus that causes AIDS. Someone who is HIV-positive may not exhibit any outward indication of the disease. Assume that this individual has no outward sign of disability— would you still consider him or her as having a disability under ADA? In the summer of 1998, the United States Supreme Court ruled on a case regarding HIV. In that particular case, a woman who was HIV-positive sought treatment from a dentist to fill a cavity. The dentist refused to treat her in his office, insisting that she be treated in a hospital, because he believed that greater precautions were necessary, despite official medical guidelines to the contrary. So what major "life activities" were limited by the plaintiff being HIV-positive? The woman argued that being HIV-positive limited her ability to conceive and reproduce a child. Thus, even though being HIV-positive did not completely rule out conceiving and reproducing, nor might you think that this was a "major life activity," the Supreme Court ruled that she was to be considered to have an actual disability under ADA.[11]

Alcoholism is another disability that is protected under ADA. However, an organization may prohibit the use of alcohol at work and may prohibit employees from working under the influence of alcohol. ADA also states that an alcoholic can be held

---

Table 2.2	**Who Is and Who Is Not Covered by ADA**

The Following Individuals Would Be Covered by ADA:	The Following Conditions Are Not Covered by ADA:
1. An individual with a physical or mental impairment that substantially limits one or more major life activities of the individual (for example, someone who uses a wheelchair).	1. Various sexual disorders, such as pedophilia and transvestitism.
2. An individual with a record of such an impairment (for example, someone who has had heart disease).	2. Compulsive gambling, kleptomania, or pyromania.
3. An individual who is regarded as having such an impairment (for example, someone the interviewer believes has a learning disability, even though the individual has no such disability).	3. Psychoactive substance-use disorders.
4. An individual who has a business, family, or social relationship with someone with a disability (for example, the individual has a physically disabled child).	4. Homosexuality and bisexuality.
	5. Current illegal drug use.
5. Former drug addicts.	6. Temporary disabilities (for example, a broken leg that will heal soon).

Source: Adapted from the U.S. Equal Employment Opportunity Commission, *Technical Assistance Manual on the Employment Provisions (Title I) of the Americans with Disabilities Act* (Washington: U.S. Government Printing Office, 1992).

to the same qualification standards and job performance requirements as are applied to other employees.[12]

Finally, an individual who suffers from attention deficit–hyperactivity disorder (ADHD) may potentially be considered to have a disability. This may be a particularly troublesome situation for an organization because no objectively verifiable standards yet exist for diagnostic purposes, and yet individuals with this condition tend to be impulsive, have trouble organizing their work, and procrastinate.[13]

Defining *Qualified*

Simply stated, according to the ADA, a *qualified* individual is someone who is able to perform the *essential* functions of the job with or without a reasonable accommodation. Typically, functions are the tasks or responsibilities the position involves. For example, the functions of a restaurant host might include greeting customers, escorting customers to an available table, maintaining a list of customers' names when there is a wait, refilling beverages, and wrapping cutlery in napkins. On occasion, when the restaurant is busy, another function may be to help remove dishes and other objects from tables. In addition, *function* seems to apply to other job requirements, such as regular attendance, overtime, and weekend work, taking directions from supervisors, and so forth, that we might think of as workplace rules and regulations.

Essential and Nonessential Functions

Now that you know what functions are, you may be wondering what "essential" functions are, as compared to "nonessential" functions. According to the EEOC, an essential function is a basic job duty. To determine whether a function is essential, the manager must consider whether the position exists primarily to perform that function (for example, a typist job exists to type, so typing would be an essential function), the number of other employees who can perform that function (for example, if only one person can perform that function, it may be an essential function), and the degree of expertise and skill required (the higher the skill level required, the more likely the function is essential). A work rule, such as regular attendance, will probably be considered essential if it makes good business sense and is required of all employees. Using the example of the restaurant host's job described above, all of the functions might be considered "essential," except for helping to remove dishes from tables, because other employees might be able to do this when necessary.

Accommodation

In addition to protecting applicants and employees from discrimination on the basis of a disability, both the Rehabilitation Act of 1973 and the ADA require that employers go one step further by offering **reasonable accommodation.** Simply put, a reasonable accommodation is "a modification or adjustment to a job, the work environment, or the way things usually are done that enables a qualified individual with a disability to enjoy an equal employment opportunity."[14] A reasonable accommodation must be provided for the following purposes:

1. To provide equal opportunity in the application process.
2. To enable a qualified individual with a disability to perform the job.

reasonable accommodation
A modification or adjustment to a job, the work environment, or the way things usually are done that enables a qualified individual with a disability to enjoy an equal employment opportunity.

Table 2.3	**Reasonable Accommodations: Some Examples**

1. Providing equal opportunity in the application process. When an applicant who is visually impaired ("blind") applies for a job, the company must provide an accommodation to enable this applicant to complete the application blank, take written tests, and fill out other necessary paperwork.
2. Enabling the applicant or employee to perform the job. The job requires the employee to read brief reports. The applicant, who is visually impaired, but qualified for the job, cannot be denied the job on the basis of the disability if access to the reports can be provided through such means as braille, tape recordings, or a reader.
3. Enabling the employee to have equal benefits and privileges of employment. The employee cannot be treated differently because of his or her disability. For example, he or she cannot be denied health insurance. Due to insurance companies' policies, this may create problems for employers and disabled employees.
4. Some specific examples and costs of accommodations enabling companies to accommodate disabled employees include the following:
   - Providing a drafting table, page turner, and special tape recorder to a sales agent paralyzed by a broken neck ($950).
   - Supplying a telephone amplifier for a computer programmer who was hard of hearing ($56).
   - Providing padded wrist-rests under a computer keyboard to alleviate repetitive motion strain ($35).

Source: Adapted from information from the Job Accommodation Network (JAN) and C. Koen, S. Hartman, and S. Crow, "Health Insurance: The ADA's Missing Link," *Personnel Journal*, November 1991, 82–7.

3. To enable an employee with a disability to have equal benefits and privileges of employment.[15]

Table 2.3 provides an example of each of these purposes.

According to the EEOC, more than half of accommodations cost companies nothing. More than 80 percent of accommodations cost a company less than $500. Under what circumstances could an employer deny an accommodation? Under ADA, a company could refuse to accommodate if it could prove that to do so would create an **undue hardship.** An undue hardship would exist if the accommodation would involve considerable expense or difficulty to the company. For example, redesigning a work area might cost hundreds of thousands of dollars, which for a small business could make the difference between profitability and bankruptcy. Just what constitutes too much expense or difficulty is not clearly defined under ADA. It will probably take several court decisions to clarify this issue. Given the previous information about the relatively low cost of many accommodations, though, it is unlikely that the EEOC will willingly accept this as a defense.[16] The President's Committee on Employment of People with Disabilities, in conjunction with a private organization, has established a free service that provides help to companies with accommodations (the telephone number is 1-800-526-7234 or see www.jan.wvu.edu).

At this point you may be wondering, "What if hiring an applicant or retaining the employee creates a danger to safety or health?" For example, what if a person with a visual impairment applies for a factory assembly-line job involving various power saws,

undue hardship
Exists if the accommodation to enable a qualified individual with a disability to enjoy an equal employment opportunity would involve considerable expense or difficulty to the company.

drills, and other dangerous equipment? Under the ADA, a company may refuse to hire or retain an employee if a direct threat exists to the health or safety of the person or to other workers. However, if the company was charged with discrimination, the employer would need to show objective evidence that a specific risk was involved, that it could result in substantial harm to individuals, and that a reasonable accommodation reducing or eliminating the risk could not be applied.[17] Figure 2.1 shows a comparison of employment-related discrimination charges filed with the EEOC.

In addition to these points, the ADA places some additional requirements and restrictions on employers. We describe four of these in more detail next.[18]

1. **ADA Differentiates Between a Pre-Job Offer Stage and a Post-Job Offer Stage.** According to ADA, a distinct difference exists between the types of questions that an organization can ask in the pre-job offer stage and in the post-job offer stage. Specifically, prior to making a job offer to the applicant, the employer is prohibited from asking a question that is disability-related (for example, what medications do you use?) or any question that is likely to lead to information about a disability (for example, how many days did you miss due to illness last year?). In addition, with few exceptions, the employer may not ask the applicant whether he or she will need a reasonable accommodation to perform the job. All of these questions, however, may be asked of applicants in the post-job offer stage; in other

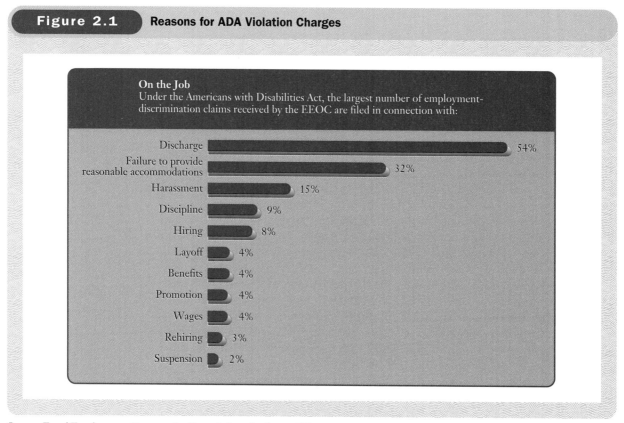

Figure 2.1   **Reasons for ADA Violation Charges**

On the Job
Under the Americans with Disabilities Act, the largest number of employment-discrimination claims received by the EEOC are filed in connection with:

Discharge	54%
Failure to provide reasonable accommodations	32%
Harassment	15%
Discipline	9%
Hiring	8%
Layoff	4%
Benefits	4%
Promotion	4%
Wages	4%
Rehiring	3%
Suspension	2%

Source: Equal Employment Opportunity Commission, fiscal year 1997.

words, once a job offer has been made, the employer can ask such questions. However, if the applicant is then denied a job, the organization must be able to show that the reason for the rejection is legitimate.

2. **ADA Prohibits Medical Examinations Prior to a Job Offer.** Although medical examinations could be given after a job offer is made, they are not permitted before making a job offer. Of concern to companies is what constitutes a medical examination. For example, is a vision test considered a medical examination? What do you think? If your answer was that it depends on how the vision test is conducted, you are right. In general, an examination conducted by a health professional (for example, a nurse), using medical equipment (for example, a stethoscope), measuring physiological responses (for example, heart rate), given in a medical setting (for example, in a doctor's office), would be considered a medical examination. On the other hand, if a police department had an obstacle course that job applicants were required to complete within a certain time limit, this would *not* be considered a medical examination, assuming that heart rate or other physiological responses were not measured. Similarly, some personality tests may be considered medical examinations, whereas others would not.

3. **ADA and Drug and Alcohol Testing.** Drug testing may be conducted under this law. Furthermore, a drug test is not considered a medical examination, so it may be performed before a job offer is made. On the other hand, alcohol testing is considered a medical examination. Therefore, an alcohol test may not be given until after a job offer is made.

4. **Employee Medical Information Must be Kept Confidential.** In general, companies may not release medical information about employees to other parties, including supervisors, coworkers, and others. The exceptions include the following:
   a. Supervisors and managers may be informed about work restrictions and necessary accommodations;
   b. First aid and safety personnel may be told if an individual with a disability might require emergency treatment.

In addition, medical information must be kept in a file separate from the regular personnel file.

Discrimination on the Basis of Age

Age discrimination was prohibited in the broader context by the **Age Discrimination in Employment Act (ADEA) of 1967** and in the federal government by **Executive Order 11141.** An *executive order* is a law passed by the president of the United States. Unlike a *congressional act*, such as the ADEA, an executive order does not require approval by Congress. Executive orders in the employment context, though, generally apply only to federal employees and companies doing business with the federal government.

When first passed, the ADEA applied only to individuals between the ages of 40 and 65, meaning that, once you turned 65, a company could require that you retire or discriminate against you in other ways (for example, pay you less). After changing the coverage to include individuals under 70 years old in 1978, Congress abolished the age cap in subsequent years for almost all jobs, with the exception of certain executives.

Under current laws then, a discrimination charge could be brought by an employee who was 102 or even older! Nonetheless, ADEA still only applies to employees

Age Discrimination in Employment Act of 1967 Prohibits age discrimination. When first passed, it applied only to individuals between the ages of 40 and 65. In 1978, it was changed to include individuals under 70 years of age. In subsequent years, Congress abolished the age cap for almost all jobs.

or applicants who are at least 40 years old. Does that mean that under ADEA your company could discriminate against you on the basis of age if you were 25? If you answered yes, you are right. However, some states (Minnesota, Florida, and Michigan, to name a few) have laws that ban discrimination on the basis of age at ages far younger than 40. This is a good example of how some states have laws that provide more protection to employees than does the federal law.[19] Box 2.1 reviews an age discrimination case that occurred in California.

Age discrimination suits can be extremely expensive for the organization. For example, in 1997, Westinghouse Electric and Northrup Grumman agreed to pay $14 million to settle an age discrimination lawsuit filed by 800 older workers who were terminated during the early 1990s. First Union, a major bank, agreed to pay over $50 million to 239 older workers at banks it had recently acquired.[20]

Although age discrimination suits have arisen for many reasons, including failure to hire and promote, one of the most common reasons for filing an age discrimination lawsuit is termination or reduction in workforce. One of the most damaging things for a company is for managers or supervisors to make either verbal or written statements that either directly or indirectly refer to the age of an employee. Take, for example, an organizational document written by the manager responsible for reducing the size of his company's workforce. The document, entitled "Young Managers," included statements such as "Top and middle managers are mostly young, well educated, and results oriented." In another case, the CEO himself noted that "people over 45, myself included, have trouble adjusting to change." These type of cases are the most damaging to organizations because written documents are hard for the organization to refute.

Oral comments, such as ones made by a supervisor who referred to an older employee as "a sleepy kind of guy, droopy, with no pizzazz" and "old and tired," were assumed by the court to be indicative of discriminatory intent. However, not all age-related comments will be viewed by the courts as indicative of age discrimination. Specifically, courts have indicated that age-related comments are not reflective of discrimination under the following conditions:

1. The comments were "stray remarks," or remarks that had no direct relationship to the HRM decision;
2. The comments were made by an employee who did not make the HRM decision at issue;
3. The comments were made by someone who made the decision at issue but the comments were unrelated to that decision.[21]

Discrimination on the Basis of Sexual Orientation

Although sex discrimination is prohibited, the Civil Rights Acts of 1964 and 1991 do not prohibit discrimination based on sexual orientation. However, using sexual orientation to treat employees differently is considered discrimination in eight states (such as Minnesota and New Jersey) and more than 100 municipalities (such as Washington, D.C.). To date, however, the courts have concluded that none of the federal civil rights acts covers sexual orientation.[22]

Discrimination on the Basis of Religion

As you should have noted above, freedom from discrimination on the basis of religion is prohibited by the Civil Rights Act of 1964. In addition, employees who work for a

TALES FROM THE TRENCHES

Box 2.1
An Age Discrimination Case

Maurice Crommie and Arthur Mangold sued their employer, the California Public Utilities Commission (PUC), on the grounds of age discrimination. Crommie and Mangold claimed that they had been held back from receiving promotions for about six years because they were both more than 40 years old. Mr. Mangold had spent his entire career with PUC and had a bachelor's degree in engineering and business administration. Mr. Crommie had an undergraduate degree in engineering, three master's degrees, and coursework for two doctoral programs. He had extensive experience in the aerospace industry. Promotions at PUC followed a multistep process. After an opening was announced, each candidate would submit a self-evaluation, which was reviewed by his or her supervisor. The supervisor would also rate the candidate on a five-point scale. This information would then pass on to the next level in the organization, followed by a "promotional readiness examination." The promotional readiness examinations consisted of somewhat subjective questions submitted and evaluated by a panel of three or four directors or assistant directors. PUC maintained that Crommie and Mangold failed to be promoted because they performed poorly on these examinations. Crommie and Mangold argued that PUC's promotion process was biased in several ways. First, they argued that the questions in the examination were based on experience in jobs at PUC that were primarily granted to younger employees. Second, they argued that supervisors rated younger employees higher on the promotion evaluations. Third, they argued that the panels consisted primarily of directors and assistant directors who supervised many of the young employees. In addition, the plaintiffs and some of their coworkers testified to various comments that had been made by various members of PUC's top management, such as the comment to Maurice Crommie by one director that "we want fresh young blood in this group." In another instance, the president/executive director of PUC was quoted as saying: "We're going into a bright new future in which we have an excellent staff of *young* (emphasis added) professional people who will be able to carry us into this bright new future. . . ." Finally, some of the panel members testified to being pressured by other panel members to lower their ratings of Mr. Crommie, while raising the rating of a younger employee. After losing the case in the trial, PUC appealed the case to the 9th Circuit Court. The Court of Appeals ruled in favor of Crommie and Mangold.

Source: Adapted from *Mangold v. California Public Utilities Commission* 67 F.3d 1470.

government organization may be protected by the First Amendment to the Constitution, which allows freedom to practice one's religion. Although relatively few discrimination charges are filed annually with the EEOC regarding religion (only 1,709 were filed in 1997), managers and organizations must be careful not to discriminate against applicants and employees on the basis of their religion or religious practices. Unlike other protected categories covered by Title VII of the Civil Rights Act of 1964, employers also have a legal obligation to try to accommodate the religious practices of workers.[23]

Most discrimination lawsuits involving religion are based on either dress codes or work scheduling. For example, Alma Dolores Reardon, who converted to Islam in the early 1980s, was barred from working as a substitute teacher in the Philadelphia public school system because she wore a head scarf and long flowing dresses. The school asserted that this was a violation of its dress code. Simcha Goldman, a Jewish officer in the U.S. Air Force, was prohibited from wearing a skullcap while on duty. The U.S. Air Force argued that use of distinctively different clothing would diminish cohesiveness and encourage disobedience. It may surprise you to know that the employees lost in both cases.[24]

Relatively more cases have involved work scheduling. In its first such discrimination case, which occurred in 1977, the Supreme Court of the United States ruled that airline TWA had done enough to accommodate Larry Hardison, a follower of the Worldwide Church of God, who refused to work on his Sabbath. In ruling on his case, the Supreme Court indicated that neither a union nor the organization is required to go beyond the collective bargaining agreement to accommodate an individual's religious preferences. In short, the Supreme Court stated what became known as "de minimis" rule, which means that the employer need exert only minimum cost and effort to accommodate the individual's religious requirements. Recent rulings indicate that organizations must be careful to try to accommodate employees' religious practices with work schedules, but at this point in time, organizations tend to win more of these cases than they lose.[25]

Discrimination Based on Genetics

Scientists have made great strides in the past ten years in identifying genetically transmitted genes, such as cystic fibrosis, Gaucher's disease, and Huntington's disease. According to one recent survey, 15 percent of companies plan to test for genetic status of applicants in the near future. The concern for applicants and employees is that such tests will be used to unfairly discriminate against them. Consider, for example, what would happen if your employer discovered that you had a 50 percent chance of having inherited sickle-cell anemia. Do you think it is possible that you would be fired? Believe it or not, stories circulate of companies that have fired people on that basis. Do employees and applicants have any legal protection from genetic discrimination? At present, we have four possible sources of legal protection from this type of discrimination:

1. The Health Insurance Portability and Accountability Act (HIPAA) prohibits group health plans from using health-related information, including genetic information, as a reason to deny or restrict eligibility for coverage;
2. The Americans with Disabilities Act (ADA) indicates that people with symptomatic genetic disorders are protected because this constitutes a disability. However, the status of people who have no symptoms of a genetic disease, but are discriminated against because of a *predisposition* for a genetic disease, is unclear under ADA;
3. The Civil Rights Act of 1964 (CRA) may potentially apply when genetic testing is used for the purpose of detecting racially or ethnically based genetic disorders. For example, Jews of Eastern European descent are more likely to be carriers of Tay-Sachs disease; African Americans have a greater susceptibility than other ethnic groups for sickle-cell anemia. Companies conducting tests to identify such predispositions might potentially be sued for religious or racial discrimination.
4. State laws have been enacted in some cases. In Oregon, for example, companies are prohibited from testing or using genetic information to make employment decisions. A similar law exists in Texas. Some states, such as Florida and North Carolina, merely ban discrimination based on specific disorders such as sickle-cell (Florida) and hemoglobin (North Carolina). Forty-six states remain without such laws.[26]

Retaliation

It is illegal for a company to retaliate against, or punish, an employee who is involved in an employment discrimination case. According to recent guidelines issued by the

EEOC, the following employee activities are protected by the law; in other words, the company may not dismiss, discipline, or otherwise warn employees who do any of the following:

1. Threaten to or actually file a discrimination charge against the company
2. Complain to coworkers, managers, or even customers about alleged discrimination against them or other employees
3. Refuse to obey an order from a supervisor or manager because they reasonably believe that the order is discriminatory

Even former employees can sue their previous employers. For example, a company can be sued if it tells another organization that the employee had filed a discrimination charge. Moreover, if the former employer refuses to give the other organization a reference, this can be grounds for a lawsuit. You should know that the number of charges of retaliation filed with the EEOC has risen considerably over the years, from 7,906 filed in 1991 to 18,113 filed in 1997. Companies must therefore be careful in how they handle and respond to employees' complaints of discrimination.[27]

Proving a Discrimination Case

Now that you have learned about the various laws banning discrimination in the workplace, and who is covered by those laws, you may be wondering how you would prove you were discriminated against. You probably are also wondering what the company would need to defend itself if you were charging discrimination. Just how one proves that discrimination has occurred is not an easy matter. Consider for a moment the company's perspective. The company may receive hundreds, perhaps thousands, of applications for a particular job. But only a handful of workers can be hired. Or, in the case of a large reduction in the workforce, hundreds of thousands of employees may work for the company, and due to business losses, the company may need to reduce the workforce by 10 percent. As a result, many people will lose their jobs. Typically, the company doing the hiring or the layoff will want to consider qualifications, such as education, work experience, skills, and other job-related factors, such as past performance. Some of these factors may be quite objective, such as a college degree; others may seem quite subjective to you, such as an applicant's communication skills. Factors such as seniority may seem best to you because of their objectivity. Subjective factors, like work motivation and customer relations, however, may be far more important to the company, even though they are less quantifiable. Therefore, what might seem to the rejected applicants or terminated employees to be a clear case of discrimination may be nothing more than the company making the best decision given limited and often subjective information.

Now consider the applicant/employee perspective. Substantial data (some of which is discussed in this chapter and some of which is reviewed in other chapters) suggest that, at least in the past, women and minorities, as well as other groups, have suffered from lower wages and limited employment opportunities. And, no doubt people of both sexes, all races, colors, religions, and backgrounds have experienced discrimination at some point in time. It is safe to say that discrimination does occur sometimes. It is also safe to say that at times what might have seemed like discrimination was not. The major point here is that it is often unclear whether discrimination has occurred or not. Over the years, several approaches have evolved for bringing and defending discrimination cases: *intentional discrimination*, *disparate treatment*, and *adverse impact*. Let us examine each of these approaches in greater detail.[28]

Intentional Discrimination

intentional discrimination
A practice where employers refuse to hire applicants of a particular race, religion, or gender simply out of prejudice; earlier referred to as *evil intent.*

bona fide occupational qualification (BFOQ)
Suitable defense against a discrimination charge only where age, religion, sex, or national origin is an actual qualification for performing the job.

In earlier times, employers often would refuse to hire applicants of a particular race, religion, or gender simply out of prejudice, a practice referred to as **intentional discrimination.** Can you think of any situations where a company might legitimately exclude people of a certain religion, sex, or national origin? What about a model for men's clothing or a women's bathroom attendant? In fact, under the Civil Rights Act of 1964, an organization may defend the decision to hire people of a certain religion, sex, or national origin where this characteristic constitutes a **bona fide occupational qualification (BFOQ).**[29] The most recent example of a BFOQ involved Hooter's, a national chain of restaurants that features young, scantily dressed women as foodservers. A man applied for a job of foodserver and was turned down. Hooter's claimed that being a woman was a BFOQ, in order to maintain their marketing strategy. The courts have accepted the BFOQ defense in cases such as a model for clothing and an Asian restaurant wishing to ensure authenticity (and therefore only hiring Asian servers). On the other hand, the courts have rejected the company's BFOQ defense in cases such as a refusal to hire men as flight attendants and the exclusion of fertile women from jobs involving contact with toxic chemicals, which potentially could harm a fetus. In general, it is safe to say that an organization that openly excludes persons on the basis of their religion, sex, or national origin will have a difficult time defending the action.

Rather than having a formal policy not to hire applicants from a certain racial group, age, gender, and so on, representatives of the company may make statements that suggest such a policy exists in a more informal fashion. In one case, for example, Otis Felton, a black machine operator, was denied a promotion to production supervisor. Witnesses testified that managerial employees responsible for the promotion decision had made various derogatory statements in the past, such as "if it was . . . [my] company, . . . [I] wouldn't hire any black people."[30] Once it can be proven that such statements were made, the plaintiff must show that there is a link between the statements and the employment decision. For example, in one case, the employer allegedly made statements that "women are not good sailors." When a woman was denied a job requiring work on a ship, this statement was used as evidence of discrimination.[31]

Finally, what would you say as the judge if a company argued that even though some discriminatory remarks had been made, the applicant would have been rejected anyhow, based on job-related factors? This was the company's response in a recent case where a woman rejected for promotion to the partnership level charged the company with making a variety of discriminatory statements about her. The company's defense was that regardless of the sexist comments, the same decision would have been made, because sufficient work-related problems prevented her promotion. Because there were both job-related, legitimate reasons as well as non-job-related, discriminatory reasons involved, this is referred to as a mixed-motive case. The Civil Rights Act of 1991 states that a company would lose a mixed-motive case, overturning a 1989 Supreme Court decision.

Turning back to the hypothetical situation posed at the beginning of this chapter, the first question to ask is what law(s) could Maria use to file a discrimination charge. If Maria believes that sex or race discrimination was occurring, she could file a charge under the Civil Rights Acts of 1964 and 1991. Second, recall that Maria did not mention that any specific discriminatory statements or comments had been made. Nevertheless, it is possible that examination of documents or statements made to others could be used to advance a discrimination case. Given the limited information presented in the opening case, it may be difficult to prove intentional discrimination. The next approach to bringing a lawsuit may therefore be more relevant.

Disparate Treatment

A classic form of discrimination involves **disparate treatment,** in which the employer treats people differently, depending on their age, sex, race, or other protected categories. For example, employers in the past often asked women if they had children, but did not ask the same question of male applicants. In general, treating people differently in the employment context is discrimination. In 1973, in the ***McDonnell-Douglas v. Green*** case, the Supreme Court of the United States described a somewhat more elaborate three-step process for examining hiring or promotion discrimination under the disparate treatment concept.[32] The three steps are as follows:

Step 1. The plaintiff (employee or applicant) must show that he or she is from a protected class (that is, a racial or ethnic minority, female, or over 40 years old), applied for a job for which a vacancy existed, was qualified for the job, was rejected, and the employer continued to seek other persons or selected a person of a different class. This is often referred to as *prima facie evidence* (meaning evidence sufficient to establish a fact or presumption of a fact). For example, a woman might establish that she applied for promotion to a midlevel management position, had three years of relevant experience, was rejected, and that ten males were promoted.

Step 2. If the plaintiff can prove all of the required points in Step 1, the defendant or company must provide a *legitimate, nondiscriminatory reason* for rejecting the plaintiff. Legitimate reasons may include seniority, education, experience, and other job-relevant factors. For example, following along with the previous example, the company might defend their failure to promote her by stating they had a policy of promoting only employees who had an MBA or equivalent graduate degree.

Step 3. If the defendant can provide an acceptable legitimate, nondiscriminatory reason for rejecting the plaintiff, the plaintiff has the opportunity in Step 3 to show that this reason was simply a pretext or cover-up for discrimination. Following the above example, the female plaintiff may show that some other employees who were promoted (for example, males) lacked an MBA or equivalent graduate degree. Alternatively, the plaintiff may show that her gender somehow played a role in the rejection decision. It is noteworthy that in a recent Supreme Court decision *(St. Mary's Honor Center v. Hicks)*, the Court concluded that even if the plaintiff can show pretext, it may still be necessary for the plaintiff to prove the company was motivated to discriminate against him or her.[33]

Returning to the opening case in this chapter, Maria would have to show that she belonged to a protected class (that she was a woman, racial or ethnic minority, or over 40 years old, for example), a vacancy existed (even though it did not advertise positions, the company made promotions, indicating vacancies existed from time to time), she was at least minimally qualified for promotion, and she was rejected for the position (that is, not promoted). Would she meet all these criteria? Even if she did, the company usually has a great deal of leeway in the legitimate, nondiscriminatory reason offered. For example, it may be able to show that the other people who were promoted

disparate treatment
When an employer treats people differently or evaluates them by different standards, depending on their age, sex, race, or other protected categories.

McDonnell-Douglas v. Green
A 1973 case that outlined a more elaborate three-step process for examining hiring or promotion discrimination under the disparate treatment concept.

had higher performance appraisal ratings. Or, perhaps the people promoted had obtained an MBA. In such a case, it would be important for Maria to try to show that the company was inconsistent in their promotion policy. Finally, a key issue is whether remarks were made suggesting they discriminated against people of Maria's protected class. Clearly, much more information would be needed to determine whether she had a reasonable chance of proving discrimination under the disparate treatment approach. Box 2.2 describes a case in which e-mail communications provided evidence in a discrimination suit.

Adverse Impact

adverse impact
The selection process or procedure has a disproportionate effect on a protected group (for example, women).

Unlike disparate treatment, which focuses on the *individual* who may have been discriminated against, **adverse impact** focuses on the plaintiff's *group* as a whole. The adverse impact approach is perhaps the most controversial way to advance a discrimination case. This concept was first articulated by the Supreme Court of the United States in the *Griggs v. Duke Power* case, shortly after the passage of the Civil Rights Act of 1964.[34] Griggs was a part of a *class action* suit, in which a large group of people in a similar situation, allow a representative to sue on their behalf. In this particular case, the suit involved charges of race discrimination against Duke Power, a power-generating facility located in North Carolina. The suit charged race discrimination with regard to hiring and job assignment: blacks were employed only in the lowest-paying department of the facility. In order to qualify for placement in the other departments, an applicant had to have a high school degree or pass two professionally developed tests: the Wonderlic Personnel test, which measures general cognitive ability, and the Bennett Mechanical Comprehension Test, which measures knowledge of mechanical principles. The first black person to be employed in the other departments was not hired until after the race discrimination charge had been filed. A lower court had ruled in favor of the company, pointing out that the Civil Rights Act of 1964 specifically allows use of professionally developed ability tests and finding no evidence of *intention* to discriminate against blacks.

The Supreme Court, however, issued a different interpretation of the Civil Rights Act of 1964 and ruled against the company. (See *Griggs v. Duke Power Co.*, 401 U.S. 424.) In explaining this decision, the Supreme Court asserted that the goal of the Civil Rights Act of 1964 was to remove discriminatory barriers that had existed in the past and to actively advance the employment opportunities of minorities. Therefore, tests or other procedures that were "neutral on their face, and even neutral in terms of intent" would be deemed discriminatory if they served to maintain the status quo of prior practices. Because the selection procedures were serving as a barrier to the employment of blacks, albeit unintentionally, the Supreme Court ruled that the company was guilty of discrimination. Over the next 25 years, in conjunction with the EEOC's Uniform Guidelines on Employee Selection Procedures and the Civil Rights Act of 1991, an adverse impact case has been determined to involve the following three steps:

applicant flow
A method of assessing whether the plaintiff's group was adversely affected by the selection procedure that involves comparison of the hiring rate of the plaintiff's group to the hiring rate of the majority group.

Step 1. The plaintiff must show that his or her protected class was disproportionately affected by the selection practice, procedure, or test. Similar to a disparate treatment case, this constitutes the prima facie evidence that must be established. Two popular approaches are used by plaintiffs to establish prima facie evidence.[35]

- **Applicant Flow.** This method of assessing whether the plaintiff's group was adversely affected by the selection procedure involves comparison of the hiring rate

YOUR TURN

Box 2.2
Sending an E-mail: Would You be Embarrassed If a Jury Read It?

Because of the heavy use of e-mail in today's workplace, many court cases have begun to use e-mails as evidence of wrongdoing. For example, Airborne Freight Corporation lost a lawsuit filed by John Kelley for age discrimination when he was discharged after 19 years of service. Among the documents produced by the company in the case was a series of e-mails regarding Kelley, including one that implied that the company knew it was doing something wrong when it terminated him. The result? The jury awarded Kelley more than $3 million. E-mails can get employees and managers in trouble for more than just violating discrimina-tion laws. They have been used in antitrust, copyright infringement, and many other work-related lawsuits. Several suggestions may help employees and managers avoid these problems: First, avoid using e-mails to communicate about sensitive topics such as suspicions of employee misconduct, employee performance, hiring, or terminations. If you are using e-mail to send jokes to other employees or even friends, consider how your boss, coworkers, or a jury would respond if that joke were read aloud in front of them. Second, realize that e-mails are rarely completely deleted; in most cases, e-mails remain on a hard disk until the space is overwrit-ten. Even then, some files may be only partially overwritten, leaving e-mail fragments that can still be read. Third, if you are responsible for human resource issues, develop a policy of how and where electronic records are stored. Some electronic records may need to be stored for a certain amount of time (for example, electronic contracts). The policy should state where records are stored and for how long; the policy should also provide instruction on how the records are to be deleted to ensure that they are truly eliminated. Just remember, once a lawsuit begins, it may be too late to try to erase any e-mails.

Source: B. Sunoo, "E-mail Ends Up in Court?" *Workforce* 77 (July 1998): 37–8, 40–1.

of the plaintiff's group to the hiring rate of the majority group. Although several means of comparing the two selection rates are applied, a commonly used rule is the four-fifths (or 80 percent) rule. A specific example of this approach is shown in Box 2.3.

- **Stock Analysis.** An alternative approach for showing that the selection procedure had an adverse effect is to compare the percentage of the protected group members in the organization's workforce to the percentage of the protected group members in the labor market. Although some ambiguity may exist regarding the calculation of the percentage of the protected group members in the organization's workforce (for example, should part-time employees be counted?), things become far more complex when trying to calculate the percentage of protected group members in the labor market. The difficulty arises when one attempts to calculate precisely what the relevant labor market is (for instance, does it cover the entire city or county, the larger metropolitan area, the state, or the nation?) and who should be included in the relevant labor market (Should it include only qualified individuals? What constitutes "qualified"?). Given that decisions about such matters could have a tremendous effect on conclusions about the disproportionate effect of a hiring procedure, such issues are the source of much argument in the courts.

stock analysis
An alternative approach for showing that the selection procedure had an adverse effect is to compare the percentage of the protected group members in the organization's workforce to the percentage of the protected group members in the labor market.

Step 2. As in a disparate treatment case, if the plaintiff is able to successfully demonstrate prima facie evidence as described in Step 1, the company must provide a defense in Step 2. In an adverse impact case, the company must show that the selection or

TALES FROM THE TRENCHES

Box 2.3

Assessing Applicant Flow Using the Four-Fifths Rule

The EEOC's *Uniform Guidelines on Employee Selection Practices* suggest that one way to establish the disproportionate effect required in Step 1 of an adverse impact case is to use the 80 percent or four-fifths rule. Briefly stated, this rule establishes that the percentage of protected group members who are hired (or, in a promotion case, promoted) should be at least 80 percent of the percentage of majority group members who are hired (or, in a promotion case, promoted). In one case, for example, a test was administered as one step in the promotion process. Of the employees taking this test, 48 were African Americans and 259 were white. Twenty-six African Americans and 206 whites passed the test. Four African Americans failing the test sued on grounds of race discrimination. To assess whether or not the test met the 80 percent rule, you

would first divide 26 by 48 to obtain the minority pass rate of .54 (54 percent), and then divide 206 by 259 to determine the majority pass rate of .80 (80 percent). Did you calculate these two figures? You should have arrived at a pass rate of .54 or 54 percent for minorities, and .80 or 80 percent for majority employees. Now, divide .54 by .80 (that is, the pass rate of minorities by the pass rate of the majority), you should get a figure of .675 or, rounding off, 68 percent. In other words, the percentage of minorities who pass the test is 68 percent of the percentage of majority group members who pass the test. Because 68 percent is *less than* 80 percent, the organization fails to meet the 80 percent rule. In turn, this provides prima facie evidence of discrimination.

In the actual case, though, the organization defended its actions by fo-

cusing on the "bottom line." That is, the organization stated that the more appropriate number to look at was the percentage of minorities who were actually promoted after going through all the stages of the process. Because 11 blacks were promoted at the end, and 35 whites were promoted, the bottom-line pass rate for minorities was .23 (11 were promoted out of 48 who took the test) and .14 (35 were promoted out of 259 who took the test) for whites. Because .23 divided by .14 is 1.6 (or 160 percent), the organization would meet the 80 percent rule based on these figures. So, in the end, which set of numbers did the court accept? Ultimately, the court felt that the first set of figures, wherein the 80 percent rule was not met, were the relevant ones, and the organization therefore lost the case.

Source: Adapted from *Connecticut v. Teal*, 102 S.Ct. 2525, 73 (1982).

validation study
A method of demonstrating that a test is valid by statistically examining its relationship with job performance.

promotion procedures are "job related for the position in question and consistent with business necessity." The law does not define precisely what this entails. However, an organization has several possible ways to demonstrate this. One way is through a **validation study.**[36] Although Chapter 5 will describe a validation study in greater detail, one way a test can be shown to be valid is by statistically examining its relationship with job performance. That is, if scores on the test vary in tandem with measures of job performance, this is evidence that the test is valid. In cases not involving a test, such as an educational requirement (for example, a college degree), the company might explain the connection between the requirement and the job on logical grounds. For example, it would probably be legally acceptable to require applicants for an attorney's position to have a law degree.[37] Other defenses might be useful here as well, including a properly implemented seniority system.[38]

Step 3. Even if the company is able to successfully prove that the procedure used is job related, the plaintiff may attempt to show that there is an alternative selection procedure that has less adverse impact and yet is equally useful to the organization. For example, if an alternative test can be shown to have less adverse impact, but is equally effective in screening applicants, the organization may be required to adopt this alternative procedure in place of the original procedure.

Organizations can, and should, take certain steps to avoid discrimination charges. To avoid disparate treatment charges, organizations must be careful to avoid inconsistent decisions. For example, personnel policies must be applied uniformly. Every personnel decision must be based upon carefully documented job-related information. Non-job-related factors, particularly those related to sex, race, age, and so forth, should play absolutely no role in personnel decisions. To avoid adverse-impact lawsuits, organizations should carefully monitor the hiring and promotion rates of classes that traditionally have suffered discrimination. In addition, organizations should compare their workforce to labor market surveys to ensure comparability.

Companies concerned about reducing the likelihood of a lawsuit should be sure that each job requirement and selection procedure can be clearly justified as to its importance. We'll discuss in Chapter 5 the legal history of many common selection procedures, as well as legally inappropriate interview questions.

Do you think that Maria, in the opening situation of this chapter, might find the adverse-impact approach an effective way to bring a lawsuit? Indeed, she might. If she could show that her protected class was underrepresented among area-level managers, the burden would shift to the company to show that a job-related procedure was being used. However, given the statistics involved, the case might require an expert witness, which could become quite expensive for Maria.

Now that you have read about the different approaches to proving a discrimination case, you will read about affirmative action, which has generated quite some controversy over the years.

Affirmative Action

Depending on with whom you talk, you may get different explanations of what **affirmative action** means, including the following:

1. Emphasis on recruitment of traditionally underrepresented groups, such as women, for executive positions
2. Altering managerial and supervisory attitudes to eliminate prejudice
3. Removing discriminatory barriers in hiring and promotions
4. Using a quota, or giving preferential treatment in hiring and promotion, to groups that have been underrepresented in the organization's workforce[39]

affirmative action
Emphasis on recruitment of traditionally underrepresented groups; altering managerial and supervisory attitudes to eliminate prejudice; removing discriminatory barriers in hiring and promotions; and using a quota, or giving preferential treatment in hiring and promotion, to groups that have been underrepresented in the organization's workforce.

None of these explanations is wrong; different companies and different people simply use the term "affirmative action" differently. The first three explanations, however, are fairly noncontroversial. You would probably agree that these three are reasonable actions for a company to undertake. The fourth explanation, on the other hand, may surprise you. After all, didn't the Civil Rights Act of 1964 bar discrimination and preferential treatment on the basis of race, sex, religion, color, and national origin? Wouldn't a quota hiring plan (for example, one female must be hired for each male hired) therefore be illegal? Because of the controversy that has arisen regarding it, this section will cover only the fourth explanation of affirmative action. As you will see, certain affirmative action programs have evoked much attention and have been addressed in several major Supreme Court cases. An affirmative action (AA) program may become part of the organization's staffing system in three ways:

1. The organization may *voluntarily* choose to implement an AA program.
2. The organization may be *required* to implement an AA program because it does business with the government.
3. The organization may be *required* to implement an AA program because it has been found guilty of discrimination or as the result of an out-of-court settlement.

We begin with a discussion of the first situation, where a company voluntarily adopts an affirmative action program. To understand this concept, it is useful to review a famous Supreme Court decision that was handed down in the late 1970s and some subsequent legal developments. Following this, you will read about the two situations where affirmative action will be required. This section concludes with a discussion of additional areas where affirmative action programs exist and some recent developments concerning them.

Affirmative Action: Can a Company Voluntarily Adopt Quota Hiring?

Perhaps the most controversial affirmative action situation is one where a company voluntarily adopts a quota hiring or promotion plan. The first major court case involving such a plan in the workplace was brought by a white male, Brian Weber. Weber was working as a production employee for Kaiser Aluminum & Chemical Corporation. As a member of the Kaiser workforce, Weber was eligible for entry into a highly sought-after, skilled-craft training program. Entry into this program was based on seniority at Kaiser. However, due to the AA plan, several black production workers with less seniority were admitted into the training program prior to Weber. From Weber's perspective, this action was a clear violation of the 1964 Civil Rights Act because the decision to deny his entry into the training program had been based solely on his race. From the company's perspective, the percentage of black crafts workers was extremely low. At the time of the lawsuit, only 1.83 percent of the skilled crafts workers were black, even though blacks constituted 39 percent of the workforce in the labor market surrounding the plant. Thus, the company's goal was to establish a more equitable workforce (and perhaps to avoid a lawsuit by blacks for racial discrimination).

Do you think Kaiser was violating the Civil Rights Act of 1964 by not admitting Weber? At the end, the Supreme Court ruled in favor of the company and against Weber. In justifying this decision, the majority opinion of the Supreme Court focused on two points. First, based on records of the debate that took place when Congress discussed the 1964 Civil Rights Act, the Supreme Court believed that the intent of Congress was to help further the employment of blacks in the workforce. Thus, the Supreme Court majority opinion asserted that the purpose of the act was not only to remove barriers and discrimination, but to also encourage the advancement of minorities in the workforce. Voluntary AA plans, such as the one implemented by Kaiser, were therefore perceived to be in keeping with the spirit of the Civil Rights Act. A second point raised by the Supreme Court was the wording of the section in the Civil Rights Act of 1964 that pertains to AA programs. The major statement regarding affirmative action here was as follows:

Nothing contained in this title shall be interpreted to require any employer . . . to grant preferential treatment to any individual or to any group because of the race, color, religion, sex, or national origin of such individual or group on account of an imbalance which may exist.

Do you see the term *require?* The majority opinion on the Supreme Court pointed out that *require* implies that an organization may choose to adopt such a plan. Had Congress intended to ban a voluntary affirmative action plan, the word *permit* would have been used. Although the Supreme Court ruled in favor of Kaiser's AA plan, the Court indicated that not just any affirmative action plan would pass muster. Specifically, the Supreme Court outlined several features of Kaiser's plan that made it acceptable:

1. The plan did not seriously violate the rights of the majority (in this case whites); one white would be admitted for each black, and no whites would be terminated as a result of the plan.
2. The plan was temporary in nature, it was designed to end when its purpose was achieved.
3. The plan had a specific, reasonable purpose in mind, namely, to correct a racial imbalance.[40]

Voluntary AA plans in other organizations have also been accepted by the courts. In cases where layoff situations have been the focus, however, the courts have generally ruled in favor of seniority systems and against AA principles. For example, in one case, the Supreme Court decided that even though a reduction in workforce based on seniority would be more harmful to blacks (most of whom were hired on the basis of a recently implemented AA plan and therefore had only worked a short time), the seniority principle was more important.[41]

In more recent times, the courts have become increasingly critical of voluntary affirmative action programs. In a lawsuit filed against the City of Birmingham and Jefferson County of Alabama, white firefighters charged that the affirmative action plan that called for 50 percent of all promotions to lieutenant be filled by qualified African Americans discriminated against them. The appeals court considered this case with regard to the three features mentioned above and concluded that the City of Birmingham and Jefferson County had seriously violated the rights of the majority, whites, because it completely excluded them from competing for 50 percent of the promotions. Conversely, African Americans were completely excluded from the other 50 percent of the promotions. Second, the court noted that this plan contained no specific point at which it would end, although it was stipulated that it would be in place for at least six years. Thus, the plan appeared to not meet the second rule noted in the Kaiser case. Third, the court failed to find a "specific, reasonable purpose" for the City of Birmingham and Jefferson County to have a 50 percent set aside of jobs for African Americans. Only nine percent of the firefighters were African Americans; African Americans represented just 28 percent of the labor market in the City of Birmingham and Jefferson County.[42]

Another recent affirmative action case, in which a white teacher was dismissed in order to cut costs, was particularly interesting because the school had an ethnically diverse workforce and explicitly stated that it was terminating Sharon Taxman, a white, because of its commitment to affirmative action. However, the parties settled the lawsuit before it reached the Supreme Court of the United States.[43]

In short, to have a successful voluntary affirmative action program, an organization must plan carefully and be ready to explain the purpose of the program and why it does not impinge on the rights of others.

Affirmative Action: Presidential Mandate

Executive Order 11246
A law passed by President Johnson in 1965 that applies to government contractors and prohibits discrimination.

Executive orders, as defined earlier, refer to laws enacted by the president of the United States. The most well-known is **Executive Order 11246,** which was initially signed into law by President Lyndon B. Johnson in 1965 and which prohibits discrimination on the basis of race, color, religion, sex, and national origin.

Private businesses that have government contracts and subcontracts of more than $10,000 are covered by this law. Firms with contracts of $50,000 or more and 50 or more employees also must engage in "affirmative action" to remedy underutilization of women and minorities. The guidelines for AA under this law are contained in a document referred to as "Revised Order No. 4," which was written and is enforced by the **Office of Federal Contract Compliance Programs (OFCCP).** A company covered by this document must engage in affirmative action planning, which involves the following steps:

Office of Federal Contract Compliance Programs (OFCCP)
Government agency that wrote and enforces a document referred to as "Revised Order No. 4," which contains the guidelines for affirmative action to remedy the underutilization of women and minorities in firms that have government contracts.
utilization analysis
A method of affirmative action planning where the employer must compare the race, sex, and ethnic composition of the workforce to the race, sex, and ethnic composition of the labor market.

1. **Utilization Analysis.** The employer must compare the race, sex, and ethnic composition of the workforce to the race, sex, and ethnic composition of the labor market; this is called a **utilization analysis.** A list of eight factors is used to determine the composition of the labor market (for example, general availability of minorities having requisite skills in the immediate labor market), which are combined using a formula. A job group in which the percentage of women or minorities in the workforce is significantly lower than in the labor market indicates underutilization.
2. **Establishment of Goals and Timetables.** For any areas in which there is an underutilization, the organization must establish a goal (such as a target percentage of women or minorities to be attained) along with a timetable for when that goal will be reached.
3. **Action Steps to Be Taken.** The organization must specify in writing the steps it will take to achieve the goals within the specified timetables. Steps may include publicizing its affirmative action plans, participating in minority outreach programs, advertising in minority newspapers and magazines, and so forth.[44]

Affirmative Action: Required Due to Court-Ordered or Out-of-Court Settlement

An affirmative action program may be court imposed if the company is found guilty of persistent and serious discrimination. Or, the company may agree to implement an affirmative action program as part of a settlement with the EEOC or OFCCP. Such programs appear to be becoming less common, however. You can conduct your own survey of employment discrimination laws and related topics. Box 2.4 provides some relevant Web sites to explore.

Affirmative Action: Other Laws

Another type of affirmative action program, referred to as a "set-aside program," is often mandated at the state or federal level. Such programs require the government office to award a certain percentage of contracts to minority-owned firms. Such programs were recently considered in a major Supreme Court case, *Adarand Constructors v. Pena,* filed by Adarand Contractors, a highway construction firm that had submitted a bid for some construction work. Although Adarand submitted the lowest bid, the contract was given to Gonzalez Construction Company, which was owned by an

WEBBING AROUND

Box 2.4

The World Wide Web can be an excellent source of information about employment discrimination laws. A major advantage of the Web is that you can find updated information on the latest laws and legal analyses, many times without any financial cost. Listed below are some of the more useful legal sites, along with comments about some of the information available.

www.eeoc.gov This is the EEOC's Web site. In it you will find information about how to file discrimination charges, along with the addresses and phone numbers of EEOC offices. You will also

find the complete text of the major laws enforced by the EEOC, such as the Civil Rights Act of 1964, the Americans with Disabilities Act, and others. You will also find current proposed and new regulations that help explain and interpret these laws.

www.lawnewsnetwork.com/ practice/employmentlaw This is an on-line version of an excellent legal newsletter, with a major section on employment law. In addition to an up-to-date section on employment law issues, ranging from sexual harassment to race discrimination, you will find memos from various law firms

covering a range of related topics, as well as information on recent court cases.

www.ahipubs.com This is an excellent resource for employment law issues and includes a section of free reports for various legal topics of interest. One of the most interesting features is a section devoted to frequently raised management issues (for example, how to reduce the workforce and avoid legal problems) and answers from experts. It also includes a section where you can ask questions and get answers from colleagues as well as lawyers, at no charge.

ethnic minority member. Because Adarand Contractors was not an employee, the company filed under the Equal Protection Clause of the 14th Amendment to the Constitution, which requires that the government treat its citizens equally, unless there is a good reason for doing otherwise. In ruling that Adarand had been discriminated against, the Supreme Court asserted that the government office would have to prove prior discrimination in the awarding of contracts and the need for remedial action to correct such problems. Furthermore, the Supreme Court stated that alternative actions, which could achieve the same objectives without creating discrimination against others, must be considered before adopting a set-aside program. If you consider these points, you will see that they are not much different from the criteria for an acceptable affirmative action program voluntarily adopted by the organization discussed above.[45]

As the mood of the United States has turned more conservative, groups have made various attempts at the state level to prohibit or restrict the use of affirmative action programs. The most publicized attempt in this regard was California's Proposition 209, approved by voters in 1996. This proposition amended the state constitution by stating that the State of California could not use "race, sex, color, ethnicity, or national origin as a criterion for either discrimination against, or granting preferential treatment to, any individual or group in the operation of the State's public employment, public education, or public contracting." Since this law passed, other states have considered similar laws and propositions. Although few such laws have been passed to date, interest remains in some states to ban affirmative action. Despite much public attention to affirmative action, however, it is safe to say that the affirmative action laws and court precedents in this area have actually changed less than one might have expected.[46]

Bringing a Lawsuit

So far, you have learned about who is covered by the laws, the procedures for proving and defending a legal charge, and the conditions under which an organization may implement an AA plan. But, what if you have had a bad experience in your job or in applying for a job, and you would like to bring a discrimination charge? Figure 2.2 shows the number of charges filed annually with the EEOC for selected categories. So what happens if you decide to take legal action against an organization? Here are the basic steps you would need to follow.[47]

1. Most of the federal fair employment laws require you to first file the complaint with the EEOC or the state agency responsible for processing such complaints. Check your phone book for the address and phone number. You should be aware of the following issues in filing your charge:
   a. You may file a charge either in person or by mail.
   b. You need not identify yourself in the charges you file, but in many cases your

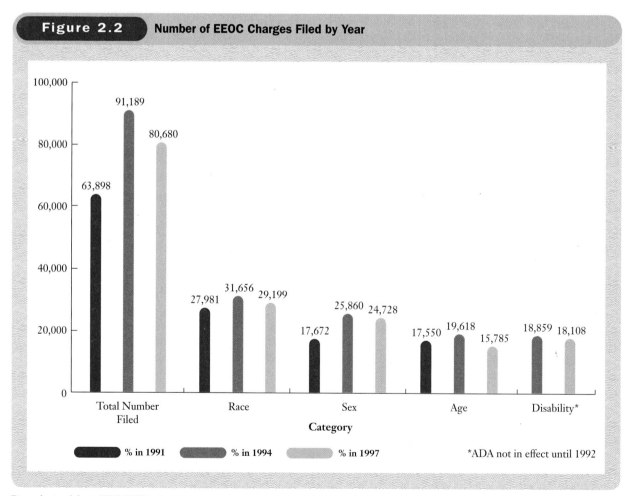

Figure 2.2   **Number of EEOC Charges Filed by Year**

Data obtained from EEOC Web site.

company may be able to figure out who you are. It is, however, against the law for your company to retaliate against you for filing a charge.

   c. Strict time limits exist for filing charges. Although the limit depends in part on whether a state agency or the EEOC is handling the complaint, it is safe to say that you should file your complaint within six months of the act you are challenging. So, if you believe you have been discriminated against and plan to file a charge, don't wait too long!

2. What will the EEOC do with your complaint?

   a. The EEOC must notify the organization within ten days that you have filed a charge.

   b. The EEOC has the authority to conduct an investigation of your charge. Toward that end, the EEOC may inspect company records, interview other employees, and request other information from the company such as job descriptions, tests, and so forth.

   c. Based on its initial investigation, the EEOC may decide that your case has merit (or **reasonable cause**). The EEOC is obliged to first try to reach a *reconciliation*, or settlement, between you and the organization.

   d. If no reconciliation can be agreed upon, the EEOC can sue the organization on your behalf. If the EEOC finds insufficient evidence of discrimination, it will issue you a **right-to-sue notice.** This gives you the right to have a lawyer take your case. Given that many discrimination charges are filed each year, the EEOC usually concentrates only on the most promising cases. Even though your charge may have merit, chances are good that the EEOC will not pursue your case.

3. If the EEOC has issued you a right-to-sue notice, or if you are filing a charge under a law not requiring you to go to the EEOC first, you will need to hire a lawyer to represent you. Here are some things you should know about hiring a lawyer:

   a. There are tens of thousands of lawyers in practice today; choosing an effective lawyer you can work with is not easy. You are encouraged to obtain a referral from a reliable source, such as the state bar association. Certain publications, such as *The Best Lawyers in America* by Steve Naifeh and Gregory White Smith or the *Martindale-Hubbell Law Directory*, provide background information on many lawyers (check www.lawyers.com for help on choosing a lawyer).

   b. Carefully interview several potential lawyers. Because they may charge an initial fee, use the time carefully to explain your case and listen to their advice. Honest lawyers won't make any promises about how much money they can win for you. Make sure you ask who would handle the case. Will it be the person you are talking with (who may be a partner) or an associate (usually a junior lawyer with less experience)?

   c. Be sure to determine the fee structure. Depending on the nature of the case, attorneys often charge an hourly fee (typically this will range between $100 to $250 per hour, depending on the cost of living in the area) or a contingency fee, which is based on winning the case. In either situation, you may also have to pay for various expenses, such as travel, filing costs, and so forth. Be sure you fully understand the fee structure.

The bottom line in hiring a lawyer is this: Choose carefully and make sure you understand what you are getting into. Box 2.5 describes employment issues for women in various countries around the world.

reasonable cause
Based on its initial investigation, the EEOC may decide that a case has merit, or reasonable cause, to pursue a settlement or a suit.

right-to-sue notice
A notice issued from the EEOC that gives you the right to have a lawyer take your case in a discrimination suit.

Box 2.5

Sex Discrimination: A Global Comparison

Although sex discrimination in the workplace occurs around the world, the experience of women differs from country to country. Consider Japan, where powerful cultural norms dictate that women should remain housekeepers, while their husbands devote both their work life and social life to the company. A majority of Japanese women continue to accept that norm, as indicated by a 1992 poll showing that 56 percent endorsed a statement that the man should be the wage earner while the wife stays home. In comparison, only 24 percent of American women and 13 percent of Swedish women approved of that statement. Thus, despite the existence of a national law banning discrimination, women in Japan continue to face many hurdles, especially in light of the current economic problems. Male college graduates, for example, are twice as likely to get jobs as females. Many newspaper job ads specify whether a man or woman is desired; being less than 35 years old is sometimes an explicit "qualification" listed in the ad. Only 1 percent of women who work hold managerial jobs.

Although different in certain ways, working women in Mexico have had a similar experience as working women in Japan. On the surface, though, women in the workplace have far more rights than in Japan. An equal rights law for women has existed for more than twenty years, and working women are legally provided three months of paid maternity leave, as well as extra rest time for nursing mothers. But companies regularly run afoul of the law by firing pregnant women and requiring married women to take pregnancy tests before being hired. Apparently, existing laws are of little or no help to women who believe they have been discriminated against. But this may change in the future, as the number of women in the Mexican Senate tripled in the most recent year, and about twice as many women serve now in the lower house.

Women in Sweden have experienced far fewer problems than in most countries of the world, but even there problems remain. On the positive side, many laws support working women in their child care efforts, including more than one year of paid maternity leave and a guaranteed equivalent job upon return. Companies must also allow working mothers to work part-time for up to twelve years after the birth of a child (men are also eligible for these benefits). At the same time, differences between men and women persist. Women hold only 8 percent of managerial jobs, and practically no women are in top management jobs. Some critics assert that the generous leave policies too often encourage working women to maintain traditional roles and forego career advancement.

Source: Adopted from V. Reitman, "Japan: She Is Free, yet She's Alone in Her World," *Wall Street Journal*, July 26, 1995, B1, B12; D. Solis, "Mexico: A Pioneer in the Land of Machismo," *Wall Street Journal*, July 26, 1995, B1, B12; and D. Milbank, "Sweden: Laws Help Mom, but They Hurt Her Career," *Wall Street Journal*, July 26, 1995, B1, B12.

Remedies for Discrimination

You may be wondering at this point whether it is worthwhile to even file a discrimination complaint or talk with a lawyer. Although the remedies you might win differ depending on the specific law you are suing under, you may be awarded the following:[48]

1. The promotion or job that you were denied as a result of discrimination
2. Back pay (the amount of money you lost as a result of being discriminated against)
3. Attorney's fees (and fees of certain other parties, such as expert witnesses who testified on your behalf)
4. In a case of intentional discrimination, punitive damages, which could amount to hundreds of thousands of dollars
5. An agreement that the organization will no longer engage in the practice(s) you have complained about

Of course, in many cases, the company simply settles out of court, so you may win something even though the case never goes to trial.

Current Issues in Workplace Discrimination

Several current issues in workplace discrimination have captured the attention of interested observers. We will address two of these in further detail, namely, the glass ceiling and sexual harassment.

Women and the Glass Ceiling

The term *glass ceiling* refers to an invisible barrier preventing women from advancing to higher levels in the organization.

glass ceiling
Refers to an invisible barrier that prevents women from advancing to higher levels within the organization.

Evidence from many different sources indicates that women continue to have their progress in the workplace stymied. For example, although many more women are in managerial positions today compared to previous years (in 1995, 42 percent of U.S. managers were women versus only 17 percent in 1972), women are underrepresented in top managerial positions, where fewer than 5 percent of the jobs are held by women.[49] Less than 2 percent of the highest-paid executives in Fortune 500 companies are women, and only .4 percent (two, to be exact) of the Fortune 500 CEOs are women. Female executives are also paid less than their male counterparts. In 1997, the average pay of female top managers in the Fortune 500 companies was $518,596, while the average pay of male top managers in these companies was $765,000.[50] The glass ceiling has become a major reason why women quit their jobs; a recent study indicated that 80 percent of the women who changed jobs did so because of run-ins with the glass ceiling. Since the U.S. Department of Labor released its reports on the glass ceiling in the mid-1990s, some insightful research has surfaced as to why the glass ceiling exists. (For a copy of the USDL report, go to http://gatekeeper.dol.gov/dol/_sec/public/media/reports/main.htm). Next, we will discuss some of this research and some strategies successful female executives and concerned organizations are using to shatter the glass ceiling.

What causes the glass ceiling? In a recent survey of Fortune 1000 companies, female executives offered the following top three reasons for the glass ceiling:[51]

1. 52 percent blamed it on male stereotyping and preconceptions of women;
2. 49 percent blamed it on exclusion from informal networks;
3. 47 percent attributed it to women having a lack of general management/line experience.

Thus, women in top management positions placed primary blame for the glass ceiling on the corporate culture and to some extent, limited experience. This same study however found that male CEOs from Fortune 1000 companies placed the blame on a different set of factors:

1. Eighty-two percent attributed it to women's lack of general management/line experience;
2. Two-thirds believed that women had insufficient time in the "pipeline" or seniority on the job;
3. Only 25 percent blamed male stereotyping and preconceptions of women.

Thus, male CEOs tended to blame women's lack of qualifications for their slow progression, while female executives placed greater emphasis on the corporate culture. Such differences in perception suggest that much work needs to be done to eliminate the glass ceiling. Next, you will read about some personal strategies successful female executives recommend for avoiding the glass ceiling problem.

Personal Strategies for Avoiding the Glass Ceiling

Here are some personal strategies successful female executives recommend for avoiding the glass-ceiling problem:

1. **Consistently Exceed Performance Expectations:** In order to succeed in a predominantly male environment, practically every female executive indicated that it was necessary to be highly effective at work. As one put it, "Always go the extra mile. It is not enough to be willing, you have to do it, even if no one is looking."
2. **Develop a Professional Style That Male Executives Accept:** Almost all of the female executives indicated that they worked hard to develop a style that was neither too masculine nor too feminine. This was clearly a challenging obligation, but one that the female executives viewed as necessary to succeed.
3. **Seek Out Stretch Assignments:** About half of the female executives perceived that taking on difficult or highly visible assignments was a critical success factor. Such assignments were deemed important in order to learn new things, gain entry into higher level positions, and create networks with influential people.
4. **Develop a Mentor:** Over 90 percent of women indicated that they had a mentor at some point in their career and 81 percent perceived a mentor to be critical or important to success. Although most of the women had male mentors (not surprising, given how few women are in senior management positions), those who had both women and men as mentors reported that each had different mentoring strengths.

What Can Organizations Do to Shatter the Glass Ceiling?

Organizations can adopt and implement various policies and practices that will help women to progress. Four of the most important ones are as follows.[52]

1. **Have a Task Force to Address Women's Issues.** Tenneco has eight advisory counsels composed only of women. Corning sponsors quality improvement teams that address issues of concern to both women and minorities.
2. **Clearly Communicate and Reward Managers for Career Progression of Women.** Tenneco has linked executives' yearly bonus to their advancement of women and minorities. American Airlines requires that top managers create highly detailed developmental plans for all middle- to upper-level women managers.
3. **Provide Assignments to Women That Will Promote Their Careers.** DuPont Company, for example, has a job rotation system for both men and women that provides them with experience in at least two or three functional areas.
4. **Convince Top Management That Something Must Be Done.** It is clear from the previous section that CEOs often fail to understand the challenges facing women in progressing to executive positions. Yet, in order to make sure the programs listed above work, top management must be supportive. When discrimination conflicts seem headed for court, some companies require other forms of dispute settlement to be tried first, as described in Box 2.6.

TALES FROM THE TRENCHES

Box 2.6
Look Before You Sue! Your Company May Require Alternative Dispute Resolution

Think your employer is discriminating against you in pay, promotions, or some other condition of employment? Some companies require that you take your complaint through an alternative dispute resolution (ADR) process instead. At Red Lobster, a restaurant chain, the company requires employees to proceed through a peer committee that reviews and reconsiders terminations and disciplinary actions. For example, Ruth Hatton was fired from her job as a waitress for stealing a guest-comment card. The termination decision was reviewed by a panel of five peers, including a hostess, a food server, and a bartender. After describing her version of the story, and listening to various witnesses, the panel overturned the termination de-cision and Ruth was returned to her job. According to Clifford Whitehill, the general counsel, the company has reduced the amount of money spent on fighting employee lawsuits by $1 million annually.

As you can guess, some employees are opposed to the idea of alternative dispute resolution. While a peer review might seem like a rather fair process, many organizations use an outside expert, or arbitrator, to decide whether an improper decision was made. In addition, some companies require employees to sign a document stating that they will abide by the decision. When employees discover that they must go through an arbitrator whom the company has chosen, and that they have given up the right to file a lawsuit, they may feel taken advantage of. For example, an employee of Smith Barney, who had signed an agreement to have any discrimination charges resolved by an arbitrator, filed a lawsuit under the Civil Rights Act of 1964 alleging that she had been sexually harassed. The company then argued in court that she had waived the right to file such a suit and that instead it must be heard and resolved by an arbitrator. The court agreed with the company. The Equal Employment Opportunity Commission strongly opposes the use of ADR requirements, which are viewed by employee advocates as a means of forcing employees to give up their rights.

Source: Adapted from M. Jones, "Red Lobster Tale: Peers Decide Fired Waitress's Fate," *Wall Street Journal*, January, 20, 1998, B1, B6.

Sexual Harassment

Almost everyone has heard of sexual harassment. Various surveys show that sexual harassment at work has, at least in the past, been quite prevalent. A random telephone survey of private-sector women in Los Angeles reported that more than half had experienced at least one incident of sexual harassment in their careers. Have you ever been sexually harassed at work? The number of sexual harassment charges filed with the EEOC has risen considerably over the past few years. In 1991, 6,883 sexual harassment charges were filed, and more than 15,000 such charges were filed in 1997. Maria's experience, as described in the opening case of this chapter, is not unique. But what exactly is considered sexual harassment? What have recent Supreme Court decisions said about sexual harassment? What can companies do to avoid sexual harassment lawsuits? These issues will be discussed in greater detail next.[53]

What Is Sexual Harassment?

One particular cause for companies' concern about sexual harassment is that the definition of this term can be quite vague. Initially, sexual harassment was understood to occur only in a **quid-pro-quo** (a Latin phrase meaning something in exchange for something) situation. This might be when a supervisor offered to provide a promotion,

quid-pro-quo sexual harassment
A Latin phrase meaning something in exchange for something else, such as a supervisor offering an employee a promotion or raise or other personnel action in exchange for sexual favors.

hostile environment sexual harassment
An environment created by unwelcome sexual advances, requests for sexual favors, and other verbal or physical conduct of a sexual nature.

raise, or other personnel action in exchange for sexual favors. But a legal case in 1986 changed that situation. In *Meritor Savings Bank v. Vinson*, the Supreme Court identified a second type of sexual harassment, known as **hostile environment.** A hostile environment is created by unwelcome sexual advances, requests for sexual favors, and other verbal or physical conduct of a sexual nature. As a result of these and other cases, the EEOC's guidelines on "Discrimination Because of Sex" provides this definition of sexual harassment:

> Unwelcome sexual advances, requests for sexual favors, and other verbal or physical conduct of a sexual nature constitute sexual harassment when
>
> **1.** Submission to such conduct is made either explicitly or implicitly a term or condition of an individual's employment;
> **2.** Submission to or rejection of such conduct by an individual is used as the basis for employment decisions affecting such individual; or
> **3.** Such conduct has the purpose or effect of unreasonably interfering with an individual's work performance or creating an intimidating, hostile, or offensive working condition.

Although the first two points seem relatively straightforward, the third point appears quite subjective. What determines, for example, when working conditions are "hostile" or "offensive?" Is it possible that what is offensive to me may not be offensive to you? Indeed, that is what makes sexual harassment charges difficult for an organization to defend. Table 2.4 gives some specific examples of hostile environment cases where the plaintiff won. As you can see from Table 2.4, a hostile environment can be created by even nonsupervisors (such as coworkers). In fact, in certain cases actions taken by a nonemployee (for example, a vending machine operator) served as grounds for a sexual harassment charge.

So, what behaviors are okay? And what behaviors should you avoid so that you are not charged with sexual harassment? Table 2.5 gives a list of do's and don'ts in this regard. Be sure to note that sexual harassment charges can be made against women as

Table 2.4	**Typical Sexual Harassment Cases Where Plaintiff Won** *Photographs, Graffiti, and Comments*

1. The shipyard in which a woman welder worked had pictures of nude and partially nude women in a variety of posters. These pictures were affixed to walls throughout the shipyard. In addition, sexually offensive words, phrases, and drawings appeared. Male employees continuously made sexually offensive comments to the woman.
2. A female police officer was subjected to frequent sexually oriented incidents by fellow officers and other local officials, including kissing and moaning noises over the police radio. Various pictures and graffiti were also written on police department walls.
3. A female agent with the Internal Revenue Service was asked to lunch by a male coworker, which she accepted. Subsequently, the coworker began to spend much time talking with the female agent, and one day he asked her to go out for a drink. She refused. A few days later, the coworker wrote a note to her, expressing his deep feelings toward her. After she refused to talk with the coworker, he sent her an emotionally charged letter in the mail, which frightened her further.

Source: Adapted from *Sexual Harassment Manual for Managers and Supervisors* (Chicago: Commerce Clearing House, 1991).

well as men. In fact, in 1997, 12 percent of sexual harassment charges were brought by men. Next, you will read about three recent Supreme Court rulings in this area, followed by a discussion of what an organization can do to avoid charges and reduce the likelihood of losing a sexual harassment suit.

Recent Supreme Court Rulings on Sexual Harassment

In 1998, the United States Supreme Court issued rulings in three separate sexual harassment suits. One case, *Faragher v. City of Boca Raton*, involved a woman, Beth Ann Faragher, who had experienced sexual harassment but never filed a formal complaint about the misconduct. Do you think the organization should still be guilty if she never formally complained to anyone? The details of this case were as follows. The plaintiff had worked as a lifeguard for the City of Boca Raton both part-time and during summers in the mid- to late 1980s. During this time, she alleged that two of her supervisors, Bill Terry and David Silverman, had created a hostile work environment for her and other lifeguards by offensive touching and lewd comments. In 1986, the City of Boca Raton had adopted a sexual harassment policy, which it provided in a letter to its employees. In 1990, the policy was revised and reissued to most of the employees. This policy, however, was not distributed to the lifeguards. Although Faragher complained about the harassment to her third immediate supervisor, Robert Gordon, she did not consider these to be formal complaints, and she did not file a formal complaint with anyone else. Although other female lifeguards talked with Robert Gordon about harassment, he never spoke with anyone else (for example, city officials) about this problem. Although the trial court ruled that the situation constituted illegal harassment, the appeals court ruled that the city was not guilty. The Supreme Court concluded that it was sexual harassment and that the city had not "exercised reasonable cause to prevent the supervisors' harassing conduct."[54] Do you agree with the Supreme Court's decision? Do you think the organization should still be guilty if the plaintiff never formally complained to anyone?

Table 2.5	The Do's and Don'ts of Sexual Harassment	
Here's What You Can Do	**Here's What Might Be Seen as Sexual Harassment**	**Here's What Probably Would Be Seen as Sexual Harassment**
1. Hug or pat on the back if the recipient doesn't flinch, scowl, or object (better yet, play it safe, and don't hug or pat anyone on the back). 2. Shake hands. 3. Request a date.	1. Sexually suggestive conversation if the other person objects. 2. Sexist remarks about the person's body, clothing, or personal activities. 3. A request for a date after the person says no. 4. A dirty joke if a person objects. 5. Leering, ogling.	1. Demands (subtle and blatant) for sexual favors. 2. Pictures of nude and seminude bodies, including possibly the swimsuit issue of *Sports Illustrated*. 3. Repeated leering or ogling. 4. Repeated requests for a date after a person says no. 5. Repeated brushing against a person's body.

Source: Adapted from R. Sharpe, "Acceptable Behavior: Sexual Harassment Message Swift and Clear," *St. Louis Post-Dispatch*, November 14, 1993, B1.

A second case involved a woman, Kimberly Ellerth, who had never filed a complaint of sexual harassment through the harassment policy and had not even suffered a loss of privileges or promotions as a result of the harassment. Should she still win a lawsuit based on harassment? In *Burlington Industries v. Ellerth*, Kimberly Ellerth had worked in sales for Burlington Industries for fifteen months before quitting because she was being harassed by one of the supervisors, Ted Slowik. Slowik was not Ellerth's immediate supervisor, nor was he considered upper management. According to Ellerth, Ted Slowik had made numerous crude sexual comments to her, including various statements suggesting that promotions would be made more difficult for her because of her lack of interest in sexual relations. Nevertheless, she received a promotion. Despite her knowledge of Burlington's sexual harassment policy, Kimberly did not file a complaint. On the basis of this information, the district court dismissed her claim without a trial, arguing that there was no way for the company to have known of the harassment. The Supreme Court, however, sent the case back to the lower court, stating that the company should have to prove that its sexual harassment policy and practices were sufficient to prevent such situations.[55]

The third case to be addressed by the Supreme Court of the United States during this time period involved a male, Joseph Oncale, who was allegedly harassed by other male coworkers. Among other acts, Oncale claimed he was physically assaulted in a sexual manner and was threatened by supervisory employees with rape. Do you think that males who are sexually harassed by other males should be protected by the law as well? You may be surprised to hear that in several previous cases, lower courts had ruled that "same sex" harassment (i.e., harassment of a man by other men and harassment of a woman by other women) was not protected under the Civil Rights Act of 1964. The Supreme Court, however, ruled that same-sex harassment was protected under the law, just as is opposite-sex harassment.[56]

Now that you understand what sexual harassment is, you are probably wondering what organizations can do to avoid legal liability. You will read next about seven highly recommended strategies for organizations.

What Can Organizations Do to Avoid Sexual Harassment Problems?

Companies employ numerous tactics to avoid sexual harassment problems. The following are seven highly recommended strategies.[57]

1. **Establish a formal, written policy regarding sexual harassment.** This policy should include a definition of sexual harassment, a statement that sexual harassment is prohibited, information on how to file a complaint, a description of the steps that will be taken if a complaint is filed, and language indicating that the company will not retaliate against someone who files a legitimate complaint of harassment.
2. **Educate employees about sexual harassment.** Particularly in light of recent cases, it will become increasingly important for companies to train employees in terms of what sexual harassment is, what actions may be taken against violators of this policy, and how employees can go about using the company procedures to file a complaint. Companies are advised to document the dates of these sessions, keep attendance records, and maintain copies of all training materials used.
3. **Establish an effective grievance procedure.** The presence of an effective grievance procedure is evidence that the company does its best to eliminate sexual harassment. An effective grievance procedure will have a designated person (other than one's direct supervisor) to handle any complaints, an alternative person if the

grievant believes the complaint was not handled fairly, and a promise of confidentiality. Organizations must be sure, however, to always follow their official grievance procedures. Failure to follow the policies that they have established can cause more harm than good.

4. **Conduct prompt, thorough investigations.** It is critical for the company to promptly conduct a complete, careful investigation of any charges of sexual harassment. Once a complaint has been received, and the details obtained (for example, who was involved, when and where the events occurred, and so forth), it is critical to interview potential witnesses and attempt to verify the events from independent sources. Of course, in many cases there are no other witnesses, and management must make the best possible judgment under the circumstances. An extended investigation can also hurt the company. In one lawsuit, for example, a sales representative claimed to have been harassed and nearly raped by a coworker. The company took three weeks to complete the investigation, which the court ruled was simply too long, given the nature of the complaint.

5. **Take quick, but carefully considered, disciplinary action against harassers.** In some court cases, the court ruled in favor of the company because it had taken immediate disciplinary action. In addition, taking the appropriate disciplinary action is a clear sign that such behavior will not be tolerated. At the same time, the organization should be sure not to unjustly punish persons. Disciplinary actions may include an oral warning, reassignment, or termination.

6. **Communicate the company's position about sexual harassment.** Employees generally model the behaviors that they believe top management would support. It is essential, therefore, that sexual harassment policies be supported and regularly reaffirmed. Top management can demonstrate their support by attending training sessions, signing written communications about sexual harassment policies, and by acting in an appropriate manner.

7. **Conduct regular assessments of the workplace.** Managers have a responsibility for ensuring that work areas, including production facilities, locker room areas, and lunchrooms are free of inappropriate pictures, conversations, and behaviors. The individuals responsible for ensuring a harassment-free workplace may need to take periodic tours of all work areas to ensure that problems are not occurring.

In sum, Maria's comments in the opening case suggest that sexual harassment is occurring in her company. She has the legal right to end the behaviors and comments that her boss, Pat, is making. Given both potential liability, as well as ethical and moral considerations, organizations must take an active role in weeding out this problem. It is also important to point out here that the law does not prohibit only sexual harassment. Indeed, harassment based on age, race, disability, religion, and other protected categories is also illegal.

❖ Conclusion

You have read about the various federal laws regarding employment discrimination, as well as the procedures relevant to proving a discrimination charge. You have also learned about affirmative action and some conditions under which it may be required. Finally, you learned about some major issues in discrimination today. You should have gathered several key points from this chapter. First, discrimination laws have a major effect on the human resource management function today. To be an effective line manager, you will need a basic understanding of the legal aspects of any personnel decisions you make. If you wish to be a successful human resource manager, of course, you will need a much more in-depth understanding of the law. Similarly, it is in your best interest as an employee to be aware of your protection from discrimination. That way, you will be better able to identify and deal with potentially unfair employment decisions. Second, employment discrimination issues are related to some major societal problems. Such issues as the glass ceiling suggest more careful consideration of our various laws, as well as various social policies. At the same time, given the trend toward reducing government regulation, a move toward changing some of these laws may gain momentum. The final result on employment discrimination will be seen in the next few years.

❖ Applying Core Concepts

1. Jose Sanchez recently applied for a job where he was one of three final candidates. Although he had the necessary skills, abilities, and education, the manager told Sanchez that he lacked the necessary experience. What type of lawsuit might Jose pursue? What would he need to show to prove discrimination? What would the company need to show to defend itself?

2. Mary Lao applied for a job as a secretary. The job involves using a personal computer to type letters and memos, answering the phone, and filing papers. Although Mary is qualified in every way, she is legally blind. What would you do if you were the hiring manager?

3. What does your company or organization do to help prepare women for senior executive positions? What steps would you recommend to your company or organization for better helping prepare women for these jobs?

4. Do you think what is happening to Maria in the opening case constitutes sexual harassment?

5. Should the United States pass a federal law protecting workers from discrimination on the basis of sexual orientation? Why or why not?

6. If you believed you were discriminated against in your job, what laws might protect you?

7. Does the company that you work for now or plan to work for in the future have an affirmative action program? Do you think that it should? Explain your answer.

❖ Key Terms

Civil Rights Act of 1866	Rehabilitation Act of 1973	Bona fide occupational
Civil Rights Act of 1964	Americans with	qualification (BFOQ)
Equal Employment	Disabilities Act of 1990	Disparate treatment
Opportunity	Reasonable	*McDonnell-Douglas v.*
Commission (EEOC)	accommodation	*Green* case standards
Pregnancy Discrimination	Undue hardship	Adverse impact
Act of 1978	Age Discrimination in	Applicant flow
Civil Rights Act of 1991	Employment Act of	Stock analysis
Immigration Reform and	1967	Validation study
Control Act	Intentional discrimination	Affirmative action

Executive Order 11246	**Utilization analysis**	**Quid-pro-quo sexual**
Office of Federal Contract	**Reasonable cause**	**harassment**
Compliance Programs	**Right-to-sue notice**	**Hostile environment**
(OFCCP)	**Glass ceiling**	**sexual harassment**

❖ **CHAPTER 2** *Experiential Exercise*

The Case of Paula Kind

Microtone Products (not its real name) is a two-hundred-employee company located in the midwest, near a large city. It produces electrical machinery. Paula Kind (not her real name) began working for the company several months ago. She is one of the maintenance staff, responsible for machine repair. Most of the workers are men, and she is the only woman in her department. During the first month, the workers would occasionally whistle at her, and once or twice, someone made a crude, sexually suggestive remark. At the end of the first month of her employment, Paula talked to you, the manufacturing manager, about the whistles and the remarks. After she told you what had happened, you replied as follows:

"Well, that's what it is like working in a predominantly male workforce, especially in a factory. Some of the men resent having a woman around, but mostly they are trying to lighten the place up. If you just ignore them, I'm sure they'll stop. If you are still having problems in a few weeks, let me know and I will do something."

Paula seemed to follow your advice, and the whistles and remarks tapered off. A few months later, however, Paula came back to you with the following story. She had been repairing some equipment on the second shift when Bill "Wild Man" Smith came over to her and said, "You look foxy tonight, Paula! I've been meaning to ask you to have a drink with me at the end of the shift."

She replied, "No, thank you, I'm busy tonight."

He then said, "How about tomorrow night?" to which she again replied, "No, thank you, I'm busy tomorrow night as well." According to Paula, Bill stood there looking her "up and down" in a suggestive way, winked, and then left. After she finished the story, you thanked her and told her that you would talk to Bill and make sure that this never happened again.

The next day, you called Bill in to your office to hear his version. He admitted asking her to have a drink with him after the shift, but said that he likes to socialize with the new employees (male and female) just to

get to know them better. When you asked him about the "suggestive look," he smiled and said that she is attractive and it's only natural to admire beauty. You firmly told him that this was not appropriate behavior and that he should avoid conversation and even looking at her, unless it was strictly job-related.

Matters seemed quiet for several months after that. Although you passed Paula on the production floor several times during that time, she seemed busy at work and work seemed to be going well for her. Then, one day, Paula asked for a meeting with you. When you arrived the next day, she began by saying, "Unless some immediate action is taken and some significant changes are made in this company as a whole, I intend to press discrimination charges against this company. I just found out that I have been given the smallest raise in the department, and I have been given some of the dirtiest tasks to do in this facility. I am also tired of having the men leer at me all the time and whisper things behind my back. I expect to hear back from you in three days or I will immediately proceed to file a lawsuit."

When the meeting with Paula was over, you immediately went over to talk with Brad, her supervisor. He stated that because Paula was the newest worker in the group, she did get the tasks no one else wanted—but all new employees were treated that way. And, in terms of pay, she received the smallest raise because she was new and was still making quite a few mistakes, just like any new person would. As for the leering and whispering things, he certainly had told the men about that, and they just said that they talked about all kinds of women, including their wives and girlfriends, just like the women in the office talked about their husbands and boyfriends. Paula's name was probably mentioned once or twice, but they were not doing it intentionally.

The questions for you to address are as follows:

1. What should you say now to Paula? Do you think that she is being discriminated against? What kind of discrimination charges could she file?

2. What should you do now? What would you have done differently in the beginning?

3. What actions could you take to avoid this situation in the future?

❖ Chapter 2 References

1. United States Equal Employment Opportunity Commission, *Legislative History of Titles VII and XI of Civil Rights Act of 1964* (Washington: U.S. Government Printing Office [no date]).
2. H. Graham, *The Civil Rights Era* (New York: Oxford University Press, 1990).
3. United States Equal Employment Opportunity Commission, *Legislative History of Titles VII and XI of Civil Rights Act of 1964* (Washington: U.S. Government Printing Office [no date]).
4. M. Hanley, "Who's the Boss? How Discrimination Law Treats Leased Employees, Independent Contractors, and Consultants," *Labor Law Journal* 48, (1997): 233–40.
5. J. Jones, W. Murphy, and R. Belton, *Discrimination in Employment* (St. Paul: West, 1987).
6. L. Joel, *Every Employee's Guide to the Law* (New York: Pantheon, 1993).
7. D. Bennett-Alexander and L. Pincus, *Employment Law for Business* (Chicago: Irwin, 1995).
8. J. Ledvinka and V. Scarpello, *Federal Regulation of Personnel and Human Resource Management* (Boston: PWS-Kent, 1991).
9. U.S. Census Bureau, *Labor Force Status and Other Characteristics of Persons with a Work Disability 1981–1988* (Washington: U.S. Government Printing Office, 1989).
10. Bennett-Alexander and Pincus, *Employment Law for Business.*
11. *Bragdon v. Abbott* 107 F.3d 934.
12. T. Holt, "Alcoholism and Misbehavior: Implication of the ADA," *Labor Law Journal* 47 (1996): 729–34.
13. S. Malko, "On the Defensive With the ADA," *HRFocus* 75 (February 1998): 5.
14. U.S. Equal Employment Opportunity Commission, *Technical Assistance Manual on the Employment Provisions (Title I) of the Americans with Disabilities Act* (Washington: U.S. Government Printing Office, 1992).
15. Ibid.
16. Equal Employment Opportunity for Individuals with Disabilities, 29 CFR Part 1630 *Federal Register*, July 26, 1991.
17. M. Wilson, "Defenses to Discrimination Actions Filed under the Americans with Disabilities Act," *Labor Law Journal* 42 (1991): 732–46.
18. Equal Employment Opportunity Commission, *ADA Enforcement Guidance: Preemployment Disability Related Questions and Medical Examinations*, Washington, D.C., 1995.
19. L. Joel, *Every Employee's Guide to the Law.*
20. S. Steinhauser, "Is Your Corporate Culture in Need of an Overhaul?" *HRMagazine* 43 (July 1998): 87–91.
21. T. Brown, "The Dirty Words of Corporate Downsizing: Impermissible Statements of Intent in Reduction-In-Force Cases," *Labor Law Journal* 48 (April 1997): 214–24.
22. Bennett-Alexander and Pincus, *Employment Law for Business.*
23. M. Malone, S. Hartman, and D. Payne, "Religion in the Workplace: How Much is Too Much?" *Labor Law Journal* 49 (June 1998): 1074–81.
24. H. Schachter, "A Case for Moving from Tolerance to Valuing Diversity," *Review of Public Personnel Administration*, Spring 1993, 29–44.
25. M. Malone, S. Hartman, and D. Payne, "Religion in the Workplace: Specific Accommodations for Scheduling and Personal Appearance," *Labor Law Journal* 49 (June 1998): 1082.
26. Department of Labor, Department of Health and Human Services, Equal Employment Opportunity Commission, and the Department of Justice, "Genetic Information in the Workplace," *Labor Law Journal* 49 (1998): 867–76.
27. L. Reynolds, "What Constitutes Protected Workplace Activity?" *HRFocus* 75 (August 1998): 8.
28. M. Player, *Federal Law of Employment Discrimination* (St. Paul: West, 1992).

29. Ibid.
30. *EEOC v. Alton Packaging Corporation*, 901 F.2d 920 (1990).
31. Player, *Federal Law of Employment Discrimination*.
32. *McDonnell-Douglas Corporation v. Green*, 93 S.Ct. 1817 (1973).
33. *St. Mary's Honor Center v. Hicks*, 113 S.Ct. 2742 (1993).
34. *Griggs v. Duke Power Co.*, 91 S.Ct. 849 (1971).
35. Ledvinka and Scarpello, *Federal Regulation of Personnel*.
36. R. Gatewood and H. Feild, *Human Resource Selection* (Fort Worth, TX: Dryden, 1998).
37. Player, *Federal Law of Employment Discrimination*.
38. Ledvinka and Scarpello, *Federal Regulation of Personnel*.
39. Ibid.
40. *Weber v. Kaiser Aluminum and Chemical Corporation*, 443 S.Ct. 193 (1979).
41. L. Kleiman and R. Faley, "Voluntary Affirmative Action and Preferential Treatment: Legal and Research Implications," *Personnel Psychology* 41 (1988): 481–96.
42. R. Robinson, J. Seydel, and H. Sloan, "Reverse Discrimination Employment Litigation: Defining the Limits of Preferential Promotion," (March 1995): 101–41.
43. J. Welch, "U.S. Affirmative Action Hangs in the Balance," *People Management* 25 (September 1997): 13.
44. Ledvinka and Scarpello, *Federal Regulation of Personnel*.
45. R. Robinson, R. Fink, and B. Allen, "*Adarand Constructors v. Pena:* New Standards Governing the Permissibility of Federal Contract Set-Asides and Affirmative Action," *Labor Law Journal* (November 1996): 661–668.
46. J. Kellough, S. Selden, and J. Legge, "Affirmative Action Under Fire: The Current Controversy and the Potential for State Policy Retrenchment," *Review of Public Personnel Administration* 17 (Fall 1997): 52–74.
47. L. Joel, *Every Employee's Guide to the Law*.
48. Player, *Federal Law of Employment Discrimination*.
49. B. R. Ragins, B. Townsend, and M. Mattis, "Gender Gap in the Executive Suite: CEOs and Female Executives Report on Breaking the Glass Ceiling," *Academy of Management Executive* 12 (February 1998): 28–42.
50. J. Lublin, "Even Top Women Earn Less, New Study Finds," *Wall Street Journal*, 10 November 1998, B18.
51. B. R. Ragins, B. Townsend, and M. Mattis, "Gender Gap in the Executive Suite: CEOs and Female Executives Report on Breaking the Glass Ceiling," *Academy of Management Executive* 12 (February 1998): 28–42.
52. A. Eyring and B. A. Stead, "Shattering the Glass Ceiling: Some Successful Corporate Practices," *Journal of Business Ethics* 17 (February 1998): 245–51.
53. S. Riger, "Gender Dilemmas in Sexual Harassment Policies and Procedures," *American Psychologist* 46 (1991) 497–505; and P. Popovich, "Controlling Sexual Harassment in the Workplace," in *Applying Psychology in Business*, ed. J. Jones, B. Steffy, and D. Bray (Lexington, MA: Lexington Books, 1991).
54. *Faragher v. City of Boca Raton* 111 F.3d 1530.
55. *Burlington Industries v. Ellerth* 123 F.3d 490.
56. D. Bennett-Alexander, "Same-Gender Sexual Harassment: The Supreme Court Allows Coverage Under Title VII," *Labor Law Journal* 49 (April 1998): 927–40.
57. M. Raphan and M. Heerman, "Eight Steps to Harassment-Proof Your Office," *HRFocus* 74 (1997): 11–12.

Human Resource Planning

Core Concepts   After reading this chapter, you should be capable of:

1. Identifying major trends that will affect human resource processes.
2. Understanding significant issues that will affect your career.
3. Using the five-step model of human resource planning.
4. Successfully implementing new human resource processes.

Opening Case

Imagine that you have been working as an assistant manager for Le-Kaim, a medium-sized chain (there are about 30 stores spread over three states) of health food stores on the West Coast. Le-Kaim sells a variety of products, including vitamins, organic fruits and vegetables, canned goods, and bulk items (for example, nuts, flours, and dried fruit). In the past year, the owner opened two new branches. One Monday morning, your boss invites you into her office and tells you to sit down. In the next ten minutes, she informs you that Le-Kaim is going to close its doors and become a virtual store (see the main page of this Web site in Figure 3.1). That is, all customers will make purchases over the Internet. Customers will no longer physically enter a store. Before you can even ask, she tells you "I don't want you worrying, so I will tell you right now that I will have you remain as the assistant store manager. Actually, I may change your job title to something like assistant virtual store manager. Oh, there is one thing I would really like your help on; that is, I'd like you to help me understand: what are some of the implications of this change for human resources?"

Figure 3.1   **Le-Kaim's Web Site Main Page**

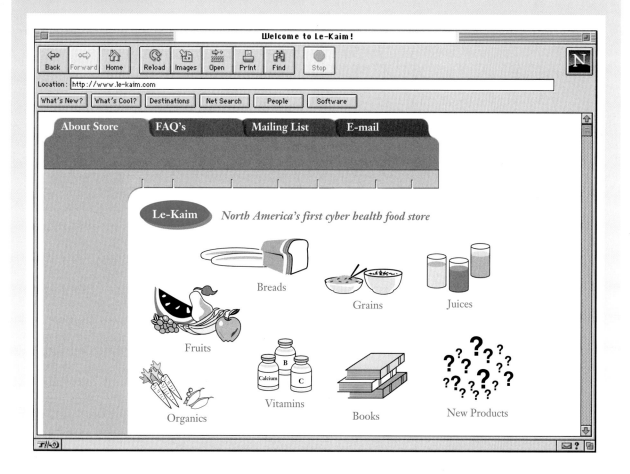

After you left her office, you began to think about some of the implications of what your boss had just told you. In terms of the effect on human resources, it would seem that there would no longer be a need for certain jobs, such as cashiers. At the same time, this would vastly increase the need for certain other employees, such as information system staff. The company will now need to have employees with Internet marketing experience. Shipping may need to be a new function in the organization. The more you think about the change, however, the more you realize that it will have a significant effect on your own career as well. For example, what new skills will you need to succeed at Le-Kaim? Will there be new opportunities for you at Le-Kaim? And should you change your major? (if you are interested in examining an on-line grocery store, see www.peapod.com or www.net-grocer.com).

This chapter is about human resource planning. As you will see, many of these concepts also apply to your own career planning. We will examine a five-step model of human resource planning and discuss some important issues that affect both organizations and employees. We will conclude with information on recent job trends. First, however, let us discuss ways in which HR planning is important.

Why Is Human Resource Planning Important?

Human resource planning is important for helping both organizations and employees to prepare for the future. But you might be thinking: isn't it difficult to even predict the future. Take for example a set of predictions published in 1966 by *The Wall Street Journal*, such as the forecast that large nuclear facilities would produce an oversupply of power by the year 2000.[1] In fact, we have relatively few nuclear facilities and the supply of petroleum is expected to be depleted by the year 2020. How about the prediction from 1966 that airplanes would fly at 4,000 miles per hour? That hasn't happened either.

So what is the value of planning? The answer is that in spite of the fallibility of predictions, even an imperfect forecast of the future can be quite helpful. Consider weather forecasts. You can probably think of occasions when it snowed, even though the television weather forecaster predicted there would be no snow. Conversely, you can probably think of times when it did not snow, even though the weather forecaster predicted a foot of snow by the next morning. You may be surprised to learn that as inaccurate as weather forecasts sometimes seem to be, many organizations pay a forecasting service for regular weather updates. The reason for this is quite simple. Even a prediction that is sometimes wrong is better than no forecast or prediction at all. And, just as importantly, some of the 1966 *Wall Street Journal* predictions were quite accurate. Take, for example, the prediction that by the year 2000, the world population would be at 6 billion—quite accurate, given that the world population was 5.9 billion at the end of 1998. Another quite accurate prediction made in 1966 was that computers would play an increasingly important role in education. The key, then, is whether one's prediction tool *improves* the chances of making the right decisions. Even though the predictive tool may not be always accurate, as long as it is more accurate than random guessing, it will result in better decisions.[2]

human resource planning
The process of examining an organization's or individual's future human resource needs compared to future human resource capabilities, and developing human resource policies and practices to address potential problems.

The basic goal of human resource planning is not just to make predictions about the future. The more general purpose is to anticipate and overcome human resource obstacles that will prevent the organization from fulfilling its stated mission and vision. In other words, **human resource planning** is the process of determining future human resource needs (for instance, what types of competencies will employees need), assessing the organization's future human resource capabilities (for instance, the types of skills employees will actually have), and developing human resource processes to address the gap between human resource needs and human resource capabilities (for example, implementing training programs to avoid competency problems). We turn now to a five-step approach to human resource planning.

A Five-Step Approach to Human Resource Planning

Human resource planning typically involves five steps, which are shown in Figure 3.2. Let us discuss each of these steps in detail.

Figure 3.2   **A Model of Human Resource Planning**

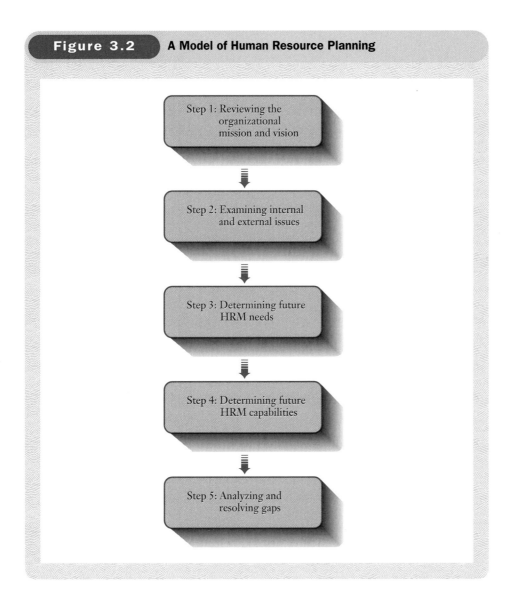

Step 1: Reviewing the Organizational Mission and Vision

Every organization, regardless of its size, should have both a mission statement and vision statement. The reason for having a mission and vision statement is that the stakeholders in an organizations including employees, supervisors, and customers, need to understand the purpose of the organization and what roles they play in the organization. A typical *mission* statement expresses three things:

1. The service or product provided
2. Who the customers are
3. The organization's purpose[3]

An organization's mission may not be quite as obvious as you first think. For example, what do you think is a typical mission for a hospital? If you answered something like "providing health care," you gave the answer that is typical for hospital executives to provide. But is the real mission of a hospital to provide health care or is it to take care of illness?[4]

An examination of the organization's customers is critical in creating a mission statement. Once the customers are identified, the organization should analyze *why* the customer uses the organization's product or service. Successful organizations must also anticipate *changes* in the customer. For example, customers may age, become more sophisticated, or go through any variety of changes. Can you think of any HR implications of a changing customer base? For example, if an organization's customers became much more computer literate, demand might increase for a company Web site. This in turn would require the company to hire or train employees in creating and maintaining a Web site.[5]

In addition to the mission statement, the organization should also decide upon a set of *measures* that will be used to determine whether the mission has been successful. For example, if a gun control lobbyist organization wishes to increase public awareness of the need for stricter gun control laws, it may choose to measure success in this mission based on a survey of public attitudes toward gun control. A hospital may measure the success of its mission by the number of patients processed, customer satisfaction ratings, profitability, and patient recovery rates.[6]

A *vision* statement indicates what the organization should look like in the future. The vision can be expressed in terms of the impact it will have (for example, becoming the leader in the software industry) or the purpose it will have (for example, to create broad support for new tax legislation).[7]

Most organizations (87 percent) today have mission and vision statements and tend to view them as useful.[8] If the organization does not have one, it is recommended that the HR planning process begin by developing a mission and vision statement for the organization. And, even if there is a mission and vision statement, once the remaining steps in this HR planning model are examined, the organization may find that a reconsideration of these statements is necessary in light of various issues that are identified.

Once the mission and vision statements are reviewed, there should be a clearer understanding of the organization's goals and objectives. With this in mind, we proceed to the second step of the HR planning process: examining internal and external issues.

Step 2: Examining Internal and External Issues

An *issue* is any factor, event, or trend that has the potential to affect human resource needs or capabilities, such as employee motivation, competencies, or the number of required employees. **External issues** are events or trends that originate primarily outside of the organization, such as globalization or workforce demographics. **Internal issues** are events or trends within the organization, such as the organizational structure and business strategy.[9]

It should be observed that while Step 2 is presented after the review of the organizational mission and vision, there may be times where examination of internal or external issues leads to reconsideration of the organizational mission and vision. In fact, the first two steps of our HRM planning model are often conducted simultaneously.

Although all of the issues you will read about next are likely to affect you as an employee, we first focus on issues that organizations are addressing, followed by issues that are likely to be of special interest to you and your career.

external issues
Events or trends outside of the organization, such as workforce demographics and technology.

internal issues
Events or trends within the organization, such as business strategy, organizational structure, and company profitability.

External Factors

Globalization. Globalization is a fact of business today. Our ability to instantly communicate through the Internet, fax, telephone, and satellite hookup has made the world a small place. As businesses become increasingly global, there will be consolidations in many industries, just as there continue to be mergers in the U.S. in banking and publishing, to name a few. Companies will continue to develop complex alliances with businesses in different countries as they seek to capitalize on the strengths of each. For example, while the best new technologies might be developed in the United States, a company may find that Japan offers the best manufacturing processes and India supplies superior information systems development. Countries other than the United States may lead in certain industries; Hong Kong, for example, is the leader in cellular phone systems. Of course, there are both positive and negative sides to globalization. On the positive side, greater globalization offers more potential markets for businesses. On the negative side, greater globalization creates more competition, as businesses from different parts of the world are able to compete with each other. Another negative is that there is greater political unrest in some countries than is typical of the Western world. While there are vast reserves of oil in Siberia, for example, there is considerable political uncertainty there, which makes the financial risk far greater than would otherwise be the case.[10]

Technology. The role and effect of technology as an HR issue cannot be overestimated. Technology has vastly increased the speed with which we can communicate and share ideas and information. Technology also has reduced some of our cultural differences (for example, U.S. and British television shows are seen around the world).[11] Predictions are that technology will continue to reduce cultural barriers. For example, experts predict that speech recognition software will become so sophisticated by the year 2008 that people will no longer need to learn foreign languages. They will only need to carry a device the size of a pocket tape recorder that will translate speech into the language of your choice. Another prediction is that by 2010, supercomputers will be able to perform as many calculations per second as the human brain. One implication is that computers will handle more and more order-taking and billing processes, which will in turn eliminate millions of jobs.[12] Internet access and use are also expected to grow dramatically over the next decade. Currently, there are about 70 million users in over 250 countries. It is predicted that certain businesses, such as automobile sales, real estate, and job placement will be conducted primarily over the Internet and that by the year 2008 there will be over 1 billion Internet users. Without doubt, even if these predictions are only partially true, computers have the potential to dramatically change many businesses and careers.[13] What are the implications of these predictions for your career?

New Competitive Landscape. The two forces of globalization and technology will create a new competitive arena for businesses. One aspect of this new landscape will be a rapidly changing, volatile business environment, characterized by constant shifts. For example, in the 1980s, Japan was perceived to have one of, if not the best, economies and business systems in the world. In the 1990s, however, Japanese business experienced a significant decline and numerous problems. A second aspect of this new landscape is the blurring of industry boundaries. As an example, television, telephone, and telecommunications companies are forming strategic alliances and mergers. Third, customer expectations have risen in many industries to expect the lowest price, the highest quality, and customization of products and services to meet their needs. Together, these three factors have created an extraordinarily competitive marketplace.[14]

Workforce Diversity. As shown in Table 3.1, the U.S. workforce has increasingly large numbers of African Americans, Hispanics, and Asians. Many organizations are realizing that their workforce should reflect this diversity or heterogeneity in terms of gender, race, ethnicity, age, physical abilities, perspectives, and backgrounds. Toward that end, organizations are beginning to pay closer attention to creating and maintaining a heterogeneous workplace, a process we will refer to as *diversity management.* The attention being given to diversity management is reflected in a recent article in *Fortune* magazine that identified the top 50 best businesses for racial minorities.[15] Despite this emphasis on diversity, a recent survey found that only 5 percent of companies felt that they were doing well at managing diversity. So why are organizations concerned about the diversity of their workforces? Besides the obvious need to avoid discrimination lawsuits, three basic reasons are cited for why diversity management is important:[16]

1. Cost Savings. Many organizations are experiencing higher rates of turnover and absenteeism for women and minorities. Mobil, the large petroleum company, re-

Table 3.1	The Changing Racial Composition of the U.S. Workforce Group		
	PERCENTAGE OF WORKFORCE IN		PERCENTAGE OF NEW EMPLOYEES IN
	1986	1996	1996–2006
African Americans	10.6	11.0	15.6
Hispanics	6.9	9.5	14.9
Asians and others	2.8	4.1	8.4

ported that high-potential women left the company at a substantially faster rate than high-potential men. Much discussion has concerned why women quit their jobs and whether those reasons differ from those given by men. A recent report by Catalyst, a research organization, indicates that women sometimes mask their reason for leaving by saying that they wish to spend more time with their families, when in fact, they are starting new jobs with a competitor. As an example, one woman left her job at a large New York bank because her requested transfer was turned down and she received a lower raise than she believed she deserved. At her exit interview, however, the human resource manager began by saying "You're leaving for lifestyle reasons, right?" Thus, organizations need to devote careful thought to addressing turnover and absenteeism issues of women, minorities, and other groups.[17]

2. **Enhanced Business Opportunities.** Companies are realizing that having a diverse workforce may be important for business opportunities. For example, when Maybelline, Inc., initiated a new makeup product geared toward women of color, the company found there were no minorities in cosmetics marketing or middle management. To ensure product success, the company hired minorities to help launch the product and subsequently captured a large portion of the market.

3. **Competing for Scarce Talent.** A final reason for the importance of diversity management is the increasing shortage of qualified workers in many areas. Consider, for example, McDonald's, the fast-food chain. After relying heavily on young workers for many years, the company recently realized that the increasingly smaller cohort of teenagers would no longer meet all of its recruiting needs and that a different cohort would have to be attracted to work in the stores. Toward this end, McDonald's has created various HR processes to attract older workers.

Finally, as globalization continues, cultural differences will become more noticeable in the workplace. It is quite common in Norway, for instance, for top managers to leave work mid-afternoon to bring their children home from school, behavior that would be considered quite inappropriate in the United States.[18]

Internal Factors

Organizational Structure. Organizational structure refers to how work tasks are assigned, who reports to whom, and how decisions are made.[19] Although there are many variations, three basic types of organizational structure exist. The *highly centralized* structure is the classic approach, in which top management retains close control over the organization, which consists of several levels of hierarchy; decisions come from the top, and there is little sharing of information. This organizational design works best for highly routine, high-volume products or services.

The second structure, the *moderately centralized* model, places greater emphasis on information flow throughout the organization, both across functional areas and to some extent up the hierarchy. Status is less important in this structure and decision making is conducted more independently than in the highly centralized approach. This structure works best for products or services that are generally standardized and routine, yet some customization and product or service changes do sometimes occur. The third model, the *highly autonomous* structure, involves an extremely flat hierarchy, with practically no difference in status between employees. All financial, customer, and performance information may be examined by any employee. Work focuses on basic processes (for example, fulfilling customer orders), and employees belong to multiple

organizational structure
Refers to how work tasks are assigned, who reports to whom, and how decisions are made.

work groups, some of which change on a regular basis. The highly autonomous structure is ideal for products and services that require innovation and creativity.[20]

Business Strategy. The approach that a company takes in conducting its business is referred to as its **business strategy.** As Table 3.2 shows, an organization may choose from three basic business strategies: innovation, quality enhancement, and cost reduction.[21]

Each business strategy, in turn, has implications for human resource practices. As an example, consider Grand Union, a large East Coast grocery chain. In terms of business, Grand Union represented the traditional small, discount-oriented 40,000 square-foot grocery store. But in the mid-1980s, Grand Union faced a new kind of competition: the superstore food market. The smallest of the competition's new superstores was double the size of Grand Union's largest store. To avoid going out of business, Grand Union's management decided to refine its business strategy by adopting a quality-enhancement strategy, which would be highly customer oriented. This new business strategy had numerous implications for human resources. Whereas previously employees could ignore customers, interaction with customers was quite important under the new business strategy. This new emphasis, in turn, required numerous changes in human resource activities such as performance appraisals (which now would incorporate customer service dimensions), training and development (which would now cover customer service), and compensation (which would now cover more than just speed and efficiency).[22]

In sum, it is important for organizations to monitor their environment in order to anticipate and understand the issues that will affect their mission and vision. Next, you will learn about some issues that are likely to have a strong effect on your career.

Issues Likely to Affect Your Career

Whether you are just beginning your career, or have worked for many years, certain issues are likely to affect you. We discuss three of these next.

1. **Fewer Traditional Jobs.** As you read in Chapter 1, some experts are predicting a major decline in traditional, full-time jobs and a corresponding rise in temporary, contract, and **outsourcing** of work. While other experts predict that there will be less radical change, it is clear that the notion of everyone having a fixed set of job

Table 3.2	**Three Business Strategies**

1. Innovation. The organization develops a product or service that is different from those offered by other organizations. Companies such as Hewlett-Packard, 3M, and PepsiCo typify this strategy.
2. Quality enhancement. The organization emphasizes improving quality of product or service. Companies such as Xerox, Corning Glassware, and Honda typify this strategy.
3. Cost reduction. The organization emphasizes tight cost controls and minimization of overhead costs. Companies such as Emerson Electric, Texas Instruments, and DuPont typify this strategy.

tasks in one organization is outdated. What are some implications for your career? One implication, of course, is that you may need to market yourself more in order to stay regularly employed. Can you think of other implications? [23]

2. **A Broken Covenant Between Organization and Employee.** Years ago, companies and employees shared a sense of covenant, or commitment to one another. In the 1990s, however, this shared commitment has all but disappeared. The 1990s saw the beginning of the DCOI (Don't Count On It) era, meaning that employees should no longer expect to receive many of the traditional rewards associated with work, such as promotions, raises, a pension plan, and even continued employment. [24]

3. **The Rise of the Cellular Organization.** A cell can live alone in an organism, but when it combines with other cells, it can create a much more sophisticated entity. Following this analogy, a cellular organization is comprised of numerous cells (for example, teams, task forces, individuals) that exist as separate entities, but are also able to interact together to produce a greater impact than their sum total. The implication for careers in a cellular organization is that employees will increasingly need cross-functional and global experience in order to effectively work with others, as well as experience in leadership of project-based teams, ability to adapt to change, and the ability to learn new things. [25]

In sum, you have read about some of the major issues that are likely to affect organizations and employees. It is critical that you stay attuned to trends in business, technology, and the world around you. You are surrounded by vehicles for learning about issues, including newspapers, trade magazines, conferences and seminars, as well as conversations and Internet discussions with suppliers, competitors, and coworkers. Returning to this chapter's opening case, can you think of some current issues that are likely to affect the cyberspace health-food business? For example, would the organizational structure need to change? Why? Would the type of rewards given to employees change? Would a different type of employee want to work for Le-Kaim's than was the case in the past? How might those issues affect the career of the employee described in the opening story?

Step 3: Determining Future HRM Needs

With the mission and vision statement in mind, and an analysis of issues completed, the organization may now proceed to Step 3, which involves considering what its human resource needs will be in the future. This includes the number of employees that will be needed, the types of skills that will be required, productivity levels needed to compete successfully, and so forth.

Organizations use several procedures for predicting the number of employees they will need in the future. Typically, this is referred to as estimating the **human resource demand.** Some of these approaches are quantitative and use mathematics, while other approaches are qualitative and are based on subjective judgments.

Two quantitative techniques for estimating human resource demand are ratio analysis and multiple regression analysis. [26] **Ratio analysis** involves comparing the number of employees to some index of workload, such as number of clients handled, number of products manufactured, or sales. For example, a study of well-managed

human resource demand
The procedure for predicting the number of employees that will be needed in the future, usually by using quantitative and qualitative methods.

ratio analysis
Involves comparison of the number of employees to some index of workload.

companies indicated that the ratio of training and development (T&D) staff to employees in the company was 4.1 to 1,000.[27] In other words, the well-managed companies averaged 4.1 T&D staff for every 1,000 employees. If your organization was planning for its future T&D staffing demand in five years, you could estimate the number of employees likely to be employed by the company in five years and, using this ratio, determine the number of T&D employees needed in five years. For example, if your company was expecting to have 5,000 employees in five years, this ratio would suggest 20.5 T&D employees would be needed. A major advantage of the ratio analysis technique is that it is easily understood and can be quickly calculated with standard spreadsheet programs. The major problem is that it may not take into account recent changes in the types of employees (for example, temporary, contract, full-time) or restructuring of the organization.[28]

multiple regression analysis
Relies on factors or predictors that determine the demand for employees, such as revenues, degree of automation, and so forth.

Multiple regression analysis relies on various factors or predictors that determine the demand for employees, such as revenues and degree of computerization. Information on these predictors from past years, as well as the number of workers employed in each of those years, is used to produce an equation or formula. The organization can then enter expected figures for the predictors, such as expected revenues and anticipated degree of automation into the formula to obtain an estimated number of employees needed in future years. Multiple regression analysis is more sophisticated than ratio analysis and should lead to more accurate predictions of employee demand. On the other hand, the use of multiple predictors may make this approach more time-consuming.[29]

bottom-up forecast
When department managers make estimates of future human resource demands based on issues such as new positions needed, positions to be eliminated, expected overtime, hours worked by temporary, part-time, or independent contractors, and expected changes in workload by department.

position allocation and control procedure
A more traditional approach to estimating the demand for employees, position allocation and control procedure uses rules determined by top management in estimating future needs.

Turning now to qualitative tools for estimating the demand for employees, the most common tool is the **bottom-up forecast** where department managers make estimates of future human resource demands based on issues described in Table 3.3. Like any other technique, bottom-up forecasting has its shortcomings. For instance, line managers may overestimate the demand in order to ensure that they don't find themselves understaffed. A more traditional approach, referred to as the **position allocation and control procedure,** uses rules determined by top management in estimating future needs. Typically, a predetermined payroll budget is the determining factor in how many employees will be hired and retained in the future. A major problem with this approach is that it is not linked to actual workload and does not incorporate differential importance of some functions or skills over others.[30]

Examining Other HRM Needs. So far in this section, you have read about ways to estimate the *number* of employees an organization will need in the future to fulfill its mission and vision. But how can an organization go about predicting the types of competencies needed or the productivity level that will be required in the future? One

---

Table 3.3   **Factors Considered in a Bottom-up Forecast**

1. New positions needed
2. Positions to be eliminated or not filled
3. Expected overtime
4. Hours to be worked by temporary, part-time, or independent contractor employees
5. Expected changes in workload by department

Source: Adapted from J. Walker, *Human Resource Strategy* (New York: McGraw-Hill, 1992).

way to help assess these kinds of organizational needs is to use a technique called "mental imagery."[31]

Mental imagery involves presenting participants with a description of a future scenario and asking them to consider the causal events and issues that led to the scenario and the responses they would make to such a situation. For example, participants may be asked to imagine the following scenario:

> Picture yourself at work in five years. The telephone suddenly rings and a person identifying herself as a customer is calling to complain about one of your subordinates. What are the complaints that she gives? When she asks you what you intend to do to solve the problems, what will you tell her? Two minutes later your phone rings again and a person identifying herself as a customer is calling to compliment you about one of your employees. What are the praises that she provides? What things have you done as a supervisor to warrant such praise?

The goal is to help members of the organization attain insight into future possible situations and to anticipate problems that may arise. Next, we turn to the fourth step of the HR planning model.

Step 4: Determining Future HRM Capabilities

The fourth step of the human resource planning process involves an analysis of future HRM capabilities. Capabilities include anticipated skill levels of employees, the number of employees the organization expects to have in the future, future productivity rates, and so forth.

Most of the focus here has been on predicting the number of employees, or **human resource supply,** the company was likely to have in the future. Organizations use various procedures to estimate the supply. Again, these procedures are generally categorized as either quantitative, which use mathematical or statistical procedures, or qualitative, which use subjective judgment approaches.[32]

human resource supply
The number of employees the company is likely to have in the future.

The quantitative procedures generally use past information about job categories and the numbers of people retiring, being terminated, leaving the organization voluntarily, and being promoted.[33] One of the most well-known quantitative procedures is the **Markov analysis.** This technique uses historical rates of promotion, transfer, and turnover to estimate future availabilities in the workforce. Based on past probabilities, one can estimate the number of employees who will be in various positions with the organization in the future. Of course, the Markov analysis is based on various assumptions, which may not necessarily be correct. One assumption is that the same patterns and probabilities will apply in the future as they have in the past, when various unforeseen events (such as new technologies) and trends may affect the actual supplies.[34] Other quantitative techniques for measuring supply include computer simulations, trend extrapolation, and various operations research techniques.

Markov analysis
A quantitative procedure of determining supply that uses historical rates of promotion, transfer, and turnover to estimate future availabilities in the workforce.

Qualitative or judgmental approaches are more popular in forecasting human resource supplies. Among the most frequently used methods are replacement planning, succession management, and vacancy analysis. **Replacement planning,** a practice that initiated in the 1970s, involves an assessment of potential candidates to replace existing executives and other high-level managers as they retire or leave for

replacement planning
A method of forecasting human resource supply, which involves an assessment of potential candidates to replace existing executives and other high-level managers as they retire or leave for other organizations.

succession management
Similar to replacement planning, except that it is more long term and developmentally oriented and is likely to involve input from several managers and the recommendation of various developmental activities for the candidates to ensure the ability to fill positions as they open.

vacancy analysis
Similar to the Markov analysis, except that it is based on managerial judgments of the probabilities of promotion, transfer, and turnover rates.

benchmarking
Involves comparing an organization's human resource practices and programs to other organizations.

other organizations. **Succession management,** an alternative approach developed in the 1990s, is used to examine existing managerial talent in light of future competencies and future business needs and challenges. The major goal of succession management is to ensure that the right talent is available when needed and that appropriate developmental experiences are provided for high-level employees. Unlike its predecessor, succession planning, which assumed that the business environment was relatively stable, succession management assumes that business needs and challenges are continually changing. At Sunoco, for example, top executives meet monthly to conduct succession management discussions.[35] Succession management also differs from succession planning in that it may track nonemployees (for example, employees of a competitor) who the organization views as viable candidates should a position open up. Finally, **vacancy analysis** is much like the Markov analysis, except that it is based on managerial judgments of the probabilities. If knowledgeable experts provide these estimates, the vacancy analysis may be quite accurate.[36]

One organization that has conducted extensive human resource planning for many years is Quebec-Telephone, one of the largest Canadian businesses. An early issue that particularly prompted the company's attention was the rapid technological change, which resulted in the need for fewer telephone operators. Based on its estimates, the task force decided to decrease the number of new operators hired and to expedite the retraining of current telephone operators. Another objective of the human resource planning committee was to develop a forecast of human resource supplies. Based on reports from various divisions of the company, the committee compiled a large database that contained information on staffing practices, turnover, and promotions for more than 20 years. This database was then used to develop early retirement programs and estimate the number of engineers needed in the future.[37]

In recent years, organizations have become concerned with a broader range of issues under the rubric of future capabilities. For example, organizations have begun to estimate their future productivity levels. Toward this end, **benchmarking** is a technique that has recently become popular. Benchmarking involves comparing an organization's human resource processes (or any process, including financial, customer service, or marketing) to those of other organizations. Security Life, an insurance company located in Denver, Colorado, used benchmarking to review its compensation system. One of the issues that prompted the benchmarking study was an internal issue, namely, a change in management philosophy that was placing much greater weight on creativity, teamwork, and performance than in the past. In conducting the study, the human resource department solicited information from outside sources, as well as from internal sources (employees, for instance). Some of the most valuable information came from Security Life's competitors.[38]

Although benchmarking often focuses on an organization's competitors, *best-practices* benchmarking focuses on the programs and policies used by outstanding organizations.[39] For example, Federal Express's leadership evaluation system, employee survey program, and total quality management efforts are frequently studied by other organizations because of their reputation.[40] Box 3.1 describes the basic steps, as well as some general advice, for conducting a benchmark study.

Yet another means of analyzing current programs and policies is to obtain reactions from various parties, such as employees, business partners, and customers. *Employee attitude surveys,* used for years for a variety of purposes, may be quite helpful for human resource planning as well. More recently, techniques such as *focus groups* have been employed to obtain feedback from suppliers and vendors.[41]

Box 3.1
Conducting a Benchmark Study

A benchmark study may be broken down into five basic steps.

Step 1. Determine what processes or functions you are going to benchmark. For a small organization using benchmarking for the first time, this may be a more challenging step than one might think. One way to determine the relevant processes or functions is to ask customers what is important to them.

Step 2. Define the appropriate measures. In other words, will you be measuring speed, error rate, quality, quantity, or other metrics? One highly recommended metric is "value-added per employee," which is sales minus expenses from materials and services, divided by the number of employees. This is an excellent measure because it differs widely from company to company and is related to other important indicators, such as profitability. And perhaps most interesting, HR-related changes will be reflected in this metric.

Step 3. Identify "best-practice" organizations. You must determine what companies are appropriate to compare with your organization. Should it be your closest competitors or organizations that are successful in other industries? Your findings could differ dramatically depending on from which organizations you obtain information. One possible source of good suggestions for best-practice organizations may be your customers.

Step 4. Obtain the information. There are many ways to collect information, including telephone calls and mail. When Bell Canada conducted a benchmarking study, the task force used both short, 45-minute phone calls and longer, 4-hour phone calls, as well as site visits.

Step 5. Analyze the information. Most organizations think that they are better than they really are. For example, a study of small manufacturers found that over 80 percent believed that they were in the top 25 percent of the industry. Top management may be surprised when the results put the organization in a worse light than expected. Be prepared to explain how matters can be improved.

Sources: E. Wiarda and D. Luria, "The Best-Practice Company and Other Benchmarking Myths," *Quality Progress* 31 (February 1998): 91–4; V. Powers, "Measuring Up," *Business Quarterly* 62 (1998): 52–7.

Step 5: Analyzing and Resolving Gaps

In Step 5, the organization must determine the gaps between future capabilities and future needs and implement the necessary human resource processes to avoid these gaps. Because much of this book is devoted to various human resource processes that organizations might use to address anticipated gaps, we will focus only on implementation issues here.

Implementing new human resource processes often sounds much easier than it actually is, because employees tend to resist change. Consider the case of Navistar International.[42] Known for more than 100 years as International Harvester, a manufacturer of engines, trucks, and related equipment for construction and farming, the company ran into serious financial problems in the late 1970s. The financial problems were caused by various issues, such as a declining farm economy, two severe recessions, and the failure of management to react properly. After selling off various parts of its businesses, closing down numerous facilities, and changing its strategic focus, Navistar's top management realized that effective human resource planning was necessary for future success. Accordingly, the CEO, Don Lennox, assigned Roxanne Decyk, vice president of administration, the responsibility of comparing future human resource capabilities with future human resource needs and determining critical gaps. Decyk came to the conclusion that the most important problem was the existing management style. That is, Navistar's management style continued to be bureaucratic and hierarchical. This was completely contrary to the organization's new mission and vision, which would require teamwork, innovation, and continuous improvement. Hence, the problem was an incompatibility between management style, human resources, and company mission. Once Decyk determined that the major problem was management style, the next step was to choose and implement the human resource processes that would enable the company to deal with the problem. But in this case, the problem lay with the people who would be involved in making the necessary changes. So the CEO could not simply tell the managers they must encourage innovation, teamwork, and worker autonomy.

In order to pave the way for such changes, then, Decyk and Lennox decided that it was critical for the top executives in the company to become actively involved in all future human resource planning. Accordingly, an outside consultant conducted a team-building program to provide the necessary communication skills and to improve trust among the top executives. Following this, the executives worked on developing a formal statement of corporate mission. Drafting such a statement might seem like a simple, straightforward task. In reality, however, it was a controversial, conflict-laden process, which nevertheless led to a highly productive airing of differences between the top executives. Moreover, by participating in creation of the mission statement, the executives had committed themselves to a greatly changed management style. Excerpts from the final mission statement are provided in Table 3.4.

In implementing a new human resource process, four basic steps are recommended to obtain employee acceptance.[43]

1. **Communicate need for the program.** Employees will want to know why the program is being introduced. Many people believe the old saying: "If it ain't broke, don't fix it." It is imperative to explain, then, exactly why the change is needed.
2. **Explain the program.** Management must explain precisely what the program is, how it will be implemented, and its potential effects on other practices and programs.
3. **Explain what is expected of the employees.** Management must discuss how the behaviors of employees are expected to change as a result of the new program. For example, implementation of a new pay-for-performance system may also redirect employee activities.
4. **Establish feedback mechanisms.** No matter how carefully planned and implemented, almost any new policy or practice is likely to lead to questions and problems. It is critical, therefore, for mechanisms to be established to resolve problems

Table 3.4	**Excerpts from Navistar's Corporate Mission Statement**

The Company will [provide] . . . an environment which . . .

- promotes teamwork and ethical behavior among its employees and dealers,
- recognizes the contribution of its employees and encourages the full use of their abilities,
- challenges all employees to achieve continuing improvement in quality, productivity, and service to customers.

Source: C. Borucki and C. Barnett, "Restructuring for Self-Renewal: Navistar International Corporation," *Academy of Management Executive* 4 (1990): 36–49.

and answer concerns that arise. Such mechanisms may include a telephone hotline, an ongoing survey program, as well as a dispute resolution policy.

Choosing and implementing new HR processes is a critical component in human resource planning. Because organizational resistance can defeat even the most effective processes, HR practitioners must pay special attention to ensure that the program is understood and accepted by all affected parties. Given the cynicism shared by many employees (just look at a few recent Dilbert cartoons as evidence), organizations must be careful to not be viewed as simply adopting the latest HR fad. One way to avoid this perception is to explain to employees how the new HR processes fit with the mission and vision statement. It is also important to avoid making frequent changes in HR processes, including mission and vision statements.

Finally, it is critical that some mention be made of expenses. Most HR processes cost money, whether it be in the form of salaries, benefits, or training. Careful thought must be given to the costs before a decision is made regarding implementation of a new human resource process or modification of an existing one. Fortunately, there are algorithms for estimating whether the financial cost of an HR process is outweighed by the dollar gain it provides. **Utility analysis** is one relatively recent approach to choosing among alternative human resource processes. Using such techniques, organizations are able to determine the best way to invest money in employees.[44]

utility analysis
A relatively recent approach to choosing which, if any, human resource programs should be implemented, utility analysis considers the financial benefits versus the costs of any human resource program and attempts to base the choice of program on its dollar value to the organization.

Applying the Human Resource Planning Model to Career Planning

So far, our emphasis has been on how organizations conduct HR planning. You can apply the same techniques, however, to your own career. Consider, for example, the first step in the model, reviewing the mission and vision statement. You should create a mission and vision statement for your career. To help you out, examine Table 3.5 and answer the questions provided there. Following that, develop a vision statement. One way to help you create a vision statement is to think about a point in time five years from now. What type of product or service will you provide in the future? How does that product or service differ from what you provide now? Who is your customer in your vision statement? Does this customer differ from the customer you listed in Table 3.5? Your mission and vision statement should remain flexible. For example, your mission may include "leading others." This term is generally preferable to "managing others," because you could be a project leader, a leader of volunteers, or any number of leadership roles, without being a full-time supervisor of employees. Also, be sure to incorporate life and family goals. Be realistic; if your work mission leads to conflicts with your family responsibilities, you may need to reconsider.[45]

Next, examine the various issues discussed earlier in this chapter, including changing technology, globalization, and increasing competition. What are the implications of these issues for your mission and vision? Are there other important issues that you should consider?

Now, consider future needs in light of your vision statement. What new competencies will you need to achieve that mission and vision? You might find out by consulting experts in the field or talking with people who work in that area. Then, continue to assess your capabilities. What are your strengths and weaknesses? What do your competitors have as their strengths? What about their weaknesses? Box 3.2 describes an exercise to help you think about some of these topics.

Table 3.5	**Treating Your Career Like a Business**

1. Define your product or service. Define your target market—in other words, who are your customers? Your customers may include your boss, coworkers, people outside of the organization, and so forth.

2. Understand why your customer does business with you. For example, are you a low-cost provider (that is, you cost less than the competition), or do you have a specialized skill that is difficult to find elsewhere? Why might your customer(s) go elsewhere? In other words, what might your competition (for example, other employees) do that threatens your business?

3. The emphasis in today's business is on quality and customer satisfaction. Even if your only customer is your boss, you need to provide these two elements. Several techniques can help you in this regard, including total quality management and continuous improvement (see Chapter 12). Apply these concepts to your career.

4. Invest in research and development (R&D), just as any business would. In the career context, this means obtaining books, magazines, training programs, and other products and services that will enhance your marketability (you may even be able to obtain a tax deduction in some cases).

5. Consider restructuring or changing businesses. Sometimes, you must change your business or seek new customers. It is unlikely you will remain with the same company or even within the same job for 30 years. Expect change and prepare for it.

Source: Adapted from W. Kiechel, "A Manager's Career in the New Economy," *Fortune*, 4 April 1994, 68–72.

Finally, how will you solve gaps between future needs and future capabilities? As you will see in a later chapter, training can happen in a variety of ways. One way may be to take a class or seminar. But some things can only be learned on the job. In that case, you might learn a new competency by volunteering for a project at a local charity, hospital, educational institution, or religious organization. Alternatively, you might take a part-time job or begin a business on the side.

Next, we discuss some predictions about job trends.

Jobs for the Future

Probably the best single source of information on job growth is the *Occupational Outlook Handbook*, published every 10 years by the U.S. Department of Labor. The most recent version of this volume, which costs about $32, was published in 1996. It provides a wealth of information, including working conditions, required training, and salaries, for about 250 occupations.

What would you guess are supposed to be the two fastest growing occupations through 2005? If you guessed health-care services and computer technology, you are right. The reasons for the growth in the former occupation will not completely surprise you. One reason, of course, is the rising number of elderly in the United States, particularly given the increasingly long life span in this day of advanced medicine and the aging baby boomer population. Yet another reason for growth is the high turnover rate; many people begin and then leave health-related occupations because of low pay and poor working conditions. Of course, different kinds of jobs exist within the health-

TALES FROM THE TRENCHES

Box 3.2

Using Mental Imagery for Career Planning

After you read this scenario a few times, close your eyes, and think about the answers. Write them down.

Scenario: It is exactly five years from today. The workday is over and you are preparing to leave your workplace. Without warning, someone you do not recognize enters your work area and informs you that there is a problem with your job performance. All you can tell is that this person is not your boss. Who is this person? What is the nature of his or her complaint? After that person leaves, you suddenly turn around and find that your boss is right next to you. She says that she is terminating you immediately. Why is she doing that? What made her say that? What can you say in your defense? When you return home, you pick up the phone and call a company or organization that you think has the highest likelihood of hiring you. What is the nature of that business? You are told that the organization will hire you. What kind of job were you hired to do? Why have they chosen to hire you? What skills, experiences, and expertise do you have that made you the top choice candidate for this job? Who were the other applicants for that job? What made them qualified for that job? What weaknesses did they have? What weaknesses did you have?

What thoughts came to mind in answer to these questions? Remember, the goal is to consider your future needs and what competencies, experiences, and other requirements you will need for success, as well as factors that may lead to failure. Only by carefully analyzing possible future situations can you effectively plan for the future.

Adapted from W. Anthony, R. Bennett, E. N. Maddox, and W. Wheatley, "Picturing the Future: Using Mental Imagery to Enrich Strategic Environmental Assessment," *Academy of Management Executive* 7 (1993): 43–56.

care field. Some jobs, such as physical therapy, are in less demand than they once were, though there will continue to be openings for physical therapists. Home health-care aides will see a rapid rise in the number of jobs available.[46]

A wide variety of computer-related jobs will also continue to be plentiful. In 1996, there were just over a half million computer scientist and computer engineer jobs, 427,000 systems analysts, and 568,000 computer programmers. By 2006, however, it is estimated that there will be over 1 million jobs for computer scientists and engineers (nearly double the current number), 912,000 system analyst positions, and 697,000 computer programmer jobs.[47]

On the other hand, it has been predicted that the mining and manufacturing sector is expected to lose jobs over the next few years. Job loss is estimated at over 3 million positions, due to changing technology.[48]

You may be wondering how much stock to put into these predictions. After all, as you read in the beginning of this chapter, predictions are sometimes wrong. How accurate has the *Occupational Handbook* been in the past? A recent study looked at this question in some detail and reported some interesting findings. Specifically, projections from the 1986 *Occupational Handbook* were compared with what really happened in those jobs, and from that the following conclusions may be drawn:

1. While 30 percent of occupations were predicted to have average growth, only 12 percent experienced average growth. The remainder either grew in greater numbers or declined in greater numbers than predicted.
2. Employment of engineers was overestimated, probably because the end of the Cold War led to unexpected declines in defense spending and research and development

of military weapons. On the other hand, occupations such as adult and vocational teachers experienced greater growth, likely due to greater demand for adult education.

3. The most accurate predictions were for occupations where there were clear trends or an obvious impact due to changing technology. Predictions that job opportunities for cashiers, registered nurses, truckdrivers, and scientists would increase were proven to be correct.

4. About 75 percent of the occupations that were predicted to have declines in employment actually declined. For example, it was correctly predicted that the number of stenographers employed would decline.

In general, then, the *Occupational Handbook* may be too conservative in its predictions. Based on a previous volume, jobs that are expected to decline may experience even greater declines than predicted, while jobs that are expected to increase may experience even more substantial growth. Events, such as political changes or new technologies, appear to have the greatest influence on actual decline or growth in jobs. Nevertheless, the *Occupational Handbook* can be a helpful guide in planning a career.[49] Box 3.3 offers some Web sites related to career and HR planning.

We conclude this chapter with a look at some possible new jobs of the century.

Futuristic Jobs: Not Butcher, Baker, or Candlestick Maker

Many novel jobs of the century are likely to revolve around the application of high technology. Here are two new jobs of that ilk:[50]

1. **Information Manager.** The deluge of information available today will only continue to grow in the century, which will create the need for information managers to collect, synthesize, and disseminate this information in a useful form. Information managers will also play a key role in designing and refining search engines to

help you locate relevant information. Is there a job today that sounds similar to this? How about librarian? It is quite likely that the future librarian's job description will be completely different in 10 or 15 years. In fact, librarians in the year 2010 may prefer the title "information manager." A related job title may be "knowledge enabler," for employees who are responsible for collecting, synthesizing, and retaining organizational information to ensure that it is not lost or forgotten.

2. **Netcaster.** You are probably already familiar with netcasting, the audiovisual shows over the Internet. Experts expect this technology to grow rapidly and to eventually converge with television until there are perhaps 50 million channels worldwide. Anyone with a video camera and telephone will be able to broadcast his or her channel. It is predicted that poetry, music, and possibly new art forms, will flourish over this medium.

   Not all of these futuristic jobs will be a direct result of high technology. Some jobs will be created as a result of many people having high disposable incomes, working long hours, and facing many alternative employment opportunities. Two predicted futuristic jobs that result are the passion architect and the personal concierge.

3. **Passion Architect.** Companies, such as computer software firms, that have employees in high demand, will experience increasing difficulty retaining those employees. Some firms are already creating a job entitled "retention consultant," which focuses on methods to keep employees from leaving the organization. The goal of the passion architect will be to maintain a highly motivated, contented employee. The position will require an understanding of how to best motivate and maintain excitement on the part of the employee.

4. **Personal concierge.** Some of the trends mentioned above will lead to increasing need for personal concierges who help people to manage their money, arrange for home services, such as dry cleaning, shopping, and car repair, and provide entertainment activities. These "person Fridays" will serve a role in many ways similar to the concierge at high-scale hotels.

❖ Conclusion

This chapter discussed a number of major issues and trends in today's workplace that will affect organizations and employees alike. We also examined a model for conducting human resource and career planning. Although rapid change is occurring in the work world, it is important for both organizations and employees to monitor issues and events continuously, and to consider the potential effects on their mission and vision.

❖ Applying Core Concepts

1. Discuss three key trends that are likely to affect the organization you currently work for or hope to work for in the future.
2. Discuss how three of the trends identified in this chapter will affect your career plans.

3. Using the five-step model of human resource planning, describe how you would go about conducting a human resource plan for the organization you work for or an organization you are familiar with (for example, the high school you attended or your college).

4. Answer the questions in Table 3.5 in terms of your career.

5. Assume your boss would like you to implement a new pay-for-performance plan at the organization you work for or hope to work for. How would you go about implementing the program so that employees accept it?

6. Discuss three ways in which you currently do or will stay abreast of issues in your chosen career field.

❖ Key Terms

Human resource planning	Ratio analysis	Markov analysis
External issues	Multiple regression	Replacement planning
Internal issues	analysis	Succession management
Organizational structure	Bottom-up forecast	Vacancy analysis
Business strategy	Position allocation and	Benchmarking
Outsourcing	control procedure	Utility analysis
Human resource demand	Human resource supply	

❖ CHAPTER 3 *Experiential Exercise*

Human Resource Planning at Le-Kaim

One week after you met with your supervisor at Le-Kaim, the company's owner, Henri, decided to form a task force to initiate a human resource planning process. You were asked to chair this committee. Henri asked if you had any questions about the company. You prepared the following list of questions and Henri returned one week later with some answers. Your task is to review the five-stage model of HR planning described in this chapter and develop answers for each stage, based on the available information. Feel free to gather additional information, such as trends in the health food business, grocery business, and Internet use.

Your Questions and Henri's Answers

1. What are Le-Kaim's mission and vision?
   Answer: Our mission statement is "Provide high-quality health products in an employee-friendly environment." I am wondering whether it should change now that we will be an on-line store. I would

like your thoughts on this. We currently do not have a vision statement. Should we?

2. What kind of competition do we face in the on-line business?
   Answer: Although other on-line companies sell some of our products (for example, vitamins), I believe that we will be the only on-line health food store in the United States. There is a similar business in Europe, but I don't think that business possesses any risk to us due to geography.

3. Will our customer base change?
   Answer: I hope not. We have some loyal customers, many of whom I have talked with and who said they will be happy to purchase products on-line instead.

4. What is our current number of employees in each job category?
   Answer: We currently employ 60 part-time stockers, 20 full-time cashiers, 30 full-time store managers, 30 part-time assistant store managers, one accountant, one finance manager, one marketing manager, two information system staff, one part-time human resource manager, one facilities man-

ager, three clerical employees, and three purchasing employees. I have hired one part-timer to develop our Web site.

5. What HR concerns do you, as the owner, have as we move on-line?

Answer:

a. I worry that our employees will have difficulty adjusting to a completely different way of doing business.

b. I worry that we will not be profitable at first, and that employees will become concerned.

c. I worry that some employees will no longer be needed, and I am not sure what will be the best way to handle that.

6. What is your timetable for switching to cyberspace? Answer: I would like to have a Web site available within six months. I hope to close all of the stores within one year.

❖ Chapter 3 References

1. R. Toth, "Keeping Us Honest," *Wall Street Journal*, 16 November 1998, R38.
2. J. Walker, *Human Resource Strategy* (New York: McGraw-Hill, 1992).
3. D. Eadie, *Beyond Strategic Planning* (Washington, D.C.: National Center For NonProfit Boards, 1993).
4. P. Drucker, *The Five Most Important Questions You Will Ever Ask About Your Nonprofit Organization* (San Francisco: Jossey-Bass, 1993).
5. Ibid.
6. Ibid.
7. Eadie, *Beyond Strategic Planning*.
8. D. Rigby, "What's Today's Special At the Consultants' Café?" *Fortune*, 7 September 1998, 162.
9. Walker, *Human Resource Strategy*.
10. M. Hitt, B. Keats, and S. DeMarie, "Navigating in the New Competitive Landscape: Building Strategic Flexibility and Competitive Advantage in the 21st Century," *Academy of Management Executive* 12 (1998): 22–42.
11. Ibid.
12. W. Bulkeley, "Peering Ahead," *Wall Street Journal*, 16 November 1998, R4.
13. R. Narisetti, "New and Improved," *Wall Street Journal*, 16 November 1998, R33.
14. Hitt, Keats, and DeMarie, "Navigating."
15. R. Johnson, "50 Best Companies for Asians, Blacks, and Hispanics," *Fortune*, 3 August 1998, 94–108.
16. G. Robinson and K. Dechant, "Building a Business Case for Diversity," *Academy of Management Executive* 11 (August 1997): 21–31.
17. C. Hymowitz, "Managing Your Career," *Wall Street Journal*, 11 November 1997, B1.
18. K. Roberts, E. Kossek, and C. Ozeki, "Managing the Global Workforce: Challenges and Strategies," *Academy of Management Executive* 12 (November 1998): 93–106.
19. S. Robbins, *Organization Theory: Structure, Design, and Applications* (Englewood Cliffs, NJ: Prentice-Hall, 1990).
20. M. Overholt, "Flexible Organizations: Using Organizational Design as a Competitive Advantage," *Human Resource Planning* 20 (1997): 22–32.
21. M. Porter, *Competitive Strategy* (New York: Free Press, 1985); R. Schuler and S. Jackson, "Linking Competitive Strategy with Human Resource Management Practices," *Academy of Management Executive* 1 (1985): 207–19.
22. R. Schuler, "Strategic Human Resources Management: Linking the People with the Strategic Needs of the Business," *Organizational Dynamics* 21 (1992): 18–32.
23. K. Brousseau, M. Driver, K. Eneroth, and R. Larsson, "Career Pandemonium: Realigning Organizations and Individuals," *Academy of Management Executive* 10 (1996): 52–66.
24. Ibid.

25. B. Allred, C. Snow, and R. Miles, "Characteristics of Managerial Careers in the 21st Century," *Academy of Management Executive* 10 (1996): 17–27.
26. H. Heneman and R. Heneman, *Staffing Organizations* (Middleton, WI: Mendota House, 1994).
27. D. Ford, "Benchmarking HRD," *Training & Development* 47 (1993): 36–41.
28. D. Ward, "Workforce Demand Forecasting Techniques," *Human Resource Planning* 19 (1996): 54–5.
29. Heneman and Heneman, *Staffing Organizations.*
30. Ward, "Workforce Demand."
31. W. Anthony, R. Bennett, E. N. Maddox, and W. Wheatley, "Picturing the Future: Using Mental Imagery to Enrich Strategic Environmental Assessment," *Academy of Management Executive* 7 (1993): 43–56.
32. C. Greer, *Strategy and Human Resources: A General Managerial Perspective* (Englewood Cliffs, NJ: Prentice-Hall, 1995).
33. Heneman and Heneman, *Staffing Organizations.*
34. Ibid.
35. M. Leibman, R. Bruer, B. Maki, "Succession Management: The Next Generation of Succession Planning," *Human Resource Planning* 19 (3) (1996):16–29.
36. Greer, *Strategy and Human Resources.*
37. T. Wils, C. Labelle, and J. Le Louarn, "Human Resource Planning at Quebec-Telephone," *Human Resource Planning* 11 (1988): 255–69.
38. S. Overman, "In Search of Best Practices," *HRMagazine,* December 1993, 48–50.
39. H. L. Richardson, "Measuring Up with Benchmarking," *Transportation and Distribution* 34 (1993): 32–5.
40. M. Harris, "The Benchmarking Boom," *HR Focus* 70 (1993): 1, 6.
41. J. Walker, "Human Resource Planning: 1990s Style," *Human Resource Planning* 13 (1990): 229–40.
42. C. Borucki, and C. Barnett, "Restructuring for Self-Renewal: Navistar International Corporation," *Academy of Management Executive* 4 (1990): 36–49.
43. Walker, "Human Resource Planning."
44. J. Boudreau, "Utility Analysis for Decisions in Human Resource Management," in *Handbook of Industrial and Organizational Psychology,* Vol. 2, ed. M. Dunnette and L. Hough (Palo Alto: CA: Consulting Psychologists Press, 1991).
45. W. Boggs, "Create A Career Vision," *Quality Progress* (May 1997): 30, 33–6.
46. K. McGuinness, "Future Jobs: From Now to 2005," *Futurist* 31 (Jan./Feb. 1997): 60–62.
47. D. Bank, "Dumb Machines, Smart Networks," *Wall Street Journal,* 16 November 1998, R8.
48. McGuinness, "Future Jobs."
49. C. Veneri, "The 1995 Employment Projections: How Accurate Were They?" *Occupational Outlook Quarterly* 41 (Fall 1997): 34–52.
50. I. MacLeod, "Taking A Look Into the Future Job Market," *Ottawa Citizen,* 5 August 1998, D1.

Part 2

Staffing

Chapter 4

Recruitment

1. Identifying different sources of job candidates.
2. Understanding the advantages and disadvantages of different recruitment sources.
3. Using the Internet to find a job.
4. Designing a recruitment strategy.
5. Developing a job-hunting strategy.
6. Creating a resume and cover letter.

Opening Case

Imagine that yesterday you realized you were beginning your third year of full-time employment since graduating from college. For the last six months, you have had the feeling that you should begin looking for a job at a different company. It's not that your current job is bad in any way. Rather, you have learned all you can from this position, you see few promotion opportunities, and even worse, the company has announced some layoffs for next year.

But how should you go about applying for other jobs? The last time you searched for a job you were graduating from college. As you think back about those times, you remember that your attempts then to find a job were not well planned and you became quite frustrated. You didn't begin applying for jobs until about one month before your graduation. As you recall, the first thing you did was go to the college placement office, where you attended a one-hour session on job hunting. Initially, someone spoke about submitting your resume to the placement office resume bank. Next, a recruiter talked about proper conduct during the campus interview, and afterward a counselor discussed other means of job hunting (such as answering newspaper ads). The assistant director then asked how many of the attendees had begun their search at least a year prior to graduation; nobody responded. She asked how many attendees had begun the job search six months prior to graduation; a few hands were raised. Incredibly, several attendees indicated they were within a week of graduation and had yet to initiate a job search. What surprised you the most was when the recruiter said, "Most experts recommend you begin your job search six months prior to graduation. But you should begin planning the job search two years before graduation!"

The job hunt did not go too well for you after that. Despite having several campus interviews, not a single job offer materialized. You also sent out 300 resumes to local companies, answered 75 newspaper ads, and called several managers at companies where you had worked during summer breaks. Although you did not end up using them, you talked with several employment agencies, who promised that over 95 percent of their clients found jobs within six months. After all of those inquiries, mailings, and telephone calls, a friend of yours who had graduated from college the previous year informed you of a job at her company. You interviewed and were made an offer the same day. You accepted this job the next day and are still employed there.

As you think about your current situation, you wonder how you should go about job hunting now. One of your best friends, Yun Taek, told you last week that he had found a job over the Internet, on the Monster Board (www.monster.com). You wonder how you should go about searching for a job over the Internet. You have heard that some people post their resumes on Web sites, and you wonder whether you should do this too. Your major concern about posting your resume on a Web site is that your boss will find out that you are on the job market. On the other hand, you wonder, perhaps it will do some good if your boss thinks you are on the job market. Alternatively, perhaps answering newspaper ads would work better this time, particularly since you have gained some valuable job experience (that was the most common explanation you were previously given for not receiving a job offer). Also, you wonder if there are other sources of job leads that you might have overlooked. What about such sources as employment agencies? Can they really help you find a good job?

You also realize that it's time to make a new resume, which you have not updated since your job hunt three years ago. How should you write a resume? What should you include on the resume? Do you need a cover letter to go with the resume?

This chapter concerns the recruitment process or—from the applicant's perspective—the job search process. The recruitment process includes those practices and activities an organization uses to identify and attract job applicants.[1] Obviously, if an organization fails to obtain applicants who are qualified for the job, it will face a problem in the selection phase. Likewise, if too few applicants apply, an organization may be unable to fill all of its vacancies. It is therefore critical for organizations to identify and properly utilize effective recruitment processes. In previous years, shortages of jobs in some fields made recruiting relatively easy for some organizations. One ad in the local newspaper may have been enough to attract a large pool of qualified applicants. In the last few years, however, there has been a shortage of qualified applicants in many fields and organizations have had a much more difficult time recruiting qualified applicants. An organization's recruitment processes therefore have become far more important in recent times than in the past.

In this chapter, we will first discuss three basic decisions an organization must make in planning a recruitment strategy, and then examine the sources companies use to obtain applicants. As you will learn, organizations must be far more proactive in their recruitment efforts than ever before. For example, it is no longer sufficient for organizations to simply offer competitive pay. In many cases, they must offer a distinctive culture in order to attract job applicants.

In addition to learning about how companies create effective recruitment processes, you will also learn how to:

- Conduct an effective job search
- Create a letter of introduction and a resume that will be useful in finding employment
- Use the Internet for finding employment

Developing a Recruitment Strategy

From the organization's perspective, developing a recruitment strategy involves three basic decisions:[2]

1. **Determining the target population.** The first question that must be considered is what type of applicant is being sought? The type of applicant refers to both the competencies that are necessary to be qualified and the employment status (for example, part-time, temporary, permanent full-time) of applicants who will be hired. Based on this information, the organization can determine geographic boundaries of the recruitment process (will we recruit from only the local area, the state, the country, the continent, or perhaps the entire world?), specific educational prerequisites (for example, recent college students), and whether recruitment should focus on a specific group (retirees, welfare recipients, or others).
2. **Determining the applicant source.** As indicated in the opening case of this chapter, organizations have many potential sources of applicants, including employee referrals, the Internet, newspaper ads, radio and television ads, to name a few.
3. **Deciding how to attract applicants to the organization.** In today's competitive market, organizations must decide how to attract qualified applicants. Toward that end, the organization considers what information to offer potential applicants (pay, benefits, work environment), the source of that information (for example, HR managers, line managers), and timing of recruitment efforts (for example, in the main hiring season or before the main hiring season).

We will discuss each of these three issues in greater detail next. For a look at how one company designed a hiring program for its expansion into another country, see Box 4.1.

Determine the Target Population

There are a number of decisions that must be made by an organization in determining the target population for a job opening. As a first step in this process, the organization

TALES FROM THE TRENCHES

Box 4.1
Recruiting for Starbucks . . . in China!

When you think of China, what beverage comes to mind? If you answered "tea," you are right! The fact that China is primarily a tea-drinking country is just one of the many challenges faced when Starbucks signed a contract to open franchises in mainland China. Another major challenge for Mei Da Coffee Company, which will operate the Starbucks stores in China, is finding enough qualified applicants who will be comfortable serving as store managers. Are you surprised that the company will have difficulty finding enough managers? After all, doesn't China have a population of over 1 billion people? According to Catherine Chau, deputy general manager of Mei Da Coffee

Company, Starbucks stores don't just offer coffee—they offer a "coffee experience." So, the difficulty is finding store managers who are capable of providing the right environment, not just making sure that the coffee is properly prepared.

In fact, Chau's company has many more positions available for Chinese employees with experience in American-run businesses than there are qualified applicants. To ensure that she hires top candidates, Starbucks is focusing on applicants who are already working for chic American-based restaurants, such as Hard Rock Café and T.G.I.Friday, that are already operating in China. To locate these applicants, Catherine Chau has

worked with headhunters and friends, as well as attended job fairs. What helps attract applicants to the Starbucks stores? One factor is the training the company is offering: the first group of applicants hired was sent to Seattle, Washington, for three months of training. Another attractive aspect of working for Starbucks is the trust that the new recruits feel the company has placed with them. As one recruit, Jimmy Dong, explains, young Chinese "are looking for dignity" in their jobs. Sherman Chin, a consultant working for Towers Perrin in Hong Kong, notes that local employees place greater value on training and development than on the salary they can make.

Source: Adapted from J. Lee-Young, "Starbucks' Expansion in China is Slated," *Wall Street Journal*, 5 October 1998, A27G.

should perform a job analysis (see Chapter 5) to determine what kind of knowledge, abilities, and other job requirements are needed for the position in question. Once this is determined, the type of employee sought must be carefully considered. A major issue pertaining to the type of worker sought is the nature of the employment relationship the organization wishes to maintain. For example, does the company seek a full-time employee, a part-time employee, or a temporary employee? It may surprise you to learn that about 3 out of every 4 workers in today's workforce is a "permanent" worker; 1 out of 4 is a temporary or part-time employee.[3] Manpower, the largest temporary employment agency in the United States, has about 600,000 employees on its payroll. That's larger than General Motors (which employs about 400,000 workers) and IBM (which employs about 255,000). In fact, more than 1.5 million U.S. workers are employed by temporary agencies.

The role of temporary employees has changed a great deal in the last decade. Consider Matthew Harrison, for example. Harrison is a temporary employee who works for Imcor, a firm that provides temporary executives. What is his current position? He heads a manufacturing operation in Queens, New York. Companies will therefore make greater use of short-term employees, at increasingly higher levels in the organization.[4]

Temporary employees, or temps, as they are often called, offer many basic advantages for companies. One major advantage for organizations is that temps usually are less expensive, partly because the employer does not pay for benefits. Although the organization must pay a higher hourly rate to the temporary agency, the savings from

temporary employees
Employees hired for short-term projects or to fill a position created by personnel who are on leave, and so on. Temporary employees often are less expensive for businesses and can be added or dropped without having to terminate them. The task of recruiting, hiring, disciplining, and so forth is the responsibility of the placement agency, not the company.

not offering health benefits, a retirement program, and other benefits can be even higher. The cost advantage is particularly attractive for a global organization, because, compared to the United States, other countries often require many more benefits, and have stricter rules regarding firing an employee.[5]

Companies usually save money on recruiting and hiring temp employees, too, and often use the temporary position as a stepping stone to a full-time position. In addition, temp employees often are already trained. A second major advantage of temporary employees is that they allow much flexibility for employers. For example, during peak times, such as the winter holiday season, many retail stores experience a major increase in business. By hiring temp workers, a retail organization can sufficiently staff its stores without having to terminate workers when the peak season is over. Temp workers also provide highly specialized skills that the organization may need only on an irregular basis. For example, an organization may have no need for security personnel, except during a special annual event. Finally, using temps may allow the employer to avoid certain legal restrictions and obligations. For example, the temporary agency is responsible for all employment taxes that must be paid. Most state and federal offices must obtain special authorization to hire a full-time employee and find that it is much simpler and quicker to hire a temporary employee.[6]

On the other hand, there are significant disadvantages to temporary employees. One disadvantage is that the turnover rate among temporary workers can be extremely high. One midwestern automobile manufacturer found that temp employees had an annual turnover rate of about 75 percent, compared to a 3 percent turnover for permanent employees. With a special program designed to reduce the turnover rate, however, the company was able to reduce turnover to 25 percent.[7] Second, mixing temporary employees and permanent full-time employees can lead to problems. For example, Kolmar Laboratories found that temporary workers, who had no share in the company's incentive program, frequently conflicted with permanent full-time employees, who participated in an incentive program based on output. Ultimately, Kolmar Laboratories found that the disadvantages of the temporary employees outweighed their advantages.[8]

Some research has shown that the presence of temporary employees may decrease the job satisfaction of permanent employees and increase the likelihood that the permanent employees will unionize.[9] Lastly, the presence of temporary employees may lead to added insecurity on the part of permanent employees. Permanent employees may fear that they too will be replaced by temps. This can work in two ways—it may motivate permanent employees to work harder or it may cause negative feelings on their part.

You should also note that some companies today prefer to outsource certain functions. For example, rather than having an information systems department and recruiting and hiring employees for this function, an organization may contract with a firm that specializes in information systems to perform all of those tasks. Such a move might eliminate the need to find scarce applicants in this area.

Another issue is whether the organization should focus on a specific population in its recruiting efforts. There are two specific populations that some organizations target. First, as discussed in Chapter 3, many large companies are focusing efforts on minority recruitment (www.minoritycareernet.com/op-board.shtml). Intel, for example, maintains a list of 10 colleges and universities with a high number of minority students majoring in certain technical areas. As a result of this focused recruiting as well as other programs, such as a mentoring system, Intel increased the number of minorities in management positions from 13 percent in 1993 to 17 percent in 1997. Mercury Computer Systems, a firm specializing in high-performance stream computing systems, uses minority trade journals and professional groups to recruit minority applicants.[10]

Second, a relatively new target population for some organizations is welfare recipients. Along with efforts to reduce the number of people on welfare, some companies are viewing this population as a potentially effective source of employees. For example, discount retail chains, who are increasingly facing a shortage of job applicants, may focus on welfare recipients as a fresh source.[11] Bank of America often uses welfare recipients for filling positions.[12]

Once an organization has decided on the target population, it is necessary to decide what recruitment sources to use. A major decision at this point is whether to use internal recruitment sources, which provide applicants who already are employed by the organization, or external recruitment sources, which tap applicants from outside of the organization. Each has both advantages and disadvantages.

Determine the Applicant Source

Internal versus External Recruitment Sources

As shown in Table 4.1, the basic advantages of internal recruitment include less expense, greater speed in completing the recruitment process, less orientation time for new employees, and an effective motivator for employees. Finally, and perhaps most importantly, because internal candidates have worked for the organization, a more accurate assessment of their job qualifications should be possible than for external candidates. On the negative side, internal recruitment reduces the influx of new ideas and encourages in-breeding. Furthermore, internal recruitment means a smaller pool of potential candidates and may hamper efforts to increase minority and female representation in the workforce.

External recruitment has a number of advantages for the organization. Employees from other organizations often bring with them a new perspective. External recruitment also offers a large pool of applicants and may be necessary for increasing minority and female representation in the workforce. In terms of its disadvantages, external recruitment may increase dissatisfaction among current employees, who will resent an outsider being hired. Moreover, external recruitment is generally more time-consuming, more expensive, and requires longer orientation time for the new hires.[13]

Table 4.1 Pros and Cons of Internal versus External Recruiting

INTERNAL RECRUITING		EXTERNAL RECRUITING	
Pros	Cons	Pros	Cons
1. Less expensive	1. Limits new ideas	1. Large pool of candidates	1. May increase employee resentment
2. Faster	2. Encourages in-breeding	2. Will help increase workforce diversity	2. More expensive and time-consuming
3. Orientation time is shorter	3. Smaller pool of potential applicants is available	3. Will encourage new ideas	3. Requires lengthier orientation period
4. Serves as a motivator	4. May hinder efforts to increase workforce diversity		
5. More accurate assessment of skills and abilities is possible			

For these reasons, many companies use both internal and external recruitment methods.[14] Regardless of whether the organization chooses to use internal or external methods for recruitment, there are many different sources that can be used. As you will see, each of the sources has its own strengths and weaknesses. We first discuss internal sources, followed by a discussion of external sources of recruitment.

Internal Recruitment Sources

internal recruitment sources Provide applicants who already are employed by the organization. Advantages include less expense, greater speed in completing the recruitment process, less orientation time for new employees, and an effective motivator for employees.

closed internal recruitment system Employees are unaware of job openings and therefore do not have the opportunity to formally apply.

open internal recruitment system Employees are made aware of potential openings and have the opportunity to formally apply.

job posting When an organization publicizes job openings on bulletin boards, electronic media, and similar outlets.

Companies rely on several commonly used **internal recruitment sources** or methods. In a **closed internal recruitment system,** employees are unaware of job openings and therefore do not have the opportunity to formally apply. The simplest, most informal closed system is based on managerial nominations, wherein employees are simply nominated by managers when there is a job opening. The major problem here is that nominations may be based on favoritism toward specific individuals or biased against various protected groups. Or, perhaps unintentionally, highly qualified candidates will be overlooked due to the capriciousness of the recruitment system. Other organizations use more systematic and objective closed systems. IBM, for example, has designed a system known as the Recruiting Information System, whereby employees complete a long questionnaire describing their background and qualifications. When a manager has an opening, he or she can access a computer base that contains these listings.[15]

Given the many problems associated with closed systems, some organizations have moved to **open internal recruitment systems,** wherein employees are made aware of potential openings. Perhaps the most well-known is **job posting,** where the organization publicizes job openings on bulletin boards, electronic media (for example, an intranet), and similar outlets. A major purpose of an open system is to avoid the "good old boy network," by providing all employees the opportunity to apply for job openings. Another advantage of job posting is that it provides employment opportunities within the company for highly qualified applicants who might otherwise leave the organization in search of external opportunities. The basic disadvantages of job posting include a great deal of administrative time and expense. Another common problem is that the job postings may be tailored to fit a particular employee. Thus, in some cases, the job posting may only increase the perceived sense of inequality among employees who are not promoted.[16]

External Recruitment Sources

external recruitment sources Tap applicants from outside of the organization. Advantages include new perspectives gained by bringing in new employees and a large pool of applicants. May be necessary for increasing minority and female representation in the workforce.

Organizations seek job applicants through many different external sources. We'll begin our discussion of external recruitment sources with newspaper ads, followed by a discussion of television and radio ads, networking, college campus recruitment, employment agencies, applicant-initiated sources, Internet, and miscellaneous sources. In each case, you will learn about the pros and cons from the company's perspective, as well as some suggestions from a job applicant's viewpoint.

Newspaper Advertisements

When you look at the Sunday edition of a major newspaper such as the *Chicago Tribune,* you will find page after page of job ads. Another major source of jobs, primarily

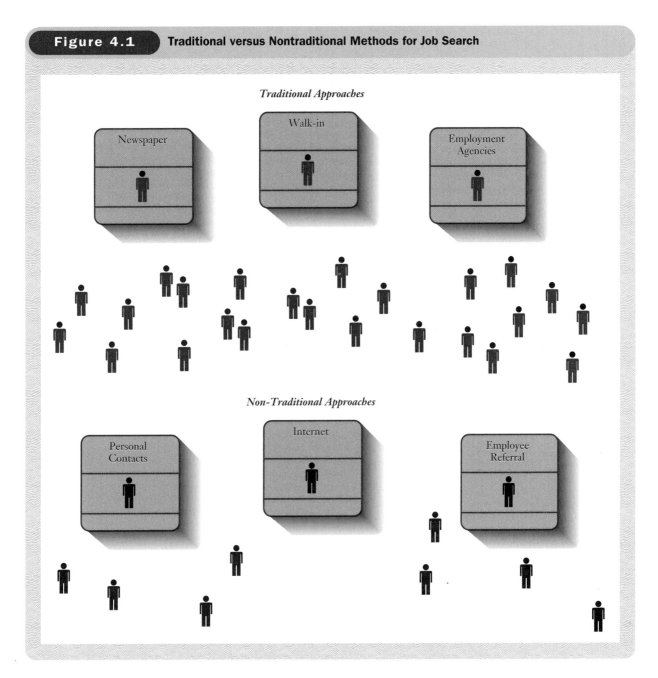

Figure 4.1   **Traditional versus Nontraditional Methods for Job Search**

Traditional Approaches

Newspaper

Walk-in

Employment Agencies

Non-Traditional Approaches

Personal Contacts

Internet

Employee Referral

for managerial and professional employees, is the *National Business Employment Weekly*, which provides ads from all regional *Wall Street Journal* editions. It has been estimated that more than $2 billion is spent annually for newspaper ads.[17]

Given the popularity of **newspaper advertisements,** it is not surprising that this source has several advantages. First, job ads can be placed quite quickly, with little lead time. Newspaper ads permit a great deal of flexibility in terms of information; they can also target a specific geographic area.[18] For example, Stegall Security and Protective Services, a small security services company, recently faced a shortage of job applicants for security guard positions. To recruit applicants, they placed an ad in a local

newspaper advertisements
A method of job recruitment by advertising in newspapers. Advantages include quick placement of ads, flexibility in terms of information, and the ads can target a specific geographic area.

newspaper serving a nearby county with a high unemployment rate. The ad generated almost 100 applicants, 12 of whom were hired within a few weeks.[19] When Mirage Resorts opened a new hotel in Las Vegas, it placed a newspaper ad that included a toll-free number. The ad generated 75,000 applicants.[20]

On the negative side, newspaper ads tend to attract only individuals who are actively seeking employment, while some of the best candidates, many of whom are well paid and challenged by their current jobs, fail to even be aware of these openings. Also, a company may get many applicants who are marginally qualified or completely unqualified for the job. Newspaper readership has also declined, so fewer people are reading newspaper ads. Moreover, more organizations are finding that newspaper ads often fail to stand out from each other. Finally, newspaper ads can be quite expensive—major newspapers may charge over $10,000 for advertising a job opening. But not all newspaper ads are that expensive. A three-inch-by-five-inch job ad in a Sunday paper in San Antonio, Texas, costs only $1,630. One company reviewed its newspaper ads over two years and found that despite the fact it had spent about $20,000 for the ads, not one person hired had come from this source. Thus, newspaper ads appear to be increasingly ineffective for organizations.[21]

In sum, newspaper advertisements are becoming a less popular source for organizations to use in conducting an external recruitment campaign. This is not to say that newspaper ads will cease any time soon; it simply means that organizations will decrease their use, particularly for technical and professional positions. From an applicant's perspective, this is not the most effective source of jobs, as a job ad may produce anywhere between 150 to several thousand resumes. A recent newspaper ad, for example, placed by Ford Motor Company for production workers in Louisville, Kentucky, produced more than 100,000 inquiries, of which the company planned to hire at most 1,300 individuals.[22] It should not surprise you, then, that somewhere between 24 percent and 5 percent of applicants find jobs this way. Like the employee in the beginning of this chapter discovered, newspaper ads are often a poor source for job hunters.[23]

Television and Radio Ads

Television and radio ads are gaining in popularity among employers such as Ford Motor Company and Six Flags over Georgia. When Dow Corning needed to hire 100 plant operators in Saginaw, Michigan, the company included radio ads and was able to attract far more qualified applicants than needed. This recruitment source offers several potential advantages, particularly compared with newspaper ads. First, television and radio ads are more likely to reach individuals who are not actively seeking employment. Likewise, because relatively few organizations use this approach, they are more likely to stand out. Radio and television ads are also perceived by applicants as demonstrating a genuine interest by the company, while newspaper ads may be regarded as only present to fulfill legal requirements. Television and radio ads also enable the organization to target the audience more carefully, by selecting the channel or station and the time of day the advertisement is aired. Another advantage is that a considerable amount of creativity can be used in designing the ad.[24] Einstein Medical Center is an example of an organization that successfully used television ads to recruit registered nurses (RNs). The organization began by surveying RNs as to what features they considered in choosing a job, and it found that three important factors were nurse-to-patient ratio, flexible scheduling, and the hospital's reputation. But the most important factor was proximity to home. Based on this survey, a recruitment campaign was designed. Because no other hospitals used television ads, Einstein Medical Center felt that these media would be particularly effective. To address the nurse-to-patient ratio issues, three 30-second television ads were designed to highlight this feature. In each ad, a nurse from the hospital described a special aspect of the job (for example, the satisfaction of seeing patients returning to health).[25] Finally, it is estimated that 95 percent of Americans listen to the radio at some point during the week, and the average person listens to the radio for 4 hours each day. Relative to other media, such as newspapers, radio and television ads get much more exposure.

On the negative side, television and radio ads may be quite expensive. In addition to design costs, airtime may be quite costly. For example, a 30-second television commercial may cost as much as $40,000. Einstein Medical Center found that its entire recruitment program for RNs (which included a variety of features besides the television ads) cost more than $1 million. On the other hand, radio ads are not quite so expensive. A standard radio campaign in San Antonio will cost about $2,000. Because the television or radio ad is only seen or heard, another disadvantage is that potential candidates may have a difficult time remembering the information, making application difficult. For this latter reason, some employers choose to use the television or radio ad as a supplement to a more traditional newspaper ad. In addition to newspaper ads, Einstein Medical Center also developed brochures and even created a 5-minute videotape for interested applicants.

Radio and television ads are not effective for all positions. For example, they are probably not an effective source for top management positions. Finally, radio and television may be limited to the local area that they serve. Thus, an organization that is conducting a national or international recruitment effort may not find this source as useful as others. All in all, some organizations have been quite successful using this approach for recruitment. Einstein Medical Center, for instance, found that, compared to alternative recruitment sources, its program saved more than $2 million.[26]

Networking

Almost everyone has heard the expression "networking," which means using personal contacts to locate job opportunities. If you have heard that networking is an effective means of finding a job, it will not surprise you that companies can also do networking. Box 4.2 lists some Web sites of job-networking interest to both employers and potential employees.

In today's world, organizations may network in two different ways. One way is to use **employee referrals,** in which employees of the organization recommend friends and acquaintances for jobs. The employee referral method has the reputation for being an excellent source of job applicants. Several reasons have been offered as to why applicants referred by employees may be superior to applicants garnered from other sources. First, employees are likely to refer only highly qualified applicants who they think will reflect well on them. Second, applicants obtain information about the organization from the employees, which enables them to self-select and to have realistic expectations about the job and organization.[27]

Because employee referrals can be so successful, many organizations will reward employees for this activity. Mitec Controls, a small fire- and life-safety company in Georgia, offers bonuses to employees who refer successful job applicants. Half the bonus is paid out after 90 days, the other half is paid out after 6 months. Exchange Applications, a Boston information technology company, pays a referral bonus of $3,000 for most positions, and $5,000 for certain jobs that need to be filled immediately.[28]

employee referrals
An excellent source of job applicants, employee referral means using personal contacts to locate job opportunities.

WEBBING AROUND

Box 4.2

Here are some useful Web sites to help you, regardless of whether you are an employer or a job applicant.

www.monster.com This is probably the most well-known job database, referred to as the Monster Board. It has over 50,000 job postings and provides a number of search engines to help organizations and applicants match up. There is no fee for job applicants. Some organizations provide detailed descriptions of company benefits and culture.

www.careermosaic.com This is another well-known job database that enables job applicants to search by zip code as well as other categories. Again, this is free for job applicants.

www.hrsjobs.com This database contains federal jobs that are available around the country. It enables you to complete a profile for your desired job type, pay, and location and this database will e-mail information about relevant job openings to you. There is no fee. However, each relevant job

posted is mentioned in a separate e-mail, so be prepared to be swamped if your profile fits in-demand jobs.

www.nationaladsearch.com This database contains over 10,000 job ads from newspapers in many major metropolitan areas. There is a nominal fee for using this database, and some lag time occurs between the jobs listed on the database and their listing in the newspapers. On the other hand, it provides an efficient way to search through many newspaper listings.

Source: Adapted from R. Quick, "Your Cyber Career: Using the Internet to Find a Job," *The Wall Street Journal*, 5 March 1998, B8.

---

college campus recruitment
A method of recruiting by visiting and participating in college campuses and their placement centers. Advantages: the placement center helps locate applicants and provides resumes to organizations, applicants can be pre-screened, applicants will not have to be enticed away from a current job, and applicants have lower salary expectations.

The college campus placement center is one method of finding a job in your career field. The center provides applicants' resumes to organizations seeking workers and sets up prescreening interviews for the organizations. Resource material is also available to help students find information about the different careers available.

A second form of networking is for top managers and human resource managers to meet potential applicants, much the way in which scouts operate for professional sports teams. Barry Broderson, cofounder and vice president for Domino Equipment, for example, followed an employee of another company he had heard about for 30 miles. When they stopped, Barry introduced himself and ended up hiring the individual. Kathi Jones, recruiting manager for Aventail in Seattle, intentionally arrives at the airport an hour early when she is traveling and looks for opportunities to meet employees of competitors (she can spot them by the luggage tags or clothing). Finally, Dave Clark, president of a technical company, began a monthly industry-networking group, which his company has used for recruitment purposes.[29]

Despite the advantages to organizations of network recruiting, this source has some potential disadvantages. First, lawsuits have involved companies with predominantly white workforces and few minority employees who heavily relied on employee referrals. In those instances, the courts have tended to rule against the company, arguing that this recruitment practice was used in a discriminatory fashion. Indeed, some research has shown that women and minorities are less likely to network in their job searches than white males.[30] Thus, employee referrals may create legal problems. Second, employee referrals may not produce enough applicants to fill job vacancies.[31]

College Campus Recruitment

If you are currently enrolled in a university or college, you are almost certain to be aware of the placement center. From the employer's perspective, **college campus recruitment** offers several advantages, as well as several shortcomings. On the positive side, many organizations find the college campus an effective source of applicants because placement offices provide much support. The placement center typically helps locate applicants and provides their resumes to organizations. Often these resumes are organized by type of work sought, and they are usually computerized. Most placement offices now allow the organization to prescreen applicants, thereby giving the organization control over which candidates will be interviewed. Because all applicants are on campus, an interviewer may be able to meet with as many as 16 candidates each day. Also, applicants have at least some qualifications, since they have demonstrated the ability and motivation to complete a college degree. Furthermore, in most cases, these applicants will not have to be enticed away from a current job. Another advantage of the college campus is that students generally have lower salary expectations than more experienced applicants. Finally, in some fields, such as the computer industry, where technology is continuously changing, the college campus may be the source with the largest number of well-qualified candidates. In fact, in recent years, 8 percent of all job offers on college campuses have gone to computer science majors.[32] Box 4.3 describes one company's college-campus recruitment program.

On the negative side, the college campus suffers from several distinct disadvantages compared with other recruitment sources. First, most of the applicants have little or no work experience. Thus, the organization must be prepared to provide some kind of training, even if informal, to the applicants they hire. This is likely to be more of a problem on some campuses than others; urban campuses with a large evening studies program will have students with more experience (though they may not necessarily be seeking jobs through the placement service). A second disadvantage to this source is the amount of timing and preplanning required. Although this too will depend on the particular college campus, in some cases organizations must register several months prior to interviewing. Third, college campus recruiting tends to depend on the season. For example, few students seek jobs during the summer. An organization that is hiring during the months of July and August may find few qualified applicants at college campuses. Fourth, college campus recruiting can be quite expensive for organizations located in another city. Costs such as airfare, hotels, and meals for recruiters as well as for applicants invited for a site visit can become quite high for organizations located at a distance from the university. On the other hand, organizations located in the same city as the university may find college campus recruiting a highly cost-effective source.[33]

In recent times, given the amount of time invested in college campus recruitment, organizations have begun to more carefully evaluate these programs and, in many cases, institute changes. One of the biggest changes in recent times has been the decline in college campus recruiting by large companies and an increase in college campus recruiting by small companies. Some organizations, such as TRW, have developed close relationships with a select number of universities by providing faculty grants and student scholarships and by donating money for equipment such as computers.[34]

In sum, college campus recruiting can be a cost-effective, efficient way to hire well-qualified candidates at readily affordable salaries. Whether the organization can utilize and train applicants with relatively little experience, however, must be considered carefully.

Employment Agencies and Search Firms

Organizations known as **employment agencies** serve as a third party by matching applicants to jobs. The U.S. Employment Service (USES), a federal agency, operates a network of public employment offices, which serve as a liaison for individuals receiving unemployment compensation. These individuals must register with the state employment agency in order to receive payments. The employment service also obtains

employment agencies
Organizations that serve as a third party, matching applicants to jobs.

TALES FROM THE TRENCHES

Box 4.3
How One Company Conducts College Campus Recruitment

Northwestern Mutual Life Agency in Northfield, Illinois, employs about 130 insurance agents, and focuses a great deal of attention on college campus recruiting. In 1993, this agency gave initial interviews to over 650 applicants at 18 different colleges and universities. Out of this number, 18 job offers were made and 12 were accepted. The agency prepares the recruiting schedule approximately six or seven months before the interviews begin. Recruiters do their best to set up schedules for top candidates ahead of time and to talk with professors to identify top students. The initial interview generally lasts about 30 minutes. The interviewer for the firm begins with the question, "Tell me about yourself." This question helps determine whether or not the candidate can make a good first impression, a skill that is necessary in order to be an effective insurance salesperson. Other common questions at this stage include, "What is the most stressful thing that has happened to you, and what did you learn from that experience," and, "If you could design your ideal career, what elements would be in it?" In the second half of the interview, the agency representative talks about careers in the company, the compensation system (the job is completely commission based), and even discusses the fact that only about 1 out of 35 candidates at this stage is hired. Candidates who do sufficiently well in the interview complete a career profile. Those who pass the profile are invited to the agency for at least three, and sometimes seven, longer interviews. During the first site visit, applicants attend another interview, meet with some of the insurance agents, and are assigned a market survey to complete. The second site visit can be scheduled when the market surveys are performed. During the second site visit, the results of the market surveys are discussed with the candidate and the candidate's reactions to this assignment are reviewed. In the third visit, a parent or spouse may even be interviewed by the agency, and the sales approach is described and explained to the candidate. Does this sound like a hiring process you would like to go through? Why or why not?

Source: Adapted from H. Hoopis, "The Old College Try: How to Recruit Outstanding College Students," *Managers Magazine* 69 (1994): 16–20.

information from the individuals regarding their work histories and abilities and attempts to find them appropriate work. Because neither the applicant nor the organization is charged a fee, this is often seen as a low-cost recruiting source. A major drawback, however, is that the available applicants often have neither the motivation nor the ability to work, and frequently they are poorly matched to the job requirements. Nevertheless, especially in high-unemployment areas, such agencies can be a useful source of job applicants. If you are an applicant, be aware that public employment agencies place only about 15 percent of those who enroll.[35]

There are two types of private employment agencies. One type charges the applicant. This type of agency will help you in your job search by training you on how to write an effective resume, coaching you on how to interview, and informing you about job opportunities. Fees can run into the thousands of dollars. A second type of private employment agency, known as a **search firm** or headhunter, is paid by the organization. Search firms often have lists of qualified candidates, many of whom may not actively be seeking a new job. They are particularly important for organizations seeking to fill high-level jobs (such as a CEO or a physician), where there is a scarcity of qualified applicants, and when the search must be conducted with a great deal of discretion to protect potential applicants who may fear their company finding out. In addition, the search firm does prescreening, which should produce better candidates. The major disadvantage of the search firm is cost: search firms tend to work either on

search firm
A private employment agency that works for the employer and maintains lists of qualified candidates.

a retainer basis, where they will fill any openings that appear within a given year, or on a contingency basis, when the need arises. In the latter case, a typical fee is between 25 and 33 percent of the hired applicant's yearly salary, plus expenses. Given the fees charged and the need to use such firms for higher-level positions, it is not surprising that nearly 2,000 search firms exist in the United States. It is estimated that nearly two-thirds of executive positions are filled by search firms.[36]

Search firms play an especially important role for companies that are recruiting globally, particularly in emerging markets and where the applicant pool is limited. In those cases, new U.S. managers often make the mistake of hiring either someone who seems extremely bright (for example, the applicant knows several languages and has an advanced degree in a technical field) or someone who seems easy to communicate with (for example, the applicant speaks English fluently and is extremely familiar with American culture). In fact, the most qualified candidate may fit neither description, which is why a search firm that is based in that country may be the best source for recruiting.[37]

Job applicants must be careful to use a reputable employment agency. Numerous employment agencies have been charged with bad business practices so you may wish to check with a consumer agency (such as the Better Business Bureau) to determine the history of the agency. Agencies that have the National Association of Personnel Consultants (NAPC) and the Certified Personnel Consultant (CPC) designations are recommended. Also, check with the National Board for Certified Counselors for information on career counselors and obtaining a list of qualified career counselors (www.nbcc.org). Be aware of company claims regarding success in placing individuals. If the company says its databases contain information about many jobs, ask how many of the jobs are from ads, how many fit your qualifications, and how many of those jobs are available from the Internet. Finally, don't be pressured into signing a contract. If you do choose to use an employment agency, you are generally advised to use a fee arrangement that charges by the hour. That way, you can stop whenever you like.[38]

Search firms that contact you are an entirely different matter, since they are paid by the company. Although they will often accept resumes, their best candidates generally come from personal contacts (referrals from others). If you choose to send your resume to such a firm, be selective. You want to make sure that your application does not get back to your current employer. On the other hand, even if a search firm doesn't have a possible position for you at the moment, keep in touch. A position may materialize later. The best way for a search firm to become interested in you is for you to establish an excellent work record and to remain visible in your field. Network and join professional organizations. Take the case of Joyce Golden, a 44-year-old African-American woman. Several years ago, Golden decided to leave the banking industry. Through her contacts with various search firms, she was able to land a job as controller with a San Francisco-based newspaper company. A short time later, she was promoted to her current position, where she earns more than $100,000 annually and supervises more than 100 employees.[39]

Applicant-Initiated Recruitment

Many applicants search for jobs either by walking into the organization and completing an application form or by mailing a resume in the hope that a position is available. Have you ever tried to get a job this way? Referred to as **applicant-initiated recruitment,** many retail, fast-food, and production facilities hire employees this way.

applicant-initiated recruitment Applying for a job by either walking in and completing an application, or by mailing in a resume in the hope that a position is available.

Some applicants have been successful in obtaining managerial and technical jobs this way as well. You should be aware that some organizations receive more than a quarter million resumes each year. Small companies may receive hundreds of resumes each year. The major advantage of this source is the relatively low cost to companies, because the company is not spending money to gather the resumes. On the other hand, there are several disadvantages. First, although there are no advertising costs, there is a cost associated with processing and storing the resumes and application forms. Second, minorities are less likely to apply for jobs that have not been advertised.[40] Thus, heavy reliance on this approach may lead to the underrepresentation of minorities in the workforce, which could result in legal problems. This source tends to favor applicants who are actively job searching; highly qualified applicants who are satisfied with their current jobs are unlikely to be applying. Given all of these reasons, companies tend to differ on the value of this recruitment source. Some organizations will simply discard any mailed resumes unless they are submitted for a specific job opening. Other organizations may save the resumes for future consideration, even if no position is open at the time.[41] With these points in mind, what percentage of job hunters would you guess obtain jobs by mailing in resumes to an organization without a specific opening in mind? According to one expert, only about 7 percent of job hunters obtain employment this way.[42]

Internet Recruitment

Perhaps the HR process that has changed the most as a result of the Internet is recruiting. The Internet is estimated to have more than 35,000 recruitment sites; millions of people are using the Internet to find jobs. Unisys Corporation, for example, posts over 1,000 jobs annually on the Internet. Texas Instruments plans to hire 15 percent of its specialized positions using the Internet.[43] A recent survey indicates that about 70 percent of companies use the Internet for at least some recruiting.[44] Figure 4.2 shows an example of a job database screen. Organizations are relying increasingly on the Internet for several reasons:[45]

1. The Internet is cost-effective, particularly compared to other recruitment sources. Beacon Application Services, for instance, recruits only from the Internet because one year of Web recruiting costs less than hiring one search firm to conduct a search. Unisys officials indicate that Internet recruiting costs less than $1,000 per applicant, compared with newspapers and trade journal ads, which cost several thousands of dollars per applicant.
2. The Internet is fast. Beacon Application Services found that candidates often reply the same day that a job is posted on the Internet.
3. The Internet enables the company and applicant to share information. Unlike a newspaper or television or radio ad, an Internet ad lets the organization provide additional information about the company, the job, interview schedules, and so forth, in one easy-to-find location. Similarly, as discussed below, the candidate can quickly and easily provide a resume and other relevant information to the organization.

In terms of disadvantages of using Internet recruiting, it is somewhat early to tell. However, there are two possible problems that may arise. First, different Web sites attract different populations. For example, a recent analysis of one Web site (www.careershop.com) found that most resumes posted there were for technical jobs (for

Figure 4.2	Job Database Screen

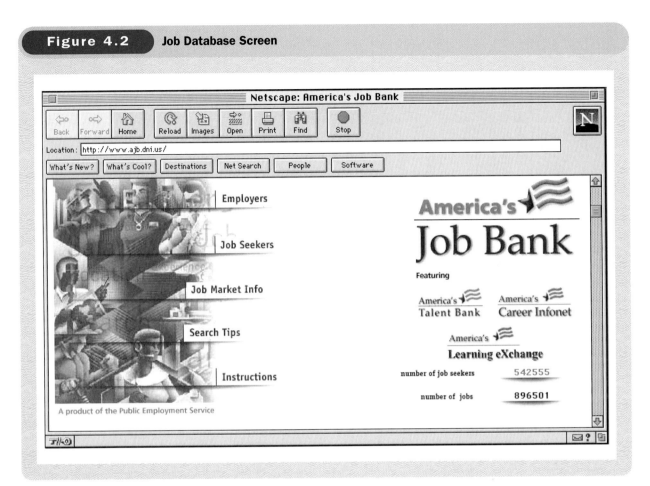

example, engineering, computers); clerical, financial, and accounting resumes were relatively rarely posted. A different Web site (www.careermosaic.com), however, reported that the jobs most sought by applicants were in sales, engineering, and human resources. It is important, then, that companies determine which Web sites are best for them. Second, the largest users of the Internet are white males under 40 years old (see www.headcount.com and www.gvu.gatech.edu for information on demographics of Internet users). An organization that wishes to develop and maintain a diverse workforce should be cautious not to rely too heavily on the Internet.[46]

So, how can organizations use the Internet for recruiting? The Internet provides three ways for organizations to recruit:[47]

1. Both general and specialized Web sites (or job databases) will post job openings from your organization. Many of these job databases also provide a place for job applicants to post their resumes (see Box 4.2, Webbing Around).
2. You or your organization can create a Web page that lists job openings and provides a means for job applicants to submit their resume through the Internet.
3. You or your organization can participate in on-line career and professional group discussions. For example, Deja News (www.dejanews.com) enables managers and supervisors to quickly locate discussion groups of interest and communicate with people who seem knowledgeable in the field.

Y_OUR_ T_URN_

Box 4.4
How to Network for Job Leads

There are many networks you can, and should, tap into when you are searching for a job. You have probably heard the saying "network, network, network." Unlike many such sayings, this one is true. Surveys indicate that about 34 percent of jobs are obtained through friends and about 27 percent through relatives. Other networking sources include acquaintances (for example, your lawyer, banker, insurance agent, and so forth), neighbors, members of professional organizations, individuals in volunteer organizations, and members of your church, synagogue, or temple. A network is also useful when you need references for potential employers to contact. You should speak with your contacts prior to beginning your job search for at least two reasons. First, it will enable you to update them on your recent experiences and accomplishments, as well as your future plans, so they are better informed in case a potential employer calls on them. Second, you can ask them if they know of any job openings or contacts.

Here are some recommended steps in talking with these contact people:

1. In most cases, you should telephone the person. Depending on your relationship, you might begin by mentioning how you know one another ("As you probably remember, we worked together for two years at company xyz"). In any case, begin with some small talk by asking the other person how he or she is doing or talking about some other topic you know is of interest to him or her (for example, sports).

2. Briefly explain your situation ("As you may have heard, John Doe and Associates had a big workforce reduction, and unfortunately, I was let go").

3. Describe why you are contacting him or her. You probably should not come out and directly ask whether the person has any openings in his or her organization; this might put your contact on the spot. Rather, you should focus on two basic things. First, you want to know if she or he has any general suggestions for you in regard to job hunting (for instance, you could say, "I'm calling to see if you have any career advice for me as to where job opportunities are or what the future holds for the profession"). Most people love being asked for advice, and you may get some excellent ideas. Second, you want to know if he or she is aware of any job openings at other companies ("I'm also wondering whether you know of any job openings or any jobs you expect

will open in the near future in any organizations"). If you word your request carefully, the person will also think of any jobs at his or her organization, without being put in an awkward position.

4. Follow through to obtain specific information from the contact person. If he or she indicates that Widget Manufacturing is hiring salespeople, ask the name of the hiring manager. Also, ask if you may use your contact person's name. Presumably, he or she will agree, but asking indicates your professionalism.

5. If you would like to use the contact person as a reference, you should ask whether he or she has any reservations about this. Even if you are disappointed by the answer, you are better off finding that out now than ruining your chances at getting a job later.

6. Next, briefly describe your accomplishments and experiences and offer to send an updated resume.

7. Thank the person, and finish the conversation on a positive note ("Let's try to get together for coffee one of these days").

8. Be sure to follow up in writing with a thank-you note, and offer to return the favor one day.

Source: Adapted from M. Yate, *Knock 'Em Dead: The Ultimate Job Seeker's Handbook* (Holbrook, MA: Bob Adams, 1994).

Managers planning to use Internet recruiting should consider the following suggestions:[48]

1. Locate effective Internet employment sites. As noted above, thousands of possible sites will advertise openings, in addition to your organization's own Web site (see Box 4.2, Webbing Around, for more information). Monitor the results of different

Web sites by examining tracking information to determine how many individuals have clicked on the ad.

2. Establish a budget for Internet recruiting. Begin by setting aside 10 percent of your recruiting budget for the Internet. If you are wondering what costs you may incur, you should realize that some Web sites charge a small fee for posting your job ads. Even more importantly, you may wish to assign an employee to coordinate your Internet recruiting efforts.

3. Create an Internet recruiting page. Many organizations have developed an informative "hard copy" recruiting brochure; you can create an effective one for the Internet as well.

4. Make use of Internet resources. Be proactive in using the Internet to seek good applicants by joining newsgroups related to your industry and by following discussions to determine who might be qualified for job openings.

Job Hunting on the Internet: An Applicant's Guide

As noted above, the Internet has quickly become a popular vehicle for job hunting. This section focuses on processes and tactics for applicants using the Internet. In certain ways, of course, Internet job searching is no different than the more traditional ways of job searching. The major advantage of using the Internet for you, the applicant, is that you can quickly and easily submit resumes to many organizations and databases, send e-mails, research companies, and locate many helpful resources. You can also post your resume in a way that many organizations will be able to quickly review it.[49] There are two major disadvantages of Internet job searches. First, there are many more job seekers posting resumes on the Internet than there are job openings. It is therefore estimated that only 10 percent of technical or computer-related jobs are obtained from the Internet, and only about 1 percent of other job seekers find employment this way (ask 10 recently employed people you know if they found jobs over the Internet and compare your findings).[50] Second, experts believe that networking is much more effective over the telephone or in person than over the Internet. So, if networking is a major component of your search strategy, which it should be, it is important to also use other job-searching means. In short, you should consider the Internet as another tool in your tool kit rather than the only way to search for a job. With this information in mind, let us examine two different strategies for job hunting on the Internet.

Strategies for Internet Searches. Job hunters rely on two common strategies for job hunting on the Internet:[51]

1. **Passive.** This strategy involves staying alert for job openings of interest, but limits the amount of time and effort you expend on the search. You should probably use this strategy if you are relatively satisfied with your job and you want to be extremely careful about other people, such as your boss, finding out that you are job searching (by the way, it is generally recommended that your boss not find out that you are job searching). If you choose to follow this strategy, follow these steps:

   A. Focus on a few *major* resume databases and have one or two send e-mail notices of job postings to you.

   B. Choose a few *specialty* resume databases and have one or two send notices of job postings to you.

    C. Post your resume on-line with selected databases, but only if you have complete confidence that you can control who will see the resume.

    D. Selectively respond to job opportunities of interest to you.

2. **Blowout.** This is the recommended strategy if you want a job immediately and don't mind 100 people calling you in one day. You also do not care if other people find out you are job searching. If you are a graduating college student, for example, this might be the strategy best suited for you. The following steps are recommended for this strategy:

    A. Post your resume on all major databases and as many niche databases as you can find.

    B. Post your resume with relevant discussion groups.

    C. Send your resume to as many relevant recruiters as possible (www.interbiznet. com/eeri/index.html and www.recruitersonline.com are two good starting points).

Tools for Internet Job Searching

Now that you have learned about some basic Internet job search strategies, you will need some basic tools, including electronic resumes and portfolios. We will discuss those and offer suggestions for conducting company research and posting your resume on the Internet.[52]

Electronic Resumes. In the not too distant past, a resume was a neatly printed, one- to two-page paper document that highlighted your work experience and achievements. In today's information world, employees use several different resume formats, depending on whether they need an electronic resume or a paper resume. The three types of electronic resumes are: Web-based, plain text, and formatted. A *Web-based resume* can vary widely, depending on your needs and circumstances. A basic Web-based resume is not much different than the traditional paper resume. It can be used to provide more detailed information about your work history than a paper resume will allow. A multimedia Web-based resume can include sound clips, video clips, and graphics, as well as other attachments (for example, papers you have written). The advantages of a multimedia Web-based resume are that it provides evidence that you are computer literate and, perhaps most importantly, it can provide valuable information about your achievements. A *plain-text, or ASCII, resume* is the basic resume you are most likely to be asked to submit to an organization. It is called plain text because it is created without any italics, underlining, bold, or other formatting. This is most commonly asked for by employers because it is easy to submit and receive. If you are unsure of what format to electronically send the resume in, use this one. Finally, a *formatted electronic resume* comes with all of the "frills" that the plain-text resume is missing. See Appendix 3 at the end of this chapter for more information on creating a resume.

Electronic Portfolios. An electronic portfolio is nothing more than a Web site that contains job-related information, similar to the multimedia Web-based resume described above. A good portfolio can demonstrate your knowledge of computers, your design abilities, and of course, your ability to design a good Web page. Also, a well-designed portfolio can show someone the personal side of you and provide additional, supporting evidence of your job qualifications. Among the elements you can include in your portfolio are drawings and writing samples (see www.byteit.com for a good example of a portfolio). Be careful about overdoing non-job-related items, such as hobbies. Employers generally are turned off by these. In general, avoid putting your picture on the portfolio, because companies usually wish to avoid any appearances that they made an employment decision based on an applicant's race, sex, age, or other such characteristic.

Researching the Organization. You can use the Internet to conduct extensive research on an organization to which you've applied. First consider investigating the industry in which the organization operates. You might search and join discussion groups (try www.liszt.com, which allows you to search for relevant discussion groups). Also, check for relevant on-line trade publications. Next, conduct research on the company itself by locating its Web page. You can find detailed financial information through the Securities and Exchange Commission (www.sec.gov/edgarhp.htm). Hoover's Online (www.hoovers.com) is an excellent way to find information about the company's products, financial information, names of top employees, and other organizational information. Lastly, get information about the company's competitors through Hoover's Online. You might find some really useful information that will impress the interviewer and give you greater insight into the company's future.

Posting Your Resume On-Line. Posting your resume on the Internet may get you a job, but you should be aware of some dangers of doing this. First, imagine someone told you to post a copy of your resume on the walls of a local bar. How would you feel? Posting your resume on-line is rather similar. Although some databases promise confidentiality, be careful. You may gain a greater degree of security from companies that offer a password-protected resume database. Second, be aware of "reverse spamming." Reverse spamming means that someone copies your resume from one database to other databases without permission (perhaps so that they can claim they have 200,000 resumes in their database). Again, this is like someone making a copy of your resume at the local bar and posting it in other bars in other cities. Finally, beware of identity bandits, who may use information from your resume to pose as you. For the same reasons, be careful about posting a home phone number or address on a resume.

Now that we have covered the major sources of job applicants, we offer a few additional sources that are less widely used, but nevertheless interesting. Specifically, we will briefly comment on billboards, kiosks, and parties.

Miscellaneous Recruitment Sources

As Table 4.2 shows, many other recruitment sources deserve at least a mention.

Some organizations have successfully used billboards for recruiting purposes. A Boston-based high technology firm, i-Cube, recently ran a series of large billboards, proclaiming the company as an "incredible place to work." As the company explained, despite the cost of $10,000 to $15,000, the billboards stay for 30 days and are more effective in attracting applicants than newspaper ads, which cost about the same amount.[53]

Adecco Personnel Services, an employment agency, has developed a strategy using job-search kiosks located in malls, where job seekers can input information and find matches with employers that are hiring.[54] But the latest source, which if you will excuse the pun, really "takes the cake," is to hold a winter holiday party. This approach is becoming more popular among Internet consulting firms, such as Cha! Technologies (www.chabang.com), which held a recent party in Manhattan that featured French wine, a heated outdoor swimming pool, and food from a chic restaurant. As the company's 23-year-old cofounder explained, "When [potential recruits] see us partying

Table 4.2	**Miscellaneous Recruitment Sources**

- Job fairs (either on-line or in person)
- Trade publications
- Transit advertisements
- Billboard advertisements
- Direct mail
- Open houses
- Professional organizations' placement rosters
- Kiosks
- Trade associations' directories

like that, jumping in the pool, and drinking, and having a good time, they want to be part of it . . . because it is a great social circle." After the party, Cha! hired two engineers that it had been recruiting, one of whom specifically mentioned the party as a factor in his decision.[55]

In sum, we have reviewed a large number of sources for applicants (see Figures 4.1 and 4.2). Each source has its advantages and disadvantages. From a company's perspective, there is no one best source of job applicants; the best source will depend on the type of employee needed, the nature of the job, and similar considerations. From the job hunter's perspective, there is no one best way to job search either. However, experts suggest that the more contacts and acquaintances you have, the more employment opportunities you will find. Personal networking, in other words, is one of the best ways to find a job. Does job searching seem like a big game? See Figure 4.3.

We now turn to the last section of this chapter and our discussion of how organizations attract applicants. The appendices at the end of this chapter provide information on the job search, how to write a letter of introduction, and how to create a resume.

Attracting Applicants to the Organization

It is one thing for an organization to identify possible sources of applicants, and it is an entirely different task to determine how to entice applicants to apply and accept job offers. In order to successfully hire qualified job applicants in tight labor markets, organizations must carefully plan just what they can do to attract employees. Job applicants take many factors into account in deciding whether to participate at each stage of the recruitment process, and those factors may even change, depending on whether the decision is to apply for a job or to accept an offer. To try to simplify matters, we will separate the factors that affect applicant attraction to an organization into three categories: job attributes, organizational fit, and recruitment practices.[56]

Job Attributes. Job attributes are pay, benefits, type of work, opportunities for advancement, and other aspects of the work and organization. So just how important are these attributes in relationship to one another? You probably won't be surprised to hear that there is a great deal of research comparing different job attributes in terms of

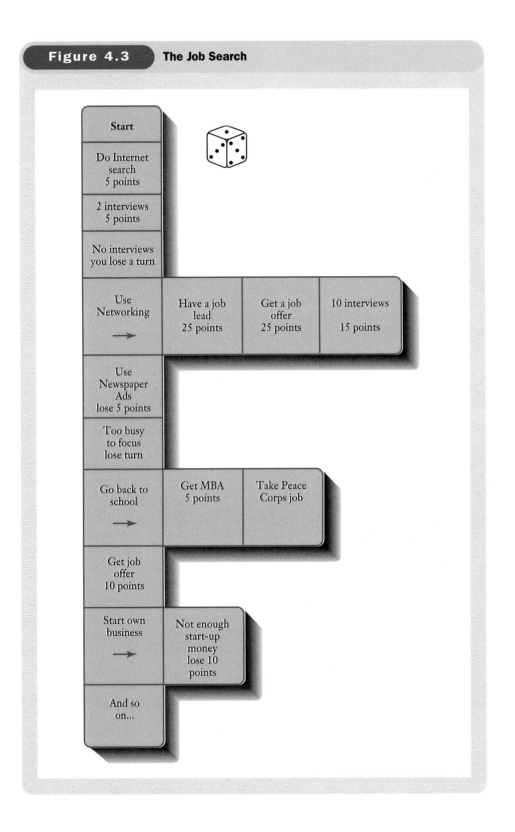

Figure 4.3   The Job Search

their importance. The bottom line is that the answer depends on many different things. First, how is the question asked? For example, one researcher asked people to rank order the importance of different attributes for themselves and then for others. Interestingly, while pay was ranked only fifth out of ten attributes in terms of importance for themselves, people ranked pay first out of ten attributes for how others would feel. Second, different people are likely to feel quite differently about the importance of various attributes. For example, if you have an extravagant lifestyle, pay may be more important to you than to someone who lives modestly. Age and experience are also likely to affect the importance of different job attributes. From an organization's perspective, managers must realize that the type of job attributes they offer will likely affect the type of applicants attracted. For example, if an organization offers low starting pay, but much opportunity for advancement, applicants who have limited experience may be much more likely to apply than well-paid, experienced employees. Finally, it is critical for the organization to provide realistic information to applicants. All too often, job candidates have an overly positive perception of the job and organization. In part, the candidate may simply have limited information or may overlook negative aspects. On the other hand, interviewers sometimes are reluctant to provide negative information for fear that applicants will reject job offers. In reality, however, employees' unrealistic expectations can create excessive turnover. This is particularly problematic if the organization has invested considerable time, effort, and money in hiring and training the employees. To reduce unrealistic expectations, organizations should develop a **realistic job preview (RJP)** program. An RJP is simply a mechanism for providing information about the more difficult or challenging aspects of a job. Merrill Lynch, for example, developed a tape recording to simulate the kind of phone calls a stockbroker can expect to receive. Included in the tape recording are responses from people answering a sales inquiry. Other ways to provide an RJP include a film, a "walk-through" of the job site, informal conversations with coworkers, and brochures describing the job.[57]

realistic job preview (RJP)
A systematic method for providing information to job applicants about the more challenging aspects of a job.

Organizational Fit. Another factor that is likely to affect applicant attraction is "fit." *Fit* is a rather ambiguous term, but we will define it here as the perceived match between the applicant's values and the organization's values. Like fit, the term *values* may be defined very differently from person to person, so we will simply say that your values refer to the importance you place on honesty, achievement, concern for people, and other similar factors. To improve perceived fit, some organizations try to create a common set of organizational values that will appeal to a wide variety of people. Perhaps one of the most interesting examples today is the emphasis that some organizations are placing on "work–life" balance. Consider the following statement from General Motors regarding this issue:

> General Motors is committed to providing a high-quality work environment that meets the diverse needs of its employees. In support of this commitment, General Motors provides a variety of policies and programs designed to help employees effectively balance their work and personal lives (www.gm.com/about/info/world/diversity/emp_env.shtml).

Does that statement affect your perceptions of how your values would fit with General Motors' values? Box 4.5 provides some suggestions for avoiding pitfalls in Internet job hunting.

TALES FROM THE TRENCHES

Box 4.5
Internet Recruiting: Applicants, Look Out!

Here are some mistakes that can cost you a job if you are searching over the Internet:

1. Ignoring the directions on the company's Web page. For example, if you send your resume or e-mail a person other than the one designated on the company's Web page, the organization is likely to eliminate your application from further consideration. Why? Among other reasons, you will have just shown that you don't follow directions well.

2. Paying to post your resume. This might surprise you. After all, if you are paying a Web site to post your resume, shouldn't you be getting better service than if you can post for free? The answer is that the best sites are free for job applicants because they have a high volume and don't need to charge you for this service. As the old saying goes, "the best things in life are free."

3. Being rude. As you may know, search engines on the Internet will enable you to search by a person's name. And many organizations will do just that. If you have ever "flamed" someone or written anything else that is inappropriate in a discussion group, it is quite possible that a potential employer will find out.

4. Not realizing the response you may receive. If you conduct an Internet job search, especially if you post a resume, realize that you may get many replies, perhaps even hundreds. Are you prepared? You may wish to have a separate e-mail account just for your job search, as well as a separate telephone line.

5. Sending attachments with your e-mail. By and large, managers involved in the hiring process dislike receiving attachments to files. Why? First of all, that takes extra work and if you have ever had to respond to a few hundred e-mails, you know what that is like. Second, managers fear receiving viruses. High-tech companies in particular receive many e-mails containing viruses. So, avoid sending e-mail attachments in your job search.

6. Making telephone calls. Most organizations prefer to receive an e-mail, snail mail, or even faxes. A telephone call can be a real nuisance. If the company is interested, you will receive a call back. Most managers prefer, at least in the early stages, to avoid the telephone.

Source: P. Dixon, *Job Searching Online for Dummies* (Foster City, CA: IDG Books), 1998.

Recruitment Practices

It probably won't surprise you that recruitment practices can affect applicants' attraction to the organization. In particular, the recruiter or line manager who first meets the applicant may leave a lasting impression, particularly if the organizational representative is rude or acts uninterested. Although the recruiting process can have a major effect on job candidates' impressions of an organization and willingness to accept a job offer, surveys indicate that few companies offer training in this area. Quite often, line managers take turns serving as a recruiter. Companies that provide training in recruitment methods go a long way toward improving the effectiveness of line managers responsible for recruiting. A training program at Exxon, for example, provides guidelines to recruiters on what information to ask of applicants, what information to share with applicants, how to plan a site visit, and other relevant issues. At a minimum, those managers responsible for recruiting should be chosen carefully, to ensure that only employees who are effective communicators and aware of basic discrimination laws participate in this process.

Research indicates that organizations make two errors in particular that cause applicants to turn away. Time delays, despite their frequency, are often seen by job applicants as a negative sign. The most highly qualified job applicants will view delays as an indication that the organization has problems. A second major problem, especially for women, is offensive recruiting incidents. Among the offensive incidents frequently encountered are letters that address women as Mr. even after an interview, being interviewed in a man's hotel room, and hearing inappropriate comments about dress or appearance.

Finally, as organizations work to devise effective recruitment processes, they have learned that it is not enough to merely attract top applicants. They must also develop and implement retention processes, which will motivate employees to continue working with the organization. Toward that end, some organizations have focused on creating a unique *organizational culture* that will stand out from their competitors. As an example, consider Bill Ziercher, CEO of Sterling Direct, Inc., a marketing and communications firm, based in Earth City, Missouri. He has created an organizational culture that emphasizes "work is fun," by giving rewards for the sloppiest desk, holding beach parties, and giving interesting rewards (for example, a free limo ride) to employees nominated for being the most helpful. Mitec Controls divided the organization into five teams, each of which is responsible for some accounts. The teams are paid based on the profits generated by their accounts, information which the company uses in recruiting new employees. Finally, Amy's Ice Creams is a chain of ice cream stores growing at a rate of 20 percent annually. The owner, Amy Miller, shares the stores' culture with applicants from the beginning of the recruitment process. How does she do that? Rather than giving out formal application forms, Amy gives applicants a plain paper bag and instructs them to do anything they want with it and to bring it back in one week. One applicant turned the bag into a pop-up jack-in-the-box, while another applicant created a globe-like sphere that perched on top of an ice-cream cone. Other organizations have emphasized sharing with and obtaining from applicants extensive information about the recruitment process. Consider Robert Charles Lesser & Company, a Los Angeles-based real-estate consulting firm. In terms of sharing information with potential and actual job applicants, the firm has created a Web site that contains extensive information on the recruiting process (see www.rclco.com). The company also publishes an annual report covering all benefits (including paid sabbatical and a training allowance), information about client-projects, and information about company revenues, which it supplies to job applicants. In order to improve its recruiting processes, the company interviewed current employees who had recently gone through the hiring process and the HR manager uses e-mail to get feedback from applicants who turn down a job offer.[59]

❖ Conclusion

Regardless of whether you are seeking to hire new employees or are trying to find a job, the recruitment process is critical to success. From a job applicant's perspective, networking is the best way to find jobs. Be sure to develop a thorough job hunt, and devote the necessary time to it. From the perspective of an employer, there are many different applicant sources; which one will be most useful depends on the nature of the job and the type of employee you seek to find. You, as a manager or supervisor, can do much to improve the effectiveness of your recruitment process, including developing an accurate job description, conducting a good interview, providing realistic information about the job and company, and creating a rewarding and unique organizational or departmental culture.

❖ Appendix 1

The Job Search: General Strategies

You can choose among many different strategies and ways to find a job. Many books, computer software packages, and businesses (such as employment agencies) also provide assistance in your job search. Your choices will depend much on your occupation, experience, education, and qualifications. Nevertheless, here are some general pointers for job hunting.[60]

1. **A Job Search Takes Much Time and Effort.** How long do you think it generally takes to find a job? Two days? Two weeks? Four weeks? Ten weeks? The truth is that it generally takes between 2 to 8 months to find a job. Because that's only the typical length of time, it can take much longer, too. How many hours each week do you think you should devote to the job search? Most experts recommend 20 or more hours, even though the majority of job searchers spend fewer than 5 hours per week. The point is that a job search takes a great deal more time and effort than most people think.

2. **Try to Talk with as Many Hiring Managers as Possible.** Because the hiring manager is the one who determines if there is a need to hire someone and whom to hire, you should find out who this person is and meet with him or her. If you have a mutual acquaintance who can serve as a contact with the person, you are even more likely to be successful in finding a job. We can draw an analogy between a job hunter and a salesperson. Who do you think is going to be the most successful— the salesperson who merely sends flyers about the product, the salesperson who talks on the phone to a receptionist without control over the purchasing, or the salesperson who meets with the purchasing manager? As you probably guessed, the salesperson who meets in person with the purchasing manager is most likely to sell the product. You, the job hunter, are similar to a salesperson—you are selling yourself as an employee.

3. **Pursue Small Businesses.** Every survey shows that large companies are downsizing and reducing their workforces. A great deal of job growth, on the other hand, is coming from small businesses. Although small businesses may seem less prestigious, they often offer many more opportunities. In a small company, you will generally have a wider variety of responsibilities, because a small company does not need and cannot afford many specialists. As a human resource employee, for instance, you may well be responsible for all compensation, benefits, hiring, and training. Such broad responsibilities would be rare in a large firm. Not only are there many more job openings in small businesses, then, but the learning and growth opportunities abound.

4. **Use All Possible Recruitment Sources.** In this chapter, we described many of the different recruitment sources companies use, ranging from newspaper advertisements to the Internet. While you need to be much more careful and discreet if

you are currently employed, if you are unemployed, throw caution to the wind. And don't forget networking. As described in the chapter, anyone can serve as a potential job lead, including friends, neighbors, doctors, professors, and so forth.

5. **Cast a Wide Net.** The worst thing you can do in today's extremely competitive job market is be narrow either in terms of the type of companies you are pursuing or in the type of job you are pursuing. You must be more willing to consider companies that are not your ideal and be willing to consider jobs that are not your "dream job."

6. **Seek Support.** If you search earnestly, you will get turned down for jobs. There is only one way to have a perfect batting average—by not going up to bat! But that's a .000 batting average. Job hunting is different from baseball in one key way. The job seeker who hits a home run (that is, gets an excellent job offer) one time out of 1,000 at bat is just as successful as the job seeker who gets 300 home runs out of 1,000 times at bat. So, like any successful salesperson, you will get rejections. What you need, therefore, is a support group, friend, or relative who will serve as a cheering squad. You will probably need to work at keeping your morale and self-esteem up. The worst mistake is to come across to a prospective employer as a frustrated person with low self-esteem. So, keep your chin up and keep hunting!

❖ Appendix 2

Writing the Cover Letter

In almost every case, you will want to include a letter with your resume. Traditionally referred to as a *cover letter*, some experts recommend that you think of this as a letter of introduction. Ask yourself this question, when you introduce yourself to someone that you meet, do you always use the same format? Probably not—if you were meeting a customer, you would probably introduce yourself differently than if you were meeting a new boss. The same idea is true here—you need to tailor your job-hunting introduction differently, depending on the situation. The basic purpose of the letter of introduction is to introduce yourself and grab the attention of the reader. While the content of the letter of introduction will depend to some degree on the particular circumstances (for example, how well you know the recipient or whether you are responding to a specific job ad or not), here are seven basic steps to assist you in writing the letter of introduction.[61]

1. Use a standard business letter for.mat, in which your name, address, and phone number appear in the top left-hand corner, followed by the date on the far right-hand side of the page, and the addressee's name and address on the left-hand corner. Begin with the salutation "Dear Ms.:" or "Dear Mr.:". Never address the person by job title (for example, "Dear HR Manager"). That signals to the reader that he or she is just another name from a mailing list.

2. In preparing your letter, put yourself in the place of the reader. The reader probably wants to know, as quickly as possible, who you are, why you are writing, what you want, and what can you offer to him or her. The best style choice is to communicate to the reader as directly as possible. In other words, use short sentences, everyday terms, and the active voice ("I have the ability to ABC") rather than the passive voice ("The abilities that I have include ABC . . .").

3. Begin the body of the letter with a strong opening sentence or two, such as, "I was recently encouraged by a mutual acquaintance, Richard Green, to write to you re-

garding a potential job opening in your firm." If you are responding to a job ad, be sure to mention that ("I am writing in response to the job advertisement in the *Wall Street Journal* for a position in financial management"). Add any other information, such as a job number, that will help the reader know which job you are applying for (for example, Job #12459696).

4. Now that you have told him or her why you are writing, you want to explain in a short paragraph why the reader should be interested in you. Emphasize what you can do for the recipient of the letter (for example, "My background in SAP will enable me to do XYZ"), not what the recipient can do for you (for example, "Your position will enable me to learn more about SAP"). Explain briefly (in one or two paragraphs) why you are qualified for the job (for instance, "In my seven years of experience in the field of financial management, I have produced a consistent track record of cost reduction . . .").

5. Be careful not to overuse sample letters that are provided in books and CD-ROMs. Those letters will often times show lack of creativity, rather than anything else.

6. To wrap up the letter, close on a strong note. In fact, the ending may be the most important part of the letter. Say something like, "I hope to speak to you further, and I will call next week to follow up."

7. Review the letter very carefully for typos, mistakes, and clarity. Get the most critical person you know to read it over carefully. You would be surprised at all of the funny and stupid mistakes that I have found reading over letters of introduction. The letter should be no more than one page long.

❖ Appendix 3

Writing the Resume

Aside from the formatting issues discussed in this chapter, job searchers tend to use one of three basic resume styles: [62]

1. The **chronological resume** is the style with which you are probably most familiar. The chronological resume lists each of your jobs, beginning with the most recent and ending with the first job you held. The chronological resume is considered ideal for someone who has worked primarily in one profession, has had few periods of unemployment, and has had few job changes. The chronological resume tends to be ineffective for someone who is changing occupations or is just out of school and has little job experience.

chronological resume
The type of resume that lists each of your jobs, beginning with the most recent and ending with the first job you held.

2. The **functional resume** emphasizes your skills and experiences. It is ideal for someone with many different jobs and areas of expertise, military employees who are applying for civilian jobs, people closer to retirement age, and individuals who are returning to the work world after a long absence (such as women who have been full-time homemakers and are now beginning to work outside the home).

functional resume
The type of resume that lists skills and experiences.

3. The **chrono-functional resume** combines both the chronological and functional approaches. It is ideal for someone with a strong career record who desires to use the advantages of both approaches. This may also work well for a recent college graduate.

chrono-functional resume
The type of resume that combines the chronological and functional resume.

Regardless of the type of resume you have, the resume should be no more than two pages long. Any longer than that, and the hiring manager will seriously question your business judgment and ability to communicate successfully. Now that you have read about the different kinds of resumes, let's talk about the basic components of any resume.

All Resumes Should Have the Following Elements

1. **Your Name.** Give your first and last names only (for example, Michael Harris); avoid initials (D. Z. Dean). Generally, there is no need to mark Mr. or Ms., though you may wish to if your name does not indicate your gender (Mr. Chris Sanders).

2. **Your Address.** Avoid abbreviations (for instance, use "Street" rather than "St."). The only exception is the state, where postal standards stipulate the use of the postal abbreviation (Missouri is MO, for example).

3. **Your Telephone and Fax Numbers.** Always include your area code, even if you apply for a local company. While you will always want to include your home phone number, the question is whether to include your work number. Including a work number might allow a prospective employer to call you at a bad time, or even more critically, may tip off your manager that you are job hunting. One recommended solution is to put your work number in the letter of introduction, with a comment about using discretion if he or she contacts you there. Regardless of which number you provide, be sure there is always someone to answer the phone or there is an answering machine. Otherwise, the recruiter may simply proceed to the next person on the list without trying again.

4. **Your Internet Information.** If you have an e-mail address, include that information as well. If you have a Web site or portfolio, include the URL (that is, Web site address) on the resume as well.

5. **Education.** Typically, this section should contain the degree awarded from each school, the name of the school, and the date of graduation (unless that will mark you as possibly too old or too young for the position). If your grade-point average was between 3.0 and 4.0, you should list that information, otherwise you are better off not listing it. If applicable, you should include any scholarships or honors you received. Whether the education section comes before or after the experience section will depend on several factors. In general, the education section should come first only if you have just graduated from school and you have a limited job history.

6. **A Summary or Key Word Paragraph.** With the popularity of resume tracking and scanning systems, medium- and large-size organizations are increasingly using computers to cull through resumes. The purpose of the summary or key-word paragraph is to list possible key words that will ensure your resume is not mistakenly eliminated in the process. For example, one job applicant included over a dozen buzz words and key terms in a paragraph, such as ultrasonics, casting, steel, and molten metal. There is some disagreement as to whether this paragraph should be the first paragraph, or should come after the job objective (see below). By the way, you need not label this the "key-word summary." The term "qualifications" or "skill summary" or something like that may look more professional.[63]

Think Carefully About Including the Following in Your Resume

1. **Job Objective.** There is considerable debate among experts as to whether you should include a job objective or desired position statement. On the positive side,

this information will help focus the resume and clarify for the company why your application is appropriate. On the other hand, a job objective that is too specific will exclude you from other opportunities. Therefore, you should keep the objective fairly general or avoid a job objective altogether on the resume. Some job hunters use two or three resumes, each with a different objective. Just don't get mixed up if you get a call!

2. **Personal Interests.** Do any of your hobbies or interests mesh with the job? If they do, you may wish to include them. If there isn't an obvious link, it's probably not worth it to include them.
3. **Personal Information.** Facts such as your marital status and relocation flexibility are often not pertinent or conceivably could hurt your chances of employment, In other circumstances, these facts may help increase your chances of employment. Generally, personal information should be avoided, since many issues, such as your marital status, are not job related.

Never Include the Following in Your Resume

There are several pieces of information that you probably should never provide in your resume. These include the following:

1. **Reasons for Leaving a Job.** It can only hurt you. This topic will be covered in the interview anyhow—so there is no value in addressing it here.
2. **References.** It is considered unprofessional to put the names of actual references on the resume. Most employers will assume you have references anyhow. But you should note at the end something like "References available upon request." If for no other reason, this forces you, the job hunter, to make sure you have informed these references of your plans.
3. **Exaggerations.** Don't lie or stretch the truth on your resume. Most likely a thorough, smart interviewer will catch it.

Now that you have read about some basic considerations, let's address the actual writing of a resume. First, we will review some general writing style considerations, followed by specific suggestions for writing a chronological resume. After that, you will learn some tips on writing a functional resume.

Writing the Resume: General Points

The writing in any resume must be clear, concise, and direct. To meet these guidelines, follow these general suggestions:

1. Use action verbs: *acted, adapted, installed, performed, edited,* and *produced.*
2. Avoid the pronoun *I* since the reader will assume that you did whatever you have described. (Write, for example, "Designed and installed new computer system.")
3. Use incomplete sentences, especially since you do not need the pronoun *I.*
4. Use quantitative terms wherever possible. It is much more convincing to have "Increased sales volume 50 percent" than to have "Greatly increased sales volume."
5. Use one long sentence rather than several short sentences, and avoid any extraneous words.

Chronological Resume: Describing the Jobs

Recall that the chronological resume focuses on each job that you have worked, in the order that you have worked in them. For each job, then, you should list the following:

1. **Job Title.** Use the most general, meaningful job title. This may not be the actual title your company used, but you want to make sure that the screening manager understands what your previous job was. For example, "Senior Associate" may be what your company called the job, but the more meaningful title might be "Account Representative." Also, avoid using titles that designate level, such as junior, intermediate, or trainee. Such titles might imply a lower status than was the case.
2. **Responsibilities.** Rather than merely providing a brief description of the basic tasks you performed, you should report the major achievements in the job. For example, rather than saying "responsible for monitoring inventory, negotiating contracts, and making purchasing decisions" you might say "implemented new JIT inventory system, negotiated 30 percent reduction in charges, and decreased purchase decision time by 20 percent." If you managed a budget or supervised people, be sure to include the actual figures ("managed a $500,000 budget").
3. **Employment Dates.** Failure to include the dates of employment for each job is an immediate red flag to the hiring manager. If you have no significant gaps in your employment record, you should probably use the month and year (such as "August 1988 to July 1992"). If there are short gaps in your employment, you may wish to insert only the years ("1988–92"). If there are gaps of several years, you probably should be using a functional resume.

Functional Resume: Describing the Skills and Experiences

The functional resume focuses on your skills and experiences. To design the functional resume, you should determine the major responsibilities and functions of the job(s) you are applying for. Then, rank the importance of each of those major responsibilities and functions. Once you have done that, determine which of those responsibilities and functions you have had experience with and your major accomplishments in each. For example, you might determine that "cost reduction" is a major responsibility for the kind of work you are seeking. Although you have never worked in the position of office manager, you may have engaged in cost reduction in other positions you had, such as production supervisor. List any related accomplishments under the cost reduction heading (for example, "reduced scrap rate, resulting in a 20 percent cost reduction").

For a combination resume, you will probably list the skills and experiences first, followed by a brief section on work history. In that case, the work history might include only the dates of employment, the name of the employers, and the positions.

Preparing the Resume for Copies

Nothing is worse than using a resume that is sloppy, contains spelling mistakes, or has a poor visual appearance. To avoid such problems, you are encouraged to do the following:

1. Have several people proofread your resume. It is easy to overlook your own spelling mistakes, typos, and missing words no matter how many times you read and reread your resume. Any one of those mistakes can cost you a job. You must therefore have as many individuals proofread your resume as possible.

2. Once you have had the resume proofread, you will need to have it typed up. If possible, use a word processor and have the resume printed on a laser printer or letter-quality printer. Above all, don't scrimp on this. Appearance is extremely important. You may even wish to have the resume typeset. The difference in cost may well be worth it. If you don't have the proper word processor or laser printer, have a printing company do it.

3. Use the proper paper. You should have the resume printed on high-quality (16 to 25 lb.) paper. In most cases, white is best, especially if it will be scanned by the organization. Again, aim for a professional business-like appearance. Be sure to obtain envelopes that match.

4. Submit the resume in the proper fashion. Faxing a resume is generally not recommended, because fax paper does not look good and it is difficult to scan properly. If the resume will be scanned, and it is best to assume that it will be, send the resume so that you do not have to fold it (in other words, use a large manila envelope). Also, be careful about stapling your resume if it is more than one page, because that may cause problems when it is being scanned.

Conclusion

Your resume is an important tool for job hunting. Many paperback books are available at a relatively low cost that provide additional information as well as examples on how to create a resume. Also, a number of computer software programs are now available for resume writing.

❖ Applying Core Concepts

1. If you were responsible for hiring someone for your job, which recruitment sources would you use? Why? Which recruitment sources would you avoid? Why?

2. Which recruitment sources described in this chapter have you used in job hunting? How well did they work?

3. Ask a friend or relative for a recent copy of his or her resume. Based on the suggestions in Appendix 3, provide comments on the resume. How can your friend or relative improve her or his resume?

4. Think about your current job or a job you were hired for previously. How effective was the employer's recruitment process? How would you have improved it?

5. Thinking about your current employer or an organization that a friend or relative works for, would internal or external recruitment sources be more valuable? Explain your thinking.

6. Design a job-hunting program for the person described in the opening vignette of this chapter.

7. Go to a job database, like the Monster Board, and examine several different descriptions of organizations. How effective were the descriptions? Were some better than others? How much information did they contain? Was some information missing that would have been useful?

❖ Key Terms

Temporary employees

Internal recruitment
  sources

Closed internal
  recruitment system

Open internal recruitment
  system

Job posting

External recruitment
  sources

Newspaper advertisements

Television and radio ads

Employee referrals

College campus
  recruitment

Employment agencies

Search firm

Applicant-initiated
  recruitment

Realistic job preview (RJP)

Chronological resume

Functional resume

Chrono-functional resume

❖ **CHAPTER 4** *Experiential Exercise*

Technosoftware Company: Part 1

On Monday morning, Walter Chipnowsky looked concerned as he took his first sip of espresso. Walter had spent the weekend examining the financial data and status reports for the small computer firm, Technosoftware, that he had founded with his two college friends, Darrell D. Rive and Benjamin B. White. Although the three of them had operated the company for the last three years with little more than part-time clerical help and the services of an occasional consultant, Walter had recently concluded that the company had grown much more rapidly than he originally expected and that they desperately needed another full-time employee. The impending release of their latest product made this need even more apparent.

    As Walter thought more about the need to hire another full-time, professional employee, he realized that this would create new concerns and potential problems. Over the years that Technosoftware had been in existence, the three partners had grown accustomed to having complete control over decisions. Moreover, they believed that this was a major strength of the company. And, although they had occasionally had major disagreements, they had known each other for many years and trusted each other completely. Bringing in an outsider could change all of that.

Company History

Technosoftware's history is not unlike that of other entrepreneurial firms. The company developed out of the dreams and frustrations of three ambitious computer experts. Walter, Darrell, and Benjamin (usually called

Ben) graduated from Purdue University in the early 1980s. Although all three had received master's degrees in mathematics or computer science, each had a somewhat different personality. Walter was the "people person," who enjoyed interacting with others and working out interpersonal problems. Darrell was the technically oriented one; he preferred to work on computer or math problems and tended to avoid dealing with people. Ben was the more business-oriented one, who enjoyed the financial aspects of Technosoftware. Even though they each had their particular strengths, none of them had any formal training or experience in areas besides computer and software development.

    After graduating from Purdue, each of the three partners began a career in a large computer company, slowly working their way up to a middle management position (Walter and Ben) or moving up to a highly regarded research and development job (Darrell). Eventually, though, all three became tired of the politics and lack of challenge in their jobs. This led to the creation of Technosoftware.

Technosoftware: Current Projects

Technosoftware focuses on software development for business applications. In the past, they have dealt primarily with other companies on a contract basis to modify existing software and to implement and train companies on various software packages. But over the last year, the partners have been spending many weekends working on a new software program, called *RavWeb*. Walter and his partners feel that *RavWeb*, which the partners are keeping a closely guarded secret, could be a revolutionary product. All they are willing to say at this point is that *RavWeb* will involve an on-line software package that will focus on the consumer market. It will combine a popular leisure activity with a fascinating learning experience, and it will be geared toward adults.

The Job

After drinking his espresso of the day, Walter began to write a brief description of the responsibilities of the person to be hired, along with some basic characteristics of the ideal candidate. His lists follow.

Responsibilities: The person would be involved in all phases of product management and product introduction, including packaging, user manual writing, pricing, product announcements, positioning strategy, promotion, advertising, and sales.

Characteristics of the Employee: Given the size of Technosoftware, the ideal candidate would be highly motivated, self-sufficient, familiar with personal computers, and be prepared to do his or her own clerical work (for example, typing, copying). Although a degree in a technical field would be nice, the right experience is more important.

Compensation: Because most of the partners' energy and time has been devoted to *RavWeb*, their cash flow is rather poor. The person they hire would not be highly paid. They prefer to set up some kind of bonus plan with the individual, so that his or her pay would be related to sales of *RavWeb*. They feel they would probably have to pay someone about $65,000 annually, but if sales of *RavWeb* were successful, they would be prepared to pay a bonus of up to 20 percent. Because they are a very small firm, they offer no health insurance or pension plan. All three have put their careers and life savings on the line for their company and work extremely long hours. It is not unusual for the three of them to work Saturdays and Sundays, as well as most legal holidays. They expect anyone they hire to do the same.

Question for You

Walter's Question: Walter's question for you to answer is how he should go about getting interested people to apply for this job. He realizes that if he does a poor job of getting qualified applicants to apply, he will not be able to hire an effective person for the job. His biggest concern, and it is shared by the other partners, is that they need to hire someone quickly. If they don't hire someone soon, the product will be late, and the partners feel the recognition they can get by being first is absolutely essential. He would like you to come up with a recruitment plan for this position. Offer as many relevant recruitment sources as possible. For each source, be prepared to explain the pros and cons. Also, write a brief description of the organization, job, and reward package for use in any recruiting sources (for example, newspaper, Internet).

❖ Chapter 4 References

1. A. Barber, *Recruiting Employees: Individual and Organizational Perspectives* (Thousand Oaks, CA: Sage, 1998).
2. Ibid.
3. D. Albrecht, "Reaching New Heights," *Workforce* 77 (1998): 42–8.
4. J. Fierman, "The Contingency Workforce," *Fortune* 24 January 1990, 30–6, 129.
5. V. Frazee, "How to Hire Locally," *Global Workforce* (1998): 19–23.
6. C. von Hippel, S. Mangum, D. Greenberger, R. Heneman, and J. Skoglind, "Temporary Employment: Can Organizations and Employees Both Win?" *Academy of Management Executive* 11 (1997): 93–104.
7. Von Hippel, Mangun, Greenberger, Heneman, and Skoglind, "Temporary Employment."
8. Fierman, "Contingency Workforce."
9. von Hippel, et al. "Temporary Employment."

10. M. Adams, "Building A Rainbow, One Stripe At A Time," *HRMagazine* 43 (1998): 72–9.
11. L. Berg, "Plant a Seed; Help It Grow," *HRMagazine* 43 (1998): 114–20.
12. Adams, "Building A Rainbow."
13. R. Heneman and H. Heneman III, *Staffing* (Middleton, WI: Mendota House, 1994).
14. J. Breaugh, *Recruitment: Science and Practice* (Boston, MA: PWS-Kent, 1992).
15. Ibid.
16. B. Schneider and N. Schmitt, *Staffing Organizations* (Glenview, IL: Scott, Foresman, 1986).
17. Breaugh, *Recruitment: Science and Practice.*
18. Ibid.
19. D. Huntley, "Security Firm Beats Bushes for Workers," *Personnel Administrator* 34 (1989): 50–2.
20. E. Gunn, "How Mirage Resorts Sifted 75,000 Applicants to Hire 9,600 in 24 Weeks," *Fortune*, 12 October 1998, 195.
21. C. Caggiano, "How to Hire: Part One: Sharpening the Old Tools," *Inc.* 20 (October 1998): 36–9.
22. N. Templin, "Dr. Goodwrench: Auto Plants, Hiring Again, Are Demanding Higher Skilled Labor," *Wall Street Journal*, 11 March 1994, A1, A4.
23. R. Bolles, *What Color Is Your Parachute?* (Berkeley, CA: Ten Speed Press, 1999).
24. Breaugh, *Recruitment: Science and Practice.*
25. R. Kimmell, "Health Care Marketing Minicase: Market Research Guides an RN Recruitment/Retention Campaign," *Journal of Health Care Marketing* 11 (1991): 69–73.
26. Kimmell, "Health Care Marketing"; Breaugh, *Recruitment: Science and Practice*; C. Johnson, "Turn Up the Radio Recruiting," *HRMagazine* 43 (September 1998): 64–70.
27. S. Rynes, "Recruitment, Job Choice, and Post-Hire Consequences: A Call for New Research Directions," in *Handbook of Industrial and Organizational Psychology*, vol. 2, ed. M. Dunnette and L. Hough (Palo Alto, CA: Consulting Psychologists Press, 1991): 399–444; Caggiano, "How to Hire: Part One."
28. Caggiano, "How To Hire: Part One."
29. Ibid.
30. Ibid.
31. Breaugh, *Recruitment: Science and Practice.*
32. J. Hawes, "How to Improve Your College Recruiting Program," *Journal of Personal Selling and Sales Management* 9 (1989): 47–52; Breaugh, *Recruitment: Science and Practice*; L. Thornburg, "The New Crop—Recruiting Today's Graduates," *HRMagazine* 42 (1997): 74–9.
33. Ibid.
34. R. Blumenthal, "Entrepreneurs Vying for Graduates the Giants Recruit," *Wall Street Journal*, 4 February 1994, B2; Breaugh, *Recruitment: Science and Practice.*
35. Bolles, *What Color is Your Parachute?*
36. Ibid.
37. Frazee, "How to Hire Locally."
38. Ibid.; B. Mende, "Should you Pay in Advance for Job-Search Assistance?" *National Business Employment Weekly*, 2–8 August 1998, 10–12.
39. S. Harrison, "Star Search," *Black Enterprise* (April 1990): 74–8; Breaugh, *Recruitment: Science and Practice.*
40. J. Kirnan, J. Farley, and K. Geisinger, "The Relationship Between Recruiting Source, Applicant, and Hire Performance: An Analysis of Sex, Ethnicity, and Age," *Personnel Psychology* 42 (1989): 293–308.
41. Breaugh, *Recruitment: Science and Practice.*
42. R. Bolles, *What Color is Your Parachute?*
43. "Work Week," *Wall Street Journal*, 4 August 1998, A1.
44. P. Dixon, *Job Searching Online for Dummies* (Foster City, CA: IDG Books, 1998).
45. Baillie, "Attracting Employees Who Surf the Net," *Personnel Management* 2 (August 1996): 46.
46. J. Stanton, "Validity and Related Issues in Web-based Hiring," *The Industrial-Organizational Psychologist* (January 1999): In press.

47. Dixon, *Job Searching.*
48. R. Schreyer and J. McCarter, "10+ Steps to Effective Internet Recruiting," *HR Focus* 75 (1998): S6.
49. Dixon, *Job Searching.*
50. Bolles, *What Color is Your Parachute?*
51. Dixon, *Job Searching.*
52. Ibid.
53. Caggiano, "How to Hire: Part One."
54. B. Sunoo and K. Wallsten, "Posting Jobs At the Mall," *Workforce* 77 (1998):19–20.
55. A. Peterson, "Have a Canape, I'll Take Your Resume," *Wall Street Journal,* 22 December 1998, B1, B8.
56. Barber, *Recruiting Employees.*
57. Breaugh, *Recruitment: Science and Practice.*
58. C. Caggiano, "How to Hire: Part Three: Your New "Marketing Mind-Set," *Inc.* 20 (October 1998): 40–42.
59. Ibid.
60. Bolles, *What Color Is Your Parachute?*
61. R. Beatty, *The New Complete Job Search* (New York: John Wiley, 1992); M. Yate, *Knock 'Em Dead: The Ultimate Job Seekers Handbook* (Holbrook, MA: Bob Adams, 1994).
62. Ibid.
63. E. Pollock, "When Computers Control Your Employment," *National Business Employment Weekly,* 13–19 September 1998, 21–2; P. Dixon, *Job Searching Online.*

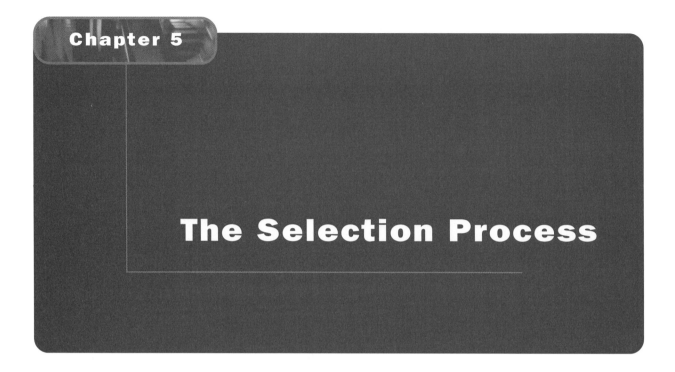

Chapter 5

The Selection Process

Core Concepts — **After reading this chapter, you should be capable of:**

1. Understanding the uses of job analysis.
2. Explaining what factors organizations use in choosing selection procedures.
3. Describing the features of different selection procedures.
4. Identifying the advantages and disadvantages of different selection procedures.

Opening Case

Five minutes ago, Tom Brown received a phone call from Mike Clayton, the human resource employment manager of Federal Bank. Mike began by saying that he was pleased to inform Tom that he was one of three finalists for the commercial loan officer job, and that he was invited to the bank for a series of interviews, tests, and background checks (including a review of his credit history). Tom was excited to get the call. Not only had he had only two interviews so far (despite applying for more than 50 jobs), but Federal Bank was one of his top choices. However, when Mike Clayton told him that he would be taking some tests and would be subject to a background check, Tom became apprehensive. Tom has always disliked taking tests, and does not feel that tests reflect what he is capable of doing. Tom believes that a face-to-face interview provides a much better assessment of his qualifications. Nonetheless, of the two interviews he has participated in so far, neither has gone particularly well for Tom. Midway through his first interview, Tom was asked to describe his greatest weakness. He was not expecting this question, and so he blurted out, without thinking: "It sometimes takes me a while to learn a new routine or procedure. But once I catch on, I really become good at it." By the look on the interviewer's face, Tom could tell that he had lost any chance of getting that job. So, before his interview with the next company, Tom went to the library and checked out a book on interviewing. But his interview with the second company was completely different. In that interview, the manager asked questions about Tom's work experiences. One question in particular really unnerved Tom. The interviewer asked if Tom had ever persuaded his boss to adopt a new technique or procedure. It was the third question in a row that Tom answered, "I never had that experience," and it was then clear to him that he didn't stand a chance of getting a job offer from that company either. So, as Tom continued to think about the upcoming interview at Federal Bank, he worried that he would not do well once again. Furthermore, he wondered, what tests would he be given? And what information would Federal Bank obtain from a background check? Is such a procedure even legal? What if his credit record has a mistake on it?

What kinds of selection procedures do companies use? Are there different kinds of interviews and tests? The purpose of this chapter is to discuss the procedures that companies use in hiring applicants and promoting employees. First, however, you will read about job analysis, which is a way to determine what qualifications employees will need. Following this, you will read about the critical factors companies look for when they choose selection procedures. After that, we will review the major features of commonly used selection procedures, including application forms, interviews, tests, background and reference checks, and drug and alcohol screens. We conclude with a discussion of selecting for two special situations: team work and global assignments.

Job Analysis

What Is Job Analysis?

Job analysis may be defined as the process of collecting information about two basic issues:

1. What the job entails (what tasks and functions employees perform).
2. What competencies (that is, knowledge, abilities, and other requirements) the work requires.

job analysis
The process of collecting information about two basic issues: What the job entails, and the knowledge, skills, abilities and other requirements needed to perform the work.

As an example of the first issue, a job analysis may reveal that the tasks performed by a commercial loan officer include generating new clients, evaluating loan applications, and maintaining relationships with existing clients. With regard to the second issue, a job analysis might reveal that the competencies or qualifications a commercial loan officer needs to effectively perform these tasks include the ability to interact with others, knowledge of financial concepts, oral communication skills, and a four-year college degree.

There are, as you will soon see, many different approaches to conducting a job analysis. Which approach is best depends on the purpose of the job analysis and the nature of the job. Before we discuss different types of job analyses, however, you will first learn why organizations conduct job analyses.

Why Conduct a Job Analysis?

While a superficial job analysis may take only an hour or so to conduct, an extensive, thorough, and detailed job analysis covering many different positions can be expensive and time-consuming. In fact, some organizations spend as much as $4 million annually for this purpose. Why do companies spend the time and money to conduct job analyses? The answer is that job analysis is a basic building block for many human resource management (HRM) processes. As you can see in Table 5.1, job analysis provides useful information for many HRM programs and practices, including training, career development, performance management, and work design, to name just a few. Job analysis is particularly helpful from a legal standpoint, because it helps to justify the qualifications upon which hiring, promotion, and termination decisions are made. A job analysis is also useful in clarifying expectations for both the employee and his or her supervisor so that both parties are clear as to what the job involves. Now that you know what job analysis is and why it is done, you will read more about how to conduct a job analysis.[1]

Table 5.1	Uses of Job Analysis

1. Hiring
2. Training
3. Career development
4. Performance management
5. Work design
6. Compensation
7. Human resource planning
8. Safety
9. Vocational guidance
10. Recruitment
11. Rehabilitation counseling
12. Engineering design

Source: Adapted from W. Cascio, *Applied Psychology in Personnel Management* (Englewood Cliffs, NJ: Prentice-Hall, 1991).

Conducting a Job Analysis

When you work for an organization you choose from among many different approaches to conducting a job analysis. These approaches differ in terms of three factors:

1. The type of information collected.
2. How the information is collected.
3. The form of the information.

What Type of Information Will Be Collected? Are you interested in determining the tasks and functions performed in the job, the competencies needed to perform the job effectively, or the basic behaviors performed in the job? The answer to this question is determined in part by the purpose of the job analysis. Suppose that the purpose of the job analysis is to clarify job responsibilities. For example, Mike Clayton from the opening case in this chapter may perform a job analysis so that the commercial loan department understands who is responsible for which tasks. In that case, Mike Clayton would determine the tasks that are performed in the department, and the final result would be a **job description** or list of the tasks and functions performed by each employee. If, however, Mike Clayton wanted to determine which candidate to hire as a commercial loan officer, he would focus on determining the competencies required for the job. The final result would be a **job specification,** or list of knowledge, abilities, credentials, and experiences candidates need to be deemed qualified. Finally, if Mike Clayton were conducting the job analysis to establish career development programs, his emphasis might be on broad behaviors (for example, dealing with outside customers) underlying performance in different jobs.[2]

job description
A list of the tasks and functions performed by each employee.

job specification
A list of competencies needed to successfully perform the job.

How Will the Information Be Collected? You can collect job analysis information in many ways. How the information is collected will in large part be determined by the nature of the work. For instance, if the job involves production work, you might simply observe workers and record the tasks that they perform over a period of a week. Thus, observing employees at work is one way to collect information. Consider, however, a computer programmer. Because a computer programmer's work is primarily mental, you would probably learn little about the tasks involved simply by observation. Instead, you may need to interview computer programmers and ask them to describe the tasks they perform. Another way to collect information is by using a questionnaire. An example of a questionnaire used to collect job analysis information is provided in Figure 5.1. Questionnaires are commonly used for job analysis because they enable one to obtain information in an efficient fashion from many different people, and if done properly they will withstand legal scrutiny.[3] Because of their popularity, we will discuss questionnaires in greater detail later.

Additional means of gathering job analysis information include using work logs, videotapes, and meetings with customers.[4] You can also purchase software programs to help you conduct a job analysis (for example, www.workscience.com).

In What Form Will the Information Be Collected? Information may be collected in either a qualitative or quantitative form. Figure 5.1 shows an example of a questionnaire used to collect *qualitative information.* As you can see, employees are asked to provide a narrative description of the tasks they perform, the tools and

| **Figure 5.1** | **Sample Job Analysis Questionnaire** |

Name: _____

Position: _____

Department: _____

Supervisor: _____

1. Briefly describe your job: _____
   _____
   _____
   _____

2. Describe the specific tasks you are responsible for in your job: _____
   _____
   _____
   _____

3. Name the person to whom you report, along with his or her job title: _____
   _____
   _____

4. List the equipment, tools, or machines you use in your job: _____
   _____
   _____
   _____

5. List any outside customers you deal with: _____
   _____
   _____
   _____

6. List any internal departments or units you deal with: _____
   _____
   _____
   _____

7. List any physical hazards you face in your work (for example, heavy lifting):
   _____
   _____
   _____

8. How many employees report to you? _____ List their names: _____
   _____
   _____
   _____

Figure 5.2	**Sample of a Quantitative Job Analysis Questionnaire**

Directions:

Step 1. Significance

Indicate how significant each activity is to your position by entering a number between 0 and 4 in the column next to it. Remember to consider both its importance in light of all the other position activities and its frequency of occurrence.

0—**Definitely not** a part of the position.
1—**Minor significance** to the position.
2—**Moderate significance** to the position.
3—**Substantial significance** to the position.
4—**Crucial significance** to the position.
Dimension: Controlling

Step 2. Comments

Use this space to clarify or comment on any aspects of **Controlling** that you feel are not adequately covered by the questions.

_____
_____
_____
_____
_____
_____
_____

The Duties of This Position Require You to

1. Review proposed plans for adequacy and consistency with corporate policies and objectives.
2. Track and adjust activities to ensure that objectives and commitments are met in a timely fashion.
3. Develop milestones, due dates, and responsibilities for projects, plans, and activities.
4. Monitor product quality and/or service effectiveness.
5. Develop evaluation criteria to measure the progress and effectiveness of a unit.
6. Evaluate and document the effectiveness of plans, projects, and/or operations upon their completion.
7. Analyze at least monthly the effectiveness of operations.
8. Analyze operating performance reports.

Source: Sample items from the *Management Position Description Questionnaire*. (Copyright 1984, Control Data Business Advisors, Inc. All rights reserved.)

equipment they use, and the conditions under which they work. Figure 5.2 shows a questionnaire used to collect *quantitative information*. A person completing the questionnaire in Figure 5.2 rates each task on a scale of 0 to 4, indicating the importance of and the frequency with which each task is performed.

The purpose of the job analysis often determines whether you'll use a qualitative or quantitative approach. If the purpose of the job analysis is to clarify what a subordinate's responsibilities are, a qualitative approach might be best. If the purpose is to determine the appropriate wage for different jobs, a quantitative approach might be best (see Chapter 8).

Now that you have learned about some ways in which job analysis procedures differ, you will read about the questionnaire method in greater detail. Because many questionnaires use a quantitative approach, we will focus our attention there. Following that section, we will discuss a new approach to job analysis, called competency modeling.

Quantitative Job Analysis Questionnaires

Although employers use many different quantitative job analysis questionnaires, we will discuss just two of them: the PAQ and the task/competency inventory.

PAQ
A standardized job analysis questionnaire that may be used for nearly any job.

PAQ. The **position analysis questionnaire,** or **PAQ,** is a standardized job analysis questionnaire that may be used for nearly any job (www.paq.com). The PAQ consists of 194 items, the majority of which concern work behaviors and use of equipment and tools. A few items concern work conditions, such as the physical environment and pay practices. The items on the PAQ are grouped into 32 specific scales and 13 overall dimensions for scoring purposes. Some examples of the items on these scales are "making decisions," "using machines/tools/equipment," and "performing service-related activities."[5]

Figure 5.3 displays some sample PAQ items. As you examine Figure 5.3, it should not surprise you that the job analyst (the person performing the job analysis) must receive training in how to use the PAQ. Indeed, the PAQ is a relatively complex job analysis tool.

The PAQ has two advantages. Because the PAQ is a standardized questionnaire, results can be compared across different organizations. To assist in this comparison, a large database with ratings of many different jobs from many different organizations has been gathered by the firm that owns the PAQ copyright. Another advantage of the PAQ is that it is scored by computer, thereby producing more objective results. In turn, these features have facilitated the use of the PAQ for several different HRM purposes.[6] We will briefly describe two applications of the PAQ.

Using the PAQ for Choosing Selection Tests. The PAQ can be a useful comparison tool in choosing tests for hiring purposes. Earlier research studies using the PAQ calculated the relationships between PAQ scores, test scores on some popular selection tests, and job performance ratings for many different jobs. By statistically comparing the PAQ scores for jobs in your organization with the PAQ scores from this database, you can estimate how useful these tests would be in hiring workers for your organization. The PAQ, then, can be used to choose tests for hiring purposes.

Using the PAQ for Compensation Decisions. The PAQ may also be used to perform an analysis of an organization's pay structure. Toward that end, PAQ scores for each job are statistically analyzed in relationship to their base pay. Deviations from what a job is actually paid to what the statistical analysis indicates the job should be paid will pinpoint where pay adjustments may be needed.

Now that you understand what the PAQ is and what it may be used for, we will discuss another quantitative job analysis questionnaire: the task/competency inventory.

task/competency inventory
A job analysis technique that focuses on both the tasks performed in the job and the competencies needed to perform them.

Task/Competency Inventory. The **task/competency inventory** is a job analysis technique that focuses on both the tasks performed in the job and the competencies needed to perform them. This approach has been widely used in both public-sector and private-sector organizations. Unlike the PAQ, we have no standardized task/competency inventory. Rather, each organization develops its own unique list of tasks and competencies for each job. Another difference from the PAQ is that the task/competency inventory is usually completed by the employees themselves, rather than by a trained job analyst.

Figure 5.3   Position Analysis Questionnaire (PAQ)

Organization of the PAQ

The job elements in the PAQ are organized in six divisions as follows (examples of two job elements from each division are included):

1. *Information input.* (Where and how does the worker get the information he or she uses in performing his or her job?)
   Examples: Use of written materials
   Near-visual differentiation
2. *Mental processes.* (What reasoning, decision-making, planning, and information-processing activities are involved in performing the job?)
   Examples: Levels of reasoning in problem solving
   Coding/decoding
3. *Work output.* (What physical activities does the worker perform and what tools or devices does he or she use?)
   Examples: Using keyboard devices
   Assembling/disassembling
4. *Relationships with other persons.* (What relationships with other people are required in performing the job?)
   Examples: Instruction
   Contact with public, customers
5. *Job context.* (In what physical or social contexts is the work performed?)
   Examples: High temperature
   Interpersonal conflict situations
6. *Other job characteristics.* (What activities, conditions, or characteristics other than those described above are relevant to the job?)

Rating Scales Used With the PAQ

There is a provision for rating each job on each job element. Six types of rating scales are used:

Letter Identification	Type of Rating Scale
U	Extent of Use
I	Importance to the Job
T	Amount of Time
P	Possibility of Occurrence
A	Applicability
S	Special Code (used in the case of a few specific job elements)

A specific rating scale is designated for use with each job element, in particular the scale considered most appropriate to the content of the element. All but the "A" (Applicability) scale are 6-point scales, and "0" (which is coded as "N") is for "Does not apply," as illustrated below:

Rating	Importance to the Job
N	Does not apply
1	Very minor (importance)
2	Low
3	Average
4	High
5	Extreme

A typical task/competency inventory consists of a list of 50 to 100 tasks and 10 to 15 competencies, which are then rated by subject matter experts (SMEs). The SMEs are usually supervisors and job incumbents. The tasks are typically rated in terms of the frequency with which they are performed and their overall importance. The competencies are usually rated on how important they are for successful job performance, as well as other aspects. Task/competency inventories are particularly helpful in developing selection procedures, as well as designing training programs.[7]

Competency Modeling

competency modeling
A recent approach to job analysis that focuses on the mission and vision statement to generate broadly defined knowledge and abilities to create an integrated HR system.

Competency modeling is the most recent approach to job analysis, although competency modeling has been defined in a number of different ways. This technique differs in several ways from the job analysis techniques described above:[8]

1. Competency modeling begins by focusing on the organizational and departmental mission and vision statement. Thus, compared to traditional job analysis, competency modeling ties in more closely with the bigger picture.
2. Competency modeling tends to use more broadly defined knowledge and abilities than does traditional job analysis. The major advantage of this approach is that the same set of competencies generated through this approach may be used for many different jobs. As an example, Anheuser-Busch identified thirteen different competencies for its employees, such as analysis and planning, professionalism, and customer focus.[9] If you would compare these results to those derived from more traditional job analyses, you would find that competency modeling contains more general knowledge and abilities.
3. Competency modeling is designed for use in an integrated HR system. In other words, competency modeling is created to serve multiple purposes, including hiring, training, compensation, and performance management processes. Competency modeling lends itself to HR planning processes in a more efficient manner than does traditional job analysis.

A list of competencies that might be necessary for members of a global work team may include interpersonal (for example, patience, coaching), communication (listening, presentation), project management (strategic planning, scheduling), conceptual (negotiating, innovation), and technical (computer, equipment) abilities.[10]

Now that you know how organizations determine the necessary competencies for a particular job, you will learn how organizations choose selection procedures to assess those competencies.

Choosing Selection Procedures

Companies consider several factors in choosing selection procedures: job relatedness, utility, legality, and practicality. In some cases, particularly in large companies, formal research studies may be conducted to examine these factors. In other cases, particularly in small companies, there may be no formal study regarding these factors. Of course, without a careful examination, a company may be in error with regard to the characteristics of its selection procedure.

Job Relatedness

Job relatedness refers to whether the selection procedure is related to job requirements (for example, professional license) or job outcomes (performance, attendance, and so forth). There are several possible ways for an organization to demonstrate that a selection procedure is job related. One way is by conducting a **criterion-related validity study.** In a criterion-related validity study, the organization uses the selection method, or *predictor*, with a large number of applicants (known as a *predictive study*) or current employees (known as a *concurrent study*). The organization would also obtain measures of job behavior, or *criteria*, such as absenteeism, turnover, accident rate, or productivity level for each hired applicant or employee.[11] Next, the organization would use statistics, usually correlation coefficients, to calculate the relationship between the predictor and the criteria. A selection procedure would be considered valid if the correlation coefficient was significantly greater than zero. Be sure that you read Table 5.2, which describes what a correlation is in greater detail, as we will be using this statistic throughout the chapter.[12]

A closely related way to demonstrate job relatedness is through a *validity generalization study*. To understand validity generalization, it is helpful to briefly review the history of criterion-related validity studies. For many years, HR experts who conducted such studies were baffled by the fact that rather different correlations were often reported for different samples, or groups of employees, even when the same test was used for the same jobs. For example, even though a criterion-related validity study had shown that this test was valid for Boeing production workers in Washington, the test was not necessarily valid for Boeing production workers in Arizona. This became known as the *situational specificity hypothesis*. These findings that indicated situational specificity led many HR experts to recommend that a criterion-related validity study be performed in each case. In other words, even if the test was shown to be valid in Washington and Arizona, this did not necessarily mean that it would be valid for Boeing production workers in Missouri. In the 1970s, however, two researchers, Frank Schmidt and John Hunter, developed a technique referred to as **meta-analysis,** which enabled them to examine the veracity of the situational specificity hypothesis. These researchers argued that correlations differed from study to study because statistical artifacts, or "white noise," made it appear as though situational specificity was occurring. By using meta-analysis, which is a statistical procedure for summarizing previous correlations, Schmidt and Hunter demonstrated that statistical artifacts frequently explained apparent differences in correlations from study to study. If, indeed, much of the difference between correlations can be explained by these statistical artifacts, and the average correlation is greater than zero, one can claim *validity generalization* for this test. The only other steps necessary would be to show that the test you were intending to use assessed the same thing as the tests in the meta-analysis and that the jobs you were applying it to were similar to the jobs in the meta-analysis. In sum, validity generalization is a systematic process for demonstrating that validity evidence found elsewhere can be applied to a new situation involving identical or similar jobs.[13]

Another way to demonstrate job relatedness is through **content validity.** While criterion-related validity is shown through statistics, content validity is primarily judgmental in nature. In order to be considered content valid, a selection procedure should meet the following stipulations:

1. Comprise a simulation of the job
2. Have scores based on concrete and observable behavior by the test taker

job relatedness
Refers to whether the selection procedure is related to job requirements or job outcomes.

criterion-related validity study
One method of demonstrating that a procedure is job related. The organization would use the selection method, or predictor, with a large number of applicants or current employees to obtain measures of job behavior, then use statistics to calculate the relationship between the predictor and the criteria.

meta-analysis
Developed by Frank Schmidt and John Hunter, this statistical procedure for summarizing past research has indicated that cognitive ability tests have adequate validity across virtually all jobs.

content validity
Another method of demonstrating job relatedness, where the selection procedure should (1) comprise a simulation of the job, (2) have scores based on concrete and observable behavior by the test taker, (3) represent important aspects of the job, and (4) assess activities for which the person will not receive training if hired.

Table 5.2   **The Magic of the Correlation Coefficient**

correlation coefficient
A statistic that summarizes the relationship between two variables or measures.

A **correlation coefficient** is a statistic that summarizes the relationship between two variables or measures. A correlation can range anywhere between (and including) +1.00 and −1.00. Let's first start with what a +1.00 correlation would mean. Figure A shows a scatterplot of average daily temperatures in St. Louis during 1998. The x axis plots the temperature in Fahrenheit; the y axis is in centigrade. Because Fahrenheit and centigrade are simply two measures of the same thing, they correlate perfectly, namely, +1.00. This *perfect correlation* means that if you know the temperature in Fahrenheit, you can completely and accurately determine the temperature in centigrade, and vice versa.

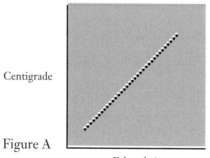

Centigrade

Figure A

Fahrenheit

A −1.00 represents a perfect inverse relationship between the two variables. Figure B shows a scatterplot of the amount of daylight for each day in St. Louis in 1998 and the length of the night during this time frame. This comprises a −1.00 correlation, indicating that the longer the daylight, the shorter the night, and vice versa. As in the previous example, a −1.00 means that you can accurately predict one variable (for instance, the amount of daylight) from the other variable (the length of the night). This is a *negative correlation*, which means that high numbers on one variable are associated with low numbers on the other variable, and vice versa.

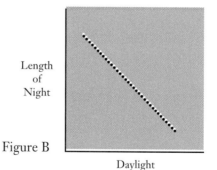

Length of Night

Figure B

Daylight

Figure C illustrates a *zero correlation* between two variables. A zero correlation means that no relationship exists between the two variables. A zero correlation also means that knowing the score on one variable is not the least bit helpful in predicting the score of the second variable. Shoe size, for example, would probably have a zero correlation with grade point average.

The examples given here representing a +1.00, a −1.00, and a zero correlation were, of course, fairly artificial. In reality, when you read about the correlations between selection methods and job outcomes, you will see that they rarely exceed .40, and they often hover around .30. In other words, job outcomes such as performance and turnover are difficult to predict with a great deal of accuracy. Nevertheless, a selection method that correlates at .30 or

(continued)

Table 5.2   (continued)

.40 with job outcomes will lead to better decisions than a selection method that has a zero correlation with job outcomes.

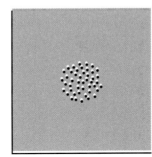

Figure C

While the predictions will not be completely accurate, a selection method with a correlation coefficient of .30 or .40 will lead to better decisions than a selection method with a zero correlation. Well, you might be wondering, since a correlation of .30 or .40 is far from perfect accuracy, of what use is a test like that? The answer is to think of a casino. Everyone knows a friend or relative who has actually won money at a casino. So, how do casinos make money? Because, on average, the casino wins. And, even though the odds only slightly favor the casino, when so many people play, the slight odds in favor of the casino can mean big earnings for "the house." The same is true for a preemployment test—even a small correlation like .30 or .40 can greatly improve the workforce. Finally, why is the correlation coefficient referred to here as "magical"? Because it is a simple statistic, one that is easy to understand, and it can be used to compare the predictive accuracy or validity of different selection methods.

3. Represent important aspects of the job
4. Assess activities for which the person will not receive training if hired[14]

A good example of a content-valid test is a typing test for a typist job. The typing test would meet the first rule, because a typing test would simulate the job. Assuming the score on the test is based on, say, the number of words typed per minute minus errors, the score would be based on highly concrete and observable behavior, thus meeting the second rule. The third rule would be met if the typist job, as suggested by the job title, involves a significant amount of typing. Finally, the fourth rule would be met if in fact the typist hired would be expected to know how to type and would not receive typing training.

Another approach, particularly for procedures other than standardized tests, is to judge the job relatedness of a particular selection procedure on the basis of logical arguments. For example, while few companies conduct a formal criterion-related validity study on their reference-checking procedure, most people would probably consider this a job-related practice on logical grounds.[15]

Now that you have read about these different methods of demonstrating the job-relatedness of a selection procedure, which do you think would be best in a discrimination lawsuit? If you answered the first, namely, criterion-related validity, you are probably right. Recall from Chapter 2 that the two basic approaches to bringing a lawsuit are *disparate treatment* and *adverse impact*. The "logical argument" may not be acceptable to the courts in an adverse-impact case, though it may well be sufficient for a disparate-treatment case, where the company only presents a "legitimate, nondiscriminatory reason."

Utility

Utility refers to the benefits versus the costs of using a particular selection procedure. As was emphasized in earlier chapters, today's focus on cost cutting and remaining competitive means that a company must ensure that each process, including HRM, provides satisfactory financial gains. Not surprisingly, most selection procedures also have a cost associated with them, whether it is direct (for example, a test may cost as much as $200 to purchase) or indirect (an interview takes a certain amount of time for the manager to conduct, for example). Utility is an increasingly important concept in HRM, not just for selection procedures. While there are several different ways to calculate the utility of a selection procedure, the commonly accepted way is to use the Brogden-Cronbach-Gleser model. Given the many factors that go into this formula, such as the number of employees being hired, the utility of any given selection procedure could vary widely from company to company. In most cases, however, systematic selection procedures such as psychological tests provide at least some financial gain over costs to organizations. An example of the utility of a drug test as calculated by one organization is provided in Box 5.1.[16]

Legal Concepts

As you know from reading previous chapters, laws have a major effect on all HRM practices. We will refer again here to some of the legal principles and regulations covered earlier and introduce some new principles and regulations as well. Our discussion will address both legally restricted and legally recommended selection practices.

Restricted Selection Procedures and Questions. There are laws that restrict or ban a variety of selection procedures and questions. Most preemployment questions and inquiries regarding age, sex, race, national origin, religion, disabilities, and marital status, for example, are directly prohibited or discouraged by federal or state laws and various court cases. Table 5.3 provides a list of questions that would probably be considered discriminatory if asked during the hiring process. However, certain questions may need to be asked at some point in the hiring process. For example, to meet the requirements of certain laws, an organization may need to ascertain that employees are old enough to meet child labor laws. Table 5.3, therefore, also lists acceptable ways to ask some of the otherwise illegal questions.[17]

Finally, lie detectors or polygraphs, which are mechanical or electrical tests designed to assess whether you are lying in response to various questions, are restricted by law. The **Employee Polygraph Protection Act of 1988** prohibits most private-sector organizations from requiring an applicant to take a polygraph test as a condition of employment (security companies and drug and pharmaceutical companies are allowed to test for certain positions). In addition, this law prohibits covered organizations from the following:

1. Discharging or disciplining an employee based on a refusal to take a polygraph test
2. Using or obtaining information about the results of a polygraph test given to an applicant or employee

YOUR TURN

Box 5.1
Utility of a Drug Test

In order to examine the utility of a preemployment drug test, the U.S. Postal Service conducted a large-scale, carefully designed predictive validation study in 21 locations nationwide. Drug tests were administered to more than 5,000 applicants, of whom 4,396 were ultimately hired. The study focused on differences between drug positives (those hired whom the test identified as drug users) and drug negatives (those hired whom the test had not identified as drug users) in absenteeism, turnover, injuries, and accidents. The statistical analyses showed that significant differences existed between drug positives and drug negatives on absenteeism and involuntary turnover. Be-cause it was possible to calculate the financial gain of reduced absenteeism and involuntary turnover, the Postal Service could determine the utility of the drug test in dollar terms. More specifically, it was estimated that more than 60,000 new employees would need to be hired each year, from a total of 180,000 applicants. Approximately 9 percent of the applicants taking the test would show up as drug positives. In addition, the benefit of the drug-test program would last beyond one year, because the average postal service employee stays for 10 years.

On the cost side, the postal service estimated that the total cost of testing each applicant would be $11. Since the test would be given to all 180,000 applicants, this would result in a total cost of nearly $2 million in any given year. Do you think the costs out-weighed the benefits? If you answered no, you are right! According to the formula, the Postal Service would gain more than $3 million the first year alone from the reduced absenteeism. With the reduction in involuntary turnover from using the drug test, the gain would be even higher in the first year, and the postal service would continue to reap benefits over the years. As you can see from this example, even an expensive test may have great utility for an organization.

Source: Adapted from J. Normand, S. Salyards, and J. Mahoney, "An Evaluation of Preemployment Drug Testing," *Journal of Applied Psychology* 75 (1990): 629–39.

3. Retaliating against an employee or applicant filing a complaint on the basis of this law

However, this law does permit organizations to require employees to undergo a lie detector examination in specific, legitimate circumstances (for example, theft has occurred, and there is reasonable suspicion that the employee was somehow involved).[18]

Legally Recommended Practices. Certain selection practices may be legally rec-ommended or even required. One legal concept that would encourage employers to conduct careful background and reference checks is known as **negligent hiring.** In a negligent-hiring lawsuit, an organization could be held liable for actions of an em-ployee that should have been foreseen. Some examples where negligent hiring charges were filed against the company are the following:

A service station employee shoots a customer to death.

A truck driver sexually assaults a hitchhiker.

An apartment manager rapes a tenant.

A doorman shoots a customer being chased by a bouncer.

negligent hiring
A finding that an employer is responsible for using poor se-lection procedures after an employee inflicts harm on the customer or other third party.

Table 5.3   Do's and Don'ts of Interviewing

Subject	Unlawful Inquiry	Lawful Inquiry[a]
Name	If your name has been legally changed, what was your former name?	Have you ever worked for this company under a different name? What is your maiden name? (May be asked of married female applicants, if necessary, to check educational or employment records.) Have you ever been convicted of a crime under another name?
Age	[Any question that tends to identify applicants age forty or older.]	Are you older than eighteen years of age? If hired, can you furnish proof of age? [Statement that employment is subject to verification that applicant's age meets legal requirements.]
Citizenship	Are you a citizen of the United States (varies by state)? Are your parents or spouse citizens of the United States? On what dates did you, your parents, or your spouse acquire U.S. citizenship? Are you, your parents, or spouse naturalized or native-born U.S. citizens?	If you are not a U.S. citizen, do you have the legal right to remain permanently in the United States? What is your visa status (If answer to above is no)? Do you intend to remain permanently in the United States? [Statement that employment is subject to verification of applicant's identity and eligibility for employment as required by immigration laws.]
National origin/ Ancestry	What is your nationality/lineage/ ancestry/ national origin/descent/ parentage? How did you acquire the ability to speak, read, or write a foreign language? How did you acquire familiarity with a foreign country? What language is spoken in your home? What is your mother tongue?	What language do you speak, read, or write fluently? Do you have special familiarity with any foreign country? What is the nature of that familiarity (If answer to above is yes)?
Race or color	[Any question that directly or indirectly relates to race or color]	[None]
Religion	Do you attend religious services or a house of worship? What is your religious denomination or affiliation, church, parish, or pastor? What religious holidays do you observe?	[None]
Sex	[Any inquiry as to sex, such as the following:] Do you wish to be addressed as Mr., Mrs., Miss, or Ms.? What are your plans regarding having children in the future? Do you have the capacity to reproduce?	[None]
Relatives/ marital status	What is your marital status (If older than age 18)? What is the name or address of relative/ spouse/children? With whom do you reside? Do you live with your parents? What are the ages of your children?	What are the names of relatives already employed by the company?

[a] Lawful only if job related.

(continued)

Table 5.3 (*continued*)

Subject	Unlawful Inquiry	Lawful Inquiry[a]
Physical condition	Do you have any physical disabilities? What is your disability? What caused your disability? What is the prognosis of your disability? Have you had any recent serious illness?	Do you understand the requirements of the job and can you perform the job with or without reasonable accommodation? Explain how you would go about doing the job applied for. [The Americans with Disabilities Act (ADA) prohibits pre-employment-offer medical examinations or inquiries into an individual's disability status. Even where a disability is evident to an employer, the employer cannot make inquiries into the nature or severity of the disability.]
Education	[Any question asking specifically the nationality, racial, or religious affiliation of a school.]	[Questions related to academic, vocational, or professional education of an applicant, including schools attended, degrees/diplomas received, dates of graduation, and courses of study.]
Experience	[Questions related to military experience in general.]	[Questions related to applicant's work history.] [Questions related to applicant's military experience in the armed forces of the United States or in a U.S. state militia.]
Organizations	To what organizations, clubs, societies, and lodges do you belong?	To what organizations, clubs, societies, and lodges do you belong? (Exclude those whose names or character indicate the race, religious creed, color, national origin, or ancestry of its members.)
Character	Have you ever been arrested?	Have you ever been convicted of any crime?[b] If so, when, where, and disposition of case? Have you been convicted under any criminal law within the past five years (excluding minor traffic violations)?
Work Schedule/ Traveling	[Any question related to child care, ages of children, or other subject that is likely to be perceived by covered group members, especially women, as discriminatory.]	Would you be able to work overtime/travel? Would you be able to consistently arrive for work on time and work according to the company's (location's) work schedule?
Relocation	[Any question related to spouse's attitudes or other subject that is likely to be perceived by covered group members, especially women, as discriminatory.]	Would you be willing to relocate?
Miscellaneous	[Any inquiry that is not job-related or necessary for determining an applicant's potential for employment.]	[Statement or notice to applicant that any misstatements or omissions of significant facts in written application forms or in an interview may be cause for dismissal.]

[a] Lawful only if job related.

[b] In some states, such as California and New York, such a question must be accompanied by a statement that a conviction will not necessarily disqualify an applicant from a job. In Delaware, one may ask if the applicant has ever been arrested; in Massachusetts, one may ask if the applicant has been arrested for a felony. Some states put a time limit on convictions that may be inquired about (for example, Massachusetts [ten years]). Minnesota suggests that the best practice may be to obtain conviction information through local police departments, rather than from applicants.

Adapted from: S. Kahn, B. B. Brown, M. Lanzarone, *Legal Guide to Human Resources* (Boston, MA: Warren, Gorham & Lamont, 1995).

A bond salesman threatens a customer into buying bonds.

A hospital orderly hurts a patient when removing a catheter.[19]

As you can see from these examples, a negligent hiring suit can arise in many different occupations. Because of the negligent hiring concept, organizations are encouraged to conduct reference and background checks much more diligently in order to screen out applicants who may present a risk. Depending on the nature of the job, organizations may also be encouraged to perform conviction record checks and drug testing.

Certain regulated industries also have substantial numbers of laws that require background checks, drug testing, and other selection procedures to be performed. For example, Executive Order 12564, also known as the Drug-Free Federal Workplace order, requires government agencies to drug-test employees in sensitive positions. Similar laws are in place for other industries, such as the transportation industry.[20]

Practicality

There are several practical matters that an organization should consider in choosing selection devices. One of these is the *face validity* of each procedure. Face validity refers to perceptions held by various affected parties as to the job relatedness of the selection procedure. For example, if hiring managers feel that a test is not really job related (that is, it lacks face validity), they may not use test results properly. Similarly, if a selection procedure is not considered face valid by applicants, the organization may have difficulty getting them to accept job offers. Other practical considerations include administration of the procedure (for instance, is it time-consuming?) and scoring procedures for tests (are the tests difficult to score?).[21]

Typical Selection Steps

Although organizations differ in terms of which selection methods they use, many companies use a fairly standard set of steps in the hiring process. The common steps are as follows:

1. Review application forms and resumes.
2. Select best applicants for interview.
3. Interview.
4. Administer tests.
5. Conduct reference and background checks.
6. Perform drug test.

Of course, not all organizations use all procedures. Other organizations may follow somewhat different steps. For example, an organization may have far too many applicants to interview first. In that situation, an organization may use a psychological test in step 3, and follow up with interviews in step 4.

Now that you have read about some of the considerations that companies use in choosing selection methods, we will discuss some of these different procedures in more detail. We begin first with a discussion of the application form and related techniques, followed by a discussion of the interview and various tests. We conclude with a discussion of background checks, drug screens, and several miscellaneous procedures.

Application Form

Nearly every organization requires you, as an applicant, to complete an application form at some point in the employment process. Figure 5.4 provides an example of an application form. Notice the sentences near the end of the form in Figure 5.4, just above the signature area. If you read this statement carefully, you will see that, among other things, the company has retained the right to terminate you at any time, for any reason. Most application forms have a similar statement, and an applicant can do little to get around this. Furthermore, as you will read in Chapter 16, even without such a statement, most employees have little protection from arbitrarily being terminated. You may also observe a warning on the application form that falsification or omission of information is grounds for dismissal. This warning is an attempt to combat applicants' attempts to misrepresent themselves, given that as many as 30 percent of all resumes and application forms contain some false information.[22]

For the most part, organizations use information from the application form as an initial screen to reduce the number of potential candidates. In larger organizations, the human resource representative may perform an initial screen of the application forms, and decide which candidates should be invited for an interview.

An alternative to the application form is the **weighted application blank (WAB).** Typically, the standard application form is reviewed in a subjective fashion. The WAB is really nothing more than an objectively scored application form. Rather than having the HRM manager or hiring manager judge the application form on the basis of "gut feel," the WAB provides a score for each applicant, based on an answer key developed through research. The WAB is best suited for jobs where there are many workers, and it is particularly useful for reducing turnover. As such, WABs appear to be most commonly used for clerical and sales jobs, which traditionally have high turnover.[23] Although research on the WAB suggests it can be a valid selection device, it is not commonly used by employers.[24]

weighted application blank (WAB)
An objectively scored application form.

Another related technique is the **biographical information blank (BIB).** The BIB extends the concept of the WAB one step further. That is, the BIB aims to utilize a broader range of questions, particularly those pertaining to past achievements and personal goals and aspirations, which are scored with a standardized key.[25] Some examples of BIB items are provided in Table 5.4.

biographical information blank (BIB)
Utilizes a broader range of questions on an application form, particularly those pertaining to past achievements and personal goals and aspirations, which are scored with a standardized key.

Research on the BIB has been generally favorable with regard to its criterion-related validity.[26] The criterion-related validity of the BIB is about .30.[27] However, a number of concerns have been raised with this selection method.[28] One criticism is that a person's employment opportunities may be permanently affected by earlier (even childhood) experiences. For example, responses to BIB items such as 1 and 2 in Table 5.4 cannot be changed, regardless of a person's subsequent accomplishments. A second criticism is that BIB items often seem rather intrusive. Do you think, for example, that item 3 in Table 5.4 constitutes an invasion of your privacy? Indeed, the face validity of biodata appears to be quite low.[29] These concerns may explain why relatively few companies use BIBs. We turn now to the interview, which is one of the most popular selection methods.

The Interview

The interview is such a common selection practice that you would probably be suspicious if a company hired you without one. It is indeed rare to find a company that does

Figure 5.4 **Sample Application Form**

Name: _____

Address: _____

Home Phone Number: _____

Education

College/University Attended: _____ Highest Degree: BA/BS MA/MS/MBA PhD

High School Attended: _____

Work Experience (List most recent jobs first)

Name of Organization: _____

Final Salary: _____ (annual; be sure to include any bonuses or commission earned)

Job Title: _____

Name of last supervisor: _____

May we contact this supervisor?   Yes   No

Reason for Leaving: _____

_____

Name of Organization: _____ Dates of Employment: from _____ to _____

Final Salary: _____ (annual; be sure to include any bonuses or commission earned)

Job Title: _____

Name of last supervisor: _____

May we contact this supervisor?   Yes   No

Reason for Leaving: _____

_____

Name of Organization: _____ Dates of Employment: from _____ to _____

Final Salary: _____ (annual; be sure to include any bonuses or commission earned)

Job Title: _____

Name of last supervisor: _____

May we contact this supervisor?   Yes   No

Reason for Leaving: _____

_____

Name of Organization: _____ Dates of Employment: from _____ to _____

Final Salary: _____ (annual; be sure to include any bonuses or commission earned)

Job Title: _____

Name of last supervisor: _____

May we contact this supervisor?   Yes   No

Reason for Leaving: _____

_____

(continued)

Figure 5.4   *(continued)*

Work skills

1. List any job-related languages you are able to speak or write: _____

2. List any job-related clerical (for example, typing) or technical skills (for example, computer programming) that you have:

   A. _____

   B. _____

   C. _____

Additional Information

In case of an emergency, please contact:

Name: _____

Address: _____

Telephone: _____

_____

_____

I understand that falsification of information is grounds for dismissal.

I understand that my employment at the company may be discontinued at any time for any reason either by myself or by the company.

I agree to submit to a drug and/or alcohol test as a condition of employment.

_____

Signature   Date

---

not use at least one interview in its selection procedure. Many companies have applicants go through two or more interviews. You may have wondered just what interviewers are trying to assess when they talk with job applicants. Most interviews address four basic issues: reliability, competencies, values, and motivation. *Reliability* refers to the applicant's likelihood of adhering to the basic rules and policies of the job and organization, such as attendance, overtime, and travel requirements. An example of a question used to assess reliability might be: "How many days of work did you miss last year?" *Competencies*, as you read earlier, are those knowledges (for example, tax laws) and abilities (for example, verbal reasoning) that are considered necessary to perform the job. A question to assess your competency in marketing might be, "Tell me how you would go about marketing a new computer software package." *Values* are applicant preferences for different aspects of the work environment (for example, supervisory style). A question to assess values might be, "How do you think people in this organization should be promoted?" And finally, *applicant motivation* refers to the different

Table 5.4   **Sample BIB Items**

1. Check each of the following activities you participated in by the time you were age eighteen.
   a. Shot a rifle
   b. Drove a car
   c. Worked on full-time job
   d. Traveled alone more than five hundred miles from home
   e. Repaired an electrical appliance
2. While growing up, did you collect coins?
3. Are you satisfied with life?
   Yes
   No
4. While in school, how often did you believe a teacher was unfair in a decision she or he made?
5. While in school, how often did you go to your parents for advice?

Source: Items 1, 2, and 3 are from R. Gatewood and H. Feild, *Human Resource Selection* (Fort Worth, TX: Dryden, 1994). Items 4 and 5 are from C. Russell, J. Mettson, S. Devlin, and D. Atwater, "Predictive Validity of Biodata Items Generated from Retrospective Life Experience Essays," *Journal of Applied Psychology* 75 (1990): 569–80.

types of rewards desired by the applicant (for example, opportunity to learn new skills, performance bonuses). A typical question here is, "What did you like most about your previous position?"[30] Box 5.2 puts together some of the more commonly asked interview questions and suggested answers.

As suggested by the opening case, interviews take many forms. Four basic kinds of interviews, namely the traditional interview, the structured interview, the stress interview, and the panel interview, are described next.

Traditional Interview

traditional interview
The most common type of interview, which allows the interviewer a great deal of discretion in terms of which questions are asked and in what order.

Most people at one time or another have experienced a **traditional interview,** or unstructured interview, which is probably the most common type of interview. Table 5.5 contains a list of questions that are often asked in the traditional interview. The traditional interview format also allows the interviewer a great deal of discretion in choosing which questions to ask and in what order. In other words, using a traditional interview, the hiring manager might ask completely different questions of each candidate.[31]

You can probably guess why an interviewer would want to ask most of the questions listed in Table 5.5. In general, the traditional interview focuses on assessing applicant reliability, values, and motivation. As you read the questions in Table 5.5, you may also note that few of them directly assess the competencies needed to perform the job. Even the question about your greatest strength is rather indirect, because it merely asks the applicant to provide information, and the accuracy of the answer is unknown. Questions that more directly assess job-related competencies are found in structured interview formats, which you will read about in the next section.

Despite its popularity, many experts have been skeptical as to the value of the traditional interview. First, from a criterion-related-validity viewpoint, the traditional interview generally is believed to have a relatively low correlation with job performance,

Box 5.2

"What Do I Say If They Ask . . . ?"

Because certain questions are commonly asked in the traditional interview, experts recommend that you prepare carefully ahead of time to answer these. Below are some suggested answers to some of these questions.

"You're just the type we're looking for."

1. "Tell me about yourself." You should have planned an answer to this question. Your answer should consist of a brief speech, containing about 300 words and taking approximately one to one-and-a-half minutes. This speech should be an oral presentation of the highlights of your resume, along with the highlights of the letter of introduction you would write for this employer. In other words, your speech should emphasize your key achievements, key strengths, and an explanation of how these achievements and strengths are pertinent to the position. If possible, you should end your speech with a question to the interviewer (for example, "What new strategic directions is the company taking?"). Experts say the key to a successful answer here is to demonstrate your confidence, communication skills, and match between the job and your qualifications.

2. "Why do you want to work for our company?" This is the kind of question that makes you pleased you did some research on the company. And this is a way for companies to see if you showed initiative. A good answer, then, reveals that you know something about the company and its products. For example, you may have read that the company is restructuring, and is in the process of redesigning the sales department into teams. You might respond by saying that you enjoy the team approach to sales (and hopefully you can demonstrate some experience working with teams) and describe why that sales approach makes sense given the company's product line.

3. "What's your greatest weakness?" Gulp! That's the question you probably dread most. This can be a "damned if you do and damned if you don't" question. If you say you have no weaknesses, the interviewer may believe you are being evasive (everybody has a weakness). If you say something like, "I work too hard" or "I'm demanding of myself" your answer may also sound artificial. Experts advise you try to offer something that won't disqualify you (for instance, if you have never supervised anyone and the job doesn't involve supervising others, you can answer, "I have not supervised anyone") or something that sounds reasonable (for example, "I offered several innovative ideas, but my boss was worried the ideas would lead to radical changes in the department").

4. "Describe the best boss and worst boss to work with." This is obviously a tough question. If you say the worst boss is one who checks on everything you do, and that's the prospective supervisor's style, your answer may not work in your favor. One response is to play it safe and say something like, "I've worked with a variety of different styles of bosses, and am able to adjust to different styles."

5. "Are you married?" or "What religion do you practice?" or "How old are you?" are questions that are probably illegal and certainly inappropriate. But how should you answer them? If you refuse to answer that kind of question, the interviewer may feel offended (he or she may not be aware such questions are inappropriate). If you challenge the interviewer by saying the question is illegal, you may be perceived as offensive. Experts suggest that you answer a question about religion or similar area by saying something like, "Do I look like I practice some unusual form of religion? I assume you are (continued)

YOUR TURN

(continued)

joking, because that is considered an illegal question." Or, perhaps more tactfully, "I am not sure how that question relates to the job, but I can assure you that I behave in a professional manner and can perform the job at issue well." Likewise, you may be able to answer a clearly illegal question in a positive way. For example, if you are confined to a wheelchair and the interviewer asks you if you are disabled, you might say: "No, I am not disabled. I am in a wheelchair, but that does not in any way pre-

vent me from successfully performing a secretarial job."
6. "What questions do YOU have?" If you don't have any questions, the interviewer may take this as a lack of interest in the company or a lack of savvy, both of which may hurt you in the hiring process. Some good questions to ask include the following:
- What is the mission of this department?
- What new products or services is the company thinking of introducing in the next few years?

- What changes do you expect in the company's business strategy over the next few years?
- How soon do you want someone to begin in this position?
- Can I get a tour of this facility or a visit to the department?
- Why is this position open?

Whatever you do, do not ask about the company's vacation plans, personal days, and so forth! It will seem as though you are most worried about time away from the organization.

Source: Adapted from H. Medley, *Sweaty Palms: The Neglected Art of Being Interviewed* (Berkeley, CA: Ten Speed Press, 1984); R. Fry, *Your First Job* (Hawthorne, NJ: Career Press, 1993); M. Dorio, *The Complete Idiot's Guide to the Perfect Interview* (New York: Alpha Books, 1997); and A. Ludmer, "Watch Out for Deadly Interview Traps," *St. Louis Post-Dispatch*, 3 October 1993, 19G.

Table 5.5	**Questions That May Be Asked in the Traditional Interview**

1. What did you like most about your last job?
2. What did you like least about your last job?
3. What are your career goals?
4. What is your greatest strength?
5. What is your greatest weakness?
6. What kind of boss do you work best with?
7. What is most important to you on the job?
8. What were your favorite courses at school?
9. What extracurricular activities did you participate in during school?
10. How did you choose this particular field of work?
11. What do you think your current supervisor's greatest strength is?
12. Why did you leave your last job?
13. Do you prefer to work alone or in a team?
14. What are your hobbies?
15. Who was your favorite teacher? Why?
16. Who paid your tuition in college?

perhaps as low as .14. Second, the traditional interview is susceptible to a wide variety of biases and errors. Hiring managers may use the traditional interview to select someone who seems similar to them or is likable, rather than the candidate most qualified for the job. Third, because the traditional interview permits complete discretion over which questions to ask, some interviewers will ask illegal or bizarre questions. HRM students have reported being asked everything from, "Are you married?" to "If you could be any item in the produce section of a grocery store, what would you be?" From the organization's standpoint, then, the traditional interview has shortcomings. Many companies have therefore turned to the structured interview approach.[32] Box 5.3 describes some of the intricacies organizations face when interviewing applicants in other countries.

Structured Interview

Although there are many ways to structure an interview, the term **structured interview,** as we use it here, refers to an interview that includes a predetermined set of questions that are clearly job related.[33] Although the interviewer may have a choice of questions from which to choose, he or she may not use a question that is not on the list. Although several different kinds of structured interviews are available, the two most popular are the *behavior description interview (BDI)* and *situational interview (SI)*.[34] BDI questions address past experiences (they may begin with, "Tell me about a time when . . ."), whereas SI questions address how the applicant would handle a situation in the future ("What would you do if . . . ?"). Table 5.6 provides an example of a BDI and SI question that assess the same topic. As you can see, the questions are clearly job related and probably more challenging to answer than many of the traditional questions found in Table 5.5. Some commonly asked BDI questions are provided in Table 5.7.

There are several advantages to the structured interview approach. As you may have guessed, structured interviews are more valid than the traditional interview. Their criterion-related validity has been estimated to be as high as .60.[35] Second, by having highly structured interviews, managers use job-related, preestablished questions, which in turn discourages biases and errors. Third, having a structured interview prevents managers from asking illegal questions. Finally, recent evidence suggests that highly structured interviews produce less adverse impact against African Americans and Hispanics compared to relatively unstructured interviews.[36] On the other hand, designing a structured interview may take a good amount of time and energy. Furthermore, some managers resent being restricted in terms of the questions they may ask.

structured interview
Uses a predetermined set of questions that are clearly job-related, such as the behavior description interview and situational interview.

Stress Interview

On occasion, you may encounter the stress interview. A **stress interview** is simply an attempt by the interviewer to see how you fare under duress. There is little evidence that such interviews are valid. An interviewer may justify them on the grounds that the job involves highly volatile situations, where it is important to remain calm. In any case, the key is to remember that nearly any interview situation involves some degree of stress, and it is always important to maintain your self-composure. So, if you think the interviewer is deliberately trying to shake you up, you may be right. Just don't become flustered.[37]

stress interview
An interview technique that is an attempt by the interviewer to see how a candidate fares under duress.

Panel Interview

In a **panel interview,** the interviewee faces a group of interviewers. Although you may think the purpose of the panel interview is to make you uncomfortable, in most cases the actual purpose is to limit the impact of the personal biases of any individual

panel interview
A group of interviewers interview a candidate at the same time. This type of interview reduces the effects of personal biases any individual interviewer may have.

Box 5.3
Interviewing Applicants in Other Countries

Depending on which country a job candidate is from, the wording of interview questions may be quite important. Consider first the Japanese. Because of cultural norms that encourage teamwork and deemphasize individual achievements, Japanese managers would be uncomfortable answering a question such as, "How do you compare your skill level to that of your coworkers?" A question such as, "From the time you were in high school through your time at the university, what skills did you exhibit that enabled you to excel?" would be far more appropriate. Nevertheless, Japanese managers tend to give brief responses to such questions, due to a concern that a lengthy answer will be less well understood. Therefore, probing questions, such as "Could you provide some more specific details on how you used those skills on a daily basis?" are usually needed to obtain further information.

If you are interviewing a Korean manager, this question would be considered highly appropriate: "What skill do you most enjoy using?" For a Japanese manager, however, this question might appear odd, because in Japan there is little concept of work enjoyment, whereas in Korea it is assumed that work should bring personal satisfaction. Another question that would be appropriate in Korea is, "What was the most difficult decision you ever had to make on your own without your boss's input?" While Korean managers must sometimes make independent decisions, this would be a very rare occurrence in Japan.

Interviewing in Europe also reveals interesting cultural differences. French managers often operate within the "Napoleonic Code," which is patterned after the famous military general. This style of management is similar to the traditional bureaucratic management approach, which emphasizes close supervision and constant reaction to problems. To assess a French manager's type of management style, an effective question is, "Which of your skills do you employ that best demonstrates your leadership ability?" Yet another request that is revealing of a French manager is, "Describe your formal education and how that helps you in your current position." The rationale here is that the French culture places tremendous value on formal education and degrees. The answer given by a French applicant will provide insight into his or her ability to learn new things and the degree to which the applicant can utilize education in the job.

Clearly, depending on the country in which an interviewer is operating, different approaches to questions may be needed.

Source: Adapted from J. Artise, "Selection, Coaching, and Evaluation of Employees in International Subsidiaries," in *Global Perspectives of Human Resource Management*, ed. O. Shenkar (Englewood Cliffs, NJ: Prentice-Hall, 1995), 71–111.

Table 5.6	Structured Interview Questions for a High School Teacher's Job
Behavioral Description Interview Questions	**Situational Interview Questions**
■ Tell me about a time when you had a student who was clearly having trouble keeping up with your class material, and was falling far behind. Describe how you handled the situation, and what the outcome was. ■ Tell me about a time when students were talking or engaging in other disruptive behaviors during class. How did you handle it?	■ What would you do if a student was having a great deal of trouble keeping up with the class, and was beginning to fall further and further behind? ■ What would you do if you were in the middle of a lecture and several students began to whisper, laugh, and generally disrupt class?

Table 5.7	**Some Commonly Asked BDI Questions**

Tell me about a time when. . . .

1. You handled a difficult situation with a coworker.
2. You were creative in solving a problem.
3. You had to deal with a difficult customer.
4. You had conflicting deadlines.
5. You had to discipline an employee.
6. You were forced to implement an unpopular policy.
7. You encountered a stressful situation.
8. You had to learn a new task.

Adapted from A. Hirsch, *The National Business Employment Weekly Premier Guide: Interviewing* (New York: Wiley, 1996).

interviewer. Nevertheless, as an applicant, a panel interview may make you feel more stressed than usual. Here are two suggestions for interviewees:

1. Imagine you are talking to only one person; in fact, in some cases, only one person on the panel will do the talking. The others may be there only to listen and take notes.[38]
2. If different people do start asking questions and do not let you finish giving your answers, pause and then say something like, "Let me answer one question at a time. First . . . ." Then, respond to the next question. In other words, don't let the questioning get out of hand, but at the same time, be polite.

Legal Considerations

In terms of legality, the interview has a mixed record. Most recent research suggests that the interview varies greatly in terms of whether protected groups, such as older workers and minorities, are adversely affected or not. Recent studies indicate that women, on average, fare no worse than men in the interview.[39] Most court cases concerning interviews have involved organizations that used discriminatory questions. For instance, in one lawsuit, an African-American woman applied for the position of kitchen helper. During the interview, she was asked about her recent pregnancy and future plans pertaining to children, her marital status, and her relationship with an employee of the company. However, such questions were not asked of other applicants, and the interviewer had a history of discriminating against women. Thus, companies seem particularly vulnerable to charges against their interviewing procedure when inappropriate questions are asked.[40] Table 5.8 provides some additional suggestions for companies that wish to increase the likelihood that their interviews will pass legal muster if challenged in court.

At some point in your human resource career you will likely be the one in the interviewer's seat. The following suggestions are offered for managers and supervisors who are conducting an employment interview:[41]

1. Plan ahead. Before the interview, determine what reliability issues, competencies, values, and motivations you are trying to assess. Determine the questions you will ask and how you will evaluate answers to them. For each question you develop, ask

Table 5.8	**How Organizations Can Avoid Legal Problems with Interviews**

1. Develop job descriptions. Using job descriptions for developing interview objectives, questioning strategies, and evaluation standards will enhance interview consistency and job relatedness. Make sure that you incorporate recent developments in the Americans with Disabilities Act.
2. Use appropriate questions. Questioning practices will be used as evidence of discrimination; be sure that illegal questions are not asked. Prepare questions in advance.
3. Review selection and training of interviewers. Consider carefully the race and gender makeup of the interviewing team, their training, and their background. Be sure that the interviewers reflect diversity in terms of race, gender, age, and other EEOC characteristics.
4. Involve other people. Frequently, the interviewer alone decides on the objectives, questions, and evaluation standards. Use additional parties as much as possible (for example, multiple interviewers, HR manager, or management committees) to review interviewer recommendations.
5. Keep documentation. A serious problem for some organizations in defending their practices is a lack of information which would have allowed them to explain the job relatedness of their selection procedures. Encourage note-taking and documenting reasons for hiring and not hiring candidates. Be aware, however, that documentation is a "double-edged sword." Inappropriate comments, such as notes about an applicant's sex, race, age, or other EEOC categories, can seriously damage an organization that is sued.

Source: Adapted from M. Roehling, J. Campion, R. Arvey, "Unfair Discrimination in the Employment Interview," In R. Eder and M. Harris (Eds.), *The Employment Interview Handbook* (Newbury Park, CA: Sage, in press).

yourself the following: (1) is it legal to ask? (2) how does it relate to the job and organization? If you are unsure of the answer to either of these, leave it out, rephrase it, or check with a knowledgeable person, such as a human resource manager or an employment lawyer.

2. Take notes during the interview. During the interview, take notes about what the applicant said. However, be aware that note-taking can tip off the candidate about your reactions. Do not write the whole time; at least some of the time you should make eye contact with the candidate. You can always ask the candidate to wait while you write things down.

3. Maintain positive rapport with the candidate. Do this by beginning the interview with small talk, maintaining a pleasant facial expression throughout the interview, and being polite. Avoid interrupting the candidate unless necessary. Keep in mind that if you maintain a good rapport, the applicant will be more likely to accept a job offer, to say positive things about the organization to other applicants, and will be less likely to file a lawsuit or badmouth the organization.

4. Provide information. Candidates usually expect you to provide some information about the job and organization; be sure to leave ample time for this phase of the interview. Also, be sure to give the candidate an opportunity to ask questions. Generally, it is better to end the interview with this phase.

5. Don't be swayed by irrelevant information. Many interviewers succumb to various errors and biases in making a decision based on the interview. For example, some candidates are good at oral communication, so we tend to rate them as being more qualified on other factors than they might be. Conversely, some quiet people are rated lower on other dimensions. Also be aware that some candidates will

try ingratiating themselves with you. Make sure you hire based on job-related factors.

Turning to the applicant, job seekers are encouraged to prepare for a variety of interview questions, some of which were provided in this section. As you participate in more interviews, you will become more comfortable and generally will perform better. Consider role-playing various possible questions with a friend. Try to anticipate all types of questions that might arise, and think ahead to how you might answer them. Finally, recall that in this chapter's opening case, Tom Brown was unable to come up with previous experiences in one of his interviews. You should know that in some cases, you may be able to use experiences outside of the workplace, including school, volunteer experiences, and possibly even family situations.

In sum, the interview is a popular selection procedure, and all signs indicate it will remain so. As an applicant, you should prepare carefully for every interview. From an organizational perspective, given the importance of the interview, selection interviews must be carefully planned and only job-related questions should be asked. Questions not directly related to the job, particularly inquiries that address sensitive areas such as age, religion, marital status, and so forth, should not be asked under any circumstances.

We now turn to a discussion of what were often referred to as "paper-and-pencil" tests. With today's technology, however, many of these tests are administered with a computer. Therefore, we will refer to them as "psychological tests."

Psychological Tests

There are many different kinds of psychological tests but most can be sorted into three basic categories: personality measures, cognitive ability measures, and job knowledge examinations.

Personality Tests

Do you think a **personality test** would be a good predictor of job performance? It seems reasonable to expect that personality tests would predict job performance at least somewhat. After all, everybody has heard of personality conflicts, "bad" personalities, and other personality-related problems that take place at work. Table 5.9 provides some examples of questions found on a typical personality test. If you want to take a personality test and obtain a score, try this Web site: www.davideck.com/links/k-disc.html.

Although you might think that personality tests would be good predictors of job performance, early studies of the validity of these tests often produced low correlations with job performance, leading many experts to conclude that such tests were of little

personality test
A test given to an applicant that will supposedly predict the type of personality a candidate has and how that personality will affect job performance.

Table 5.9	**Typical Personality Test Items**

1. I like to win in any activity I try.
2. I have many friends.
3. I sometimes get upset when I'm criticized.
4. I prefer working in a team to working alone.
5. It's more important to me to do a thorough job on one thing than to complete many things.

value in the workplace. Using validity generalization methods, however, there has been a change in conclusions about the validity of personality tests. A recent estimate placed the validity of personality tests at .24, but it found that when the personality test was chosen on the basis of a careful job analysis, the validity of the personality test climbed to .38.[42]

There are many personality tests available for companies to use, and most personality tests contain multiple scales. Most of these scales fall into one of five dimensions: extroversion, emotional stability, openness to experience, agreeableness, and conscientiousness. Which of these dimensions do you think is the most predictive of job performance? If you guessed conscientiousness, you are right. This scale is the most consistently predictive of job performance. People who are persistent and who feel a sense of obligation generally perform better on the job.[43]

One of the more interesting types of personality tests, which has received some attention in the past few years, allegedly measures honesty. Because **honesty tests** are not considered polygraph tests, companies in most states may use them as part of the selection process. Two types of honesty tests are used: the overt test and the personality-based test. The *overt honesty test* asks questions that directly address the test-taker's perceptions and feelings about honesty, such as, "Do you ever think about stealing?" "Do you know people who steal?" and "Should someone who steals from his or her company be fired?" *Personality-based honesty tests* tend to be somewhat less obvious as to what they are assessing and to focus on personality traits associated with dishonesty. Typical items include, "Do you like to do dangerous things?" and "Do you sometimes do things without thinking?" Do you think such tests demonstrate good validity? A recent summary of research found a criterion-related validity of .55 for overt tests and .32 for personality-based tests. Such tests appear to have utility, then, particularly when the cost (which is only about $10 per test) is considered.[44]

Legally, personality tests have generally fared well, particularly because they produce little, if any, adverse impact.[45] The same is true for honesty tests. Another advantage of both personality and honesty tests is that they are easy to administer and score.[46]

The face validity of personality tests, on the other hand, may be somewhat low.[47] All in all, personality tests appear to be making a comeback, though they may never become as popular as cognitive ability tests, which are reviewed next.

Cognitive Ability Tests

Cognitive ability tests, or intelligence tests, have a long history of use in the workplace. An example of a cognitive ability test that you can take and receive a score for is provided in this Web site: www.apsoft.com/~anduin/gentest/iqtest.shtml. The use of cognitive ability tests in the United States for selection purposes goes back to the early part of the 20th century. Both private- and public-sector employers began using such tests extensively in the 1950s and 1960s. But in the 1970s, public outcry against such tests in educational settings, as well as in business settings, led many organizations to reduce their reliance on them. Even more importantly, court cases based on the Civil Rights Act of 1964 (for example, *Griggs v. Duke Power*, 1971), in which cognitive ability tests fared poorly, led to a marked decline in their use.[48] A major problem, which continues even today, is that on average, African Americans and Hispanics obtain lower scores on these tests than do whites, which in turn often creates adverse impact.[49] To compound the problem, early researchers found contradictory results regarding the criterion-related validity of such tests. Sometimes the tests appeared to

---

honesty test
Two types of honest tests: overt and personality-based. The overt test asks questions that directly address test takers' perceptions and feelings about honesty. Personality-based tests tend to be somewhat less obvious as to what they are assessing and focus on personality traits associated with dishonesty.

cognitive ability test
Intelligence test given to applicants.

have sufficient criterion-related validity, while at other times they did not, making it difficult for companies to defend the job relatedness of such tests. As a result, the use of cognitive ability tests began to wane in the 1970s. Two developments created a revival in the use of cognitive ability tests in the 1980s. First, validity generalization studies indicated that cognitive ability tests have adequate validity across virtually all jobs. Situational specificity, in other words, is not a problem for these tests. In fact, this research suggested that when used properly, cognitive ability tests would have a criterion-related validity of .53.[50] The validity of cognitive ability tests therefore is much higher than earlier HRM experts had thought. Second, experts suggested that one way to avoid potential adverse impact problems with these tests would be to use **race norming:** separate norms for different racial and gender groups.[51]

race norming
A method used to eliminate adverse impact by separate norms for different racial and gender groups.

Many companies continue to use cognitive ability tests today. In addition to their validity, they are fairly inexpensive and relatively easy to administer and score. Thus, their utility is likely to be high. The major shortcoming of these tests is that the Civil Rights Act of 1991 explicitly prohibits the use of race and gender norming. Companies that had previously used race or gender norming to eliminate adverse impact must therefore decide whether they have sufficient validity evidence to defend a lawsuit if one arises. In spite of their general validity, then, cognitive ability tests may create a legal problem. Table 5.10 provides some sample items from a cognitive ability test. Figure 5.5 provides examples of a nonverbal cognitive ability test.

Job Knowledge Examination

When you applied for a driver's permit, you probably took a test of your knowledge of the rules of the road. That is a kind of **job knowledge test,** which is a measure of your comprehension of basic facts and information pertinent to the job. To practice law or psychology, for example, you would have to pass a job knowledge test. Research shows that job knowledge tests, if developed properly, have a relatively high correlation with job performance. In fact, the average correlation is .48, which compared to other procedures, such as personality tests, is relatively high. In addition, content validity is also high for properly designed job knowledge tests. There are, however, two major shortcomings of job knowledge tests. First, a properly designed test can be expensive and time-consuming to design. Second, a job knowledge test assumes that the applicant has been trained to perform the job. If a company is planning to train the hired applicants to perform the job, a test of knowledge is probably irrelevant.[52]

job knowledge test
Measures comprehension of basic facts.

Work Samples

Most managers will tell you that the best way to assess someone's job qualifications is to hire him or her to work on a trial basis for a few weeks. In fact, many organizations do just that when they hire a temporary worker. Hiring an employee on a trial basis may not always be feasible for two reasons. First, hiring someone on a trial basis might pose significant risks for the organization. For example, a poorly qualified production worker might be injured while operating a drill press. An unqualified salesperson could lose valued customers. Second, many applicants would be reluctant to accept a job that they may lose shortly after they begin. Therefore, some organizations and businesses use **work samples,** which are basically a brief simulation of major job activities. Work samples are commonly used for secretarial and clerical positions, where typing skills

work samples
A brief simulation of major job activities.

Table 5.10	Typical Cognitive Ability Test Items

1. Which of the following is the opposite of *sanguine?*
   a. pessimistic   b. happy   c. melodic   d. rapid
2. If it takes three employees to complete each widget produced, how many employees would it take to complete 120 widgets?
   a. 300   b. 360   c. 36   d. 40
3. What is the next number in the following series of numbers: 1 3 7 15 31?
   a. 4   b. 63   c. 92   d. 103

Figure 5.5	Typical Nonverbal Cognitive Ability Test Items

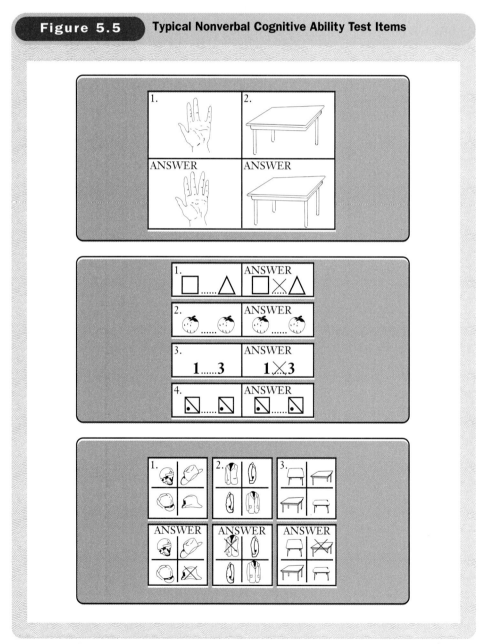

Source: From the Beta-II Examination. Copyright by the Psychological Corporation (Harcourt-Brace).

can be assessed using an objective method. The actual work sample depends on the particular job one is being hired for. An applicant for a sales position, for example, might be asked to simulate a meeting with a potential customer. A well-designed work sample would provide information about a hypothetical organization and product. Following a brief preparation period, the applicant would be given an opportunity to meet with the prospective "buyer," usually role-played by the interviewer. After the role-play, the interviewer would rate the applicant on job-related abilities, such as communication skills and persuasiveness. Work samples have been developed for every imaginable job, including bakers, auto mechanics, managers, army recruiters, customer service personnel, supervisors, police officers, and computer programmers, to mention just a few.[53]

An **assessment center** is an extended work sample. A typical assessment center consists of several different exercises, measuring various competencies, such as oral communication, decision making, and leadership. Several assessors, usually employees from the organization, observe the applicant's behavior. In many organizations, assessors meet together after the exercises are completed to make consensus-based ratings on the competencies and to make an overall assessment rating.[54]

assessment center
An extended work sample.

In terms of the validity of work samples and assessment centers, findings have generally been quite positive. A recent review of assessment centers reported that the average criterion-related validity was .37.[55] The assessment center technique has several additional advantages. First, the assessment center may also be content valid. Second, the assessment center has an excellent legal history. In at least one case, the court even recommended the use of assessment centers. Overall, the evidence suggests that assessment centers do not produce adverse impact on the basis of sex or race.[56] Third, when the assessment center closely simulates the actual jobs of the organization, it may provide a realistic job preview (see Chapter 4). Finally, because the assessment center relies on ratings by multiple assessors from different parts of the organization, rather than one supervisor, it is often viewed as a more objective procedure than interviews and performance ratings. The assessment center may therefore be an excellent device for promotion decisions, as well as for career development purposes.

Despite many virtues, the assessment center method has two potentially significant drawbacks. First, it is expensive to design and administer. In fact, it can cost thousands of dollars to assess each applicant. Second, although it is valid, other selection methods reviewed earlier, such as cognitive ability tests, interviews, and BIBs, appear to be equally valid. Viewed in this light, it may be difficult to justify the expense of the assessment center.[57]

In sum, work samples, and particularly assessment centers, offer several major advantages to organizations as a selection device. The major drawback is that the assessment center is likely to be more expensive and more time-consuming than other selection devices that are equally valid. But, if the organization is worried about discrimination lawsuits, a properly designed assessment center is probably the safest tactic. We now move to two selection methods that are usually reserved only for candidates to whom the organization plans to make a job offer: background and reference checks and drug and alcohol screening.

Reference and Record Checking

In today's highly litigious workplace, employers are increasingly interested in uncovering information about such factors as an applicant's prior employment history, past criminal convictions, and possibly other records, such as motor vehicle history. Recall

Fair Credit Reporting Act
A modified act that allows an employer to collect third-party information about an employee or applicant within certain specific guidelines of consent and disclosure.

in the opening case that Tom Brown expressed concern as to what information would be obtained from the credit check. Indeed, credit checks are notorious for errors; when the author was buying a house, the credit check incorrectly indicated an unpaid bill from a major retailer that supposedly was more than four years past due! However, recent changes in the law are providing even more protection for the job applicant and employee than in the past. The **Fair Credit Reporting Act,** which was modified by the Consumer Credit Reporting Reform Act in 1997 (www.instant-info.com/fcra-comparison.htm), requires the following: [58]

1. An employer who is going to have any third party collect information about an applicant or employee, regardless of whether it is to examine the person's credit history, or even to check references, is covered by these laws.
2. If the information gathering is covered by this law, the employer must obtain consent from the applicant or employee in a separate document;
3. The employer must share that consent with the third party;
4. If, based on the report, the organization is going to take some adverse action (for example, decides not to hire the applicant), the organization must supply the applicant with a copy of the report, along with a summary of the person's rights *before* the action.
5. After the action is taken, the organization must issue a form to the person, indicating among other things, contact information, the right to a free copy of the third-party report, and an acknowledgment of the right to dispute the accuracy of the report.

Another popular selection method is the reference check. While many organizations conduct a reference check on their own, some organizations will contract with another party to do this (for example, see www.letr.com). This procedure involves contacting previous employers to verify employment information and obtain independent assessments of an applicant's qualifications. In recent years, reference checking has become much less useful to companies. This is the result of **defamation** lawsuits, which may be filed if a past supervisor makes statements about a former employee that cannot be proved to be true and that damage the reputation of the former employee. If such information is provided in writing (such as on a written reference form), it is called libel. If such information is given in oral form (for example, over the telephone), it is referred to as slander. In order to win a defamation case, the past employee would have to show the following:

defamation
Slander or libel that can result in a lawsuit.

1. The statement was made to another party.
2. The statement is false. Generally, the defendant has the burden of proving the statement was true.
3. The employee's reputation was harmed. [59]

Occasionally, employers and employees part on unfavorable terms. A bad reference can make future job hunting difficult. Box 5.4 discusses options open to employees to counter erroneous or negative references.

In the mid-1990s, several well-publicized lawsuits affected employers' liability once again. One of these lawsuits involved a former vice principal who applied for a job at another school. Several officials from the previous school wrote positive letters about him, none of which mentioned the reason that he had left the school, namely, a

TALES FROM THE TRENCHES

Box 5.4
Former Boss Giving a Bad Reference?

What Employees Can Do to Fight Back

Ever wonder if a former boss is giving an employee a negative reference? Documented Reference Check (DRC), a company located in California, now offers employees a way to fight back. DRC uses the same procedure as any HRM manager would in contacting past employers. The company calls or writes former employers and obtains information regarding an employee's employment dates, salary, and job title, as well as any other information that a past employer releases. DRC then provides the employee with a written report. If the report reveals negative or erroneous information, DRC will offer additional services so that the employee can prevent the information from being given to others (www.badreferences.com).

Some former employees are fighting the effects of bad references by invoking a legal concept known as "compelled self-publication." A lawsuit of this nature would arise if the prospective employer asked the employee why he or she was terminated. In certain industries, applicants are even required to explain in writing why they left a particular job. Applicants may then claim they were forced to provide the reason, which they felt was untrue, thus creating a kind of self-slander. In a 1986 lawsuit in Minnesota, for example, several claims processors were awarded nearly half a million dollars in such a case.

Source: Adapted from J. Woo, "Quirky Slander Actions Threaten Employers," *Wall Street Journal*, 26 November 1993, B1, B5.

history of sexual misconduct charges. When the new employer found out that he had this history, the past employer was sued on grounds of intentional misrepresentation. A second major case involved a man, Paul Calden, who was terminated by Allstate Insurance Company. Although Calden had been forced to resign by Allstate, they informed a prospective employer, Firemen's Fund Insurance Company, that his resignation had been due to corporate restructuring. In fact, Allstate dismissed Calden because he had carried a weapon to work, threatened coworkers, and acted inappropriately in other ways. After Firemen's Fund dismissed Calden, he returned to the building with a weapon and killed several workers. Allstate was sued by the estates of several of the victims as a result.[60]

These types of lawsuits, coupled with the defamation lawsuits described above, appeared to put companies in a double-bind; if they presented a negative reference about an employee, he or she could sue for defamation. If the company failed to include negative information, the prospective employer could potentially sue for misrepresentation. To address that problem, about 19 state legislatures (such as Alaska, Colorado, and Ohio) have passed laws aimed at limiting employers' liability for giving out accurate reference information. Nevertheless, some experts maintain that the legislation that has been passed has not really made it easier for companies to protect themselves.[61]

In order to avoid lawsuits, companies should be cautious about providing information to other parties. Many companies have written policies that prohibit managers from discussing past employees with other individuals. Companies may also require that the HRM department handle all reference requests, and in many cases to limit information to verifying employment dates and perhaps final salary. In cases where past supervisors do provide information about former employees, they tend to say little that is negative. If you are a supervisor, be extremely careful concerning the information you release to other parties about past employees. As indicated above, even a glowing reference letter could create problems for you, a manager or supervisor, if the new employer sues you for misrepresentation.[62] On the other hand, you should attempt to get as much information about a prospective employee as you can from past companies, in order to avoid a negligent hiring lawsuit. Thus, the advice about reference information may seem contradictory to you, but it really does make sense.

In terms of criterion-related validity, the reference check has not fared well. Typical estimates of the criterion-related validity range between .13 and .26.[63] The relatively low validity is probably due to the reluctance on the part of supervisors to provide negative information. With regard to adverse impact, the reference check has been examined in few court cases.[64] One lawsuit, though, found no evidence of adverse impact.[65] Moreover, most people would probably say that reference checking seems like a reasonable selection procedure.

Drug and Alcohol Testing

In the last 10 years, drug testing, and to a lesser extent alcohol testing, has become much more popular. Although our focus here is on preemployment uses of drug and alcohol tests, such testing is often used for other HR decisions as well. We begin with a discussion of drug testing.

Drug screening is commonly used in business, industry, and government today. About two-thirds of medium to large companies use drug screening as part of their preemployment procedures and approximately one-third of medium to large companies conduct random drug testing of current employees. Drug screening has become widespread for several reasons, including industry laws, the belief that such programs help combat drug abuse in the United States, and concern with company safety and productivity. Drug testing has also received some negative publicity, particularly from such groups as the American Civil Liberties Union (ACLU), who feel that this procedure is an unfair invasion of people's privacy.[66] (Check this Web site for more information: www.aclu.org/library/pbr5.html.)

Drug Screening Procedures

urinalysis
A urine sample test for drugs.

Have you ever applied for a job where a drug screen was administered? Chances are that if you were drug-tested, you were administered a **urinalysis**—that is, you were asked for a urine sample. You may have had several questions about this test:

1. How long will the presence of drug traces (or, as they are usually called, metabolites) stay in urine?

false positive
Occurs when drug test mistakenly identifies the subject as a drug user.

2. What is the likelihood of a **false positive?** A false positive occurs when you are mistakenly identified as a drug user even though you do not use drugs.
3. About what percentage of job applicants are identified as drug users?

What did you guess about question 1? You may be surprised to learn that most drug metabolites, including cocaine and heroin, leave your urine within one to four days. Only marijuana can remain as long as several weeks, particularly for a heavy drug user.[67] Question 2 has led to controversy as a result of some widely publicized stories in which people eating a poppy-seed bagel or taking over-the-counter cold medicines were mistakenly identified as drug users when they took a drug test. Also, several early studies on the accuracy of drug tests found a great many false positives; in one test, as many as 66 percent of the drug samples were false positives! How could the false positive rate be so high? We have at least two answers. One, some laboratories are not careful and may make mistakes. Two, certain drug tests are not highly accurate. To get around this problem, many companies use a two-step drug screening procedure. In the first step, an initial screen is used; that is, a relatively inexpensive, but occasionally fallible test is employed (for example, the Enzyme Multiplied Immunoassay Test [EMIT] test). If the urine sample indicates drug use, a second, confirmatory procedure is applied, such as the gas chromatography/mass spectrometry (GC/MS) test, which when used properly is extremely accurate. However, not all companies use the two-step procedure.[68]

Finally, if you guessed about 4 percent in answering the third question, you are right. Although the number of drug positives varies from location to location, nationwide about 4 percent of job applicants are identified as drug users. The number of current employees who are drug positive is much lower—about 2 percent.[69]

Validity of Drug Testing

Because drug testing seems to make so much sense to many employers who accept its validity as a matter of faith, there have actually been few good criterion-related validity studies of drug tests. The few good validation studies that have been conducted indicate that drug testing seems to have fairly low validity (perhaps a correlation of .10).[70] You may be rather surprised by this low validity. One reason it is probably so low is that relatively few people in the working population are found to be drug users. As you read earlier, only about 4 percent of applicants and employees tested are drug positive. In this type of situation, a test will have limited validity. Moreover, the cost of drug testing is not inexpensive. A recent American Management Association survey reported that companies spent on average about $50,000 annually on such programs. Companies considering implementing a preemployment drug testing program should therefore consider carefully whether the benefits of such a program will outweigh the costs. In some cases, however, industry or customer regulations will require the organization to perform such tests.

Legal Considerations in Drug Testing

Given the popularity of drug testing, it is not surprising that there have been legal challenges. In terms of discrimination laws, practically all permit drug testing. Most of the legal challenges to drug testing, then, have come from other laws and regulations. The most well-known lawsuits involving drug testing focused on constitutional rights to privacy and due process. Basically, these laws place restrictions on the use of drug screening by organizations, especially for government employees. Because of their complexity, however, we will discuss these laws in greater detail in Chapter 16. You should be aware, however, that myriad industry, state, and government laws regulate drug testing. Some states, for example, require that companies conducting drug tests use a confirmatory test, inform applicants ahead of time that they will be tested, and employ a properly certified laboratory.[71]

Alcohol Testing

Some organizations also test for alcohol use. In fact, companies with 50 or more commercial-license drivers (for example, trucking companies) are required to conduct both drug and alcohol tests. The law, written by the Federal Highway Administration, also covers aviation, rail, and mass-transit companies (see the Web site at mcregis. fhwa.dot.gov/382menu.htm). This law mandates alcohol testing on a random basis, as well as after an accident, on reasonable suspicion, upon return for duty, as well as for preemployment screening. Will such testing make a difference in safety or profitability? Some say it will. Bud Cuca, legal counsel for a drug and alcohol testing business, says that a large percentage of work time missed is due to substance abuse. Robert Montgomery, safety manager for a transportation company, says that the returns from such testing are tenfold over the costs. It is estimated that organizations spend on average $64 to $98 annually per driver to comply with this law.[72]

Although these laws exist in the United States, our northern neighbor, Canada, has a rather different attitude toward drug and alcohol testing. In a recent court case, the Ontario Division Court ruled that preemployment and random drug testing were prohibited, as was random alcohol testing. However, the Division Court did acknowledge that drug testing would be permitted if there was a drug-related incident, to fill a safety-sensitive position, or **"for cause"** (for example, an accident). In a similar ruling, the Canadian Federal Court of Appeal ruled that Toronto-Dominion Bank's preemployment drug testing policy, which required all new and returning employees to be tested, was illegal because it was not tied to job performance and there was no evidence of a drug problem at the bank. How do you feel about such testing programs? Do you think the United States response or the Canadian response is more appropriate?[73]

"for cause"
If good reason exists to believe an employee may have been under the influence of drugs during work, the company may require the employee to take a drug test.

Miscellaneous Selection Devices

In addition to the selection methods described above, companies use several others, including medical examinations and physical strength and agility tests. Two particularly interesting ones are individual assessments and graphology.

Individual Assessment

individual assessment
Conducted by a psychologist, this assessment lasts four to eight hours and involves a ninety-minute interview as well as personality and cognitive ability tests.

Many companies, particularly in manufacturing and banking, use an **individual assessment** to evaluate candidates for middle- and upper-level management positions. Generally, this assessment is conducted by a psychologist, and the average fee per candidate is more than $500. A typical session lasts from 4 to 8 hours and involves a 90-minute interview, as well as personality and cognitive ability tests. Information gathered is generally used to produce a written summary of the candidate's strengths and weaknesses, with a specific recommendation regarding the hiring or promotion decision. If you are ever assessed in this fashion, you should know that the majority of psychologists in this business will provide individual feedback to you, and in some cases, they may even share a copy of the report they gave the organization. Little research has been done regarding the validity and adverse impact of individual assessments.[74] Box 5.5 offers some Web sites that explore interviewing and testing issues.

Graphology

Graphology, or handwriting analysis, was first developed in 1622, but the most well-known work on this technique was published in France in 1875. It may surprise you to learn that while only a few companies in the United States use graphology as a selection device, it is quite popular in Europe. One estimate indicates that as many as 80 percent of companies in Western Europe use graphology as a selection tool. Although there are different approaches to analyzing handwriting, most focus on the size of letters, the slant, width, pressure, and spacing of letters, and connections between letters.[75] Despite its popularity in some circles, graphology has not fared well in carefully designed research studies. One well-designed study found that although the two handwriting analysts were in reasonably high agreement on their ratings of personality traits of employees, correlations of their ratings with employees' job performance ratings were practically zero.[76] Most HRM experts in the United States, at least, do not favor graphology as a selection device.

We now turn to two special applications of selection procedures: team work and global assignments.

graphology
Handwriting analysis.

Selecting for Team Work

Many companies have had to reconsider their selection practices in light of the growing use of teams. The first step in deciding what selection instruments to use when hiring people to work in teams is to determine the relevant competencies. In an extensive study, five basic competencies and fourteen subcompetencies were identified as necessary for success as a team member. The five basic competencies and some sample subcompetencies were[77]

1. Conflict resolution (for example, ability to recognize and address desirable team conflict and discourage undesirable team conflict).

2. Collaborative problem solving (for example, ability to identify and eliminate obstacles to effective group problem solving).
3. Communication (for example, ability to listen effectively).
4. Goal setting and performance management (for example, ability to help develop effective team goals).
5. Planning and task coordination (for example, ability to coordinate work among team members).

   With these competencies in mind and given some of the selection techniques and procedures described earlier, how do you think organizations would assess these competencies? Some experts recently devised a 35-item job knowledge test to assess these competencies. A sample item asks what a team should do to improve the quality of discussions and provides four alternative answers, ranging from setting a specific order for team members to speak, to using comments that build upon what others have said. Other procedures that organizations have used to assess these competencies include structured interviews, assessment centers, and personality tests.[78]

Selecting for a Global Assignment

Many factors need to be considered in selecting an employee for a global assignment. In this particular case, we are referring to a situation where the organization is choosing a current employee to spend a significant amount of time in another country. In many ways, the process for this decision differs from the processes discussed throughout this chapter. One approach for selecting an employee for a global assignment is to use the following four steps:[79]

1. **Self-Selection.** Approximately one year prior to the assignment, have employees consider whether they are interested in and capable of taking a global assignment. The self-selection tool should cover such areas as personality traits (for example, flexibility), career issues, and, where relevant, family issues. Some organizations have developed a formal instrument to help employees decide whether a global assignment is appropriate for them.
2. **Generating a Candidate Pool.** In the second step, the organization should generate a database containing information about which employees are interested, what languages they speak, when they would be available, and which countries they prefer. Only employees who meet the minimum qualifications for success in this position should be included.
3. **Assess Skills.** The organization should at this point assess the relevant skills needed to perform successfully in the assignment and compare the relative strengths and weaknesses of the different candidates.
4. **Preparation for the Move.** After a final decision has been made and before the assignment begins, certain activities such as training, must take place. For example, many organizations have the employee and his or her family meet with other families that have experienced a global assignment. You will read more about the training employees undertake in preparing for a global assignment in Chapter 11.

❖ Conclusion

You have read about the factors that companies consider in deciding which employee selection methods to use. To be beneficial, the selection method should be practical to use, job related, legally acceptable, and provide sufficient utility. As you have seen, many different selection procedures are available to organizations. Although interviews, reference and background checks, and application forms are the most common methods, each has its limitation. Some suggestions were also provided for improving the value of the interview. Many companies supplement their hiring decisions with various additional methods, including paper-and-pencil tests, work samples, and individual assessments. Only with careful selection procedures will organizations be assured of hiring and promoting the most qualified candidates.

❖ Applying Core Concepts

1. Describe how you would go about conducting a job analysis for either your own job or a job with which you are familiar.
2. What selection process was used to hire you or a friend of yours for a recent job? What selection procedures described in this chapter might have been used to improve the process?
3. Develop a structured interview to hire people for a job with which you are familiar.
4. If you were hiring a college instructor, would you use any psychological tests? Why or why not?
5. Do you think that a drug screen should be used to hire people for a job? Can you think of some jobs where a drug test might be irrelevant?
6. How would you feel if a company asked you to complete an honesty test? Would you feel insulted? Why or why not?
7. Do you think that psychological tests are more fair or less compared to an interview? Explain your answer.

❖ Key Terms

Job analysis
Job description
Job specification
PAQ
Task/competency inventory
Competency modeling
Job relatedness
Criterion-related validity study

Meta-analysis
Content validity
Correlation coefficient
Utility
Employee Polygraph Protection Act of 1988
Negligent hiring
Weighted application blank (WAB)

Biographical information blank (BIB)
Traditional interview
Structured interview
Stress interview
Panel interview
Personality test
Honesty test
Cognitive ability test

Race norming   Fair Credit Reporting Act   "For cause"
Job Knowledge Test   Defamation   Individual assessment
Work samples   Urinalysis   Graphology
Assessment center   False positive

❖ CHAPTER 5 *Experiential Exercise*

Technosoftware Company: Part 2

Two Months Later . . . Based on his recruiting effort, Walter received a total of 150 resumes. He managed to narrow down the list of potential applicants to three. Walter, Darrell, and Ben reviewed the resumes, conducted brief telephone interviews, panel interviews, and gave several paper-and-pencil tests to the three candidates. In order not to affect your judgments, Walter, Darrell, and Ben have tried to be as objective as possible in writing up this information. The results of these selection devices are summarized next.

Background Information. Based on an examination of resumes, an initial phone conversation, and preliminary questions in the interviews, the company obtained educational, work, and experience information from each candidate. This information is summarized below.

Candidate 1: Jack Smith. Has B.S. in engineering and M.B.A. from Harvard (1970); worked for last 20 years in a large computer products firm (both hardware and software). Began as product manager, ended as assistant vice president, business-to-business marketing. Terminated due to restructuring of the workforce. Prior to this worked as salesperson for several manufacturers. Has had broad range of experience in all phases of marketing to businesses. Familiar with Internet marketing and basic spreadsheets. Appears to be about 50 years old.

Candidate 2: Ann Real. Has B.S. in mathematics; M.S. in information systems (1992) from Purdue University. Also took some business courses in marketing. From 1996 to present has worked in developing computer software for large computer firm. During last year worked with a team responsible for designing and marketing of a new PC statistics package. Experience and familiarity with popular computer software is extensive. Appears to be about 30 years old.

Candidate 3: Tom VanFleet. Has B.S. in computers; M.B.A. with concentration in marketing (1988) from California State University at Fresno. From 1988 to present has worked in marketing positions at five different firms. Each job involved slightly broader responsibilities. Second job was for a computer products firm, which involved marketing of computer hardware; other jobs have been with office supply companies. Appears to be about 35 years old.

Interview Results. Each of the three candidates was interviewed in a panel session with Walter, Darrell, and Ben. Each candidate was asked the same set of questions, with follow-up probes. A summary of each candidate's responses follows.

The key questions were

1. What strengths can you bring to this company?
2. Describe your managerial style.
3. Describe your ideal job.
4. What are your career plans?
5. Describe a time when you had a major disagreement with a coworker. How did you resolve the conflict?
6. Why are you interested in this job?
7. What salary would you expect to make?
8. What is your current (or most recent) salary?

Candidate 1

1. A great deal of experience in the marketing of computer products (but primarily hardware); many contacts in the marketing world, which will help in the introduction and promotion of a new product; exposure to other functions, including production and accounting.
2. Believes in open communication, delegation, ongoing feedback, and frequent goal-setting sessions.
3. Ideal job would be one with a great deal of responsibility, challenging assignments, and a great deal of influence over marketing decisions.

4. (Candidate chuckled when asked this question.) "To stay employed."

5. Several years ago, candidate had a major disagreement with vice president of sales regarding some promotional plan. After days of heated debate, they agreed to present their arguments in a one-hour session to the executive vice president of sales and marketing. He agreed, listened carefully to their arguments, and candidate lost.

6. Job offers many of the points raised in response to question 3.

7. Salary less important than potential share in company. Willing even to forego base pay for first year or two as long as can get ownership in company.

8. Earned $120,000 plus "substantial" bonus ($20,000–$30,000).

Candidate 2

1. Great knowledge of computer software products; well versed in user needs.

2. Although she never has managed anyone . . . open style, judge on the basis of results, democratic, encourage participation in all areas.

3. Ideal job would have lots of responsibility, challenging assignments, involve computer software in some way, lots of opportunity to learn.

4. Career plan is to be involved in all aspects of computer software, including marketing, design, R&D, etc.

5. Got into major disagreement with a coworker regarding a software development project. Had ongoing debate for weeks about it; finally, came to work over an entire weekend to resolve disagreement. In the end, found they were both wrong.

6. Allows candidate to devote full time to marketing. Also, want opportunity to work for small firm, where one can have much impact.

7. At least $75,000.

8. $59,000.

Candidate 3

1. Has worked several phases of product management and introduction as they relate to software, including pricing, product announcement, market research, and positioning strategy. "Outstanding performance in every job."

2. Establish close supervision, careful monitoring of subordinate performance, give ongoing feedback.

3. Ability to achieve ongoing advancement in the marketing area through increasing responsibility, continuous development of new products, and innovation.

4. Advance into a senior marketing position in a small computer software firm.

5. "Have never had such a situation. . . . Always able to deal with such situations before they became major conflicts."

6. Position offers a "fast track" opportunity to learn about a whole lot of marketing tasks that a larger company cannot offer.

7. Negotiable, but at least $50,000, depending on opportunities for bonus or stock ownership.

8. $50,000 plus "large bonus" that he agreed to keep confidential.

Test Scores. Each of the three candidates was then sent to a management psychologist, who administered to each candidate three tests. One test, the Thurstone Cognitive Ability Test, provides a verbal ability (V) and mathematical ability score (M). The second text, the Guilford-Zimmerman Temperament Survey (GZTS) is a standard personality measure—the psychologist relies on only four scales, so only four scales are reported here, namely, energy (E), emotional stability (ES), thoughtfulness (T), and personal relations (PR). Finally, the psychologist had each candidate complete the Computer Programmer Aptitude Battery, which measures one's ability to write computer programs (CP). Provided below are the scores for each candidate, in terms of their percentile (a percentile score indicates the percentage of test takers that the individual did as well as, or better than. For example, a percentile score of 50 indicates that the individual did as well as or better than about half the people who have taken the test).

Candidate	V	M	E	ES	T	PR	CP
1	80	15	50	99	40	95	5
2	90	99	99	50	99	70	99
3	80	50	80	40	25	90	40

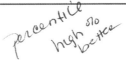
percentile %
high
better

❖ Questions

1. Rank order your choices from best candidate for the job to worst candidate for the job.
2. Be prepared to defend your rank order; you may choose to ignore any information you want, but be prepared to explain why you did not use that information.
3. What additional information would you have obtained from the candidates (for example, additional interview questions, tests)?

❖ Chapter 5 References

1. E. Levine, F. Sistrunk, K. McNutt, and S. Gael, "Exemplary Job Analysis Systems in Selected Organizations," in *Applying Psychology in Business*, ed. J. Jones, B. Steffy, and D. Bray (Lexington, MA: Lexington Books, 1991).
2. W. Cascio, *Applied Psychology in Personnel Management* (Englewood Cliffs, NJ: Prentice Hall, 1991).
3. R. J. Harvey, "Job Analysis," in *Handbook of Industrial and Organizational Psychology*, vol. 2, ed. M. Dunnette and L. Hough (Palo Alto, CA: Consulting Psychologists Press, 1991).
4. Cascio, *Applied Psychology.*
5. R. Gatewood and H. Feild, "Job Analysis Methods: A Description and Comparison of the Alternatives," in *Applying Psychology in Business*, ed. J. Jones, B. Steffy, and D. Bray (Lexington, MA: Lexington Books, 1991).
6. R. Gatewood and H. Feild, *Human Resource Selection* (Fort Worth, TX: Dryden, 1998).
7. B. Schneider and N. Schmitt, *Staffing Organizations* (Glenview, IL: Scott, Foresman, 1986).
8. M. Harris, "Competency Modeling: Viagraized Job Analysis Or Impotent Imposter," *The Industrial-Organizational Psychologist* (January 1999): In press.
9. Gatewood and Feild, *Human Resource Selection.*
10. S. Odenwald, "Global Work Teams," *Training & Development* 50 (February 1996): 54–57.
11. Gatewood and Feild, *Human Resource Selection.*
12. R. Guion, "Personnel Assessment, Selection, and Placement," in *Handbook of Industrial and Organizational Psychology*, vol. 2, M. Dunnette and L. Hough ed. (Palo Alto, CA: Consulting Psychologists Press, 1991).
13. Gatewood and Feild, *Human Resource Selection.*
14. *Uniform Guidelines on Employee Selection Procedures*, 29 CFR, Part 1607.
15. M. Player, *Federal Law of Employment Discrimination* (St. Paul, MN: West, 1999).
16. J. Boudreau, "Utility Analysis for Decisions in Human Resource Management," in *Handbook of Industrial and Organizational Psychology*, vol. 2, ed. M. Dunnette and L. Hough (Palo Alto, CA: Consulting Psychologists Press, 1991); F. Schmidt, J. Hunter, R. McKenzie, and T. Muldrow, "Impact of Valid Selection Procedures on Work-Force Productivity," *Journal of Applied Psychology* 64 (1979): 609–26.
17. L. Joel, *Every Employee's Guide to the Law* (New York: Pantheon, 1993).
18. J. Bible, "When Employers Look for Things Other Than Drugs: The Legality of AIDS, Genetic, Intelligence, and Honesty Testing in the Workplace," *Labor Law Journal* 41 (1990): 195–221.
19. A. Ryan and M. Lasek, "Negligent Hiring and Defamation: Areas of Liability Related to Pre-Employment Inquiries," *Personnel Psychology* 44 (1991): 293–319.
20. Joel, *Every Employee's Guide to the Law.*
21. Schneider and Schmitt, *Staffing Organizations.*
22. Gatewood and Feild, *Human Resource Selection.*

23. F. Mael, "A Conceptual Rationale for the Domain and Attributes of Biodata Items," *Personnel Psychology* 44 (1991): 763–92; G. England, *Development and Use of Weighted Application Blanks*, rev. ed. (Minneapolis: University of Minnesota, 1991).

24. E. Hammer and L. Kleiman, "Getting to Know You," *Personnel Administrator* 34 (1988): 86–92.

25. C. Russell, J. Mettson, S. Devlin, and D. Atwater, "Predictive Validity of Biodata Items Generated from Retrospective Life Experience Essays," *Journal of Applied Psychology* 75 (1990): 569–80.

26. J. Hunter and R. Hunter, "Validity and Utility of Alternate Predictors of Job Performance," *Psychological Bulletin* 96 (1984): 72–98.

27. H. Rothstein et al., "Biographical Data in Employment Selection: Can Validities Be Generalizable?" *Journal of Applied Psychology* 75 (1990): 175–84.

28. Gatewood and Feild, *Human Resource Selection.*

29. J. Smither et al., "Applicant Reactions to Selection Procedures," *Personnel Psychology* 46 (1993): 49–76.

30. R. Eder and M. Harris, "Employment Interview Research: Historical Update and Introduction," In R. Eder and M. Harris (Eds.), *The Employment Interview Handbook* (Newbury Park, CA: Sage, in press).

31. R. Fear, *The Evaluation Interview* (New York: McGraw-Hill, 1984); B. Smart, *Selection Interviewing* (New York: Wiley, 1983).

32. R. Eder and G. Ferris, *The Employment Interview: Theory, Research, and Practice* (Newbury Park, CA: Sage, 1989); M. Harris, "Reconsidering the Employment Interview: A Review of Recent Literature and Suggestions for Future Research," *Personnel Psychology* 42 (1989): 691–726.

33. M. Campion, D. Palmer and J. Campion, "A Review of Structure in the Selection Interview," *Personnel Psychology* 50 (1997): 655–702.

34. T. Janz, L. Hellervik, and D. Gilmore, *Behavior Description Interviewing* (Boston: Allyn & Bacon, 1986); G. Latham, L. Saari, E. Pursell, and M. Campion, "The Situational Interview," *Journal of Applied Psychology* 65 (1980): 422–27; M. Campion, E. Pursell, and B. Brown, "Structured Interviewing: Raising the Psychometric Properties of the Employment Interview," *Personnel Psychology* 41 (1988): 25–42.

35. W. Wiesner and S. Cronshaw, "A Meta-Analytic Investigation of the Impact of Interview Format and Degree of Structure on the Validity of the Employment Interview," *Journal of Occupational Psychology* 61 (1988): 275–90.

36. A. Huffcutt and P. Roth, "Racial Group Differences in Employment Interview Evaluations," *Journal of Applied Psychology* 83 (1998): 179–89.

37. H. Medley, *Sweaty Palms: The Neglected Art of Being Interviewed* (Berkeley, CA: Ten Speed Press, 1984).

38. Ibid.

39. J. Campion and R. Arvey, "Unfair Discrimination in the Employment Interview," in *The Employment Interview: Theory, Research, and Practice*, ed. R. Eder and G. Ferris (Newbury, CA: Sage, 1989).

40. M. Roehling, J. Campion, and R. Arvey, "Unfair Discrimination in the Employment Interview," In R. Eder and M. Harris (Eds.), *The Employment Interview Handbook* (Newbury Park, CA: Sage, in press).

41. M. Harris and R. Eder, "The State of Interview Practice: Commentary and Extension," In R. Eder and M. Harris (Eds.), *The Employment Interview Handbook* (Newbury Park, CA: Sage, in press).

42. R. Tett, D. Jackson, and M. Rothstein, "Personality Measures as Predictors of Job Performance: A Meta-Analytic Review," *Personnel Psychology* 44 (1991): 703–42.

43. M. Barrick and M. Mount, "The Big Five Personality Dimensions and Job Performance: A Meta-Analysis," *Personnel Psychology* 44 (1991): 1–26.

44. D. Ones, C. Viswesvaran, and F. Schmidt, "Comprehensive Meta-Analysis of Integrity Test Validities: Findings and Implications for Personnel Selection and Theories of Job

Performance," *Journal of Applied Psychology* 78 (1993): 679–703; P. Sackett, L. Burris, and C. Callahan, "Integrity Testing for Personnel Selection: An Update," *Personnel Psychology* 42 (1989): 491–529.

45. Joel, *Every Employee's Guide to the Law.*
46. Ryan and Lasek, "Negligent Hiring and Defamation."
47. Gatewood and Feild, *Human Resource Selection.*
48. M. Tenopyr, "The Realities of Employment Testing," *American Psychologist* 36 (1981): 1120–27.
49. F. Schmidt, "The Problem of Group Differences in Ability Test Scores in Employment Selection," *Journal of Vocational Behavior* 33 (1988) 272–92.
50. Hunter and Hunter, "Validity and Utility."
51. Schmidt, "The Problem of Group Differences in Ability Test Scores."
52. F. L. Schmidt and J. E. Hunter, "The Validity and Utility of Selection Methods in Personnel Psychology: Practical and Theoretical Implications of 85 Years of Research Findings," *Psychological Bulletin* 124 (1998): 262–74.
53. J. Asher and J. Sciarrino, "Realistic Work Sample Tests: A Review," *Personnel Psychology* 27 (1974): 519–33.
54. G. Thornton, *Assessment Centers in Human Resource Management* (Reading, MA: Addison-Wesley, 1992).
55. B. Gaugler, D. Rosenthal, G. Thornton, and C. Bentson, "Meta-Analysis of Assessment Center Validity," *Journal of Applied Psychology* 72 (1987): 493–511.
56. R. Arvey and R. Faley, *Fairness in Selecting Employees* (Reading, MA: Addison-Wesley, 1988).
57. Gatewood and Feild, *Human Resource Selection.*
58. G. Flynn, "Are You Legal Under the Fair Credit Reporting Act?" *Workforce* 77 (March 1998): 79, 81+.
59. Ryan and Lasek, "Negligent Hiring and Defamation."
60. A. Long, "Note: Addressing the Cloud Over Employee References: A Survey of Recently Enacted State Legislation," *William and Mary Law Review* 39 (October 1997): 177–228.
61. J. H. Verkerke, "Legal Regulation of Employment Reference Practices," *University of Chicago Law Review* 65 (Winter 1998): 115–78.
62. Joel, *Every Employee's Guide to the Law.*
63. P. Muchinsky, "The Use of Reference Reports in Personnel Selection: A Review and Evaluation," *Journal of Occupational Psychology* 52 (1979): 287–97; Hunter and Hunter, "Validity and Utility."
64. Arvey and Faley, *Fairness in Selecting Employees.*
65. *EEOC vs. National Academy of Sciences,* 12 FEP 1690 (1976).
66. M. Harris and L. Greising, "Alcohol and Drug Use as Dysfunctional Workplace Behaviors," In R. Griffin, A. O'Leary-Kelly, and J. Collins (Eds.), *Dysfunctional Behavior in Organizations: Non-Violent Dysfunctional Behavior* (Greenwich, CT: JAI Press, 1998).
67. B. Potter and J. Orfali, *Drug Testing at Work* (Berkeley, CA: Ronin, 1990).
68. Harris and Greising, "Alcohol and Drug Use."
69. Ibid.
70. M. Harris and L. Heft, "Preemployment Urinalysis Drug Testing: A Critical Review of Psychometric and Legal Issues and Effects on Applicants," *Human Resource Management Review* 3 (1993): 271–91.
71. Ibid.
72. J. Candler, "A Sobering Law For Truckers," *Nations Business* 84 (January 1996): 26–8.
73. Anonymous, "Courts Overrule Drug and Alcohol Testing Policies," *Worklife Report* 11 (1998): Number 2, 6, 9.
74. A. M. Ryan and P. Sackett, "A Survey of Individual Assessment Practices by I/O Psychologists," *Personnel Psychology* 40 (1987): 455–88.
75. Gatewood and Feild, *Human Resource Selection.*
76. A. Rafaeli and R. Klimoski, "Predicting Sales Success Through Handwriting Analysis: An Evaluation of the Effects of Training and Handwriting Sample Content," *Journal of Applied Psychology* 68 (1983): 212–17.

77. M. Stevens and M. Campion, "The Knowledge, Skill, and Ability Requirements for Teamwork: Implications for Human Resource Management," *Journal of Management* 20 (1994): 503–30.

78. H. Heneman, R. Heneman, and T. Judge, *Staffing Organizations* (Middleton, WI: Mendota House, 1997).

79. V. Frazee, "Selecting Global Assignees," *Global Workforce* (July 1998): 28–30.

Career Management

After reading this chapter, you should be capable of:

1. Understanding why career patterns have changed in the last 25 years.
2. Defining the three basic career stages.
3. Explaining various strategies both organizations and individuals can use to maximize effectiveness at different career stages.
4. Discussing the four types of career advancement systems that organizations use.
5. Addressing some common career issues.

Yesterday, on her first day at Drafco, Julie Cheng attended an orientation program for new employees. As she thought back over things, it wasn't much different from what she had expected. First, Julie and about 25 other new management trainees had breakfast together. All wore badges with their names on them and introduced themselves. After 30 minutes, the human resource manager introduced the CEO of Drafco, who welcomed them and wished the group much luck and success. Next, the human resource manager showed a film about the company, which described the company's history, including when it was founded (1957), its original business (selling chocolate novelties), and the original owners (Mary and Beth Townsend). Mr. Gooden, vice president in charge of the management trainee program, spoke next. He described the type of job the management trainees would have, the assignments they would experience, and typical career paths in the company. Most of what he had to say Julie had already heard when she interviewed for the job. When he was done, several of the new employees asked questions regarding the company's performance expectations, the new computer system, and current business conditions.

The presentation that followed was the most intriguing. Employees who had been through the management trainee program last year, 10 years ago, 20 years ago, and even one who had gone through the program 30 years ago took turns talking about their careers in the company. While it was interesting to hear what the different employees had to say, Julie began to wonder about several things. First, what did one really have to do to succeed in this company? While the 30-year employee was now second in charge (only the CEO had a higher position),

none of the speakers had explained what they had done to get ahead. Second, Julie wondered if there were some common career problems people encountered at Drafco and how they were handled. All of the speakers had been very upbeat about the company and talked enthusiastically about their personal successes, but had said virtually nothing about difficulties or frustrations that they had experienced.

These and other questions continued to circulate in her mind as the final part of the program began. Perhaps, she thought, this would be the part where she would learn some answers to these questions. Much to her disappointment, however, the remainder of the program dealt with such things as choosing the most suitable benefit program and learning more about different departments in the company. The program concluded with a walking tour of the entire facility.

This chapter concerns career management issues. Career management is important both for organizations and employees. From an organizational standpoint, an understanding of these issues is helpful in managing employees and providing appropriate programs to support productive careers. From an employee perspective, an understanding of career stages and common career issues will help you perform more effectively. The remainder of this chapter, then, is divided into four sections. First, you will read about why careers have changed a great deal over the last 20 years. Next, you will learn about typical career stages. Third, you will read about career advancement systems that companies use. The chapter concludes with information on several common career issues, such as gaining global work experience, and provides strategies for dealing with them.

Why Have Career Patterns Changed?

Prior to the 1980s, careers in the United States were characterized by stability and continuity. Managerial and professional employees, in particular, often worked their entire careers in the same organization. In the 1980s, however, careers became much less stable and subject to far more disruption. Next is a discussion of some factors that have led to these changes.

Organizational Layoffs

It is almost commonplace now to hear about mass layoffs in organizations. Regardless of whether they call it *downsizing, reduction in force* or *rightsizing*, nearly every large organization in the United States has terminated workers for reasons other than poor performance during the last five years. Nor do layoffs only happen when organizations report a decline in profits. In 1998, despite a booming economy, over 500,000 U.S. employees lost their jobs. In fact, the number of layoffs nearly equaled the number of layoffs during the 1991 recession, when more than 550,000 jobs were lost. It is particularly common for organizations to eliminate middle management and staff jobs, while maintaining production and customer service positions. As a result of these layoffs, many employees have had successful careers end abruptly and have been forced to start their careers over again. Clearly, one implication is that even working for a highly successful organization is no guarantee of employment.[1] Box 6.1 lists motivations, or "anchors," for many people's choices of careers. Having several motivations for work can help keep a career going or restart one that has ended.

Changing Nature of Work

Careers in most organizations have been defined in terms of a ladder or set of steps. Take, for example, a traditional human resource career pattern. One might begin in the HRM field as an interviewer, followed by a promotion to HRM staffing supervisor. Next, one might be promoted to manager of college placement, followed by a promotion to manager of human resources, and then to vice president of human resources. At the dawn of the 21st century, however, work is less frequently designed along specific job responsibilities and more and more commonly designed around projects. In the human resources area, for example, projects might include redesigning the pay-for-performance plan, developing an integrated training program, and conducting an annual employee satisfaction survey. The workers assigned to these projects would depend far less on position in the hierarchy, and much more on their abilities and experience as well as developmental needs. In turn, position in the hierarchy has become less important than in the past, thereby changing the way in which careers progress.[2]

Changing Nature of Organizations

A third factor that has changed careers is the design of organizations today. Organizations in the 21st century typically have far fewer managers and supervisors than organizations did 20 years ago. The organization of today, therefore, is usually far flatter than organizations in the past and so in general offers far less room for advancement. Many companies therefore are downplaying promotions and are rethinking their fundamental assumptions about careers. Later in this chapter you will read about a career advancement system that almost completely eliminates the notion of promotions.[3]

Box 6.1

Career Anchors: What Makes You Tick?

Experts have suggested that people have one or more career anchors or orientations that characterize their work interests. Below, eight primary anchors are identified, defined, and accompanied by some predictions for the success of each. Which career anchor or set of career anchors fits you best?

1. **Technical and Functional Competence.** If this is your anchor, your career interests focus on working in a specific technical or functional area, such as finance, marketing, accounting, and so forth. People with this interest tend to avoid supervising others. They generally prefer to develop their skills rather than be promoted for the sake of a higher-level position. In today's world, obsolescence comes quickly as technologies change rapidly in many fields. If this is your anchor, be sure that you are constantly retraining.

2. **General Managerial Competence.** If this is your anchor, your career focuses on climbing to the highest level possible and being responsible for output of a specific business unit. You desire accountability for results and view your experiences in specific functions or technical area as a means to that end. The danger of having this as your main anchor is that pure managerial work is becoming increasingly rare with the proliferation of teamwork and greater autonomy throughout the organization. Plan carefully to determine how best to maximize your marketability.

3. **Autonomy and Independence.** If this is your anchor, you strive to be independent at work and prefer minimal rules and regulations concerning your work. You like to establish your own hours and dress code and dislike supervision. This career anchor will work well for you in today's workplace.

4. **Security and Stability.** If this is your anchor, you prefer stability in your job. You avoid taking risks at work and seek as secure a working future as possible. In today's world of change, this is the most difficult career anchor to satisfy. If this characterizes you, you need to reconsider your goals and needs.

5. **Entrepreneurial Creativity.** If this is your anchor, your desire is to create a business of your own. You work for others only insofar as you feel you are gaining important experience. You seek risks and enjoy overcoming obstacles. This is another career anchor that will be in much demand as companies continually strive for new creative products and services.

6. **Dedication to a Cause.** If this is your anchor, you focus on a cause that you believe is important, such as discovering a cure for a disease or helping bring about world peace. This, too, is a career anchor that should serve you well in the 21st century. The world is recognizing the importance of such issues as world starvation, disease, global warming, and pollution, and governmental concern over such problems will lead to increased employment opportunities.

7. **Pure Challenge.** If this is your anchor, you seek to meet and overcome difficult barriers or obstacles. For a medical researcher, this may be finding a cure for the common cold; for a business consultant, this may be taking over companies going through bankruptcy. You seek novelty and variety in your work. There will always be challenges in the world that provide continuing demand for people with this career anchor.

8. **Lifestyle.** If this is your career anchor, you seek to integrate personal, career, and family goals. You define success in terms greater than just your career. You choose jobs that enable you to fit all parts of your life together. People who anchor themselves in terms of this model have begun to blur the distinction between jobs, family, and leisure. One of the biggest shifts over the last few decades has been the increased number of people who center their career in terms of lifestyle.

Which career anchor fits you best? Of course, it is possible that a combination of two or three anchors describes you.

Source: E. Schein, "Career Anchors Revisited: Implications for Career Development in the 21st Century," *Academy of Management Executive* (November 1996): 80–8.

In sum, several factors have changed careers. As a result, many successful career management practices of the past are no longer appropriate today. What you will read about next is a description of typical career stages that many employees go through today, along with a brief discussion of how these stages differ from the past.

Career Stages

Career stages refer to points or phases in one's career. Career stages today differ in several fundamental ways from career stages of earlier times. One difference is that many people today will change occupations numerous times in the course of their lifetime. Within the 61 to 65 age group, where you would expect the least amount of occupational change, 22 percent of people in the United States in this age group have changed occupations.[4] This experience is not unique to the United States; most British managers experience a major job change every three years, and fewer than 10 percent work for a single company through their entire career.[5]

A second difference is that achievement today is defined much more broadly than in years past. Today, employees must define career success at least in terms of degree of preparation for the next job or career, balance between personal and work life issues, and the extent to which one experiences a sense of personal fulfillment. Are there other factors that you would include if someone asked you to define career success?

A third difference between today's career stages and those of previous years is that these days many of us cycle through the career stages repeatedly. In the past, one would enter through each stage only once.[6]

Figure 6.1 displays the three career stages, each of which we will describe in greater detail next.

Entry Stage

entry stage
The point at which the individual begins a new job.

The **entry stage** is the point at which the individual begins a new job. In the past, the entry stage was populated primarily by young workers, typically in their early 20s. Today, however, individuals may pass through the entry stage several times as they make radical transitions into completely different jobs. Workers in the entry stage face several challenges. First, particularly for young and inexperienced employees, the entry stage is fraught with unrealistic expectations regarding the type of work they will per-

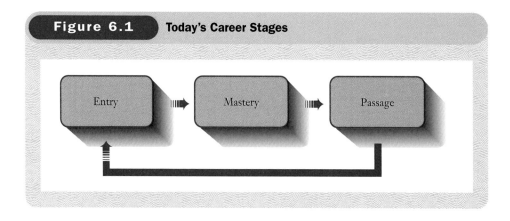

Figure 6.1   **Today's Career Stages**

Entry → Mastery → Passage

Table 6.1	Typical Entry-Level Employee Expectations versus Reality

Expectation	Reality
"I will have much freedom to work as I please."	"My boss tells me what to do and how to do it."
"Most of my work projects will be fun."	"Much of my work is boring and routine."
"I will receive a lot of helpful feedback from my boss."	"I really don't know how well I'm doing."
"If I do well at work, I will get good raises and promotions."	"Money and promotions are limited, and factors other than performance count."
"I can apply the latest techniques that I learned at school."	"People resist the new ideas I suggest."
"I will be able to balance my personal needs and work life."	"My job and personal goals often conflict."

Source: Adapted from J. Greenhaus, *Career Management* (Fort Worth, TX: Dryden, 1987).

form, the amount of feedback they will receive, the rewards they will obtain, their capacity to apply on the job what they have learned at school, and the balance between personal goals and organizational demands. Table 6.1 lists some typical expectations that young and inexperienced employees have and how they compare to the reality that the employees often find. Hence, one important challenge in the entry stage is for the individual to adopt more realistic expectations of work.[7]

A second challenge in this stage is for employees to learn more about their career goals and interests as they discover what they enjoy and what competencies they have. Finally, a major challenge employees face during this stage is to determine the important goals of the organization and to become accepted by their peers and supervisors.[8] Box 6.2 offers an interesting comparison of the Japanese career model to the U.S. career model.

Next, you will read about some steps that organizations can take to help employees in the entry stage.

Entry Stage: Suggestions for Organizations

Organizations and managers can help their employees to succeed in the entry stage in several ways.

1. **Early Interactions with the Organization Have Lasting Effects.** Research shows that a new employee's earliest encounters with the organization, perhaps as early as the recruitment phase, have a lasting effect on the employee's experience of the entry stage. Organizations and managers must do as much as possible to help employees even before they formally begin work. Early opportunities for contact with the new employee's coworkers and supervisor become important in this regard.[9]
2. **Emphasize Informal Orientation Programs.** While the opening case described a formal, structured orientation session for new hires, employees tend to rate such

INTERCULTURAL ISSUES IN HUMAN RESOURCES

Box 6.2
Comparing Japanese and U.S. Career Models: The Latest Results

Over the past few decades, many pundits have compared the typical Japanese career model to the typical U.S. career model. The Japanese model is characterized by its emphasis on job security through lifetime employment and promotions based on seniority, rather than performance. By contrast, the U.S. career model minimizes job security and heavily weights performance rather than seniority in promotions. To understand the pros and cons of each, it is helpful to briefly review the history of the Japanese model. Contrary to what you might think, Japanese workers were considered quite unreliable prior to World War II. The 1920s, for example, were characterized by many work stoppages, and turnover was often a significant problem. All of this changed after World War II, as business and political leaders realized that a stable workforce was a prerequisite for Japan to compete globally. To increase stability, Japan passed many laws that reduced companies' power over employees in such areas as firing. Hence, one reason for the lifetime employment practice is that Japanese companies have many legal restrictions regarding terminations. During the 1980s, as Japan flourished, some management experts argued for implementing the Japanese career system in the United States. These experts argued that one reason for the widespread embrace of robotics and automation in Japan was that employees knew they would not lose their jobs. In fact, they argued that the job security would be advantageous to firms because employees would understand that new technology improves competitive advantage, thereby benefiting them in the long run. Furthermore, while many U.S. companies refrain from expensive training and development programs on the grounds that workers often leave, Japanese companies knew their employees would stay. Not surprisingly, then, Japanese companies provided far more training than did U.S. companies. What about seniority-based promotions? Again, some experts argued that a seniority-based system had some advantages. First, Japan experiences less intergenerational conflict than does the United States. Second, because supervisors felt less threatened by younger, possibly more current, employees, they would be more likely to mentor an employee than in the United States.

In the late 1990s, however, the Japanese unemployment rate increased to 4.4 percent, a rate unheard of for Japan and one that matched that of the United States. Unlike the United States, however, which reported annual job growth of 1.7 percent, Japan in the later 1990s suffered a much lower job growth rate of 1 percent. As a result, Japanese workers who were laid off or forced to accept early retirement programs had a much more difficult time finding new employment than did laid-off U.S. workers. According to many experts, the U.S. job market is far more efficient than the Japanese market. In other words, because of different laws and cultural values, U.S. businesses can terminate workers in one area and hire workers in other areas. Furthermore, the workers benefit because the United States permits greater mobility and distributes information about job opportunities far better than does Japan. As just one example, few workers in Japan use the Internet to seek employment; many middle-aged workers do not know how to use a computer. Even though terminations are for the most part illegal in Japan, many companies simply give workers meaningless tasks or in some cases, no work at all, when the demand for products or services declines. Thus, the Japanese career system in some instances is quite wasteful and inefficient. The new economic reality has led some Japanese leaders to declare that their country will need to adopt the U.S. career system. In the late 1990s, at least, the U.S. career system appears to have many advantages for businesses, and perhaps in the long-run, even for employees.

Source: Adapted from E. Fingleton, "Jobs for Life," *Fortune*, 20 March 1995, 119–25; Y. Ono and J. Schlesinger, "Parity's Paradox," *Wall Street Journal*, 28 December 1998, A1, A8.

programs as being of little help.[10] Instead, orientation programs that provide significant early, informal on-the-job interaction with peers or experienced co-workers appear to be far more effective in facilitating the transition for entry stage employees.[11]

3. **Provide Opportunities to Learn about Other Areas in the Organization.** General Electric, which is famous for its employee development programs, sends new employees to its education unit located near New York City. As part of the extensive training program, new employees meet in small groups with top managers from different parts of the company. Not only does this enable the new employees to learn about different segments of the organization, but it also enables them to develop networks.[12]

4. **Establish Formal Mentoring Relationships.** Although some employees will establish mentoring relationships on their own (see the next discussion), in other cases, a mentoring relationship will only develop if the organization establishes a formal program. Mentoring programs are particularly helpful in increasing workplace diversity. Consider Dianna Green, an African-American woman in her 40s, formerly employed at Xerox Corporation. A key reason Green left her job at Xerox to join DQE, a small, male-dominated utility, was the person who recruited her, Wesley von Schack, CEO of the company. From the start of her employment at DQE, von Schack made it clear that he would play a key role as her mentor. In that role, von Schack has enhanced Green's career by praising her to outsiders, helping her secure various board of director positions, and making sure that she received key assignments at DQE.[13]

Entry Stage: Suggestions for Employees

Now that you know what organizations can do, here are some suggestions for you, as an employee, to achieve success in the entry stage.[14]

1. **Actively Seek Information.** There are two sources of information you need to draw from in learning about the people and the organization: written, formal sources and unwritten, informal sources. Take, for example, your assigned responsibilities. While you may have been shown a job description that listed your responsibilities, do not assume that it was completely accurate. Many organizations have outdated or incomplete job descriptions, and you need to determine what your actual job responsibilities are. If you want to learn about the written rules, seek out the relevant documents or sources (for instance, the employee handbook). To learn the unwritten rules, however, you will need to ask the appropriate questions. For example, if there are two different ways to order equipment, ask your boss about the advantages and disadvantages of both. You may also wish to check with a few coworkers. Be careful when you seek out information that you do not naively accept everything you are told. Sometimes you may intentionally be given the wrong information.

2. **Develop Networks.** Networks within the organization are useful for obtaining information, equipment, key assignments, as well as other resources. Again, organizations will have formal, written networks and informal, unwritten networks that you may be able to tap. Identify those individuals who control important resources, and develop effective relationships with them.

3. **Learn about Your Boss, Coworkers, and Department.** Determine early on the needs of each of these parties and how to meet those needs. Actively seek out this information. You may need to do some careful detective work, because these parties may not fully recognize their own needs.

4. **Develop Mentors.** Although some organizations have formal mentoring programs, most organizations do not, and you must acquire a mentor on your own. A

mentor is a person who is higher up the organization and who can provide career advice and support to you. The mentor might be your immediate supervisor; but in many cases, it is advantageous to have a mentor to whom you do not report. An effective mentor will help in many ways, including recommending you for important assignments, protecting you from controversial issues, and coaching you for better performance.[15]

Individuals who have a mentor report higher salaries than individuals who do not have a mentor.[16] Those employees who have mentors also experience greater career success.[17] Hence, mentoring relationships are helpful in a variety of ways.

While there are many advantages to having a mentor, particularly in the entry stage, beware of some problems that may arise from a mentoring relationship. These include the following:

1. **The Mentor May Experience Disappointment or Even Anger When the Relationship Ends.** Typically, the protege outgrows the relationship after two to five years. This can create a sense of disappointment or even anger on the part of the mentor. In the worst case, the mentor may turn against the protege.[18]
2. **Cross-Gender Relationships Create Difficulties.** Tension sometimes arises when the mentor is a man and the protege is a woman. One source of tension is that mutual liking may lead to issues of intimacy and romantic involvement. Second, there may be a tendency for both the mentor and the protege to assume stereotypical roles within the relationship. Third, other employees may look upon the relationship with greater suspicion than a relationship where the two parties are of the same gender.
3. **Your Mentor May Have a Poor Reputation.** Your mentor may have or develop a poor reputation in the organization, as a result of performance problems or unethical behavior. As his or her protege, your reputation may become tarnished as well.[19]

In sum, both organizations and employees can take many steps to ease the transition in the entry stage. Assuming the individual demonstrates basic competency in the entry stage, he or she moves to the next phase: the mastery stage.

Mastery Stage

In the **mastery stage,** employees seek to attain a high degree of success in their work. This stage represents a major departure from careers of the past. In years past, this stage consisted of two separate stages: an achievement stage and a mid-career stage. The achievement stage typically involved workers in their late 20s and 30s, and marked the period of time during which one was most likely to achieve success and advance up the organization hierarchy. Success in this stage was typically measured by and rewarded with promotions to higher positions, and employees assessed their level of achievement by how high they climbed the staircase toward the penthouse (the CEO's office). The mid-career stage, on the other hand, was characterized by a period of career reassessment, frequently marked by self-doubt and uncertainty on the part of the employee. That stage was typically experienced by employees between the ages of 40 and 55 who had stopped advancing in the hierarchy, and sometimes were experiencing diminished motivation. The phenomenon was often referred to as *plateauing*.[20] Mid-career employees often experienced this reassessment phase for three basic reasons:[21]

1. **Fewer Career Opportunities.** Unlike entry, which typically featured more jobs, as an individual moved up the organizational hierarchy, he or she often found fewer and fewer job opportunities.
2. **Greater Uncertainty about the Future.** In the past, many companies focused resources on early career stages, but devoted far less effort to mid-career development activities.
3. **Changing Perspective toward Careers.** In the past, employees in the mid-career stage began to explore different definitions of career success. Furthermore, unlike the entry stage, where new employees often experienced a set of concerns shared by many other new employees, mid-career employees often perceived their concerns to be unique.

The mastery stage of today is not associated with any specific age nor is it closely associated with promotions. Instead, success is measured by and rewarded in a wide variety of ways including assignment to important or special projects, receiving training opportunities, and being granted time off to pursue other work-related interests.[22] Unlike the career ladder of the past, success in many companies today may be thought of as a moving sidewalk, with exits to various outlets. Thus, career success is measured not by how high you have climbed, but by how many different outlets (projects, assignments, learning opportunities, and so on) you have experienced. This model has long been common in some occupations, such as consulting, law, and research and development. In these occupations, star performers often earn handsome rewards and large bonuses. As Mel Warriner, the head of human resources at Walt Disney Imagineering, explains, performance is assessed in terms of successful projects. Success at an important project is rewarded with an opportunity to participate in the next project.[23]

Mastery Stage: Suggestions for Organizations

Organizations can take several steps to facilitate employees' progress in the mastery stage.

1. **Develop Effective Promotion Systems.** Although we observed earlier that fewer promotion opportunities exist today than in years past, organizations continue to promote employees, albeit in fewer numbers and at a slower rate. Accurate promotion systems are notoriously difficult to develop because favoritism and politics often abound. Attempts to build objectivity into promotions, using, for example, seniority as an explicit factor, may lead to promotion of less qualified individuals. At the same time, candidates who are skilled in dealing with organizational politics may be more successful in their jobs than candidates who are ineffective at organizational politics. One manager described the ideal candidate for promotion as someone who can successfully navigate the politics of the organization. Who you know and who knows you is important.[24]

General Electric has one of the most thorough and well-regarded promotion systems in the world. As part of the process, the organization has internal consultants whose job involves assessing top managers, designing development plans, and disseminating this information when a promotion is being considered. To assess the candidates, the consultants spend many hours talking with a candidate's current supervisor, past supervisors, and subordinates, and then they write a lengthy report of their findings. This information becomes part of each top manager's record and plays a prominent role in promotion decisions.[25] Finally, several of the selection methods described in Chapter 5, such as structured interviews, job knowledge tests, and assessment centers have been used successfully for promotion purposes. Organizations that are designing promotion systems should carefully consider the use of such standardized, well-regarded practices.

2. **Organizations Must Provide Appropriate Developmental Experiences.** Research has identified a number of employee assignments and experiences that are useful in developing employee abilities. You may be surprised to hear that some of the most valuable learning experiences involve difficult, stressful situations.[26] Table 6.2 shows two important developmental experiences and the abilities each affects.

3. **Provide Effective Career Programs That Reflect New Reality.** To facilitate their employees' success in the mastery stage, some organizations offer career programs that emphasize many of the new career concepts described above. Chase Manhattan Bank, for example, recently initiated the Career Vision Program, which offers employees such services as confidential assessment tests and training in the competencies needed for team project work. Sun Microsystems provides information to new hires about its Career Resilience program. Initially an outplacement program, it has evolved into a career counseling system that provides help regarding career issues as well.[27] Chevron contracted with Beverly Kaye, a consultant, to implement a career guidance program to help redefine career objectives for employees. Among the suggestions her program gives to employees is that they can move through the organization in ways other than up, including sideways (such as to a more interesting department, but in a job with the same pay and prestige), out of the organization, or down (to a job that has lower pay and status, but more opportunity for growth).[28]

Mastery Stage: Suggestions for Employees

As an employee, you must acquire three basic competencies during the mastery stage:[29]

1. **Advanced Knowledge in a Specialty Area.** This may be marketing, finance, computer programming, or whatever. You probably have such an expertise if you were hired, but you must update and improve upon it during the mastery stage.

Table 6.2	Examples of Two Developmental Experiences and the Abilities They Affect
Experience	**Abilities Affected**
1. Stabilizing or correcting a troubled business operation or unit	Learning how business works, being decisive, motivating others, gaining cooperation, negotiating, persevering, ability to confront others
2. Starting a new career to deal with dissatisfaction with a previous job	Coping with new situations; persevering; self-awareness, handling new relationships

Source: From M. W. McCall, "Developing Executives through Work Experiences," *Human Resource Planning* 11 (1988): 1–11.

2. **An Understanding of How Your Business Operates and Succeeds.** It is critical to learn this during the mastery stage. One of the common criticisms employers make is that inexperienced workers fail to comprehend how their specialty area can contribute to the business.

3. **The Ability to Work with Others.** This includes effective communication, the ability to resolve conflicts, and networking. While you begin learning some of these competencies in the entry stage, you need to become an expert in them during the mastery stage.

The new rules in the mastery stage, then, emphasize success in projects. The most successful workers are those in greatest demand to work on projects; in turn, they not only receive the highest rewards (pay, bonuses, and so forth), but they are asked to participate in the most interesting and challenging assignments. Seniority and favoritism play a smaller role than in the past. Box 6.3 offers advice on succeeding in your chosen career.

Passage Stage

The **passage stage** is the point during which the employee prepares to change jobs or employers. This may involve a complete change of occupation. Sydney Wood-Cahusac, for example, worked as a treasurer for several organizations, and finally concluded that what he wished to do was become a clergyman. Ten years after retiring from business, he is an ordained priest and says he finally feels fulfilled.[30]

In previous years, the passage stage was often known as the late career phase. Employees in that stage were usually past age 55. Traditionally, they would be planning for retirement while combating issues of declining productivity and growing technical obsolescence. Today, however, as a result of many organizational layoffs and other factors affecting careers, employees are likely to enter the passage stage more than once.[31]

One may enter the passage stage either voluntarily (the employee chooses to change jobs or companies) or involuntarily (the organization terminates the employee). Voluntarily exiting a job or career and beginning afresh is something many people dream of but often hesitate to do out of fear of failure and concerns over loss of pay. But as Stephen Paskoff, formerly a partner in a successful law firm and now owner of a supervisor-training business, explains, "In the long run would you rather have the risk in your own enterprise or that your company lays you off?" In today's world working for even a large, established organization is certainly no guarantee of a job.[32]

passage stage
Refers to the point during which the employee prepares to change jobs or employers.

Passage Stage: Suggestions for Organizations

Although layoffs create a stressful and unpleasant situation for organizations and managers, a number of recommendations are offered here to help organizations facilitate this process.[33]

1. **Involve All Employees in the Downsizing Process.** Although top management initiates the downsizing, all levels of employees can have input. Some organizations, for example, have had employees form task forces for the purpose of identifying unnecessary expenses, redundant positions, and other cost-savings changes. In one organization, employees were informed that their jobs were being eliminated, but they were told that they would receive full pay for one more year. During that time,

YOUR TURN ───

Box 6.3
General Tips for Career Success

Everyone has some favorite career tips. Here are some career tips you might find of use.

1. **Take reasonable risks.** To succeed in today's world, you must take some risks. But make sure that you have alternative plans if things don't go as planned. As an example, you may consider changing companies in order to improve your career options. But if you are worried that the change won't work out, consider first whether the job market is good enough that you will have alternative opportunities with other organizations.

2. **Compensation should be much less important in the beginning of your career.** Think of the first ten or so years of your career as a learning process; the major reward should be the opportunity to learn and develop your skills and pay should be of less importance. Some experts suggest that you not even consider the compensation offered for the first few years and concentrate solely on what you can learn and the experience you can acquire.

3. **Focus on making your boss successful.** If your boss is successful, he or she will help you. This doesn't mean you should neglect your own career. But it does mean that you need to be attuned to your boss's goals and what it takes to achieve those.

4. **Recognize the contribution of others.** Giving credit to others does not reduce your contributions. People tend to remember and to reciprocate when their contributions are recognized by others. This is especially true today, when many companies emphasize teams and alliances. Giving credit when it is due is critical in developing a team spirit.

Source: Adapted from G. Graen, *Unwritten Rules for Your Career* (New York: Wiley, 1989).

they were asked to create another job for themselves within the organization that would make a contribution, or seek a position elsewhere.

2. **Develop Plans for Both the Employees Who Will Remain and Those Who Will Leave.** Organizations should consider a variety of programs to assist employees who are being terminated in their job search. Providing outplacement support to help employees in writing resumes and locating alternative jobs is a common practice for organizations that are conducting large layoffs. Organizations must also consider the needs of employees who will remain at the organization. Given all of the sympathy for the employees who are being asked to leave, it is not uncommon for the remaining employees to develop "survivor syndrome." They may experience feelings of anxiety about potential job loss, guilty feelings regarding departing workers, and loss of commitment to the organization. To combat such feelings, organizations must be sure to provide frequent, detailed communication with remaining workers, and develop programs and practices to signal a new start.

3. **Organizations Should Develop Alternative Work Arrangements to Help Individual Employees in the Passage Stage.** Programs such as sabbaticals, job sharing, and leaves of absence to pursue different opportunities may be helpful for individuals in the passage stage. Rank Xerox, for example, developed a formal program to enable employees in its human resources and purchasing departments to become consultants. As part of this program, the company helped employees to become independent contractors by hiring them part time at their current salary,

while saving money by not paying benefits. Employees were also able to consult with other companies.[34]

4. **Organizations Should Be Aware of Legal Requirements.** Most of the laws discussed in Chapter 2, including the Civil Rights Act of 1964, the Americans with Disabilities Act, and the Age Discrimination in Employment Act, cover terminations and layoffs. In addition to those, the **Worker Adjustment and Retraining Notification (WARN) Act of 1988** requires companies with 100 or more employees to give notice to their workers of a facility closure or mass layoff at least 60 days before taking action. Because employees are most likely to sue if they are being fired or terminated, organizations involved in these decisions must be extremely careful not to violate relevant laws.[35]

<aside>
Worker Adjustment and Retraining Notification Act
Requires certain companies to give notice to employees of closure or layoff.
</aside>

Passage Stage: Suggestions for Employees

Here are some suggestions for you as an employee in the passage stage:[36]

1. **Do Not Be Tempted by Jobs That Conflict with Your Career Plan.** Although occasionally apparent mismatches turn into positive situations, be wary of them. The wrong move may be extremely costly. On the other hand, Mike Hernacki, currently a freelance writer, has had five different careers, ranging from schoolteacher to lawyer. Some of these careers lasted only two years. Although you might think none of these careers relates to freelance writing, Mike would completely disagree. As he explains, his business and legal experience helps him when he writes about financial issues, and his experience in advertising is useful for promotional writing.[37]

2. **Keep Moving Around in Order to Acquire Your Targeted Experiences and Competencies.** Although it's important not to appear as a job hopper, you also want to make sure that you attain your goals. Kathy Reed, who worked for several years at Xerox Corporation, found that the program manager position at the company enabled her to acquire a wide variety of competencies, including marketing experience and conflict resolution ability.

3. **What Seems Bad May Not Be Bad After All.** Kathy Reed was laid off less than one year after being hired by Compaq Computer. Although she was devastated at first, she ultimately was hired at Recognition International, which manufactures document-processing materials. As she describes the experience, "it was scary as hell. . . . But it was terrific to learn there is life after a layoff."

4. **Handling the Termination.** Given the number of mass layoffs in recent times, don't be surprised if you are terminated in a workforce reduction. Below are some suggestions of what to do if you are fired:

Stay Calm. Quite understandably, you may feel extremely upset when you lose your job. If you lose your cool, however, you may end up saying things (such as, threatening to sue your supervisor) or doing things (like badmouthing the company) that you will regret later. Don't be so concerned about how other companies will view the termination. Employers' perceptions of terminated workers have changed quite a bit in the last 25 years. In the past, being terminated had much stigma attached to it; but given the many layoffs during the last decade or so, many highly qualified employees are now fired for reasons other than their job performance. Dennis Lunder, an executive director of marketing communications for a large greeting card company, has lost his job six times in almost 30 years.[38]

Avoid the Emotional Roller Coaster. Once you accept the fact that you must find a new job, adopt a regular schedule and continue engaging in outside activities. Keeping a regular schedule and maintaining your outside interests will help prevent you from becoming depressed and will help you to keep a balanced perspective.[39]

Negotiate with Your Company. You may discover many benefits that either your company may offer you or that you may be able to obtain through negotiation. The number and amount of the benefits will depend in part on why you were fired (was it poor performance on your part, or was the company simply reducing the size of the workforce). One of the most important benefits is severance pay—money above and beyond that which the company owes you. A common rule of thumb is a minimum of one week's pay for each year of service. Your company may offer you the amount as a lump sum or as a continuation of salary. There are pros and cons to each of these arrangements. The conditions under which you leave the organization also have implications. If the company asks you to resign, you may be forfeiting unemployment compensation. However, unemployment compensation may not provide much money, and your organization may even fight your claim. Chances are, your health and life insurance will end when you are terminated; but you may even be able to negotiate continuation of these benefits for some period of time. Even if your company does not continue your health benefits, you have the right to pay to continue them (see Chapter 10). Finally, the company may decide to hire you as a consultant to do the same job you were doing. It pays, then, not to "burn the bridges" as you leave.[40]

In sum, the passage stage can be a difficult one for employees, particularly if entry into this stage was involuntary; it can take months to find a new job. According to a major outplacement consulting firm, it took an average of 5 months to find a job in 1998 (http://outplacement-chalenger.com/index.html). By comparisons, in 1989, executives who were terminated took on average 6 months to become reemployed. During the 1991 recession, the average was more than 8 months. Individuals who are most able to cope with a termination tend to maintain their regular activities, have strong social support (including from their family) and financial resources to draw from, and limit the amount of time they are without a job.[41]

Organizational Advancement Systems

In this section, you will read about four different career advancement systems that organizations use. To help better understand the different career advancement systems, we will use the jungle gym as an analogy. Each rung on the jungle gym represents a work position, and managers succeed by climbing up the rungs (with the exception of the fourth jungle gym). We will describe four different kinds of jungle gyms. We begin with the jungle gym most often associated with large, hierarchical organizations: the command-centered jungle gym.[42]

Command-Centered Jungle Gym

As shown in Figure 6.2, the command-centered jungle gym looks somewhat like a three-dimensional image of a traditional organization structure. The example portrays three basic ports of entry into the jungle gym, each of which represents a different

| **Figure 6.2** | **Command-Centered Jungle Gym** |

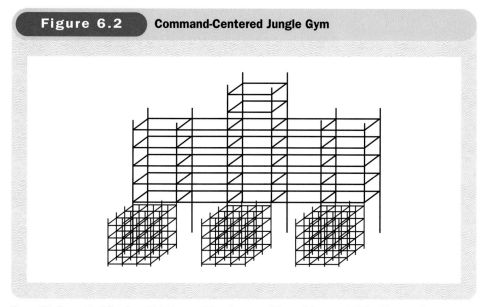

From: H. Gunz, R. Jalland, and M. Evans, "New Strategy, Wrong Managers? What You Need to Know About Career Streams," *Academy of Management Executive* 12 (May 1998): 21–37.

| **Table 6.3** | **Advantages and Disadvantages of the Command-Centered Jungle Gym** |

Advantages	Disadvantages
1. Employees have a clear idea of promotion steps.	1. If the organization is not growing or is in decline, employees have limited promotion opportunities.
2. If the organization is growing, employees have promotion opportunities.	2. Many employees may be competing for the few positions available.
3. Managers understand subordinates' jobs and can be helpful to them.	3. Some lines of progression may be short, limiting promotion opportunities.
4. The system provides reliable and thorough competency development.	

Source: Adapted from H. D. Dewhirst, "Career Patterns: Mobility, Specialization, and Related Career Issues," in *Contemporary Career Development Issues*, ed. R. F. Morrison and J. Adams (Hillsdale, NJ: Erlbaum, 1991): 73–107.

functional area. The key concept in the command-centered jungle gym is that managers move up through a series of similar rungs. For example, an employee may begin in the organization as a product manager, then be promoted to a group product manager, followed by a move to vice president of marketing. Each promotion entails greater responsibility, but the job essentially remains the same. The command-centered jungle gym approach works best in an organization that focuses on being effective in one market or product. The business strategy is to be consistent and reliable, and to retain continuity. By putting all employees through identical experiences and assignments in a functional area, the organization instills a common purpose and understanding. Table 6.3 describes some of the advantages and disadvantages of this system.

Figure 6.3	Evolutionary Jungle Gym

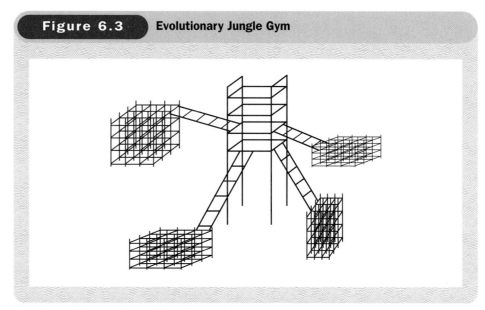

From Gunz, Jalland, and Evans, "New Strategy."

Evolutionary Jungle Gym

The evolutionary jungle gym, depicted in Figure 6.3, is almost the opposite of the well-planned and clearly demarcated command-center jungle gym. This system is referred to as the evolutionary jungle gym because the organization is always changing, or evolving, by entering new businesses or markets. As managers grow their own projects or ventures, which expand or die, the firm experiences an unpredictable pattern of growth. In other words, the organization evolves, as do the managers who work there. As an example, a large electronics firm hired a college physics professor to help design transistors when they first came out, a completely new product for the firm. The professor's product was successful, and eventually the professor was managing a large division within the company. Not surprisingly, this career model works best for organizations that regularly change and develop new businesses. The advantages of the system include opportunities for employees to learn new things and experience tremendous autonomy and variety. On the negative side is the pervasive ambiguity and uncertainty as to what career moves will be successful and which will fail. With the autonomy comes more room for failure, so the risks are probably much higher.

Constructional Jungle Gym

The constructional jungle gym is depicted in Figure 6.4. This career system falls somewhere between the command-center and evolutionary jungle gyms. It is referred to as the constructional jungle gym because employees in this kind of system speak of constructing careers from a set of experiences. The key to success in this type of organization is to create as many diverse experiences or, to use our analogy, climb as many *different* rungs as possible. In some organizations, the goal is to have exposure to as many different functional areas as possible in as many different divisions and countries as possible. In one chemical company, for example, an employee started as an engineer,

| **Figure 6.4** | **Constructional Jungle Gym** |

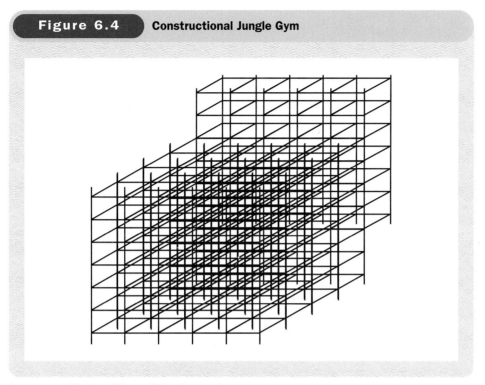

From Gunz, Jalland, and Evans, "New Strategy."

became expert in a number of engineering positions, moved to a top-level HR position, and then advanced to vice president of engineering. In this system, career movement is the way to success. Staying in the same functional area (for example, engineering) is viewed negatively. In fact, the greater the change in functional areas, as indicated in the previous example, the more valuable the move. Some organizations use a more carefully planned version of the constructional gym, often referred to as *planned job rotations*, for managerial and professional employees. The aim of planned job rotations is a more systematic method to career moves.

The constructional jungle gym system functions best in an organization that has excelled in a particular business, but is always on the lookout for new opportunities that fit within its general business strategy. The successful manager therefore must have a broad understanding of the business. Like the two previous systems, this one has advantages and disadvantages. A primary advantage is that employees have numerous opportunities; they are far less likely to get stuck waiting for someone to leave the organization or take a different position. On the other hand, this system creates uncertainty as to what positions will be more helpful in getting ahead. In addition, because of the frequent moves across functional areas, employees will be learning new competencies all the time and may experience difficulty, or even failure, in some assignments.

Protean Jungle Gym

The protean jungle gym, depicted in Figure 6.5, is named after Proteus, the Greek god who could change his shape at will. This term has been used in career literature to refer to employees' careers, but we use it here to refer to an organizational

| **Figure 6.5** | Protean Jungle Gym |

advancement system.[43] The protean jungle gym structure changes at will, depending on the particular needs and challenges the organization is facing. The structure may include both internal pieces (that is, people employed by the organization) and external pieces (that is, people employed by other organizations).[44] For example, Nike, the athletic shoe company, does not manufacture shoes; that work is done by firms in Asia. Nike partners closely with major retailing chains and other distribution business to sell their shoes (see www.nikebiz.com/jobs/jobs_nj.html for more information on Nike's organizational structure). Some Silicon Valley research and development businesses take on external partners to help them market and distribute new products. A completely protean jungle gym has little room for hierarchy or status differences between workers. In fact, the protean jungle gym system is highly project based (see the section "Changed Nature of Work" earlier in this chapter). Unlike the other systems, where employees progress in an upward fashion, the protean jungle gym involves few upward moves, but potentially many sideways moves. In fact, as shown in Figure 6.5, some upward moves (a climb up a small tower) will logically be followed by a downward move (a ride down a slide). The protean jungle gym has four basic job types:[45]

1. **Project Manager.** Project managers are responsible for overseeing projects. They coordinate the work, obtain the necessary resources, and interact with others, including clients and resource managers. Project managers perform many of the tasks that managers and supervisors perform in a traditional organization.
2. **Strategist.** Strategists are responsible for the "big picture" issues, such as the organization's vision. They also have contact with major clients and external partners. These employees are relatively few in number. They perform the work that CEOs and top executives do in a traditional organization.
3. **Resource Manager.** Resource managers are responsible for obtaining, developing, and allocating the resources that project teams need, such as people, money, equipment and materials. The employees who serve in this capacity do the tasks that human resources, finance, accounting and procurement staff perform in a traditional organization.

4. Talent. These are the people who perform the projects. Depending on the nature of the work, they may be computer programmers, scientists, statisticians, or other technical, professional, production, or clerical employees.

Another feature of the protean jungle gym is that employees easily move around. The strategist, for example, probably has had experience as a resource manager or project manager. There may even be flux between some of these roles; that is, the talent in one project may be project managers in the next project. Unlike the other systems reviewed above, however, employees do not advance in any traditional sense. The major advantage of the protean jungle gym is its flexibility and adaptability to change. Thus, in a rapidly changing business, such as the Internet industry, this may be the ideal career system. Another major advantage is that, because the protean jungle gym largely deemphasizes hierarchy and status, employees should feel a greater sense of fairness. Also, the variety and change will please many, but not all, employees. The disadvantage of this system is that some employees may be uncomfortable with the amount of change and lack of clear rules. In addition, the change and flexibility this model allows will not be efficient in businesses where consistency and reliability are essential. For example, this model probably would not be effective in a large retail chain such as Wal-Mart, which emphasizes continuity and efficiency. Box 6.4 describes changes in the kinds of organization structure and employment experiences demanded by today's graduates.

We next turn to consideration of some common career issues that many employees encounter, and discuss ways to handle them.

Common Career Issues

Four common issues faced by many employees are (1) gaining global experience, (2) being a specialist versus generalist, (3) job burnout, and (4) prioritizing managerial activities for success. Each is discussed in greater detail next, along with ways to address them.

Gaining Global Experience

As you probably know, the need for global exposure is more important in careers than ever before. So, how do organizations, and you as an employee, ensure that you obtain global experience? Organizations have developed four basic strategies for providing their employees with global exposure. By learning about these strategies, you will be able to suggest ways for your company to provide global experience, even if it currently is not doing so. The four strategies are described in greater detail next.[46]

Borderless Career. Some employees will work in several different countries over the span of their careers. One employee, for instance, served as a health care expert in France for several years, then spent several years in London, Tokyo, and finally in Switzerland. If you use this strategy in your career, you will acquire significant cross-cultural knowledge. Typically, organizations have only a small part of their workforce using this model, because, among other problems, a borderless career can create family problems. Only about 1 percent of Merck's workforce has pursued a borderless career.

The next three strategies, then, are more commonly used.

YOUR TURN

Box 6.4
The Move Away from Corporate Careers

One recent career trend is the move away from large corporations. In fact, a recent survey indicated that only 1 percent of adults indicated they would like to work as a corporate manager. The trend is particularly pronounced among recent MBA graduates from top programs. At Stanford University, for example, six years ago almost 70 percent of graduating MBAs went to work for large manufacturing businesses; in 1994 only about 50 percent chose this career. While many MBAs from top schools become consultants or investment bankers, their real aim often is to save a lot of money so that they can become entrepreneurs at a later date.

The trend against working for a large corporation has in some cases created difficulties for university officials. In recent years, for example, recruiters from large corporations have arrived at campuses, only to find far fewer interested students than expected. Some manufacturers no longer recruit at Harvard University because so few students accepted their job offers. On the other hand, university officials are finding extremely strong demand for certain courses with a small-business focus, such as entrepreneurial financing. At the University of Chicago, more than 300 students signed up for a course in this area. The school could only admit 130 of them.

Why the move away from corporate careers? Several reasons have been offered. First, large organizations have acquired a reputation for bureaucracy, limited autonomy, and minimal impact. In the past, however, these negatives were often outweighed by several positives, such as implicit job security and frequent promotions. In light of many layoffs and flattened organizational structure, though, the benefits of working for a large corporation have greatly diminished.

Robert Berg, who recently graduated with an MBA and now works for a large consulting firm, commented as follows about his former large employer: "When the time came to close the division I was working with, management left us with the feeling that they were going to take care of us. They didn't. Basically, they lied to us."

Another reason for the decline in corporate careers lies with having more women in the workforce. As Kristin Snowden, a second-year MBA student, explains, "There is a way people are supposed to behave at work at large companies, and it's based on a male model that is hundreds of years old. Women cry more often than men, for example; we find that it is an effective way to relieve stress. But you are never, ever supposed to cry on the job if you work at a large company."

Finally, the newest generation heading into the work world (the "Net Generation") seems to value independence and interesting work much more than previous generations did; yet these are the very characteristics that jobs in large corporations usually lack. Whether the trend against large companies will change remains to be seen.

Source: Adapted from K. Labich, "Kissing Off Corporate America," *Fortune*, 20 February 1995, 44–52.

Awareness Building. The primary goal of an awareness-building strategy is to develop a sensitivity to, rather than a specialty in, global issues. Thus, the awareness-building approach is *not* meant to provide an in-depth knowledge of global concerns. Typically, an awareness-building assignment is performed early in one's career. It lasts for only a brief period of time, usually only 3 to 12 months. Baxter, which manufactures medical equipment, began using an awareness-building strategy when the company developed products for sale in Japan that were sized for U.S. patients. Amoco Oil often uses this approach in developing local nationals who work for the organization. The local nationals spend some time in the U.S. headquarters and then are sent to various global production sites. This is a relatively common approach for gaining global exposure.

SWAT Teams. As the name suggests, SWAT teams are mobile teams of trouble-shooting experts who solve a specific problem or finish a well-defined project in another country. Unlike the borderless career and awareness-building strategies, the major purpose of the SWAT team is to solve a problem or complete a project; the immediate goal is *not* to develop the employee. However, the indirect payoff for an employee can be high. Amoco Oil, for example, uses this approach in deciding whether to base an operation in a new country, a decision that relies on knowledge from a number of different areas (for example, legal, drilling, human resources, and so on). General Motors uses SWAT teams to design global benefits programs, which also require a mix of expertise. As an employee, then, you can gain a great deal from involvement in a SWAT team, with relatively little cost, since it usually does not involve a major relocation or permanent change in your job duties.

Virtual Teams. As the name implies, the virtual-team approach relies on groups of employees from around the world, who communicate using a variety of means, including e-mail, Instant Messaging, and videoconferencing. The major advantage of this strategy is that employees can obtain global exposure with minimal cost and disruption. A second advantage is that a virtual team, due to time-zone differences, can conceivably work and communicate around the clock. One virtual team from IBM, for instance, included programmers from the United States, Russia, and India. When the group in the United States ended its day, their work was sent through the Intranet to Russia, where it was worked on until the end of the workday there. The work was then shipped to India. NASA, the U.S. space agency, conducted training over several countries using virtual reality. The major advantage, then, of the virtual team is that it enables employees to have some global exposure at a relatively low cost and investment. On the other hand, the contact is limited and even small misunderstandings can create major problems, which are difficult to solve without the opportunity to meet face-to-face.

As you can see from the above discussion, there is no one best way to obtain global exposure in the workplace. However, there are several different ways that differ in terms of cost and commitment. Given that the workplace is increasingly global, you will only enhance your career by participating in such opportunities as they become available. Box 6.5 offers some Web sites that may offer additional advice on career enhancement.

Being a Specialist versus a Generalist

In many fields, such as computer programming and law, one begins working in one specific area, but after a few years one is faced with the question of whether to remain a specialist, and know a great deal about one topic, or to become a generalist, competent of handling several different areas. Research with scientists and engineers indicates that no one right answer tells us which is best—some individuals have highly effective careers as specialists, while others have highly effective careers as generalists.

So, what are some considerations that you should take into account in deciding whether to remain a narrow specialist or become more of a generalist? First, you can remain a specialist if you are in a highly sought-after field, especially where there is a shortage of qualified people. Certain computer fields, for example, are likely to always have a high demand for workers. You also need to evaluate the long-term picture, of course, in deciding how much demand there will be for your specialty. Is your specialty an area that is constantly changing or takes a high degree of training? Second, are you

WEBBING AROUND

Box 6.5

A lot of career advice is available on the Internet, but not all of it is useful. Presented below are only a few of the better links.

http://cdc.stuaff.duke.edu/ CDC/Planning/Assess.html This Web site contains self-assessment tools, including a vocational interest survey that provides a score and some suggested occupations, to help you determine an appropriate career.

www.careermag.com This is an on-line magazine covering career issues, including information on job fairs and recruiters, as well as articles and other useful information relating to careers.

www.cweb.com/doctor This Web site contains brief articles, as well as an e-mail address for a career counselor.

http://205.134.174.109/career. htm Now, on a more humorous note, if you have no idea what career to choose, you might try this Web site!

willing to work as a consultant, either independently or for a firm? If the answer is yes, you may be able to succeed as a specialist. The reason why specialists will be more successful as consultants is that they will need more customers than someone who is a generalist. In other words, someone who is an expert on the Family and Medical Leave Act is unlikely to have enough work to do if she is employed by one organization; but she may have plenty of work if she is employed by a consulting firm that provides services to 100 organizations that need help with this law. If you specialize, then, you should make sure of sufficient demand for your skill over the long term, that you are extremely effective at what you do, and that you are willing to work as a consultant. If you don't meet these criteria, you should probably become more of a generalist. As Gary Kniser, an executive recruiter, says, "Never narrow your options. To the extent that technical expertise narrows your market, you've made a bad career decision."[47] To avoid becoming a specialist, you need to learn new things and acquire new competencies. You can do this by participating in task forces, special projects, or even volunteer organizations.

Burnout

Have you ever had a sense of emotional exhaustion, including a lack of energy and a perception that you were emotionally drained? How about a feeling of depersonalization toward coworkers or clients, or a sense of personal failure and limited progress at work? Practically everyone has had some of these feelings from time to time, but if you had one or more of those feelings for a longer period (such as a few weeks), you may be suffering from job burnout. Certain jobs are particularly susceptible to job burnout, particularly the helping professions, such as social workers, schoolteachers, and customer service representatives. Jobs that tend to create relatively little job burnout include laboratory technicians, researchers, and people who work alone. You will read next about some of the factors that contribute to job burnout, as well as some things you can do to avoid this symptom.[48]

job burnout
A sense of emotional exhaustion, lack of energy, feeling of depersonalization toward coworkers or clients. A sense of personal failure and limited progress at work are all characteristics of burnout. One cause lies within the individual employee, whereas a second cause lies within the nature of the work.

Causes of Job Burnout. Job burnout has two primary causes. One cause lies within the individual employee; a second cause lies in the nature of the work. To understand the first cause, consider Nancy Parker, a new business graduate, eager to make her mark in the business world. She has set a number of goals for herself, including earning at least $100,000 by the time she is 30 and owning a BMW. She also expects to be a top executive by the time she is 35. Do you think these are realistic goals? Unless Nancy Parker is extremely talented, or works for a family-owned business, there is a good chance that she will not achieve these goals. She may begin to suffer from job burnout as she encounters setbacks. Job burnout, then, is particularly common for young employees who have set unrealistic goals for themselves and have inflated expectations as to what the organization will provide in the way of rewards and opportunities.

In order to understand work factors that contribute to burnout, consider Tom Richardson, a newly graduated business student who works for a collection agency. His job will be to try to get people to pay their debts. The people he is trying to collect from respond in a variety of ways, ranging from open hostility to crying. Because of the intensity (many people resist paying their debts to a collection agency) and frequency of these interactions, Tom Richardson also is likely to experience job burnout. Jobs with frequent, intensive contact with clients often lead to burnout. Other factors that contribute to burnout include having too much work to do and reporting to different supervisors with different expectations for work.

Avoiding Burnout. One of the most important ways to avoid burnout is to have access to social support. Social support means having one or more people who will listen to you when you want to complain, provide advice about issues that concern you, and generally make you feel valued as a person. Social support can come from several different sources, including your spouse, friends, and even your supervisor. Although there are also instances where your coworkers can provide social support to alleviate your feelings of burnout, at times social support from coworkers can actually increase your feelings of being burned out. Perhaps in talking with coworkers you may begin to feel even more negative about the situation than you did before.[49]

From the organizational perspective, another way to reduce burnout is to rotate jobs so that employees have a break from constant interaction with clients. Perhaps paperwork or other needed assignments can be performed each day by different employees, thereby providing a brief break from the tension associated with client contact. Similarly, reducing the workload to more manageable levels and reducing role conflict can in the long run save a great deal of turnover, and the necessary recruiting, hiring, and training that goes along with turnover.

In sum, burnout is a common problem. Be sure to set reasonable, achievable goals for yourself, and develop sources of social support. Finally, remember that there is more to life than just work.

Prioritizing Managerial Activities for Success

One question that often arises for managers is how to set priorities among their supervisory activities to achieve maximum effectiveness. To answer this question, we need to first distinguish between four types of managerial activities:

1. Communication Activities. These involve such things as writing reports, answering telephone inquiries, contacting others, and so forth.

2. **Traditional Management Activities.** These include such activities as setting goals for employees, completing work schedules, inspecting work, assigning work tasks, and so forth.
3. **Human Resource Activities.** These include training employees, giving rewards (for instance, compliments), managing conflict between employees, mentoring employees, and so forth.
4. **Networking.** Activities in this category involve interacting, socializing, and politicking with others. It includes all types of informal interactions with others, including joking, gossiping, and discussing rumors.

Before we discuss which of these four activities is most related to success as a manager, it is important to note that there are at least two ways to define managerial success. One way, which we will refer to as career advancement, is based on how rapidly the manager has advanced in the organization. The second way, which we will refer to as unit performance, is based on how productive the manager's unit is in terms of quality and quantity of work, as well as subordinates' measure of job satisfaction. Interestingly enough, research has indicated that few managers rate highly on both career advancement and unit performance.

Given this information, on which of the four managerial activities do you think managers who demonstrate rapid career advancement spend most of their time? If you answered networking, you are correct. So, if you want to advance rapidly in the organization, spending your time on networking seems to be the key. On the other hand, in what activities do you think the managers who have the highest unit performance tend to engage most? If you answered communication and human resource management, you are right. Interestingly, the activity least related to unit performance was networking. Which activities you prioritize, then, will affect the type of success you experience. Based on earlier comments in this chapter, however, as organizations focus less on promotions and more on project management, it is likely that unit performance will become more important than career advancement. Given the choice between these activities, then, communication and human resource management should be given your highest priority as a manager.[50]

❖ Conclusion

The nature of careers has changed dramatically in the last 25 years for several reasons, including the large number of corporate layoffs, the changed nature of work, and the changed nature of organizations. Accordingly, career stages are also different than in the past. Many individuals today will experience a three-phase cycle of entry, mastery, and passage several times around. Each stage will involve different challenges. There are several different types of organization advancement systems, ranging from the traditional command-centered approach to the relatively new protean jungle gym. You also read about several common career issues, including gaining global experience, specializing versus generalizing, job burnout, and prioritizing managerial activities. With careful planning and foresight, organizations and employees should be able to foster career effectiveness. For employees, the future is clear: You need to take complete responsibility for your career.

❖ Applying Core Concepts

1. Discuss how the career of someone 30 years ago may have differed from the career you are likely to have.
2. What career stage do you think you are in now? What issues have you dealt with so far? What issues do you expect to come up in the near future?
3. What types of programs and practices does your company or a company that a close friend works for offer to deal with transitions to different career stages?
4. What advancement system does your company or a company that a close friend works for use? Which would you prefer? Why?
5. Which of the following career issues do you think you may experience in the career you have chosen or the career you hope to choose: being a specialist versus generalist, job burnout, and prioritizing managerial activities for success. Choose the one you think you are most likely to face, and explain how you would deal with it.
6. How important do you think global experience is for your career? What have you done so far, or plan to do in the future, to gain global exposure in the workplace?

❖ Key Terms

Entry stage	Passage stage	Job burnout
Mentor	Worker Adjustment and	
Mastery stage	Retraining Notification	
	Act	

❖ CHAPTER 6 *Experiential Exercise*

The Controversial Promotion

Your instructor will assign you into groups of three people; each of you will be given a specific role. The exercise involves Kitchy Kitchens, Inc., a company that sells consumer appliances, such as kitchen sinks, faucets, garbage compactors, and various other major kitchen appliances and hardware. Historically, Kitchy Kitchens has sold high-quality, high-cost products. With the advent of the Internet, the marketplace has become far more competitive. The company's long-term customers are able to make extensive price comparisons, and on-line-only companies have sprung up that offer the same products at a lower cost. The company has just developed a Web page, but it is too early to tell what impact that will have.

The Issue

The Issue: Should Bill or should Mary be promoted to manager of marketing? Because your company has a policy of promoting from within, a list was generated of possible employees qualified for the job. The two top contenders are Bill Smith and Mary Wells. Both have worked at the company for 10 years. There are some differences between them. Bill Smith is a few years older and has had several years of prior marketing experience with a competitor. Bill also has had more varied experience than Mary. Besides his experience in product design, Bill has had more varied experience in the marketing function, working on several different products in various different markets, including stores and individuals. Mary, on the other hand, has an undergraduate degree in marketing (Bill's degree is in philosophy) and has worked the entire time on marketing to retail stores, which is where the growth is. Neither candidate has experience with Internet marketing.

In addition to the information above, read your role carefully before beginning the exercise; *do not read any other role besides the one given to you.* After you have concluded your discussion and decided whom to promote, your group should generate career development suggestions for *both* Mary and Bill. The suggestions could include training programs, task forces, or any other developmental experiences that would enhance their careers. Also, when you are done discussing this case, prepare to answer the following questions:

1. What additional information would you like to have had here? Is there any information about the company that you wish you had? What type of career advancement system does your decision reflect? Would your decision be different if there were a different career advancement system?

2. Should discrimination issues be considered in making promotion decisions?

3. Do you think a disagreement between the HRM manager and the VP is inevitable here? Why or why not?

HRM Manager's Role

Additional Information: In addition to the background information above, your examination of the personnel files indicates that Mary and Bill have received on average identical performance ratings over the last 3 years, which is when performance ratings were first formalized.

The vice president of marketing and sales, to whom the person would report, wants to promote Bill. As far as you can tell, Mary and Bill are fairly evenly matched in certain ways. You interviewed both Mary and Bill and were convinced that both are good communicators and both would be effective with subordinates. Given that they are fairly evenly matched, you felt *strongly* that Mary should be promoted because

there are far too few females in management at Kitchy Kitchens. In fact, you have heard recent rumblings about a lawsuit regarding sex bias in promotions. Given the new law, Kitchy Kitchens could lose some actual money if such a lawsuit were successful. You are not quite sure what the vice president's reasoning is, so you and the vice president are going to meet to discuss this matter. Your task, then, is to explain why Mary should be promoted over Bill.

Vice President of Marketing and Sales Role

Additional Information: In addition to the background information above, for the past three years the company has had a yearly formal performance appraisal for all employees. You took an active role in monitoring those conducted by the previous manager of marketing, even attending some of the feedback sessions. From your observations, Bill is the more qualified of the two top candidates.

As the manager to whom the position reports, you believe it is your "call." You have met with all five candidates. You even called the prior manager of marketing, who said Bill and Mary were both well qualified (but from the tone of his voice, you were pretty certain he would pick Bill). You have no doubt that Bill should be promoted. However, rumor has it that the HRM manager would like to promote Mary and has called a meeting with you to discuss whether Bill or Mary should be promoted. Given that you are going to be the one who has to work with the manager of marketing, it seems logical that you should be the one to make the decision. Your task, then, is to explain why Bill should be promoted.

President's Role

Additional Information: In addition to the background information above, the company has had a yearly formal performance appraisal for all employees. The ratings indicate that Bill and Mary have had nearly identical ratings; sometimes Bill was rated a shade higher, sometimes Mary was rated a shade higher.

Since you are not directly involved in the decision of who gets hired, you have not interviewed any of the candidates. You assume that the vice president of marketing and sales will make the final decision, with the approval of the HRM manager. However, in this case, you have heard there may be some disagreement between the two. The HRM manager has requested that you attend a meeting with them, where this issue will be discussed. Both the HRM manager and vice president have been with the company for years, and you have a high regard for both. Though you are less familiar with the HRM manager's work, you know that the vice president is one of the best in the business. You also know that lawsuits are on the rise, and that the HRM function is critical in avoiding such things.

❖ Chapter 6 References

1. Y. Ono and J. Schlesinger, "Parity's Paradox," *Wall Street Journal*, 28 December 1998, A1, A8.
2. T. Stewart, "Planning a Career in a World Without Managers," *Fortune*, 20 March 1995, 72–80.
3. W. Kiechel, "How We Will Work in the Year 2000," *Fortune*, 17 May 1993, 38–52.
4. H. D. Dewhirst, "Career Patterns: Mobility, Specialization, and Related Career Issues," in *Contemporary Career Development Issues*, ed. R. F. Morrison and J. Adams (Hillsdale, NJ: Erlbaum, 1991).
5. N. Nicholson, "The Transition Cycle: A Conceptual Framework for the Analysis of Change and Human Resources Management," in *Research in Personnel and Human Resources Management*, ed. K. Rowland and G. Ferris (Greenwich, CT: JAI Press, 1987).
6. E. Schein. *Career Survival: Strategic Job and Role Planning* (San Diego, CA: Pfeiffer, 1993).
7. J. Greenhaus, *Career Management* (Fort Worth, TX: Dryden, 1987).
8. Ibid.
9. T. Bauer and S. Green, "Effect of Newcomer Involvement in Work-Related Activities: A Longitudinal Study of Socialization," *Journal of Applied Psychology* 79 (1994): 211–23.
10. M. Louis, B. Posner, and G. Powell, "The Availability and Helpfulness of Socialization Practices," *Personnel Psychology* 36 (1983): 857–66.
11. G. Jones, "Socialization Tactics, Self-Efficacy, and Newcomers' Adjustments to Organizations," *Academy of Management Journal* 29 (1986): 262–79.
12. R. Morrison, "Meshing Corporate and Career Development Strategies," in *Contemporary Career Development Issues*, ed. R. Morrison and J. Adams (Hillsdale, NJ: Erlbaum, 1991).
13. C. Hymowitz, "How a Dedicated Mentor Gave Momentum to a Woman's Career," *Wall Street Journal*, 24 April 1995, B1.
14. G. Graen, *Unwritten Rules for Your Career* (New York: Wiley, 1989).
15. R. Noe, "An Investigation of the Determinants of Successful Assigned Mentoring Relationships," *Personnel Psychology* 41 (1988): 457–79.
16. G. Dreher and R. Ash, "A Comparative Study of Mentoring Among Men and Women in Managerial, Professional, and Technical Positions," *Journal of Applied Psychology* 75 (1990): 539–46.
17. D. Turban and T. Dougherty, "Role of Protege Personality in Receipt of Mentoring and Career Success," *Academy of Management Journal* 37 (1994): 688–702.
18. K. Kram, *Mentoring at Work* (Glenview, IL: Scott, Foresman, 1985).
19. R. Noe, "Mentoring Relationships for Employee Development," in *Applying Psychology in Business*, ed. J. Jones, B. Steffy, and D. Bray (Lexington, MA: Lexington Books, 1991).
20. Greenhaus, *Career Management*.
21. D. Hall, "Breaking Career Routines: Midcareer Choice and Identity Development," in *Career Development in Organizations*, ed. D. Hall and Associates (San Francisco, CA: Jossey-Bass, 1986).
22. J. Fierman, "Beating the Midlife Career Crisis," *Fortune*, 6 September 1993, 52–62.
23. Stewart, *Planning a Career*.
24. G. Ferris, M. R. Buckley, and G. Allen, "Promotion Systems in Organizations," *Human Resource Planning* 15 (1992): 47–68, 95.

25. S. Friedman and T. LeVino, "Strategic Appraisal and Development at General Electric Company," in *Strategic Human Resource Management*, ed. C. Fombrun, N. Tichy, and M. A. DeVanna (New York: Wiley, 1984).

26. M. W. McCall, "Developing Executives Through Work Experiences," *Human Resource Planning* 11 (1988): 1–11.

27. Stewart, *Planning a Career.*

28. Ibid.

29. Ibid.

30. J. Connelly, "How to Choose Your Next Career," *Fortune*, 6 February 1995, 145–46.

31. Greenhaus, *Career Management.*

32. Connelly, *How to Choose.*

33. K. Cameron, S. Freeman, and A. Mishra, "Best Practices in White-Collar Downsizing: Managing Contradictions," *The Executive* 5 (1991): 57–73.

34. T. Gilmore and L. Hirschhorn, "Managing Human Resources in a Declining Context," in *Strategic Human Resource Management*, ed. C. Fombrun, N. Tichy, and M. A. DeVanna (New York: Wiley, 1984).

35. D. Twomey, *Employment Discrimination Law: A Manager's Guide* (Cincinnati: West, 1998).

36. H. Lancaster, "Managing Your Career," *Wall Street Journal*, 14 February 1995, B1.

37. Connelly, *How to Choose.*

38. D. Kirkpatrick, "The New Executive Unemployed," *Fortune*, 8 April 1991, 36–48; K. Salwen, "Decade of Downsizing Eases Stigma of Layoffs," *Wall Street Journal*, 8 February 1994, B1.

39. Kirkpatrick, "The New Executive Unemployed."

40. L. Asinof, "If Ax Falls, Know Your Benefits, Rights, and Don't Forget the Art of Negotiation," *Wall Street Journal*, 17 January 1992, C1, C4.

41. Kirkpatrick, "The New Executive Unemployed"; J. Latack, A. Kinicki, and G. Prussia, "An Integrative Process Model of Coping with Job Loss," *Academy of Management Review* 20 (1995): 311–42.

42. H. Gunz, R. Jalland, and M. Evans, "New Strategy, Wrong Managers? What You Need to Know About Career Streams," *Academy of Management Executive* 12 (1998): 21–37.

43. D. Hall, "Protean Careers of the 21st Century," *Academy of Management Executive* 12 (1998): 8–16.

44. B. Allred, C. Snow, and R. Miles, "Characteristics of Managerial Careers in the 21st Century," *Academy of Management Executive* 10 (1996): 17–27.

45. Stewart, *Planning a Career.*

46. K. Roberts, E. Kossek, and C. Ozeki, "Managing the Global Workforce: Challenges and Strategies," *AME* 12 (1998): 93–106.

47. Stewart, *Planning a Career.*

48. C. Cordes and T. Dougherty, "A Review and Integration of Research on Job Burnout," *Academy of Management Review* 18 (1993): 621–56.

49. G. Kaufmann and T. Beehr,. "Interactions between Job Stressors and Social Support: Some Counterintuitive Results," *Journal of Applied Psychology* 71 (1986): 522–26.

50. F. Luthans, "Successful vs. Effective Real Managers," *Academy of Management Executive* 11 (1988): 127–32.

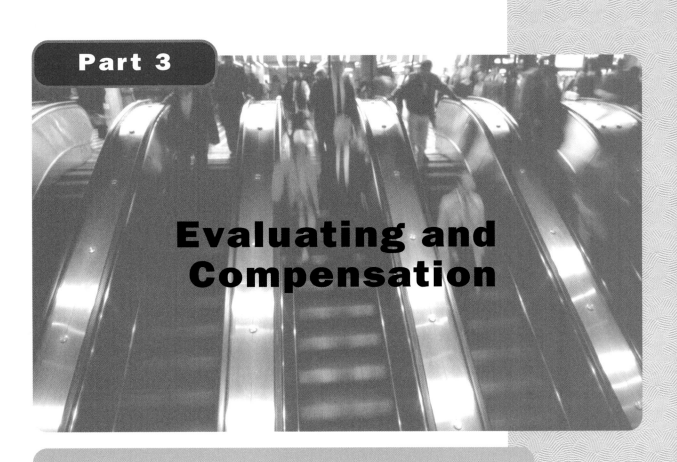

Part 3

Evaluating and Compensation

Chapter 7

Performance Management

1. Identifying major uses of performance management processes.
2. Understanding strengths and weaknesses associated with different performance measures.
3. Developing solutions to problems associated with different performance measures.
4. Understanding current issues in performance management.
5. Giving performance feedback to an employee.
6. Receiving performance feedback in an effective manner.
7. Designing a performance management process that will withstand legal scrutiny.

Opening Case

Nicholas has been working as an inventory specialist at Runners' Gear, a company that designs and manufactures jogging apparel and equipment, for almost three years. Although he has worked there longer than many others, Nicholas has never been given much feedback about his work. He finds this particularly frustrating because he has always sought feedback from others. As far as he can guess, his performance must be at least adequate, because he has not been fired or demoted. In addition, his pay raises seem to be about what other employees are getting, assuming the office gossip is correct.

So far, the few formal performance appraisal meetings Nicholas has had have been practically fruitless. On all three occasions, his manager began by showing him the rating form (see Figure 7.1). Each time, Nicholas had been rated "average" on all aspects of performance. Although there was room for written comments, each time the manager had written: "Employee performs satisfactorily." Near the bottom of the page was an area for the employee's signature, indicating that he or she had seen the ratings. After showing Nicholas the form, the manager inevitably said, "You seem to have done a satisfactory job during the past year. Do you have

any questions?" Nicholas would have liked to ask for some more specific feedback, but from the tone of the manager's voice, Nicholas could tell that his manager was thinking about other things he had to do and was hoping that Nicholas would simply say no.

What concerns Nicholas the most about the performance appraisals is his feeling that the ratings do affect promotions. Although no one has actually told him this, Nicholas also feels that if there were any layoffs, the performance ratings might be used to make decisions. Even though Nicholas' ratings have always been satisfactory, he is certain that some employees are getting higher ratings. Nicholas also receives practically no informal feedback. Occasionally, after a particularly tough project is completed, his manager has said "nice work." The time when he received the most feedback was when he turned in a managerial report that apparently had not been well received by the department vice president. In that case, Nicholas' manager provided written comments about the report and talked about his concerns for almost 20 minutes. Although the feedback was negative, he was glad to get some helpful input. As a result, Nicholas attended a 10-week writing program

Figure 7.1 A Performance Appraisal Form

Employee's Name: Nicholas Rozincksi

For each dimension, mark a number from 1–5, where 1 means poor, 2 means below average, 3 means average, 4 means above average, and 5 means outstanding. Provide written comments to support each rating.

A. Quality of work _3_ Comments:
B. Quantity of work _3_ Comments:
C. Customer service _3_ Comments:
D. Initiative _3_ Comments:
E. Leadership potential _3_ Comments:
F. Attendance _3_ Comments:
G. Overall _3_ Comments:

Additional Comments: *Employee performs satisfactorily.*

I have seen my performance ratings _____ (employee signature) and a one-day seminar on multimedia presentations, both of which he felt would be helpful for his career.

Given all of the shortcomings that Nicholas indicated, why would Runners' Gear bother to maintain a performance management process? If the company wants to continue to have a performance management process, isn't there a better approach than the one used? Further, why does the manager seem so reluctant to give Nicholas feedback? If you were in Nicholas' place, how would you go about getting more feedback?

This chapter will discuss performance management processes. Performance management refers to those activities that measure job performance and provide feedback to employees about their performances. This chapter will discuss why organizations use performance ratings, how organizations assess employee performance, the strengths and weaknesses of performance ratings, how organizations attempt to overcome problems in performance management processes, and current issues in performance management processes. You will also read about difficulties associated with giving and receiving feedback, and you will look at some solutions to these issues. As you will see, performance management processes play an important role in organizations; perhaps because of their importance, they produce a great deal of anxiety and concern for both managers and employees alike. We begin first with a discussion of why organizations have performance management processes.

Performance Management: Organizational Uses

Organizations use performance management processes for four basic purposes: [1]

1. Human resource decisions, such as pay increases, promotions, and terminations.
2. Feedback to and development of employees.
3. Design and evaluation of various human resource systems, such as company training programs and human resource planning.
4. Documentation of personnel decisions.

Depending on the organization's needs and issues, the performance management process may function better for some of these purposes than others. For example, as you will see below, 360-degree feedback systems may work best for feedback and development of employees. However, this system may not be as effective for making HR decisions. Similarly, a rating form that relies on the comparative approach is not likely to be particularly helpful for feedback and development purposes. Organizations therefore need to carefully consider the purpose of the system as they design the performance management process.

Because all of these purposes are important, an effective performance management process take considerable time and effort to develop and operate. We now turn to a discussion of performance measures and the shortcomings associated with them.

Performance Measures: Objective and Subjective Approaches

There are many different measures of individual job performance. Generally these can be divided into two groups: objective measures and subjective measures. Although objective measures may seem as though they would be the best, they often have serious limitations.

Objective Performance Measures

For certain jobs, objective measures of performance, such as sales, units produced, or papers published, do exist. What about your current job? Are there objective measures of your performance? Certain occupations, such as those in production and sales, lend themselves to objective measures of performance. But if you have ever worked in these fields, you are probably aware that these seemingly objective measures often fail to accurately reflect an individual's performance. Consider, for example, a sales job. Although most sales organizations use an index such as sales volume or number of sales per unit time, other factors often play a role. In any given location, sales may be affected by the local economy, the nature of the businesses in the area, and so on. To take such differences into account, organizations often include a market potential factor in assessing an individual's performance. But the market potential is based on various subjective judgments, which may have shortcomings. Further, the sales volume or the number of sales is separate from the identification of new customers and the maintenance of relationships with existing customers. Even though the identification of new customers and the maintenance of existing customers may be difficult to measure in any objective way, they may be extremely important aspects of the job. In short, despite their apparent objectivity, measures such as sales volume and units produced may have serious shortcomings.[2]

Subjective Performance Measures

For many jobs, there simply is no objective measure of job performance. Particularly in the knowledge-based, service-oriented business world of today, relatively few employees produce a tangible, quantifiable product or service. Instead, they generate knowledge, handle customer complaints, or perform various other intangible services. Or, in the case of an individual production worker, performance is affected by factors such as the machinery and other employees, over which he or she has no control. In these and many other cases, organizations must rely on subjective judgments of an employee's performance, usually made by the employee's supervisor, but more and more frequently, made by customers, peers, and subordinates. It is not surprising, then, that almost all organizations rely on subjective ratings to at least some extent. Box 7.1 offers a global perspective on performance appraisal practices. Despite their popularity, subjective performance ratings are also vulnerable to myriad problems. Next, you will read about these problems and some solutions to them.

Problems with Subjective Performance Appraisals

The problems inherent in subjective performance appraisals can be divided into four categories: judgment errors, poor appraisal forms, lack of rater preparedness, and ineffective organizational policies and practices.

Judgment Errors

People are notoriously poor judges and decision makers, and we are subject to many biases and **"judgment errors."**[3]

1. Halo. The **"halo"** error occurs when one aspect of the subordinate's performance affects the rater's evaluation of other performance dimensions. An employee with

judgment errors
Errors made due to poor judgment, poor decision making, and biases.
halo
This error occurs when one aspect of the subordinate's performance affects the rater's evaluation of other performance dimensions.

INTERCULTURAL ISSUES IN HUMAN RESOURCES

Box 7.1
Performance Management Practices in the Pacific Rim

Contrary to what you might think, performance appraisal practices in Pacific Rim countries differ substantially from one another. Take Singapore and Hong Kong, for example. In an effort to bolster productivity, both of these countries emphasize the importance of performance appraisals, and, like the United States, utilize the reviews for both HRM decisions and developmental feedback. The performance management processes in these countries are often more sophisticated than those found in some U.S. firms. The Fraser Neave and Malayan Brewery Company, headquartered in Singapore, uses a self-appraisal system, which the employee completes at least three days prior to the formal meeting. The self-appraisal form includes such questions as "What are the most important things you have achieved in the past twelve months?" and "In what way would you like to see your career develop within the next three years?"

The Sime Darby company in Singapore uses performance appraisal forms geared toward the specific job. The dimensions on the form are behaviorally defined so that it is clear what high and low performance on each dimension represents. Goals are set for all areas of performance. Managers receive four hours of training in giving performance feedback, as well as training on how to avoid common human judgment errors.

Like the United States, however, most companies in Hong Kong and Singapore use graphic scales, and most small companies have no mechanism for formal performance appraisals. As Yip Yu Bun, owner of a small company in Hong Kong observed, "My 40 employees have worked too long with one another to need a formal appraisal. We know each other extremely well."

Japan has traditionally taken a much different approach to perfor-

mance appraisals than the United States has. The typical system used until recently in Japan focused on personality factors, especially cooperation, and the ability to perform different jobs within the individual's work group. Both of these emphases are in keeping with the Japanese team culture. More recently, however, with Japan's changing economy as well as the increasing Westernization of its culture, there has been an increasing emphasis on individual job performance. Even here, however, there is a difference from many Western approaches—and indeed the approaches taken in other Pacific Rim countries—in that measures of individual job performance often take into account employee effort as well as achievement. In recent times, many Japanese companies have begun incorporating such measures into salary raise decisions.

Source: Adapted from G. Latham and N. Napier, "Chinese Human Resource Management Practices in Hong Kong and Singapore: An Exploratory Study," in *Research in Personnel/Human Resources Management* (Supplement 1; International Human Resources Management), ed. A. Nedd, G. Ferris, and K. Rowland (Greenwich, CT: JAI Press, 1989), 173–99; M. A. Von Glinow and B. J. Chung, "Comparative Human Resource Management Practices in the United States, Japan, Korea, and the People's Republic of China," in *Research in Personnel/Human Resources Management* (Supplement 1; International Human Resources Management), ed. A. Nedd, G. Ferris, and K. Rowland (Greenwich, CT: JAI Press, 1989), 153–71; and T. Mroczkowski and M. Hanaoka, "Continuity and Change in Japanese Management," *California Management Review* 31 (1989): 39–53.

leniency
Many raters give higher performance evaluations than deserved, a practice often created by organizational policies and practices.

severity
A bias in the opposite direction, in which a supervisor has a tendency to rate too harshly.

central tendency
An alternative to the leniency effect where raters rate practically all employees about average.

highly effective interpersonal skills, for example, may be rated higher on other performance dimensions, such as written communication skills, than is appropriate. Conversely, an employee with poor interpersonal skills may be rated lower on other performance dimensions than he or she deserves.[4]

2. **Leniency/Severity.** Many raters routinely give higher performance evaluations than are deserved. If the rating scale ranges from 1 to 5, with 5 being highest, it is not uncommon for 90 percent or more of the employees to be rated either a 4 or 5. This error, referred to as the **"leniency"** effect, is often created by organizational policies and practices, as described later. The **"severity"** effect refers to a bias in the other direction, in which a supervisor has a tendency to rate too harshly.

3. **Central Tendency.** An alternative to the leniency effect is the **central tendency,** which occurs when raters rate practically all employees about average. This way, the manager "plays it safe" because all employees are rated the same.

4. **Fallible Memory.** What were you doing yesterday at this time? What were you doing a week ago at this time? For most of us, including supervisors, our memories tend to focus only on the most important issues and concerns. We usually forget the details of any situation. When asked to recall the minor (or perhaps even major) details, we may fill in the missing gaps based on how we think things ought to be. For example, if someone asked you today what you ate while watching television two months ago, you might say, "potato chips," if that is what you generally eat while watching television, even though you had actually eaten popcorn that time. The same thing tends to happen to managers and supervisors when they are asked to rate a subordinate's performance. Moreover, managers and supervisors tend to remember more recent behaviors and results (known as the recency effect) and therefore more recent events generally have a greater effect on performance ratings. If your performance is going to be rated soon, it may be in your best interests to perform particularly well in the time frame prior to the performance appraisal.

5. **First Impressions.** Almost everyone has experienced a first impression of someone, whereby your subsequent interactions with this person were affected by things he or she said or did when you initially met. In the performance appraisal context, a manager may have a first impression (or primacy effect) that biases his or her evaluation of all subsequent behavior. In the case of a negative primacy effect, the employee may seem to do nothing right; in the case of a positive primacy effect, the employee can do no wrong.

6. **Affect.** Both the rater's general mood and his or her liking or disliking of the employee can affect the performance rating. In terms of general mood, a person who is in a bad mood often rates more harshly than someone in a good mood. There is also evidence that someone in a bad mood will give good performers even higher ratings than they deserve. In terms of your manager's liking for you, not surprisingly, your ratings are likely to be higher if your manager likes you and lower if he or she does not like you.[5]

Poor Appraisal Forms

As you will see in a later section, many types of appraisal forms are available. Some of these forms are more useful than others, but to a large degree, the best form will depend on the situation. Many appraisal forms, however, suffer from the following problems:[6]

1. **Ambiguity.** The scales may be quite vague and unclear. For an example of **ambiguity,** ask three people how they define leadership. You are likely to get three different answers as to what leadership is and what an effective leader does.

2. **Deficiency.** Sometimes a performance appraisal form is missing key aspects of job performance. As you will see near the end of the chapter, one organization almost lost a lawsuit because of such a **deficiency;** only a few aspects of job performance were included on the rating form.

3. **Contamination.** On occasion, a rating form may have additional, irrelevant performance dimensions. Particularly in today's legal environment, where companies must be sure to include only job-related criteria in making personnel decisions, **contamination** with extraneous considerations can be problematic.

4. **Complexity.** If the rating forms are too long and complex, managers may choose to either not fill them out or to complete them in a haphazard fashion.

ambiguity
The rating scales are vague or unclear.

deficiency
When a performance appraisal form is missing key aspects of job performance.

contamination
When a rating form has additional, irrelevant performance dimensions that may contaminate the performance appraisal.

Lack of Rater Preparedness

Managers and supervisors may be unprepared to conduct performance appraisals. Lack of preparedness can come about in several ways:[7]

1. **Low Self-Confidence.** Some raters feel they are not competent to engage in performance management activities and therefore are reluctant to participate. Managers who have low self-confidence in this area will be particularly reluctant to give negative feedback.
2. **Limited Familiarity.** Particularly in today's workplace, with far fewer managers and supervisors than ever before, many raters have limited knowledge of how their subordinates are performing. If you work in a highly technical field, for example, you may report to an individual who has little more than a cursory understanding of your work. Your manager or supervisor therefore may have little knowledge as to your performance. It is therefore often incumbent upon you, the employee, to keep accurate records of your performance and achievements.
3. **Lack of Time.** Given that managers often have many responsibilities and numerous subordinates, they may lack the time to gather sufficient information and to conduct thorough feedback sessions.

Ineffective Organizational Policies and Practices

Many problems with subjective performance appraisals are due to ineffective organizational policies and practices, which undermine performance management processes. Key issues here include the following:[8]

1. **Lack of Rewards.** What motivation does your supervisor have to conduct thorough and careful performance appraisals? In many organizations, there are few, if any, rewards for this activity. Given their many other responsibilities, then, doing performance appraisals may have low priority for managers and supervisors. Recall that in the opening case, Nicholas' manager seemed unwilling to spend much, if any, time giving feedback. Do you think that manager was rewarded for doing performance appraisals? Probably not. Most organizations offer few, if any, tangible rewards, such as pay raises, that are directly attached to performance management processes.
2. **Company Culture Supports Leniency.** Rather than rewards for doing thorough and accurate performance appraisals, the company culture often penalizes supervisors for giving low ratings. Low ratings may be viewed as a sign of managerial failure or as promoting employee discontent. As a result, most employees receive satisfactory ratings, even if they don't deserve them.
3. **Lack of Appropriate Accountability.** Although in most companies the rater's immediate supervisor must approve the ratings, the ratings are rarely challenged. As a result, the rater has little incentive to make accurate ratings, especially when subordinates are likely to become upset with low ratings.

Solutions to Performance Appraisal Problems

Because subjective performance ratings are popular, organizations have applied a variety of tactics to reduce the above problems.

Provide Training to Raters

To increase raters' self-confidence and reduce judgment errors, many companies train raters on how to conduct more effective performance appraisals. Effective training programs include help in understanding how to use the forms, how to give feedback, and so forth.[9]

Involve Users in the Development of Rating Forms

To make the rating forms more usable, some organizations have users participate in their development. In fact, some of the forms described later, such as the BARS, rely heavily on input from managers and supervisors. By being involved in their development, users will be more committed to the final product.[10]

Educate Managers on the Importance of Performance Appraisals

It is important to explain to managers *why* accurate ratings and thorough feedback are important. For example, managers must be persuaded that effective performance appraisals will improve their department's performance. Moreover, managers must be convinced that by giving the best performers the highest ratings, employees who are working hard will be motivated to continue. By the same token, managers must be informed that legal requirements (discussed later in greater detail) dictate that poorly performing employees must be given specific feedback and correspondingly low ratings.

Reward Managers for Performance Appraisals

Managers must be rewarded for conducting effective performance appraisals. At General Electric, for example, managers are held responsible for the development of their subordinates, which includes providing effective feedback. General Electric uses several mechanisms for monitoring a subordinate's development, including the independent evaluations of subordinates and tracking a subordinate's performance as he or she moves to different positions. Because subordinate development affects bonuses, a financial incentive is attached to performance management processes.[11]

Choose Appropriate Raters

Although most organizations involve only the employee's immediate supervisor in the performance evaluation, some organizations have begun to use other raters. In organizations that use teams, for example, coworkers may be the primary source of performance appraisals. Some organizations seek input from customers as well, much as universities and colleges obtain student evaluations of their instructors. Many companies have recently begun using a technique referred to as 360-degree feedback, which you will read about in greater detail later in this chapter.[12]

Even if your company only uses supervisors to give performance ratings, you might consider soliciting feedback from other sources on an informal basis. For example, the employee in the opening case might have sought feedback from other department managers or perhaps other coworkers.

Rating Forms

The popularity of subjective performance ratings has led to development of many different types of rating scales. We will divide them into four categories:

1. Comparative approaches
2. Graphic scales
3. Behaviorally based scales
4. Management-by-objectives

Each of these is described in greater detail next.[13]

Comparative Approaches

comparative approaches
Rating forms that require the rater to compare each employee to the other employees, also known as the bell-shaped curve that is particularly common in freshman and sophomore college courses.

Comparative approaches require the rater to compare each employee to the other employees. Practically everyone has heard of this type of approach in a school setting—the infamous bell-shaped curve that is particularly common in freshman and sophomore college courses is an example of the comparative approach. If you were in a class that used the bell-shaped curve, it meant that a certain percentage of the class would receive Fs, a certain percentage would receive Ds, and so on. Some companies use this type of approach for performance appraisals as well. In a *forced distribution*, a certain fixed percentage of employees must be given the highest rating, a certain percentage the next highest rating, and so forth. An even simpler procedure, the *rank order method*, merely requires the manager to rank order his or her employees from best to worst. The comparative approach has both advantages and disadvantages. The basic advantages include the fact that these systems force managers to assign low ratings or rankings to some employees. As you read earlier, managers are often too lenient in their ratings of employees. Use of comparative rating forms is one way to circumvent this problem. A second advantage is their basic simplicity and ease with which they are developed. The comparative approach has numerous disadvantages as well. A chief disadvantage is that this method tends to produce resentment and bickering among the employees and supervisors, and it makes comparisons between different departments difficult if not impossible. Another disadvantage is that the comparative approach usually provides little concrete information on which to make the comparisons. In terms of providing feedback to employees, then, this method is generally of limited use.

Graphic Scales

graphic scales
A type of performance evaluation form that uses broad, relatively ambiguous work dimensions, such as quality, leadership, and reliability.

A **graphic scale** is a type of form that uses broad, relatively ambiguous work dimensions, such as quality, leadership, and reliability. A good example is shown in Figure 7.2. The major advantage of graphic scales is the ease in developing and using them. You could quickly and easily design four or five graphic scales—such as scales that rate quality of work, quantity of work, managerial effectiveness, and attendance—to rate all the employees in your company. Because the same scales could be used for nearly all jobs, comparisons between different departments, and even employees in different jobs, could be easily made. Given these advantages, it is not surprising that graphic scales are the most commonly used form.[14] These scales also have some potentially serious shortcomings. Due to the ambiguous nature of the scales, different supervisors may ascribe quite different meanings to the dimensions and may have dif-

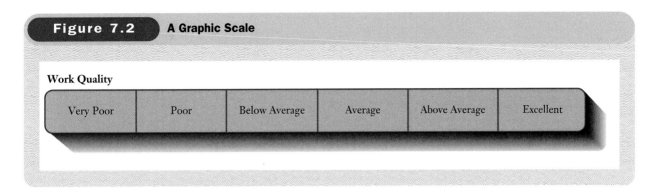

Figure 7.2   A Graphic Scale

Work Quality

Very Poor	Poor	Below Average	Average	Above Average	Excellent

ferent standards for what average, poor, and good performance is. These scales tend to be less useful for feedback purposes as well, because they do not specify what good, average, and poor performance entails.[15]

If you are creating your own graphic scales, a good Web site to go to with a variety of examples with definitions is: www.hr.arizona.edu/ratingfactors.html.

Behaviorally Based Scales

Behaviorally based scales were developed as a response to the shortcomings of the graphic scale approach described above. The major aim of behaviorally based scales is to provide a set of scales that is defined in a precise, behavioral fashion. As an example, consider Figure 7.3, which displays a **behaviorally anchored rating scale,** or BARS.

behaviorally based scales
Developed as a response to the shortcomings of the graphic scale approach, the behaviorally based scale provides a set of scales that are defined in a precise, behavioral fashion.

behaviorally anchored rating scales
A rating system that defines the dimension in terms of behavior and where the points on the scale are defined, or anchored, in behavioral terms.

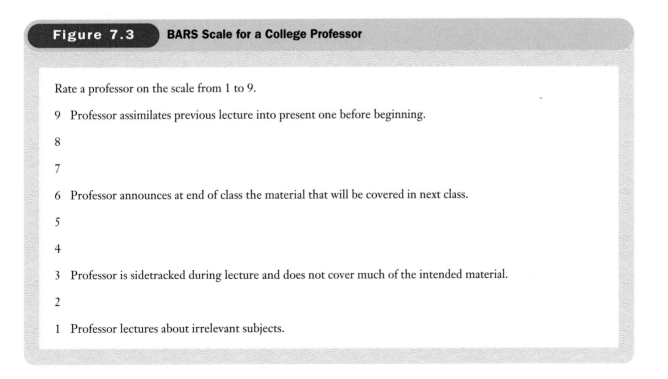

Figure 7.3   BARS Scale for a College Professor

Rate a professor on the scale from 1 to 9.

9   Professor assimilates previous lecture into present one before beginning.

8

7

6   Professor announces at end of class the material that will be covered in next class.

5

4

3   Professor is sidetracked during lecture and does not cover much of the intended material.

2

1   Professor lectures about irrelevant subjects.

Note that several points on the scale are defined, or anchored, in behavioral terms. For example, the instructor who is rated a 9 would be one who assimilates the present lecture into the previous one, an instructor rated somewhere between a 1 and a 2 would be one who spends a great deal of time talking about irrelevant topics. Raters should have a much clearer idea as to what is meant by good, average, and poor performance, which in turn should reduce differences caused by raters using different definitions and standards.[16]

There are several different behaviorally based approaches besides the BARS. With **behavior observation scales (BOS)**, the rater evaluates the frequency with which the employee engages in various behaviors. An overall rating for each dimension is obtained by adding the points assigned to each of the items that fall under that dimension. An example of the BOS form is provided in Table 7.1. If you examine Table 7.1, you will see that the items are nearly identical to the behavioral anchors in the BARS scale in Figure 7.3.[17]

The major advantage of the behaviorally based approach is that the scales are more specific and less ambiguous. In turn, this should result in greater equivalence in the ratings of different supervisors. In practice, however, there is little evidence that behaviorally based ratings produce more accurate, or better, ratings than other approaches. That is, supervisors appear to assign the same ratings, regardless of the specific form used. On the other hand, behaviorally based scales should facilitate feedback to the ratees, because they force the supervisor to be more specific. Similarly, such scales should increase communication between subordinates and supervisors, because expectations and job requirements are more clearly delineated. On the negative side, the development of behaviorally based scales is much more time-consuming than the other forms discussed so far. And, because different scales and standards will exist for different jobs, it may become more difficult to compare employees with different jobs than it is when graphic scales are used.[18]

behavior observation scales
A behaviorally based approach that has the rater evaluate the frequency with which the employee engages in various behaviors.

Management-by-Objectives

Management-by-objectives (MBO) became popular in the 1970s as a means of removing much of the subjectivity in performance appraisals. Essentially, this form uses clearly defined objectives or goals and a specified time frame in which they will be

management-by-objectives
An evaluation system that uses clearly defined objectives or goals, with a specified time frame in which they will be reached.

Table 7.1	BOS Scale for College Professor

Rate how often the professor engages in each of these behaviors using the following scale (1=never; 2=occasionally; 3=sometimes; 4=often; 5=all of the time):

1. Professor assimilates previous lecture into present one before beginning.

2. Professor announces at end of class the material that will be covered in next class.

3. Professor is sidetracked during lecture and does not cover much of the intended material.

4. Professor lectures about irrelevant subjects.

reached. For example, a salesperson may have a goal of increasing sales volume by 20 percent within 9 months, as well as visiting 15 new customers and revisiting 200 previous customers. In many cases, the objectives are established by a joint planning session involving both the subordinate and the supervisor. It is strongly recommended that the objectives be tied to the organization's and department's mission and vision statements. The MBO approach aims to minimize the subjective judgments associated with other forms. Because the objectives are clearly defined and have a specified time frame, it should be clear to any observer at the end of the time period whether or not the goals were met. Moreover, the form encourages extensive employee participation, which should increase employee commitment to the objectives. For some examples of an MBO form that might be used here, see this Web site: http://hrntserver1.lanl.gov/Performance/forms/.

The MBO method is particularly popular for managerial and professional employees because they have considerable control over the objectives to be achieved and the specific behaviors needed to succeed are often ambiguous. Research shows that use of an MBO program can greatly increase productivity, particularly if top management actively supports and participates in the program.[19] Despite MBO's potential advantages, such programs have several weaknesses.[20] One weakness is that different objectives may be set for different individuals doing the same job. Therefore, MBO probably would not be appropriate for determining promotions or pay raises. Second, the objectives may be set too low. Third, use of MBO tends to encourage short-term objectives that are simple to quantify, when in fact a longer-term perspective with more qualitative goals may be appropriate. Nonetheless, with proper modifications, MBO may be an important component in a performance management process. For example, by combining behaviorally based scales with an MBO approach, a thorough performance management process might be developed.[21]

In conclusion, measuring job performance is a complex undertaking. Although there are both objective and subjective methods for measuring job performance, no one method is perfect. As difficult as obtaining accurate measures of performance is, providing effective performance feedback is typically even more challenging. The next section describes some current issues in performance management. Following that, we will discuss why managers and subordinates generally dislike performance feedback and make some suggestions for both receiving feedback and giving feedback. The chapter concludes with some guidelines for maintaining a legally sound performance management process.

Current Issues in Performance Management

In the past few years, 360-degree feedback processes and electronic surveillance have become increasingly popular in organizations. We begin with an explanation of, and some guidelines for, 360-degree processes, followed by a discussion of several critical issues in electronic surveillance systems.

360-Degree Feedback Systems

A **360-degree feedback** system is a performance management process that gathers performance information from multiple parties, including one's subordinates, peers,

360-degree feedback
Information is gathered from a variety of sources, including subordinates who complete performance appraisals, then the results are summarized for the employee and areas needing improvement are discussed.

supervisor, and customers. According to recent estimates, 12 percent of U.S. organizations are using a 360-degree feedback system, while about one-fourth of U.S. organizations are using a part of this kind of system (for example, an upward appraisal system, where subordinates rate their supervisors).[22] See Box 7.2 for an example of how a 360-degree feedback program worked in one small, family-owned organization.

A major advantage of this system is that the feedback comes from multiple sources. If a manager has five subordinates, the manager does not know which subordinate said what, as the results are summarized and averaged. A related assumption is that if there is congruence among the different sources, the feedback will be much more convincing to the recipient. For example, one manager was informed through the 360-degree feedback process that he had a bad habit of standing too close to people. Another major advantage of the 360-degree feedback program is that people give the ratings anonymously, which is likely to reduce some of the reluctance to give negative feedback. In addition, in many organizations, a summary of the feedback is provided by a trained consultant, who will be more comfortable and skilled in this task.[23]

An organization considering adoption of a 360-degree feedback program must make a number of decisions in order for the process to be successful. Some of the most important decisions are as follows:[24]

1. **Decide What Type of Form to Use.** Typical dimensions evaluated in a 360-degree feedback program for supervisors include fairness, coaching, communication, and creating a team environment. The organization must decide whether to use a standardized instrument or to develop its own form. Just as important, while many organizations only use numerical ratings, it is strongly recommended that raters be allowed room for written comments. For a sample form and additional information on 360-degree feedback issues, see this Web site: www.ccl.org/products/benchmarks/benchsamp.htm

2. **Ensure Anonymity of Raters.** It is critical that raters remain anonymous to encourage honest feedback. Because anonymity will not be preserved with only one or two raters, most experts suggest at least five raters in each category (for example, five peers). Research shows that when the raters are not anonymous, they tend to give ratings more positive than they would otherwise give.

3. **Select Raters Carefully.** Many employees would prefer to give the forms to people they know will give them good ratings. This, of course, may defeat the purpose of the process. It is helpful that the employees and their supervisors work together to select raters.

4. **Consider the Purpose of the Process.** It is essential that organizations consider the purpose and goals of the 360-degree feedback process. While the major purpose of this process is strictly used for development and growth purposes, some organizations have begun to use it for HR decisions (for example, pay raises). What problems do you see with using the ratings for HR decisions? Some companies found that employees developed negative attitudes toward the process when it became used to make such decisions, and ratings tended to be higher and presumably less accurate. At the very least, organizations should begin by using the results only for development and growth, and decide later whether the results should be used for other purposes as well.

5. **Train for Effective Use of the System.** All relevant participants in the process must be given appropriate training. The same issues described earlier that plague more traditional subjective performance appraisal systems (for example, judgment

Box 7.2
Using Subordinate Ratings at a Small, Family-Owned Business

Not only medium and large companies use 360-degree feedback programs for developmental purposes. Take the Brownstein Group, a successful advertising and public relations firm based in Philadelphia that has about 20 employees. Marc Brownstein, the president of this firm, and his father, the CEO, were happy with the company's growth and felt all was going well, until Marc took an executive development course several years ago. As a result of the course, he asked his top managers to anonymously evaluate his performance. To Marc's complete surprise, the feedback was not positive. Criticisms included that he was a poor listener, gave little feedback, provided little structure, and offered scant business information.

In light of Brownstein's high turnover rate, Marc realized that he needed to make some changes to ensure the business's survival. One change that he implemented was monthly meetings for the entire company to discuss any issues of concern and to provide information about company trends and news. But a much more difficult and expensive issue raised by employees was the nature of their benefits program. Employees wanted a life insurance program, a retirement plan, and more vacation time. Although reluctant at first, Marc eventually agreed to most of the requests, despite the fact that it would take about 2 percent of the company's budget in the first year. Perhaps the most difficult change for

Marc to accept was giving up the authority that he had shared with his father, in deciding which customers to solicit and to accept. Now, these decisions are based on a vote by the managers. This change was recently tested when a company offered to pay the Brownstein group $1.5 million to create a film. Despite the CEO's desire to accept this contract, the employees voted against it. Marc is still struggling with ways to create more structure for the firm. In the meantime, the feedback seems to have paid off: turnover has been reduced by 50 percent, billings are the highest ever, and the agency recently won a coveted award.

Source: Adapted from H. Stout, "Self-Evaluation Brings Change to a Family's Ad Agency," *Wall Street Journal*, 6 January 1998, B2.

errors) can affect a 360-degree feedback program. Raters, for example, should be trained to avoid halo, central tendency, and other errors. The person giving the feedback summary must be trained. And finally, employees must be given training so that they understand the results and most importantly, are able to effectively use the results to improve and develop.

6. **Maintain Follow-Up.** It is essential for organizations to create a follow-up process after the results are presented to the employees. One organization conducts smaller-scale 360-degree processes so that employees receive ratings of their performance several times each year. IBM makes it clear to managers that poor ratings must improve within two or three years, or they will be demoted. The employees' managers become critical agents in the follow-up process and must be trained to provide positive recognition for improvements that have occurred.

The question that you may be asking at this point is: "Does 360-degree feedback really work?" It may surprise you to learn that despite the relatively large number of companies conducting 360-degree feedback, relatively few have conducted any scientific research on this question. Nonetheless, one recent study found that managers who received low or average ratings from their subordinates experienced an improvement in performance over a six-month period.[25] Thus there is some evidence that 360-degree programs can work effectively. Other organizations have implemented this process because of its current popularity and found that the program did not lead to improvement.[26] Like most HRM processes, the way it is implemented and used can have a large impact on its effectiveness.

Electronic Performance Monitoring

Probably anyone who has ever talked on the telephone with a customer service representative has heard the message at least once that "this telephone call may be monitored." Indeed, it is estimated that the number of employees whose performance is electronically monitored has risen from about 8 million to 30 million in the past few years. It is estimated that companies spend upwards of $1 billion annually for this purpose.[27] Businesses argue that the ability to electronically monitor employees has great payoffs. For example, John Gerdelman, senior vice president for consumer markets at MCI, argues that the ability to listen in on phone calls helps a company train workers and improve customer service. MCI, Pacific Bell, and other phone companies assert that they have been able to vastly improve their service because of the use of electronic monitoring. A California insurance company attributes its 15 percent productivity improvement to the implementation of electronic performance monitoring. Michael Tamer, president of an electronic performance monitoring system company, argues that the benefits of these programs extend to everyone, including the customer. (To learn more about such products, check this Web site: www.teknekron.com)[28]

Critics of electronic performance monitoring argue that these systems constitute a violation of employee privacy. They argue that electronic performance monitoring can lead to misuse, such as videotaping employees in their dressing areas. Most importantly, however, critics argue that electronic monitoring leads to increased stress, more health problems, and greater dissatisfaction with the job. For example, one survey found that 81 percent of respondents indicated that such systems made their jobs more stressful.[29]

The American Civil Liberties Union (ACLU) is one of the most outspoken critics of electronic performance monitoring. They advocate that companies use the following guidelines for the electronic performance monitoring system:

1. Send a notice to employees of the company's electronic monitoring practices;
2. Use a signal to let an employee know when he or she is being monitored;
3. Ensure employee access to all personal electronic data collected through monitoring;
4. Forbid monitoring of areas designed for the health or comfort of employees;
5. Ensure the right to dispute and delete inaccurate data;
6. Ban the collection of data unrelated to work performance; and
7. Restrict disclosure of personal data to others without the employee's consent.[30]

You can find more information on the ACLU position at this Web site: www.aclu.org/library/pbr2.html. Box 7.3 lists additional Web sites that discuss performance management.

One recent, carefully designed and conducted study reported intriguing results regarding the effects of electronic performance monitoring as follows:[31]

1. High-ability workers performed better with the monitoring, while low-ability workers performed worse with monitoring;

Box 7.3

Here are four useful Web sites for performance management issues. They range between examples of on-line rating forms, practical advice, and software that you can examine or purchase to conduct performance management processes.

www.people.memphis.edu/~hresources/employ-pa/pahome.htm This Web site contains a performance appraisal rating form that can be used on-line and printed off to make a report. It also provides a useable format that can be adapted to other organizations.

www.performance-appraisal.com/archer.htm This Web site contains a complete performance management process, including forms, training guidelines, and so forth. Look at the information provided. Do you think it is a good system?

http://hr2.hr.arizona.edu/HRInfoSeries3.htm#E This Web site contains a wealth of information about why performance management processes are important, what information should be contained on the form, and general procedures and policies from a large organization.

http://www.austin-hayne.com/index4.htm This Web site allows you to download interesting and handy software that will enable you to conduct performance management processes from your computer. The software contains many samples to help a manager to write out narrative reports.

2. Monitoring increased the stress levels reported by participants in the study;

3. Working in a group alleviated the stress to some degree.

Based on this study, then, the results of electronic performance monitoring are not simple. In the mid-1990s, Senator Paul Simon of Illinois introduced legislation in Congress to restrict the use of such systems. This bill, however, has since lain dormant and shows no sign of being revived any time soon.[32] In sum, all trends point to electronic performance monitoring being here to stay. We turn now to an examination of how to give and get helpful performance feedback. We begin this with a discussion of why people find it difficult to give and to get feedback about their work.

Performance Feedback: Why Is It So Difficult?

While it may be difficult to obtain accurate measures of job performance, giving performance feedback poses an even greater difficulty for many managers and supervisors. As one expert stated it, providing performance feedback is like approaching someone and saying "Here's what I think of your baby."[33] Recall that the manager in the opening case seemed to have no interest in giving feedback. Some possible reasons were already mentioned for this, including the lack of any rewards. It is also possible that the manager was uncomfortable at the mere thought of giving feedback. Why is giving feedback such an uncomfortable task for most managers? If you examine Figure 7.4, you will see that for both the supervisor and the employee, the performance feedback context contains certain inherent conflicts. Recall that from the supervisor's perspective, performance appraisals serve several major purposes, including helping the supervisor to make HRM decisions and develop employees. A manager may experience conflict between his or her role in developing an employee and the need to reprimand the employee for poor performance. From the employee's perspective, there is conflict

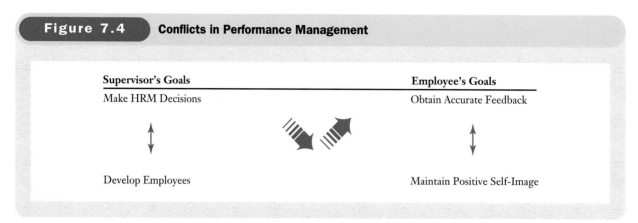

Figure 7.4   **Conflicts in Performance Management**

Supervisor's Goals   Employee's Goals

Make HRM Decisions   Obtain Accurate Feedback

Develop Employees   Maintain Positive Self-Image

Source: Adapted from M. Beer, "Performance Appraisal: Dilemmas and Possibilities," *Organizational Dynamics* 27 (1981): 24–36.

in receiving performance feedback as well. On the one hand, most people do desire feedback about how they are doing. However, this desire may conflict with the need to maintain positive self-esteem. Most employees, then, look forward to getting positive feedback but often dread the negative feedback they may hear. Coupled with the fact that many managers are not well prepared to give effective feedback, it is hardly surprising that conducting a performance feedback session is considered one of the most dreaded managerial tasks. In many cases, employees receive little constructive feedback and leave the feedback session even more confused than before. Moreover, employees often perceive their supervisors more negatively after the feedback session than they did before the session. The situation described in the opening case, then, is certainly not unusual.[34]

Now that you have read about some reasons as to why the feedback process is often difficult for both parties, you will learn some strategies for improving these sessions. First, we will discuss what managers and supervisors can do to increase the effectiveness of the feedback process. Next, we will examine some suggestions for employees preparing to receive feedback.

Handling Performance Reviews: The Managerial Perspective

This section provides guidelines for supervisors and managers conducting feedback reviews. You will read first about some general suggestions, followed by specific steps for giving feedback. In addition, Box 7.4 offers a quiz for trying your hand at handling performance feedback situations.

General Suggestions for Conducting Feedback Reviews

1. **Distinguish between Formal and Informal Feedback Sessions.** Effective managers use informal feedback sessions on an "as needed" basis. The primary purpose of an informal feedback session is to help a subordinate who is having performance problems. Most organizations also require the manager to meet with his or her sub-

YOUR TURN

Box 7.4
Handling Performance Feedback: A Quiz

Read each of the following situations. Make notes on what you would recommend the manager do. Compare your suggestions to those of Andrew Grove, president and CEO of Intel Corporation, which follow the situations.

Situation 1. Whenever criticized about job performance, the manager's assistant begins to look stubborn and upset, so the manager hesitates to continue. Instead, the manager simply corrects the assistant's work by himself.

Situation 2. A recently hired manager made some passing comments criticizing the quality of the work in her department. These comments have circulated throughout the department, and the manager is concerned that she has alienated the staff.

Situation 3. In a recent feedback situation, the manager's subordinate began to cry. Since then, the manager has acquired the reputation of being an SOB. That didn't seem to be a problem until the manager's boss told him that his style was too abrasive and his promotion chances could be adversely affected. What should the manager do now?

Situation 4. An employee's supervisor recently got married and as a result is spending less time and focusing less on the workplace. The department's productivity has fallen somewhat as a result. What should the employee say to her supervisor?

Answers According to Andrew Grove

Situation 1. When discussing the employee's performance, ignore the assistant's facial expressions and deal with the issues at hand. Find a later time, when things are going well, to bring up the matter of the employee's facial expressions, focusing on specific details (for example, "When we were discussing an error in the report last time, you began to frown and your face began to show anger") and discuss the implications for work (you might say, "That kind of expression sends a message to the other party that you don't really want to get the feedback, even though it may be crucial for work effectiveness"). Since the assistant's expression seems to affect the manager's ability to give needed feedback, it is important to discuss this.

Situation 2. Do not take back the comments. If indeed there are problems with the work quality, it is important that the feedback be given and the problems corrected. The manager must, however, plan a procedure for giving the feedback in a more effective, professional manner.

Situation 3. Having tough standards does not mean that one is an SOB. The manager must focus on giving feedback in a constructive and fair fashion. It is important to be consistent; being the "nice guy" won't work either. The expression "tough but fair" is where it's at.

Situation 4. The employee should have a private meeting with her supervisor and share these observations, using some specific examples. If the supervisor doesn't realize what's happening, there is no point in trying again. If the supervisor doesn't change, the employee shouldn't worry. Let the supervisor's boss take care of the problem.

Source: Adapted from A. Grove, "Criticism: Giving It Effectively," *Working Woman*, June 1993, 18–20.

ordinates once a year in a more formal manner to review their performances. As a manager, you should use the annual, formal session as an opportunity to summarize the employee's performance for the year, set goals for the next year, and discuss any general issues or concerns. If done properly, there should be no unpleasant surprises for the employee in this meeting.[35]

2. **Focus on Behavioral Examples.** In giving performance feedback, be sure to use specific, behaviorally based examples of the employee's performance. Criticizing employees in terms of their personality traits or attitudes has two disadvantages. To

understand this, imagine that someone told you that you were lazy. How would you feel? Compare that to someone saying that you completed your orders a day later than most of the other employees. How would you feel then? Do you see the difference? In the first approach, you probably took the criticism as a personal attack. The latter approach was not an attack on you; it was a criticism of your behavior. In all likelihood, you would take the latter statement far less personally. Perhaps just as importantly, if someone tells you that you are lazy, it may not be at all clear to you why you are getting this feedback and what you need to change. If you were told that your orders are later than most of your coworkers, you would have a far better idea of what to change. Whenever you give feedback, it is critical to state the negatives, as well as the positives, using specific, behavioral examples.[36]

3. **Seek the Employee's Input.** No matter what the focus of the performance review session, it is critical for the manager to obtain input from the employee. There are several reasons for this, but two stand out. First, in today's workplace, most employees actively seek to participate in a variety of ways. Active participation in the performance review session is viewed by many employees as important. Second, active participation will help build commitment to the results of the review session. An effective manager is able to provide many participation opportunities during the feedback session.[37]

4. **Carefully Plan the Feedback Session.** As with any business activity, you should plan carefully and determine an agenda before the session. Be sure to obtain as much information about the person you are evaluating as possible. Consider what questions, issues, or even challenges he or she might raise. Of course, be sure to provide sufficient time and opportunity to address any issues your subordinate may bring up. Sometimes, particularly when there are many issues to discuss, it may be best to schedule a second or even third meeting.[38]

5. **Use Effective Communication Skills During the Feedback Session.** Good communication skills are essential to an effective review session. Given the discomfort and awkwardness typically felt by both the appraiser and the ratee, it is critical that both parties fully understand what has been said. One way to do this is to make frequent use of summary statements. By restating your point and paraphrasing the employee's reaction, you will ensure that you understand each other. Be certain to also use good nonverbal communication skills, such as nodding, leaning forward, and much eye contact. Those behaviors indicate that you are listening and taking the session seriously.[39]

6. **Emphasize the Developmental Aspect as Much as Possible.** To the greatest extent possible, you should emphasize the development and growth opportunities for the employee. This is just as important in the United States as it is in other parts of the world. For example, a major complaint of Mexican workers is that their supervisors tend to treat them as mere numbers, rather than as people. One way to avoid this problem is to emphasize the developmental nature of performance management processes.[40]

7. **Document Everything.** Recall that our memories, especially in the long term, are quite limited. It therefore is helpful if you keep careful notes about the employee's performance and the discussion that you held. As you will also see later in this chapter, proper documentation is helpful if there is a legal challenge.[41]

Now that you have read some general guidelines, we will discuss specific steps for giving feedback. As you will see, the approach a manager takes should depend on the nature of the situation.

Conducting Performance Reviews: Specific Steps for Managers

The nature of the performance review session depends heavily on the employee's general performance, as well as on the purpose of the session (that is, is this the formal, end-of-the-year session or an informal meeting for immediate feedback?). Generally speaking, the informal session is used to solve specific performance problems, while the formal session is used more to summarize the employee's performance for the year and discuss future goals and developmental needs. Let's first start with a set of steps for an informal feedback session.[42]

Conducting the Informal Feedback Session

1. **Summarize General Performance.** If the employee is generally satisfactory, you may begin by informing the employee that you are generally quite satisfied with his or her work. Give specific examples of the employee's strengths or major achievements. In more serious cases (for example, the employee's overall performance is not satisfactory), you should skip this step.

2. **Introduce Problem Area.** If the employee's performance is generally acceptable, move to the problem area by saying something like, "But there is an area where there is room for improvement. . . ." If the employee's general performance is generally not acceptable, begin with a general statement like, "There are some job performance concerns that we need to discuss. Let me begin here. . . ." Give some specific examples of the employee's performance, then explain the company's expectations or standards (for instance, you might say, "As you know, the company maintains a scrap rate level of 1 percent or less, and your work clearly is above that"). This step is easier described than done; see Box 7.5 for handling two common employee reactions.

3. **Determine Cause of Problem.** In this step, the manager asks the subordinate what he or she thinks is the cause or source of the problem. Although you may have your own ideas as to what the causes are, there are several reasons to have the employee provide explanations. First, you may be wrong. Second, having the employee determine the causes will begin to establish commitment to the next steps. As the manager, feel free to probe the employee about the alleged causes, and clearly state your concerns to the employee if you disagree with the reasons brought forth. In some cases, the employee may say, "I didn't know that was the expectation." In most cases, however, once the possible causes are determined, you should go to the next step, which focuses on solutions to the problem. Be aware that if an employee discusses a cause that could be a disability, you need to be extremely careful so that you do not violate the Americans with Disabilities Act.

4. **Obtain Solutions.** Once you have determined the probable causes of the problem, it is time to address solutions. As in Step 3, it is helpful to turn to the employee for possible solutions. The manager should say something like, "Now that we've discussed the causes, what can we do to solve the problem?" Again, if the employee comes up with the solution, he or she will be more likely to accept and follow through with it than if you come up with the solution. On the other hand, you should participate fully in discussing possible solutions. The final solution must be something that is acceptable to you, the manager, as well. If, for example, the proposed solution is going to be too costly or cause resentment among other employees, you may need to reject it. Be reasonable, though, and if you must reject it, don't

YOUR TURN

Box 7.5
Handling Employee Responses to Criticism

Employees react differently to criticism. Although some employees readily accept negative feedback and will initiate a discussion on how to improve, some employees will respond either by denying the problem exists or by becoming angry. In the former case, the employee may respond by saying, "That's not my fault; that problem is caused by stations further down the production line!" In the latter case, the employee might respond by saying something like, "For what the job pays, you certainly can't expect perfection!" Here are some suggestions for dealing with those reactions.

Handling Denial
Provide additional evidence (such as specific examples) of the problem. Explain exactly why the employee's performance constitutes a problem and what the implications of the problem are for the organization (lost customers, more waste, and so on). If the employee persists in denying the problem, you may have to explain the consequences of not improving ("Given the importance of this issue, I may be forced to take disciplinary action if change is not forthcoming").

Handling Anger
You definitely do not want to get into a shouting match and say things you will regret later. Although it may be easy for you to lose your temper when the employee is hostile toward you (after all, the employee might really be affecting your department's success, so how dare the employee get angry?), it is most important that you stay calm. Further, you should try to calm the employee down and let him or her vent anger. Saying something like, "I can tell you're pretty angry. Why don't you give me your perspective in more detail" may be helpful.

Or, you might say, "I'm rather surprised by your strong reaction. Perhaps there are some issues I'm not aware of that you would like to discuss." If the employee can't seem to calm down, you might consider requesting another time in the near future to discuss the issue. A statement like, "You seem pretty upset by this. I'd rather schedule a meeting first thing tomorrow when we have both had more time to think about the issues." You can choose to meet at a later time, but don't back off. Delaying the meeting more than 24 hours is only going to work against you. Be sure to explain your persistence in dealing with the problem by emphasizing the importance to the department and organization. If the employee remains angry even after these attempts, you will have to consider possible disciplinary action.

Source: Adapted from S. Pollan and M. Levine, "Finding the Right Words: Criticizing an Employee's Work," *Working Woman*, November 1993, 18, 80.

sound overbearing. Say something like, "I think that you have proposed a good solution, but other employees will be resentful if you are always coming to work later. Is there some other way we can modify the solution to avoid such problems?"

Recall that under the Americans with Disabilities Act, an employee has the right to request a reasonable accommodation to perform the essential functions of the job. Be aware that if the employee asks for such an accommodation, you may have a legal requirement to provide one. What constitutes a request for a reasonable accommodation? EEOC guidelines note that to request accommodation, an individual may use "plain English" and need not mention the ADA or use the phrase "reasonable accommodation."[43] Thus, you need to be careful if you are a manager or supervisor to properly understand when and if a request for accommodation has been made.

5. **Establish Goals.** Now that you have agreed to a solution, set a goal to achieve the improved performance within a short, but reasonable, time frame. Be sure to have the employee participate in this phase as well. Finally, summarize your agreements, and set a time for a follow-up meeting. You will probably want to write down the solution and the goals, and consider having the employee sign this document and

keep a copy for himself or herself. Arrange for another meeting in the near future so that you can both evaluate the improvement.

6. **Encourage the Employee.** End the meeting on a positive, upbeat note by indicating your confidence in the employee. Saying something like, "I have confidence that you will succeed, and I look forward to meeting you again on the date we've set" is usually a good way to end.

7. **Document the Meeting.** Take careful notes on everything said. This will be particularly critical if improvement does not occur and you need to discipline the individual.

8. **If the Problem Persists.** If the employee's performance has not come up to standards by the next meeting, you will need to decide what to do next. If you think that the employee simply needs a little more time to improve, you may indicate that his or her performance is still unsatisfactory, but you would like to know what could be done to bring it up to par. If, on the other hand, you see little or no improvement, you should summarize what you said at the initial meeting and go through the above steps once again. This time, however, you will probably need to mention that if improvement is not forthcoming, you will need to take disciplinary action (disciplinary action is discussed in greater detail in Chapter 16).

Conducting the Formal Performance Review Session

There are many different ways to conduct the formal annual performance review session. Some organizations have specific procedures that managers must follow; other organizations leave the conduct of this session largely to the manager. The more effectively you handle this session, the more productive your subordinates will be. As you read earlier, there should be no major surprises for the employee during the formal review if you have given appropriate informal feedback throughout the year. This session should focus on summarizing the employee's performance and setting an agenda for the next year. Here are some basic steps to follow:[44]

1. **Summarize the Employee's Performance.** Regardless of the specific rating form used, you should begin by summarizing how the employee has done. Be sure to provide specific examples of the employee's performance. Assuming the employee's performance is at least minimally acceptable, begin with the positives. After that, discuss any problem areas. You may also wish to ask how the employee feels about his or her performance.

2. **Establish Objectives and Areas for Improvement for the Next Year.** No matter how successful the employee, there are always areas for improvement and it is always helpful to focus on future objectives. The organization's and department's mission and vision statement can be extremely helpful here in determining those objectives, even if they are not part of the performance appraisal form. Ask the employee for input in setting those goals, and make sure that the employee actively participates in setting them. Share the mission and vision statement with the employee, using it as a guide. Depending on the nature of the job and organization, this may be a large or small part of the focus of the session.

3. **Discuss the Employee's Developmental Needs.** In the case of an outstanding employee, this area might consume most of the feedback session. For an average employee in a job where there is little opportunity for promotion and advancement, this topic may take up far less time. Regardless, the focus here should be on further opportunities for career development, skills enhancement, and so forth. You might

begin this part of the review session by turning to the employee and saying something like, "We've talked about your overall performance for the year, and established some directions for the next year. Now I'd like to talk about your career development plans. What activities or opportunities would be useful for you?"

4. **Summarize the Session.** This is a final opportunity to be sure that both the manager and the employee understood what has been said. As a manager, then, take the lead by summarizing the key issues that were covered in the session. Then, ask the employee if he or she has any additional comments or questions to ask.

In sum, despite its importance to successful organizations, performance feedback is often one of the most neglected aspects of management. Failure to successfully provide useful feedback will hurt the most effective organization.

Handling Performance Reviews: The Employee Perspective

Perhaps the best way for you, as an employee, to understand the importance of the performance management process is to compare it to visiting the dentist. Consider, for a moment, the consequences of skipping the annual visit to the dentist or waiting for your toothache to disappear by itself. In almost every situation, as uncomfortable and unpleasant as the visit may be, the alternatives (for instance, a root canal procedure) are far more painful. Similarly, although many employees dread the performance feedback sessions, the alternatives are only worse. Quite the contrary, an effective performance appraisal session can provide much information on other opportunities in the company, as well as a chance to get some accurate and helpful feedback about an employee's strengths and weaknesses. Here are some suggestions for how employees can enhance the value of the performance management process:[45]

1. **The Performance Management Process Is a Joint Responsibility.** As an employee you shouldn't view this session as only your manager's responsibility. Rather, view the performance appraisal as a joint effort. Take an active role in setting up meetings, establishing goals, and reviewing your performance.

2. **Plan Carefully.** Once you accept joint responsibility, you become equally responsible for planning. Some organizations have a formal mechanism to facilitate your preparation, such as a self-rating form. Even if your organization does not have a formal mechanism, it is important for you to make a list of your accomplishments, achievements, and any training programs you have completed during the last year. You should also conduct an honest evaluation of your own performance. That way, you will be prepared if your manager asks you for input on how you did or if he or she seems to have overlooked some aspect of your performance. Don't be surprised, however, if your self-rating is higher than your manager's rating of your performance. Research indicates that most people rate their performance higher than others rate it.

3. **Take an Active Role.** While some managers will run an effective session, you can't always count on that happening; you may need to ensure that key issues are covered. For example, if the manager fails to provide clear goals, you should raise this issue with the manager. Be sure that you understand what the goals are, how performance will be measured, and what resources (such as training) are available to meet those goals. Do not be embarrassed by or too humble about your performance. Because performance reviews are often used to make salary and promotion recom-

mendations, it is important that your performance be properly evaluated. Be careful, though, in how you go about addressing these issues. You certainly do not want your supervisor to think you are being too aggressive or undermining his or her authority. Returning to the opening case of this chapter, recall that the employee wanted to get more feedback, but felt the manager was simply not interested. One suggestion would be for the employee to try to schedule a different time, perhaps after work, to get more specific feedback. Another suggestion would be for the employee to explain why getting feedback would be useful (for example, "With some more specific feedback, I could contribute much more to the department and organization").

4. **Handle Negative Feedback Effectively.** Most managers are extremely uncomfortable giving negative feedback, and they usually are ineffective in handling such situations. Frequently, a manager will delay giving critical feedback, which may create more problems than advantages for the employee. In that sense, it is better to be told the negative feedback than to have your manager hide it from you. But many of us find negative feedback difficult to accept, and we have a tendency to become defensive when we hear it. Rather than learning from such feedback, many people tend to explain it in some way ("My boss doesn't like me, so she finds reasons to criticize my work"). Box 7.6 provides suggestions for dealing with criticism.

Performance Management and the Law

Like any other HRM practice, performance appraisals are subject to legal scrutiny. Many court cases, involving alleged violations of civil rights laws, have focused on the appropriateness of the performance appraisals. Following are recommendations to organizations and managers to improve the chances the performance appraisal system will pass legal muster.[46]

1. **Be Sure the Performance Measures Are Job Related.** Although this may sound obvious, some organizations are ineffective in measuring work performance. For example, in one case, a rank-order comparison was used that was based on only three performance areas. Although the organization eventually won the case, the court criticized the performance appraisal as being too narrowly focused. Clearly, all relevant aspects of the job should be addressed in a performance appraisal system.[47] One of the best ways to ensure this is to use job analysis (see Chapter 5) as the basis for developing a performance management process.[48]

2. **Use a Clearly Defined Form with Written Standards.** While the use of behaviorally based forms is recommended by professionals, the court system does not appear to prefer them over other approaches, nor do the courts consider objective measures to be inherently superior. For example, in one lawsuit, an investigator was terminated by the Equal Employment Opportunity Commission (even the EEOC can be charged with discrimination!) for poor performance. The EEOC's defense was that it used an objective system whereby each investigator was required to complete four investigations per month. Upon careful examination, however, it was determined that the plaintiff had been given the most difficult assignments, and he ultimately won the case. Hence, no system is necessarily perfect; it will depend on the particular situation.[49] Nonetheless, organizations will be legally safer if the forms include specific, written instructions for supervisors responsible for the ratings.[50]

YOUR TURN

Box 7.6

Suggestions for How Employees Can Deal with Negative Feedback

1. **Avoid Being Defensive.** Even though the criticisms may be hurtful when you hear them, the negative feedback you receive may well contain important information that you are completely unaware of. It is therefore critical that you listen carefully and stay calm. Above all, don't get angry. Becoming hostile or aggressive toward the person giving the criticism will only work against you.

2. **Check Your Self-Esteem.** If you do feel humiliated by the feedback, consider why you feel that way. Do you view the criticism as a threat to your self-esteem? Again, given that many managers are ineffective in giving criticism, your manager may simply be handling the situation poorly. But that does not mean that the feedback is unjustified.

3. **Get Enough Information.** You may have difficulty concentrating when you first hear the negative information, causing you to miss key points. Be sure you understand the feedback and ask clarifying questions if you do not. It may be useful to request follow-up discussions, particularly after you have a chance to think about the feedback. So, one way to handle the feedback is to say something like, "You have given me some critical, but constructive, feedback. I'd like to spend some time thinking about it more carefully and considering some ways to improve. Afterward, I would like to meet with you again to discuss some strategies and work out a mutually agreeable plan. Can we meet in, say, two days?"

4. **Develop a Strategy.** You will probably need some time to think privately about the feedback and develop a strategy for dealing with the information you have received. Along these lines, you may want to verify the criticism. For example, are there other individuals (for example, a coworker, a mentor outside of work) whom you can go to for a "reality check"? Is this the first time anyone has ever mentioned the problem(s), or have you received similar feedback before? Once you have determined whether there is merit to the feedback, you should begin to develop a plan. Focus on the most important issues first, and decide what you can do to change. Perhaps some type of training program or seminar would be helpful; your manager may even be willing to pay the costs. Whatever the case, be sure you respond to the person who provided the feedback.

The critical comments you get may be the most useful feedback you ever receive. Demonstrating to your manager that you are able to accept the feedback in a professional, effective manner may really change his or her mind about your abilities.

Source: Adapted from J. James, "Dealing with Criticism during an Evaluation," *Nursing*, vol. 21, (September 1991): 103–104.

3. **Have the Performance Ratings Scrutinized by Other Parties.** In several court cases, a major factor in a favorable decision for the organization has been the use of reviews by parties other than the supervisor. In one instance, the organization had terminated two employees for poor performance after they had completed a training program. In the courtroom, the organization demonstrated that the decision was based on reviews by four separate parties: the training supervisor, the line supervisor, the training director, and an executive board. Independent reviews by several different parties are often viewed as a vehicle for eliminating bias by any one individual. It is recommended that the manager's supervisor, as well as the HRM department, serve as independent checks.[51]

4. **Require Documentation.** It is essential to properly document the basis for performance ratings and the reasons why HRM decisions, particularly terminations, were made. Given that a lawsuit will generally require the managers involved in

these activities to explain their decision, careful, accurate, and detailed notes are invaluable.

5. **Provide Guidance and Counseling to Poor Performers.** In some court cases, the judges have considered whether the plaintiff was provided an opportunity to improve his or her performance. For example, in one case, a sales representative working for Xerox was given written warnings regarding customer complaints and was placed on a one-month performance improvement program, which was extended an additional month at his request. When the performance was not forthcoming, the plaintiff was warned that he would be terminated if his performance did not improve. Although the employee sued after being terminated, the court ruled in favor of Xerox, given the attempts to improve his performance.

At the other extreme, in some cases the plaintiffs have argued that they were completely unaware of any performance deficiencies up until the day they were fired. A recent review of federal appeals court decisions found that employees won the vast majority of cases where the organization failed to provide them with information about the performance ratings they had received.[52] It is therefore critical that employees see their evaluations. One way many companies ensure awareness is to have each employee sign the form, indicating the ratings have been seen. That way, if the employee later claims that he or she did not see the ratings, the organization can prove that the employee did in fact know about them.

❖ Conclusion

Performance management processes play an integral role in human resources. As you read, performance management processes are used for a variety of purposes, including salary raises, terminations, employee development, and program evaluation. Subjective rating approaches, which are quite popular, suffer from various problems, including rating errors, poor forms, lack of rater preparedness, and ineffective organizational policies and practices. A variety of suggestions were offered to overcome these problems. Recent approaches to performance management have involved more parties, including customers, subordinates, and coworkers, as well as newer electronic technologies. Although giving and receiving performance feedback can be difficult, numerous suggestions were offered for handling the review process. If done properly, both organization and employee will profit.

❖ Applying Core Concepts

1. Explain why organizations use performance management processes.
2. What performance management process does the company you work for (or a close friend works for) use? What are some problems the company has with the system? What could the company do to solve those problems?

3. Think of a time when an employee you supervised or interacted with as a customer did something wrong. How would you have given him or her feedback?
4. Think of a time when someone gave you feedback in an ineffective fashion. Given what you read in this chapter, how could you have reacted to improve the usefulness of the feedback?
5. What advantages do you see in gathering performance ratings over the Internet? What disadvantages do you see? What about giving performance feedback over the Internet, using either e-mail or Instant Messenger? Do you think you would be more comfortable this way than in a face-to-face meeting? Why?
6. What are your feelings about electronic performance monitoring? Would you like or dislike it? Explain your answer.

❖ Key Terms

Judgment errors	Contamination	Behavior observation
Halo	Comparative approaches	scales
Leniency	Graphic scales	Management-by-
Severity	Behaviorally based scales	objectives
Central tendency	Behaviorally anchored	360-degree feedback
Ambiguity	rating scales	
Deficiency		

❖ CHAPTER 7 *Experiential Exercise 1:*

Completing Performance Appraisal Forms
Performance Management

Your task is to complete the performance appraisal form for both of the employees described below and prepare to give feedback to each employee. Also, make recommendations as to how you would change the rating form for next time you need to make ratings. Be prepared to explain your reasoning. Here are several things you should know about Mary Wilson and Jack Smith:

1. They have both worked for the company for three years.
2. They have roughly the same experience and education; although they are both administrative assistants, they have somewhat different responsibilities.
3. They are paid the same ($29,000), and this is average compared to other administrative assistants in the company.

4. Their previous supervisor never criticized their work and seemed to have been satisfied with their performance.
5. You have been their supervisor for one year.
6. Finally, assume the employees are likely to talk together about whatever you tell them.

Jack Smith

Jack Smith has worked as an administrative assistant for five years with the company. He is responsible for scheduling meetings, filing correspondence, responding to customer inquiries, and completing reports. On the negative side, he has had some disagreements with customers. In one situation, he became noticeably irate over the phone with a customer and ended up slamming the phone down. On another occasion, a customer demanded to speak with Jack's supervisor. When you got on the phone, the customer said that Jack had tried to cut her call off and refused to answer some of her questions. When you asked Jack about the incident, he said that he was busy that day and was rushing to go to a meeting. Another shortcoming appears to be in filing correspondence. Jack seems to make more mistakes than other administrative assistants. On at least three occasions, a file was totally misplaced in the drawers, and Jack took several hours to locate it. On the positive side, Jack has come up with several creative ideas for the reports. One of the most innovative contributions he made was the computerization of the reports, which saves the company hundreds of hours. He has also developed a customer satisfaction survey, which is now used by several other departments. He developed these ideas on his own, although he sought your approval when he completed them. In other areas, Jack seems about average, and there have been no complaints about his performance from other employees. Jack seems to really like his job, and has told you that he has no interest in moving to other jobs or other departments. As he said when you first met, "I really like working here, I do a good job, and I have zero interest in moving elsewhere."

Mary Wilson

Mary's responsibilities include typing papers and reports. She has been with the company for 10 years. She is also responsible for handling customer inquiries and serving as a coordinator between different departments. Mary is a conscientious, hard-working employee who puts a great deal of effort into her job (she frequently takes only a short lunch, sitting at her desk). She is extremely pleasant with everyone, offers to help people when they are too busy, and is a great writer. She even volunteered to help write the departmental newsletter, although that is not part of her job. She is now the editor and sometimes stays late to finish it. She has a great deal of experience with several different companies and is familiar with just about every word-processing package (for example, *Word*, *WordPerfect*, *WordStar*, *Wordiest*). She almost never makes a mistake and proofreads her typing carefully. On the negative side, she was late in completing three important projects this year, and on at least ten different occasions she asked for an extension of time on an assignment (which you reluctantly agreed to provide). At times, she is unable to return a customer's call until two days later, even though your organization has a policy of returning phone calls within 24 hours. Finally, she will sometimes take a half hour or more to explain something to a coworker, which would take anyone else five minutes. Group meetings also seem to take about 20 percent longer than normal when she attends. In terms of future plans, Mary has told you that she really would like to become a supervisor and help run another department.

The Rating Form

Employee's Name:

Use the following scale to make your ratings:
1-*failed to meet standards*
2-*some improvement*
3-*fully met standards*
4-*consistently exceeded standards*
5-*significantly exceeded standards*

1. Quantity of Performance   1   2   3   4   5
   Justification for rating:

2. Quality of Performance   1   2   3   4   5
   Justification for rating:

(continued)

3. Customer Service Justification for rating:	1	2	3	4	5
4. Work Effort Justification for rating:	1	2	3	4	5
5. Overall Rating Justification for rating:	1	2	3	4	5

❖ CHAPTER 7 *Experiential Exercise 2:*

Role-Playing Situations

This exercise involves a role-play of two different situations. In each situation, the supervisor must deal with an employee who has exhibited performance problems. Both situations pose somewhat different problems. The person who is the supervisor in situation A should take the role of the employee in situation B.

Situation A

Employee: A

You, CHRIS, have worked in the warehouse area for 25 years now, and have been doing a conscientious job the entire time. You know almost everyone in the company and have not missed a day of work for 10 years. Your work has been regularly praised by different bosses, and you know that it is mostly because of you that the warehouse area has been as effective as it has been. In the past few years, however, you have been upset that you keep getting passed over for promotion to supervisor of the warehouse area. In your opinion, this is probably due to favoritism by the plant manager, who does not get along with you at all. Three months ago, someone much younger than you was hired from outside the company to be the warehouse manager. Now you're really upset! Who can blame you for occasionally complaining to the other employees about the new supervisor, JEAN, who has no idea as to how the warehouse operates? After all, you know your job performance is excellent.

When Jean meets with you, you should really blow off some "steam" about Jean's lousy job performance so far!

Supervisor: A

You are JEAN, the new supervisor of the warehouse area. You are new to the company and job. Recently, you heard Chris complaining loudly to other workers about your performance. This appears to be undermining the morale of the area, and you can tell that other workers are beginning to challenge your authority. You have decided to talk with Chris about this issue, because it is important that morale not become a problem. In general, Chris is effective and knows a lot about the operation. So, just this one area seems to be a problem.

Situation B

Employee: B

You have been working with this organization for 28 years now. Your job consists of routing customer telephone calls to the appropriate department within the organization. For years you have been reliably performing your job, but for the past few months, things seem different. The pay isn't great, the work isn't at all interesting—but then it never has been. What is really bothersome is the way management communicates. Occasionally, you are abrupt with a caller who is annoying and irritating, and you are always blamed by the area manager, who says something like, "You have a real attitude problem, and you'd better shape up or else." Your attitude is one of "What does it matter if you are curt to rude people?" You cannot just pretend to be nice to everyone. If someone is rude to you, you can't just roll over and play dead. The majority of callers you handle promptly and nicely. Besides, you are retiring in two years, and work does not matter as much to you anymore. Finally, given your age and closeness to retirement, what can the company do to you anyhow? Your supervisor is new to this company and has called you to attend a meeting.

Supervisor: B

You were recently hired to serve as a supervisor of receptionists and customer-call handlers. The person you are meeting with has been with the company for 28 years now and has informed the company of plans to retire in two years. This person's job consists of routing customer telephone calls to the appropriate department within the organization. This person's performance ratings have been satisfactory for years, but your boss (the area manager) discussed the fact that this person recently has been rude to a large number of callers, who have complained to the customer service reps.

❖ Chapter 7 References

1. J. Cleveland, K. Murphy, and R. E. Williams, "Multiple Uses of Performance Appraisal: Prevalence and Correlates," *Journal of Applied Psychology* 74 (1989): 130–35.
2. W. C. Borman, "Job Behavior, Performance, and Effectiveness," in *Handbook of Industrial and Organizational Psychology*, vol. 2, ed. M. D. Dunnette and L. M. Hough (Palo Alto, CA: Consulting Psychologists Press, 1991): 271–336.
3. M. Stevenson, J. Busemeyer, and J. Naylor, "Judgment and Decision-making Theory," in *Handbook of Industrial and Organizational Psychology*, vol. 1, ed. M. D. Dunnette and L. M. Hough (Palo Alto, CA: Consulting Psychologists Press, 1991): 283–374.
4. H. J. Bernardin, and R. W. Beatty, *Performance Appraisal: Assessing Human Behavior at Work* (Boston, MA: PWS-Kent, 1984).
5. M. M. Harris, "Rater Motivation in the Performance Appraisal Context: A Theoretical Framework," *Journal of Management*, 20 (1994): 737–56.
6. R. D. Gatewood, and H. S. Feild, *Human Resource Selection* (Orlando, FL: Dryden, 1998).
7. Bernardin and Beatty, *Performance Appraisal*; and H. J. Bernardin, and P. Villanova, "Performance Appraisal," in *Generalizing from Laboratory to Field Settings*, ed. E. A. Locke (Lexington, MA: Lexington Books, 1986).
8. A. M. Mohrman, and E. E. Lawler, "Motivation and Performance Appraisal Behavior," in *Performance Measurement and Theory*, ed. F. J. Landy and J. Cleveland (Hillsdale, NJ: Erlbaum, 1983): 173–89; and C. O. Longenecker, D. A. Gioia, and H. P. Sims, "Behind the Mask: The Politics of Employee Appraisal," *Academy of Management Executive* 1 (1987): 183–93.
9. D. E. Smith, "Training Programs for Performance Appraisal: A Review," *Academy of Management Review* 11 (1986), 22–40.
10. Bernardin and Beatty, *Performance Appraisal*.
11. S. D. Friedman, and T. P. LeVino, "Strategic Appraisal and Development at General Electric Company," *Strategic Human Resource Management*, ed C. Fombrun, N. M. Tichy, and M. A. DeVanna (New York: Wiley, 1984): 183–201.
12. B. O'Reilly, "360 Feedback Can Change Your Life," *Fortune*, 17 October 1994, 93–100.
13. Bernardin and Beatty, *Performance Appraisal*.
14. R. D. Bretz, G. T. Milkovich, and W. Read, "The Current State of Performance Appraisal Research and Practice: Concerns, Directions, and Implications," *Journal of Management* 18 (1992): 321–52.
15. K. R. Murphy, and J. Cleveland, *Performance Appraisal: An Organizational Perspective* (Boston, MA: Allyn & Bacon, 1991).

16. E. Pulakos, "Behavioral Performance Measures" in *Applying Psychology in Business,* ed. J. Jones, B. Steffy, and D. Bray (Lexington, MA: Lexington Books, 1991).
17. G. Latham and K. Wexley, *Increasing Productivity through Performance Appraisal* (Reading, MA: Addison-Wesley, 1981).
18. R. Cardy and G. Dobbins, *Performance Appraisal: Alternative Perspectives* (Cincinnati, OH: South-Western Publishing, 1994); Borman, "Job Behavior, Performance, and Effectiveness."
19. R. Rodgers and J. Hunter, "Impact of Management by Objectives on Organizational Productivity," *Journal of Applied Psychology* 76 (1991): 322–36; Bernardin and Beatty, *Performance Appraisal.*
20. Murphy and Cleveland, *Performance Appraisal.*
21. C. Schneier and R. Beatty, "Developing Behaviorally Anchored Rating Scales (BARS)," *Personnel Administrator* (August 1979): 59–68.
22. D. Waldman, L. Atwater, and D. Antonioni. "Has 360-Degree Feedback Gone Amok?" *Academy of Management Executive* 12 (1998): 86–94.
23. B. O'Reilly, "360 Feedback Can Change your Life," *Fortune* 17 October 1994, 93–100.
24. D. Antonioni, "Designing an Effective 360-Degree Appraisal Feedback Process," *Organizational Dynamics* 25 (Autumn 1996): 24–38.
25. J. Smither, M. London, N. Vasilopoulos, R. Reilly, R. Millsap, and N. Salvemini, "An Examination of the Effects of An Upward Feedback Program Over Time," *Personnel Psychology* 48 (1995): 1–32.
26. Waldman, Atwater, and Antonioni, "360-Degree Feedback."
27. L. Reynolds, "Washington Update: Does Technology Mean Big Brother?" *HR Focus* 73 (November 1996): 10.
28. G. S. Alder, "Ethical Issues in Electronic Performance Monitoring: A Consideration of Deontological and Teleological Perspectives." *Journal of Business Ethics* 17 (1998): 729–43.
29. Ibid.
30. Web site of the American Civil Liberties Union (www.aclu.org).
31. J. Aiello and K. Kolb, "Electronic Performance Monitoring and Social Context: Impact on Productivity and Stress," *Journal of Applied Psychology* 80 (1995): 339–53.
32. Reynolds "Washington Update."
33. B. Rice, "Performance Review: The Job Nobody Likes," *Psychology Today* 19 (1985): 30–36.
34. R. Henderson, *Performance Appraisal* (Englewood Cliffs, NJ: Prentice-Hall, 1984).
35. C. Green, "How to Turn Your Staff into Star Performers," *Black Enterprise* (July 1991): 61.
36. B. Armentrout, "Eight Keys to Effective Performance Appraisals," *HR Focus* 70 (1993): 13.
37. S. Bushardt, J. Jenkins, and P. Cumbest, "Less Odious Performance Appraisals," *Training and Development Journal* 44 (1990): 29–35.
38. Ibid.
39. Ibid.
40. M. Teagarden, M. A. Von Glinow, M. Butler, and E. Drost, "Human Resource Management in Mexico's Maquiladora Industry," in O. Shenkar, (Ed.), *Global Perspectives of Human Resource Management* (Englewood Cliffs, NJ: Prentice-Hall, 1995).
41. M. Smith, "Documenting Employee Performance," *Supervisory Management* 24 (1979): 30–37.
42. W. Mahler, *How Effective Executives Interview* (Homewood, IL: Dow-Jones, 1976).
43. Web site of the Equal Employment Opportunity Commission (www.eeoc.gov).
44. D. Pennock, "Effective Performance Appraisals (Really!)," *Supervision* (1992):14–16.
45. A. LaPlante, "Making Performance Reviews Work for You," *Computerworld* 26 (1992): 119.
46. G. Barrett and M. Kernan, "Performance Appraisal and Terminations: A Review of Court Decisions Since *Brito v. Zia* with Implications for Personnel Practices," *Personnel Psychology* 40 (1987): 489–503.
47. C. Miller, J. Kaspin, and M. Schuster, "The Impact of Performance Appraisal Methods on Age Discrimination in Employment Act Cases," *Personnel Psychology* 43 (1990): 555–78.

48. J. Werner and M. Bolino, "Explaining U.S. Courts of Appeals Decisions Involving Performance Appraisal: Accuracy, Fairness, and Validation." *Personnel Psychology* 50 (1997): 1–24.
49. Barrett and Kernan, "Performance Appraisal and Terminations."
50. Werner and Bolino, "Explaining U.S. Courts."
51. Barrett and Kernan, "Performance Appraisal and Terminations."
52. Werner and Bolino, "Explaining U.S. Courts."

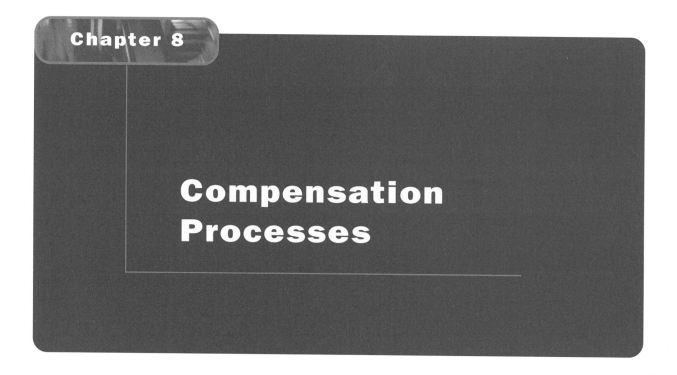

Compensation Processes

Core Concepts   After reading this chapter, you should be capable of:

1. Explaining the laws that apply to compensation processes.
2. Discussing how organizations determine internal pay fairness.
3. Discussing how organizations determine external pay fairness.
4. Describing how organizations combine job evaluations and wage surveys to develop a pay structure.
5. Identifying alternative approaches to the traditional pay structure.
6. Developing a strategy for seeking a pay increase.

Opening Case

Laurie has been working at the same company for two years. Although she is satisfied with her situation at work, she cannot stop wondering whether she is underpaid. The most recent event that made her wonder is a conversation that she had with an old high school friend last week. Much to her surprise, both Edward and she were in the same field of work. As they began talking, Laurie discovered that while their job titles differed, they both worked for different divisions of the same corporation and the actual work they performed was quite similar. Edward casually stated to Laurie that he made more than $35,000 annually. Laurie was so astonished that she blurted out, "What? More than $35,000? How do you make that much?" Edward responded by saying, "Even new employees in my department start off making about $31,000." After an embarrassing silence, another friend from high school came over and the conversation switched to another topic.

The next day, Laurie continued to think about her salary. She had once asked Dolly, a coworker who had been employed with the company for 20 years, what she thought about pay policies and practices, and Dolly replied in a whisper, "I don't talk about pay with anyone else. A number of years ago I asked another supervisor about pay raise policies, and he told me that they are a confidential issue that should only be discussed with your own supervisor. If you have questions, you are probably better off keeping them to yourself."

As Laurie thought more about her pay, she could not help remembering a question that came up during her interview with this company two years ago. Near the end of the interview, the human resource representative asked her, "What are your salary expectations?" She was so unprepared for the question that she paused and then said, "I don't really know. I guess I haven't thought that much about it." The human resource representative smiled and said, "Well, how does $23,000 sound?" That seemed like so much more money than Laurie was earning in her part-time job that she nodded her head and said, "That sounds reasonable to me." The actual salary offer was slightly more ($24,000), but Laurie now wonders whether she handled the question properly. Should she have negotiated for a higher salary? Is she being paid fairly now? Could Edward really be making so much more in a different division of the company? And what can she do now to obtain a higher salary?

This chapter, and the next two chapters, address compensation issues. Total compensation packages for employees may be broken into three parts: (1) base pay, or the set amount for a given time period; (2) performance-based pay, or the part of one's pay that is based on job performance; and (3) benefits, or indirect pay, which would include such company-paid additions as medical benefits, contributions to the pension plan, and so forth. This chapter only addresses base pay. In particular, you will read about the goals of an organization's pay system, relevant laws, and how companies go about determining base pay. You will see that many of the concepts are useful for employees and job applicants, as well as supervisors and managers who are responsible for determining pay. We begin now with a discussion of the basic objectives that organizations consider in designing a compensation process.

Goals of Compensation Processes

What does an organization try to achieve in its compensation process? Understanding the answer to that question may help both the employee and the organization operate more effectively. As an employee, if you understand what the organization is trying to achieve, you may be able to concentrate your efforts better and therefore receive higher compensation. From an organization's perspective, the better the match between what is desired and what is actually rewarded, the more likely the business objectives will be met. Organizations attempt to achieve six basic goals with their compensation programs:

1. Complying with legal requirements.
2. Maintaining a sense of equity and fairness among employees.
3. Attracting new highly qualified employees.
4. Retaining current employees.
5. Motivating employees.
6. Controlling costs.[1]

Most organizations will use other means, besides their compensation processes, to achieve these goals. Nonmonetary rewards, such as the nature of the work, interesting assignments, and flexible hours, are likely to be used as well. For most organizations, though, the compensation process is an important factor in recruiting, retaining, and motivating employees. But the compensation process is also a large part of most organizations' operating expenses. In fact, for most organizations, the payroll accounts for anywhere between 25 and 60 percent of operating expenses.[2] So, if not managed properly, an organization's payroll can severely reduce its profitability.

We now turn to a discussion of the first goal, complying with legal requirements.

Compensation Laws: Complying with Legal Requirements

Virtually all compensation decisions—including starting pay, pay raises, and benefits—are covered by the discrimination laws. So, rather than repeat them here, you may wish to review those laws as described in Chapter 2. In addition to those laws, however, certain other laws pertain to the compensation area specifically. These can be divided into three areas:

1. The Fair Labor Standards Act of 1938
2. Comparable worth
3. Prevailing wage laws

Fair Labor Standards Act of 1938

Fair Labor Standards Act of 1938
A congressional law passed with the intent of improving working conditions and living standards.

The **Fair Labor Standards Act (FLSA) of 1938** was a congressional law passed with the intent of improving working conditions and living standards. Prior to this law, long work weeks, low pay, and young children working in extremely hazardous conditions were common occurrences in the United States. In addition to requiring substantial record keeping and reporting to the government, the Fair Labor Standards Act of 1938 requires companies to do the following:

1. Provide overtime pay.
2. Pay a minimum wage.
3. Restrict the number of hours and the types of jobs children may work.
4. Pay equal wages to men and women doing the same job.

Each of these provisions can get quite complex, and organizations often get into trouble for alleged violations. Hence, whether you are a manager or an employee, it is useful to have a basic understanding of these provisions.

Overtime Pay. This provision requires you as an employee to be paid time and a half (one and one-half of your regular pay) for each hour that you work more than 40 hours per week, as long as your job is covered by the law. A major determinant of whether your job is covered by the law—that is, whether your job is **nonexempt**—is the nature of your job. Specifically, executive, administrative, and professional employees are not covered, or are **"exempt"** from this law, as are certain other jobs (such as car salespeople and agricultural workers). If you are employed in a hospital or other health care institution, a two-week period may be used to calculate overtime, such that you would not receive overtime wages unless you worked more than eighty hours during a two-week period. In today's world, many companies would rather have employees work overtime than hire additional workers. You may wonder whether there is a maximum number of hours your company can require you to work. The answer is that many states do limit the maximum number of hours certain employees, such as bus drivers and mine workers, may work in a given time period.[3]

Minimum Wages. The FLSA requires that companies pay employees no less than the minimum wage.[4] As stipulated by federal law, the minimum wage is $5.15 per hour as of September 1, 1997.[5] Six states and the District of Columbia have a higher rate. You should note, however, that not all jobs are covered by this provision. Similar to the overtime provisions, if your job is considered an executive, administrative, or professional job, your company would not be required to pay you a minimum wage. Likewise, you would not be covered by this provision if you were employed as an apprentice (for example you were learning a skilled trade, such as electrician), trainee, or independent contractor. Some people believe that the minimum wage should be raised even higher, to as much as perhaps $7.25 per hour by the year 2002.[6] What do you think?

For more information on the overtime and minimum wage laws under FLSA, see this Web site: www.dol.gov/dol/asp/public/programs/handbook/minwage.htm

Child Labor Laws. Although technically not related to compensation, the FLSA also regulates the work hours and type of jobs employees under the age of 18 may work. This law focuses on three age groups: people between the ages of 16 and 18; people between the ages of 14 and 16; and people under the age of 14. Children between the ages of 14 and 16 are not allowed to work in a variety of dangerous occupations, including mining, manufacturing, and work involving heavy machinery. Children this age also have restrictions in the number of hours and the times they may work. People between the ages of 16 and 18 are restricted from certain hazardous jobs, such as meat packing, working with bakery machines, and coal mining.[7]

For more information on this law, you should check this Web site: www.dol.gov/dol/asp/public/programs/handbook/childlbr.htm

Equal Wages to Men and Women Doing the Same Job. The fourth provision of the Fair Labor Standards Act of 1938 was actually an amendment passed by Congress in 1963. This amendment, known as the **Equal Pay Act of 1963,** attempts to eliminate sex discrimination in pay. Although the primary intent was to help women who were frequently discriminated against on the basis of pay, men can sue for discrimination as well.

In order to bring a lawsuit under the Equal Pay Act of 1963, the plaintiff would need to show the following:

1. That his or her work was essentially the same as the work performed by another employee of the opposite sex working in the same facility.
2. That his or her pay was less than that of the other employee.

nonexempt employees
Employees who are covered by the law's provision that requires companies to pay time and a half for each hour that an employee works more than 40 hours per week.

exempt employees
Employees who are not covered by the law's provision that requires companies to pay time and a half for overtime; often applies to executive, administrative, and professional employees.

Equal Pay Act of 1963
An amendment to the Fair Labor Standards Act of 1938 that attempts to eliminate sex discrimination in pay.

If the plaintiff is able to successfully prove these two facts, the burden would shift to the organization to defend the pay difference in terms of one of the following factors:

1. Seniority (the lower paid employee has less seniority)
2. Merit or job performance (the lower paid employee is not as productive)
3. Differences other than sex[8]

The third option, differences other than sex, allows the company many possible alternative defenses, some examples of which are provided in Box 8.1.

Recall in the opening case that Laurie wondered whether she was being paid fairly. If men were making more money in the same job, she might have grounds for a lawsuit. On the other hand, given that the friend from high school was working in a different division, the company would be able to defend the pay difference on the grounds that it was a "different facility." Unless she could prove gender-related pay differences within the same division and facility, the employee in the opening case would probably fail to win a lawsuit under the Equal Pay Act.

Despite the Equal Pay Act of 1963, gender-related differences in salaries and wages persist (if you want to learn more about gender-related differences in pay, try this Web site: www.aflcio.org/women/equalpay.htm). Women continue to earn significantly less than men in a wide variety of occupations and jobs. As you can see from Table 8.1, women's earnings on average in 1997 were only about 74 percent of those of men, a ratio that has persisted for years. In other words, for each $1.00 the average man earns, the average woman earns only 74 cents. Some critics assert that this is evidence that the Equal Pay Act of 1963 is of limited use in correcting sex discrimination pay, which only covers situations where women and men are working in the same job. These critics maintain that jobs that are stereotypically female (such as registered nurses) are systematically undervalued and therefore underpaid in our society, as compared to stereotypically male jobs (such as production supervisors). According to some, then, the only meaningful way to eliminate sex bias in pay is to pass comparable worth laws. As you will see next, the comparable worth concept is controversial. Can you think of other reasons, besides discrimination, for the differences in pay in Table 8.1? What about seniority, training, and years of work experience? Are there differences in personal responsibilities between men and women that might explain the gap in pay?

Comparable Worth

comparable worth
The concept that jobs of equal worth or value should be paid the same, even if the jobs are completely different.

According to the **comparable worth** principle, jobs of equal worth or value should be paid the same, even if the jobs are completely different. This concept, then, is more sweeping than the Equal Pay Act, which requires that pay be the same only if the jobs are the same. As an example, consider two jobs in the state of Washington in the late 1970s, namely, a dental assistant and a stockroom attendant. The average monthly salary for a dental assistant, most of whom were women, was $608. The average monthly salary for a stockroom attendant, most of whom were men, was $816. But according to a study conducted for the state of Washington, there was evidence that the job of dental assistant and the job of stockroom attendant were equal in worth to the state. Based on the comparable worth principle, the average pay for dental assistants should have been the same as that for stockroom attendants. Comparable worth proponents advocate that each organization conduct an objective, unbiased

TALES FROM THE TRENCHES

Box 8.1
How Companies Defend against Equal Pay Act Lawsuits

Organizations have used many different arguments to defend themselves in Equal Pay Act lawsuits. A common approach for organizations is to make use of the "differences other than sex" defense. Some of the following possibilities have been used here:

1. **Shift Differentials.** Different wages for different shifts (for example, night workers versus day workers) will be accepted by the courts, as long as they are applied equally to both men and women.
2. **Salary Matching.** It is legal for an organization to match or exceed salaries offered or provided by other organizations, even if this results in sex differences in pay. For example, if you had a competing offer from another employer, your company could choose to match the offer, even if it created

a situation in which a member of the opposite sex doing the same job was paid less than you.

3. **Profits.** An organization may establish different commission rates for different products or services, even if this results in different earnings for men and women, as long as both men and women are permitted to sell the product or services. Likewise, different salaries can be paid for people in departments or units of different profitability. So, if men are working in a department that is profitable, their salaries may be higher than women working in a department that is losing money.

A completely different defense used by companies in some cases is to demonstrate that the jobs held by men and women are not really the same. For in-

stance, in one court case involving a lawsuit by female janitors, the organization argued that male custodians (who were paid more) spent at least one-third of their time doing additional duties involving heavy lifting and moving. In a court case involving hospital orderlies, the organization successfully demonstrated that the men spent 70 percent of their time doing heavy work, unlike the women. One rule of thumb used by the courts is the frequency of the extra work being performed: if the extra duties are performed on a regular and frequent basis, the jobs may be deemed different. If, on the other hand, the extra duties are only performed occasionally (for example, less than 10 percent of the time), the courts may consider the jobs to be essentially the same.

Source: Adapted from E. Cooper and G. Barrett, "Equal Pay and Gender: Implications of Court Cases for Personnel Practices," *Academy of Management Review* 9 (1984): 84–94; and G. Milkovich and J. Newman, *Compensation* (Homewood, IL: Irwin, 1996).

analysis of the worth of every job that has a large majority of female employees. Then, for those jobs that are not paid according to their worth, the company would raise their wages or salaries to the proper levels (comparable worth proponents would oppose reducing the wages in male-dominated jobs to achieve equality).[9]

Not surprisingly, the comparable worth principle has generated a great deal of controversy. Critics of this principle raise several concerns, including the inherent additional pay costs, the difficulty of objectively determining the worth of jobs, the need to take into account other considerations besides job worth (for example, what other companies are paying for this job) and the additional litigation that would be generated if extensive comparable worth laws were passed.[10] The critics of comparable worth appear, in the United States at least, to hold the upper hand. To date, no comparable worth laws cover private-sector businesses in the United States and court cases have ruled against this concept. It is safe to say that, with one exception, comparable worth is not a concept that U.S. employers need to worry about. The one exception is state governments. Presently, nearly 20 states have made comparable worth pay adjustments, and require by law that state employees be paid in accordance with comparable worth principles.[11] Most of the legal activity in terms of gender-related differences in pay has come from OFCCP (see Chapter 2) investigations of

Table 8.1	Median 1997 Weekly Earnings for Selected Occupations	
	Men	**Women**
Overall	$579	$431
Financial managers	991	660
Accountants/auditors	791	590
Sales	603	352
Real estate sales	685	523
Mail carriers	691	610
Police	628	547
General office supervisors	754	513

Source: U.S. Bureau of Labor Statistics Web page.

federal contractors. After a recent examination of U.S. Airways Corporation, which the OFCCP charged with sex discrimination in pay, the company agreed to a settlement that included a sum of $400,000 being paid to 30 professional and managerial women to remedy unfair pay.[12]

Prevailing Wage Laws

prevailing wage laws
Require companies with certain government contracts to pay workers the standard wage for the area, either the wage paid to a majority of workers in the area or a wage based on a weighted formula, which may be used if there is no single wage for the area.

Prevailing wage laws require companies with government contracts to pay workers the standard wage for the area. The original purpose was to prevent companies with large government contracts from unfairly depressing workers' wages. As of 1982, a prevailing wage is either (1) the wage paid to a majority of workers in the area, or (2) a wage based on a weighted formula, which may be used if there is no single wage for the area.[13] The following are the major prevailing wage laws:[14]

1. The Davis-Bacon Act of 1931, which covers public construction projects.
2. The Walsh-Healy Public Contracts Act of 1936, which covers manufacturers and suppliers of goods to the government.
3. The Service Contract Act of 1965, which covers services (for instance, janitorial) to the government.
4. The National Foundation Arts and Humanities Act of 1965, which covers employees working on projects funded by the foundation.

If you are a manager employed by an organization with such a contract, be sure that your compensation practices are in compliance. You can find more information on these laws in the following Web site: www.dol.gov/dol/asp/public/programs/handbook/contents.htm

To summarize, organizations must conform to a great number of regulations and laws in administering their compensation programs. As was mentioned in Chapter 2, other discrimination laws—such as the Age Discrimination in Employment Act, the Americans with Disabilities Act, and the Civil Rights Acts of 1866, 1964, and 1991—also apply to pay issues. Comparable worth laws apply only to certain state governments. Finally, prevailing wage laws pertain to many companies with government contracts. As in other aspects of human resources, the laws play a major role in compensation processes. We now turn to a discussion of the second goal, maintaining a sense of fairness among employees, which also relates to our third, fourth, and fifth goals of attracting, retaining, and motivating employees.

Maintaining a Sense of Fairness among Employees

What is Fairness? Fairness can be a subjective term. Nevertheless, if you talk with anyone about what is fair and what is not fair, you are quite likely to hear that person refer to two somewhat separate aspects of fairness: outcome fairness and procedural fairness. The first type, outcome fairness, is probably the one you would mention first because that is obviously important. Outcome fairness refers to the fairness of *what* you received. For example, if we are talking about your base pay, outcome fairness would refer to the amount of money you receive. There are different theories as to how you determine whether the amount of money you earn is fair or not. Most of these assume that you somehow compare the amount of money that you earn to what other people earn, while at the same time, considering the amount of time, effort, and other inputs (such as differences in skill) that other people have put into the job. In other words, even though some professional athletes earn millions of dollars annually, when you compare your salary to theirs, you may still believe you are earning a fair wage because you take into account the differences in physical skills most of us have compared to these athletes.

Procedural fairness refers to *how* that amount of money that you earn was decided, in other words, the process that was used to make that pay decision. Some rules that employees will use in determining procedural fairness include whether the decision rules are applied consistently, whether an appeals process is available, and whether they have had an opportunity to participate in the decision making. It becomes important, then, that the company be able to explain how compensation decisions are made.[15]

Do people think their pay is fair? With that background in mind, you may wonder just how satisfied employees are with their compensation. What would you guess is the percentage of workers who indicate that they are satisfied with their pay? If you guessed about half, you are right. In a recent survey, 49 percent of the workers said they were satisfied with their pay. Not surprisingly, higher paid workers were more satisfied with their pay; only about a third of those workers making less than $25,000 annually were satisfied with their pay (32 percent). More than two-thirds of workers making more than $60,000 annually were satisfied with their pay. Interestingly enough, more than half of the respondents to the survey felt that their CEO was overpaid (56 percent) (for more information about CEO pay, see Box 8.2), but a nearly equal number (45 percent) thought that entry-level employees were also not worth the amount of money they were paid. By and large, employees in the survey were not pleased with the role their supervisor plays in the pay process—only 30 percent were satisfied with their supervisor's influence. Information on the pay process was also viewed negatively—only 35 percent were happy with the amount of information they have on the pay process.[16] How would you have answered these questions?

So, how would you go about determining whether your base pay was fair? In the opening case, Laurie seemed particularly troubled when she found out that a friend from high school who worked in a different division of the same company doing what seemed to be the same job appeared to be earning much more money than she was. Do you think Laurie was making an appropriate comparison? After all, the friend did work for a different division. What would you have done if you were in that situation? Would you have tried to find out what other employees in your department with the same job title were making? If that is what you would have done, be aware that some organizations have strict policies that prohibit employees from discussing salaries with

YOUR TURN

Box 8.2
Are CEOs Overpaid?

Who do you think was the highest paid U.S. CEO in 1996 and how much did he or she make? If you guessed Sanford Weill of Travelers Group, you were right. Weill earned $93.9 million that year, the bulk of which ($83.2 million) was from exercising stock options. The next highest-paid CEO was Anthony O'Reilly, of the H. J. Heinz Company, who earned $64.1 million, the majority of which again was from stock options. Overall, CEOs from the 350 largest U.S. firms received salary increases of 5.2 percent from the previous year. Do you think that is a good increase or not? Compared to the average increase of 4 percent of white-collar workers, that average is slightly better, but not quite as good as the 10.4 percent average increase CEOs received in 1995. The median compensation, including salary, bonus, gains from exercised stock options, and other rewards, for these CEOs from the 350 largest firms was $2.38 million. When you take all of these sources of compensation into consideration, CEO pay increased an average 18 percent in 1996. So, do you think that CEOs are paid too much? If you are not sure, or would like more information about what other CEOs have earned, try this Web site: www.aflcio.org/paywatch/index.htm

Current critics of CEO pay have argued that the pay often does not reflect the performance of the company. In fact, research suggests that in fact little or no correlation exists between CEO pay and company performance. A response to this criticism that some make is that organizations have to pay a lot to retain good CEOs, so that forces besides company performance drive CEO pay. A second criticism has to do with the large stock options that many CEOs receive. Companies provide such programs in order to motivate CEOs to increase the value of stock. But critics argue that in many cases, the stock options are priced so low that the CEOs are almost guaranteed to make hefty windfalls. For example, when Eastman Kodak gave its CEO a contract to buy 2 million shares at $90.125 each, plus some 50,000 restricted shares, Alan Johnson, a compensation consultant, determined that Kodak's stock had only to increase 5 percent annually for four years for the CEO to earn more than $33 million. Thus, even though much of CEOs' compensation may be performance-based, the hurdle may be set too low. In response, many companies are setting the bar higher. For example, at DuPont, top executives will lose out on certain stock awards unless the price reaches a certain level for five straight days by the year 2002. Finally, some companies are reducing their CEOs' salary, such as Masco did when it cut top officers' pay by 10 percent, and replacing raises with various stock options. It appears that complaints about CEO pay that began in the early 1990s have had some effect on the nature of their compensation, although as you can see from the figures presented above, CEOs are still well-paid for their efforts. Given all of these points, do *you* think CEOs are overpaid?

Source: J. Lublin, "Raising the Bar," *Wall Street Journal*, 10 April 1997, R1, R4; Anonymous, "The Boss's Pay," *Wall Street Journal*, 10 April 1997, R15.

coworkers. Some organizations might even terminate you for such discussions. So the coworker's refusal to discuss pay in the opening case is realistic. Would you have instead attempted to find out what other organizations pay employees doing your job? One way to do this would be to visit some of the Web sites in Box 8.3 to find out how other employees in your field are paid. Would you try to get information only from organizations in the same industry and same geographic location that you work in? You might even arrive at different conclusions regarding the fairness of your pay, depending on which comparison you use, because there is no one "right" comparison. From an individual's perspective, then, pay fairness may depend on whose salary you are comparing your pay with.[17]

Organizations face a similar dilemma in determining base pay. Organizations must determine what jobs are appropriate to compare to each other and what aspects of the jobs should be analyzed. By comparing jobs to one another within the organization, pay can be made *internally* fair. Organizations must also decide who the relevant companies are that should be used for comparison purposes. By basing compensation on

WEBBING AROUND

Box 8.3

You can search various Web sites to help you determine more precisely what an appropriate wage would be for the job you or your employees perform. Although most of these Web sites charge a fee, the information you get may be well worth it. Consider the case of Holly Peckham, a communications specialist earning $28,000. When she examined an on-line wage survey for her profession, she discovered that she was earning about $9,000 less than the average for her profession. After receiving a job offer for $32,000, she used her on-line information to convince her company to offer her more. Peter Reed of Korn/Ferry, an executive recruiting firm,

discovered from his company's wage survey Web site that his salary was 18 percent below the average and used this information to negotiate a higher salary. Good luck in using these salary survey Web sites to increase your pay:

www.jobsmart.org: This Web site provides free information from many different salary surveys, especially those from California.

www.wageweb.com: This site provides salary survey information for over 100 different jobs. For about $100, you can get breakdowns by industry, geographic location, and others.

members.aol.com/payraises: This site will give you individualized pay figures, based on experience, job, industry, and other categories. The fee for the first set of figures is about $100.

www.futurestep.com: This is an interesting collaborative Web site, combining resources from Korn/Ferry, the executive search firm, and the *Wall Street Journal*. If you register, you will not only obtain salary survey information, but career advice as well, and possible job opportunities.

Source: J. Lublin, "Web Transforms Art of Negotiating Raises," *Wall Street Journal*, 22 September 1998, B1, B16.

what other companies are paying for the same job, an organization can make its wages and salaries *externally* fair. As the 21st century begins, many companies are also taking a careful look at what wages and salaries are in other parts of the world. As shown in Figure 8.1, wages for U.S. production workers are lower than some of our major competitors, such as Japan and Germany, but higher than Mexico. However, there is more than just pay to consider. As shown in Figure 8.2, productivity levels also may differ from country to country. Just because wages are lower does not necessarily mean that productivity will be higher. As shown in Figure 8.2, U.S. manufacturing workers actually have higher productivity levels than workers in either Japan or Germany, despite the fact that U.S. production workers earn on average less than their counterparts in Japan and Germany.

As you might guess, internal and external fairness are determined quite differently. Internal fairness is determined by a job evaluation; external value is assessed using salary surveys. Each of these procedures is reviewed in greater detail next, followed by a discussion of how organizations combine the two approaches to determine the actual base pay for their employees.

Determining Internal Fairness: Conducting a Job Evaluation

A **job evaluation** is a systematic, objective procedure for determining the value of a group of jobs for the organization. A job evaluation may serve several purposes, some of which may be more important than others, depending on the organization's needs. Specifically, a job evaluation may be useful for the following:[18]

job evaluation
A systematic, objective procedure for determining the value of a group of jobs for the organization.

1. Explaining to employees how the base pay is determined.
2. Ascertaining the appropriate pay for jobs that are unique to the organization.

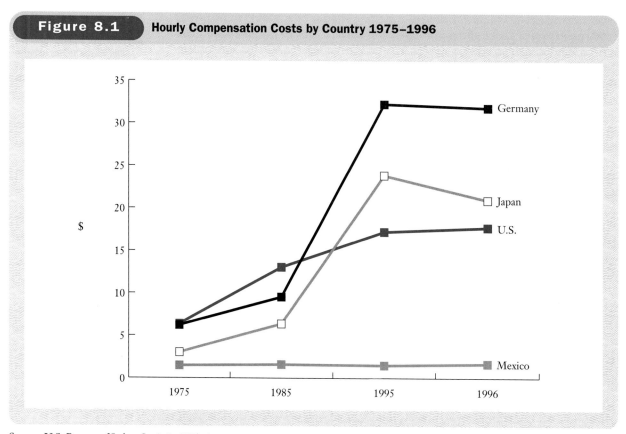

| Figure 8.1 | **Hourly Compensation Costs by Country 1975–1996** |

Source: U.S. Bureau of Labor Statistics Web site.

3. Defending the pay system from a legal challenge.
4. Helping design career paths.
5. Performing a comparable worth study.

Many different job evaluation procedures exist. You have read about one of these (the position analysis questionnaire, or PAQ) in an earlier chapter; we will discuss two additional procedures in some detail: the point method system and the Hay system. Following that, the rank order and job classification methods are briefly mentioned.

Point Method System of Job Evaluation

The **point method job evaluation** is one of the most commonly used procedures. It involves the following basic steps: [19]

1. **Form a Job Evaluation Committee.** The committee should include compensation experts, as well as managers, supervisors, and others who are familiar with the jobs being evaluated. Generally, anywhere between three to ten individuals should work on the committee.

2. **Select and Define Compensable Factors. Compensable factors** are the determinants of job worth. As an analogy, if you were considering how much to pay for

point method job evaluation
One of the most commonly used job evaluation procedures that involves forming a committee, selecting and defining compensable factors, establishing and defining levels for each compensable factor, determining the total number of points for the system, dividing total points among compensable factors, distributing points to each level on every factor, and evaluating the jobs.
compensable factors
The determinants of job worth.

| **Figure 8.2** | **Output Per Hour in Manufacturing by Country 1975–1996** |

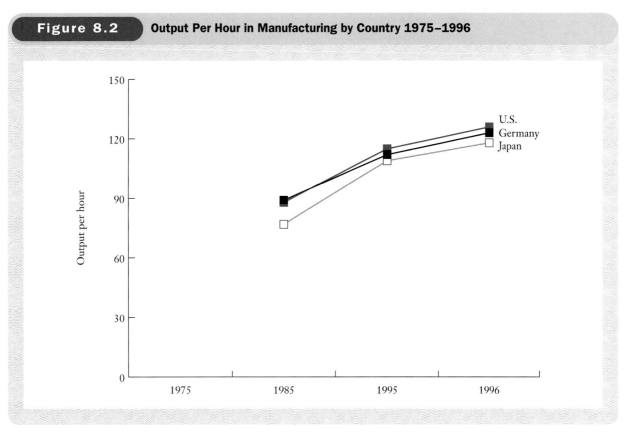

Source: U.S. Bureau of Labor Statistics Web site.

an automobile, the relevant compensable factors might include safety ratings, fuel economy, resale value, and available options (such as antilock brakes). In the job evaluation domain, compensable factors often include the education required to perform the job, the amount of decision making performed on the job, the amount of responsibility involved in the job (such as budgetary responsibility), and the dangerousness of the work. In practice, the number of compensable factors used in the job evaluation can vary from 3 or 4 to as many as 15 or 20. Once determined, the compensable factors must be carefully defined.

3. **Establish and Define Levels on Each Compensable Factor.** It is not sufficient to merely define each compensable factor. Rather, like a ruler, each level or step must be clearly delineated. This is best explained by examining Table 8.2, which provides an example of the levels on education, a commonly used compensable factor. As you can see in Table 8.2, this compensable factor has four levels, ranging from a four-year college degree to an eighth-grade education. There is nothing magical about the number of levels or the particular levels chosen. The number of levels and the particular levels used should be a function of the jobs being evaluated. The levels should also be chosen such that each job to be evaluated will fall on one and only one level. While the levels in Table 8.2 might be appropriate for office workers, if the job evaluation was going to be used for a scientific laboratory, a different set of levels might be more appropriate, perhaps with the highest level being a Ph.D., and the lowest level being a two-year college degree.

Table 8.2	Levels of the Compensable Factor of Education

Level 1: Eighth-grade education

Level 2: High school diploma or equivalent

Level 3: Two-year college degree; technical/vocational school diploma

Level 4: Four-year college degree

4. **Determine the Total Number of Points for the System.** In this step, the committee must determine the total number of points (not dollars) to be allocated in the job evaluation. This step is similar to your course instructor assigning a total number of points that can be earned through tests, projects, and class participation. Although this is an arbitrary number, it must be large enough to accommodate differences among even highly valued jobs. Many experts recommend that 1,000 points be used.[20]

5. **Divide Total Points among Compensable Factors.** In this step, the committee must decide how many points to assign to each compensable factor. This essentially weights the different factors, much as an instructor assigns a number of points for each test, quiz, and project in a course. The more important a given compensable factor is to the organization, the more points it should receive. For example, if our compensable factors were education, decision making, responsibility, and dangerousness, we might assign 200 points to education, 300 points to decision making, 350 points to responsibility, and 150 points to dangerousness. All things being equal, then, the job with a great deal of responsibility is likely to have a higher overall worth than a job with a great deal of danger.

6. **Distribute Points to Each Level on Every Factor.** Now that a total number of points has been assigned to each factor, the committee must determine the number of points each level will receive. There are several ways to do this, but the simplest way is to divide the number of points assigned to the factor by the number of levels on the factor and assign this value to the lowest level. For example, since education was assigned 200 points and there are four levels, an eighth-grade education would receive 50 points. Each level receives 50 points more than the previous level. Thus, a high school diploma would receive 100 points, a two-year college degree 150 points, and a four-year college degree would receive 200 points. The development of the job evaluation system is now complete. All that needs to be done is to create a job evaluation manual or computer program to use in evaluating the jobs.

7. **Evaluate the Jobs.** In this step, relevant information must be gathered about the jobs so that they can be evaluated on each of the compensable factors. There are many ways to obtain this information, but among the most common are written questionnaires completed by supervisors and job incumbents that contain questions relevant to the compensable factors. The job evaluation committee may also interview supervisors and incumbents and observe the jobs being performed. Committee members should first independently rate the jobs on each compensable factor, then discuss their ratings to reach agreement. Once the points on each compensable factor are determined, the points can be added up for each job to determine its overall value.

As you can guess, a properly performed point method job evaluation can take a great deal of time and energy to complete. On the positive side, the careful, systematic thinking involved should help employees to feel that the resulting pay decisions are fair.

Finally, it is important to note that most organizations will perform a separate job evaluation for different occupational groups. For example, most organizations will perform one job evaluation for clerical and office staff, a different job evaluation for managerial and professional staff, and yet a third job evaluation for other employees (for instance, manufacturing workers).

Hay Plan

The **Hay Plan,** or Hay Guide Chart-Profile method, is a preestablished job evaluation plan owned and copyrighted by the Hay Group, a management consulting firm. The Hay Plan is widely used for evaluating executive, managerial, and professional positions, but it can also be used for other positions, such as clerical jobs. A chief advantage of the Hay Plan is that it is based on preestablished compensable factors and points. A company choosing the Hay Plan will probably be able to complete the evaluation of jobs much more quickly than if a point method system was used.

The Hay Plan assumes that three universal compensable factors can be used to evaluate all jobs.[21]

1. Know-how, which represents all skills, knowledge domains, and abilities that are required by the job.
2. Problem solving, which represents the degree to which analyzing, creating, and reasoning are required by the job.
3. Accountability, which represents the job's responsibility and impact on the organization.

Each of these three compensable factors is a function of several subfactors. For example, know-how is broken down into three subfactors: (1) breadth and depth of knowledge; (2) degree of integration of different functions, and (3) amount of human relations skill required for the job. An example of the know-how factor is provided in Figure 8.3.

To use the Hay Plan, a trained analyst would carefully review the jobs being evaluated (that is, the analyst would examine job descriptions, talk with supervisors, and so forth). Next, the analyst would find the appropriate levels on each of the subfactors underlying each of the three compensable factors.

A major advantage of the Hay Plan is that it is ready for immediate use. Another advantage of this method is that it was initially designed for executive, managerial, and professional positions, which by their very nature are difficult to evaluate. On the other hand, because employees will have less involvement, they may be less inclined to accept the results than they would be with the point method plan.

Other Job Evaluation Procedures

In addition to the job evaluation procedures already mentioned, two other noteworthy procedures are ranking and job classification. The **ranking method** is among the simplest procedures. With this method, a committee ranks the jobs from most valued

Hay Plan
A preestablished job evaluation plan that is widely used for evaluating executive, managerial, and professional positions.

ranking method of job evaluation
Involves a committee ranking jobs from most valued to least valued by the organization.

Figure 8.3 — JMS Master Guide Chart

DEFINITION—Know-How is the sum total of every kind of skill, however acquired, needed for acceptable job performance. This sum total, which comprises the overall fund of knowledge, has three dimensions, the requirements for:

- Depth and breadth of knowledge, ranging from basic knowledge of the most simple work routines, to unique and authoritative knowledge within learned disciplines.
- •• Know-How of integrating and harmonizing the diversified functions involved in managerial situations (operating, supporting, and administrative). This Know-How may be exercised consultatively as well as executively and involves, in some combination, the areas of organizing, planning, executing, controlling, and evaluating.
- ••• Active, practicing person-to-person skills in the area of human relationships.

MEASURING KNOW-HOW: Know-How has both scope (variety) and depth (thoroughness). Thus, a job may require some knowledge about a lot of things, or a lot of knowledge about a few things. The total Know-How is the combination of scope and depth. This concept makes practical the comparison and weighing of the total Know-How content of different jobs in terms of: "HOW MUCH KNOWLEDGE ABOUT MANY THINGS."

JMS MASTER GUIDE CHART
1992
KNOW-HOW
GUIDE CHART

HAY MANAGEMENT CONSULTANTS 1991

		••KNOW HOW OF										
		T. Performance of a task or tasks highly specific as to objective and content with limited awareness of surrounding circumstances and events.			**I.** Performance or supervision of an activity or activities specific as to objective and content, with appropriate awareness of related activities.			**II.** Operational or conceptual integration or coordination of activities which are relatively homogenous in nature and objective.			**III.** Operational or conceptual integration of activities which are diverse in nature and objectives in an important management area of a company-wide coordination of a function.		
••• Human Relations Skills →		1	2	3	1	2	3	1	2	3	1	2	3
PRACTICAL PROCEDURES	**L. LIMITED** Basic instructions and simple work routines to carry out manual tasks.	29	33	38	38	43	50	50	57	66	66	76	87
		33	38	43	43	50	57	57	66	76	76	87	100
		38	43	50	50	57	66	66	76	87	87	100	115
	A. PRIMARY Basic literacy and/or ciphering skills plus work indoctrination for performance of repetitive operational or clerical routines which may involve use of common tools and standard single purpose machines.	38	43	50	50	57	66	66	76	87	87	100	115
		43	50	57	57	66	76	76	87	100	100	115	132
		50	57	66	66	76	87	87	100	115	115	132	152
	B. ELEMENTARY VOCATIONAL Familiarization with an uninvolved, standardized work routines and/or use of equipment and machines.	50	57	66	66	76	87	87	100	115	115	132	152
		57	66	76	76	87	100	100	115	132	132	152	175
		66	76	87	87	100	115	115	132	152	152	175	200
SPECIALIZED PROCEDURES	**C. VOCATIONAL** Procedural or systematic proficiency, which may involve a facility in the use of specialized equipment.	66	76	87	87	100	115	115	132	152	152	175	200
		76	87	100	100	115	132	132	152	175	175	200	230
		87	100	115	115	132	152	152	175	200	200	230	264
	D. ADVANCED VOCATIONAL Some specialized (generally non-theoretical) skill(s), acquired on or off the job, giving additional breadth or depth to a generally single function.	87	100	115	115	132	152	152	175	200	200	230	264
		100	115	132	132	152	175	175	200	230	230	264	304
		115	132	152	152	175	200	200	230	264	264	304	350
	E. BASIC SPECIALIZED Sufficiency in a technique which requires a grasp either of involved practices and precedents, or of scientific theory and principles, or both.	115	132	152	152	175	200	200	230	264	264	304	350
		132	152	175	175	200	230	230	264	304	304	350	400
		152	175	200	200	230	264	264	304	350	350	400	460
	F. SEASONED SPECIALIZED Proficiency, gained through wide exposure, in a technique which combines a broad understanding either of involved practices and precedents, or of scientific theory and principles, or both.	152	175	200	200	230	264	264	304	350	350	400	460
		175	200	230	230	264	304	304	350	400	400	460	528
		200	230	264	264	304	350	350	400	460	460	528	608
	G. SPECIALIZED MASTERY Determinative mastery of techniques, practices, and theories gained through wide seasoning and/or special development.	200	230	264	264	304	350	350	400	460	460	528	608
		230	264	304	304	350	400	400	460	528	528	608	700
		264	304	350	350	400	460	460	528	608	608	700	800
LEARNED DISCIPLINES	**H. PROFESSIONAL MASTERY** Externally recognized mastery of a complex professional or scientific field.	264	304	350	350	400	460	460	528	608	608	700	800
		304	350	400	400	460	528	528	608	700	700	800	920
		350	400	460	460	528	608	608	700	800	800	920	1056
	I. AUTHORITATIVE MASTERY Internationally recognized authority in an unusually complex professional or scientific field.	350	400	460	460	528	608	608	700	800	800	920	1056
		400	460	528	528	608	700	700	800	920	920	1056	1216
		460	528	608	608	700	800	800	920	1056	1056	1216	1400
	J. PREEMINENT AUTHORITY Unique command of theory and principles at the pinnacle of an unusually complex professional or scientific field.	460	528	608	608	700	800	800	920	1056	1056	1216	1400
		528	608	700	700	800	920	920	1056	1216	1216	1400	1600
		608	700	800	800	920	1056	1056	1216	1400	1400	1600	1840

HayGroup

INTEGRATING AND HARMONIZING DIVERSIFIED FUNCTIONS

SCOPE OF TOTAL MANAGEMENT OF THE CHIEF EXECUTIVE OFFICER POSITION IS ESTABLISHED AFTER CONSIDERATION OF:

DIVERSITY (degree of integration; number of different businesses; dispersion of operations; organizational complexity; size)
POSITION IN INDUSTRY (degree of dominance and leadership—pace setter for the industry)
CHARACTER OF INDUSTRY (degree of regulation; effect on economy)
BUSINESS STRATEGY (response to challenge and environment; rate of change and growth)

IV. Integration of major functions in an operating complex; or company-wide coordination of a strategic function which significantly affects corporate planning or operations.			V. Administration of an operating unit where size and character significantly augment managerial complexity or a corporate sub-function of wide and deep penetration or integration and coordination of a major function(s) in a major operating complex.			VI. Administration of a major operating unit or of a major corporate function of wide and deep penetration.			VII. Administration of a major operating complex or a major function which uniquely and comprehensively affects corporate planning and results.			VIII. Integration and coordination of the overall corporate activity with primary concern for assigned major operating complex and/or multiple function components.			IX. Total management of the enterprise.			
1	2	3	1	2	3	1	2	3	1	2	3	1	2	3	1	2	3	
87	100	115	115	132	152	152	175	200	200	230	264	264	304	350	350	400	460	
100	115	132	132	152	175	175	200	230	230	264	304	304	350	400	400	460	528	L.
115	132	152	152	175	200	200	230	264	264	304	350	350	400	460	460	528	608	
115	132	152	152	175	200	200	230	264	264	304	350	350	400	460	460	528	608	
132	152	175	175	200	230	230	264	304	304	350	400	400	460	528	528	608	700	A.
152	175	200	200	230	264	264	304	350	350	400	460	460	528	608	608	700	800	
152	175	200	200	230	264	264	304	350	350	400	460	460	528	608	608	700	800	
175	200	230	230	264	304	304	350	400	400	460	528	528	608	700	700	800	920	B.
200	230	264	264	304	350	350	400	460	460	528	608	608	700	800	800	920	1056	
200	230	264	264	304	350	350	400	460	460	528	608	608	700	800	800	920	1056	
230	264	304	304	350	400	400	460	528	528	608	700	700	800	920	920	1056	1216	C.
264	304	350	350	400	460	460	528	608	608	700	800	800	920	1056	1056	1216	1400	
264	304	350	350	400	460	460	528	608	608	700	800	800	920	1056	1056	1216	1400	
304	350	400	400	460	528	528	608	700	700	800	920	920	1056	1216	1216	1400	1600	D.
350	400	460	460	528	608	608	700	800	800	920	1056	1056	1216	1400	1400	1600	1840	
350	400	460	460	528	608	608	700	800	800	920	1056	1056	1216	1400	1400	1600	1840	
400	460	528	528	608	700	700	800	920	920	1056	1216	1216	1400	1600	1600	1840	2112	E.
460	528	608	608	700	800	800	920	1056	1056	1216	1400	1400	1600	1840	1840	2112	2432	
460	528	608	608	700	800	800	920	1056	1056	1216	1400	1400	1600	1840	1840	2112	2432	
528	608	700	700	800	920	920	1056	1216	1216	1400	1600	1600	1840	2112	2112	2432	2800	F.
608	700	800	800	920	1056	1056	1216	1400	1400	1600	1840	1840	2112	2432	2432	2800	3200	
608	700	800	800	920	1056	1056	1216	1400	1400	1600	1840	1840	2112	2432	2432	2800	3200	
700	800	920	920	1056	1216	1216	1400	1600	1600	1840	2112	2112	2432	2800	2800	3200	3680	G.
800	920	1056	1056	1216	1400	1400	1600	1840	1840	2112	2432	2432	2800	3200	3200	3680	4224	
800	920	1056	1056	1216	1400	1400	1600	1840	1840	2112	2432	2432	2800	3200	3200	3680	4224	
920	1056	1216	1216	1400	1600	1600	1840	2112	2112	2432	2800	2800	3200	3680	3680	4224	4864	H.
1056	1216	1400	1400	1600	1840	1840	2112	2432	2432	2800	3200	3200	3680	4224	4224	4864	5600	
1056	1216	1400	1400	1600	1840	1840	2112	2432	2432	2800	3200	3200	3680	4224	4224	4864	5600	
1216	1400	1600	1600	1840	2112	2112	2432	2800	2800	3200	3680	3680	4224	4864	4864	5600	6400	I.
1400	1600	1840	1840	2112	2432	2432	2800	3200	3200	3680	4224	4224	4864	5600	5600	6400	7360	
1400	1600	1840	1840	2112	2432	2432	2800	3200	3200	3680	4224	4224	4864	5600	5600	6400	7360	
1600	1840	2112	2112	2432	2800	2800	3200	3680	3680	4224	4864	4864	5600	6400	6400	7360	8448	J.
1840	2112	2432	2432	2800	3200	3200	3680	4224	4224	4864	5600	5600	6400	7360	7360	8448	9728	

•••HUMAN RELATIONS SKILLS		
1. BASIC: Courtesy, tact and effectiveness in dealing with others in every day working relationships, including contacts to request or provide information.	2. IMPORTANT: Alternative or combined skills in understanding and/or influencing people are important to achieving job objectives, causing action or understanding in others.	3. CRITICAL: Alternative or combined slills in understanding, selecting, developing, and motivating people are important in the highest degree.

Source: 1992 Know-How Guide Chart from Hay Group © Hay Management Consultants. Reprinted by permission.

to least valued by the organization. No compensable factors are used; rank is based on the overall worth of the jobs to the organization. Although this method is quick and relatively easy to use, it suffers from several shortcomings. First, because it uses no compensable factors and no standards by which jobs are evaluated, bias may arise, particularly against stereotypical female jobs. Likewise, there is little documentation to explain why the jobs have been ranked as such. Therefore, this method may be of little value in convincing employees of the fairness of the pay system. Second, while a committee may have no difficulty deciding which are the most valuable and which are the least valuable jobs, the jobs in the middle may spark much more disagreement. Without clear standards, such disagreements may be difficult or impossible to resolve in a satisfactory manner.[22]

job classification
Categories or classes are defined in terms of responsibility for subordinates, contact with other departments, amount of education required, and technical skills involved.

If you have ever worked in a government position, you are probably familiar with the **job classification** method. With this method, categories or classes are defined. A simple example of classes is provided in Table 8.3. As you can see in Table 8.3, each class is defined in terms of responsibility for subordinates, contact with other departments, amount of education required, and technical skills involved. Typically, there are about eight categories or classes, but some organizations will have as few as five and as many as fifteen. Because class definitions may be ambiguous, and disagreement may arise as to the proper class, it may become difficult to classify some jobs. In addition, the rationale for pay differences between classes is often limited, making such plans vulnerable to lawsuits.[23]

After reading about these various job evaluation methods you may be wondering whether different job evaluation procedures will produce different results, or whether the conclusions would be the same regardless of which procedure you used. If different procedures do in fact produce different results, the job evaluation system used could have major policy implications, particularly in the case of comparable worth adjustments. One study that compared the PAQ to the point method found relatively large differences in estimates of the underpayment of traditionally female jobs. Moreover, the way in which weights for the compensable factors for the PAQ and point method systems were developed made a difference.[24] Other studies have found similar results.[25] Thus, the job evaluation method used could have a large effect on one's conclusions. Unfortunately, we have no way to determine the "right" job evaluation procedure. As in beauty, it is ultimately in the eye of the beholder.

Table 8.3	Sample Classes in a Job Classification System

Class 1: No supervisory responsibility; minimal contact with other departments; high school diploma required, minimal technical skills.

Class 2: No supervisory responsibility; minimal contact with other departments; two-year college degree required; moderate technical skills.

Class 3: No supervisory responsibility; some contact with other departments; four-year college degree required; extensive technical skills.

Class 4: Supervisory responsibility; significant contact with other departments; four-year college degree required; extensive technical skills.

Determining External Fairness: Using Wage and Salary Surveys

In order to assess external fairness, organizations use wage and salary surveys, which report what other companies are paying their employees. An example of a page from a wage and salary survey is shown in Table 8.4. Organizations use wage and salary surveys for two purposes. A **labor market survey** provides information as to what other organizations that compete for employees are paying. The labor market survey, then, is used to help an organization effectively recruit and retain its workers. A **product market survey** provides information as to what other organizations providing the same product or service are paying their employees. The product market survey, then, is used to make sure that the organization's payroll costs are not higher than its business competitors. Because the labor market and product market surveys have different purposes, the information they contain may be based on completely different organizations. Consider, for example, the wage and salary surveys used by an automobile manufacturer located in central Indiana. The labor market survey may include all businesses within 100 miles of this factory, because those might be the organizations the automobile manufacturer competes with for employees. The product market survey, however, may be based on all automobile manufacturers worldwide, because those companies represent the business competition. Choosing the appropriate organizations to survey is critical. It might be completely irrelevant for you to compare what manufacturing firms in New York City are paying accounting clerks if your organization is a retail chain in the rural South.[26]

Wage and salary surveys can be obtained from several sources. Most organizations will use one or more of the following sources:

1. **Federal Government.** The federal government routinely conducts salary and wage surveys for major metropolitan areas in the United States. A potentially valuable salary survey that you can access over the Internet, the National Compensation Survey, is conducted by the Bureau of Labor Statistics (BLS), a federal government office. Although the BLS has conducted similar surveys for many years, the National Compensation Survey is more extensive and more readily available to the public than previous programs. (The actual information is available at the following Web site: http://stats.bls.gov./compub.htm.)

   If you go to this Web site, you will find that this survey is used to collect pay information from about 150 cities throughout the United States. For each of these cities, data are gathered for nearly 500 occupations, including sales jobs, service employees, executive, managerial, and administrative positions, and transportation workers. If you were interested in finding out how much financial managers in Columbus, Ohio earned, you could look it up at this Web site. (The most recent survey figures indicate that the median pay for these employees was $28.57 per hour.) If you were in charge of salary decisions for a hospital in Columbus, Ohio, it might be useful to find out that registered nurses earned on average $18.31 per hour. To obtain this information, the BLS collects pay data from thousands of businesses. In addition to pay information, this survey contains information about benefits.[27]

2. **Professional Associations.** Many professional associations conduct wage and salary surveys as a service for their members. Graduating college students might be particularly interested in obtaining a copy of the Endicott Report, published by Northwestern University in Evanston, Illinois, which surveys starting salaries offered to graduating college students.

labor market survey
Provides information as to what other organizations that compete for employees are paying; used to determine what other companies are paying employees so that an organization can effectively recruit and retain its workers.

product market survey
Provides information as to what other organizations providing the same product or service are paying their employees; used to make sure that the organization's payroll costs are not higher than its business competitors.

Table 8.4 Page from a Salary Survey

Survey Report Prepared by Compensation Consulting Firm

REPORT PREPARED FOR COMPANY   P844   LOMELI PHARMACEUTICALS

Modifier
(A = stronger match; B = exact match; C = weaker match)

SIRS job family   *SIRS subfamily*   *Level of job (3 = senior)*

Company's salary grade or job evaluation points

Salary range minimum, midpoint or control point (*), maximum

Status under Fair Labor Standards Act

Benchmark job code and title

Company number

CO NO / MOD	JOB TITLE/INTERNAL JOB CODE	NO OF INC	ACTUAL SALARIES— AVG	LOW	HIGH	RANGE MIN	MIDPT/ CNTRL	RANGE MAX	% SP	GR/ PTS	FL SA	TOTAL COMP
E067 B	PROG/ANALYST BUSINESS-SR	2	32396	32240	32500	25220	31564	37908	50	53	E	33692
E008 C	SR DATA PROC ANALYST	5	32656	28288	35464	25584	35464	45344	77	A4	E	34145
P023 B	PROGRAMMER ANALYST SR	13	34892	31980	39156	25584	37310	49036	92	45	E	34892
D032 B	MGMT SYSTEMS ANALYST SR	2	34892	33852	35880	31460	39520	47580	51	11	E	34892
E009 B	PROGRAMMER/ANALYST BUS	8	35388	31500	38400	29160	37860	46560	60	07	E	35388
E017 B	MCS 2-BUSINESS	297	35620	28756	45604	29380	39468	49556	69	12	E	35620
G002 B	PRINCIPAL BUSINESS PROG	1	36240	36240	36240	31740	39360	46980	48	A4	E	36240
P019 B	PRGRMMR/ANLYST SENIOR	12	36868	32240	43836	31460	41678	51896	65	73	E	36868
E231 B	PROGRAMMER ANALYST SR	3	37260	33000	39540	28896	37596*	45096	56	08	E	38750
E111 C	PROGRAMMER ANALYST SR	3	37536	34560	41520	28896	37002	45108	56	08	E	37536
P221 B	PROG/ANALY III	1	37980	37980	37980	30936	39600	48264	56	26	E	37980
E008 B	ADP ANALYST	4	38948	34840	43160	27144	39364	51584	90	A5	E	38948
E035 B	SR SYS ANALYST GEN	22	39204	27000	48195	33600	42000	50400	50	10	E	39204

SIRS job family: 09   04   TQ14   LEVEL 3

PROGRAMMING/ANALY-BUSINESS APPLICATIONS

Job Code	Mod	Job Title	No. Inc.	Avg	Low	High	Min	Mid	Max	Spread %			Base + Bonus
P844	B	SYSTEMS DEV SPEC III 4821	3	39252	37392	42300	27744	39636	51528	86	28	E	39252
A012	B	ADMIN INFO SYS PROG/ANL	9	40040	35776	43628	33436	43498	53560	60	06	E	42442
K215	B	COMPUTING ANL SR	7	40196	31200	44096	31096	39676	48204	55	75	E	40196
E020	B	PROGRAMMER/ANALYST SR	1	40352	40352	40352	35880	46254	56628	58	14	E	40352
E015	C	PROGRAMMER ANALYST II	4	40417	39000	44200	31252	39052	46852	50	47	E	40417
C026	B	SR SYSTEMS ANALYST	13	40760	36312	47944	31100	40400	49700	60	09	E	40760
E003	B	PROGRAMMER/ANALYST SR	6	40812	37560	44100	31920	39900	47880	50	46	E	40812
E017	A	MCS 3-BUSINESS	125	41392	32916	50960	32136	42510	52884	65	13	E	41392
E111	B	PROG/SYS ANALYST (SR)	3	41520	40800	42600	32496	41646	50796	56	09	E	41520
B110	B	PROGRAMMER ANALYST III	103	41772	34560	51240	34560	43200	51840	50	09	E	41772
F007	A	SR PROGRAMMER/ANALYST	24	41988	29784	52740	34416	44748	55068	60	05	E	41988
P122	B	SR PROGRAMMER/ANALYST	1	42840	42840	42840	32400	41500	50600	56	13	E	42840
E009	A	PROGRAMMER ANALYST BUS	10	43080	39852	49116	33120	43260	53400	61	08	E	44803
S037	B	MGMT SYS ANALYST SR	2	43160	42276	43992	30680	40820	50960	66	47	E	43160
E034	B	ANALYST BUS SYSTEMS SR	1	44720	44720	44720	31564	42458	53352	69	17	E	44720
Q154	A	PROGRAMMER ANALYST SR	1	45032	45032	45032	35828	45136	54444	52	18	E	45032
E231	A	PROGRAMMER ANALYST STAFF	4	47436	44580	53040	36600	47604*	57096	56	10	E	47436
Q018	A	INFO SYS ANALYST SR	4	47700	46644	49008	32700	44790	56880	74	23	E	47700
E015	B	PROGRAMMER ANALYST I	1	48308	48308	48308	33540	41912	50284	50	49	E	48308
P005	B	SR MIS SPEC	1	50492	50492	50492	34216	45604*	54704	60	10	E	50492
		TOTAL INCUMBENTS 26 COMPANIES	696										
		COMPANY P844 AVERAGE	3	39252	37392	42300	27744	39636	51528	86	28		39252
		MARKET WEIGHTED AVERAGE	693	38570			31179	40999	50801	63	06		38647
		MARKET SIMPLE AVERAGE		40360	36314	44659	31667	41143	50475	59			40596
		MARKET ARITHMETIC AVERAGE MIDPOINT						41071					
		LOW		32396	27000	32500	25220	31564	37908	48			33692
		HIGH		50492	50492	53040	36600	47604	57096	92			50492
		3 COMPANIES MATCHING MODIFIER C	12	36463	33949	40394	28577	37172	45768	60			37083
		23 COMPANIES MATCHING MODIFIER B	513	37531	36731	42817	31194	40530	49712	59			37587
		6 COMPANIES MATCHING MODIFIER A	168	41893	39801	49982	34133	44675	54962	61			41996

Your company's data, including internal job code, in boldface for easy reference

Number of incumbents reported to job

Salary range percentage spread minimum to maximum

Base salary plus bonus or incentive compensation

Source: Organization Resources Counselors, Inc. From G. Milkovich and J. Newman, *Compensation* (Chicago: Irwin, 1993).

3. **Consulting Firms.** Various well-known consulting firms conduct wage and salary surveys, including Hay Associates (www.haygroup.com), and William Mercer (www.wmmercer.com). Some consulting firms focus on a particular industry, such as health care, while others specialize in a particular occupational group, such as middle and top management. Prices for these surveys vary, but they generally cost between a few hundred to several thousand dollars.

Once you have salary survey information, what do you do with it? Assume for a moment that you have salary survey information from three different surveys for several job titles. The following steps describe what you should do next:

1. **Age the Data.** The salary survey data you gathered are likely to be somewhat old, if only by six to nine months. Nevertheless, given that salaries tend to increase over time, you will need to take this into account by adding a constant to the numbers. For example, if the survey data are 12 months old, and you determine that salaries have risen about 4 percent over that time, you may wish to multiply the figures by 1.04 to match what the salaries are currently likely to be.
2. **Combine the Information.** Given that we assumed you have salary survey information from three different surveys, you will want to combine this information in some way. If you believe that each survey is equally accurate and appropriate, you could just take a simple average. However, you may place more weight on one survey than the other two, perhaps because it is based on a much larger number of individuals. If that is the case, you might calculate a weighted mean, which gives greater weight to one survey than the other two.
3. **Incorporate Any Adjustments.** You may wish to adjust the salary survey averages in order to take into account job differences (for example, the same job in your organization has somewhat greater responsibilities than the salary survey jobs). Therefore, you might modify those numbers slightly. Be sure to document and explain all of these decisions in writing in case you are asked about this at a later time.[28]

The Traditional Pay Structure: Merging Job Evaluation and Salary and Wage Surveys

You may be wondering at this point why organizations do not simply conduct a salary and wage survey to determine how to pay their jobs. The answer is that wage and salary surveys have several limitations. First, most organizations have jobs for which there is no close match in the salary surveys. Second, even with a relatively close match for a particular job in the salary surveys, there may be some differences (for example, your organization uses the same job title, but the incumbent has additional duties and responsibilities not covered in the survey jobs). Third, for most jobs there is a range of pay across companies. Thus, a secretary may be paid as little as $6 per hour or as much as $15 per hour at different companies. Fourth, your organization may value some jobs more than the external market does.

For all of these reasons, most companies use the wage and salary surveys only to obtain information for benchmark jobs, and then use the results from a job evaluation to determine the pay for nonbenchmark jobs. **Benchmark jobs** have the following basic characteristics:[29]

benchmark jobs
Jobs that are similar or comparable in content across firms.

1. Many workers in other companies have these jobs.
2. They will not be changing in the foreseeable future in terms of tasks, responsibilities, and so forth.
3. They represent the full range in terms of salary, such that some are among the lowest paid in the group of jobs, others are in the middle range, and some are at the high end of the pay scale.

At this point, the manager in charge of developing the pay structure has sufficient information to complete the system. For example, let us assume that the manager has both salary information for 30 benchmark jobs and job evaluation points for all 100 managerial and professional jobs within the organization. Now the task is to determine the appropriate pay for all of these 100 jobs, not just the 30 benchmark jobs. In other words, the manager must determine the **pay structure,** which designates the base pay for each job. (For an example of a completed pay structure that includes information about pay grades, pay range, and other information, see this Web site: portfolio.stanford.edu/104788.) Thus, consider the job of administrative assistant. When hiring a new administrative assistant, the manager would be able to look up which grade this job was in, and then determine what the minimum starting pay and the maximum starting pay for the job would be.

pay structure
Designates the base pay for each job.

In designing the pay structure, the manager must make five decisions.

1. **What Should the Pay Level Be Compared to Other Organizations?** This question concerns how the organization's average salary or wage should compare to the average salary or wage paid by other organizations. Should the organization match (pay about average), lead (pay more), or lag (pay less) relative to other organizations? In deciding which of these three courses of action to follow, the manager must consider several factors, one of which will be the organization's ability to pay. If, for example, the organization is losing money it may be difficult to lead the market. Conversely, given evidence that pay level can increase the number of job applicants, the likelihood of an applicant's accepting a job offer, and the performance of employees, the benefits of higher salaries may outweigh the costs.[30]
2. **Should Each Job Be Considered Separately or Should Jobs Be Broken Down into Grades?** In most cases, the manager will choose to sort the jobs into a smaller number of **job grades** or **classes.** Otherwise, it would be quite confusing administratively to try to establish pay rules for each job in the organization when there may be hundreds or even thousands of different jobs. It is simpler to divide the jobs into anywhere from 10 to 20 different grades. The number of grades needed for a particular set of jobs depends on many factors, such as the number of managerial levels within the organization and how quickly employees are expected to progress from grade to grade. Depending on how many grades are desired, the manager may

job grades
A manager may choose to sort jobs into a smaller number of grades or classes, usually into ten to twenty different grades.

place all jobs rated between 100 and 120 points in grade 1, all jobs rated between 121 and 140 points in grade 2, and so forth.

pay range
The range of pay a manager chooses for each grade.

3. **Should Each Grade Be Paid a Single Salary or Should There Be a Range of Pay for Each Grade?** In most cases, the manager will choose to have a **pay range** within each grade. The logic behind that choice is that even within the same job, two people may need to be paid differently, depending on their seniority, performance, or other relevant factors. How large the range is depends on various factors, such as the amount of variation in job performance and the length of time a worker is likely to stay within the grade. To operationalize the range, each grade will have a minimum as well as a maximum salary. From an employee's perspective, this can be good news or bad news, depending on where you place in the grade. The good news is that within a grade, you will earn at least the minimum wage designated for that grade. The bad news is that if you are at the top of your grade, you will not make more money, unless adjustments are made for inflation, the maximum is raised, or you are promoted to a higher grade. The grade range is usually expressed as the percentage difference between the minimum pay in the grade and the maximum pay in the grade. For clerical employees, a typical range is between 30 and 40 percent. For managers and executives, the typical range is about 50 percent.[31]

grade overlap
The amount of overlap that exists between grades.

4. **How Much Overlap Is Acceptable between Grades?** The amount of grade overlap, or the overlap that exists between grades, affects whether salaries in one grade will be more or less equivalent to salaries in higher grades. As shown in Figure 8.4, for any given set of grades there may be no overlap (as shown in Figure 8.4a) between grades, some overlap between grades (as shown in Figure 8.4b), or nearly complete overlap between grades (as shown in Figure 8.4c). All else being equal, the less overlap between grades, the greater the incentive for the employee to move from grade to grade. Companies that wish to use promotions to motivate employees will have less overlap between grades.[32]

Figure 8.4 **Different Overlap Between Pay Grades**

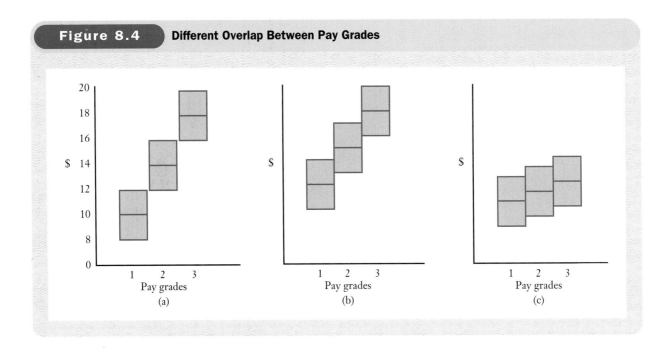

5. **What Is the Midpoint Salary for Each Grade?** The midpoint or salary corresponding to the middle point of the grade, must be determined. A quantitative approach is to use regression analysis, a statistical technique that relates two variables. In the present situation, one could use job evaluation points and salary data from the benchmark jobs as the two variables. The regression analysis provides a formula based on this data. For example, the following formula might be produced by the regression analysis: weekly salary is equal to: 410 + the number of job evaluation points multiplied by 2. To use the formula to determine the midpoint salary in each grade, the manager could take the average number of job evaluation points for each grade and insert this number into the formula. For example, if jobs in grade 1 were worth an average of 110 points, the manager would multiply 2 by 110 and add 410, for a total of 630. Thus, the midpoint weekly salary for grade 1 would be $630. Based on the range that had been decided in decision 3, the manager could then determine the minimum and maximum wage of grade 1. A similar procedure would be used for the remaining grades.[33]

Depending on the organization's particular objectives, quite different pay structures may be developed. Consider, for example, Organization A, whose pay structure is shown in Figure 8.5a. Assume that all new employees are hired at grade 1. As they demonstrate effective performance, they are eligible for promotions to higher grades. As shown there, the pay in the entry-level grade is higher compared to Organization B, whose pay structure is presented in Figure 8.5b. All things being equal, Organization A may be more effective in attracting new employees than Organization B, because of the higher pay in grade 1. At the same time, Organization A's grades have more overlap than Organization B's grades. That means employees in Organization A will be less motivated to get promoted than employees in Organization B. Furthermore, all things being equal, Organization A will be less able to retain existing

Figure 8.5 **Pay Structures from Two Different Organizations**

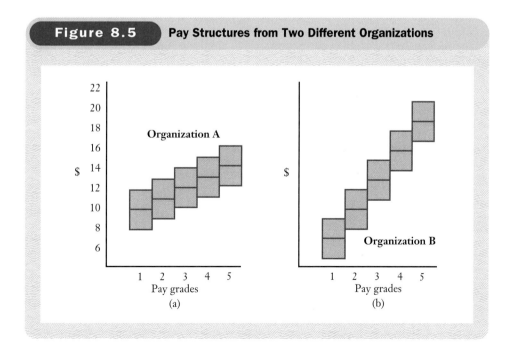

employees than Organization B, which on average pays employees in grades 4 and 5 more.

From an employees' perspective, you should be careful about accepting an entry-level job merely because it pays more than other companies. It is quite possible that another company offering lower pay initially will pay potentially much more for higher level jobs.[34]

Once the pay structure is designed, adjustments are nearly always required. For example, unless the pay structure is being developed for an organization that does not yet exist, chances are some employees' salaries will be outside of their newly established grade. **Green circle rates** apply to employees whose salaries are below the minimum of their grades. Depending on the company's financial constraints, their pay may be increased immediately to the minimum of the grade, or it is more rapidly increased than that of other employees over a period of several years. **Red circle rates** apply to employees whose salaries exceed the maximum of their respective grades. Because of adverse reactions to pay being cut, most organizations will refrain from immediately reducing an employee's pay. Rather, over time, raises may be much smaller or nonexistent until the employee's pay is within the grade range. Another often needed adjustment is in regard to the grade a job is assigned. Sometimes a job will be misclassified, or its duties and responsibilities will change. A formal procedure for requesting a job grade review is therefore recommended to avoid perceived inequities that might otherwise result. As an employee, this might be one avenue for pursuing a pay raise.[35]

Returning to our previous example of a manager hiring an administrative assistant, assume the job fell into grade 3 in Figure 8.5a. According to this chart, the minimum pay for a job in grade 3 is $10 per hour, the maximum is $14 per hour. Thus, the starting pay could be less than $10 per hour and no more than $14 per hour. Depending on the applicant's experience and qualifications, the manager might wish to start the new administrative assistant near the bottom or near the top of the pay grade.

In conclusion, an organization's pay structure can have an important effect on its ability to attract, retain, and motivate employees. Without a formal pay structure, an organization may face much confusion and make many mistakes in pay decisions. In turn, these matters can affect the organization's ability to survive and prosper. Despite the popularity of the traditional pay structure as described here, several alternative approaches are available, including broadbanding, market pricing, and skill-based pay. These three approaches are described in greater detail next.

green circle rates
Apply to employees whose salaries are below the minimum of their respective grade.

red circle rates
Apply to employees whose salaries exceed the maximum of their respective grades.

Alternatives to Traditional Pay Structures

Broadbanding

broadbanding
A pay structure that contains relatively few grades, with much greater range in each as compared to the traditional pay structure.

Broadbanding may be defined as a pay structure that contains relatively few grades, with much greater range in each. As compared to the traditional pay structure, which consists of 10 to 20 pay grades, each with relatively little range, the broadbanding approach may use as few as three pay grades, with a great deal of range within each grade. The difference between the traditional pay structure and the broadbanding approach is illustrated in Figure 8.6.[36]

To understand why broadbanding may be preferred over the traditional system, recall from Chapter 6 that changes have occurred in the workplace in recent years that include far fewer promotion opportunities and an increased emphasis on cross-

| Figure 8.6 | **Traditional versus Broadbanding Pay Structure** |

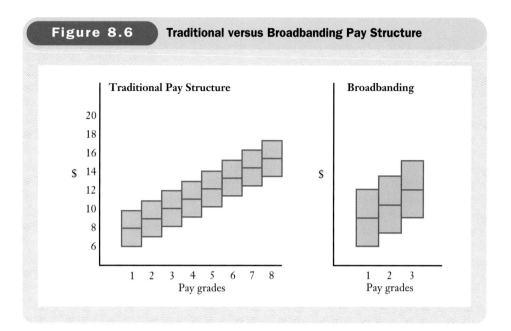

training. Considering first the limited number of promotions in organizations, recall that the traditional pay structure emphasizes the value of promotions. The broadbanding approach, by having relatively few job grades, downplays the value of promotions. This is further reinforced by having a large range within each grade, allowing for considerable room for rewarding performance. With regard to the emphasis on cross-training, it may sometimes be critical for an employee to take a lower-level position as part of a developmental experience. With the traditional system, moving to a lower grade might require a pay cut. With the broadbanding approach, because there are few job grades, there is less of a chance that the other job is in a lower grade. Hence, the broadbanding approach facilitates job transfers and similar developmental experiences. Finally, broadbanding helps reduce the emphasis on hierarchy and status.

Although broadbanding has several advantages, it is not without problems. One problem that can arise is increased difficulty in controlling costs. Because jobs that might otherwise be in two or three different job grades are now all in the same grade, managers may be inclined to press for higher salaries for jobs that are not worth quite so much. Communication of the new "rules of the game" may also become more difficult, as the rules for obtaining a bigger salary are less clear. Employee reactions can also be negative. For example, when a major bank in Scotland introduced broadbanding for managerial and professional employees, the number of job grades was reduced from 15 to 5, with much larger pay ranges. Cost of living raises were eliminated and managers had far more discretion to determine raises than in the past. Employees raised concerns over loss of promotion opportunities, concerns about fairness of the raises, and fears that their new work responsibilities would not be rewarded.[37]

A recent survey indicated that nearly 20 percent of U.S. companies have adopted broadbanding and 27 percent of U.S. companies plan to introduce or expand their use.[38] IBM is one U.S. firm that switched to a broadbanding approach in the mid-1990s as part of a major organizational change. In doing so, IBM reduced its 24 grades to 10 grades, while going from over 5,000 different job titles to fewer than 1,200 job titles. The previous job evaluation system used 10 compensable factors and required a two-inch binder of documentation. The new system used only three compensable factors (skills, leadership, and job scope), requiring only a single page to explain. Under the new system, some employees were in the same band as employees who previously had been in lower bands. Some of the other components of a traditional pay structure, such as the midpoint, have been eliminated, providing much more flexibility to managers in determining salaries.[39]

About 20 percent of companies in the United Kingdom have also implemented broadbanding. A recent survey of these companies, however, indicated that many used a relatively conservative approach in changing their pay structure. In terms of the reduction of grades, the median number of grades went from 17 to 8, although one firm had gone from 24 grades to 3. Likewise, the increase in the range of grades was relatively modest. In sum, broadbanding is basically a means of reducing hierarchy and increasing flexibility compared to the traditional pay structure. Although its impact can be great, it is more a modification of, rather than a radical alternative to, the traditional pay structure. Box 8.4 offers a look into compensation overseas.

Market Pricing

market pricing
An approach to developing a pay structure that essentially downplays internal value and relies almost exclusively on external value to determine pay.

The **market pricing** approach to developing a pay structure essentially downplays internal value. Instead, this approach relies almost exclusively on external value to determine pay. The underlying premise is that the organization should pay employees what it must in order to hire and retain them, with much less regard for internal fairness.[40]

Organizations that use this system obtain as much information as possible on benchmark jobs. Once that process is completed, the nonbenchmark jobs are priced in between, based on logical relationships. For example, assume the vice president of human resources and the compensation analyst positions are two benchmark jobs for which we have external salary data. Now, we must decide how to "price" the manager of compensation job. Because this position reports to the vice president of human resources, while the compensation analyst reports to the manager of compensation, it is reasonable to "price" this position somewhere between the two benchmark jobs.

A market pricing strategy is likely to be particularly appropriate for an organization that is concerned with keeping costs down and does a great deal of hiring from the external labor market. Thus, this system should work best to attract new employees and retain high performers. Its potential disadvantage is an increased likelihood that current employees will perceive internal unfairness. Like broadbanding, then, market pricing is more a modification to the traditional pay structure approach than a radical alternative to it. In essence, market pricing merely emphasizes external fairness over internal fairness. Small organizations, as well as some medium-size firms, rely more heavily on this approach, in part because it eliminates the need for expensive and time-consuming job evaluation systems.

Skill-Based and Competency-Based Pay

Unlike the two alternatives described above, skill-based and competency-based pay represents a significant departure from the traditional pay structure. Essentially, these procedures focus on skills or competencies that the individual is capable of performing; the traditional pay structure focuses on the job being performed. Under skill- or competency-based pay, the more skills or knowledge an employee has mastered, the

YOUR TURN

Box 8.4
Compensation: U.S. Expatriates versus Chinese Locals

Although average salaries have increased only modestly in the United States for the past few years, rising only 4 percent, local employees in China are experiencing much faster increases in their pay. Annual increases for qualified Chinese working for U.S. firms are rising as much as 15 to 50 percent. Nonetheless, compared to expatriates, locals are still much cheaper to employ: it estimated that an expatriate can cost the company as much as $300,000 a year, including housing, education of children, and other expenses. A local employee, then, is still a bargain, considering the average compensation is only $19,400 for a finance manager and $16,200 for a sales manager of a high-tech firm. So, even with double-digit salary increases, the local employee costs the company far less. With the shortage of local talent in China, some U.S. firms are seeking other types of compensation that will attract mobile professionals. One new incentive is housing; the shortage of housing is so severe in China that many Chinese in their 20s and 30s live with their parents. As a way of attracting new employees, Motorola is developing and selling apartments at low prices. Coca-Cola is providing zero-interest housing loans to their local employees in China. The danger for companies providing housing is that companies become involved in complicated contractual issues (for example, who really owns the home) and need expertise in real-estate to make appropriate decisions.

Adapted from: B. Hagerty, "Asian Scramble," *Wall Street Journal*, 10 April 1997, R12, R19; and F. Hansen, "Currents in Compensation and Benefits," *Compensation and Benefits* 30 (September/October 1998): 6–15.

higher his or her pay. For now, we will focus on skill-based pay because it has been more commonly used and has been available for about 25 years; following that we will discuss competency-based pay.

It is important to note that in a **skill-based pay program,** workers can only use one skill at a time; so skill-based pay is not job enlargement. Although relatively few companies use skill-based pay plans, new plants operated by Procter & Gamble, Honeywell, and TRW, to name a few, have adopted this kind of pay system.[41]

There are several different ways to set up this kind of pay plan. One way is to divide the relevant jobs into separate functions or modules. For example, suppose construction of a handmade suit involves four functions: arranging materials in accordance with the pattern, cutting materials, sewing materials, and assembling the finished product for packaging and shipping. Under a traditional pay plan, the person who sews might be paid the most, followed by the cutter. Perhaps the person who arranges the materials and the person who assembles the finished product for packaging and shipping are paid the least. Under the skill-based pay plan, however, employees will be paid for each job that they are capable of doing. The person who is capable of sewing and cutting would be paid more than the person who is able only to sew.

Companies that use the skill-based pay system cite several advantages to this approach. One advantage is greater workforce flexibility. If, for example, an employee is absent, it will be easier to move other workers around to fill the position. Similarly, if a bottleneck occurs in one section (perhaps the cutting stage in the example above), everyone who is capable of doing that function can help complete the work. Another advantage is a complete understanding of the product or service being performed. Advocates of skill-based pay argue that the greater an employee's understanding of the work, the more likely the employee will be to offer work innovations and suggestions.

skill-based pay
An approach that represents a significant departure from the traditional pay structure, this procedure rewards workers for the skills or knowledge they have mastered.

Third, the ability to perform different jobs will enable the workers to use a variety of skills and rotate jobs. In turn, this should increase satisfaction with the work and help relieve boredom.[42]

Of course, there are several potential disadvantages to skill-based pay. One potentially unavoidable concern is that most skill-based pay plans will cost more than a traditional plan. In many cases, the company is paying people for what they know, not what they do. So the person who is capable of doing more than one job is paid more, even though he or she can only perform one job at a time. A second disadvantage is that the company will be required to spend a great deal of time training and developing employees to enable them to perform additional jobs. Finally, skill-based pay should be avoided in certain situations. Perhaps the worst situation for skill-based pay would be one that requires highly trained specialists. Would you want surgeons, for example, to be on a skill-based pay system? Probably not.[43]

One manufacturing organization that implemented skill-based pay introduced this system primarily because not all of the 21 production tasks were performed everyday. Thus, to have regular employees knowledgeable in only one task would have been wasteful, and at other times, when more people were needed to perform a specific task, there would be inefficiencies. The organization had an employee task force determine the appropriate skill modules. The employees decided to give the same $0.20 hourly pay increase for each module mastered by an employee, except for the skill module covering basic knowledge (for example, equipment, forms) for which mastery would lead to a $0.30 hourly raise. The employees also decided to eliminate a ceiling or maximum hourly pay; however, when a skill module would become obsolete, the employee would have his or her pay reduced by $0.20. New workers would start at $9.81 an hour. Existing employees had the option of participating in the new pay system or leaving the department.

After implementing the system, the organization found a major problem. There was no gain for the organization in having all employees learn certain skill modules. In fact, there was a loss to the organization in training all employees, because a novice in the task is less proficient. If the organization did not really need many people capable of performing that module, the payoff for the company may be nonexistent. One way the company has addressed this issue is by focusing training on the most important skill modules and modifying the simple rule that "the more skill modules mastered, the higher one's pay." Overall, however, the organization has been pleased with the outcome.[44]

competency-based pay
A system where managerial and professional employees are paid for their level on key competencies.

Competency-based pay is a term that has been in use for only a few years. As you may recall from Chapter 5, *competency modeling* is used to develop a set of broadly defined competencies, such as leadership, flexibility, and initiative, that may be used for a variety of HRM processes, including pay determination. Although competency-based pay programs have been used differently in various organizations, competency-based pay is probably best understood as skill-based pay applied to managerial and professional employees. In other words, in a competency-based pay system, employees are placed in a "band," where, depending on their level of competencies, pay can increase by as much as 150 percent as an employee moves from one level within the band to the highest level within the band.[45] For example, Frito-Lay bases managerial pay on four competencies: leveraging technical and business systems, leading for results, building workforce effectiveness, and meeting customer needs. For each competency, there are three levels of effectiveness.[46] At this point, competency-based pay is too new to evaluate its advantages or disadvantages.

In sum, various alternatives exist to the traditional pay structure. Just as there are disadvantages to the traditional pay structure, however, the alternatives have short-comings. The specific pay plan your organization uses will depend much upon the particular circumstances involved.

Compensation Processes: Implications for Employees

You have read a great deal about compensation processes such as legal requirements, job evaluations, salary and wage surveys, and pay structures. As you read about salary negotiations next, you will see that an understanding of these topics will be helpful to you as an employee.

Negotiating a Pay Increase in Your Current Job

Negotiating for a large pay increase in your current job requires a great deal of careful planning and skillful negotiation. Let's start with the planning aspect. There are several issues that you must address carefully if you are to be successful in obtaining your desired pay increase:[47]

1. **How Much of a Pay Raise Should You Try For?** Numerous factors come into play here, including what other people in your field are making, your worth to the company in terms of your performance and the importance of your position, the probability that you could get a job elsewhere, and the company's pay policies and practices. With regard to what other people in the field are earning, be sure to gather salary survey information from reliable sources (see Box 8.3 for some Web sources) so that you have a good idea as to what other companies are paying, as well as information with regard to what other employees in your organization are being paid. Research shows that people often overestimate the amount of money both lower-level and same-level employees are being paid, so you may mistakenly believe that you are being underpaid. Check your facts carefully! A major consideration is how much your company needs you. To help assess how important you are to your organization, rate yourself on a five-point scale on the following questions:[48]

   a. If you left the company, how easy or hard would it be for the company to replace you (1=easy, 5=hard)?
   b. To what extent do you have abilities or possess knowledge that most others—both inside and outside the company—lack (1=none, 5=plenty)?
   c. If your company had to eliminate departments, what would happen to yours (1=first to go, 5=last to go)?
   d. Is your department respected by other parts of the company (1=not at all, 5=highly)?
   e. How much does your business or division contribute to the profitability of the company (1=the least, 5=the most)?
   f. Does it look as if your business will grow or shrink in coming years (1=shrink, 5=grow)?

   Scores of 26 to 30 indicate you are in a good position to ask for a nice raise; scores of 21 to 25 indicate you are in a reasonable position to ask for a nice raise;

scores of 17 to 20 indicate you are in a questionable position to ask for a raise; and scores 16 or less suggest your request is probably not going to be taken too seriously. Keep in mind that just because you work long hours, it does not mean that you are being a productive member of the organization.

Try your best to learn about the company pay policies and practices. For example, you may be at the top of your grade level. In that case, your boss may simply respond that you have reached the maximum of your grade, and there is nothing else he or she can do. Finally, be careful that you don't ask for a raise that puts you at or above what your supervisor is making.

2. **Evaluate Your Supervisor's Style.** Perhaps almost as important as the issues mentioned above is to understand your supervisor's style. Some supervisors, for instance, enjoy give-and-take negotiations and will expect you to bargain hard for your raise. This type of supervisor may be impressed by an aggressive style. Others dislike conflict and will avoid confrontations. This type of supervisor might be more convinced by a rational and quiet approach.

3. **Consider Any Objections Your Supervisor May Have and How You Will Respond to Them.** Here are some common objections and possible responses:

   a. "I can't give you that much of an increase; the maximum allowed is x." Your response: "I can accept that this year. But only if I can have a written promise that next year I will be raised by y amount" or "I understand that in exceptional cases, higher raises can be allocated."
   b. "No one else in your position makes that much money—I can't justify you making more than other employees." (Remember, as noted above, surveys show that people typically overestimate the salaries their coworkers are earning.) Your response: "Let me review for you the reasons why I should be making a higher salary." Be sure to emphasize your achievements—not your coworker's shortcomings—or your supervisor may conclude that you think he or she isn't monitoring your coworker's performance properly.
   c. "No." If the answer is a clear "no," don't be shy. Ask your boss, "Why?" Particularly if you scored high on the questions above, one tactic may simply be to keep on asking for a raise.[49]

While most experts suggest that you set up a meeting to present your arguments in a coherent, logical fashion, other experts suggest that you drop some hints over a period of several weeks, like, "Do you think I am in the appropriate job grade for the work that I do?" to indicate to your manager that you are thinking about a pay increase.[50]

If you choose to focus on a meeting to introduce the topic, here are some suggestions:

1. **Start by Explaining Several Reasons, All Equally Important, That Should Merit You Your Desired Pay Increase.** These may include what other people are being paid, but you must primarily emphasize your worth to the organization. That is your key bargaining chip; focusing too much on comparisons with other employees may work against you. Also, make sure that you cover all of your points. Avoid letting the supervisor cut you off; on the other hand, you don't want to appear rude by ignoring him or her. If at all possible, bring documentation of your accomplishments, pay surveys, and other relevant information. This way, after the meeting, your supervisor can examine supporting evidence more carefully.[51]

2. **Give the Supervisor an Opportunity to Respond or Think about Your Request.** Offering your supervisor some time to consider your request might be a good way for handling a response like, "No way!" Another approach might be, "You might want time to consider my counteroffer."

3. **Work Toward Agreement and Compromise.** Most supervisors are used to negotiating toward a compromise. A particularly effective way to proceed toward a compromise is to summarize the supervisor's position, including any objections he or she has raised, and then summarize your position. This will be particularly helpful when the supervisor has made a counteroffer on the salary increase. Another tool to help come to a compromise is to include more than one reward in the discussion. For example, you may wish to talk about increasing your pay, as well as taking a training program that will require the company to pay for it and allow you to take time off. Your supervisor may feel obliged to agree to one of those two matters.

4. **Avoid the Most Common Mistakes.** During the meeting, beware of the following missteps:[52]

   a. Settling on a counteroffer too quickly. If you are even a little hesitant to accept the counteroffer, you may get more than you bargained for.
   b. Negotiating when you are not completely prepared. If you don't have all of the facts in front of you, don't negotiate.
   c. Getting upset. It is imperative that you stay calm and relaxed. Getting upset or losing your temper will work against you.
   d. Meeting at a bad time in a bad place. Always arrange for a private meeting with the supervisor where there will be no interruptions (such as phone calls). Choose a time when your supervisor will be receptive to your request. You probably know the times when your supervisor is not in a good mood or is under pressure (for example, Monday mornings are usually not a good time).

Finally, be careful not to let your request for a salary raise backfire. Although research indicates that negotiating can increase your salary, being overly aggressive or demanding could negatively affect your relationship with your supervisor and your company, and it makes matters even worse over the long term. With current trends toward pay-for-performance, you might consider trying to develop some kind of bonus plan instead of focusing on your base pay increasing.

❖ Conclusion

Compensation processes are important to every organization. In addition to the discrimination laws described in Chapter 2, several additional laws affect compensation practices, including the Fair Labor Standards Act and prevailing wage laws. In determining base wages, organizations use a combination of job evaluation, which focuses on internal fairness, and wage and salary surveys, which address external fairness. A pay structure is ultimately developed, which establishes the wages that an organization will pay each job. Alternatives to the traditional pay structure include broadbanding, market pricing, skill-based pay and competency-based pay. With this basic information in mind, both organizations and individual employees should be able to make effective decisions about pay.

❖ Applying Core Concepts

1. A commercial bakery that has a large contract to produce baked goods for a local army base has asked you what laws are likely to apply in terms of compensation. List all that may apply.
2. A company has asked you to design a job evaluation system. How would you go about this task?
3. The company you or a friend works for has decided to conduct a wage and salary survey. What organizations do you think should be included in the survey? Why?
4. Think of an organization you are familiar with (if you are not familiar with any organization, use the university setting). Do you think a traditional pay structure, broadbanding, market pricing, or a skill-based/competency-based pay system would be best? Why?
5. If Laurie from the opening case asked you how she should go about asking her boss for a pay raise, what would you suggest?
6. Using the Internet, find pay information from three different salary surveys for a specific job that you would like to have or currently have (for example, marketing manager). List the three figures you found. How close are they? If they differ by more than 10 percent from each other, can you think of some reasons why they may differ? Which do you think is the most reliable figure? Why?

❖ Key Terms

Fair Labor Standards Act of 1938	Compensable factors	Pay range
Nonexempt employees	Hay Plan	Grade overlap
Exempt employees	Ranking method of job evaluation	Green circle rates
Equal Pay Act of 1963	Job classification	Red circle rates
Comparable worth	Labor market survey	Broadbanding
Prevailing wage laws	Product market survey	Market pricing
Job evaluation	Benchmark jobs	Skill-based pay
Point method job evaluation	Pay structure	Competency-based pay
	Job grades	

❖ CHAPTER 8 *Experiential Exercise*

Bhatt, Frank, Lee, & Associates

Adamsville is a town of about 30,000 residents, located in a major metropolitan area in the Midwest. Last year, Clark Inglis was hired to serve as the new city manager. Clark was hired largely for his capability to implement innovative new programs in Adamsville. In the past few years, Adamsville has experienced declining revenues and more residents have complained about the quality of service. Moreover, there has been a great deal of turnover among homeowners as more and more of the population moves away to find newer homes. Clark has been attempting to cut costs where possible while improving service quality, in an attempt to stop the turnover.

One of the first things that Clark did when he was hired was to conduct an employee satisfaction survey. After reviewing the results, he discovered that a significant portion of employees was dissatisfied with their pay and how pay decisions were made. He then decided, with approval from the mayor and the board of aldermen, to contract with a consulting firm for an analysis of the pay structure. The consulting firm, Bhatt, Frank, Lee, & Associates, was recommended by the mayor of a nearby town and ended up making the lowest bid. In this exercise, you will see a copy of the initial draft report presented by Bhatt, Frank, Lee, & Associates, and you should prepare for a meeting with the city manager, who would like your opinion about this report. To prepare for the meeting, be ready to answer the following questions:

1. What questions do you have for the consultants?
2. Do you think the report is well done? Be specific.
3. What additional information should be provided?
4. Would you have done this analysis differently? How?

The Report

Background: Adamsville has approximately 75 employees and 20 different job titles. Most of these employees are police patrol officers. Our consulting firm was asked to examine both the internal and external fairness of the pay of these employees. Toward that end, we performed the following steps:

1. We obtained job descriptions for all positions. We then met with all supervisors and asked them to modify and update the job descriptions as needed.
2. We met with the Mayor and three top elected officials and asked them to rank-order the 20 different job titles in terms of importance based on the job descriptions. We correlated the average ranking with the average pay for the jobs.

3. We obtained salary survey data from various sources to compare with the pay at Adamsville.

The results from steps 2 and 3 are provided next, followed by a summary of our recommendations.

Internal Fairness

We calculated a correlation between the rank order of the jobs and their average pay. The correlation was .75, which indicates a high agreement between the rank-order and their pay. Two jobs were paid more than they were judged to be worth in the rank-order. These were police officer and clerk 1. Two jobs were paid less than the rank-order indicated they were worth: receptionist and supervisor of parks and recreation. The pay for all other jobs was in the same rank order as their importance.

External Fairness

We obtained pay information from four salary surveys:

1. BLS: A federal government source.
2. State Municipal League: A state salary survey that is used by many local and municipal governments. We used the overall state pay figures.
3. Federal Employee Survey: A survey containing salaries for federal employees, averaged for the country.
4. BFLA: Our firm's salary survey, which is based on information from both public and private sector companies in our metropolitan area.

Tables 1 and 2 include the jobs that are either 10 percent above or 10 percent below the market rate, that is, the jobs that are either overpaid or underpaid relative to what people in these jobs are paid elsewhere.

Table 1	Salary Survey Results For Selected Jobs			
Job Title	BLS	State Munic.	Federal Survey	BFLA
City Manager	N.A.	75,000	N.A.	82,000
Police Officer	28,000	26,005	27,005	30,100
Maintenance	22,000	29,000	27,100	31,000
Clerk I	16,000	18,000	19,000	19,900
Supervisor	24,000	28,000	29,000	21,000
Director of Public Works	N.A.	50,000	52,000	57,000

N.A. means salary survey is not available for this job.

Table 2	Actual Pay Versus Average Salary Survey Pay for Selected Jobs	
Job Title	**Actual Pay**	**Avg. Salary Survey**
City Manager	70,300	78,500
Police Officer	32,333	27,750
Maintenance	24,222	27,250
Clerk I	22,010	18,250
Supervisor	30,000	25,500
Director of Public Works	65,000	53,000

As you can see from Tables 1 and 2, two jobs are underpaid and four jobs are overpaid.

Conclusions

1. Increase the pay of supervisor of parks and recreation by $5,000 and the receptionist by $3,000 in order to increase the internal fairness of their pay so that their pay is commensurate with their internal worth.

2. Immediately increase the pay for the city manager by $8,000 and maintenance employees by $3,000.

3. Freeze the pay for director of public works, supervisors, clerk I, and police officers for two years. At that time, determine whether their pay levels have caught up with the external labor market pay. If they are still 10 percent above the market, freeze their pay for one additional year.

❖ Chapter 8 References

1. F. Hills, T. J. Bergmann, and V. Scarpello. *Compensation Decision-Making* (Fort Worth, TX: Dryden, 1994).
2. M. Wallace and C. Fay, *Compensation Theory and Practice* (Boston, PWS-Kent, 1988).
3. L. Joel, *Every Employee's Guide to the Law* (New York: Pantheon, 1993).
4. Ibid.
5. F. Hansen, "Currents in Compensation and Benefits," *Compensation and Benefits Review* 29 (November/December 1997): 6–15.
6. Ibid.
7. Joel, *Employee's Guide.*
8. M. Player, *Federal Law of Employment Discrimination* (St. Paul, MN: West, 1999).
9. E. Livernash, *Comparable Worth: Issues and Alternatives* (Washington: Equal Employment Advisory Council, 1980).
10. G. Milkovich and J. Newman. *Compensation* (Chicago: Irwin, 1996).
11. Ibid.
12. Web site of the Department of Labor (www.dol.gov).
13. Milkovich and Newman, *Compensation.*
14. Ibid.
15. Ibid.
16. P. LeBlanc and P. Mulvey, "How American Workers See the Rewards of Work," *Compensation and Benefits Review* 30 (January/February 1998): 24–28.
17. R. Scholl, E. Cooper, and J. McKenna, "Referent Selection in Determining Equity Perceptions: Differential Effects on Behavioral and Attitudinal Outcomes," *Personnel Psychology* 40 (1987), 113–24.

18. R. Henderson, *Compensation Management in a Knowledge-Based World* (Englewood Cliffs, NJ: Prentice-Hall, 1998).

19. Ibid.

20. Wallace and Fay, *Compensation Theory and Practice.*

21. Henderson, *Compensation Management.*

22. Wallace and Fay, *Compensation Theory and Practice.*

23. Milkovich and Newman, *Compensation.*

24. R. Madigan and D. Hoover, "Effects of Alternative Job Evaluation Methods on Decisions Involving Pay Equity," *Academy of Management Journal* 29 (1986): 84–100.

25. J. Collins and P. Muchinsky, "An Assessment of the Construct Validity of Three Job Evaluation Methods: A Field Experiment," *Academy of Management Journal* 36 (1993): 895–904.

26. Henderson, *Compensation Management.*

27. W. Wiatrowski, "A Formidable New Compensation Tool: Bureau of Labor Statistics' New National Compensation Survey," *Compensation and Benefits Review* 30 (September/October 1998): 29–41.

28. L. K. Beatty, "The Use and Abuse of Salary Surveys," in W. Caldwell (Ed.), *Compensation Guide* (Boston, MA: Warren, Gorham & Lamont, 1994).

29. Wallace and Fay, *Compensation Theory and Practice.*

30. B. Gerhart and G. Milkovich, "Employee Compensation: Research and Practice," in *Handbook of Industrial and Organizational Psychology*, ed. M. Dunnette and L. Hough (Palo Alto, CA: Consulting Psychologists Press, 1992).

31. J. Dantico, "Developing a Base Pay Structure," in W. Caldwell (Ed.), *Compensation Guide* (Boston, MA: Warren, Gorham & Lamont, 1994).

32. N. Bereman and M. Lengnick-Hall, *Compensation Decision Making: A Computer-Based Approach* (Fort Worth, TX: Dryden, 1994).

33. Ibid.

34. Milkovich and Newman, *Compensation.*

35. Henderson, *Compensation Management.*

36. D. Hofrichter, "Broadbanding: A 'Second Generation' Approach," *Compensation and Benefits Review* 25 (1993): 53–8.

37. D. Brown, "Broadbanding: A Study of Company Practices in the United Kingdom," *Compensation and Benefits Review* 28 (November/December 1996): 41–9.

38. Ibid.

39. A. Richter, "Paying the People in Black at Big Blue," *Compensation and Benefits Review* 30 (May/June 1998): 51–9.

40. Wallace and Fay, *Compensation Theory and Practice.*

41. E. Lawler, *Strategic Pay* (San Francisco: Jossey-Bass, 1990).

42. Ibid.

43. H. Tosi and L. Tosi, "What Managers Need to Know about Knowledge-Based Pay," *Organizational Dynamics* 14 (1986): 52–64.

44. G. Klein, "Case Study: A Pay-For-Knowledge Compensation Program that Works," *Compensation and Benefits Review* 30 (March/April 1998): 69–75.

45. D. Cira and E. Benjamin, "Competency-based Pay: A Concept in Evolution," *Compensation and Benefits Review* 30 (September/October 1998): 21–8.

46. Milkovich and Newman, *Compensation.*

47. G. Hartman, *How to Negotiate a Bigger Raise* (Hauppauge, NY: Barron's Educational Services, 1991).

48. A. Fisher and M. O'Malley, "How to Get the Raise You Deserve," *Fortune*, 7 September 1998, 169.

49. Ibid.

50. Ibid.

51. J. Traina, "Negotiating the Salary You Deserve," *Denver Post*, 2 June 1996, G11.

52. J. Rigdon, "I Want More: In Hard Times, the Old Rules on Pay Raises No Longer Apply," *Wall Street Journal*, 22 April 1992, R5.

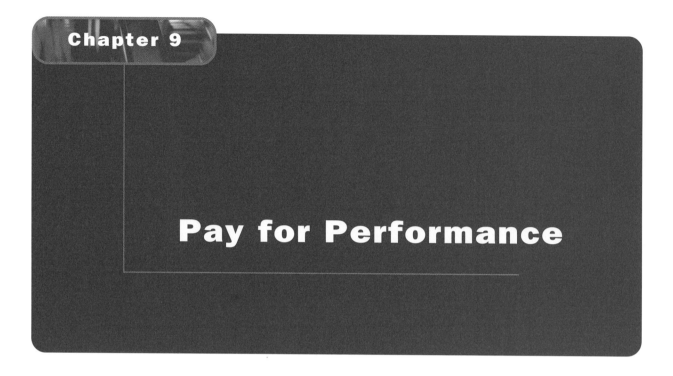

Pay for Performance

Core Concepts | **After reading this chapter, you should be capable of:**

1. Explaining why companies are using pay-for-performance plans.
2. Defining the four basic kinds of pay-for-performance plans.
3. Discussing the conditions under which employees receive the lowest and highest merit raises.
4. Identifying the advantages and disadvantages of different pay-for-performance plans.

Opening Case

During the past month, Ricardo has received job offers from four different companies. Each job involves software sales for a medium-size computer products company, and in each case, the work is the same, the benefits are the same, and the coworkers seem quite similar. Even the type of software Ricardo would be selling is the same. The only difference between the jobs is the pay policy.

Stable Works, Inc., provides a fairly generous base pay. The company told Ricardo that pay increases will depend on the area manager's yearly review of Ricardo's work.

The second company, Fire Cracker Software, bases pay primarily on the salesperson's sales volume. Although Ricardo would be paid at least a minimum wage every month, he would earn a higher salary only to the degree that he is successful selling the software. This company even showed him the highest and lowest monthly salaries earned by sales associates for the past two years. While the average monthly salary was somewhat lower than the base salary at Stable Works, in some months a few sales associates earned double or even triple the monthly salary earned at Stable Works.

The third company, TeamWare Limited, offered yet a third type of pay plan. Under this plan, Ricardo would earn a modest base salary, roughly half of what Stable Works offered him. He would be part of a four-person sales team. The commission, based on sales volume, will depend on the team's performance. The team also decides how to distribute the commission. Usually, said Vanessa Williams (the area manager), everyone shares equally in the bonus, which, she added, typically ranges from roughly one-quarter to double the base salary.

The fourth firm, Corporate Solutions, offered Ricardo a starting salary roughly 20 percent lower than what Stable Works offered, but had a profit-sharing plan based on company profitability. Over the past five years, the company has done extremely well, paying out yearly amounts equivalent to anywhere between 15 percent to 35 percent of sales associates' yearly salaries.

Clearly, each of these companies has a different pay policy, and Ricardo realizes that the policies have different consequences for him. While he likes the assurance of the high base pay offered by Stable Works, Inc., it seems as though he would have the most influence over his pay at Fire Cracker Software. But, under this plan his salary could change from month to month, and some months he might only get a minimum wage. TeamWare sounds as though it might be a nice mix of base and bonus pay, but Ricardo wonders what would happen if conflicts occurred within the team. And at Corporate Solutions, it seems as though many different factors, many of which would be out of Ricardo's control, would affect his pay.

What would you do if you were in this situation? As you can probably guess, each of these pay-for-performance (P-f-P) policies has advantages as well as disadvantages for both the organization and the employee. Many organizations are trying to find the P-f-P plan that works best for them. The purpose of this chapter, then, is to examine why companies would implement a P-f-P plan, to identify the various kinds of P-f-P plans, and to review some of the advantages and disadvantages for each plan. We begin first with a discussion of why companies implement P-f-P plans.

Why Do Companies Implement Pay-for-Performance Plans?

A **P-f-P plan** is a program in which the employee's pay is at least in part dependent upon job performance. As you will see a little bit later, P-f-P plans differ widely in terms of whether performance refers to the individual employee's success, his or her work group's success, or the success of the division, plant, or company.

Companies use pay-for-performance plans for several reasons. Each of these is described in greater detail next.[1]

Pay-for-Performance plan
A program where some pay is based on the individual, the team, or the organization's performance.

1. **Pay Is a Powerful Motivator for Employees.** Not surprisingly, a properly designed and implemented P-f-P plan will be a strong motivator for employees. For example, a review of one type of P-f-P plan, profit-sharing, estimated an average productivity increase of 7.4 percent.[2] A study of gain sharing, a different kind of P-f-P plan, found that defects per 1,000 units fell from 20.93 to 2.31 once the plan was implemented.[3]

2. **Many Employees Support the Pay-for-Performance Concept.** Many employees believe that job performance should be a major determinant of pay. In one survey, for instance, respondents rated level of job performance as being the most important factor in determining the size of a salary increase. In contrast, seniority was rated the least important factor.[4] Thus, employees generally support the pay-for-performance concept.

3. **Pay-for-Performance Plans Attract and Retain Top Performers.** A successful P-f-P plan will attract and retain highly qualified applicants, who will view the plan as offering excellent opportunities for financial rewards. For example, one survey indicated that professional employees in U.S. Navy laboratories were less likely to quit when a pay-for-performance plan was in place.[5]

4. **Pay-for-Performance Plans Provide a Clear Signal.** An often overlooked advantage of a well-designed P-f-P plan is that it clearly defines what performance is desired and what the standards for performance are in the organization. As described in Chapter 7, performance dimensions and standards are often ambiguous. By developing a P-f-P plan, two things happen. First, the organization must decide what employee behaviors, processes, and goals are important, and it must communicate those expectations to the employees. Thus, the organization is compelled to consider its mission and goals. Second, employees will have a better understanding of what the company desires, and therefore should be more successful in their jobs.

In sum, an effective P-f-P plan may be useful for an organization for several reasons. Of course, much depends on how well designed and implemented the plan is. A poorly designed P-f-P plan can do more harm than no P-f-P plan at all.

Alternatives to Pay for Performance

Not all companies have a P-f-P plan. In some companies, seniority is the sole determinant of pay increases. Do you think that two employees doing the same job, with equal skills and identical job performance, should be paid differently if one has worked longer with the company? As noted earlier, one survey indicated that people consider seniority the least important factor in salary raises. Can you think of any logical reasons as to why seniority should be a determinant of pay increases? One answer might be that employees would be encouraged to stay with a company if their pay was related to seniority. Critics, however, would question what value seniority provides to the company, and they would probably argue that pay should be based on performance, not longevity on the job. Another alternative is to compensate employees for mastering additional skills or competencies; this approach was discussed in Chapter 8. What other factors should affect pay increases? What about cost-of-living increases? Does it seem fair to you that your wages should increase in proportion to the inflation rate? It may surprise you to learn that fewer companies today than in the past would agree that salaries should be affected by the cost of living. In fact, many companies would consider this a minor or even irrelevant factor. In the remainder of this chapter,

INTERCULTURAL ISSUES IN HUMAN RESOURCES

Box 9.1
Pay-for-Performance: Global Considerations

In the United States there is a deeply ingrained notion that high performers should receive greater pay than low performers. In Pacific Rim countries, that concept traditionally has been considered quite alien. In fact, the entire pay-for-performance concept, even at the group or organization level, is hardly widespread. However, signs indicate that this is beginning to change. Countries such as Hong Kong, Taiwan, and Singapore have made extensive use of individual incentive plans in the manufacturing sector for some time. The recent economic downturn in Japan has led to some changed thinking there about the need for pay-for-performance plans, despite the traditional emphasis on seniority-based pay. Some of the biggest and best-known Japanese companies are moving to pay-for-performance plans. Tanada Kyoichi, a human resource manager for Toyota Motor, states that seniority-based systems in his company have been eliminated and that merit-based pay will be used instead. Fujitsu began a goal management and evaluation system in 1993 to help determine pay; the company now has a policy that 30 percent of employee pay should be tied to performance.

Pay-for-performance plans in the United Kingdom have generally not followed U.S. approaches. Innovations such as team pay, skill-based pay, and competency-based pay, for example, have not been widely used in the United Kingdom, despite the fact that since the mid-1990s, about 40 percent of companies have made changes in their pay programs. Merit pay, which has been adopted relatively slowly in the United Kingdom, has been viewed as helpful in improving organizational performance. Organizations in the United Kingdom are beginning to make more use of 360-degree feedback systems and are adopting a wider set of performance measures in order to enhance their pay systems. Clearly, U.S. managers working in global assignments should not assume that what works at home will automatically work elsewhere in the world.

Sources: F. Hansen, "Currents in Compensation and Benefits," *Compensation and Benefits Review* 30 (September/October 1998): 6–15; G. McEvoy and W. Cascio, "The United States and Taiwan: Two Different Cultures Look at Performance Appraisal." in *Research in Personnel/Human Resource Management* (International Human Resources Management), Supplement 2, ed. B. Shaw and J. Beck (Greenwich, CT: JAI Press, 1990); C. Hitoshi, I. Ryuko, and S. Osamu, "Salaryman Today and Into Tomorrow," *Compensation and Benefits Review* 29 (September/October 1997): 67–75.

then, we will discuss only performance-related pay differences. For a discussion of how other countries view pay-for-performance plans, see Box 9.1. Next, you will read about different kinds of P-f-P plans and the advantages and disadvantages of each.

Kinds of Pay-for-Performance Plans

You have probably heard of many kinds of P-f-P plans, such as commission plans, individual incentive plans, bonuses, and so forth. For sake of simplicity, we will organize P-f-P plans into four basic categories. As shown in Figure 9.1, these categories are merit, individual incentive, team incentive, and organization-wide incentives. Before describing each of these categories in greater detail, however, several points are worth noting about P-f-P plans.

General Principles

1. **The Best Plan Depends on the Context.** As you will see in the next few sections, there is no one best P-f-P plan. Rather, the best P-f-P plan will depend on the nature of the job, the organization's business strategy, and other factors.

2. **Many Organizations Use a Combination of P-f-P Plans.** Although each type of P-f-P plan will be described separately, in reality, many companies use a combination of P-f-P plans. The reason, as you will see, is that no one P-f-P plan is perfect. In combination, however, many of the potential problems can be reduced.

3. **Pay Is Not the Only Motivator.** Some critics of pay-for-performance systems have noted that an overemphasis on pay detracts from high performance and may even reduce certain desirable behaviors. Certainly, there is more to motivation than pay, and effective organizations use several means of motivating their employees. Nonfinancial rewards, such as flexible hours and interesting work assignments, may also be highly motivating. Keep in mind the following aphorism: "Men and women do not work for money only."

Now that you have read about some general principles of P-f-P plans, we will define the four P-f-P plan categories.

Merit

merit pay
The payout is based on the individual employee's performance, performance is evaluated in a subjective fashion, and the payout is added to the employee's base salary.

Have you ever worked for an organization where you received a yearly salary increase based on your supervisor's recommendation? If you have, you were covered by a **merit pay** plan. This is the plan Stable Works used in the opening case of this chapter. Merit plans are quite common in the United States—at least 80 percent of organizations use them.[6] Essentially, a merit P-f-P plan has these features:

1. The payout is based on the individual employee's performance.
2. Performance is evaluated in a subjective fashion.
3. The payout is added to the employee's base salary.

Individual Incentive

individual incentive
The payout is based on the individual employee's performance, and performance is evaluated using an objective standard.

Have you ever worked in a sales job? If you have, was your pay based on how much merchandise you sold? In certain industries, such as automobile sales, an employee's pay is directly tied to an objective measure of performance. This type of pay arrangement is referred to as an **individual incentive,** which is the approach Fire Cracker Software used in the opening case. An individual incentive plan, then, has two basic features:

1. The payout is based on the individual employee's performance.
2. Performance is evaluated using an objective standard.

Sales employees and production workers represent the occupations most likely to be covered by an individual incentive plan. This is not surprising, given that these jobs usually have an objective measure of performance.

Team Incentive

team incentive
The payout is based on the team's level of performance, and performance is evaluated using an objective standard.

Have you ever been part of a classroom project in which you were a member of a team? If your answer is yes, how was the grade assigned? Typically, all members receive the same grade in a school team project. The same logic applies to a **team incentive**

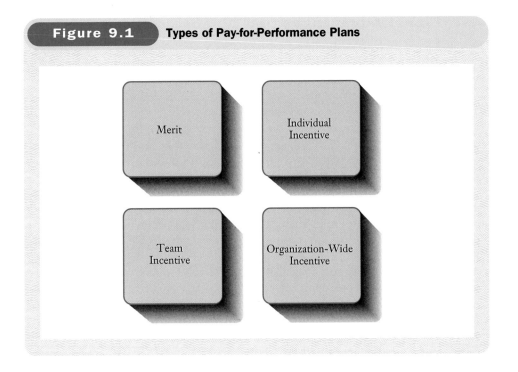

Figure 9.1   **Types of Pay-for-Performance Plans**

Merit

Individual Incentive

Team Incentive

Organization-Wide Incentive

P-f-P plan. This is also the plan TeamWare used in the opening case. A team incentive plan, then, has these major characteristics:

1. The payout is based on the team's level of performance.
2. Performance is evaluated using an objective standard.

Organization-Wide Incentive

An **organization-wide incentive** is based on how one's plant, division, or company performs. This is the plan Corporate Solutions used in the opening case. The major characteristics of an organization-wide incentive plan are as follows:

1. The payout is based on the performance of the plant, division, or organization.
2. Performance is evaluated using an objective standard.

There are two basic types of organization-wide incentive plans. In a **profit-sharing plan,** performance is linked to some index of profitability. Typically, the payout is provided on a yearly basis and, in some cases, part of the payout is placed into a retirement fund for employees (see Chapter 10). In comparison, a **gain-sharing plan** provides a payout when productivity improvements occur. The assumption is that employees can increase productivity by suggesting improvements or by working more efficiently. Gain-sharing plans generally provide cash payouts. The payout is usually made on a frequent, sometimes monthly, basis.[7]

Next, you will read about some advantages and disadvantages of each of these basic P-f-P plans.

organization-wide incentive
The payout is based on the performance of the plant, division, or organization; performance is evaluated using an objective standard.

profit-sharing plan
Pay is linked to some index of profitability.

gain-sharing plan
Provides a payout when productivity improvements occur.

Merit Plans: Advantages and Disadvantages

Merit P-f-P plans have a number of advantages and disadvantages. As shown in Table 9.1, from an organization's perspective, the merit approach is relatively easy to develop and implement. This is especially true if an effective performance management system is already in place, which can then be used to determine salary raises. Furthermore, because the merit system relies on a subjective performance evaluation, all aspects of the job can be considered in assigning raises. Take, for example, the sales job offered in the opening case of this chapter. One of the major problems many companies face is motivating salespeople to perform activities besides straight selling. For example, salespeople may be reluctant to devote time to acquiring new product information if they have an established customer base, particularly when a large portion of their pay is based on sales volume. A company such as Stable Works (which uses a merit system) should be more effective in motivating salespeople to learn about new products than companies like Fire Cracker that reward salespeople primarily for sales volume.

Another advantage of a merit pay plan is that it can be applied to all jobs. The reason for this will become apparent when you realize that a subjective evaluation can be made for any job. An objective measure of job performance, however, cannot be provided for every job, which is a limitation of the individual incentive method. Finally, because of the way in which merit plans are typically developed, in the short term at least, such plans are advantageous in that they can be designed to fit within a company's budget. For instance, an organization can decide how much of its budget to allocate to salaries and then divide this amount among employees based on their individual performances.

Despite the many strengths of a merit pay plan, it has several significant shortcomings that limit its effectiveness. One major shortcoming of this plan from the employer's perspective is that costs snowball from year to year as each year's payout becomes part of the base salary. In the long term, then, use of a merit pay plan may create significant financial problems for an organization, particularly if profits are down at some point in time. This is one reason companies have begun to move away from merit pay plans toward other plans. A second major problem with this approach is that managers often dislike it. Recall from Chapter 7 that many managers are uncomfortable giving low performance ratings; leniency or central tendency is frequently the result. Managers frequently use the "peanut butter" approach to merit raises: pay increases are spread evenly so that relatively poor performers often receive raises that are similar if not identical to those obtained by top performers.

Table 9.1	Advantages and Disadvantages of Merit Plans

Advantages	Disadvantages
1. Easy to develop	1. Costs snowball
2. Offer the ability to reward all aspects of job	2. Managers may not favor them
3. May be applied to any job	3. May not be highly motivating
4. Allow for flexibility within the company's budget	

Finally, a likely outcome of these and related issues is that merit pay systems often are not effective motivators of employees. In many companies, the top worker receives a 5 or 6 percent raise, while the worst performer gets a 3 percent raise. For a typical worker, this may work out to a difference of only $10 to $20 weekly, before taxes.[8] Not only are raise differences between the best and worst workers likely to be small under most merit pay plans, but many employees see little relationship between job performance and pay raises. One report indicated that fewer than half of the managers and professionals surveyed believed that top performers received higher raises than poor performers.[9] In more recent times, when raises have averaged close to 4 percent, the difference in pay raises between top and poor performers has become small.

Merit Pay Plans: Do They Work?

Given both the advantages and the disadvantages of merit pay plans, you may wonder if they are effective. There is some evidence that merit pay plans do improve both employee attitudes and job performance. Not all companies, however, report gains.[10] One large public transportation company, for instance, reported mixed results—employee performance improved; however, many participants reported dissatisfaction with their pay raises, further evidence that merit pay systems are not always effective in motivating employees.[11] Where is a merit plan likely to work best? It would appear that this P-f-P plan is most likely to be effective in a large, traditional organization, particularly for employees where objective measures of job performance are not available.[12] Much of the success of a merit plan hinges on how well the performance management system works.

Maximizing Merit Raises: Tips for Employees

You may now be wondering what factors will affect the size of raises you, as an employee, receive. Scientific research suggests that certain factors do affect pay raises. In discussing these factors, it is simplest to organize them into three categories: employee characteristics, supervisor characteristics, and organizational characteristics.[13]

Employee Characteristics Affecting Merit Raises

Contrary to what you might think, research has found at least some relationship between job performance and merit pay raises in many organizations.[14] Thus, although it may not seem apparent to you as an employee, merit plans often do provide higher raises for superior performance. Furthermore, as you will see, even small raises can translate over time into big payouts. So, despite the negative comments earlier about the small size of pay differences, when considered over a long period of time, receiving even a slightly larger raise than your coworker's can mean much more money in your pocket.

What about seniority? Recall from earlier that merit pay plans supposedly do not take seniority into account. Although research indicates that, in some companies, seniority is related to higher raises, in other organizations seniority may work against the employee, as more senior employees are likely to be closer to the grade maximum. On the whole, though, more companies are ignoring seniority in making raise determinations than in the past.[15]

Other employee characteristics have been linked to higher pay raises. One such factor, which you will not find surprising, is the difficulty in replacing the employee. If, for example, you have a unique skill that would be difficult for the organization to replace, you are likely to obtain a higher raise than if you are easily replaceable.[16] Some evidence also suggests that "whom you know" in the organization will improve the raise that you receive, but only if it appears that you have other job opportunities.[17]

Finally, do you think that such factors as your sex, race, and age are related to size of raise? Contrary to what you might believe, few scientific studies have found evidence for such a relationship. You should also be aware that basing salary raises on sex, race, age, and certain other demographic characteristics is illegal and that organizations have been sued on this basis.

In sum, if you want to receive the highest raise possible, you will need to demonstrate superior job performance and provide a unique skill or experience that the organization will have a difficult time replacing. Knowing the right people will not hurt either.

Supervisor Characteristics Affecting Merit Raises

Do some managers provide higher raises than other managers? The answer appears to be yes. Your chances for a higher raise are best under the following conditions:[18]

1. **Your Manager Has Relatively Little Experience Giving Raises.** Inexperienced managers are less comfortable giving raises and, to avoid controversy, will provide larger raises than will more experienced managers.
2. **Your Manager Is Relatively Well Paid and Receives High Raises.** Though it is not entirely clear why this would help you receive a higher raise, there is some evidence for a positive relationship between your raise and your manager's raise.
3. **Your Manager Is More Altruistic and People Oriented.** Logically, managers who are more concerned with the welfare of others are also more generous at salary raise time.

Despite the relationship between these managerial factors and the size of your merit raise, you should not overemphasize their importance. It is clear that the employee factors described previously are much more critical.

Organizational Characteristics Affecting Merit Raises

Certain characteristics of the company or organization for which you work will affect the size of your raise as well. These include the following:

1. **The Other Employees in Your Department or Group.** Would you rather be a big fish in a small pond, or a small fish in a large ocean? At least in some organizations, you will receive a higher raise if the other members of your department or group are less effective, suggesting that it is better to be a big fish in a small pond. In other companies, however, a highly effective work group may get a higher raise than an ineffective work group. The effect found in your organization may well depend on the nature of the work and the way the merit plan is implemented.
2. **The Merit Pay Policies.** Certain pay policies will affect the magnitude of your raise, depending on whether you are a top performer or a poor performer. Specifi-

cally, when salary increase information is available to workers, and managers are attempting to promote work team harmony, there is less spread between the highest and lowest raises. If you are a top performer in this case, you will get a smaller raise. Conversely, if you are a poor performer, you would receive a higher raise under these circumstances.

3. **The Objectivity of the Performance Measures.** The more objective and precise the performance measures, the greater the difference between highest and lowest raises, because the managers will have more confidence in making pay raise decisions. The effect on your raise will again depend on whether your performance was relatively high or low. Poor performers will, all things being equal, receive higher raises the less objective and clear the performance measures are. Higher performers will, all things being equal, receive higher raises the more objective and clear the performance measures are.

Recall from the opening case that the applicant had a choice between four different jobs, each of which offered a different pay plan. One of the organizations, Stable Works, Inc., offered a merit pay plan. Now that you have read about merit pay plans, do you think this would be the best pay plan for Ricardo? You have read about the advantages and disadvantages from the organization's perspective. Let's now consider the employee's perspective. In terms of the advantages, because the payout becomes part of one's base pay, compensation will be much more stable from month to month and from year to year than other plans. Second, because the payout becomes part of one's base pay, Ricardo will continue to reap the rewards each year. Even a small difference in pay raises (for example, a 9.8 percent raise versus a 9.0 percent raise over a 20-year period) will therefore lead to major salary differences between two employees (a cumulative earnings difference of more than $200,000 if both employees begin with an annual salary of $40,000). The lesson for employees is that even small raise differences can add up to large differences over time. On the negative side, perhaps the biggest problem of the merit approach for employees is that the payout may not be quite as big compared to an individual incentive plan. Merit pay plans, for the many reasons described earlier, tend to be fairly conservative in the size of the payout. So, if Ricardo is an outstanding salesperson, he may find Stable Work's plan to be less rewarding than Fire Cracker Software's plan.

The British Broadcasting Company (BBC) employs over 20,000 workers and uses a merit pay system. Despite its name, the BBC is a public-sector organization. In the late 1990s, the BBC adopted a merit system to reward individual performance that bases pay increases on three factors: union negotiations, individual performance, and other factors, such as market conditions, increased responsibilities, and new skills learned. The process begins with corporate salary planning guidelines issued at the beginning of a business cycle, which take into account the three factors mentioned above. Only staff who are rated as "consistently high performers" receive raises above those negotiated by the unions. Poor performers can face a pay reduction of as much as 4.5 percent for a maximum of six months. However, this is rarely done.[19] In two recent years, the unions negotiated a pay raise of 2.6 percent and 3.0 percent for the employees and an additional 1 percent and .5 percent was earmarked for performance and other factors.[20] Do you think that merit-based raises of that magnitude are meaningful motivators?

In sum, many organizations use merit pay plans. Despite their simplicity and frequency of use, however, they have limited motivational value. Not surprisingly, many organizations are developing and implementing P-f-P plans based on more objective

YOUR TURN

Box 9.2
Combining Pay-for-Performance Plans

The NRL Federal Credit Union (NRLFCU) in Washington, D.C., is one organization that uses a combination of P-f-P plans to motivate employees. Designed by a seven-person multilevel task force, the plan provides monetary rewards beyond base pay for performance at the organizational, team, and individual levels. The organizational-level component ties employee bonuses to three factors: the credit union's income, the number of eligible members using the credit union, and growth in assets. Each year, target figures are established for these three components. If the minimum figure is not reached for income, no payout is provided. Interestingly, any payout is distributed among employees based on the number of hours they have worked (overtime hours do not count), rather than the more typical approach, which uses a percentage of salary. Why do you think the credit union bases the payout on number of hours worked rather than salary? The answer is that top management believes that the em-

ployees who deal directly with the customer (for example, the tellers) have at least as great an effect on success as do the managers and supervisors who do not deal as directly with customers. Basing the payout on the number of hours worked provides a proportionately greater payout to the direct service jobs than would a payout based on salary (which would provide a greater payout to managers and supervisors).

At the team level, a payout is based on measurable goals that are consistent with the organization's mission. An organizational incentive committee reviews each team's goals on a quarterly basis and frequently adjusts them. The goals must be approved by top management. A by-product of this process is that employees learn a great deal about how their department's work meshes with other departments and with the organization as a whole, which has also led to productivity improvements.

Finally, the individual incentive program is geared toward rewarding

exemplary customer service. The program has established several criteria that may result in an individual reward, such as solving a unique or complex problem, proposing an innovative solution to a significant dilemma, or effectively handling a customer with a difficult problem. To be given an individual incentive award, employees must submit a self-nomination form, which requires a detailed description of the situation and the solution. The submissions are reviewed by the incentive committee, which makes the final decision regarding awards.

According to the president of the NRLFCU, the P-f-P plan has been extremely important to the success of this organization. From an employee perspective, the program has been successful as well, given that employees generally receive an additional 12 percent to 15 percent of their salaries. One employee even received a 20 percent increase during one quarter. NRLFCU demonstrates how multiple P-f-P plans can be used to achieve optimal results

Source: Adapted from K. Cooke, "CU-Wide Incentive System Reaps Substantial Rewards," *Credit Union Management* 15 (1992): 14–17.

results. In a recent survey, for example, more than one-third of responding companies indicated they would implement a new or additional objective-based pay plan in the near future, while almost 75 percent of the respondents indicated that their company already had this kind of plan. Moreover, organizations were setting aside increasing amounts of payroll for objective-based P-f-P plans.[21] Clearly, many companies are giving other P-f-P plans more attention, and some companies are beginning to abandon the merit approach. Box 9.2 discusses one organization's efforts to customize a P-f-P plan to suit specific goals.

Individual Incentive Plans: Advantages and Disadvantages

As shown in Table 9.2, individual incentive plans provide several advantages over merit pay plans, but they also have disadvantages compared to the merit pay system. In terms

Table 9.2	Advantages and Disadvantages of Individual Incentive Plans	
Advantages	**Disadvantages**	
1. Highly motivating	1. Require much preplanning	
2. Control costs	2. May lead to the neglect of other desirable aspects of work	
3. Reduce subjectivity	3. Encourage intragroup conflict	
	4. May lead to burnout	

of their motivational impact, individual incentive programs are considered the most effective type of pay plan. Their motivational power stems from the fact that employees are in direct control of their performance and have a clear understanding of how they can attain rewards.[22] An equally important feature of these plans from a management viewpoint is that they allow the company to control costs over the long term. Compared to a merit pay plan, where each payout becomes part of the base salary, the individual incentive payout depends on the employee's performance within a given time period. As a result, an individual incentive plan can produce great savings for the organization.[23]

Finally, employees tend to embrace such plans because of their objectivity. Subjectivity will play much less of a role than it does in a merit pay plan, because the rules and standards are clearly spelled out in an individual incentive plan.[24] In turn, managers generally are more comfortable with individual incentive programs, because their judgments will only come into play in designing the plan. For the same reason, employees may view the system as being more fair.

Individual incentive plans also have several significant disadvantages. A critical feature is that they require a great deal of careful preplanning by the company.[25] The major issue that must be determined in the planning stages is what level of performance produces what amount of payout. Consider the following situation in which production workers assemble electrical parts. For the last three years, the average worker has produced 100 circuit boards per day. Should the bonus plan be established whereby 100 boards per day is the average? Or should the average be set at 120 boards per day? If you believe workers are easily capable of producing 150 boards per day, you may wish to set 150 as the standard. In many cases, the company will monitor workers prior to implementation to determine an appropriate rate. But workers may find out what is going on and deliberately reduce their pace in order to lower the standard. If preplanning is not carefully conducted, significant problems may result when the plan is implemented.

A second significant problem with the individual incentive plan is that it also motivates employees to neglect areas not directly linked to the incentives. In one large retail organization, the compensation for sales clerks was changed to an individual incentive plan linked to sales volume. Management discovered that the plan was indeed effective in increasing sales, but, at the same time, both inventory work and merchandise display activities were neglected. Realizing that additional income would be granted only through sales volume, the clerks had diminished the effort and time they devoted to nonselling activities. Another area that may suffer when an individual incentive is in place is product quality. Safety problems may also become more prevalent.

A third major problem with the individual incentive approach is that it may promote counterproductive intragroup competition. Use of an individual incentive plan encourages the "each man and woman for himself or herself" type of thinking. In the case of the retail clerks just mentioned, the use of the individual incentive plan also increased the number of times a sale was unfairly taken away from another retail clerk, as well as other problems. Internal conflict, then, can be a serious problem with an individual incentive plan.

Finally, in the long run, individual incentives may lead to employee burnout. One can be highly motivated only for so long; eventually, the value of an incentive tends to wear out.[26]

Given the potential problems associated with individual incentive plans, it is not surprising that their use is limited. Experts suggest that they are most effective for simple, highly structured jobs, where the objectives are not affected by other employees or departments and effective performance is quantifiable and clear.[27] In light of today's emphasis on teamwork and quality in manufacturing, it is not surprising that individual incentive programs have declined in popularity in manufacturing facilities, to a point where they are used by only about 20 percent of companies.[28]

On the other hand, many salespeople continue to be covered by individual incentive plans. Moreover, some organizations are beginning to use individual incentives for jobs other than sales and production, linking the payouts to broader organizational objectives. Consider, for example, Taco Bell, the fast-food chain, which starts 500 new restaurants a year. To choose sites for these new restaurants, the company employs real estate managers, who do everything from locating appropriate sites to obtaining building permits. Prior to 1990, the real estate managers had a base salary in the mid-50s, with a bonus of about 20 percent. In 1990, the company changed the compensation program by cutting the base pay by about one-third, while increasing the incentive pay. Rather than having a single bonus, the company switched to a two-part incentive. First, for each new restaurant opened, the manager would receive a flat fee of $4,000. Once opened, the real estate manager would receive a second payout if the restaurant's return on investment (ROI) exceeded 15 percent. The higher the ROI, the higher the payout, which can be as high as $50,000. The result? Amy McConnell, whose area covers North and South Carolina, earned well over $300,000 annually under the new program. If properly designed then, individual incentive plans can be highly effective.[29]

Probably the best example of individual incentive pay is in a company that has been cited by a U.S. president and a speaker of the U.S. House of Representatives as being one of the best firms in the world. Approximately 25 production workers at this company earned over $100,000, and about 100 production workers earned more than $75,000 in 1996. The company is one you may never have heard of, Lincoln Electric Company, whose biggest product is arc welding equipment. Lincoln Electric is headquartered in Cleveland, Ohio. It employs just under 6,000 workers worldwide, with facilities in 11 countries. It has the best-known pay-for-performance plan in existence, and probably the longest running. In practice, the plan is really quite simple. All production workers are paid on an individual incentive plan; there is no base wage for these employees. For example, if an employee produces some work that is not acceptable because the machinery did not work properly, the employee would be paid nothing, unless he or she is able to repair the work.[30]

Because Lincoln Electric makes many parts for many different products, there are many different individual incentive plans. Although management makes changes in the rate as production methods are modified, workers have the right to question the alterations. Many of the rates have stayed the same for years (to maintain pace with inflation, a cost of living index is used to make annual adjustments). In addition to the number of parts produced, production workers are also eligible for an annual bonus, which is a function of a merit rating and company profits. The merit rating is determined by the worker's output (assessed by the production department), a measure of quality (evaluated by the quality-assurance department), dependability (based on absenteeism, tardiness, and other criteria), and ideas and cooperation. The merit rating system is designed so that each department is allocated 100 points per employee; if one employee receives 120 points, other employees must receive less than 100 points. Once the available bonus pool is determined, a formula is used to calculate the amount of money given to each worker.[31] In 1996, the bonus pool was $64 million. The company also has a suggestion system for employees. Employees who make suggestions have their names placed in a drawing and the winner has lunch with the president. The company rewards each individual who makes a cost-savings idea, which could amount to hundreds or even thousands of dollars.[32]

Lincoln Electric faced an interesting challenge implementing its pay-for-performance program on a global basis. The company found that the individual incentive approach did not work well in France. When Lincoln Electric opened a plant in Mexico, the company experienced a concern from Mexican nationals that they would exploit the workers. The lack of a base wage seemed to reinforce that idea. Therefore, the company added a base wage in its Mexico facility, to assure employees that even if they didn't make money on the incentive plan, they would earn close to the standard hourly rate. Once a few of the workers tried the incentive system and found that they were well rewarded, the other employees became interested and almost all are now on the incentive system. Moreover, turnover at the plant has declined dramatically.[33] Box 9.3 describes how changes in the business environment affected another company's change in pay structures.

Now that you have read about some of the advantages and disadvantages of individual incentives from a company's perspective, you may be wondering what the advantages and disadvantages of this plan are from an employee's perspective. What were your reactions to Fire Cracker Software, which, as you may recall from the opening case, used this kind of plan? Probably one of the most significant advantages from your perspective would be the potential to really do well. That is, many individual incentive plans are set up so that the sky's the limit, as in the case of Amy McConnell described earlier. Had she been covered by a merit pay plan, she could not possibly have earned that much. Another advantage of the individual incentive plan is that your pay will be less influenced by your supervisor. If you have interpersonal conflicts with your manager, an individual incentive plan will be less affected. This plan has several disadvantages for an employee, however. A major disadvantage is, of course, that success in one month or year does not affect the next pay period. You must perform well continually. Relatedly, your pay may fluctuate; at times it may be high, at other times low. This may make financial planning difficult. Finally, although the individual incentive plan is more objective, inequities and unfairness can arise. For example, some sales territories may be far more profitable than others. In a manufacturing context, some machines or product lines may be superior. Because turnover is likely to be lower in lucrative territories or product lines, most hiring is likely to be for openings in the less lucrative areas.

In sum, individual incentive plans can be highly motivating. If properly designed, an individual incentive program can be quite effective. At the same time, a poorly conceived individual incentive plan can wreak havoc on the organization.

Team Incentive Plans: Advantages and Disadvantages

As you read in previous chapters, work teams are quite popular in industry today. Not surprisingly, then, many organizations are modifying their P-f-P plans to motivate

Box 9.3
Changing from an Individual Incentive to a Unit Profit-Sharing Plan

Making changes is never easy, especially when workers' pay is affected. But sometimes, organizations are required to make changes in compensation, as was the case at West Bend Company. West Bend Company, located in Wisconsin, produces consumer appliances, including crock pots and woks. For many years, production workers were paid on an individual incentive basis. But, as in practically every industry, West Bend Company was affected in several ways by the increased global competition and the emphasis on quality. Now, objectives other than quantity were important, such as cost containment and speed. West Bend introduced several changes to meet these new objectives. One of these changes was to move to *just-in-time* production, whereby production would only work on existing orders. In many cases, paychecks fell because workers could only produce as much product as was needed at that particular time. In fact, some workers' pay fell as much as $2 per hour. To address the workers' frustration with their decreasing pay, management formed a committee with the union to design and implement a new pay-for-performance plan. Management even permitted the committee to review accounting information. After one year, the committee agreed to a pay-for-performance plan that would focus on units (for instance, the beverage operation was a separate unit). Each unit established objectives regarding quality, costs, customer service, and so forth, which were put into a formula. A substantial amount of employees' pay was made "at risk," such that if the objectives were met, the employees would receive 100 percent of their pay. To date, workers have received an average of 4 percent more than their base pay. According to management, inventory has been reduced 50 percent, scrap has been cut 70 percent, and quality has improved 70 percent.

Source: D. B. Hogarty, "New Ways to Pay," *Management Review* 83 (1994): 34–36.

employees to work in teams. In the opening case, TeamWare used a team incentive to compensate salespeople. While the team incentive approach has some advantages over the individual incentive approach, it also has several disadvantages.

As shown in Table 9.3, a major advantage of the team approach is that it rewards work-team cooperation. Recall that a significant disadvantage of the individual incentive approach is that it may encourage team conflict; the team incentive plan is the antidote to this problem. A second advantage of the team approach is that it is effective when performance differences between members of a team cannot be identified. Consider again the example provided earlier of the class team project. One person on the team may have conducted the library search, another member of the team may have contacted business professionals, and yet a third member of the team may have syn-

Table 9.3	Advantages and Disadvantages of Team Incentive Plans

Advantages	Disadvantages
1. Encourage team cooperation	1. Encourage social loafing
2. Useful when the supervisor cannot identify individual performance levels	2. Repeat the other disadvantages of individual incentive programs
3. Reasonably motivating	

thesized the information and written the report. Because each member of the team had a different task, it would not be possible to assess which person did better. Further, the instructor would have no way of knowing exactly who did what, so individual grades could not be assigned; all the instructor would be able to assess is the final product. And, if individual grades were assigned, there would be little incentive for one team member to assist another team member. Assignment of an overall grade or payout will motivate team members to help one another. Finally, in terms of motivational force, on average the team incentive plan is still relatively effective, although perhaps not quite as effective as the individual incentive approach. On the one hand, depending on the team's norms, some teams may be capable of developing an excellent esprit-de-corps that far exceeds the enthusiasm of any single individual. In that way, a team incentive plan can be highly motivating. On the other hand, a team with poor morale can significantly discourage even the most enthusiastic individual. The effect of the team incentive will depend heavily on group norms.

Turning to the disadvantages of the team approach, almost everyone has worked on a class team project in which one or two team members failed to do their fair share. If you have ever been in this situation, you were probably pretty upset because not only would their behavior hurt your grade, but you might have had to do extra work to compensate for their lack of performance. Often referred to as **social loafing,** it has long been known that individuals are less motivated when they are part of a team or group than when they are working alone. Social loafing is a common problem and represents a major disadvantage of the team incentive plan. To avoid social loafing problems, the team must have the ability to either formally or informally penalize the culprit. Like the individual incentive plan, other disadvantages of the team incentive plan include much preplanning, possible neglect of other work responsibilities, and increased chances of burnout.

social loafing
The phenomenon in which one or two team members fail to do their fair share, leaving other team members to compensate for their lack of performance.

The major advantage of the team incentive plan is that it pulls the team together by providing the incentive for cooperation. This will be particularly important when individual contributions cannot be readily identified.

Viking Freight is an example of a company that has effectively used a team-based pay-for-performance system. The company created the plan in response to deregulation in the late 1980s, which greatly increased competition from other businesses. The plan is designed around work groups within a terminal location, each of which has its own objectives that vary according to the nature of the work. Objectives are determined for each work group by an executive committee and an engineering group. All of the employees, except for some clerical and secretarial staff, have work-group goals. The objectives take into consideration the individuals in the group, as well as the market conditions of the particular terminal. The payout period is four weeks; at the end of each four-week period, a determination is made as to whether the work groups' goals were met.

If the work group meets its goals, the employees are eligible for a bonus, the size of which depends on the terminal's performance. The terminal's performance is, in turn, based on four criteria: the amount of revenue earned, the percent of performance achieved, on-time service (at least 98 percent of the shipments must be on time), and the claims ratio (the cost of damaged or lost freight must be below a certain level). These criteria are entered into an objective formula to calculate the bonus. Assuming that both the work group and the company as a whole meet their objectives, employees receive a payout based on their salaries. The maximum amount of payout that employees can earn is a function of the job. For example, hourly employees can receive bonuses as high as 7.5 percent of their pay, while the terminal manager may earn a bonus worth up to 20 percent of his or her pay. These percentages were based on the impact top management felt each job has on the company's success.

Top management has instituted several practices to maintain the motivational value of the program. One such practice is the way in which the payout is distributed. The payout is presented at a meeting, which is led by top management. The meeting begins with a review of the company's performance over the last four weeks and provides an opportunity for employees to raise any concerns or problems. The payout, which is separate from the regular paycheck, is handed out at the end of the meeting. At the same time, a chart containing information on the base pay, the payout level, and employees' total compensation is displayed. A second practice involves the weekly posting of the performance of each terminal, so that all employees can see how well they are doing. This, too, reinforces the importance of the objectives.[34]

NCR, formerly AT&T Global Information Solutions, is another organization that has developed a team incentive program. The company defines "team" as colleagues the employee works with to meet the organization's mission, and links 50 percent of the pay-for-performance compensation to managers' team performance.[35]

Now that you have read about the advantages and disadvantages of the team incentive from the company's perspective, what do you think some of the advantages and disadvantages are from an employee's perspective? Recall that, in the opening case of this chapter, TeamWare used a team incentive plan. What were your reactions to their plan? Perhaps the two most important issues from the employee's perspective are the nature of the team and one's reaction to teamwork. First, an effective team has the advantage of pooling skills. For example, if Ricardo has good sales skills but is weak in technical knowledge, being part of a team with people with strong technical knowledge would allow him to compensate for this weakness. If he worked on an ineffective team, however, his personal strengths might be obscured by other members' weaknesses. Second, some people don't like working on teams. If Ricardo prefers to work by himself, he may view the team as a hindrance. So, the success or failure of a team incentive plan will depend much on the functioning of the team and Ricardo's desire to work with a team.

Organization-Wide Incentive Plans: Advantages and Disadvantages

Organization-wide incentive plans have several advantages over the plans that have been reviewed so far. As shown in Table 9.4, a major advantage is that by basing the payout on organization performance, employees will more closely identify with the organization. Moreover, this type of plan encourages cooperation throughout the orga-

Table 9.4	**Advantages and Disadvantages of Organization-Wide Incentive Plans**
Advantages	**Disadvantages**
1. Encourage identification with the organization	1. Encourage social loafing
2. Increase cooperation throughout the organization	2. May not be motivating
3. Objective	3. Equity concerns when targets not met
	4. The formula may be difficult to understand

nization, not just at a team or department level. A third advantage is that, like the individual incentive or team incentive approach, an objective formula will be used, so that determining whether or not the goals have been met will be relatively simple.

On the negative side, organization-wide plans are quite susceptible to social loafing. Compared with the team incentive approach, employees are likely to feel even less responsible for and in control of success. Also, as described earlier, the payout from a profit-sharing plan is frequently issued on an annual basis, and some or even all of the payout may be put into a retirement fund. The motivational value of such plans is therefore likely to be lower than it is for the individual or team incentive plan. Another problem is that equity or fairness issues are likely to be raised when an organization does not meet its goals. For example, when DuPont's fibers division adopted a variable pay plan in the late 1980s in which 6 percent of employee pay was put "at risk," depending on the division's profits, many of the employees worried about whether the profit target would be manipulated by top management. As one employee stated it, "There are so many loopholes for management, how do we know if we've reached our goal?"[36] Finally, in a related vein, the formulas for these plans may be complex and difficult for employees to understand. As a consequence, they may believe the P-f-P is simply a management plan to take advantage of the employees. Many companies, such as General Electric, do in fact use a variety of accounting tactics to avoid swings in year-to-year profitability.[37] For more information about pay issues, check out the Web sites in Box 9.4.

Kinds of Organization-Wide Incentive Plans

Recall that there are two kinds of organization-wide incentive plans: gain-sharing and profit-sharing. Because they are rather different in the way they operate, each will be discussed separately.

Gain-sharing. Gain-sharing plans emphasize improving productivity by decreasing costs. These plans work best in small organizations, in organizations where there is a great deal of trust between the workers and management, and where the market and product are quite stable and sales are good. Such plans will be less successful when the company manufactures a new product, because there are likely to be major fluctuations in sales.[38] There are three basic types of gain-sharing plans: the Scanlon plan, the Rucker plan, and Improshare.

Scanlon plan. The **Scanlon plan** is named after Joseph Scanlon, who popularized this approach. Scanlon initiated this plan during the 1930s when his steel mill was on the verge of going out of business. As the union leader, he convinced workers in the plant to refrain from demanding wage increases and persuaded management to increase pay when productivity improved. As a result of this agreement, the company's business improved, and ultimately the workers prospered.[39]

Scanlon plan
Relies on a formula that contains two factors: a monetary index of output, reflecting how much was produced, and a measure of input or what it might cost the company to produce this output. The goal of the plan is to lower the input relative to output.

The Scanlon plan relies on a formula that contains two factors: a monetary index of output, reflecting how much was produced, and a measure of input, or what it cost the company to produce this output (such as labor costs). The goal of the plan is to lower the input relative to output. In other words, the lower costs are, the higher the productivity level will be. The assumption is that the workers have the capacity to lower the cost of labor.[40] Under the Scanlon plan, workers can lower the cost of labor by making money-saving suggestions. In one facility that implemented a Scanlon plan, suggestions in the first year of the plan fell into four categories: (1) those focusing on ways to improve quantity, (2) those focusing on ways to improve quality, (3) those

focusing on ways to reduce costs, and (4) those focusing on nonproductivity related problems, such as management complaints.[41]

Table 9.5 contains an example of how a payout is derived in a typical Scanlon plan. Steps 1 through 4 show how output is calculated. Note that sales dollars are not the only factor included in the total output figure. Such things as discounts are factored in as well (Step 2). Step 6 indicates the allowed payroll costs, as determined when the plan was designed. As shown in Table 9.5, the formula stipulated that costs should not exceed 20 percent of the output. Given the output was valued at $1,200,000, 20 percent of this figure, or $240,000, is the expected or allowed cost of labor. The payout will be the difference between the actual cost and the allowed cost, after various adjustments are made. Step 7 indicates that the actual cost of labor in this time period was $210,000, which is $30,000 less than the allowable amount. The bonus pool, then, is $30,000 (Step 8). The next few steps involve adjustments to this figure. In this example, the company takes a 25 percent share of the bonus pool (Step 9), leaving $22,500. A

Table 9.5	**Sample Scanlon Plan Formula**
1. Quarterly sales	$1,100,000
2. Minus sales returns, discounts, etc.	25,000
3. Net sales	$1,075,000
4. Add increased inventory	125,000
5. Total output	$1,200,000
6. Allowed payroll costs (20 percent of output)	240,000
7. Actual payroll costs	210,000
8. Bonus pool	30,000
9. Company share (25 percent)	7,500
Subtotal	22,500
10. Reserve for deficit quarters (25 percent)	5,625
11. Employee share to be distributed (75 percent)	16,875
(See text for explanation.)	

small portion of this remaining pool is then set aside for periods of low production (Step 10). The remaining portion, $16,875 is divided among the employees.[42]

Rucker plan. A variant to the Scanlon plan, the **Rucker plan** (named after its developer, Allan Rucker) replaces sales as the measure of output with "value added." Value added is simply the sales value of production, after subtracting nonlabor costs (materials, supplies, electricity, and so on). In most other ways, the Rucker plan is quite similar to the Scanlon plan. The major advantage of the Rucker plan is that it takes into account inflation increases in nonlabor costs. On the negative side, because nonlabor costs are factored out, employees can only make productivity improvements by reducing direct labor costs. In addition, the formula is even more difficult to communicate to employees than the Scanlon plan! The Rucker plan, then, probably is most effective when inflationary pressures pose a problem.[43]

Rucker plan
A variant to the Scanlon plan, this plan replaces sales as the measure of output with "value added," which is the sales value of production after subtracting nonlabor costs.

Improshare. **Improshare,** which stands for "improved productivity through sharing," was created by Mitchell Fein in the early 1970s. Unlike the Scanlon or Rucker plans, Improshare focuses on the number of hours of work. The Improshare plan, like the Scanlon and Rucker plans, also involves a formula that compares input to output. Under the Improshare approach, though, input is the number of hours that it should take to complete the work compared with the number of hours it actually took to do the work. If, for example, management estimated it would take 240 hours to complete a production run, yet it only took 160 hours, employees would be accorded a predetermined bonus for the number of hours saved.

Improshare
Stands for "improved productivity through sharing," and focuses on the number of hours of work. Improshare also involves a formula that compares input to output, where input is the number of hours that it should take to complete the work compared with the number of hours it actually took to do the work.

Proponents of Improshare point to a number of potential advantages of this approach over the Scanlon and Rucker plans. In particular, Improshare has greater flexibility and is easier to implement. In terms of disadvantages, however, Improshare tends to emphasize quantity over quality and excludes the possibility of producing savings from anything other than number of hours worked.[44]

In sum, gain-sharing plans can be effective motivators. Although most of the applications of these programs have been in manufacturing facilities, they are equally applicable in the service sector, including hospitals, libraries, and consulting firms. Which of the approaches suits best will depend on several considerations, such as the degree to which employee involvement is desired and the importance of product quality.[45]

Finally, this is an appropriate point to mention that, while these plans have the aura of objectivity and precision, they require numerous judgment calls in the development stages. Ultimately, then, even the gain-sharing plans are affected by subjectivity. Next, you will read about some suggestions for helping to create a successful gain-sharing plan.

Guidelines for Successful Gain-sharing Plans

Here are some guidelines for successful gain-sharing plans, based on a review of 17 facilities that implemented these plans.

1. Customize the Plan. Don't try to use a specific gain-sharing plan just because it was successful in another facility. You need to set up a plan that will work best in your facility.

2. **Use a Task Force.** If you involve only the HR department in setting up the gain-sharing plan, it is likely to fail. Use employees from different functions, at all levels (including hourly employees, salaried employees, and management) of the facility. A typical task force for this purpose is composed of anywhere between 7 to 28 members, and takes four to seven months from start to beginning of the program.

3. **There Is No One Best Formula.** As described above, there is no perfect or best formula to use. The formula itself is not the most important factor, either. Employee trust and involvement, along with management support and commitment, are the key factors.

4. **Establish a Fair Formula.** The formula must be set so that both employees and the company stand to gain from it. Most companies use historical information, plus an improvement factor, to establish the formula.

5. **Give Frequent Recognition.** Success must be celebrated to maintain interest. However, management must be careful not to overemphasize individuals, as the program depends on the entire facility.

6. **Timing Is Critical.** The best time to start a gain-sharing program is when profits are good, so that employees can quickly see a payoff.

7. **Payouts Should Be Frequent and Significant.** Among reviewed organizations, gain-sharing was most successful when the payouts were monthly, not quarterly. As a general rule of thumb, for new plans, a payout of between 2.5 percent to 3.0 percent of wages was considered significant. Over the long haul, it was estimated that payouts of 4 percent to 5 percent are reasonable for acceptable performance, and 6 percent to 7 percent was reasonable for good performance.

8. **Training Is Critical for Success.** Facilities that provided more training experienced more success with their gain-sharing programs. In addition to training on the formula and program, training was provided for group problem-solving, communication skills, and job skills.[46]

Profit Sharing. Many large, well-known organizations either currently use or have used profit-sharing plans in the past, including General Motors, Monsanto, Ford, Hewlett-Packard, to name just a few.[47] Essentially, profit sharing provides a payout to employees when the company, plant, or unit reaches a certain financial target.

Depending on the nature of the job and the company, a profit-sharing plan may be quite lucrative. For example, Figure 9.2 illustrates the profit-sharing plan for Deryck Maughan, chairman of Salomon Brothers, the investment banking firm. As you can see, the plan resembles a bingo card. If the company does extremely well, Maughan receives a bonus of up to $24 million (his base pay is $1 million)! According to the company, Maughan would have to turn in a "very extraordinary" performance to earn that bonus. Most profit-sharing plans are not quite so rewarding.[48]

Consider Colorado Memory Systems (CMS), a computer component manufacturer purchased by Hewlett-Packard in late 1992. After the purchase, employees at CMS expressed concern that their individual performance would go unrewarded now that they were owned by a giant. In addition, employees of Colorado Memory Systems were paid much less than their counterparts at H-P. To deal with these problems, the company began a profit-sharing plan that put 10 percent of the employees' pay "at risk." If profits were high, employees would get as much as 20 percent of their pay back. If profits were only satisfactory, they would get the full 10 percent back.[49]

There are many different indices that a company can use to measure profits or financial success. Traditionally, organizations have used standard accounting measures, such as net income, earnings per share (EPS), and return on net assets (RONA). Such measures are relatively easy to understand by employees, but tend to focus on

| Figure 9.2 | One CEO's Profit-Sharing Plan |

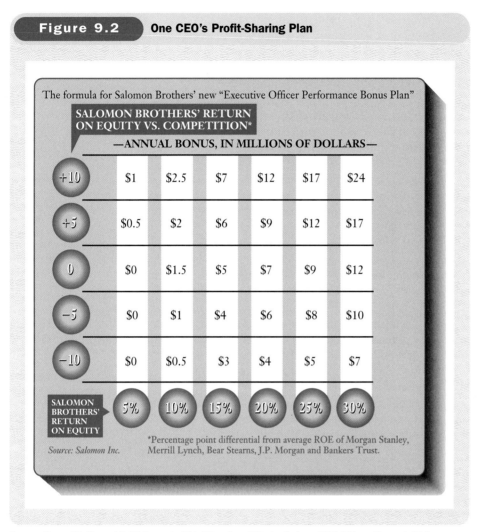

The formula for Salomon Brothers' new "Executive Officer Performance Bonus Plan"

SALOMON BROTHERS' RETURN ON EQUITY VS. COMPETITION*

—ANNUAL BONUS, IN MILLIONS OF DOLLARS—

	5%	10%	15%	20%	25%	30%
+10	$1	$2.5	$7	$12	$17	$24
+5	$0.5	$2	$6	$9	$12	$17
0	$0	$1.5	$5	$7	$9	$12
−5	$0	$1	$4	$6	$8	$10
−10	$0	$0.5	$3	$4	$5	$7

SALOMON BROTHERS' RETURN ON EQUITY

*Percentage point differential from average ROE of Morgan Stanley, Merrill Lynch, Bear Stearns, J.P. Morgan and Bankers Trust.

Source: Salomon Inc.

Source: From M. Siconolfi, "Salomon's Chief Stands to Hit the Jackpot," *Wall Street Journal*, 5 May 1994, C1.

short-term goals that, in the long run, may even have a negative effect on the company. Some companies have begun to adopt *value-based* measures of performance, which assess a company's financial performance relative to the cost of capital to determine if value has been added to the organization. Under a *value-added* system, for example, a research and development project could be treated as an "investment," rather than as a mere expense. Companies such as Eli Lilly and Coca-Cola have stated that their success in part is due to focus on value-added systems. Value-added systems have weaknesses, as well, including greater complexity and difficulty in applying them to certain businesses, such as consulting, where intellectual capital is difficult to measure. A third type of index is referred to as the *balanced scorecard*, which incorporates four different aspects of performance: financial, customer, learning and growth, and internal processes. Each of these aspects can be assessed using such things as financial data, customer ratings, and so forth. Of course, like the others, the balanced scorecard has weaknesses, including a potential lack of focus.[50] Like the gain-sharing formula, then, the index that is used must be chosen carefully for the program to be successful.

By now you are probably wondering whether profit-sharing programs are effective. Despite their widespread use, there is little hard scientific evidence regarding the effectiveness of profit-sharing plans. However, the available studies do suggest that profit sharing on average increases productivity 7 percent. If that figure seems rather low to you, consider the following points:[51]

1. In many profit-sharing plans, anywhere from some to all of the payout goes into a retirement fund, rather than into the employees' paycheck. Would you be highly motivated if the payout went into a fund you could not utilize until you retired, quit the company, or were disabled?
2. In many cases, employees perceive little or no control or influence over the objectives. If, for example, you were a customer service employee in a company with 5,000 employees, you might suspect, quite correctly, that your efforts have only the smallest influence on the company's profits for that year.
3. Remember that a distinguishing characteristic of these plans is that payouts are distributed only once each year. There is a considerable time lag, therefore, between each payout, which serves to reduce motivation.

One organization that has done a great deal with its pay-for-performance plans is Saturn Corporation. As you may know, Saturn was heralded as "a different kind of company, a different kind of car." As part of its strategy to differentiate itself from GM, as well as other automobile manufacturers, Saturn introduced a pay-for-performance plan that was relatively unique for a unionized facility. Specifically, Saturn established a base wage that was below the industry average and provided an organization incentive that would allow employees to surpass the industry average if goals were met. When it first began in 1992, 5 percent of employee pay was set "at risk," such that employees could get none of it, all of it, or more than 5 percent of their pay in a bonus. In the first year of the plan, Saturn used an individual incentive version of the program, for which each employee had to devote 92 hours of their time to learning new skills in order to earn the bonus (with an average payout of $1,800). In 1997, the amount of at-risk pay increased to 12 percent. It is now based on three factors: 5 percent is for training (that is, amount of time spent by the employee training), 5 percent is for quality, and 2 percent is for team skills. The quality factor is based on the *Uniform Vehicle Evaluation system*, an international standard that involves independent judges randomly examining about 25 cars and rating them on various defects. Thus, Saturn has designed an organization-wide component that requires the entire company to work together. To earn the bonus for "team skills," each team must meet quarterly to examine its success in meeting business goals and developing a plan for achieving these goals. Each team must also participate in a team-building activity at least once a year. The future may be tougher, however, as U.S. sales of small cars have declined and GM announced that fewer cars would be produced in 1998. Saturn may need to change the program to emphasize cost-savings, which might force a switch to a gain-sharing plan.[52]

Now that you have read about the general advantages and disadvantages of organization-wide incentive programs, it is time to consider the advantages and disadvantages from an employee perspective. Recall that in the opening case of this chapter, Corporate Solutions had a profit-sharing plan. What would you tell Ricardo about this type of plan? In many ways, like the team incentive, much will depend on the effectiveness of the other employees. In a large organization, particularly for employees other than the top executives, Ricardo's efforts will have little effect. If Ricardo is an extremely hard-working and highly successful individual, he may become quite frustrated working for such an organization. On the other hand, the pressures of this organization may be less, and he may enjoy the camaraderie and organizational cooperation that such programs encourage.

Not surprisingly then, many organizations combine the strengths of two or three approaches to eliminate the weaknesses inherent in any one P-f-P plan. To return to our opening case, none of the four pay plans is clearly superior to the others. Much will depend on the nature of the organization, and Ricardo's own personal preferences, as to which is the best plan.

❖ Conclusion

Pay-for-performance plans are an important motivational tool for organizations. As such, they play an important role in the human resources area. Although merit pay plans are among the most common P-f-P approaches, they have significant weaknesses, which in turn weaken their motivational value. Individual incentive programs, perhaps the most motivating, have several serious disadvantages, particularly in light of today's emphasis on teams and quality. Accordingly, more companies have designed and implemented team incentives and organization-wide incentive plans. Although these plans are not perfect, in tandem with other rewards, they can clearly improve organizational performance.

❖ Applying Core Concepts

1. Think about your current job (or a previous job). Does the company use a pay-for-performance plan? Why or why not? Would it be helpful for the organization if it did use a pay-for-performance plan? Why?
2. Which kind of pay-for-performance plan do you think universities and colleges should use for faculty? Explain your answer.
3. If you were Ricardo in the opening case of this chapter, which company would you choose to work for? Why?
4. Think of a job for which a pay-for-performance plan probably would *not* work. Explain why it would not work. On what other basis should pay differences occur in this job (for example, seniority)?
5. As a manager of a staff of customer service representatives in a service business, what type of pay-for-performance plan do you think would work best? What about for automobile mechanics at a car dealership?

❖ Key Terms

Pay-for-performance	Organization-wide	Social loafing
Merit pay	incentive	Scanlon plan
Individual incentive	Profit-sharing plan	Rucker plan
Team incentive	Gain-sharing plan	Improshare

After examining the pay structure, the next thing on Clark Inglis' list of projects was to revamp the pay-for-performance system. He chose to try a different way to replace the traditional merit pay system at Adamsville, one that would combine a different performance measurement technique with a somewhat different approach to pay allocations. Key excerpts from the memo that Clark wrote describing the new program, as well as a sample exhibit are provided next. The questions you should prepare to address are

1. Do you think Clark's plan is a sound one?
2. What problems do you see with his plan? How would you prepare to address them?
3. Could you implement his plan in other organizations? Why or why not?

The Memo: Customer Service Contracts

Attached is an overview of my new Customer Service Contracts (CSCs) and the pay-for-performance plan that I have promised to develop.

The CSC is a replacement for our traditional performance appraisal forms that, if you recall, rated each employee on four dimensions (quality, quantity, attitude, and attendance). The CSC will be used to evaluate employees on goals and objectives that our customers will find important, rather than on the subjective and intangible "personal" characteristics of the previous form. As you can see from the sample CSC in Exhibit 1, employee performance will no longer rely on subjective measures of performance made by a supervisor; rather, supervisors will simply be examining outcomes or output. Subjectivity will be for the most part eliminated.

The CSCs were developed by examining each employee's responsibilities and then translating those responsibilities into performance levels and time requirements (time requirements were not included in cases where safety or liability might be questioned). Although the CSCs emphasize customer service, some of the items are essential job functions that have no obvious customer, but are critical for the city.

I have developed the CSCs with considerable input from each employee, as well as from the heads of each department. All of the employees have agreed to their CSCs and I can assure you that every question or concern that they had was considered carefully and addressed completely.

New Pay Raise System

As you undoubtedly know, our merit pay system, like most others, suffers from what I considered two major flaws, which I intend to eliminate. One flaw is that "the rich always get richer." That is, employees with the highest salary tend to get larger pay increases, simply because merit raises are done on a percentage basis. What I propose to do here is to base pay increases on employees' *relative* performance to others in their department. Suppose, for example, that three employees work in Department X. Lou, who earns $50,000 annually, is performing at 81 percent of his expected performance; Debbie, who earns $25,000 annually, is performing at 98 percent of her expected performance; and Rob, who earns $35,000 annually, is performing at 89 percent of his expected level. Assume that the raise pool is 4 percent, or $4,400. Now, under the old system, assume that George got a 3.7 percent raise, which means a $1,850 annual increase. Debbie got the biggest raise, 4.5 percent, which means only a $1,125 annual increase, while Rob got a 4.1 percent raise, which means a $1,425 raise. But what if we looked at those numbers a different way, namely, that Debbie was responsible for 37 percent (that is, 98/265) of the department's performance, Rob was responsible for 33 percent (that is, 89/265) of the department's performance, and George was responsible for only 30 percent (that is, 81/265) of the department's performance, the picture looks rather different. Debbie should earn 37 percent of that $4,400 raise pool or $1,628, Rob should earn 33 percent or $1,452, and George should only earn 30 percent or $1,320 of that raise pool. In addition to basing pay increases this way, I will work with the employees to improve their performance levels. I consider anyone performing under 80 percent to be in need of some remedial work.

An important question is how will measures be kept of performance. I do not feel that this will be a problem. Currently, 75 percent of our workforce (for example, police) complete daily work reports. For example, when a police officer completes commercial building checks on his or her shift, it will be a simple matter to radio a code to his or her commander at that point. Prior to the end of the shift, the commander can initial the logbook to document the number of buildings checked. Although this system will depend to some degree on employee honesty, I have informed the em-

ployees of the stiff penalties for cheating. I have purchased logbooks for the employees to keep track of their performance on a daily basis. There is no "perfect system," as you know. But, this system will be a big improvement over the traditional performance management/merit pay system that we have used for many years.

Exhibit 1   **Sample Police Detective CSC**

1. Respond to all internal staff and external customer inquiries for information within time frame negotiated with requestor. Information should be accurate and provided by date for at least 93 percent of all inquiries.
2. Will begin a working file on 93 percent of all criminal investigations assigned within 10 working days. Upon opening the case, the crime victim will be contacted and recontacted with each new development. This will be achieved for 96 percent of all cases.
3. Ensure that 100 percent of all relevant evidence and film is sent to county crime lab and that all results are received at least once per week, every week.
4. Ensure that 100 percent of all crime suspects who are arrested in reference to assigned cases are given thorough interviews and follow relevant rules.
5. Respond to all special investigation requests, special projects, or crime scenes within the time frame requested or negotiated with the requestor. Reports should be complete, accurate, and provided by the date signified for at least 97 percent of all requests.
6. Maintain a 70 percent clearance rate on all criminal cases investigated.

Employee signature _____

CHAPTER 9 *Experiential Exercise 2*

I-C-U, Inc.[53]

I-C-U, an eye-care provider, has been in business for many years. Originally owned by a national health maintenance organization (HMO), I-C-U was sold to a local hospital network which now operates the company. Each office of I-C-U has one or two optometrists and three to six opticians. The optometrists have an advanced degree; opticians have far less training. Opticians, therefore, can conduct some of the preliminary and basic eye tests, but mostly sell eyeglasses. More skilled opticians can conduct more of the tests. Opticians also show customers how to put contact lenses on and how to remove them. The optometrists conduct most of the advanced tests and can fit contact lenses. The optometrists are also responsible

for most of the paperwork. I-C-U has approximately 10 offices, scattered around a major southwestern metropolitan area.

Compensation and Pay-for-Performance Plan for Optometrists Under the HMO

When I-C-U was owned by the HMO, optometrists were paid between $40,000 and $60,000 annually, along with reimbursement for licensing fees, sick leave, insurance, and a 401(k) plan. These fees were comparable to salary surveys, which showed optometrists in the area earning between $45,000 and $60,000 annually.

In terms of the pay-for-performance plan, an annual bonus was provided to the optometrists, using a little understood and ambiguous system supposedly based on one's performance appraisal ratings, productivity (measured, presumably, by the number of patients treated, number of glasses and contacts sold, and perhaps other measures), and other subjective factors. These bonuses were determined by the CEO, with some advice from the accounting department. Although the bonus was initially about 8 percent of the optometrist's base salary, over time, the bonus fell to about 5 percent of the base salary. Opticians' bonus pay was based simply on the number of glasses sold, regardless of the price.

Compensation and Pay-for-Performance Plan for Optometrists Under the Practice Network

When I-C-U was sold to the practice network, optometrists' pay was nearly frozen to a range of between $45,000 and $54,000, along with reimbursement for licensing fees, sick leave, insurance, and a 401(k) plan. However, to provide more incentive, the practice network changed the pay-for-performance system to a different formula and set it at a level so that optometrists would earn about $10,000 annually beyond their base pay. The new system, which has a quarterly payout, was based on the following:

1. The number of routine vision visits;
2. The number of partial vision examinations (for example, to follow-up on specific problems or concerns);
3. The number of emergency vision visits;
4. The number of eyeglass and contact lens prescriptions filled.

Note that in each case, the basis was the *number* of those items (for example, how many eyeglasses were purchased during the quarter), not the *cost* of the item (for example, not the cost of the eyeglasses purchased). This was because in some locations most of the patients were members of a Medicare program that paid a low, flat fee for all eye care services (for example, these patients purchased glasses from a limited selection for a flat fee of $5). Other locations were in areas with no patients on Medicare, and their patients demanded highly fashionable glasses and high quality contact lenses.

In the last year, however, the pay-for-performance system has been modified somewhat. Now, it is based only on two factors:

1. The number of routine eye vision examinations conducted;
2. The number of eyeglass and contact lens prescriptions filled.

The optometrists have noticed that the quarterly sum paid out has also dropped slightly, with the payout averaging only about $9,000 annually (or $2,300 quarterly).

Compensation and Pay-for-Performance Plan for Opticians

Opticians were paid between $5.50 and $10.00 per hour under both the HMO and the practice network. These fees were comparable to salary surveys, which showed opticians earning between $7.00 and $12.00 per hour. The pay-for-performance plan for opticians has also remained the same throughout this time and is based primarily on the number of eyeglasses sold, though a small amount of the bonus (about 10 percent of the total) is based on the cost of the eyeglasses.

The Problem

Under the HMO system, the optometrists felt underpaid and confused about how to get a bigger bonus. When the practice network purchased I-C-U and changed the compensation program, optometrists felt adequately paid relative to their peers in other companies. The major complaint now for the optometrists is the nature of the opticians. They concur that the skill level of the opticians has declined, so that they, the optometrists, are responsible for more of the work that the opticians used to perform. The really good opticians are able to quickly move to the two premier offices, which offer the biggest monetary incentives due to high volume and wealthy customers. The most mediocre opticians therefore stay where they are, leading to increasingly strained relationships between many of the optometrists and the opticians.

From the top management's perspective, there is a need to modify the pay-for-performance system to address the issues mentioned above and to give a greater incentive to the optometrists. Top management feels that optometrists could be more motivated and that way earn more for themselves and the organization. To get things started, the vice president of administration, Amy Blake, has proposed two possible pay-for-performance plans, and she would like your comments on them. She would also like you to come up with your own plan. The two options she has proposed are

1. Retain the current system, but add a customer rating form, to be completed by each customer, to rate the optometrist and staff. Fifty percent of the bonus would be based on the customer ratings. Base pay will continue to be frozen for the next two years.

2. Set a profit-sharing plan for each store. Top management will determine an expected profit target, based on financial projections, and the store's bonus will be based on the degree to which that target is exceeded. The bonus would be distributed among the optometrists and opticians, based on their salary. Base pay will continue to be frozen for the next two years.

Your task, then, is to evaluate these two proposals, develop your own proposal and be prepared to explain the problems with all three as well as a description of how you would address any problems that arise.

❖ Chapter 9 References

1. M. Beer, P. Spector, P. Lawrence, D. Q. Mills, and R. Walton, *Managing Human Assets* (New York: The Free Press, 1984).
2. M. Weitzman and D. Kruse, "Profit Sharing and Productivity," in *Paying for Productivity*, ed. A. S. Binder (Washington: The Brookings Institute, 1990).
3. L. Hatcher and T. Ross, "From Individual Incentives to an Organization-Wide Gain-Sharing Plan: Effects on Team-Work and Product Quality," *Journal of Organizational Behavior* 12 (1991): 169–83.
4. L. Dyer, D. Schwab, and R. Theriault, "Managerial Perceptions Regarding Salary Increase Criteria," *Personnel Psychology* 29 (1976): 233–42.
5. B. Gerhart and G. Milkovich, "Employee Compensation: Research and Practice," in *Handbook of Industrial and Organizational Psychology*, vol. 3, ed. M. D. Dunnette and L. M. Hough (Palo Alto, CA: Consulting Psychologists Press, 1992).
6. R. Heneman, "Merit Pay Research," in *Research in Personnel/Human Resource Management*, ed. G. Ferris and K. Rowland (Greenwich, CT: JAI Press, 1990).
7. Gerhart and Milkovich, "Employee Compensation."
8. M. Budman, "Is There Merit in Merit Pay?" *Across the Board* 34 (June 1997): 33–36.
9. Gerhart and Milkovich, "Employee Compensation."
10. Heneman, "Merit Pay Research."
11. D. Scott, F. Hills, S. Markham, and M. Vest, *Evaluating a Pay-for-Performance Program at a Transit Authority.* Paper presented at the National Academy of Management meetings, New Orleans, 1987.
12. Heneman, "Merit Pay Research."
13. Ibid.
14. S. Markham, "Pay-for-Performance Dilemma Revisited: Empirical Example of the Importance of Group Effects," *Journal of Applied Psychology* 73 (1988): 172–80.
15. Heneman, "Merit Pay Research."
16. K. Bartol and D. Martin, "Effects of Dependence, Dependency Threats, and Pay Secrecy on Managerial Pay Allocations," *Journal of Applied Psychology* 74 (1989): 105–13.
17. K. Bartol and D. Martin, "When Politics Pays: Factors Influencing Managerial Compensation Decisions," *Personnel Psychology* 43 (1990): 599–614.
18. Heneman, "Merit Pay Research."
19. Anonymous, "Merit Pay and Grading at the BBC," *IRS Employment Review* (March 1996): S6–S9.

20. Anonymous, "BBC: 2.6 percent with L260 Minimum and 1 percent for Merit and Increments," *IRS Employment Review* (November 1996): S11.
21. C. Carey, "Motivation Can Be Managerial Dilemma," *St. Louis Post-Dispatch*, 7 September 1992, 11BP.
22. G. Milkovich and A. Wigdor, *Pay for Performance: Evaluating Performance Appraisal and Merit Pay* (Washington: National Academy Press, 1991).
23. B. MacLean, "Value Added Pay Beats Traditional Merit Programs," *Personnel Journal* 69 (1992): 46–52.
24. Milkovich and Wigdor, "Pay for Performance."
25. F. Hills, T. Bergmann, & V. Scarpello, *Compensation Decision Making* (Fort Worth: Dryden, 1994).
26. J. Rigdon, "More Firms Try to Reward Good Service, but Incentives May Backfire in Long Run," *Wall Street Journal*, 5 December 1990, B1, B7.
27. Milkovich and Wigdor, "Pay for Performance."
28. B. Graham-Moore and T. Ross, "Introduction to PG: A Theoretical Model," in *Productivity Gainsharing*, ed. B. Graham-Moore and T. Ross (Englewood Cliffs, NJ: Prentice-Hall, 1983).
29. S. Tully, "Your Paycheck Gets Exciting," *Fortune*, 1 November 1993, 83–98.
30. R. Hodgetts, "Discussing Incentive Compensation with Donald Hastings of Lincoln Electric," *Compensation and Benefits Review* 29 (September/October 1997): 60–66.
31. C. Wiley, "Incentive Plan Pushes Production," *Personnel Journal* 72 (1993): 86–91.
32. Hodgetts, "Discussing Incentive Compensation."
33. Ibid.
34. T. Stambaugh, "An Incentive Pay Success Story," *Personnel Journal* 71 (1992): 48–54.
35 K. Abosch, "Variable Pay: Do We Have the Basics in Place?" *Compensation and Benefits Review* 30 (July/August 1998): 12–22.
36. L. Hays, "All Eyes on Du Pont's Incentive Pay Plan," *Wall Street Journal*, 5 December 1988, B1.
37. R. Smith, S. Lipin, and A. K. Naj, "Managing Profits," *Wall Street Journal*, 3 November 1994, A1, A11.
38. B. Graham-Moore, "The Literature of PG," in *Productivity Gainsharing*, ed. B. Graham-Moore and T. Ross (Englewood Cliffs, NJ: Prentice-Hall, 1983).
39. C. Frost, R. Wakeley, and R. Ruh, *The Scanlon Plan for Organizational Development: Identity, Participation, and Equity* (East Lansing, MI: Michigan State University Press, 1974).
40. M. Bazerman and B. Graham-Moore, "PG Formulas: Developing a Reward Structure to Achieve Organizational Goals," in *Productivity Gainsharing*, ed. B. Graham-Moore and T. Ross (Englewood Cliffs, NJ: Prentice-Hall, 1983).
41. B. Graham-Moore, "Ten Years of Experience with the Scanlon Plan: DeSoto Revisited," in *Productivity Gainsharing*, ed. B. Graham-Moore and T. Ross (Englewood Cliffs, NJ: Prentice-Hall, 1983).
42. Bazerman and Graham-Moore, "PG Formulas."
43. Graham-Moore, "The Literature of PG"; and Bazerman and Graham-Moore, "PG Formulas."
44. Ibid.
45. W. Hauck and T. Ross, "Is PG Applicable to Service Sector Firms?" in *Productivity Gainsharing*, ed. B. Graham-Moore and T. Ross (Englewood Cliffs, NJ: Prentice-Hall, 1983).
46. R. Maternak, "How to Make Gainsharing Successful: The Collective Experience of 17 Facilities," *Compensation and Benefits Review* 29 (September/October 1997): 43–52.
47. Gerhart and Milkovich, "Employee Compensation."
48. M. Siconolfi, "Salomon's Chief Stands to Hit the Jackpot," *Wall Street Journal*, 5 May 1994, C1, C19.
49. D. Hogarty, "New Ways to Pay," *Management Review* 83 (1994): 34–36.
50. F. McKenzie, and M. Shilling, "Avoiding Performance Measurement Traps: Ensuring Effective Incentive Design and Implementation," *Compensation and Benefits Review* 30 (July/August 1998): 57–65.

51. Gerhart and Milkovich, "Employee Compensation."
52. D. Bohl, "Case Study: Saturn Corp.—A Different Kind of Pay." *Compensation and Benefits Review* 29 (November/December 1997): 51–56.
53. This case was developed by Emily Lane.

Employee Benefits

Core Concepts **After reading this chapter, you should be capable of:**

1. Identifying the legally required benefits a company must provide.
2. Explaining how different health insurance plans operate.
3. Discussing the differences between a defined benefit pension and a defined contribution benefit plan.
4. Describing additional employee benefits that an organization may offer.
5. Explaining various paid time-off programs companies use.

Opening Case

Imagine you have job offers from three different companies. All three jobs seem identical in terms of the type of work, the opportunities for advancement, and the boss who would be supervising you. The pay is identical for two of the companies, NewForm and Tradition; however, the third company, FreeStyle, made you a job offer for $2,000 more per year than both NewForm and Tradition. The only difference that you can see between NewForm and Tradition is the nature of the benefit programs offered by each company. NewForm offers a cafeteria benefits program, which as the human resources manager explained it, may even provide you with additional money or vacation time. That sounds almost too good to be true. NewForm also offers a 401(k) retirement program, which allows you to set aside some of your salary into a retirement fund. The human resources manager smiled when she described the 401(k) plan to you and then added, "You get to pretend you are in Las Vegas, because employees are able to invest this money as they choose. Options include various stock funds, bonds, money market funds, as well as other alternatives. In fact," she added with a laugh, "some employees have even asked whether they can use the funds for state lottery tickets or poker tables. We also match 50 cents for each dollar you set aside, up to 2 percent of your salary."

Tradition, on the other hand, seems to offer a more standard benefits program. The personnel assistant emphasized its advantages: "We offer the alternative of two different health maintenance organizations (HMOs), and we have a preferred-provider organization (PPO) option as well. We also offer flexible spending accounts." You noticed that Tradition provides a retirement program, called a "defined benefit" program. This program seems different from the one offered by NewForm, but you are not quite sure how it works.

Finally, FreeStyle offers no benefits as far as you can tell. There is no health insurance program and no retirement program. You wonder whether this is even legal—isn't every company required to offer a health insurance program? But a salary that is $2,000 higher than the other two companies sounds appealing. What should you do?

This chapter explains different types of employee benefits, how they work, why companies provide certain kinds of benefits, and some of the implications of these different benefits for you as an employee. As you will see, employee benefit regulations and programs are continuously changing. As we begin the 21st century, many organizations are beginning to offer what are called "work/life" benefits—programs designed to reduce conflict between employees' work and life activities. Work/life benefits include flexible schedules (see Chapter 16), child-care programs, and convenience benefits, such as dry-cleaning pick-up services, on-site car washes, and take-home meals.[1] To make the most out of your employment situation, you will need to become knowledgeable about your benefits program. Whether you are choosing among different job offers, changing your family status (for example, getting married, becoming divorced, or having a child), preparing for retirement, or being laid off from work, it is important to fully understand your rights, privileges, and requirements as they pertain to benefits. This chapter is divided into four sections: (1) legally required payments (such as Social Security), (2) pension and health insurance plans, (3) miscellaneous benefits (such as tuition reimbursement and child care), and (4) pay for time not worked (such as vacation).

The chapter focuses on how benefits affect you as an employee. Although you may not be aware of what your benefits are worth, businesses are becoming increasingly aware of their costs associated with benefits. In 1997, companies spent on average 28 percent of their total compensation costs on benefits.[2] As you can see in Figure 10.1, the four most expensive benefits were: legally required benefits (for example, Social Security payments), paid time off (for example, vacation), medical care, and retirement programs. It is no wonder that companies nowadays are carefully examining and introducing many changes in their benefits program. It is therefore increasingly important for employees to understand how their benefits work.

| Figure 10.1 | **Percentage of Payroll Costs Associated with Different Benefits** |

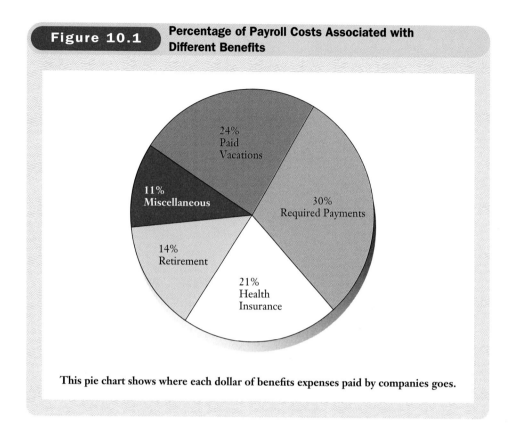

This pie chart shows where each dollar of benefits expenses paid by companies goes.

Legally Required Benefits

You may be surprised to learn that only a few benefits are required by law. Most of the benefits provided by private companies are optional. You may even question whether some of the legally required benefits are really "benefits" at all. The four legally required benefits are the following:[3]

1. Social Security/Medicare
2. Unemployment compensation
3. Workers' compensation
4. Unpaid time off from work

Next, you will learn about each of these four benefits in greater detail, and what they provide for employees.

Social Security/Medicare

Social Security/Medicare
Two government programs that receive funding from employees and their companies, which are used for retirement, disability, survivor benefits, and health-care expenses.

The basis for the **Social Security/Medicare** law is the Social Security Act of 1935. If you are a paid employee, you may find two entries in your pay stub labeled "FICA," which stands for the Federal Insurance Contribution Act. The funds received under this act are used for two purposes: Social Security payments and Medicare payments.

In 1999, employees paid 7.65 percent of up to $72,600 of their earnings to the Social Security fund, and 1.45 percent of their earnings to the Medicare fund. You may now be wondering, "If this is considered a legally required company benefit, why will money be deducted from my paycheck for it?" This is considered a company-sponsored benefit because the company matches your payments; in other words, the company pays an additional 7.65 percent of up to $72,600 (as of 1999) of your earnings into the Social Security fund and an additional 1.45 percent of your earnings into a Medicare fund. You are probably now thinking, "So, what benefit do I receive from all this?" First, if your company was not paying the matching amount (for example, if you were self-employed or serving as a consultant to the company), you would be paying the additional amount. In other words, if you were self-employed, you would be paying the full amount (15.3 percent and 2.9 percent of the salary stated earlier). Second, Social Security and Medicare funds are used for four purposes that you may not be eligible for now, but probably will be eligible for one day:[4]

1. **Retirement Income.** When you retire, you will be eligible for monthly payments for the rest of your life. The size of the payments will depend on how much money you earned during your career. A common rule of thumb is that Social Security payments will replace approximately 30 percent of your final-year earnings. The maximum monthly payment for a worker retiring at age 65 in 1993 was approximately $1,200. Social Security payments, therefore, may comprise a substantial part of your income when you retire.
2. **Disability Income.** If you become completely disabled and unable to work, you may be eligible for monthly Social Security payments.
3. **Survivor Benefits.** Depending on the age and status of your spouse and children, they may be eligible for certain Social Security benefits if you die.
4. **Health-Care Expenses.** If you are at least age 65 or older or are receiving Social Security disability payments for 24 months, you will be eligible for Medicare coverage. Medicare coverage pays for such needs as hospital stays.[5]

For more information on these and related programs, check the following Web site: www.ssa.gov.

Unemployment Compensation

Unemployment compensation provides payments to an employee who is terminated. Although it may seem odd that you would receive this legally required benefit only if you are no longer working for the company, in today's workplace, layoffs are rather common. It pays to be aware of the regulations affecting unemployment compensation. This benefit was initially established by the Social Security Act of 1935, but each state administers its own program. Accordingly, the amount of money an individual is eligible for differs from state to state. In Missouri, for example, the maximum weekly amount an individual would receive is about $170; in New Jersey, the maximum one could receive is over $300, which is about the highest in the nation.[6]

Because the purpose of unemployment compensation is to provide financial support for employees who have been laid off due to a poor economy or stagnant business conditions, a company has the right to deny unemployment compensation to an employee who was terminated for other reasons. Accordingly, employees who were terminated for poor performance, voluntarily quit, or became unemployed because of a labor dispute may not be eligible for unemployment compensation. Most states

disability income
If an employee were to become completely disabled and unable to work, Social Security would provide monthly payments.

survivor benefits
Depending on the age and status of an employee's spouse and children, they may be eligible for monthly Social Security benefits if the employee dies.

unemployment compensation
Provides payments to an employee who is terminated by such means as a layoff (not for being fired or quitting).

provide for unemployment benefits for up to 26 weeks; in some states, however, un-employment benefits may continue even longer. Unemployment compensation is not intended to provide a paid vacation for recipients—those receiving unemployment compensation must register for work at the state employment office, prove their availability for work, and be actively seeking employment. Further, recipients must not refuse an offer of suitable work without good reason.

Finally, in addition to government-mandated programs, some companies offer a program called supplemental unemployment benefits (SUB), which provides additional payments to workers who are on a temporary layoff. A SUB program is often part of a union contract. Box 10.1 lists Web addresses that will provide further information about employee benefits.

Workers' Compensation

workers' compensation
A benefit that provides income and payments for workers or survivors of workers injured, disabled, or killed on the job.

Workers' compensation is a benefit that provides income and payments for workers or survivors of workers who are injured, disabled, or killed on the job. Because such programs are administered entirely by the state, without any federal involvement, they differ greatly from state to state. In all states, however, workers' compensation is designed to provide income to workers in cases of total or partial disability (or, in cases of death, to provide income to their survivors), coverage for medical expenses (such as hospitalization), and coverage for rehabilitation costs (such as occupational therapy).

When most people think of workers' compensation, they consider the traditional cases in which a construction or production worker is injured while working. However, other interesting cases have involved different kinds of situations for which employees have received workers' compensation. For example, would an employee who is injured at the company picnic during a relay race be eligible for workers' compensation? In some cases, the company may in fact be required to make workers' compensation payments. In the past few years, there have also been large numbers of workers' compensation claims regarding mental distress produced by work-related problems. Depending on the state in which you work, if you can demonstrate that you were unable to work because of mental distress caused by the job, you may be eligible for workers' compensation.[7]

Unpaid Time Off

Family and Medical Leave Act (FMLA)
Passed in 1993, this act requires companies that have at least 50 employees to grant an unpaid leave to employees who meet any of the following conditions: the employee has become responsible for a child; the employee is providing care for a child, parent, or spouse with a serious health condition; or the employee is experiencing a serious health condition that leaves him or her unable to perform the job.

The **Family and Medical Leave Act (FMLA),** passed by Congress in 1993, requires companies to provide unpaid time off from work. Briefly, this law requires companies that have at least 50 employees to grant an unpaid leave to employees who meet any of the following conditions:[8]

1. The employee has become responsible for a child through birth, adoption, or foster care.
2. The employee is providing care for a child, parent, or spouse with a serious health condition.
3. The employee is experiencing a serious health condition that leaves him or her unable to perform the job.

For any of these three conditions, the employee can elect to take up to 12 weeks of unpaid leave within a 12-month period. Under certain conditions, the employee can take intermittent leave; that is, the employee may be able to take the leave one day each

WEBBING AROUND

Box 10.1

A great deal of information regarding employee benefits is available on the Internet. Listed below are a few interesting addresses.

http://www.state.oh.us/das/dhr/ebhindex.html. This is an example of an on-line employee benefits manual. What are some advantages of providing this information on-line instead of in "hard copy?"

http://www.pensionconsultant.com/library.htm. This Web site provides extensive information about different kinds of pension plans.

http://www.zinezone.com/Magazines/partners/tc/business/money/Retire/. Thinking about retirement? How much will you need to save in or-

der to retire? Find this and much more information at this Web site.

http://stats.bls.gov/ebshome.htm. Want to learn more about benefits programs other companies offer? Look here for updated and detailed information and compare your company to others.

week of the year. The law permits companies to request documentation of the need for leave from a health professional. The company can even require a second opinion.

Although the law does not require the company to pay the employee during the leave, the company must continue to include him or her under the health insurance plan. Upon return from the leave, the company must provide an equivalent job with the equivalent benefits, pay, and other terms and conditions of employment.

It may come as a surprise to you that Social Security/Medicare, unemployment compensation, workers' compensation, and unpaid time off from work are the only benefits a company is legally required to offer. There are, however, trends suggesting that over the next few years, your company will be required to provide more benefits. For example, some states (California, for one) require companies to provide short-term disability coverage. Thus, while relatively few benefits are required today, the list may be longer in the future.

Returning to the three companies described in the beginning of this chapter, do not assume that FreeStyle will provide even these required benefits. The reason is that if you are hired as an independent contractor or consultant, the company may not have to provide even the required benefits. Therefore, you should check to see exactly what your employment status would be if you were hired by FreeStyle. Otherwise, you might have to pay the FICA taxes on your own. Next, we will discuss two commonly offered, but not legally required, benefits that can be quite valuable to you as an employee: pension and health insurance plans.

Pension and Health Insurance Programs

Pension Plans

Recall that one purpose of the Social Security Act of 1935 was to provide retirement funds for workers. You may therefore wonder why an additional, optional pension program is even necessary or important to you. The answer is that Social Security is designed to replace only about 30 percent of the final income of the average worker;

if you are able to reduce your expenses dramatically when you retire, this may be sufficient. If, however, you intend to continue living the lifestyle that you had while you worked, you will need to substantially supplement any Social Security payments you receive.[9] In addition, many experts are predicting that Social Security will run out of funds for retirees sometime in the early part of the 21st century unless significant changes are made in the way in which the money is invested. Participation in a company-sponsored pension program may therefore be of great value. It may come as a surprise to you, then, that only 79 percent of employees in medium and large firms are covered by some type of company-sponsored retirement program, and even fewer (only 46 percent) employees in small firms (companies with fewer than 100 employees) are covered by a retirement program.[10]

There are several different kinds of company-sponsored pension programs, but they may be divided into two types: defined benefit and defined contribution. Defined benefit pension plans are becoming less prevalent in business and industry than they once were. Defined contribution plans require you to play a much greater role in the management of pension funds, and therefore it is important that you thoroughly understand how this type of plan works.[11] You will first read about defined benefit programs, followed by information about defined contribution programs. We will conclude this section with a discussion of the major law governing pension plans, ERISA, and a discussion of a relatively new, increasingly popular hybrid plan, called a "cash balance plan."

Defined Benefit Pension Programs

defined benefit pension program
Described in terms of what the employee will receive upon retirement, the plan relies on a formula that determines exactly what the employee will receive upon retirement.

A **defined benefit pension program** is described in terms of what the employee will receive upon retirement. In other words, the plan relies on a formula, which determines exactly what this retirement income will be. As shown in Figure 10.2, only 50 percent of employees working for medium and large companies are covered by this type of plan, while only 15 percent of employees in small companies (with fewer than 100 employees) are covered by this type of plan.[12] Although different formulas are used, one of the most common is the "percentage of earnings per year of service" formula. This formula is also regarded as among the fairest. It has three components to it, which generally are multiplied together to give an annual sum of money upon retirement. The three components are: (1) an index of yearly earnings or salary, often the average of one's salary for the last five years of employment; (2) years of service, or the number of years an employee has worked for the company; and (3) a constant, to reflect a percentage of salary. The typical constant is 1.5 percent. An example of such a formula is provided in Table 10.1.

One important issue related to a defined benefit pension is that, as presented here, there is no automatic change in the formula once an employee has retired. Therefore, a retiree would not necessarily receive any increase in the amount of money over the years. Inflation is likely to diminish the buying power of a retirement check over time. Even at a relatively low rate of inflation, say, 4 percent, one dollar would be worth only 69 cents after 10 years. It is, therefore, important to find out whether the pension plan provides an adjustment for cost of living. For example, the University of Missouri– St. Louis offers its retirees the option of having an automatic annual increase of either 2 percent or 4 percent, in exchange for a reduced annual retirement check.

The defined benefit pension plan has several possible advantages for the employee. First, it provides a guaranteed portion of money to an employee upon retirement. No

Figure 10.2   **Percentages of Employees Receiving Different Pension Plans**

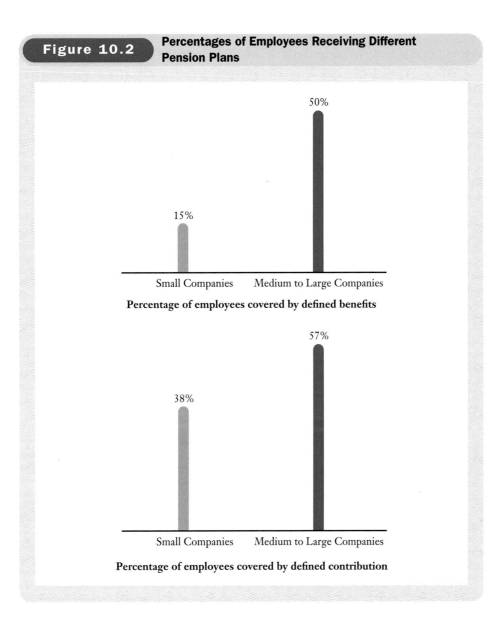

50%

15%

Small Companies   Medium to Large Companies

Percentage of employees covered by defined benefits

57%

38%

Small Companies   Medium to Large Companies

Percentage of employees covered by defined contribution

Table 10.1   **Typical Defined Benefit Formula**

Example of a Defined Benefit Pension Formula

Annual yearly retirement pay = (a) final yearly salary × (b) years of service × (c) .015

Based on this formula, an employee who earned $40,000 in his or her last year of employment and had worked with the company for 40 years would receive an annual yearly retirement check of $24,000. This would not include any Social Security payments to which the employee was entitled.

matter what happens, the employee is ensured at least some portion of money (the effect of a company declaring bankruptcy will be discussed later). A second advantage of the defined pension plan is that for plans with formulas that take into account years of service, long-term employees will be rewarded more than short-term employees. As shown in Table 10.2, all other things being equal, the employee who stays with the same company for his or her entire career would receive a larger annual pension payment than an employee who works for four different companies in his or her career. Finally, the employee in a defined benefit plan has little or no risk involved. It is the company's responsibility to make sure that the plan has enough money (or, in technical terms, is properly funded) to pay retirees.[13]

Defined Contribution Pension Programs

defined contribution pension program
In this program, each participating employee has an individual fund into which contributions may be made by the company, the employee, or both, depending on the specific type of plan.

In a **defined contribution pension program,** each participating employee has an individual fund into which contributions may be made by the company, the employee, or both, depending on the specific plan. This type of plan describes how contributions are made, not how much the employee will get upon retirement. A defined contribution plan, therefore, provides no promises as to how much money an employee will get when he or she retires. As shown in Figure 10.2, 57 percent of employees in medium and large companies are covered by this kind of pension plan, while 38 percent of employees in small (fewer than 100 employees) companies are covered by this type of plan.[14]

Guaranteed Investment Contract (GIC)
A type of fund offered by most companies that is similar to bank-sponsored accounts, guaranteed investment contracts have one major difference: GICs are usually held by insurance companies.

There are several other common features of a defined contribution pension program. One distinct feature is that, in most cases, employees have a choice of where to invest their retirement fund. Most companies, for example, offer mutual funds, company stock, bonds, and similar investment vehicles. One type of fund that is quite popular with employees is the **guaranteed investment contract (GIC).** GICs are similar to bank-sponsored accounts, such as money markets, with one major difference: GICs

---

Table 10.2	**Effects of Seniority on Employee Pensions**

The following table compares pension benefits under a defined benefit program for Jean, a worker who stayed with one company for her entire career, to those of Sam, who worked for four different companies.

Using the formula in Table 10.1, assume that Jean has worked for the same company for 40 years, and Sam has worked 10 years each for four different companies (salaries and pension formulas are assumed to be the same for both employees).

Jean	Sam
Years	
1–10	Company A: $20,000 × 10 × .015 = $3,000
11–20	Company B: $30,000 × 10 × .015 = $4,500
21–30	Company C: $40,000 × 10 × .015 = $6,000
31–40 $50,000 × 40 × .015 = $30,000	Company D: $50,000 × 10 × .015 = $7,500
Total annual check: $30,000	Total annual check: $21,000

Note that Jean receives a higher annual retirement check because the defined benefit formula rewards long-term seniority. Sam receives $9,000 less each year of retirement than Jean, which can be a considerable difference.

are usually held by insurance companies. Given that some insurance companies have recently had financial difficulties, GICs are probably a riskier investment than the name suggests.[15] Most employees are far too conservative in their investment strategies and tend to place most of their funds into relatively secure, but poorly paying investments. You should be aware that in some companies, the funds are being invested in extremely risky investments, including rare coins, antiques, and even real estate.[16]

A second feature of most defined contribution pension plans is the option to use the funds for various purposes. Specifically, most of these plans allow the employee to withdraw the monies when he or she leaves the company. Unless the employee is careful, however, not only will he or she have to pay income tax, but there may be additional monetary penalties as well. Similarly, some defined contribution plans permit the employee to borrow from the fund for such purposes as making a down payment on a home. Thus, in many ways, the defined contribution plan permits greater flexibility for the employee than does the defined benefit program.

There are several different types of defined contribution programs. Only a few will be described here.

401(k).

401(k). A **401(k)** is a savings program that has become quite popular since its introduction in 1981. A recent survey showed that more than 95 percent of large companies offered this type of pension plan. The 401(k) program permits employees to place $10,000 each year into a retirement fund. This money is not taxed. Moreover, most companies will match the employees' contributions; a typical match is that the company adds 50 cents to the fund for each $1 that the employee sets aside, up to 2 percent of the employee's salary. Hence, if an employee was earning $30,000 and puts aside $600, the company would add another $300 to the fund, resulting in a total tax-free accumulation of $900 for the year.[17]

> **401(k)**
> A type of savings program that has become quite popular since its introduction in 1981. The 401(k) program permits employees to place $10,000 each year into a retirement fund tax-free until it is withdrawn.

Despite the large number of companies offering 401(k) plans, it is estimated that only 55 percent of eligible employees in medium to large companies actually participate. The value of participating early in your career can be shown with the following figures. If you begin putting away $2,000 each year at age 21 and continue until age 64, you will have more than $1 million by age 65 (assuming an annual rate of return of 9 percent). In comparison, if you waited until you were 40 years old, you would have less than $200,000 by age 65.[18]

Although many large companies offer a 401(k), Household International has one of the best plans. This company matches 100 percent of employees' contributions for up to 6 percent of the employee's salary. Although not quite as lucrative, Ford Motor Company matches 50 cents for each dollar contributed by employees for up to 5 percent of salary. Finally, General Electric matches 50 cents for every dollar contributed by employees for up to 6 percent of salary. The percentage of salary moves up to 7 percent after the employee contributes for three years.[19]

Deferred Profit Sharing.

Deferred Profit Sharing. In another kind of defined contribution plan, known as **deferred profit sharing,** contributions are usually made only by the employer and are determined by the profitability of the company. Just over 10 percent of employees in the United States are eligible to participate in this type of plan. There are two basic approaches that a company can use for determining contributions. One approach is to use a predetermined formula. Just over half (60 percent) of employees who participate in such a plan have this kind of formula. In the second approach, contributions are determined by the board of directors each year (40 percent of employees who participate in deferred profit sharing have this kind of approach). Among other attributes, the

> **deferred profit sharing**
> The retirement fund contributions are usually made only by the employer and are determined by the profitability of the company.

second approach permits much greater flexibility for the company. From the company's standpoint, the deferred profit-sharing plan makes good business sense—if a company is doing poorly, it may have a difficult time paying for employee benefits. Furthermore, it may motivate employees to work harder. From an employee's or applicant's perspective, however, this means a poorly performing company may provide little or no pension contribution.[20]

Employee Stock Ownership Plans. **Employee Stock Ownership Plans (ESOPs)** became popular during the 1970s and 1980s. The two major reasons for companies instituting this type of plan are tax advantages and the potential to increase employee motivation. Approximately 10 million employees in the United States are covered by ESOPs. Briefly, the ESOP provides employees with company stock and at the same time allows the company to borrow money from a bank at a reduced tax rate. Because contributions to the employees' funds are in the form of company stock, employees should be motivated to work hard in order to increase the value of the company stock and therefore the value of their retirement fund. The principal disadvantage of this retirement program is that employees' retirement funds are directly tied to the stock value of the company. At one brokerage firm, Thomson McKinnon, employees owned about 75 percent of the company's stock, which was valued at $140 million in 1986. As a result of the stock market crash in 1987, the value of Thomson's stock fell, and in mid-1989, employees were sent a letter telling them it was possible that their ESOP funds would have no value whatsoever in the future.[21]

What are the basic advantages of a defined contribution program for employees? In general, such programs tend to benefit younger employees, who are more likely to leave companies after a short tenure. Also, for the employee who invests funds wisely, the defined contribution retirement program may be quite rewarding. Finally, you may be able to borrow from your fund at a low interest rate or even withdraw money under certain circumstances. On the negative side, depending on the type of plan, poor business conditions or a weak economy may lower the amount of money your company contributes. Similarly, poor investment choices can have a devastating effect on your retirement funds. From the company's perspective, there are fewer government requirements and, perhaps most importantly, no promises are made about the future, which in turn reduces the company's obligations. For organizations, then, a defined contribution plan is generally superior.

Cash Balance Plans: A Hybrid Approach

Because there are advantages as well as disadvantages to both defined benefit and defined contribution plans, many organizations have tried to develop hybrid forms, that attempt to take the best of each approach. One of these, the cash balance plan, has recently become quite popular and has been adopted by such companies as AT&T, Bell Atlantic, and Xerox Corporation. In fact, it is predicted that by the year 2010, at least 80 percent of large U.S. businesses will use this approach. While it may not seem important to you now, the cash balance plan has some important features that may be important to know as you plan for retirement.

The cash balance plan is best understood as a defined benefit plan that looks like a defined contribution plan. It is designed to look like an individual account, much like a 401(k), but it does not require employees to make contributions; all of the contributions are provided by the company. The contribution put in the cash balance is usually a percentage of the employee's annual pay—typically about 5 percent. The account is fixed to grow at an established interest rate, often set to the rate of U.S. treasury bills.

One potential advantage to employees is a clearly-defined value to their cash balance plans. Unlike the traditional defined benefit plan, where employees can only estimate what they will get when they retire, the cash balance plan is like a bank account where one can check to find the precise amount of money.

So why do you think organizations prefer the cash balance plan over the traditional defined benefit approach? One reason is that companies often save money when they convert a traditional plan to these plans. For example, Commonwealth Industries found that by converting over, the company instantly saved $11.5 million. Another advantage to companies is that the financial department has an easier time determining how much money to set aside for the accounts. And, if the company is investing its assets successfully, it may be able to easily fund its cash balance program.[22]

Are there disadvantages to employees? Well, if the organization is saving money by converting to this system, it won't surprise you to learn that some long-term employees are losing out on pension money. In general, long-term employees do better under the traditional defined benefit plan. On the other hand, younger employees, who are likely to change jobs, will do better under the cash balance plan. And, of course, employees will have a more accurate picture of what amount of money is in their retirement fund.

ERISA

Aside from the many tax laws that pertain to pension plans, there is one major federal law that governs pension plans: **Employee Retirement Income Security Act** (ERISA). Enacted in 1974, ERISA was instituted to eliminate pension mismanagement and abuse. Although intended as a reform act, some pension practitioners felt it would impose many costly and confusing regulations and joked that ERISA stood for "Everything Ridiculous Invented Since Adam!" While some of the regulations established by ERISA have no visible effect on you as an employee, all of the provisions are important for organizations to follow. ERISA contains six basic provisions:[23]

1. Reporting and disclosure rules.
2. Fiduciary standards.
3. Funding rules.
4. Plan participation rules.
5. Vesting standards.
6. Plan termination insurance.

Let us look more closely at each of these provisions.

Reporting and Disclosure Rules. Under ERISA, companies must provide reports on the fiscal health of the pension plan to a variety of parties, including the participating employees. One of these reports is the **Summary Plan Description,** which outlines the company's pension plan. This must be provided to all new participants. Employees who are concerned about the financial health of the pension plan should ask for a copy of Form 5500, which the company must provide on written request. Finally, each employee must receive a summary annual report of the pension plan, which describes what he or she would receive upon retirement at age 65.[24]

Fiduciary Standards. A **fiduciary** is a person to whom property or power is entrusted for the benefit of another. In the present context, a fiduciary is any person who has authority over the pension plan management, assets, or administration. Typically,

Employee Retirement Income Security Act (ERISA)
An act instituted in 1974 to eliminate pension mismanagement and abuse.

summary plan description
A certain type of report that details the fiscal health and outlines the company's pension plan and that must be available to all new participants.

fiduciary
A person to whom property or power is entrusted for the benefit of another, such as a person who has authority over pension plan management, assets, or administration.

a company will have an employee who helps administer or invest the pension funds, who in turn is a fiduciary. ERISA established responsibilities and legal requirements for such an individual, including the requirement to diversify pension plan investments to minimize risk of large losses, to act with proper skill, and to operate solely in the interest of the plan participants.[25]

funding rules
Requires the pension plan to have sufficient funds so that promised benefits will be available to employees when they retire.

Funding Rules. Simply stated, **funding rules** require the pension plan to have sufficient funds so that promised benefits will be available to employees when they retire. The use of the term "promised benefits" is quite deliberate here. Recall that defined contribution programs make no promises as to how much money you will have at the time of retirement. Therefore, there are no funding regulations for such plans. This is one ERISA regulation that does not pertain to defined contribution programs.

Plan Participation Rules. Initially, companies had tremendous latitude as to when a new employee would become eligible to participate in the pension plan. ERISA established the maximum time a new employee had to wait. That is, once an employee reaches age 21 and completes one year of service, he or she must be allowed to participate within six months. A year of service is defined by the law to mean 1,000 hours or more of work during a 12-month period. Thus, part-time employees might not become eligible for the pension plan.[26]

vesting
Refers to the rights an employee has to the pension benefits if employment is terminated prior to retirement.

Vesting Standards. **Vesting** refers to the rights an employee has to his or her pension benefits if employment is terminated prior to retirement. In other words, if an employee leaves the company prior to a certain time period, he or she may automatically lose some or all of the pension funds. This regulation is important to understand, because it could lead to a significant loss of pension funds. The vesting rules provide the standards by which a participating employee must gain the rights to his or her pension funds. The Tax Reform Act of 1986 stipulates that a company may use either of the following:[27]

A. An employee will be fully vested in five years of service.
B. An employee will be vested 20 percent in the first three years of service and 20 percent for each following year (this means the employee is fully vested in seven years).

Regardless of which of these plans is used, an employee must become fully vested when he or she reaches normal retirement age. Knowing the vesting rules is important for you, as an employee, because leaving a company before being fully vested means you would forfeit some or all of your pension funds. For example, if your company used plan A, and you left the organization four years after you began, you would never receive any company-provided pension funds. If your company used plan B, and you left the organization after six years, you would receive only 80 percent of the pension funds for which you were eligible. If you were to quit or were terminated from several companies over a period of a number of years, you may lose out on large sums of pension money.

Plan Termination Insurance. Similar to the stock market crash of 1929 when numerous banks failed, leaving depositors penniless, companies would sometimes go bankrupt, leaving pensioners with little or no company-sponsored pension. One such case was the Studebaker plant in South Bend, Indiana, which closed in 1963. Because of severe underfunding, a typical 40-year-old worker with 20 years of service received a lump-sum payment of only $350 instead of a lifetime monthly pension check. This and similar cases resulted in the establishment of the **Pension Benefit Guaranty Corporation (PBGC).** The PBGC serves as an insurance program whereby pension plan participants are guaranteed at least some benefits, even if the fund is terminated before being fully funded. The employer pays a premium to participate in this program; currently the rate is $19 per participating employees (the rate goes higher for underfunded programs). While this program serves to guarantee a basic pension, the maximum monthly payment a participant may get is $3,051 per month. For highly paid participants, this may be far less than they would otherwise receive. Does participation in the PBGC apply to all pension programs? The answer is no. Only companies providing a defined benefit pension program participate, because defined contribution programs make no promises as to what participants will end up with. For more information on PBGC, go to the following Web site: www.pbgc.gov.[28]

Pension Benefit Guaranty Corporation
Serves as an insurance program whereby pension plan participants are guaranteed at least some benefits even if the fund is depleted.

In addition to ERISA, certain other laws affect pension plans. The Civil Rights Act of 1964, for example, was used to sue the City of Los Angeles Department of Water & Power on the grounds that it required women to make higher contributions to the pension plan. The department's argument was that because women on average live longer, they should be required to give larger contributions than men in order for both sexes to have the same payments upon retirement. The Supreme Court, however, ruled against the department and argued that this method led women to be treated as a group, which in turn was discriminatory.

Finally, you should be aware that there are other pension programs, such as an individual retirement account (IRA), which employees can use as a tax-deferred retirement savings program. Some companies have also implemented a simplified employee pension (SEP) program, which requires little paperwork and low administrative costs. Certain workers, such as employees in a public school system, may be eligible to participate in a 403(b) plan or tax-deferred annuity, which allows them to contribute money to a pension fund. A major advantage of all of these programs is that they enable you, as an employee, to lower your present taxes, while saving for retirement.

Returning to the three companies you read about in the beginning of this chapter, you probably realize that NewForm's and Tradition's different pension plans have quite different implications. NewForm has a 401(k) plan, which, depending on how much money you are able to set aside, could be quite valuable. However, it will take discipline on your part to participate in the plan and set aside money for the 401(k). It would be useful to find out what investment options the plan offers. Tradition has a defined benefit plan. It would be helpful to find out just what type of formula is used. Because Tradition has a defined benefit plan, it will require far less effort on your part to participate. Thus, each plan has its own strengths and weaknesses. Which plan do you prefer?

In closing, retirement may be the furthest thing from your mind. Nevertheless, lack of careful planning and consideration may leave you with insufficient income when retirement does occur. Experts point out that women in particular must plan their retirement carefully; their life expectancy is longer than men's, they are less likely to have a company-sponsored pension plan, and their pension benefit tends to be smaller.[29] Next, you will learn more about health insurance programs and some critical issues pertaining to them. Box 10.2 suggests ways in which companies may be able to lower health-care benefit costs.

Health Insurance

Americans spend more than $800 billion per year on health care, which amounts to 14 percent of the gross domestic product. As you probably know, medical services are

TALES FROM THE TRENCHES ───────────

Box 10.2
Cutting Health Insurance Costs: Suggestions for Companies

Here are some suggestions for ways in which companies can cut their health insurance costs:

1. Use an insurance plan that fits the organization's needs: In some cases, an organization needs an above-average, relatively expensive plan in order to attract job applicants in a tight job market. In other situations, however, a company can offer an average health insurance program and not diminish its ability to attract candidates. In any case, careful planning must be done to ensure that the company gets a reasonable return on the health insurance program used.

2. Select the different components of a health insurance plan carefully: Prescription drug programs can be extremely expensive if not chosen properly. You may choose to have different companies provide different programs, such as one company providing behavior health (for example, psychiatric care), a different company providing basic health insurance, and a third company providing prescription drugs.

3. Don't just announce cutbacks to employees—provide gains at the same time: Employees generally know that health insurance is costly, so if an organization announces changes such as increased premiums, employees won't be surprised. But it will also help if the organization provides improvements in other areas of the program.

4. Monitor the program carefully. Companies need to develop a health-care-management strategy and take steps to meet their goals. They also need to regularly monitor their costs and find ways to address increases.

Source: Adapted from J. Fraser, "Unhealthy Increases," *Inc.* (September 1998): 132–33.

quite expensive. The national average charge for open-heart surgery, for example, is $7,280, and that figure is only for the physicians' charges—it does not include the hospital room and other service fees. The average annual cost per employee for health insurance was $1.26 per hour work in 1997, representing 6.1 percent of total compensation costs. This was a slight decline from 1995, when the average cost was $1.34 per hour worked, representing 6.9 percent of total compensation costs.[30] Although the inflation rate for medical services has come down to a point where it roughly matches the general rate of inflation, there are signs as we approach the 21st century that health-care costs may once again rise. In a recent survey, 50 percent of small businesses indicated that their health insurance premiums were rising, with an average increase of 13 percent.[31] Do you know how much your employer pays for your medical insurance, or how much it would cost to obtain medical insurance on your own? You may be surprised to learn that if you had to purchase medical insurance on your own, you would probably pay $3,000 per year for even minimum coverage. In comparison, the average monthly premium paid by employees was $39 for individual coverage and $130 for family coverage. Most medium and large companies sponsor some form of health insurance. In fact, 76 percent of employees working in medium to large businesses are covered, but only 64 percent of employees in small businesses are covered. Furthermore, many part-time workers are not eligible to participate in a company's health insurance program: only 6 percent of such employees participate in small companies, while 21 percent of part-time employees participate in medium to large size businesses.[32]

Health insurance plans typically cover services that include hospital stays, physician treatment, mental and nervous disorders treatment, surgery, and in some cases, routine medical services (such as annual physical exams).

The following section describes different kinds of company-sponsored health insurance programs, along with several important regulations that you should be aware of. Before discussing the different types of programs, however, it is important to define several basic terms associated with health insurance programs. Because health insurance operates much like car or home insurance, you are likely to have heard these terms before. *Premiums* are payments that you as an employee make for the insurance coverage; they are similar to the car insurance payments that you make on a regular basis to an insurance company. Unless your company pays for your entire health insurance program, money is likely to be automatically taken from your paycheck to pay health insurance premiums. The *deductible* is the amount of money you must pay before the insurance company reimburses you for expenses. For example, your health insurance plan may have a $250 deductible, which means that you will pay the first $250 on health insurance claims, after which the insurance company will begin to make payments. The **copayment** is the amount of money the employee must pay for the specific health service. For example, after the deductible has been paid, the health insurance program may pay only 80 percent of the costs; your copayment, then, would be 20 percent. Finally, the **maximum out-of-pocket annual payment** is the most that an employee would have to pay for medical expenses in a single year.

copayment
The amount of money an employee must pay for a specific health service.

maximum out-of-pocket annual payment
The most that an employee would have to pay for medical expenses in a single year.

Kinds of Health Insurance Programs

There are several types of health insurance programs that a company may offer to employees. Fee for service, HMOs, PPOs, and POSs are among the most common. Let us examine some important differences between these plans.

Fee for Service. This is the traditional health insurance program. In a **fee-for-service program,** either your company or you and your company pay for each medical service provided to you. A typical fee-for-service program would permit the employee to use any medical professional or facility he or she wishes, would have a deductible (which, much like car insurance, might be higher or lower, depending on the size of the premium), and a copayment of 20 percent. Like automobile insurance, your company may offer different levels of coverage. For example, AT&T offered employees three levels of coverage, ranging from a plan with a $2,500 deductible, a copayment of 30 percent, and a maximum out-of-pocket annual payment of $3,000 to a plan with a deductible of $150 to $300, a copayment of 0 percent to 20 percent (depending on the treatment), and a maximum out-of-pocket annual payment of $1,000. The employee premiums would, of course, be highest for the latter plan.[33]

fee-for-service program
The traditional health-insurance program in which the employee or the employer or both pay for each medical service provided.

A few problems are associated with the traditional fee-for-service approach, particularly from the employer's point of view. First, it provides little incentive for medical professionals and facilities to keep costs down. Because, in most cases you, the employee, pay a relatively small copayment, such a program provides little pressure and even less opportunity for you to shop around for the least costly medical professional. (Have you ever asked a doctor how much he or she charges for a particular procedure?) Second, fee-for-service programs generate a great deal of paperwork and administrative work to keep track of the bills and reimbursements, which in turn creates additional expenses. It should not surprise you, then, that the number of employees enrolled in a fee-for-service plan plummeted from 67 percent in 1991 to less than half of that number, 27 percent, in 1997.

Other programs, such as HMOs and PPOs, have been developed in response to these problems. These alternatives are discussed next.[34]

Health Maintenance Organization (HMO)
A network of medical professionals and hospitals that provide health care for participants.

primary-care physician
The physician chosen through an HMO that decides what kind of treatment is needed and provides referrals to the appropriate specialists within the HMO.

HMOs. Although **health maintenance organizations (HMOs)** have been in existence for more than 40 years, they received their biggest boost with the passage of the HMO Act of 1973, which may require a company to offer an HMO. HMOs are rapidly gaining popularity, as this system uses a variety of cost-saving techniques. Basically, an HMO is a network of medical professionals and hospitals that provide health care for participants. If you enroll in an HMO, you usually must select a **primary-care physician** who works for the HMO. The primary-care physician decides what kind of treatment you need and will refer you (if necessary) to the appropriate specialist within the HMO. The basic advantages to employees who enroll in the HMO are as follows. Unlike traditional fee-for-service health insurance plans, HMO participants usually pay no deductible and only a small copayment, usually $10 to $15, per office visit. If you use health-care services with at least some regularity, HMOs may be less expensive for you than the fee-for-service plan. Second, HMOs often provide coverage for health expenses not covered by traditional fee-for-service plans, such as the annual physical exam. Finally, HMOs typically require employees to complete little or no paperwork.[35]

While the HMO offers several advantages to companies and to employees, there are some drawbacks, particularly from the employee viewpoint. First, most HMOs require the employee to use a medical professional who is part of the network; you would not be reimbursed if you used professionals or services outside of the network. Also, most HMOs require that you first seek treatment from the primary-care physician. Only if the primary-care physician cannot treat you will you be permitted to see a specialist. The degree to which this creates a problem may depend upon the number of specialists associated with the HMO and how important it is to you to be seen by a specialist. A recent survey indicated that 14 percent of HMO participants were dissatisfied with the choice of specialists made available to them. Second, the same survey found large differences in waiting time to obtain an appointment and to see the doctor. Nevertheless, respondents in HMOs were on average just as satisfied with their medical experiences as were respondents in other types of programs.[36]

All in all, it should not surprise you that the number of employees participating in HMOs has increased a great deal over the last decade. Specifically, the number of employees enrolled in HMOs rose from 17 percent in 1991 to 33 percent in 1997, primarily because of lower costs compared with the fee-for-service plans.

Preferred-Provider Organization (PPO)
A network of medical professionals and hospitals that have agreed to give discounted services. Unlike the HMO, participants may go to any medical professional or hospital they wish.

PPOs. A **preferred-provider organization (PPO)** is simply a network of medical professionals and hospitals that have agreed to give discounted services. Unlike the HMO, participants may go to any medical professional or hospital they wish; participants merely pay less for PPO services than they do for non-PPO services. For example, you may have a copayment of only 10 percent for a PPO doctor, with a deductible of only $100. Conversely, you might have a copayment of 20 percent for a non-PPO doctor, with an annual deductible of $250. Compared to an HMO, then, participants have far greater choice with the PPO system. However, the PPO plan may cost you more than an HMO, and companies find that this approach does little to cut expenses.[37]

Point-Of-Service (POS) plan
A plan that attempts to combine the advantages of the HMO with the advantages of the PPO.

POS. The **point-of-service plan (POS)** attempts to combine the advantages of the HMO with the advantages of the PPO. Typically, the POS operates like the HMO in that you must first check with your primary-care physician. Only if the primary-care physician gives you a referral can you see a specialist. On the other hand, like the PPO, you can use any medical professional or service you would like. However, you will be reimbursed at different rates, depending on whether you use a professional associated with the POS (an **in-network** professional) or whether you use a professional not associated with the POS (an **out-of-network** professional). Obviously, the charge for seeing an in-network professional will be much lower. Thus, the POS tries to combine both the HMO and the PPO concepts to best serve the employees.[38] The number of employees who are enrolled in either a PPO or POS soared from 16 percent in 1991 to 40 percent in 1997. Clearly, the PPO and POS options have proved to be the most popular in the last few years.

As you can see, your company may choose from a variety of insurance plans. In the past few years, emphasis has increased on developing measures or report cards of the effectiveness of different health care providers. Certain organizations now conduct independent evaluations of hospitals, HMOs, and other health care providers. See the following Web site for an example of such evaluations; you may even find your health care provider listed here: http://www.ncqa.org/apps/searchableasl/main.asp[39] Carefully examining the alternatives, in conjunction with your particular needs, will help you choose the best options. The next section explains some additional terms and conditions associated with health insurance plans.

Additional Terms Associated with Health Insurance Plans

Several terms and conditions of health insurance plans are important to know. A complete understanding of these terms will help you, as an employee, make better decisions with regard to health care.

Preexisting Condition. An important term in the health insurance field, a **preexisting condition** is generally defined as an illness, injury, or pregnancy that an individual has prior to becoming covered by the health insurance plan. Many health insurance plans will not cover charges related to a preexisting condition until a set time period has passed. For example, imagine you were receiving treatment for a heart condition. When you switch jobs, you may become covered by a new health insurance plan. Your new plan may have a preexisting condition clause that states that you must complete three months of coverage under the new company's insurance plan without receiving treatment for the condition, or you might have to complete twelve months of coverage. If you needed emergency treatment for your heart condition, for example, prior to three months being completed, your new insurance might not pay anything. Obviously, this could result in considerable expense to you. Although the preexisting condition concept may seem fairly straightforward, in fact it is quite complex. There are at least three ways to avoid problems with a preexisting condition clause. One, some health insurance plans do not contain such a clause; HMOs in particular often do not have a preexisting condition clause. So, check carefully to see if you are switching to a plan that has a preexisting condition clause. Second, as explained next, using the COBRA option may help protect you from a preexisting condition. Third, a new law, HIPAA, described below, may help you. In any case, read the clause carefully, and make sure you fully understand all of the implications.

COBRA. COBRA refers to the Consolidated Omnibus Budget Reconciliation Act of 1985. Although the act addresses many other issues, for our purposes it is important

---

in-network
A list of medical professionals that are associated with the plan (POS, HMO, or PPO).

out-of-network
Any medical professional not associated with the plan (POS, HMO, or PPO). If an employee chooses a doctor that is out-of-network, the cost will be higher than using an in-network professional.

preexisting condition
An illness, injury, or pregnancy that an individual has prior to becoming covered by the health insurance plan.

COBRA
The Consolidated Omnibus Budget Reconciliation Act (COBRA) of 1985 requires companies with 20 or more employees to offer continued coverage of health insurance to participants who would otherwise no longer be eligible to participate in the health insurance plan.

to know that COBRA requires companies with 20 or more employees to offer continued health insurance coverage to participants who would otherwise no longer be eligible to participate in the health insurance plan. Imagine, for example, you were terminated from a company or that you were covered under your father's or mother's health insurance plan, which you will no longer be eligible for now that you are graduating from college. For both of these situations, you or your parent should be able to continue your coverage for some period of time (the maximum amount of time you will be able to continue coverage depends on the situation). For example, if you were terminated, you would be able to continue coverage for up to 18 months. Of course, such continued coverage is not free; your company can require you to pay all of the costs, plus an additional 2 percent to cover administrative charges. Returning to preexisting conditions, use of COBRA would permit you to continue your previous health insurance until the preexisting condition clause expired. You should plan carefully to ensure that you are covered in case of expensive health-care treatment. COBRA may be a useful option toward meeting this goal.[40]

The Health Insurance Portability and Accountability Act (HIPAA) of 1996. HIPAA was designed to help employees and their families avoid losing health insurance. It was believed that many U.S. employees remained in jobs they did not like because if they left their jobs and the health insurance that was provided, they would be prevented from having effective coverage due to a preexisting condition. To combat that problem, HIPAA prohibits group health plans from having a preexisting condition that lasts more than 12 months and requires that workers who were covered under a different health plan get "credit" for the preexisting condition when they change employers with a different health insurance plan. Employees going from one group health insurance plan at one company cannot be denied coverage by a different group health insurance plan at a different company. However, problems have occurred when employees leave a group health insurance plan and then seek individual health insurance (for example, they are now self-employed). Insurance companies have, in the views of some, charged excessive fees for such coverage—in some cases, these fees have been reported to be 4 to 20 times what a "healthy" person would be charged. In some cases, the states have stepped in to regulate the fees charged. For more information on this law, see this Web site: http://www.hcfa.gov/regs/hipaacer.htm.[41]

utilization review
A process by which medical services are analyzed and reviewed.

Utilization Review. In an effort to reduce continuously growing costs of health care, many insurance companies are turning to use of the **utilization review,** a process by which medical services are analyzed and reviewed. The utilization review may require the use of second opinions (in which a second medical professional's opinion is required before a particular planned surgical procedure is performed), concurrent reviews (in which an independent medical professional monitors your hospital stay), and review of medical bills. Utilization reviews may prevent unnecessary surgeries and cut down on the length of time you spend in a hospital. At the same time, a utilization review may result in your hospital stay being shorter than you would like or additional expenses for you if the insurance company refuses to pay the entire bill. As a consumer, you can do little about utilization reviews. Be sure, however, that you learn the requirements of your health insurance program (for example, is a second opinion necessary in order to have a surgical procedure reimbursed?) and be sure to carefully review all documents concerning your health insurance. Ask your company benefits representative any questions you might have. An appeal process may allow you to request reconsideration if you believe you have been treated unfairly.[42]

Flexible Spending Accounts. Flexible spending accounts (FSAs) allow an employee to pay for health-care expenses or dependent-care assistance expenses on a before-tax basis. A *before-tax basis* means that you, as an employee, would not pay any federal, state, or Social Security/Medicare taxes on that money. If you spend a fairly large sum of money on either health care or dependent care (such as payments to a day care center), an FSA may save you considerable money. An FSA works thus: each year your company (if it has set up an FSA program) will ask you how much money you wish to set aside for the health-care and dependent-care assistance funds (there is, of course, a limit to how much you can set aside for each). The major potential disadvantage of the FSA system is that it is a "use it or lose it" program; you forfeit any money you set aside that you do not use. Only about one out of three employees in medium to large companies are eligible to participate in an FSA; in small companies the numbers fall to slightly more than 1 out of 10.

> **Flexible Spending Account (FSA)**
> FSAs allow an employee to pay for health-care expenses or dependent-care assistance expenses on a before-tax basis.

Returning to the three companies described in the opening case, it is beginning to look as though FreeStyle may not be quite the deal you might have at first thought. Even though the starting salary is $2,000 more than the other two companies, it is clear that health insurance alone might cost more than $2,000 each year. In comparing the other two companies, Tradition seems to have some of the features discussed, including the FSAs, HMO, and PPO options. NewForm, as you may recall, has a cafeteria benefits plan, which we will discuss in the next section. For now, though, it would be useful to seek more information from NewForm to find out what type of health insurance options they offer. Likewise, it may be worth getting information from both companies as to the specific details of the health insurance plans and how much the premium is for each plan. Next, you will read about other benefits, such as long-term disability insurance, and elder care.

Miscellaneous Employee Benefits

Many companies offer other types of benefits in addition to health insurance and pension plans. As with health insurance, you may be able to purchase some of these additional benefits from an insurance company on your own, but your company may pay part or all of your premiums and obtain a better rate than you would on your own. It is important, therefore, to find out about these other benefits as well. This section discusses disability insurance, elder care and long-term care, and dental insurance, and briefly mentions other benefits such as tuition reimbursement and child-care facilities. The section concludes with an explanation of a cafeteria benefits plan.

Disability Insurance

Disability insurance provides income in case you become unable to work due to an accident or illness. You may ask, "Doesn't Social Security or workers' compensation cover this situation?" They may, but those mandatory programs typically pay a far lower percentage of one's salary; even though they may provide some income, it may be too little to cover your living expenses. That is why it is important to have additional coverage through disability insurance.

Generally, disability insurance is divided into **short-term disability (STD)** insurance and **long-term disability (LTD)** insurance. As suggested by the names, STD covers short-term disabilities, usually for a period of six months or less. LTD refers to long-term disabilities, usually for periods of time greater than six months. LTD plans

> **Short-Term Disability (STD) insurance**
> Insurance that covers short-term disabilities, usually for a period of six months or less.
> **Long-Term Disability (LTD) insurance**
> Insurance that covers long-term disabilities, usually for periods of time greater than six months.

generally have a two-stage period. In the first stage, LTD benefits are paid to an employee who, due to the disability, is unable to perform his or her regular job. In the second stage, which typically occurs two or three years later, benefits may continue only if the individual is unable to perform any occupation for which the person is qualified for by training or experience. A recent survey of medium and large companies found that 43 percent of employees participated in this disability insurance, but only 22 percent of employees in small firms participated.[43]

Because most people mistakenly assume they will never experience a disabling condition, LTD insurance is often ignored by employees. Indeed, one expert refers to disability coverage as the "Rodney Dangerfield of insurance," because it gets limited respect and little attention. It is probably a wise idea to at least consider the option of obtaining such insurance. A recent estimate indicates that a typical 40-year-old professional employee should pay roughly $39 per month in premiums for each $1,000 of monthly disability coverage. You should carefully review the terms and conditions of the disability insurance policy. For example, the ideal policy would continue paying until you are 65, when you would become eligible for Social Security payments; but many policies end after three to five years of disability. Another consideration is the renewability and cancellation clauses in the policy. The best policies guarantee you the right to continue coverage as long as you pay your premiums (thereby preventing the insurer from arbitrarily canceling your policy). Finally, just as with certain pension plans, inflation gradually reduces the value of a fixed disability income. The best policies offer some kind of adjustment for cost-of-living increases.[44] Box 10.3 describes recent changes in health insurance for retirees.

Elder Care and Long-term Care

elder-care insurance
An insurance program that pays for medical care at home or in a nursing home.

Elder-care insurance is a program that pays for medical services for an elderly relative. It is estimated that nearly one-quarter of U.S. households are taking care of an elderly person. A recent study showed that about one-third of U.S. dual-income families changed their work schedules to help an elderly relative. It has been estimated that lost productivity due to workers helping elderly friends or relatives is close to $30 billion annually. To address these issues, more organizations are offering elder-care insurance programs. These programs offer a variety of services, ranging from counselors to help employees find the best services to day-care center services. At present, only about one-third of companies provide elder-care insurance and of those companies, only 6 percent of employees were enrolled. Nevertheless, as the U.S. population continues to age, more employees will need to avail themselves of an elder-care insurance program. Long-term care covers an employee who needs home-care health services or a long-term care facility stay. Many employees fail to anticipate a need for such services only to discover when the need arises that the services are not covered by insurance. Check your organization to see if such a program is provided.[45]

Dental Insurance

Most large companies today sponsor dental insurance plans. These are similar in most ways to health insurance plans. Typically, preventive dental services (such as routine exams, cleaning, and standard X-rays) are completely covered, while basic services (such as fillings) have a deductible and small copayment (perhaps 20 percent). Major services (for example, inlays) have a deductible and a much larger copayment (maybe 50 percent).

YOUR TURN

Box 10.3
The Changing Rules for Retirees' Health Insurance

As a result of recent accounting rule changes, many companies are reducing or even eliminating their retirees' health insurance program. One company that is involved in a legal battle over retiree health benefits is John Morrell & Company, a meatpacker based in Sioux Falls, South Dakota. The legal battle began when the company sent a letter to its retirees in early 1992, indicating that the retirees would pay more for the cost of prescription drugs, have a higher premium, and face higher maximum annual out-of-pocket costs. According to the company, when combined with the federal Medicare program, retirees would still have a better benefits program than most companies provide. Somewhat surprisingly, the company, not the retirees, began the legal contest by suing the retirees in court. What was the purpose of the company's lawsuit? To have the judge declare that the company could alter the health benefits of retirees at any time. Although Medicare still covers many of the retirees' costs, changes in the company-sponsored health insurance program mean higher costs to the retirees in such areas as prescription drugs. Previously, for example, the retirees paid a flat $2 for prescription drugs. Under the new retiree health insurance policy, Gerrit Zwak (one of the retirees) will pay as much as 30 percent for his wife's heart drug, which costs $105 retail. The retirees' biggest concern was that in the next year the company would reduce the health insurance plan even further. In a subsequent trial, the company won.

Source: Adapted from R. Rose, "Chilly Sunset," *Wall Street Journal*, 2 February 1993, A1, A6.

Additional Benefits

A great many other benefits exist that a company may provide or sponsor. Although not all of these can be described or even mentioned here, two are worth mentioning in somewhat greater detail: tuition reimbursement and child-care centers.

Tuition Reimbursement. Tuition reimbursement is becoming a much sought-after benefit because many full-time employees are returning to (or beginning) college for further education. Although more than two-thirds of medium and large companies offer some tuition aid, just about one-third of eligible employees usually participate. Tuition-aid programs vary in terms of the amount of reimbursement they provide. The norm today is for companies to provide anywhere between 75 percent and 100 percent reimbursement. Most companies require the employee to "successfully" complete the course (for example, obtain a passing grade); some companies reimburse the employee in proportion to the grade obtained (such as 100 percent reimbursement for an A, 75 percent reimbursement for a B and so on)—and you thought good grades never paid off! Many companies also subsidize related educational expenses, including textbooks, registration fees, and laboratory fees. A few companies will even reimburse for graduation fees, entrance exams, and similar costs.

tuition reimbursement
Tuition reimbursement programs vary in terms of the amount of reimbursement they provide, but they usually provide 75 to 100 percent reimbursement contingent on a passing grade.

Child Care. Today, a majority of women with children are working in the labor force. Yet, only about 10 percent of employees in medium to large companies are eligible to receive child-care assistance. Even fewer (2 percent) are eligible in small companies. Working women with young children often must find a full-time baby-sitter or arrange for some type of day care. Accordingly, an increasingly valuable benefit is some type of child-care support. The best, of course, is an on-site day-care center. SAS, a computer software firm, is one of the few firms that provides free on-site day care. SAS provides this service to any employee with one or more years of service. What do you think the estimated yearly value of this benefit is? If you guessed about $4,200 you are right.[46] In fact, employees must pay taxes to the IRS as if they received this money from the company. As you can imagine, the day-care center is quite popular. More than 300 children are enrolled, with a waiting list of 80 children. From an employee perspective, there is at least one potential advantage of an on-site day-care center: proximity to work. Not only does this mean that both the child and the employee commute back and forth to the same area, but the parent may be able to visit the child during lunch breaks.

From a company's perspective, a company-sponsored day-care center can be a considerable expense. In addition to obtaining qualified staff, the company will have to pay considerable liability insurance, facilities costs, and so forth. Some research as to the benefit of on-site child-care centers has shown that employees of organizations that provide on-site child care indicate greater organizational commitment and less willingness to change jobs than employees of those that do not provide such programs. However, within the same organization, employees who are currently using or are planning to use the on-site child care exhibit no differences in job satisfaction or intentions to quit. Nevertheless, these employees did believe that the on-site child care affected their attraction to the company. These findings suggest that the presence of an on-site child-care center could be helpful in hiring and retaining employees if the alternative employers do not have one.[47]

Finally, some additional benefits that a company may offer include vision care, legal and financial advice, employee discounts on goods and services, and free or reduced costs for meals. Many companies offer additional benefits to top executives, including the use of a company car and membership in country clubs. One of the best companies for benefits is IBM, which provides home mortgage assistance, as well as up to $50,000 for the care of disabled children. An emerging trend is to offer emergency and sick-child care programs.[48] The next section discusses one way to offer a wide choice of benefits to an employee, while allowing the company to control its costs: the cafeteria or flexible benefits plan.

Cafeteria Benefits

cafeteria benefits
A benefits plan that provides a choice between taxable (usually cash) and nontaxable elements of compensation (such as health insurance).

Perhaps the best way to understand a **cafeteria benefits** plan is to think of a lunch cafeteria, to which the customer pays a flat monthly fee. The menu consists of a choice of soup or salad, three different main courses, a soft drink or hot beverage (coffee, tea, or hot chocolate), and a dessert. If, however, the customer chooses to not select a dessert, he or she receives a refund of 50 cents each day. An advantage of this type of plan is that the cafeteria could add additional offerings, without incurring much, if any, additional cost. For example, in addition to choosing between soup and salad, the menu could be modified so that the customer could choose either soup, salad, or an appetizer. The cost to the company would remain the same, since the customer can only pick one of the three items. The assumption is that with greater choice, customers will be more satisfied with their selection and better able to meet their own needs. The logic of the cafeteria benefits plan is much the same. Essentially, a cafeteria plan allows employees to choose between taxable (usually cash) and nontaxable elements of compensation (such as health insurance).[49]

Why would companies develop a cafeteria benefits plan? First, as described in an earlier chapter, the characteristics of the workforce are changing. As one benefits expert remarked, "The 'prototypical employee' (a married male, age 35 to 45, two children preparing for college, with a heavily mortgaged home and two cars) for whom most group benefit programs were designed . . . [is] starting to become a demographic dinosaur." In other words, different employees need different benefits. Just as some people prefer salad over soup, or would rather forgo dessert, the single employee with no children, for example, may prefer more vacation time or simply cash, while the single-wage earner with several children may prefer greater health insurance coverage. Second, use of a cafeteria plan allows companies to add new options at little or no cost. Thus, a plan may provide 100 credits to each participant to spend on the benefits plan. Just as with the cafeteria lunch plan wherein selection of a new dish means the customer must forgo a different dish, the cafeteria benefits plan means the employee will need to forgo some amount of another benefit, or pay more, if he or she chooses a new offering. Finally, another reason companies may adopt a cafeteria plan is to reduce increasing costs. For example, Educational Testing Service, one of the original adopters, bases its contributions on the same percentage of salary as it did when it first introduced its cafeteria plan in the mid-1970s. United Hospitals, Inc. (UHI), successfully changed to a cafeteria benefits plan in the late 1980s. Not only was the company able to contain or even reduce the cost of health benefits, but employees in many cases received extra money. Some employees took home as much as an additional $100 per month. Most UHI employees paid no more than $20 per month for their benefits. A critical factor in the success of UHI's program was that employees received much information about the plan, and it changed their approach to medical services.[50]

There are several different types of cafeteria benefit plans. For example, the plan adopted by Educational Testing Service in the mid-1970s is referred to as an **add-on plan.** In this plan, all existing benefits are maintained. The benefit plan is supplemented by additional optional benefits. An example of a **modular plan** is illustrated in Table 10.3. In this type of cafeteria plan, the employee is offered a choice of several benefit "packages" or modules. An employee chooses one of the packages and cannot substitute. As you look at Table 10.3, observe that if the employee chooses Module B, he or she would get either $300 cash or $300 in a flexible spending account to be used for day care.

add-on plan
A cafeteria plan in which all existing benefits are maintained and new ones added.
modular plan
A cafeteria plan in which the employee is offered a choice of several benefit "packages" or modules.

What should you be careful about if you work for a company with flexible cafeteria benefits? First, you should consider your choices carefully. For example, although you may think you would rather have cash than participate in the LTD insurance plan, think twice. Second, pay careful attention to any changes that your company announces. Third, when you are completing your forms to select your choices, be sure you complete the forms accurately.[51] For more information on different types of cafeteria benefit plans, see this Web site: http://www.flex-plan.com.

Returning to the three companies described in the opening case, it would be helpful to carefully examine any additional benefits provided by each company. Depending on your own needs and interests, some of the additional benefits offered by one of the three companies may be particularly valuable. If, for example, you were planning to go to graduate school while working, a company offering total tuition reimbursement might provide tremendous savings over a company that does not offer this benefit. Conversely, if you had young children and were part of a dual-career family, you might value a company that provides an on-site day-care center. Therefore, it is important that you thoroughly investigate all of the benefits that each company offers. However, before you make a definite choice based on current differences among the three companies, you should realize that companies have considerable latitude in changing or eliminating benefits; so if your choice of jobs varies on several factors (such as the opportunity for promotions, pay, type of work), do not let the benefits program be the only deciding factor. Box 10.4 addresses our next topic: paid time off.

Table 10.3	Example of a Modular Cafeteria Benefits Plan			
Medical	**Dental**	**Life**		**FSA/Cash**
A: Comprehensive Plan: $200 deductible per person, then plan pays 90 percent of expenses and you pay 10 percent. Maximum you could pay— $1,000 excluding deductible.	100 percent preventive care 50 percent other care $1,000 lifetime max. for orthodontia. You pay for dependent dental coverage.	Company-paid: 2 × pay with $50K max. Employee-paid life: 1 ×, 2 ×, or 3 × Company-paid with $150K max. Employee-paid dependent life: Spouse—$10,000 Children—$5,000		Not available.
B: Comprehensive Plan: $300 deductible per person, then plan pays 80 percent of expenses and you pay 20 percent. Maximum you could pay— $1,000 excluding deductible.	100 percent preventive care 75 percent other care 60 percent orthodontia $1,500 lifetime max. for orthodontia. Company-paid dental coverage for employees and dependents.	Company-paid: 2 × pay with no max. Employee-paid life: 1 × or 2 × pay with no max. Employee-paid dependent life: Spouse—$10,000 Children—$5,000		$300 per year from company available for dependent day care or health care or as cash. Salary reduction: up to $5,000 for dependent day care.
C: Comprehensive Plan: $600 deductible per person, then plan pays 80 percent of expenses and you pay 20 percent. Maximum you could pay— $3,000 excluding deductible.	Not available.	Company-paid: $10,000 Employee-paid life: 1 × or 2 × pay with no max. Employee-paid dependent life: Spouse—$10,000 Children—$5,000		$800 per year from company available for dependent day care or health care or as cash. Salary reduction: up to $5,000 for dependent day care.

Adapted from McCaffery (1992).

Paid Time Off

paid time off
Includes vacation, holidays, and personal absences.

Paid time off from work is the last benefits area that you will read about here. Compared to previous centuries, when employees often worked six or seven days every week, employees now work far fewer days. There are three categories of paid time off from work: vacation, holidays, and personal absences. Why companies provide these benefits, and some typical policies concerning them, are described in greater detail next.

Vacations

Companies provide vacations to employees for two basic reasons. First, it is widely recognized that employees need occasional breaks from the physical and mental demands of work. Second, it is widely believed that employees should be rewarded for staying with the company; most companies therefore offer longer vacation periods for more senior employees. Quaker Oats, for example, offers two weeks of vacation time to employees. After 25 years of service, Quaker Oats employees are entitled to five weeks of

YOUR TURN

Box 10.4
Extended Paid Time Off from Work

A few companies, particularly computer and high-tech companies, have begun to offer employees a kind of extended paid vacation, called a sabbatical (many universities offer a similar program for faculty members). Such companies may offer paid time away from work for up to one year, not so much as a vacation, but usually to provide an opportunity for self-development. Sabbaticals are often highly valued benefits. For example, in the late 1970s, Tandem Computers surveyed its employees and found that sabbaticals were more highly desired than pensions. Less than 10 years later, almost one-quarter of Tandem's eligible workforce had participated in the sabbatical program. On a somewhat smaller scale, Eastman Kodak provides up to 1-week sabbaticals each year for community service. McDonald's provides paid 8-week sabbaticals every 10 years for full-time employees. In 1992, Pace Harrington, McDonald's' vice president of personnel, took his sabbatical to spend time with his family. As he explained, "Our employees work hard. We're a global company and we travel a lot. Our employees welcome the time simply to reflect on what they've accomplished and to prioritize their futures."

Sources: Adapted from C. Kleiman, "More Firms Add up Pluses of Sabbaticals," *Chicago Tribune*, 6 December 1992; and L. Lucian, "The Good News About Employee Benefits," June 1992, 91–94.

vacation. One of the most generous vacation policies is offered by Anheuser-Busch, where employees with 15 or more years of tenure receive ten weeks of vacation each year. Levi Strauss, however, has an even more unusual policy: employees may take every Friday afternoon off! That is equivalent to more than five weeks of vacation per year. In addition, employees are allowed up to seven additional weeks off after 20 years of service.[52] A recent survey indicates that on average, after 10 years of service, employee receive 2 weeks of paid vacation.[53]

Holidays

Most of us believe that certain days on the calendar are a time for family and friends to celebrate and spend time together. Companies have also recognized and accepted this belief, and, through the 20th and into the 21st century, more and more days are being treated as paid holidays. Recent surveys show that companies provide an average of about eight or nine paid holidays per year. Some companies give even more; Johnson & Johnson gives eleven paid holidays. The following six holidays are recognized and paid for by nearly all companies in the United States: New Year's Day, Memorial Day, Independence Day, Labor Day, Thanksgiving Day, and Christmas Day. Other days that may be included are Martin Luther King's birthday, Presidents' Day, and Columbus Day.[54]

Personal Absences

Companies realize that on certain occasions, employees are unable to come to work for reasons beyond their control and therefore deserve to be paid despite their not being at work. Such reasons may include jury duty, family death, military duty, divorce hearings, and doctor visits. Rather than the employee simply not coming to work, companies offer **personal absences** as a way to have some advance notice (in the case of doctor visits, divorce hearings, or other appointments that can be anticipated) and still

personal absences
Allowed on certain days in which the employee is unable to come to work for reasons beyond his or her control, such as jury duty, family death, military duty, divorce hearings, and doctor visits.

compensate employees. Many companies today provide two to five personal days per year and let the employee decide when such a day is needed. One should be careful not to use such days frivolously, though, as you may not have any remaining when you really need them.[55]

Most companies offer a fairly standard policy of paid time off from work. Some companies, such as the ones mentioned earlier, offer excellent vacation time. While it is useful to examine a potential employer's paid time off, you will probably find the policies quite similar from company to company.

❖ Conclusion

Returning to the three companies discussed in the opening case, given what has been discussed here, which company do you think has the better benefits program? Do you think your answer will differ depending on your particular circumstances and needs? Employee benefits is a complicated area, but one that is critical for both companies and employees. Whether you are beginning your first full-time job, changing jobs, becoming unemployed, or changing your family status (such as having a child), it is imperative that you learn just what the implications are regarding your benefits.

❖ Applying Core Concepts

1. Did you ever have a job in which the company did not provide Social Security/Medicare payments? Why didn't the company pay? Ask friends or relatives if they ever filed a workers' compensation claim. Ask them to tell you what the process was like.
2. What type of health insurance plan are you covered by now? How satisfied are you with the plan? If you currently have no such plan, discuss why not. What would you do if you had a serious medical problem needing professional help?
3. What type of pension plan do you think is best? What type of plan do you have now or do you expect to have soon?
4. Of the different additional benefits companies provide, which would you consider most valuable to you? Why?
5. Ask a few friends or relatives about the paid time off they have in their jobs. How do their plans compare to the ones you read about in this chapter?

❖ Key Terms

Social Security/Medicare
Disability income
Survivor benefits
Unemployment compensation
Workers' compensation

Family and Medical Leave Act (FMLA)
Defined benefit pension program
Defined contribution pension program

Guaranteed investment contract (GIC)
401(k)
Deferred profit sharing
Employee stock ownership plan (ESOP)

Employee Retirement
    Income Security Act
    (ERISA)
Summary plan description
Fiduciary
Funding rules
Vesting
Pension Benefit Guaranty
    Corporation
Copayment
Maximum out-of-pocket
    annual payment
Fee-for-service program

Health maintenance
    organization (HMO)
Primary-care physician
Preferred-provider
    organization (PPO)
Point-of-service (POS)
    plan
In-network
Out-of-network
Preexisting condition
COBRA
Utilization review

Flexible spending account
    (FSA)
Short-term disability
    (STD) insurance
Long-term disability
    (LTD) insurance
Elder-care insurance
Tuition reimbursement
Cafeteria benefits
Add-on plan
Modular plan
Paid time off
Personal absence

❖ CHAPTER 10 *Experiential Exercise*

Choosing a Benefit Program at Emmett Press

"I want you to tell me the truth," said Mr. V. Emunah, owner and president of Emmett Press. Mr. Emunah, or V, as he prefers to be called by his employees, recently called this meeting of his 75 employees to discuss his latest ideas. Emmett Press publishes mystery and science fiction books. Many of the employees have been with the company for more than 20 years, though in the last few years there has been much more turnover among the newer hires. Because the company is a specialty business and barely makes a profit, salaries are fairly low and the benefits program has been confined to those required by law. Today, however, as he has done for the last 50 years, Mr. Emunah is seeking a consensus as to what he considers an important human resources decision. Specifically, he has decided that he should further develop a benefits program.

After talking with his insurance company last month and reading an article in *Press Magazine* (a publishing industry professional magazine), Mr. Emunah decided that offering employees a benefit program would not only be good for tax purposes, but would provide employees with a valuable supplement to their compensation. However, he is not sure what type of plan to offer. The four options are as follows:

1. A defined contribution pension plan;
2. A defined benefit pension plan;
3. A medical insurance program.
4. In lieu of any of the above, a lump sum addition of $2,000 annually to each employee's pay.

Although the fourth option is not a benefit plan, Mr. Emunah feels that if the employees would really prefer cash over a benefit program, they should have that option.

Mr. Emunah plans to spend approximately $2,000 per employee per year, regardless of which plan is chosen. As always, Mr. Emunah has called this meeting to discuss the options and have employees vote on which one they prefer. The procedure that is always followed is to have an initial vote by the employees, followed by each employee giving an explanation for his or her vote. After each employee expresses his or her current opinion, a final vote is taken and the majority wins.

Accordingly, you must do the following:

1. Discuss which of the four options described above you would vote for and why.
2. Be prepared to convince others in your class as to why they should vote the way you did.

❖ Chapter 10 References

1. R. Federico and H. Goldsmith, "Linking Work/Life Benefits to Performance," *Compensation and Benefits Review* 30 (July/August 1998): 66–70.
2. Bureau of Labor Statistics (BLS) Web page.
3. R. McCaffery, *Employee Benefit Programs: A Total Compensation Perspective* (Boston: PWS-Kent, 1992).
4. U.S. Department of Health and Human Services, *Your Social Security Taxes . . . What They're Paying for, Where the Money Goes* (Social Security Administration, Publication No. 05-10010, January, 1995).
5. McCaffery, *Employee Benefit Programs.*
6. J. Hood and B. Hardy, *Workers' Compensation and Employee Protection Laws* (St. Paul, MN: West, 1984).
7. Ibid.
8. M. Rothstein, C. Craver, E. Schroeder, E. Shoben, and L. VanderVelde, *Employment Law* (St. Paul, MN: West, 1994).
9. D. Kirkpatrick, "Will You Be Able to Retire?" *Fortune* (July 1989): 56–66.
10. BLS Web page.
11. E. T. Allen, J. Melone, and J. VanDerhei, *Pension Planning* (Homewood, IL: Irwin, 1988).
12. BLS Web page.
13. Congressional Research Service, *Retirement Income for an Aging Population* (Washington: Library of Congress, 1987).
14. BLS Web page.
15. Allen, Melone, and VanDerhei, *Pension Planning.*
16. E. Schultz, "Frittered Away," *Wall Street Journal,* 5 June 1996, A1, A9.
17. "Take Care of Your 401(k), and It'll Take Care of You," *St. Louis Post-Dispatch,* 19 January 1993, 12C.
18. J. Fierman, "How Secure Is Your Nest Egg?" *Fortune,* 12 August 1991, 50–54.
19. V. T. Pare, "Is Your 401(k) Plan Good Enough?" *Fortune,* 28 December 1992, 78–83.
20. BLS Web page.
21. W. Lambert, "ESOP at Thomson McKinnon Is Focus of Employees' Suit," *Wall Street Journal,* 25 September 1989, A7C.
22. M. Boitano, "Companies' Pension Plans Looking More like 401(k)s," *Star Tribune,* 23 August 1998, 1D.
23. McCaffery, *Employee Benefit Programs.*
24. Ibid.
25. Allen et al. *Pension Planning.*
26. Ibid.
27. Ibid.
28. Ibid.
29. Anonymous, "Gender Gap Is Wide in Retirement," *St. Louis Post-Dispatch,* 25 November 1997, C8.
30. BLS Web page.
31. J. Fraser, "Unhealthy Increases," *Inc.* (September 1998): 132–33.
32. BLS Web page.
33. L. Luciano, "Getting the Most from Your Company Benefits," *Money* (May 1991): 109–120.
34. "Wasted Health Care Dollars," *Consumer Reports* (July 1992): 435–48.
35. "Are HMOs the Answer?" *Consumer Reports* (August 1992): 519–27.
36. Ibid.
37. Ibid.
38. Ibid.
39. A. Bell, "HMO Report Cards Get an Incomplete," *National Underwriter* (life/health/financial services), 10 August 1998, 30–31.
40. McCaffery, *Employee Benefit Programs.*

41. S. Silverstein, "Work & Careers; On the Job," *Los Angeles Times*, 30 August 1998, D5.
42. "Are HMOs the Answer?"
43. McCaffery, *Employee Benefit Programs*.
44. M. Brown, "Disability Insurance Seldom Receives High Priority," *St. Louis Post-Dispatch*, 15 June 1992, 23BP.
45. M. Rachor, "When Worlds Collide: Elder Caregiving Poses New Challenges for Balancing Work and Life," *Employee Benefits Journal* (September 1998): 20–23.
46. McCaffery, *Employee Benefit Programs*.
47. T. Rothausen, J. Gonzalez, N. Clarke, and L. O'Dell, "Family-Friendly Backlash—Fact or Fiction? The Case of Organizations' On-Site Child Care Centers," *Personnel Psychology* 51 (1998): 685–706.
48. B. Leonard, "Family-Friendly Benefits Trend Gaining Momentum," *HRMagazine* (October 1998): 24–28.
49. McCaffery, *Employee Benefit Programs*.
50. Ibid.
51. M. Markowich, "Flex Still Works," *Personnel Journal* (December 1990): 62.
52. McCaffery, *Employee Benefit Programs*.
53. BLS Web page.
54. McCaffery, *Employee Benefit Programs*.
55. Ibid.

Part 4

Improving the Workplace

Chapter 11

Employee Training and Development

Core Concepts   After reading this chapter, you should be capable of:

1. Identifying current trends in employee training and development.
2. Conducting a training needs analysis.
3. Describing different training techniques.
4. Discussing the advantages and disadvantages of different training techniques.
5. Applying basic learning principles in developing a training program.
6. Explaining how to examine training program success.

Opening Case

Sally Andrews has been working part-time for her present company, In-Sync Corporation, one year now, and she will soon be moving to full-time status. As part of this arrangement, Sally will continue to work in her present position (as a customer service representative) for about 12 months. After that, she will become the area supervisor. Yesterday, Sheila, the customer service area manager, called Sally back into her office to discuss the matter further.

"As you know," Sheila began, "In-Sync is going through a number of changes. One of the biggest adjustments involves our management style—we must become more participative, open, and, above all, capable of handling a racially and ethnically diverse workforce. Our supervisors can therefore no longer simply be promoted through the ranks. They must receive appropriate training and development so that they can deal with the many challenges and changes in this business."

Next, she talked about Sally's advancement into the supervisory position and the need for her to be properly prepared. Sheila concluded by saying, "It's imperative, then, that you receive training in certain key areas, such as conflict resolution, managing the diverse workforce, delegating work, and so forth. I want you to do two things in this regard. First, find out what key areas you need to know in order to become a highly effective supervisor. Second, once you have identified those areas, determine what kind of training program you would like to use."

After Sally discussed this assignment further with her manager, Sheila described several training methods Sally might use. "In the past, we have hired faculty from the college you are attending to conduct training for us. Or, you might use Internet training or videotapes, which we could purchase from a training company. Another idea, which might work well and save money, would be for you to receive one-on-one instruction from Jean and Chris. Both of them have been supervisors for many years,

and have an excellent reputation with the managers. They probably could provide some fine on-the-job training. Why don't you come back with a written proposal, indicating what training techniques you would like to use and how much they would cost."

That night, when Sally returned home from work, she began thinking about her area manager's assignment. How would she determine what supervisory skills she currently had and what supervisory skills she might need in the future? Moreover, once she determined the answer to this question, what training methods would work best for her? The more she thought about this second question, the more confusing it became. After all, many colleges and universities offer training programs and, based on the catalogs Sheila showed her, there are many videotapes to choose from. The idea of learning on the job from Chris and Jean sounds like an inexpensive approach. Chris and Jean will be able to tell Sally what works at In-Sync and what does not work. On the other hand, both of them always seem busy. From what Sally has heard from other part-timers who work in their sections, Chris and Jean do not have the best reputation among their subordinates either. Despite these concerns, it seems as though on-the-job training might be the most practical, cost-effective way to learn needed supervisory skills.

This chapter explores more about training and development in the workplace. As you will see, training and development programs are quite important both to you as an employee and to organizations. You will learn how organizations determine training needs, the advantages and disadvantages of different training techniques, and how to increase the application of training to actual job situations. Finally, you will learn how to evaluate the success of a training program. First, however, we will discuss what training is, why it is important, and what organizations are doing in this regard.

What Is Training and Development and Why Is It Important?

training and development
Planned efforts by organizations to increase employees' competencies.

Training and development may be defined as planned efforts by organizations to increase employees' competencies.[1] So why is training and development so important for both employees and organizations? There are several reasons:

1. **Changes in the Workplace and the Workforce.** As you have read in other chapters, both the workplace and the workforce are going through many changes. In terms of the workplace, increased use of high technology (for example, computer-aided design, robotics, and the Internet), the continuing shift from a manufacturing to a service economy, and the increasingly global business world necessitate ongoing employee training and development programs. The U.S. workforce is changing as increasing numbers of immigrants with limited educational background and continuing problems in the primary and secondary educational systems force organizations to provide training and development programs, often for the purpose of improving basic writing and reading skills.[2]

2. **Maintaining Competitiveness and Improving Productivity.** Training and development are essential for maintaining global competitiveness. Japan and Germany, two of our major business competitors, have outstanding training and development programs that help them maintain high levels of productivity and flexibility.[3] From an organizational perspective, training and development programs can have a large payoff in productivity improvement. Consider, for example, Will-Burt Company, a small manufacturing plant in Ohio. Several years ago, Will-Burt was on the brink of bankruptcy. Because the company was losing $700,000 annually due to defective products, the owner decided that only a major improvement in quality would enable the company to survive. After several other approaches failed, the owner turned to a training program that cost the company almost $200,000 the first year. What was the end result? After one year of training, the company's expenditures for defective products declined more than $500,000 annually.[4] Many other companies have experienced similar productivity gains from their training and development programs.

3. **Regulatory Requirements.** Various laws require companies to provide training. For example, the Occupational Safety and Health Act of 1970 (see Chapter 13) requires companies to provide training for a variety of purposes.[5] Certain industries, such as the nuclear waste industry, also require employees to receive training for a variety of purposes, especially safety-related issues.

In short, training and development are important for several reasons. Next, you will read about some current trends and practices in training and development.

Current Trends and Practices in Training and Development

Companies spend enormous amounts of money on employee training and development. Although estimates vary, $55 billion (or $504 per employee) is probably a reasonable estimate of the amount spent by U.S. companies on formal training annually.[6] Although this might seem like a great deal of money, some experts have argued that companies do not spend enough money on employee training. First, the vast amount of this money is spent by a small number of large companies, such as GTE, Xerox, Federal Express, and Boeing. Second, the amount of money spent on training is only about

1.5 percent of organizational budgets. While the companies spending the most on training (high technology) paid on average $911 annually per employee, companies spending the least on training (customer service) expended only $162 annually per employee. Thus, the majority of companies, particularly small businesses, spend relatively little money on training and development. A typical firm has about 1 trainer for 500 employees. Cutting edge firms employ 1 trainer for 135 workers.[7]

Table 11.1 reports the average number of hours spent training different groups of employees. As you can see, about three-fourths or more of companies provide training to professional and technical employees, managerial employees, and sales and clerical employees, while about half provide training to service employees. About two-thirds of companies provide training to production and construction workers. Of the companies that provide training, the average number of hours annually provided ranges between 44 to 8.

Table 11.2 provides a summary of the most common areas of training provided by companies. The most popular categories, besides new-employee orientation, management skills, and computer skills, are job-specific technical skills and safety-related and team skills.

Table 11.1	Types of Workers Receiving Training and Average Number of Hours	
Job Group	**Percentage of Employees Receiving Training**	**Average Number of Hours Annually per Employee**
Professional and technical	84	44
Sales and clerical	73	20
Production and construction	66	30
Service	50	11
Managerial	80	8

Source: Adapted from H. Frazis, M. Gittleman, M. Horrigan, and M. Joyce, "Results from the 1995 Survey of Employer-Provided Training," *Monthly Labor Review* (June 1998): 3–12.

Table 11.2	Types of Training Provided by Companies
Type of Training	**Percentage of Companies Providing Training**
New-employee orientation	94
Management skills	93
Basic computer skills	91
Job-specific technical skills	88
Safety-related skills	84
Team skills	77
Customer service	76
Sales	53
Remedial and basic education	50

Source: Adapted from H. Frazis, M. Gittleman, M. Horrigan, and M. Joyce, "Results from the 1995 Survey of Employer-Provided Training," *Monthly Labor Review* (June 1998): 3–12.

Some research has looked at whether demographic characteristics affect which employees are most likely to receive training. First, college-educated employees are more likely to receive company training than are employees with less education. The likely reason for this is that college-educated employees are more likely to hold professional and technical jobs. Also, employees between the ages of 25 and 44 are more likely to receive training than either younger or older employees. Interestingly, although women were slightly more likely to receive training, men had more hours of training than women.[8]

In addition to company-sponsored training programs, there are many government and union-sponsored training programs. Most states provide some kind of training program for workers. These programs primarily serve small manufacturing businesses. Most recently, some states have offered training grants, enabling each business to determine how to best provide needed training. Many states contract with community colleges or vocational schools to provide training. When an IBM plant in Colorado, for example, switched from manufacturing to software development, Front Range Community College retrained more than half of the 2,000 employees.[9]

Unions are another source of training programs, generally through an apprenticeship system. Apprenticeship programs are particularly popular in mechanical and electrical trades, as well as other skilled crafts. Nevertheless, industry cost-cutting measures in the 1970s and 1980s reduced the number of apprenticeships in the United States, and only a small fraction of U.S. employees have worked as apprentices. In recent years, some unions have forged joint apprenticeship programs with management, such as the UAW-Chrysler National Training Center. In 1989, the five largest joint union–management training programs provided training for more than 700,000 workers.[10] If you want to learn more about apprenticeship programs, contact the U.S. Department of Labor at http://www.doleta.gov/individ/apprent.htm or (202) 523-6666.

Now that you have a basic idea of the kinds of training and development activities that are being provided in the workplace, we will turn to the steps used to develop a training program. There are three basic steps in this process:

1. Analyzing the organization's training needs and the objectives of the training program.
2. Deciding which training techniques and principles to use.
3. Evaluating the training program.

We turn now to the process of analyzing the organization's training needs and setting objectives for the training program. As you will see, training needs are determined by an analysis of the organization, the tasks and competencies, and the employees. Box 11.1 discusses the effects of training and development on your paycheck.

Training Needs Analysis

training needs analysis
An assessment by the organization of its employees' training needs.

A **training needs analysis** answers the following three questions:[11]

1. What competencies do employees need?
2. Are some employees deficient in these competencies?
3. Will training solve the deficiencies?[12]

Your Turn ————————————

Box 11.1
Training and Development Programs: Their Impact on Your Pay

Even though company training and development programs may help your company, you might be wondering whether such programs are worth it to you as an employee. First, let's talk about how many employees participate in training programs. A survey conducted in 1991 found that 41 percent of all employees had participated in some type of training program since starting work in their current job. More than 60 percent of college graduates reported participating in at least one training program. This reflects a significant increase from 1983, when only 35 percent of all workers reported some type of job-related training. Many more employees these days participate in training programs to improve their work skills.

Now, does participation in training affect your salary? This same survey examined average salaries earned by different groups of employees in 1991. To simplify matters, we will consider only college graduates. When college graduates whose job required special training were considered, those who took additional training to improve their skills made, on average, $2,000 more annually than those employees who did *not* take additional training. The gap was even larger for those college graduates whose job did not require special training. For those employees who did *not* take training to improve their skills, the average annual salary was approximately $31,000. For those employees who *did* take training to improve their skills, the average annual salary was about $35,000—a difference of $4,000. Clearly, company-sponsored training programs have a financial payoff for you.

Source: Adapted from A. Eck, "Job-related Education and Training: Their Impact on Earnings," *Monthly Labor Review*, October 1993, 21–38.

A training needs analysis is a three-step process:

1. An organizational analysis.
2. A task/competency analysis.
3. A person analysis.

We turn now to a more detailed discussion of each of these steps.

Step 1: Organizational Analysis

The purpose of Step 1, the **organizational analysis,** is to examine the organization, unit, or department and determine its basic business strategy, objectives, and goals.[13] In today's constantly changing business environment, the organizational analysis may focus on the company's mission and the implications for jobs.[14] One company conducting an organizational analysis, for example, found that recent changes in its business environment led to

organizational analysis
The purpose of this analysis is to examine the organization, unit, or department and determine its basic business strategy, objectives, and goals.

1. Large contracts not being replaced.
2. Increased competition for old and new business.
3. More demands for customized products.
4. Greater emphasis on efficiency and cost reduction.
5. Increased emphasis on cooperation among companies.

Some of the key points to address in conducting an organizational analysis, then, are the following:[15]

1. What is the organization's mission? Has this changed from the past?
2. How does the organization interface with the external environment? Is the external environment stable or turbulent?

3. Have the organization's culture, climate, and norms changed?
4. What are the implications of these answers for jobs in the organization?

As an example of an organizational analysis, consider Honeywell Company's plant in Ontario, Canada. In 1987, top executives of Honeywell decided to concentrate on a much smaller number of select products. As part of that strategy, each plant was to manufacture fewer products and to achieve high quality and cost efficiencies for those products. Toward that end, Honeywell's Ontario plant embarked on a series of changes that included the adoption of a total quality management (TQM) program and implementation of self-managed teams (see Chapter 12 for a description of TQM and self-managed teams). An analysis of these changes, and their implications for jobs, would constitute an organizational analysis.[16]

So far, we have described the organizational analysis from a company's perspective. But what about from your perspective as an employee? If you recall from Chapter 3, it was recommended that you, as an employee, think of yourself as a business. Put in this light, you should also conduct an organizational analysis, where the organization is you. What is your mission? How has this changed from the past? What is the nature of your external environment? For example, do you have a new supervisor? Do you have a new set of external customers? You should consider both short- and long-term perspectives. Also, do not focus solely on your present employer. Find out what other companies are seeking from their employees as well. Your present employer, for example, may not make much use of computer technology. But other employers may use computers to a far greater extent. It is important, then, to be familiar with trends in your industry, not just conditions in your current company.

In sum, an organizational analysis considers the broad perspective. Based on the findings from the organizational analysis, you are ready to go to the next step: a task/competency analysis.

Step 2: Task/Competency Analysis

task/competency analysis
Involves obtaining information from the organizational analysis to examine the tasks performed in each job and determining the competencies needed to perform these tasks effectively.

The second step, the **task/competency analysis,** involves obtaining information from the organizational analysis to evaluate the tasks performed in each job and then determining the competencies needed to perform these tasks effectively. Recall the previous example in which a company had found changes in its business environment, including large contracts not being replaced, increased competition for old and new business, and increased demands for customized products. Based on those changes, the company determined that various work tasks had been modified or added, which meant greater need for competencies such as effective communication, time-management skills, and the ability to delegate work.

As a second example, recall the Honeywell Canada plant, which introduced TQM and a self-managed team approach. These changes, in turn, led to the identification of four new important job functions: achieving low costs, high product and process quality, on-time delivery, and team membership. These new job functions meant that certain additional tasks were added to each job, such as preparing an annual budget and developing and implementing cost-cutting ideas. Employees would now need various new competencies, including basic reading skills and knowledge of accounting and financial principles, in order to succeed in their jobs.

In many ways, the task/competency analysis is similar to a job analysis (see Chapter 5). Like a job analysis, one can use different procedures to conduct a task/competency analysis. The following steps, however, are generally recommended for a task/competency analysis.[17]

1. **Develop a List of Task Statements.** Using observation, interviews with workers and supervisors, and other techniques, develop a list of tasks performed in the relevant job(s).
2. **Develop a List of Task Clusters.** Once Step 1 is completed, categorize the tasks into task clusters. For example, a supervisory job might include four or five task statements pertaining to interacting with other departments. Interacting with other departments, then, might constitute one task cluster. Developing task clusters is particularly useful for organizing large numbers of tasks.
3. **Develop a List of Competencies.** Although there are several ways to obtain a list of competencies, one of the more effective ways is to conduct focus panels with groups of supervisors and knowledgeable workers. The panels should be shown the task clusters, along with the task statements, and asked to generate competencies that are needed to perform each task cluster successfully.
4. **Assess the Importance of Tasks and Competencies.** Now that both the *relevant* tasks and competencies have been determined, it is necessary to focus on the *important* tasks and competencies. This step establishes training priorities. Typically, a structured format is used. Both the task clusters and the competencies are rated by supervisors and knowledgeable incumbents. Table 11.3 provides an example of a simple five-point rating scale that might be used for rating task importance.[18]

As before, we have emphasized the organization's perspective in conducting a task/competency analysis. It is important, however, to apply this process to your own situation as an employee. That is, given the organizational analysis you conducted for your own career, what tasks are important for success? What new tasks do you anticipate will become important? For example, if the Internet is changing how your business is conducted, you must consider how this will affect the tasks you perform now and in the future. What competencies will you need to perform the new or revised tasks successfully? All of these considerations should be carefully examined.

In sum, the task/competency analysis is a critical step in determining the likely content of a training program. Not only is this important from an organization's perspective, but it is important from your perspective as an employee. We now discuss the third step in a training needs analysis, generally referred to as a person analysis.

Table 11.3   A Rating Scale for Task Importance

1 = Not important (Improper task performance has no negative consequences.)
2 = Slightly important (Improper task performance can create some minor problems or negative consequences.)
3 = Important (Improper task performance can create significant problems or negative consequences.)
4 = Very important (Improper task performance can create serious consequences or problems, including extensive damage to equipment, serious injury to humans, or injury to the reputation of the company.)
5 = Critical (Improper task performance will create serious consequences or problems, including major loss of equipment, possible death to humans, and major injury to the reputation of the company.)

Source: Adapted from I. Goldstein, "Training in Work Organizations," in *Handbook of Industrial and Organizational Psychology*, (vol. 2), ed. M. Dunnette and L. Hough (Palo Alto, CA: Consulting Psychologists Press, 1991): 535.

Step 3: Person Analysis

person analysis
Addresses the question of
whether employees are
deficient in important tasks
and competencies and
whether training would address these deficiencies.

The final step of a training needs analysis, the **person analysis,** addresses the question of whether certain employees are deficient in the important tasks/competencies, and whether training would treat the deficiencies. There are several ways to determine employee deficiencies. One of the most popular ways is to examine measures of job performance. For example, any employee who received a less than satisfactory rating on any job dimension might be considered deficient in that area. This approach has several potential weaknesses. First, as discussed in Chapter 7, supervisor ratings are often subject to a variety of errors, including leniency. Some workers who are actually performing below average may be rated acceptable. Second, certain competencies that will be needed in the future might not be currently in use; there will be little or no information with regard to those competencies.[19] Third, the intended purpose of the performance ratings may affect how they are made; ratings made for salary-raise purposes may differ from ratings made for a training needs analysis.[20] One possible way to overcome some of these problems is to have employees complete self-ratings to establish their need for training on each of the competencies.[21] However, employees may not be aware of or willing to admit a possible shortcoming.[22] Research indeed shows that there is little relationship between an employee's self-rating of training needs and the supervisor's rating of the employee's training needs.[23]

An alternative approach is to use proficiency tests or simulations. For example, rather than having the supervisor rate an employee's typing skills, the employee could be given a typing test. That way, an employee's competencies can be measured in a far more objective fashion. Despite the potential advantages, this approach has several basic problems. First, proficiency tests may not completely reflect job performance. Second, for many areas (such as time-management skills) proficiency tests may not exist. Third, the costs associated with proficiency testing may be quite high.[24]

Ultimately, there is no simple answer regarding the best way to conduct a person analysis. Ideally, you would use several approaches, perhaps a combination of self-ratings, supervisor ratings, and, where possible, proficiency tests to determine who needs training. You should also be aware that trainees who feel that the needs assessment was properly conducted will have a better reaction to the actual training program and will be more motivated to learn.[25]

Even though employees may be deficient in certain competencies, training is not necessarily the correct solution. For example, one company decided that a one-time incentive program would be far more effective in improving the employees' knowledge than would a training program. Employees ended up learning the material far better than they would have, had the company sponsored a formal training program. It is important to realize that training programs are not a guaranteed cure-all for performance problems.[26] The solution to performance deficiencies may lie in improving the reward systems, selecting better employees, or purchasing better equipment. Figure 11.1 provides some suggestions as to when a training program might be used to ameliorate a performance deficiency or when other supervisory responses are needed. It is critical that you determine the objectives of the training program before you proceed with the design of the program. The objectives that you specify for the training program may be less ambitious than you initially intended. Remember that training programs cannot address every problem.

In terms of your own person analysis, it is critical that you try to get as much feedback from other sources as possible. As described elsewhere in this book, mentors, peers, and your supervisor may be of help by giving you feedback. While it is often difficult to be self-critical, your ability to conduct an accurate self-analysis of your

A. Is there a problem? _____
What do you observe that indicates there is a problem?
1. How long has this been a problem?
2. How general a problem is it?
   ▪ Where does it occur?
   ▪ When does it occur?
   ▪ How frequently does it occur?
   ▪ Does it ever not occur in some locations or at some times?
3. How will you know when the problem is solved?
   ▪ How will things look different?
   ▪ What numbers will increase or decrease?

B. What is the problem? _____
1. Who is the performer in question?
2. What is the desired action?
3. What specifically does he perform incorrectly?
4. Does he ever perform correctly?
   If yes: When?
   If no: Has anyone ever performed correctly?
              When?
              Where?

C. Is the problem important? _____
What impact does the incorrect performance have on:
1. The product or service?
   Quality   Cost   Quantity
2. The company?
   Procedures   Image
3. The performer or his department?
   Safety   Ease of work
4. Other workers or departments?
   Safety   Ease of work

D. Where has the performance system broken down? _____

Questions	Action	
Does the performer:		
1. Know he is supposed to take the desired action? ▪ How do you know?	If no:	Instruct him.
2. Know what the desired action is? ▪ How do you know?	If no:	Instruct him.
3. Know when to take the desired action? ▪ How do you know?	If no:	Instruct him.
4. Know how to take the desired action? ▪ How do you know?	If no:	Instruct him.
5. Know the standard or level of performance expected? ▪ Are there standards? ▪ Does everybody agree on them? ▪ Is anyone meeting them now?	If no standards: If standards:	Set them. Instruct in them.
6. Know whether he is taking the desired action or not? ▪ How can he tell whether he is acting correctly?	If no:	Redesign job. Instruct in observing. Provide feedback.
7. Have adequate resources (e.g., time, equipment) to take the desired action?	If no:	Provide resources.

(continued)

Figure 11.1 (continued)

Questions	Action	
Does the performer:		
8. Receive negative consequences for taking the desired action?	If yes:	Remove negative consequences.
■ Consider such sources of consequences as superiors, peers, subordinates, and the system.		
9. Receive no consequences for taking the desired action?	If yes:	Provide positive consequences.
10. Receive immediate, positive consequences for doing something other than the desired action?	If yes:	Remove positive consequences.
■ Do "good" things happen to him if he doesn't do it?		
11. Receive no information on the consequences of taking the desired action?	If no:	Provide feedback.
■ Does he know it makes a difference to do it right?		
12. Receive wrong information on the consequences of his actions?	If yes:	Correct feedback.
■ Does information lead him to conclude he's doing okay when he is not?		
13. Receive information on consequences that is not sufficient for him to correct his performance (i.e., not clear, not specific, too late, too infrequent)?	If yes:	Provide better feedback.
■ Does he receive enough information to know how to correct?		
14. Know how to interpret information in order to correct his performance?		Instruct on how to interpret data.
■ Given good information, can he figure out how to change?		

Source: G. Rummler, "Human Performance Problems and Their Solutions," *Human Resource Management* (Winter 1972): 2–10.

deficiencies may be one of the most important factors for a successful career. So, take a hard look at yourself and think about where improvements or new competencies are needed.

Recall that in the opening case of this chapter, Sally was asked to determine what competencies she would need training for. A training needs analysis would be quite useful in this regard. For example, Sally could conduct interviews with In-Sync's top executives and managers to get their input about the business goals, strategies, and related changes, and how these would affect the job of an area supervisor. She could supplement this information by searching a library for newspaper and magazine articles on the impact of these changes on the supervisory job. Based on this information, Sally could then conduct a task/competency analysis. Again, this information might be best obtained from top executives, human resource staff, and the area managers who have some ideas as to how the supervisor job will change. Finally, in terms of person analysis, the employee might be best off assuming that training in all key competencies would be helpful. An additional advantage of going through a formal procedure of this

INTERCULTURAL ISSUES IN HUMAN RESOURCES

Box 11.2
Training and Education Programs: An International Perspective

How do you think the United States compares to other major industrial nations in terms of training and educating the workforce? Not surprisingly, the answer depends on which countries you choose for comparison. In general, though, U.S. primary and secondary education varies greatly in quality, as does vocational training. Company-sponsored training focuses on managers and technicians (though this is changing in recent years); the quality tends to vary widely.

The training and educational systems of our two major competitors, Germany and Japan, are far more consistent in quality and availability. Germany's major strength is that primary and secondary schooling is closely integrated with subsequent training programs, and, in general, educational programs have high quality. Vocational training is also good; but Germany is best known for its outstanding

apprenticeship program. In fact, more than half of the German workforce has completed an apprenticeship program. Many workers also participate in postapprenticeship programs, and businesses help sponsor a variety of high-quality training programs.

Although Japan's approach to education is somewhat different from Germany's, the result is much the same. Japan, as is widely known, boasts one of the best primary and secondary educational systems in the world. Once employed, Japanese workers receive extensive, ongoing, company-sponsored training. As one example, workers in Japanese automobile plants average almost 90 hours of training annually, while workers in U.S. automobile plants average about 30 hours of training annually.

Our northern neighbor, Canada, has a training and education system quite similar to ours. Primary and sec-

ondary education varies greatly in terms of quality, as does the vocational education system. Companies provide relatively little training—by some estimates, about half as much as in the United States.

Korea's training and educational system has made great strides in the last few years. A strong primary and secondary school system has increased the quality of workers' basic skills, and vocational education has become remarkably strong in Korea. Nevertheless, company-sponsored training programs are scarce, and their quality is generally poor.

All in all, then, U.S. training and education programs could be improved. According to experts, the overall effectiveness of such efforts will greatly affect a country's ability to compete globally.

Source: Adapted from U.S. Congress, Office of Technology Assessment, *Worker Training: Competing in the New International Economy* (Washington: U.S. Government Printing Office, 1990), OTA-ITE-457.

nature is that the employee could demonstrate that he or she took the assignment seriously and conducted a thorough investigation. In fact, it is possible that the organization would adopt the program for training other supervisors as well.

Now that you have learned how to go about determining which employees need training in what areas, we will turn to the techniques and principles used to provide the needed training. As you will see, many different training techniques and principles are available. We begin with a discussion of different training techniques, followed by a description of some basic principles of training. Box 11.2 provides a global look at training and education programs.

Training Techniques and Principles

Figure 11.2 indicates the popularity of different training techniques used in industry. As you can see, classroom or lecture training is the most popular, followed by videotape, audiovisual, and role-play techniques. Because there are so many different methods, it is helpful to divide training techniques into two broad categories: on-the-job

| Figure 11.2 | **Overview of Use of Instructional Methods** |

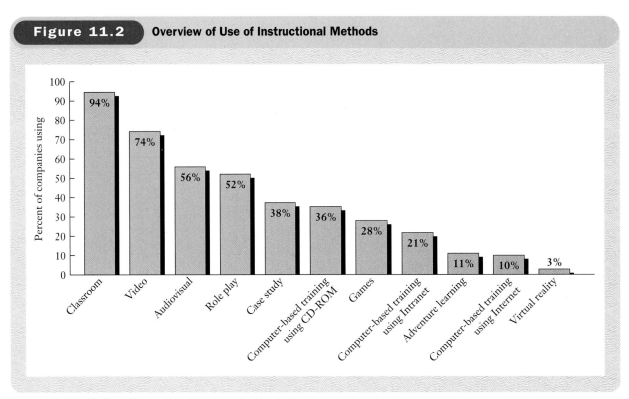

Source: Based on "Industry Report 1997," *Training* (October 1997): 56.

and off-the job approaches. On-the-job training is provided at the worksite. Off-the-job training is conducted away from the worksite. We begin first with a review of on-the-job methods, followed by a discussion of off-the-job approaches.

On-the-Job Training Techniques

on-the-job training
Training provided at the worksite.

There are four basic kinds of **on-the-job training:**

1. One-on-one instruction
2. Coaching
3. Job rotation
4. Apprenticeship and internship

Each of these methods is described in greater detail next, along with their strengths and weaknesses.

one-on-one instruction
A person who serves as a trainer for the organization meets with and instructs a trainee at the workplace.

One-on-One Instruction. One-on-one instruction is a popular approach to training and development. In one-on-one instruction, a person who serves as a trainer for the organization meets with the employee at the workplace (though perhaps in a separate area) and instructs the trainee. Generally, the instructional method involves a description of the procedures, along with a visual demonstration by the instructor. Following this, the trainee practices, under the supervision of the trainer. Of course, various texts, videos, and other materials might be used to supplement this training method.

It is important to point out that one-on-one instruction differs greatly from other, seemingly similar approaches, such as the **SAWNOF ("Sit and Watch Nellie or Fred") approach.** In the SAWNOF method, the employee is instructed to go sit and watch "Nellie" or "Fred" (usually, experienced workers). There are several major problems with the SAWNOF approach. First, while Nellie and Fred may be quite effective in their jobs, this does not necessarily mean they are effective trainers. In some cases, they may feel their own job is threatened, so Nellie and Fred may intentionally give wrong advice. Or, Nellie and Fred may be excellent trainers, but they may fear their own work will suffer if they spend too much time training other employees. Finally, the SAWNOF approach is generally informal and unplanned, so Nellie and Fred spend little or no time designing the training program. For these reasons, the SAWNOF approach often is ineffective.[27]

Recall in the opening case of this chapter that the employee considered using two supervisors for one-on-one instruction. Do you think this would be appropriate? Particularly in light of the changing nature of the supervisory job, Sally should be wary of receiving one-on-one instruction from long-term supervisors, whose perspective and approach may reflect ineffective methods. One-on-one instruction therefore may not be useful in the In-Sync situation. Box 11.3 provides brief directions for providing one-on-one instruction.

An effective one-on-one instruction program has several positive benefits, including cost-effectiveness, because workers learn while they produce, and there is little need for expensive facilities or equipment. Another advantage is that the training is directly job related, because actual equipment is used to learn and practice. Third, the trainees will get immediate feedback on their performance.[28] Fourth, this training method is flexible—as the equipment or job changes, modifications are easily made in the training.[29]

One-on-one instruction has two basic disadvantages. First, in many companies, one-on-one instruction is not carefully designed or systematically delivered. In other words, in many companies, it takes on more of the characteristics of the SAWNOF approach than the one-on-one instruction method. Second, one-on-one instruction generally works best for jobs or tasks that are fairly simple, routine, and motor oriented. For example, operating simple machinery, filing correspondence, and simple cleaning tasks may be well suited to one-on-one instruction. Other tasks, such as writing computer programs and piloting an airplane are probably not well served by this method. Third, no one in the organization may be knowledgeable enough to train others. For example, a company that wishes to train employees in the use of computer-aided design (CAD) cannot use this method if no one in the organization is knowledgeable in this area.[30]

Coaching. Although different people use the term **coaching** to mean different things, coaching is defined here as informal, unplanned training and development activities provided by supervisors and peers. While coaching may provide valuable help for employees, it should be viewed strictly as a supplement to, rather than a substitute for, formal training and development programs.[31] There are many occasions for which the coaching method is most usefully applied:

1. When an employee demonstrates a new competency.
2. When an employee expresses interest in a different job within the organization.

Your Turn

Box 11.3
A Mini-Guide to Providing One-on-One Instruction

Have you been asked to serve as a trainer to provide one-on-one instruction? If so, here are some helpful suggestions for conducting the training session. First, get ready for instruction by doing the following:

1. Make a timetable indicating how long the instruction will last. Determine how long it should take the trainee to acquire each skill.
2. Break down the job into simple steps. Be sure to determine the key steps for each task.
3. Assemble all materials, including equipment and supplies, and be sure that everything is in proper order.

Now that you are prepared, here are some simple steps you can use in conducting the training:

1. **Introduce Your Training Program.** Be sure to put the worker at ease, determine what he or she knows about the task, and encourage the worker's participation.
2. **Present the Task.** A common approach is to begin by explaining what the machine, equipment, or task is, along with its related processes and operations. Then slowly demonstrate operation of the task or machine while giving a step-by-step description of what is happening. Ask questions to determine if the trainee is understanding. Next, repeat the demonstration, skipping the description.
3. **Have the Trainee Try the Task.** The trainee should continue to perform the task while you ob-serve. Correct any mistakes along the way, and return to Step 2 (presenting the task) as needed. Have the trainee repeat the task until it is completed without any mistakes. Be sure the trainee can perform the task successfully.
4. **Monitor the Worker While He or She Performs the Task Independently.** You should encourage the trainee to continue to ask questions. At first, you should check the worker's performance carefully. Once the employee's performance has been adequate for a while, you should decrease your monitoring.

Source: Adapted from K. Wexley and G. Latham, *Developing and Training Human Resources in Organizations* (Glenview, IL: Scott, Foresman, 1981).

3. When an employee seeks feedback.
4. When an employee is expressing low morale, violating company policies or practices, or having performance problems.
5. When an employee needs help with a new skill following a formal training program.

In the right situations, then, coaching can be an effective supplement to formal training methods. When used by itself, however, coaching is likely to be inadequate.

job rotation
A formal, planned program involving the assignment of trainees to varying jobs in different parts of the organization.

Job Rotation. Job rotation is a formal, planned program that involves assigning trainees to various jobs in different parts of the organization. Eli Lilly, the pharmaceutical company headquartered in Indiana, has one of the most well-known job rotation programs. The purpose of job rotation is to provide trainees with a larger organizational perspective and a greater understanding of different functional areas, as well as a better sense of their own career objectives and interests.[32] Not surprisingly, employees in a job rotation program tend to be in the early phase of their careers and are usually top performers.[33]

In terms of advantages, job rotation appears to improve the participants' job skills, increase job satisfaction, and provide valuable opportunities for networking within the organization. From a personal perspective, employees who participate in job rotations

experience faster promotions and higher salaries than employees who do not participate. In terms of disadvantages, job rotations may create an increased workload for the
participants due to the constant job change. Job rotation may also cause dissatisfaction
in those employees who did not participate in the program. Whether this is due to
their increased workload or due to resentment for not participating is unclear.[34]

Apprenticeship and Internship. An **apprenticeship** is a formal program that involves a combination of classroom instruction and hands-on practice and training, primarily in the skilled crafts (such as carpentry). An apprenticeship, then, includes more
than just on-the-job training.[35] Although internships are included here with apprenticeships, they are rather different: an **internship** is a program that provides work
experience to students prior to graduation from an academic program. Typically,
internships are completed by students in business, law, and the health professions.
Therefore, an apprenticeship constitutes a complete program, while an internship is
merely one part of a larger educational program.

Most workers who have passed apprenticeships are satisfied with their training and
tend to earn significantly higher wages than employees who did not have an apprenticeship. There are some disadvantages to an apprenticeship program, however. First,
there is a high dropout rate among trainees; it is estimated that fewer than 50 percent
actually complete the apprenticeship. A second disadvantage of the apprenticeship
program is the high cost.[36] As noted in the introduction, the number of employees undertaking an apprenticeship has fallen over the years in the United States, which has
led to shortages of qualified applicants in the skilled crafts.

Because internships are far less formalized than apprenticeships, we know less
about them. Research does, however, indicate that students who have been through an
internship experience have several advantages over students who have not had one, including superior performance ratings in subsequent jobs, higher starting salaries, and
greater satisfaction with their jobs. Students with internships characterized by much
freedom to make decisions tend to be more successful in making the transition from
school to work. As a student, then, an internship provides advantages, and organizations find that an internship program is helpful in training future employees.[37]

In sum, an organization can choose among a variety of on-the-job training techniques. Returning to the opening case of this chapter, because of the need to learn
competencies that other employees may not know either, the employee might be best
off by using some type of off-the-job training program. These techniques are described
next in greater detail. Box 11.4 discusses the advantages to employees of one such technique, the business seminar.

Off-the-Job Training Techniques

Before you read about **off-the-job training** techniques, it is useful to consider
whether this training is provided by external providers, (for example, private consulting firms or universities), or internal providers (that is, permanent employees). In general, it is safe to say that use of external providers is growing in popularity. A recent
survey showed that organizations now spend approximately 27 percent of their training payroll on external providers.[38]

This section provides a brief description of some of the most popular off-the-job
training techniques, followed by a discussion of their advantages and disadvantages.
We begin first with the lecture method, followed by videotape, distance learning,
equipment simulators, and conclude with some additional approaches.

apprenticeship
A formal program involving
a combination of classroom
instruction and hands-on
practice and training, primarily in skilled crafts such as
carpentry.

internship
A program providing work
experience to students prior
to their graduation from an
academic program.

off-the-job training
Training conducted away
from the worksite.

TALES FROM THE TRENCHES

Box 11.4
Benefiting from Business Seminars: Tips for Participants

Many companies give their employees the opportunity to attend business seminars. Here are some suggestions for you, as a participant:

1. **Plan Ahead.** Learn what attire is appropriate for the seminar; you don't want to be too casual or too formal. Find out who will be presenting and what topics will be presented, and plan your schedule ahead of time. Write down specific questions that you have. Make sure that you assess ahead of time what you would like to learn from the seminar *and* what your supervisor and company would like you to learn from the seminar.

2. **Network at the Seminar.** A major reason, aside from the learning experience, for attending business seminars is to network and make contacts with other people in your field. You should probably bring business cards. If you get business cards from others, jot notes on the back of each one (for example, you might note that you promised to send some materials to the person).

3. **Meet People before Each Session.** If you arrive at a session before it begins, you may break the ice by asking people why they attended the seminar. If they attend the same session as you, chances are they have interests similar to yours. Also, if possible, introduce yourself to the presenter. This may give you a chance to ask a question or two that might then be addressed in the session.

4. **Bring Information Back to the Company.** The best way to justify your attendance at the session is to return with information that you then share with your organization. Be sure to offer to make either an oral presentation or a written report about what you learned. This way, the company will be willing to send you again.

Source: Adapted from P. Lee, "Getting the Most Out of Conferences," *Training and Development* (May 1993): 10, 12.

---

classroom training
An instructor addresses and presents material to a group of trainees.

Classroom training. When you think of off-the-job training, do the terms *classroom* or *lecture* immediately come to mind? As the term is used here, **classroom** or **lecture training** involves an instructor verbally presenting material to a group of trainees. The expert may encourage discussion and questions, but the majority of the information is delivered through one-way communication. There is little, if any, time set aside to practice skills. As shown in Figure 11.2, classroom training is the most commonly used training techniques. Only videotapes are more popular.

If you were asked to describe the strengths and weaknesses of the classroom technique, you would probably have no trouble thinking of some weaknesses of this method. But what about the advantages of the lecture? First, the lecture method is quite effective for providing basic information (such as new product features or changes in a company's benefit program).[39] A second advantage is that it is a familiar training method; trainees will not be uncomfortable or intimidated by this method. Third, it is adaptable to nearly any topic. Fourth, a highly skilled lecturer can provide excellent training.[40]

Of course, the classroom method has numerous disadvantages. First, while a highly skilled lecturer can use this technique effectively, you have probably had one or two college instructors who talked in a monotone and presented the material in an extremely dull fashion. Some trainers are not effective lecturers, and as a result, participants become quickly bored.[41] Second, a lecture proceeds at a single speed; differences in the trainees' ability to comprehend are ignored. Third, scheduling all trainees to be present at the same time can be quite difficult, if not impossible. Fourth, the costs can be quite high—trainers can cost hundreds of dollars an hour, and trainees must miss work. Fifth, the lecture method is quite ineffective in some areas, such as for improving interpersonal skills.[42]

As with other techniques, the classroom method has both advantages and disadvantages. Next, you will read about another popular training method, the videotape.

Videotape. **Videotape training** is one of the most popular training techniques used today. There are many mail-order companies (for example, http://www.crmfilms.com) that market and sell training videotapes on every conceivable topic, including managing diversity, customer relations, communication skills, to name just a few. Some organizations prefer to create their own videotapes, tailored to specific needs and approaches.

Videotapes have several basic advantages. First, visually presented information is generally interesting and motivating to viewers. Second, videotapes allow for a wide range of content, such as experts demonstrating complex skills and behaviors. Videotapes are useful for showing skills and behaviors that might be difficult or impossible to observe otherwise (such as extinguishing fires). Third, because individuals can use the videotapes when they desire, they offer the capacity for self-pacing.[43] Fourth, scheduling is flexible, because the videotapes may be viewed privately or in small groups. Fifth, the costs may be quite reasonable, particularly since most of the expense is in development and a videotape can be reused. Commercially available videotapes may cost as little as a few hundred dollars.[44]

The disadvantages of videotapes include a lack of scientific evidence that videotapes actually are more effective than any other technique, including lectures. Moreover, just as movies can be boring, videotapes can be quite boring. Like the lecture, trainees are generally passive observers. In fact, there is even less opportunity to interact with the trainer. Further, like the lecture, the videotape method involves one-way communication, with no opportunity for questions. Finally, for companies wishing to create their own videotapes, development costs can add up to hundreds of thousands of dollars.[45]

In sum, despite what you might think, videotapes are not necessarily any better as a training technique than a lecture. Much will depend on how well designed the videotape is—some are excellent, others are quite ineffective for training purposes.

Distance Learning

Distance learning is a broad term that covers any training conducted in a physically remote site from the participants. Distance learning can be provided over two-way satellite, videoconferencing, radio, CD-ROM, Internet, or Intranet. Each of these techniques has its own advantages and disadvantages compared to the others. We focus here on Internet/Intranet-based training, because it has the widest applicability and is the most rapidly growing and changing approach to distance learning.[46]

Internet/Intranet-Based Training. There are actually several different ways to conduct **Internet/Intranet training.** (Intranet is accessible with company authorization.) For example, the training can be conducted so that all participants are on-line at the same time with the instructor (see www.ichat.com, for hardware). Alternately, the training can be conducted such that people are not on-line at the same time. To permit "interaction" in this situation, an electronic message board can be used or a listserv can be created to allow people to respond to one another (see www.eshare.com for more information on message boards). Internet/Intranet training can use slides, along

videotape training
A videotape is used to present material to a group of trainees.

Internet/Intranet training
A computer is used to present material to trainees either on a need-to-know basis, at their own pace, or in their own offices.

with speakers, and provides a way for participants to use their keyboards to chat with each other or with the speaker (see www.placeware.com). Internet/Intranet training allows for a wide variety of graphical, audio, and visual components. Thus, sophisticated multimedia training programs can be created (see www.realaudio.com). Many companies now offer self-directed on-line training programs for employees to learn at their leisure (see www.trainingpros.com for examples of free on-line training programs).[47]

As you can probably guess, there are many advantages to using Internet/Intranet-based training. Some of the advantages are[48]

1. Reduced travel expenses, because people don't have to travel anywhere;
2. Easy access to training;
3. Reduced cost due to absence of print materials and CD-ROMs;
4. Control by the trainer of revisions and updates;
5. Participants can have much control over the timing and pace of the learning;
6. Potential for much feedback through tests administered and scored instantaneously;
7. Training can make use of many different resources, including reference materials, databases, technical experts on-line, and so forth.

All of these advantages lead to potential large cost-savings for the company. One expert has said that compared to classroom training, Internet/Intranet-based training costs are 50 percent lower. However, there is a large, up-front investment of money to buy the necessary hardware, software, and to create the programs. For a company such as Days Inn of America, this cost-savings can be enormous because the high turnover rate (about 120 percent annually) means that training is a never-ending task. Days Inn, not surprisingly, has turned to Internet/Intranet-based training for many of its employees.[49]

Of course, there are also disadvantages to using Internet/Intranet-based training. First, this type of training requires the appropriate infrastructure, including various computer system requirements, network capacity, and network access. More sophisticated forms of training require even greater amounts of bandwidth and other technical requirements. Second, Internet/Intranet-based training requires participants to be capable of using the technology. Not all participants will be able to do so. Third, although certain competencies, such as learning how to complete a tax form, can be learned more readily through Internet/Intranet-based training other competencies, such as how to drive an automobile, cannot. It is also difficult to change attitudes this way; diversity-awareness training is probably not best taught this way. Fourth, designing and creating a training program requires a diverse set of competencies. In most cases, to create and conduct Internet/Intranet-based training requires a team of experts, including programmers, design artists, and technical support staff. Box 11.5 provides Web addresses that you can explore and gather information about various training tools.

equipment simulators
Used for jobs or tasks where improper use of actual equipment would pose a danger to the trainee (or others) or where risk of substantial financial loss exists.

Equipment Simulators. You probably have either heard of or actually used an equipment simulator at one time or another. **Equipment simulators** are most frequently used for jobs or tasks where the use of actual equipment would pose a danger to the trainee (or others) or where the risk of substantial financial loss exists. Air crews, naval officers, and space shuttle crews usually receive extensive training using

this technique. Another example is using a car simulator as part of a driver's education course.[50]

There are several basic advantages to equipment simulators. First, it may be the only safe way to train. Second, this technique requires a great deal of interaction with the equipment; third, the skills learned in training should be readily transferable to the workplace. The basic disadvantage of equipment simulators is the high cost associated with them, particularly in the development phase. Nonetheless, compared with the safety risks and possible financial loss of using the actual equipment, an equipment simulator may seem like a real bargain.[51]

Additional Tools: Role Plays and Cases. In addition to the techniques described so far, there are several other commonly used training tools, such as role plays and cases. These often serve as an adjunct to a lecture or videotape.

Role plays require the trainee to act out an assigned role in a hypothetical situation. In many instances, the trainee is given feedback regarding his or her performance. The basic advantage of a role play is that it enables trainees to practice new behaviors in a safe environment. The primary disadvantage of this technique is that many trainees are uncomfortable doing role plays.[52]

role plays
A technique whereby trainees act out an assigned role in a hypothetical situation.

As part of a course in the business school, you may have used a case. **Cases** involve written descriptions of an organizational situation. Trainees must analyze the information and make a decision as to what they would do in the situation. A human resources case, for example, might describe an organization choosing between different kinds of pay-for-performance plans. The primary advantage of a case is that it provides a context for applying basic principles that might have been covered in a lecture or videotape. It also may offer an opportunity for interaction between the trainees and the trainer. The basic disadvantage of the case method is that a trainer who is not skilled in this technique can undermine its usefulness. Also, the case method may have little or nothing in common with the trainees' workplace, which may limit its effectiveness. To avoid this problem, it is recommended that the case be as similar as possible to the trainees' organization and that the trainees be encouraged to discuss its application to their own workplace.[53]

cases
Written descriptions of organizational situations.

Now that you have read about many different training techniques, you will learn about basic principles that facilitate learning.

Principles of Learning: General Guidelines

Over the years, experts have identified some basic principles that are important in designing a training program. Some of the more important ones are described next. We will conclude with some suggestions for conducting effective Internet/Intranet-based training.[54]

Provide for Active Practice. Trainees must be provided an opportunity to practice and utilize the concepts being covered in the training program. For example, in the opening case, Sally must have an opportunity to practice the new skills and abilities in order for her to learn them properly.

Choose between Massed versus Distributed Learning Sessions. A major question in designing and conducting a training program is whether to use **massed training** (conducted in a compacted timetable, such as in a lengthy two-day program) or **distributed training** sessions (conducted over a longer period of time, such as one hour per week for sixteen weeks). It is generally believed that conducting too much training in too short a time period leads to less learning than occurs when the training program is spread out. However, time constraints may require that the training be completed in a short time frame.

Provide Feedback to Trainees. Helpful feedback is important in training for several reasons. First, feedback helps trainees to correct mistakes. Second, feedback makes the learning more interesting for trainees. Third, having feedback enables trainees to set goals for improving their performance. As a trainer, though, be careful about wording your feedback so that it is perceived as positive and helpful. Trainees tend to shun feedback that criticizes them. Above all, maintain a positive atmosphere. Too much criticism will turn your audience against you.

Maximize Application of Training to the Job. One of the biggest problems associated with training programs is the lack of a **transfer of training.** In other words, many trainees, even if they have effectively learned the competencies in the training program, refrain from using them on the job. Although U.S. companies spend billions of dollars on training, it has been estimated that only a small portion of the competencies learned in programs are actually used on the job.[55] Why does transfer so frequently fail to take place? There are three key factors:[56]

1. Lack of support for use of the new competencies on the job.
2. Trainees are uncomfortable with using new competencies.
3. Trainees perceive the training program to be impractical or irrelevant.

Now that you know some of the primary causes of the problem, let us review some techniques for increasing the transfer of training. What follows are some suggestions that can be used before, during, and after the training program, regardless of whether you are the trainer or trainee.[57]

1. Participants Should Be Actively Involved in Planning the Training Program. Even if you, as an employee, are not invited to participate in the planning, you should ask to be involved. A nonthreatening way to do this is to say something like, "I've heard that the human resources department is planning a training program, and I have some suggestions I would like to share."

massed training
A training program conducted in long sessions and a compacted timetable, such as a two-day program that includes four four-hour sessions.

distributed training
A training program conducted in short sessions over a longer period of time, such as one hour per week for 16 weeks.

transfer of training
The principle that employees transfer the competencies learned in the training period onto their jobs.

2. **Develop a Written Contract Between Trainees and Their Supervisors.** The contract will stipulate what the employee will bring back from the training program (for example, it might specify that the employees create action plans with their supervisors and coworkers and review training highlights with them) and what the supervisor agrees to do in return (such as minimizing interruptions to the training program, providing encouragement and support for the new competencies, or meeting with the trainee to discuss the program). This way, both trainees and their supervisors explicitly agree to work together to maximize training transfer. This is probably an excellent idea for Sally, the employee in the opening case, to ensure that new supervisory approaches are not discouraged.

3. **Use Realistic Work-Related Situations.** It is critical for the training to demonstrate, illustrate, and explain the competencies in the most realistic, work-related situations as possible. The trainer should choose films, exercises, role plays, and other techniques with this in mind. Another way to do this is to have the trainees generate work situations where they can apply the principles and competencies being taught.

4. **Facilitate Trainee Participation.** As a general rule, people learn more when they actively participate in the training process. In fact, the most interesting aspects of the training program are often the discussion and interaction between trainees. As a trainee, if you wonder how the concepts being taught apply to your job, ask. Don't be embarrassed.

5. **Arrange Refresher Sessions.** Employees may forget or experience difficulty using the competencies. One way to reduce such problems is to plan a refresher session a few months after the training program ends. This might also offer trainees an opportunity to recommend changes for the next time the program is conducted.

6. **Support Training.** Trainers can be actively involved in supporting the training after the program is over. As a trainer, you can offer assistance via e-mail or a Web site. A listserv can also be a helpful source for past participants for discussion of concerns that arise.

Conducting Effective Interactive Internet/Intranet-based Training

Because Internet/Intranet-based training is relatively new, if you are responsible for conducting sessions over this medium, you need to plan especially carefully. Here are some suggestions to follow:[58]

1. Help your participants prepare by encouraging them to become familiar with the technology before they begin your session. Make sure that all participants can use the materials.

2. Use high-quality technology. Confirm that your program complies with industry standards, that you are using the most updated software (for example, currently *Java* is highly favored), and that the vendor supplying your materials knows what you need.

3. Maintain learner interest. Just because the training is delivered through a computer does not guarantee that it will be interesting. To maintain interest, use graphics, examples, and other techniques (for example, audiovisuals) to enhance the delivery. Encourage participation.

4. Begin with short classes of 20 to 30 minutes in length. As you become more expert at conducting such sessions, you can create longer classes. You will find, however, that people learn less when the class is long.

5. Help the class develop relationships. To avoid making the class an impersonal experience, have participants introduce themselves if at all possible. The introductions may be on-line or in person in a preliminary meeting.

Returning to the opening case, recall that Sally needed to recommend training techniques. Based on what you read in this section, what suggestions might you make as to which techniques would best suit her? One possibility would be to take some training programs offered by a local university, community college, or consulting firm that addresses the necessary skills, such as communication, delegation, and so forth. These programs might be particularly helpful because they typically have a live trainer who can provide feedback. Videotapes might be useful as well, but only if they provide practice and offer feedback. Lectures alone, without opportunity to practice, would probably be of little value. Should she consider Internet/Intranet-based training? That might work as well, if such packages exist.

Evaluating Training Program Success

The final step in conducting a training program is to evaluate its success. We will first discuss why program evaluation is important, followed by a review of different measures of success.

Why Training Program Evaluation Is Important. You might be wondering why you should evaluate the success of a training program. After all, if it seemed to go well, why bother? There are four basic reasons why you should assess the program's success:

1. **Justifying Expenses.** Because any human resources program takes money and time, it is important to justify the expense, particularly given today's emphasis on cost cutting and accountability. Failure to prove the cost-effectiveness of a program can come back to haunt even the best-run program; for example, the Michigan Public Service Commission recently prohibited the gas company from increasing customer charges to pay for a training program addressing quality and corporate culture. The Public Service Commission reasoned that the company had failed to show that the program would save money or improve service.[59] In addition, demonstrating the cost-effectiveness of your training program will enhance your own credibility.
2. **Making Decisions about Future Programs.** Once you have run a program, your company might question whether the program should be repeated, changed, or discontinued. By evaluating its success, a much more informed choice can be made.[60]
3. **Making Decisions about Individual Trainees.** Depending on the purpose, trainees may need to pass the program in order to be certified or qualified for a particular task or job. In many cases, passing the program will involve more than simply attending all sessions. The trainee may need to have a certain grade or score on some type of test. Formal evaluation of each participant's performance may therefore be necessary.[61]
4. **Reducing Professional Liability.** If you design or deliver a training program, you or your organization might be held legally responsible if a trainee subsequently becomes injured or killed in the course of performing the task or job. Thus, it is important to evaluate a training program to ensure that it can be defended against legal charges.[62]

Now that you know why evaluating a training program is important, we will discuss how to measure success. As you will see, success can be evaluated several different ways.

Defining Training Program Success

There are four basic measures of training program success:[63]

1. Trainee reactions.
2. The amount of learning that took place.
3. Behavioral change on the job.
4. Concrete results.

Each of these measures will be discussed in greater detail next.

Trainee Reactions. The simplest way to measure success is to examine **trainee reactions** to the training program. Figure 11.3 is an example of a questionnaire from a supervisory training workshop that is used to assess trainee reactions. There are several reasons why trainee reactions should be formally documented (perhaps with a questionnaire at the end of the training program). First, they can be used as evidence of the popularity of the training if the value of the program is challenged by other parties. Second, trainee reactions can be used to identify where changes should be made for future programs. Third, eliciting reactions enables the trainees to feel they have input into the training program.[64]

Although trainee reactions are an important index of program success, they have several limitations. Most importantly, just because trainees enjoyed a training program does not necessarily mean they learned anything. Other indicators of the success of the program are therefore important.

trainee reactions
An important index of program success, trainees are asked to record their reactions by means of a survey or questionnaire at the end of the training session.

Amount of Learning. **Amount of learning** refers to the competencies that the trainees acquired from the program. The amount of learning is measured in the context of the training program, not on the job. There are different ways of assessing the amount of learning, depending on the nature of the competencies taught and the training technique used. Many of the Internet/Intranet methods described earlier, for example, include a means of assessing the amount of learning. Other means of measuring how much the trainees learned include written tests and role-play exercises, which may then be evaluated by independent judges.[65]

While the amount of learning may be an important index of a program's success, particularly when trainees must pass the course to perform a certain task or job, its major limitation is that it only assesses success within the training context. Whether the trainees actually use the competencies on the job is a separate issue, which is addressed by behavioral change.

amount of learning
Refers to the competencies that trainees acquired from the program; the amount of learning is measured in the context of the training program, not on the job.

Behavioral Change. This aspect of program success refers to the degree to which the trainees' behavior on the job has been affected by the training program. Generally, you can assess **behavioral change** by measuring trainees' performance on the relevant tasks. While this approach to measuring program success addresses whether the training has actually affected the way the job is done, it is often difficult to gather this information. Most important, however, is whether the training program affects the bottom line. This is the focus of the fourth measure: concrete results.

behavioral change
This aspect of program success refers to the degree to which the trainees' behavior on the job has been affected by the training program.

Figure 11.3   **A Questionnaire to Assess Trainee Reactions**

PROGRAM LEADER EVALUATION FORM
Supervisory Certificate Training Program

Program/Topic Leader(s)	Employee Staffing, Parts I & II		
	Michael Harris	Date(s)	March 6–13, 1999

1. Was the topic pertinent to your needs and interests?

☐ Very much so   ☐ To some extent   ☐ No

2. Ratio of lecture to discussion.

☐ Too much lecture   ☐ O.K.   ☐ Too much discussion

3. Please rate the instructor by checking the appropriate box below:

	Excellent	Very Good	Good	Fair	Poor
A. How well did the instructor state objectives?					
B. How well did the instructor keep the session alive and interesting?					
C. How well did the instructor use audio/visual materials?					
D. How helpful were the handout materials?					
E. How well did the instructor summarize during the session?					
F. How well did the instructor maintain a friendly and helpful manner?					
G. To what extent did the instructor involve the group?					
H. How was the summary at the close of the session?					

What is your overall rating of the instructor?

☐ Excellent   ☐ Very Good   ☐ Good   ☐ Fair   ☐ Poor

Source: The University of Missouri–St. Louis Continuing Education.

Concrete Results. Concrete results address training program success in terms of bottom-line outcomes such as increased productivity, reduced accident rate, or other training program objectives. Although this constitutes the best way to prove training program success, it can be difficult to assess accurately. As an example, consider a training program designed to improve the presentation skills of sales employees. Even though sales revenue may have increased after the program, it may not be entirely clear why sales revenues increased. Is it due to an improved economy, increased advertising, or some other factor? NCR, the computer and teller-machine manufacturer, attempts to evaluate its training programs based on concrete results. A training course in new technical approaches for field engineers helped to cut the average number of hours for a service call in half—a clear savings in monetary terms.[66]

To conduct a completely scientific evaluation of a training program, you should be careful to address alternative explanations for any improvements. For example, as mentioned earlier, if you simply measure sales revenues for a group of trainees before the training and compare their sales revenues after the training, any increase may merely be due to general economic improvement rather than to the training. To avoid this type of problem, you should gather information on two groups of salespeople: one group that received the training and a second group that did not receive the training. If the training was effective, the group that received the training should have a larger increase in sales than the group that did not receive training. You should also use statistical analysis to show that the gains are statistically significant and are not simply due to chance improvement.

concrete results
Training-program success is rated in terms of the bottom-line outcomes, such as increased productivity, reduced accident rate, or whatever the objectives of the training program were.

❖ Conclusion

As a way of summarizing the information in this chapter, let us apply the material to an actual situation. Assume that your boss has asked you to design and conduct a training program for your department (if you are not currently working, think about how you would do this for a department you used to work for or a friend's department). You have three months to design and conduct the program. For each of the following recommended steps, consider what you would do to complete this assignment.[67]

1. **Conduct a Training Needs Analysis.** Determine who needs training in which areas. Given what you read in this chapter, how would you go about this task? What would you do to increase employee acceptance of your training program?
2. **Choose the Appropriate Training Techniques and Principles.** Many different training techniques, along with their advantages and disadvantages, were described in this chapter. Which would you use for your training program? Why? Would the Internet/Intranet be effective? Explain your answer.
3. **Discuss the Program with Supervisors and Other Relevant Parties.** If your training is to succeed, you will need relevant parties to accept and endorse the program. Failure to do so may doom even the best training program. Identify the relevant parties to consult in your department.
4. **Release Course Objectives to Trainees before the Program.** Don't forget that the trainees need to accept the program and must be motivated if they are to learn. What can you do to encourage the trainees to accept the program?

5. **Use Action Plans at the End of Each Training Course.** At the end of a training program, have the trainees write down four or five basic points they learned. That way, they can show (both themselves and their supervisors) what they accomplished.

6. **Encourage Participation throughout the Training Sessions.** Trainees learn best when they actively participate in the program. What types of training techniques described in this chapter can you include that will be helpful in this regard?

7. **Spread Out the Training Program.** In most cases, a five-part training program is best spread out over several weeks, rather than being delivered all at once. By spreading out the program, you can review previous lessons, reduce disruptions to work, and provide time for trainees to try out what they have learned. How would you most effectively spread out the training?

8. **Encourage the Application of Training.** Depending on the training area, it may be critical that you take steps to encourage trainees to use the competencies that you developed the training program to enhance. What would you do in this regard?

9. **Evaluate the Results.** You read about several ways to evaluate the cost benefits of training programs. Which would you use in your department? Why? Do not underplay the importance of this step; it will increase your credibility if you can demonstrate the success of the training program.

10. **Establish a Long-Term Training and Development Program.** Although you had only limited time to design and run the program, it is important to establish a long-term plan for training and development. With a long-term perspective in mind, what would you do differently? How can you use the Internet/Intranet to support the accomplishment of those goals?

❖ Applying Core Concepts

1. If your supervisor (or a friend's supervisor if you are not currently working) asked you to conduct a training needs analysis, how would you go about this assignment?

2. Assume you were asked to develop a training program to improve customer sales skills. What training techniques would you use? Why?

3. Apply the learning principles to help Sally Andrews develop a training program for all of the supervisors at In-Sync.

4. If Sally Andrews implemented a training program for all of the supervisors at In-Sync, how would you suggest she demonstrate that the program was successful?

5. Think about a recent training program at work. Was it delivered via the Internet/Intranet? Would it have been better if it was? If you have not recently had such a program, consider a course you recently took (what about this course?). Would it have been better over the Internet? Why or why not?

❖ Key Terms

Training and development	One-on-one instruction	Off-the-job training
Training needs analysis	SAWNOF approach	Classroom training
Organizational analysis	Coaching	Videotape training
Task/competency analysis	Job rotation	Internet/Intranet training
Person analysis	Apprenticeship	Equipment simulators
On-the-job training	Internship	Role plays

Cases

Massed training

Distributed training

Transfer of training

Trainee reactions

Amount of learning

Behavioral change

Concrete results

❖ **CHAPTER 11** *Experiential Exercise*

Training at Central Collection Agency

Central Collection Agency (CCA) is a collection agency. Businesses pay CCA to collect overdue payments from consumers. Including all managers, supervisors, and collection agents, CCA employs about 500 workers (30 are supervisors). The job of a collection agent is rather stressful; consumers contacted by CCA are under great stress and will do anything to avoid payment. Collection agents may even be threatened with physical violence. Many legal regulations restrict what the collection agent may do and say. Coupled with the fact that the pay for collection agents is low and the turnover is high, a supervisor must be effective in hiring, training, supervising, and monitoring his or her subordinates.

When CCA first started 20 years ago, the company created a separate training department composed of three people: a training specialist, who had a B.A. in education, and two former collection-agency supervisors who had years of experience managing collection agents. However, because of a low turnover rate among supervisors, the supervisory staff became increasingly skilled in managing the collection agents and there was less and less need for the training and development department to conduct sessions for the collection agents. As a result, the need for training declined to a point where a separate department was no longer needed. When a new CEO was hired three years ago, he eliminated the training department and contracted with Impact Trainers, a local training firm, to conduct any necessary training for the supervisors. All training of collection agents remains the responsibility of the supervisors.

Over the last three years, however, CCA has hired twenty new supervisors. Most of the new supervisors were hired from other agencies, but about five were collection agents who were promoted. Because of the large number of new supervisors, Impact Trainers has conducted three programs in the last two years.

Impact Trainers' Program. Impact Trainers' supervisory program contains the following six modules, which are delivered over a five-day period:

- Collection Agencies and the Law
- Coaching and Training Subordinates
- Giving Performance Feedback
- How to Hire Effectively
- Communication Skills
- Telephone Courtesy

Impact Trainers uses a variety of materials and techniques in the program, including role plays, cases, short lectures, and films. At the end of each program, Impact Trainers also collects evaluations from the trainees. According to the owner of Impact Trainers, two key questions are, "Overall, how useful will the program be in your job?" and "Overall, how much did you learn from this program?" The average rating on each question was over 8 on a 9-point scale, which is extremely high for a training program. Some of the written comments by the supervisors included "Excellent training—wish I had gone through the program years ago" and "Worth every minute of the time." Not a single negative comment has appeared yet.

The Problem. The problem that has come to the CEO's attention is that the new supervisors appear to be having difficulty in managing their collection agents. While it was first thought to merely be the result of hiring relatively large numbers of new supervisors three years ago, matters appear only to have worsened in the past year. The turnover rate among collection agents is much higher than it was four years ago; their record of receiving payment within thirty days has declined noticeably over the past three years; and the number of complaints filed by consumers has increased dramatically. The CEO and the top executives believe that the training program is not effective. However, they do *not* want to reinstitute a training department. They would like you to answer the following:

1. Why do you think the training is not effective? Are there other explanations, besides the training program, for the problems described here? Because the

CEO likes concrete evidence for any recommendations, be sure to describe how you could document your conclusions.

2. What would you do to ensure that the training is more effective? Remember, you cannot reinstate a training department and the CEO is unlikely to approve expensive changes.

3. The CEO has heard that Intranet training is popular. He would like your thoughts on the application of Intranet training here. What do you think?

❖ Chapter 11 References

1. K. Wexley and G. Latham, *Developing and Training Human Resources in Organizations* (Glenview, IL: Scott, Foresman, 1981).
2. I. Goldstein, "Critical Training Issues: Past, Present, and Future," in *Training and Development in Organizations* (San Francisco: Jossey-Bass, 1989).
3. U.S. Congress, Office of Technology Assessment, *Worker Training: Competing in the New International Economy* (Washington: U.S. Government Printing Office, 1990), OTA-ITE-457.
4. D. Hogarty, "A Little Education Goes a Long Way," *Management Review* (June 1993): 24–28.
5. B. Mintz, *OSHA: History, Law, and Policy* (Washington: Bureau of National Affairs, 1984).
6. L. Bassi and M. Van Buren, "The 1998 ASTD State of the Industry Report," *Training & Development* (January 1998): 21, 23+.
7. G. Kimmerling, "Gathering Best Practices," *Training & Development* (September 1993): 28–36.
8. H. Frazis, M. Gittleman, M. Horrigan, and M. Joyce, "Results from the 1995 Survey of Employer-Provided Training," *Monthly Labor Review* (June 1998): 3–12.
9. U.S. Congress, *Worker Training*.
10. Ibid.
11. Wexley and Latham, *Developing and Training*.
12. Ibid.
13. Ibid.
14. M. Berger, "A Market-Led Training Needs Analysis," *Industrial and Commercial Training* 25, no. 1, (1993): 27–30.
15. Ibid.
16. N. Nopper, "Reinventing the Factory with Lifelong Learning," *Training* (May 1993): 55–58.
17. I. Goldstein, "Training in Work Organizations," in *Handbook of Industrial and Organizational Psychology*, vol. 2, ed. M. Dunnette and L. Hough (Palo Alto, CA: Consulting Psychologists Press, 1991).
18. Ibid.
19. Wexley and Latham, *Developing and Training*.
20. M. Harris, D. Smith, and D. Champagne, "A Field Study of Performance Appraisal Purpose: Research versus Administrative-Based Ratings," *Personnel Psychology* 48 (1995): 151–160.
21. J. K. Ford, and R. Noe, "Self-Assessed Training Needs: The Effects of Attitude Toward Training, Marginal Level, and Function," *Personnel Psychology* 40 (1987): 39–53.
22. M. Harris and J. Schaubroeck, "A Meta-Analysis of Self-Supervisor, Self-Peer, and Peer-Supervisor Ratings," *Personnel Psychology* 41 (1988): 43–62.
23. J. McEnery and J. McEnery, "Self-Rating in Management Training Needs Assessment: A Neglected Opportunity," *Journal of Occupational Psychology* 60 (1987): 49–60.
24. Wexley and Latham, *Developing and Training*.
25. R. Noe and N. Schmitt, "The Influence of Trainee Attitudes on Training Effectiveness: Test of a Model," *Personnel Psychology* 39 (1986): 497–523.

26. P. Thayer and W. McGhee, "On the Effectiveness of Not Holding a Formal Training Course," *Personnel Psychology* 30 (1977): 455–56.

27. L. Rae, "Training 101: Choose Your Method," *Training & Development* (April 1994(: 19–25.

28. Wexley and Latham, *Developing and Training*.

29. S. Gordon, *Systematic Training Program Design* (Englewood Cliffs, NJ: PTR Prentice-Hall, 1994).

30. Ibid.

31. B. Kaye, "Career Development—Anytime, Anyplace," *Training & Development* (December 1993): 46–49.

32. Wexley and Latham, *Developing and Training*.

33. M. Campion, L. Cheraskin, and M. Stevens, "Career-Related Antecedents and Outcomes of Job Rotation," *Academy of Management Journal* 37 (1994): 1518–42.

34. Ibid.

35. U.S. Congress, *Worker Training*.

36. Ibid.

37. M. S. Taylor, "Effects of College Internships on Individual Participants," *Journal of Applied Psychology* 73 (1988): 393–401.

38. Bassi and Van Buren, "The 1998 ASTD State."

39. Wexley and Latham, *Developing and Training*.

40. U.S. Congress, *Worker Training*.

41. Ibid.

42. Wexley and Latham, *Developing and Training*.

43. Gordon, *Systematic Training*.

44. U.S. Congress, *Worker Training*.

45. Gordon, *Systematic Training*.

46. D. Abernathy, "A Start-Up Guide to Distance Learning, " *Training & Development* (December 1997): 39–47.

47. D. Fox, "How to Enliven Online Interaction," *Training & Development* (December 1997): 48–49.

48. M. Driscoll, *Web-based Training* (San Francisco, CA: Jossey-Bass, 1998).

49. B. Roberts, "Via the Desktop://," *HRMagazine* (August 1998): 99–104.

50. Wexley and Latham, *Developing and Training*.

51. U.S. Congress, *Worker Training*.

52. D. Swink, "Role-Play Your Way to Learning," *Training & Development* (May 1993): 91–97.

53. Wexley and Latham, *Developing and Training*.

54. Ibid.

55. T. Baldwin and J. K. Ford, "Transfer of Training: A Review and Directions for Future Research," *Personnel Psychology* 41 (1988): 63–105.

56. M. Broad and J. Newstrom, *Transfer of Training* (Reading, MA: Addison-Wesley, 1992).

57. Ibid.

58. D. Black, "Live and Online: A WBT Primer," *Training & Development* (September 1998): 34, 36.

59. "Michigan Disallows Corporate Culture Program," *Fortnightly* 131 (1993): 45.

60. P. Sackett and E. Mullen, "Beyond Formal Experimental Design: Towards an Expanded View of the Training Evaluation Process," *Personnel Psychology* 46 (1993): 613–27.

61. Ibid.

62. Gordon, *Systematic Training*.

63. G. Alliger and E. Janak, "Kirkpatrick's Levels of Training Criteria: Thirty Years Later," *Personnel Psychology* 42 (1989): 331–42.

64. Wexley and Latham, *Developing and Training*.

65. W. Hicks and R. Klimoski, "Entry into Training Programs and Its Effects on Training Outcomes: A Field Experiment," *Academy of Management Journal* 30 (1987): 542–52.

66. B. Filipczak, "The Business of Training at NCR," *Training* (February 1992): 55–60.

67. "12 Steps to Better Training," *Training* (June 1993): 14–151.

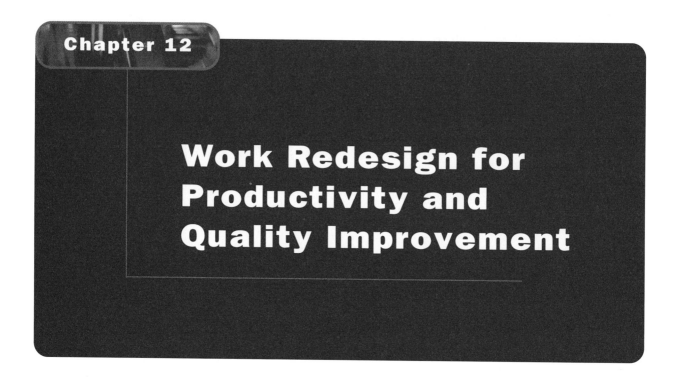

Work Redesign for Productivity and Quality Improvement

Core Concepts   **After reading this chapter, you should be capable of:**

1. Explaining the classical (scientific management) approach to work design.
2. Explaining the alternative approaches to classical work design, including job enlargement, job enrichment, quality circles, team concept, total quality management, reengineering, and the virtual organization.
3. Describing the advantages and disadvantages of different work design approaches.
4. Outlining the factors in deciding whether work redesign is the solution to an organization's problems.

Opening Case

Fiona has worked for several years now as an order processor in the customer service department of Myra's Mystery, a large mail-order company specializing in lingerie and sleepwear. Her responsibilities include opening customer mail-in orders and entering the orders into a computer terminal. Once the order is entered, the billing department must review the payment method and approve shipment. Approved orders are filled in the warehouse area by an employee who retrieves the items from shelves. The order is then given to another employee in the packaging area, who packs the materials into the appropriate container. Every hour or so, another employee collects the packages and brings them to the mailroom, where the necessary postage is added. The packages are then taken to United Parcel Service or the post office for shipment.

Over the years, Fiona has observed several problems with the way orders are processed. One problem is that it takes quite a lot of time between when she enters the order into the computer and the actual mailing of the order. A second problem is that mistakes seem rather frequent. Sometimes she enters the wrong items into the computer (usually when the customer wrote an illegible number), other times warehouse personnel pack the wrong items. A third problem is that many questions come up that, according to company regulations, a supervisor must answer. For example, Fiona must ask her supervisor how to handle an order that is missing payment. Although she knows the right answer (always call the customer), the company requires order processors to have the supervisor sign a form to allow them to proceed. This of course slows down the speed with which the order can be filled.

When Fiona began working this job, business was booming. Thirty new order processors were hired the same month she was hired. But since that time, orders have slowed down somewhat. This is probably due to increased competition from other companies as well as a slump in the general economy. Just yesterday, top management announced a major restructuring of the company's operations. When Fiona asked her supervisor about this, he answered, "The company may be reengineering. Another rumor I heard was that the company was going to go virtual. Who knows what will happen!" Before

Fiona had the chance to ask her supervisor what that all meant, he had to go to a meeting, which lasted the rest of the day.

Fiona is particularly concerned about how these changes will be made and how they will affect her future in the company. She wonders whether changing to a virtual company means that she will work at home on a computer. Although she has access to e-mail and the Web at home, her computer is about four years old and crashes frequently. She wonders whether she will need to upgrade her computer if the company goes "virtual." One of her friends worked for a company that implemented work teams. As a result, her friend's job changed dramatically. In addition, far fewer supervisor or managerial positions remained, and opportunities for advancement were reduced. Fiona wonders whether layoffs will take place at Myra's Mystery, and how any changes will affect her job.

This chapter discusses the design of jobs and work. In the last few years, many companies have changed the design of their jobs for several reasons. First, many companies have used job and work design changes as a means of increasing productivity and improving quality. Second, the nature of work itself has changed in many ways. Consider, as an example, the increasingly widespread use of personal computers (PCs), which has changed the speed and ease with which information can be obtained. In turn, PCs have led to the elimination of certain traditional tasks (such as completing paper reports) and the addition of new tasks (for example, performing statistical analyses) for many employees. Third, more people today are likely to seek interesting and challenging work. Many employees quickly become bored performing the same task over and over.

The remainder of this chapter will discuss ways to design jobs and work. First, you will read about the classical approach to work design, often referred to as scientific management. Following that section, you will read about a variety of alternative approaches, including job enrichment, the team concept, total quality management, reengineering, and virtual teams. You will see that there is no one best approach to work design. Rather, each method has its own potential strengths and weaknesses.

Work Design: Classical Approach

scientific management
The classical approach to job design, which concentrates on such principles as specialization and simplification, repetitiveness, mechanical pacing, limited interpersonal interaction, and predetermined work techniques.

The classical approach to job design, often referred to as **scientific management**, is associated with names you may have heard before in other management courses, such as Frederick Taylor and Henri Fayol, both of whom lived in the beginning of this century. Although the term *scientific management* often has a negative connotation attached to it, many organizations base their work design on this approach. The classical approach to work design rests on several basic principles listed in Table 12.1. A good example of an organization that uses the classical approach would be a large automobile manufacturer, such as General Motors, particularly as it existed 15 or 20 years ago. Cars would be produced using a traditional assembly line, in which each worker is assigned one or two simple tasks to perform over and over again. For example, one worker might be assigned the task of affixing the side mirrors, another worker might affix the rearview mirror, and yet a third worker might attach the side mirror sticker (one that reads "Images are closer than they appear in the mirror"). The speed or pace of the assembly line, as well as the equipment, layout, and other decisions, would be determined by employees other than the production workers themselves, generally by industrial engineers. There would be little or no need for the workers to interact with one another. Turning to the opening case, it should not surprise you that the jobs at Myra's Mystery are based on the classic work-design approach. In particular, each job appears quite simple and specialized. Although there was no description of the work techniques, it is likely that the pace, methods, and other aspects are determined by someone other than the employees who perform the work.[1]

Although the classical approach began to wane in popularity by the 1940s, it is still widely used, albeit in a somewhat modified fashion, by many companies. Box 12.1 describes United Parcel Service's approach to classical job design. The primary advantage of this approach is that it is highly efficient, especially for simple production jobs, with high quantity output.[2] A second advantage is that classical work design makes it easy to replace workers who leave, because each job is simple and easy to learn. There are two primary disadvantages to the classical work design. First, many workers react negatively to this kind of work; boredom and dissatisfaction are common reactions. Unless these kinds of reactions are held in check, productivity can ultimately suffer. Second, the classical work design provides little opportunity for innovation by employees. As a result of these disadvantages, several alternatives to the classical work de-

---

> ### Table 12.1   Selected Principles of Classical Job Design

1. *Specialization and Simplification.* Each job consists of a few simple sets of tasks.
2. *Repetitiveness.* Each job involves repeating the same tasks over and over again.
3. *Mechanical Pacing.* Employees work at a speed determined by engineers who focus on the nature of the product rather than the employees' natural rhythm or pace.
4. *Limited Interpersonal Interaction.* There is limited need for job-related interaction between employees.
5. *Predetermined Work Techniques.* Staff specialists determine what tools to use, how to use them, and other work technique decisions; employees have little or no influence over these decisions.

Source: Adapted from R. Griffin, *Task Design: An Integrative Approach* (Glenview, IL: Scott, Foresman, 1982).

TALES FROM THE TRENCHES

Box 12.1
Classical Job Design and United Parcel Service

Perhaps the most successful organization in the United States using classical job design is United Parcel Service (UPS). Best known for its boxy brown trucks, UPS is the largest transportation company in the United States. UPS is based on the classical job design model and, in fact, employs more than 3,000 industrial engineers to ensure maximum efficiency. As stipulated by the classical approach, extensive, detailed regulations exist to ensure maximum efficiency. For example, delivery personnel must walk at a specific pace (three feet per second) and pick up and deliver a predetermined number of packages (on average, 400 per day). In return, em-

ployees (who are unionized) are well paid; delivery personnel earn between $40,000 and $50,000 annually, making them among the highest paid truck drivers in the United States. As a result of increased competition, however, UPS has been forced to implement several changes in its service. First, UPS has expanded its guaranteed 10:30 A.M. delivery time to most of the country. Second, UPS has started a package tracing system, so that the location of each package can be readily determined as it moves from one point to the next. Third, the company has increased the services and products it offers customers. All of these changes have begun to ad-

versely affect the delivery personnel, who complain about conflicts between achieving high-quality customer service, meeting deadlines, and following safety rules. The company has responded by hiring better skilled, often college-educated, workers. But this may have only added to the problems, as higher-educated workers may be less content with this highly structured job. In light of the increasing competition from other companies, though, more changes in UPS may be coming soon. One interesting question, as you read further in this chapter, is whether a different job design would be more effective in adapting to current and future changes at UPS.

Source: Adapted from R. Frank, "Driving Harder," *Wall Street Journal*, 23 May 1994, A1, A5.

sign approach have been introduced over the last 40 years. You will now read about these in greater detail.[3]

Alternatives to Classical Work Design: An Overview

Organizations can choose among a variety of alternatives to classical work design. We will discuss the following: job enlargement, job enrichment, quality circles, total quality management, the work team, reengineering, and virtual organizations. Although these programs differ from one another in a number of ways, they can be compared and contrasted with regard to three important factors:

1. Degree of overall impact
2. Degree of employee empowerment
3. Linkage to technology

Degree of overall impact refers to the extent of their effects on overall organizational practices, policies, and norms. As you can see in Table 12.2, some work designs (for instance, quality circles) have little overall impact, while other approaches (such as reengineering) produce much greater overall impact. **Employee empowerment** refers to how much decision-making power and authority employees at the lowest level of the organization acquire as a result of the program. Job enlargement, for example, provides little empowerment, while work teams produce high levels of empowerment. Finally, the *link to technology* category refers to the degree of impact the design has on

employee empowerment
Refers to how much decision-making power and authority employees at the lowest level of the organization acquire as a result of the work design available to organizations.

Table 12.2	Characteristics of Work Design Programs		
Program	**Impact**	**Empowerment**	**Link to Technology**
Job enlargement	Low	Low	Low
Job enrichment	Modest	Modest	Modest
Quality circles	Low	Low	Modest
Work teams	High	High	High
TQM	Modest-High	Low-High	Modest-High
Reengineering	Very High	Modest-High	Very High
Virtual Organization	Very High	High	Very High

workplace technology (that is, the processes, equipment, and methods of performing the work). Programs that have a high link to technology, such as reengineering, are likely to require major changes in the technology. For programs with little linkage, such as job enlargement, technology is unlikely to be affected by the program.

Early Approaches to Alternative Work Design: Job Enlargement and Job Enrichment

Job enlargement and job enrichment were among the earliest alternatives proposed to the classical work design. Recall the two basic disadvantages mentioned regarding the classical work design, namely, negative worker reactions and lack of worker innovation. Both job enlargement and job enrichment attempt to overcome the disadvantages of the classical work design by increasing the scope of an employee's job.

Job Enlargement

job enlargement
Involves increasing the number of tasks performed by each employee and having jobs that are somewhat less specialized.

Job enlargement was an approach developed in the 1950s. As suggested by the term, job enlargement involves increasing the number of tasks performed by each employee.[4] Figure 12.1 demonstrates how this works. Let us consider the previous example of an automobile production line: rather than having one worker affixing the side mirror and another worker attaching the rearview mirror, one worker might be assigned the task of attaching both the side and rearview mirrors. In essence, then, job enlargement differs from the classical approach of job design in one way: jobs are somewhat less specialized. Rather than doing one simple task, the workers may perform three or four simple tasks. Returning to the opening case, the company might implement job enlargement by increasing the number of responsibilities assigned to the workers. Rather than having one employee retrieve the necessary items from the shelves and a different employee package the items, for example, the company might have the same employee do both tasks.

Although some evidence suggests that job enlargement can somewhat improve worker satisfaction and productivity may increase, this approach did not become a popular workplace trend. There are probably two reasons for this:[5]

1. Job enlargement results in only small improvements, since workers merely have more assigned tasks.

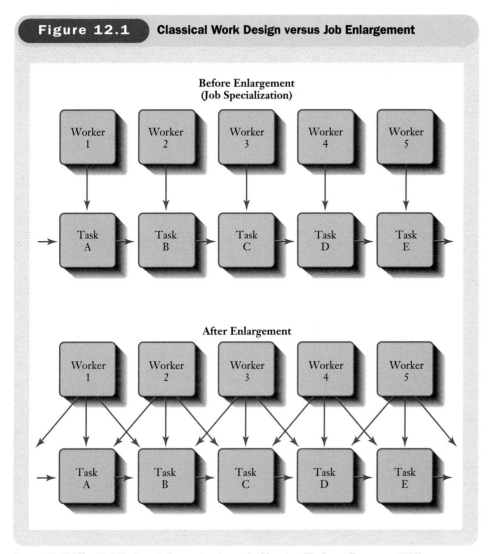

Figure 12.1 Classical Work Design versus Job Enlargement

Source: R. Griffin, *Task Design: An Integrative Approach* (Glenview, IL: Scott, Foresman, 1982).

2. Some view job enlargement as a ruse by management to increase productivity of workers, while cutting back on the number of employees.

Although job enlargement as a specific approach is rarely used in industry today, it did increase awareness of the danger of work oversimplification. As such, job enlargement constitutes an important step in work design.

Job Enrichment

The **job enrichment** approach was popularized in the 1960s and 1970s by two separate proponents. One proponent, Frederick Herzberg, developed the job enrichment notion as a result of a study of accountants and engineers conducted in the late 1950s. In this study, Herzberg asked participants to describe a work situation where they felt exceptionally satisfied or exceptionally dissatisfied with their work. Herzberg and his

job enrichment
Increasing job satisfaction by using such intrinsic factors as achievement, recognition, and the work itself of enforcing extrinsic factors such as company policy and supervision.

colleagues then sorted the responses into broad categories, such as those involving the work itself, those involving supervisors, and so forth. Herzberg found that the majority of satisfying situations involved intrinsic factors, such as achievement, recognition, and the work itself. He concluded that intrinsic factors therefore increase job satisfaction. On the other hand, Herzberg found that extrinsic factors, such as company policy and supervision, were associated primarily with dissatisfying situations. Herzberg interpreted this to mean that extrinsic factors primarily cause dissatisfaction, but contribute little or nothing to satisfaction.[6] The implication of this theory, known as the *two-factor theory*, is that motivation can be improved by increasing the intrinsic satisfaction associated with the job. Rather than merely adding additional tasks, as suggested by job enlargement, Herzberg advocated adding tasks that involve greater recognition, responsibility, and growth opportunities.[7]

In the 1970s, Richard Hackman and Greg Oldham jointly developed the *job characteristics model*, which in many ways is similar to the two-factor theory. According to Hackman and Oldham, five characteristics of a job (skill variety, task identity, task significance, autonomy, and feedback) affect key psychological states (meaningfulness of work, responsibility for work, and knowledge of results), which in turn affect internal work motivation, satisfaction, and work effectiveness. To increase work motivation, jobs must be designed to incorporate high levels of the five job characteristics.[8]

Job enrichment has four major features:

1. Each employee is made responsible for a complete unit of work.
2. Each employee is accountable to the customer.
3. The work should be designed to provide feedback to the employee.
4. Employees should have greater opportunities to make decisions regarding their work.

If you compare these points to those outlined in Table 12.1, which contains the principles of classical job design, you will note several significant differences between the two approaches. As an illustration of how job enrichment principles might be used to design a job, consider Myra's Mystery, the company described in the opening case. A job enrichment approach would require that the same employee complete as much of the entire order as possible. The employee who opens the order, for example, might proceed to retrieve the necessary goods from the shelves and package the materials. This employee might also include in the package a card with his or her name, so that the consumer could directly contact him or her regarding any problems, thereby increasing accountability to the customer. And, rather than asking the supervisor what to do for every special situation, the employees might be trained to deal with many of the common problems.

The job enrichment approach to work design has, like all of the work design programs, both advantages and disadvantages. One advantage is that research has shown the method to be effective in improving worker attitudes (such as job satisfaction) as well as worker productivity.[9] Additionally, as indicated in Table 12.2, job enrichment is less disruptive than other work redesign approaches. Such programs, then, may be easier to implement successfully than some others. In terms of disadvantages, however, job enrichment programs lead to relatively modest productivity improvements. Yet, at the same time, job enrichment can still create upheaval. For example, when employees become more empowered, there may be less need for supervisors. Consequently, supervisors may be laid off or forced to move to different (perhaps lower paying) jobs. The costs of the program, then, may outweigh the benefits.[10]

Quality Circles

Although **quality circles** are less an approach to work design than an addition to the existing organizational structure, we will discuss them here. First initiated in Japan in the early 1960s, quality circles did not debut in the United States until 1974. A quality circle typically has the following characteristics:

1. Between 3 and 15 members participate voluntarily.
2. Meetings take place on a regular basis, usually for an hour per week.
3. Their purpose is to identify, discuss, and solve production or business-related problems within the members' work area.

In most quality circles, the group chooses the problems to examine. As a rule of thumb, the group will generate a list of 50 problems, and solve 2 to 4 problems per year.[11] Generally, quality circles do not consider human resource and management issues (such as pay or supervision).

Advantages and Disadvantages of Quality Circles

Quality circles grew rapidly in popularity during the late 1970s, but began to wane almost as quickly by the mid-1980s. Currently, slightly more than half of the Fortune 1,000 companies use some type of quality circles.[12] There are both advantages and disadvantages to quality circles. Because they have only a small overall impact, quality circles are easier to implement in organizations than most other work redesign programs. Moreover, they appear to be useful in solving minor productivity problems.[13] Quality circles also have a number of disadvantages. First, they tend to die within one and a half years of implementation.[14] A major difficulty in maintaining quality circles is that companies do not provide significant rewards (such as pay raises) for participation. Also, because most quality circles do not permit discussion of human resource and management issues (such as supervision), employees may become frustrated. A "honeymoon" effect is therefore quite common with quality circles: initially, employee attitudes significantly improve and many suggestions for improvements are offered. After one or two years, however, the romance is over, and attitudes and suggestions decline. Thus, the value of a quality circle program tends to be rather short term.[15] A final disadvantage is recent legal rulings, which indicate that quality circle programs may constitute an illegally formed union. In the future, then, there may be legal restrictions on their usage.[16]

Because of these disadvantages, some experts feel that the major value of quality circles is that they may serve as a transition step in changing over to the work team approach. This approach is described in greater detail next.

quality circle
Originating in Japan in the early 1960s, the quality circle usually has between three and fifteen members who meet on a regular basis. Their purpose is to identify, discuss, and solve production or business-related problems within the members' work area.

Work Teams

The **work team** approach gained popularity in the United States during the mid-1980s and continues to be popular in the early part of the 21st century. As shown in Table 12.3, there are several different kinds of teams. For present purposes, however, we will focus on only one kind of team: the work team. The typical work team consists of 3 to 30 employees, with one person assigned as the team leader. The team may have anywhere from some control over decisions that affect it to virtually complete control over decisions that affect it. A team with limited control over decisions may, for

work team
The typical work team consists of between 3 and 30 employees, with one person assigned as the team leader; the team may have anywhere from some control to complete control over the project or problem.

Table 12.3	Kinds of Teams

Name	Definition
1. Problem-solving team	Group of knowledgeable workers gathered temporarily to solve a specific problem
2. Management team	Group of managers from a variety of functions that coordinates work teams
3. Work team	Group of workers who function on a permanent team to perform basic tasks

Source: Adapted from B. Dumaine, "The Trouble with Teams," *Fortune*, 5 September 1994, 86–92.

example, have the authority to make staff scheduling and assignment decisions. Any other decision (for example, hiring) must be made by the manager. At the other end of the spectrum, a self-managed or autonomous work team has control over such things as who gets hired, who gets promoted, and who gets terminated, as well as staff scheduling and assignments. The function of the team leader in a self-managed work team differs significantly from that of the traditional supervisor (see Box 12.2 for further discussion of the differences).[17] Next, you will read about some common stages that teams go through and how teams should go about making decisions.

Team Stages

Most teams go through three common phases as they mature. The first phase, formation, involves the group deciding what their goals are and how they will achieve those goals. For example, the team must decide on many rules in terms of how they will operate and function. While top management may give the primary goals to the team, many details the team usually must decide for itself. (See Experiential Exercise 2 of this chapter for an example of the issues raised by one work team in its formation stage.) Later in the formation stage, many teams go through an "adjustment period." Essentially, this stage occurs when the team begins to operate on a regular basis and certain problems arise. Typical issues concern deadlines and work scope. Power struggles are also common at this stage. The second stage, if the team survives, is referred to as the "development stage." At this point, progress is being made and successes are met with enthusiasm and renewed energy on the part of team members. A major crisis that often arises is that the team turns inward and begins to feel somewhat separated from other teams and functions in the organization. In order to break out of this phase, the team must reconnect with other teams and functions and focus more on exploration and trying new approaches. In the third phase, renewal, the team must try new ideas and set new goals, with an emphasis on reaching outside of itself.[18]

Next, you will read about how teams should make decisions. In order for a team to be successful, it must become effective in making decisions.

Effective Decision-Making for Teams

As shown in Figure 12.2, there are four major categories of decisions that teams will make. Decisions vary from major and minor in terms of their importance and decisions may involve either people or tasks. The way in which the decision is to be made

Box 12.2
So You Want to Be a Team Leader?

Now that you have read about work teams and found that many companies are either using them or are considering their use, you may be thinking that you would like to be a team leader. To begin with, you should realize that the tasks of a team leader in a self-managed work team are considerably different from the tasks performed by the traditional supervisor. Therefore, your motivations for being a team leader are likely to differ, as are the abilities and experiences that will be required. Let's look first at the motivations you think a traditional supervisor or manager might need to succeed. What would you guess? If you said motivations such as the need to be in control, the need for prestige, the need for respect, and the need for power you are on the right track. Now, if you have been carefully reading, what might you guess are some of the motivations a team leader should have? If you said the need for helping others make decisions, the need for seeing people challenge themselves, and the need for helping others learn, you are correct. If you want to be a team leader, then, you should think more carefully about what motivates you and where your interests and strengths lie.

Now let's consider the tasks performed by a typical team leader:

1. Coaching and training of team members
2. Team building (such as facilitating team decision making and mediating conflicts within the team)
3. Serving as liaison with other teams, departments, and units
4. Traditional supervisory activities (scheduling, disciplining, and so forth)

Typically, the first three tasks take considerably more time than the fourth, since the team often has taken over many of the activities traditionally performed by the supervisor. The reverse is true for the traditional supervisor, who probably spends relatively less time on the first three tasks. Which mix of the above listed tasks would you like most?

Now that you know what the team leader does, what should you do if you are appointed a team leader for a newly formed team? Here are some suggestions:

1. **Establish and Communicate Clear Objectives for the Team.** Make sure you emphasize the urgency and importance of these objectives. Remember, if your organization has recently implemented teams, employees will have many questions and concerns about what it is they should be doing now.
2. **Carefully Plan and Guide Initial Meetings and Activities of the Team.** Decisions, events, and behaviors early on in the life of the team often set the tone and determine the success or failure of the team. Early mistakes can cause irreparable damage. But be sure not to adopt the role of the traditional supervisor by dominating the meetings. Your goal as a team leader is to facilitate the decisions, not make the decisions.
3. **Facilitate Early Development of Rules, Responsibilities, and Norms.** *Norms*, or unwritten rules, develop quite quickly in any social context. It is important, therefore, that you as a team leader facilitate the establishment of those norms early on. One important norm, for example, concerns how conflict will be handled by the team. If you convey the message, either intentionally or unintentionally, that conflict is avoided, subsequent disagreements may be ignored, even when they need to be addressed by the team.

4. **Encourage the Team to Interact Extensively.** It is important for the team members to get to know one another quickly and to form team cohesiveness as early as possible. Having the team interact together at work, after work hours, and on the weekend is important.
5. **Utilize Positive Reinforcement.** It is critical for the team leader to establish a norm of frequent positive feedback, particularly in the beginning when the team is starting off. Remember, positive reinforcement is much more than just money; it includes verbal praise, written commendations, free movie tickets, and many other things. Be particularly willing to reward members who enhance group functioning. For example, the team member who helps coach another employee must be rewarded for this effort.

The following suggestions apply to the team leader of a more mature, established team:

1. **Establish Yourself as a Source of Inspiration for the Team.** You must encourage the team, as well as individuals, when there are problems and challenges. You must also motivate the team to work to its fullest capacity. Think of a cheerleader; that is a critical role as a team leader.
2. **Effectively Represent the Team to Other Parties.** A major component of the team leader's role will involve interactions with

(continued)

(continued)

other teams, departments, and managers. You will serve as an important filter of information spreading from the team to other units, as well as a critical interface for information coming from

other units to the team. The more effective you are in these roles, the more effective your team will be.

3. **Develop Your Team Members.** One of the most important roles played by the team leader is that

of a coach. By providing opportunities for team members to learn new skills and participate in appropriate training programs and related activities, you will be seen as a more effective team leader.

Source: Adopted from J. Katzenbach and D. Smith, *The Wisdom of Teams* (Boston: Harvard Business School Press, 1993); and R. Wellins, W. Byham, and J. Wilson, *Empowered Teams* (San Francisco: Jossey-Bass, 1993).

should depend on the nature of the decision. A minor decision should be made using a different process than a major decision. Figure 12.2 provides suggestions for how decisions should be made, depending on which category they belong in. For example, decisions that can be categorized as "minor task decisions," such as where to hold the team retreat should involve a simpler decision process than a major decision involving people, such as how to pick a team leader. As you can see in Figure 12.2, the decision as to where to hold the team retreat has five basic steps, with the last step being "move on." On the other hand, if you examine Figure 12.2, you will see that a major decision such as how to pick a team leader involves seven steps, with the last step being follow-up for learning and development. There are negative implications if the team chooses the wrong decision-making process in any particular situation. For example, if the team uses a lengthy process for making a simple, trivial decision, it can waste a great deal of valuable work time and create a sense of discouragement on the part of the team members. On the other hand, if a quick and superficial process is used to make an important "people decision," such as how will team leaders be chosen, team members may feel that they did not really participate and that the process is unfair.[19]

Advantages and Disadvantages of the Work Team

In terms of the advantages of the work team, companies have demonstrated phenomenal increases in productivity. Federal Express, for example, reported a 40 percent increase in productivity after adopting work teams. Another potential advantage is the increased innovation that follows. Two work teams at Boeing, the giant aerospace company, for instance, discovered a blueprint plan conflict in where to place the passenger oxygen and fresh-air nozzles (both teams had placed their component in the same place). Within hours of the discovery, a solution had been worked out (a special clamp was designed to hold both). Without the teams, the problem may not have been discovered until production began.[20]

While the work team can produce major boosts in productivity, it is not without its disadvantages. The primary disadvantage of this technique is that it takes a great deal of time and effort to implement properly. For example, a reopened Owens-Corning Fiberglass plant using autonomous work teams experienced many production problems early on. As a result, employees were required to work overtime, and their shifts were constantly changing. Another result was that employee training lagged far behind.[21] A

| Figure 12.2 | Categories of Team Decisions |

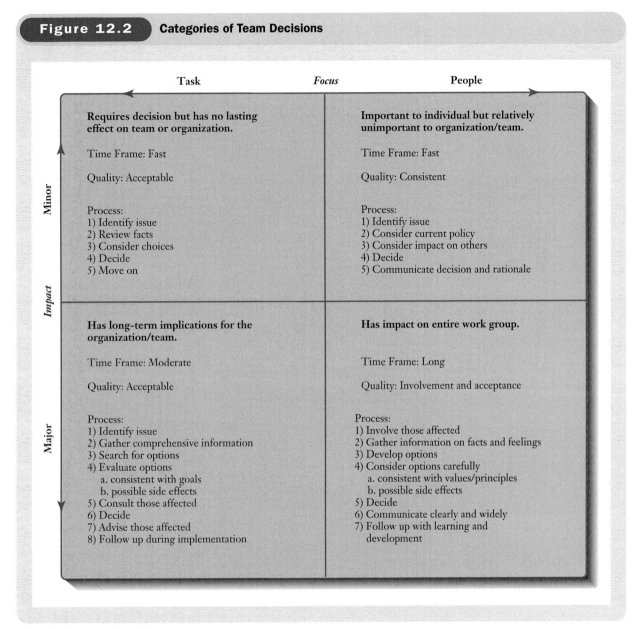

Task   *Focus*   People

Minor

Requires decision but has no lasting effect on team or organization.

Time Frame: Fast

Quality: Acceptable

Process:
1) Identify issue
2) Review facts
3) Consider choices
4) Decide
5) Move on

Important to individual but relatively unimportant to organization/team.

Time Frame: Fast

Quality: Consistent

Process:
1) Identify issue
2) Consider current policy
3) Consider impact on others
4) Decide
5) Communicate decision and rationale

Impact

Major

Has long-term implications for the organization/team.

Time Frame: Moderate

Quality: Acceptable

Process:
1) Identify issue
2) Gather comprehensive information
3) Search for options
4) Evaluate options
   a. consistent with goals
   b. possible side effects
5) Consult those affected
6) Decide
7) Advise those affected
8) Follow up during implementation

Has impact on entire work group.

Time Frame: Long

Quality: Involvement and acceptance

Process:
1) Involve those affected
2) Gather information on facts and feelings
3) Develop options
4) Consider options carefully
   a. consistent with values/principles
   b. possible side effects
5) Decide
6) Communicate clearly and widely
7) Follow up with learning and
   development

Source: Adapted from E. Aranda, L. Aranda, and K. Conlon, *Teams: Structure, Process, Culture, and Politics* (Upper Saddle River, NJ: Prentice-Hall, 1998).

second primary disadvantage is that work teams will not work in all situations. Can you think of any jobs like this? One example would be cross-country truck drivers. Work teams would probably not be helpful there because the job involves a solo effort. In certain other jobs and situations the work team would simply take more time and effort than it is worth.[22] Box 12.3 describes Levi Strauss's trouble-ridden transition into team work.

Box 12.3
Teams Sometimes Fail, Too

Despite the many advantages associated with teams, this approach does not always work. As an example, consider Levi Strauss & Company. For years, Levi Strauss used a classical work design to produce its world-famous blue jeans, under which employees were paid on an individual incentive plan for performing highly repetitive tasks, such as attaching belt loops. But in 1992, the company decided to switch to a team approach in order to reduce boredom and cut down on the number of injuries due to repetitive motions. The company also felt that the team method would increase productivity. The teams consisted of 10 to 35 workers and the pay would be based on the number of trousers completed by the team. Unfortunately, matters were more complicated than the company anticipated. The major problem seemed to be vast differences between employee skill levels. Thus, the most productive employees found that their pay actually decreased when they moved to teams, which demotivated them. The problem was compounded when a team member was absent from work or was new on the job. This would cause further delays, again lowering the productivity rate. Moreover, the team would have to decide who would make up the losses. In other cases, workers would get angry when teammates took too long in the bathroom or came to work injured. Some experts believe that Levi Strauss failed to pay sufficient attention to the transition and that managers used different approaches to implementing the teams. For example, most employees received minimal amounts of team-building training and in some cases were given insufficient training on technical details, such as measuring quality. The end result was that for a few years after the move to teams, costs actually went up by as much as 25 percent and the number of pants produced declined early on to 77 percent of the previous level. The company claims these figures have since improved, but the company is still less efficient than before the transition to teams. One response by the company has been to relocate more of the production outside of the U.S. Approximately 45 percent of Levi's pants are now produced in other countries, compared to only 15 percent in 1991.

Source: Adapted from R. King, "Jeans Therapy," *Wall Street Journal*, 20 May 1998, A1, A6.

We turn now to a work design approach that was popularized in the United States in the mid-1980s and that continues to have a major influence over organizations: total quality management.

Total Quality Management

total quality management
TQM emphasizes a business objective (quality) and articulates various policies, practices, and management philosophies to support that objective and to enhance product or service quality.

Total quality management (TQM) was introduced in the United States in the mid-1980s. Originally adopted by Japan in the 1950s, the establishment of the Malcolm Baldrige National Quality Award has solidified TQM's presence in the U.S. business world (for more information on this prestigious award, go to the following Web site: http://www.quality.nist.gov/tos.htm). In a nutshell, TQM emphasizes a business objective (quality), and it articulates various policies, practices, and management philosophies to support that objective. Because of the importance of TQM today, you will next learn in greater detail what TQM is, along with its common features and characteristics.

What Is TQM?

As suggested by the name, the goal of total quality management is to enhance product or service quality. In the quest for high quality, management's role is to design and implement systems that will facilitate quality enhancements. The role of employees is to make decisions, build customer relationships, and improve quality in all processes. TQM, then, introduces work design changes. Perhaps most importantly, however, TQM involves several significant changes in our assumptions about work. Some of the more interesting principles are discussed next.[23]

TQM Principles

Although there are several different approaches to TQM, we will focus on the principles developed by W. Edwards Deming. Some of the highlights of Deming's philosophy are presented in Table 12.4.[24]

As you look at Table 12.4, the first four principles should fit well with material that you have read in this or in other chapters. Certainly, an emphasis on teams, as suggested in the third principle, would be consistent with concepts described earlier. The last three principles listed in Table 12.4, however, may seem rather puzzling. In fact, the seventh principle, the elimination of quotas and quantitative objectives, may appear completely contrary to what you have read elsewhere in this book.[25]

To understand the fifth principle in Table 12.4 (increase consistency in production), consider the following example. Suppose you were trying to buy a car and were considering the Sphinx, manufactured by Giza Motor. After reading *Consumer Reports* and other magazines, you identify a concern with the quality of the car. The concern is that the quality of the Sphinx varies considerably; some of these cars have shoddy quality, others have outstanding quality. Would you be willing to buy a Sphinx? You would probably say no, primarily because you would be worried about getting a lemon. Deming's TQM approach would be to eliminate the variation as much as possible. In the end, the Sphinx may have just average quality (though the company would continue to try to improve quality), but at least you as a customer would know what to expect. This is one reason Deming's principles emphasize the need for consistency in production.

The sixth principle may also seem somewhat surprising in that it shifts blame for work-related problems from the workers to the machinery and equipment. This principle stems from Deming's experience in the manufacturing arena, where he found that many problems were due to the machinery or equipment, not the employees.

Table 12.4   **Selected Highlights of Deming's TQM Principles**

1. Constantly improve production and service systems by increasing quality and productivity, thereby reducing costs.
2. The purpose of supervision is to help people and technology to work better.
3. Eliminate departmental barriers and emphasize teams representing different areas.
4. Implement ongoing training and education programs.
5. Increase consistency in production.
6. The majority of quality and productivity problems lie with the technology, not the employees.
7. Eliminate work standards, quotas, and quantitative objectives in the production and service areas. Eliminate performance ratings.

Source: Based on R. Schuler and D. Harris, "Deming Quality Improvement: Implications for Human Resource Management as Illustrated in a Small Company," *Human Resource Planning* 14 (1991): 191–207.

Whether, in fact, equipment is the most common source of productivity problems is still questionable.

What do you think accounts for the seventh principle in Table 12.4, namely, that companies should avoid use of objective quotas and individual performance ratings? According to Deming, it is most important that companies achieve consistency in production and service. Using individually based performance ratings encourages less consistency. Perhaps even more importantly, though, Deming argues that it is technological differences, not human differences, that account for differential performance by different employees. Using a performance evaluation system that assumes some employees are more productive than others is therefore inappropriate, according to Deming. Further, emphasis on individual performance may hamper quality improvement efforts.

continuous improvement
Emphasizes ongoing efforts to improve productivity and quality.

One of the most important TQM practices is **continuous improvement,** which emphasizes ongoing efforts to improve productivity and quality. Only by stressing the continuous nature of quality improvement will organizations be able to make major improvements.

Advantages and Disadvantages of TQM

In terms of basic advantages of TQM, a focus on quality is certainly important in many organizations. TQM can be credited with helping U.S. manufacturers greatly improve quality, an area that had previously been quite problematic. Thus, for a company concerned about quality, a TQM program may be quite helpful. TQM is particularly appropriate when the company is basically sound but wishes to introduce change, albeit in a gradual way.[26]

With regard to disadvantages, TQM certainly does not guarantee organizational success. As an example, The Wallace Company won the 1990 Malcolm Baldrige National Quality Award on the basis of its TQM program. In early 1992, this same company filed for bankruptcy under Chapter 11.[27] A TQM program often results in the creation of many committees, programs, and policies with unknown goals and purposes.[28] Florida Power & Light found that the application of TQM principles stifled innovation and created a new bureaucracy. One quality improvement team went through an entire seven-step process to determine where to relocate a water cooler![29]

Despite the potential gains from a TQM program, some experts have felt that a more radical approach to work redesign is sometimes needed. As you will see next, reengineering is a work design program that incorporates many of the possibilities that have been mentioned in this chapter so far, while fundamentally redesigning the entire organization.

Reengineering

reengineering
A radical process of redesigning business procedures and structures.

Reengineering was the work design approach of the mid-1990s. The basic principles of this approach were first described in a book entitled *Reengineering the Corporation: A Manifesto for Business Revolution*, published in 1993 by Michael Hammer and James Champy.[30] As a result of this book, reengineering was a major trend in 1993 and 1994. By 1995, however, the popularity of this technique begin to wane.[31] Unlike most of the other work design approaches described here, reengineering offers little in the way of specific guidelines as to how to design work. Rather, reengineering is defined as a radical redesign of business processes, procedures, and structures.[32] The best way to understand reengineering, then, is to imagine someone said to you, "If you could be anything or any person in the world what or who would you want to be? Write a description on this piece of paper." By the same token, reengineering involves the company asking itself, "If we could start all over again, how would the company's business processes look?" (*Business processes* refer to the activities that support valued customer outcomes, such as order fulfillment.) Once this vision is determined, the company begins to redesign itself. In some reengineering programs, organizations involved customers throughout all stages.

Although not required, many reengineering efforts have involved changing the organizational structure from a functional arrangement to a process arrangement. The difference between the two types of work arrangements is illustrated in Figure 12.3. As shown in Figure 12.3, the **functional,** or **traditional, arrangement** is structured along departments such as sales and billing. Work is organized by task and job similarity. The **process arrangement,** on the other hand, is organized by activities that provide value to the customer. As shown in Figure 12.3, order fulfillment is one business process, which includes receiving, processing, and shipping of customer orders. Under the functional arrangement, separate departments would be created for receiving, processing, and shipping orders.[33]

functional arrangement
The traditional arrangement of organizational structure that is organized by departments and work is organized by task and job similarity.
process arrangement
The arrangement of an organization that is organized by activities that provide value to the customer.

Because reengineering does not contain any specific guidelines that must be followed, a variety of changes may be implemented as part of this program. In many cases, work teams are introduced and the number of supervisors reduced. TQM practices may be adopted.[34]

Advantages and Disadvantages of Reengineering

Reengineering appears to have several advantages and disadvantages. In terms of its effectiveness, reengineering is a powerful tool, capable of vastly improving the organization. If reengineering is effective, a major advantage is that it will have a widespread impact. Unlike other organizational change efforts that often neglect to consider the implications for other aspects of the organization, reengineering emphasizes the need to modify the entire unit or organization. In turn, this may reduce subsequent problems that result from failure to consider the ramifications of any change program.[35]

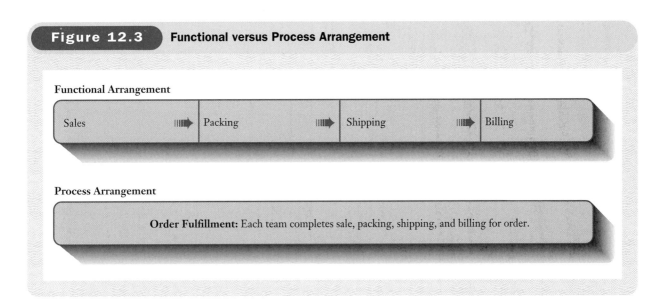

Figure 12.3 **Functional versus Process Arrangement**

Functional Arrangement

| Sales | ⮕ | Packing | ⮕ | Shipping | ⮕ | Billing |

Process Arrangement

Order Fulfillment: Each team completes sale, packing, shipping, and billing for order.

On the negative side, many companies have used consultants to help with the reengineering, which sometimes resulted in charges of as much as $250,000 each month. Experts recommended that between 20 percent to 50 percent of the CEO's time be devoted to the reengineering process. Clearly, reengineering can be an expensive procedure.[36] A second major problem with reengineering is that it can cause a great deal of upheaval and strife in the organization, particularly because reengineering efforts often have led to layoffs. In fact, popular media often have used the term *reengineering* synonymously with the word *layoff*. Reengineering, then, often has led to problems in employee morale, trust, and cooperation.[37] Even the proponents of reengineering estimate that the technique fails to achieve expected goals in at least 50 percent of cases.[38]

Although reengineering is no longer a fad as we move into the 21st century, the basic premise of reengineering—that functions can be completely redesigned—continues to attract interest. Although more frequently referred to today as "business-process redesign," or a similar term, organizations continue to redesign their basic functions and processes. The move to redesign basic processes in the last few years has been fueled by the growth of *enterprise resource planning (ERP)* software, such as *SAP*, that enables companies to integrate different databases. As a result of this potentially powerful tool, many large organizations are actually redesigning their work processes around the software they are implementing.[39] (This Web site offers more information on ERP implementation issues: www.datamation.com/PlugIn/erp/stories/survive. htm.) Also take a look at Box 12.4 for additional Web sites of interest in work redesign. Next, you will read about what is perhaps the most radical work redesign approach: the virtual organization.

The Virtual Organization

virtual organization
A network of companies or employees connected by computers.

The most recent approach to work design is the **virtual organization.** Consider, for example, ILAN Systems, a 5-year-old virtual computer-services business employing more than 50 people with nearly $6 million in sales. The corporate office operates out of Tom Reynold's 1,500-square-foot house. Tom is not the only person who works out of his house; in fact, all of the employees work out of their own homes or at their customers' facilities. Although ILAN is composed primarily of permanent employees, other virtual companies are comprised primarily of free-lance workers, who operate on a project basis from their own homes. Brian Goggin, who runs a small job-training and education business from a village in Ireland, is the owner of the latter type of virtual company. He has no permanent employees; instead, he contracts with freelance employees from Ireland, England, and the United States. He has never had a face-to-face meeting with some of the people he works most frequently with.[40] (For an interesting example of a virtual contract employer, see this Web site: http://www.willowcsn.com.)

With these two examples in mind, how would you define a "virtual organization?" The answer is not simple. One reasonably simple definition of a virtual organization is a network of companies or employees that are connected by computers or similar technology to perform work.[41] With this definition in mind, why do you think virtual organizations are becoming more common? Experts say that virtual organizations have become more common for three reasons:

1. Current technologies, especially e-mail, and the capacity to quickly and easily transmit video, audio, and text information;
2. Widespread use of computer networks throughout the world;
3. The growth of telecommuting.[42]

Challenges in Creating a Virtual Workforce

Creating and maintaining a virtual workforce is a major undertaking, especially if the organization is changing from a traditional structure. Oticon, a hearing aid manufacturer based in Denmark, went through that process in an effort to improve productivity. An organization faces the following challenges in this case:[43]

1. Employees may experience many more assignments than in a traditional structure where they meet face to face;
2. Employees are likely to work with individuals from functional areas and locations they have never worked with before;
3. Employees' roles will change much more rapidly than in a traditional organizational structure;
4. Employees must learn new ways to interact and communicate particularly because face-to-face meetings are rarely possible;
5. Employees often must learn to interact with colleagues from different cultures;
6. Employees must become proficient with new and constantly changing technologies.

All of the challenges listed above mean that managers and leaders in a virtual organization play an important role in the success of the business. To be successful, managers and leaders must do the following:[44]

1. **Establish Clear Expectations and Criteria for Evaluation.** Although having a "virtual" operation may seem to make it harder to monitor performance, in many cases, it may be easier. For example, many technologies allow for the recording of interactions, thus enabling managers to review virtual meetings and monitor effectiveness.
2. **Develop and Maintain Technology.** The leaders of the organization must stay abreast of new developments and technology and be prepared to adopt new technologies. For example, Desktop Videoconferencing Systems (DVCS) enables

members of the organization to communicate together in such a way that it simulates a face-to-face meeting.

3. **Develop and Maintain Organizational Structure and Members.** In a virtual organization, employees interact in ways similar to a team. But a virtual organization is more than just a traditional work team. First, the technology required to be an effective organizational member is far more complex. Second, unlike a traditional work team, where there can be a great deal of opportunity to get to know one another, in a virtual system, teams will rapidly develop, with little or no time to socialize.

4. **Address Unique Challenges and Obstacles.** It won't surprise you that a virtual organization has some common issues that must be addressed, including fear of technology in some employees, increased trust and cohesion issues, and the potential for increased stress due to more assignments.

The Role of Human Resources in a Virtual Organization

The human resource function plays a critical role in any work redesign program. But this role becomes even more vital in a virtual organization. The human resource function can do the following in this situation:[45]

1. **Psychological Fit.** Determine the psychological fit between different units of the virtual organization. Before creating new business partnerships, HR should assess psychological fit. While psychological differences can present problems in a traditional organization, they can be amplified in a virtual organization, due to the lack of face-to-face interaction.

2. **System Alignment.** Given the lack of physical proximity, it becomes even more critical that the organization's mission, vision, and measures (see Chapter 3) be aligned and that all parties are familiar with these considerations. The HR function can play an important part in this task.

3. **Reconsider Rewards.** A virtual organization is likely to have fewer permanent, full-time employees. In many cases, the organization will be staffed with workers having different motivational forces. In that case, it becomes even more important that every entity is rewarded in an effective way.

4. **Reconsider Staffing Needs.** The virtual organization operates in a different way from a traditional organization. In the virtual organization, many of the employees work on a contractual basis. The concepts "recruitment" and "selection" become quite different in this scenario, as do concepts such as "career advancement." The human resource function operates as more of a talent scout. What may once have been an obstacle to hiring someone (for example, an applicant refusing to relocate) may today be an irrelevant factor.

5. **Build Partnerships.** In the virtual organization, the concept of employment changes. In its place is the concept of "partnership." Trust and respect become far more important, especially as the "partners" work largely independently and physically removed from the "permanent" employees or owners of the organization.

6. **Develop Leaders.** Leadership becomes increasingly important in the virtual organization. Leaders become the major forces for building trust, creating a mission, and instilling a sense of belonging to the organization. The HR function can play an important role in ensuring that leaders take on these responsibilities and meet them in an effective way.

Advantages and Disadvantages of a Virtual Organization

What about the advantages and disadvantages of a virtual organization? It is really much too early to tell. However, it would seem that the virtual organization allows for a great deal of flexibility and potential reduction in costs (for example, the company no longer needs a physical location). On the negative side, there may be problems of cohesion and lack of direction for employees.

Is Work Redesign the Answer?

Now that you have read about various work design programs, you may be wondering whether work redesign can solve all of your organization's problems. The answer is, of course, that work redesign is not always the solution to problems within your organization. Before you recommend such a program, consider the following points.[46]

1. **Is There Sufficient Reason to Believe that the Work Design Program Will Accomplish Its Objectives?** A top executive or manager may sometimes suggest implementation of a work redesign program simply because he or she attended a seminar or read an article, without consideration of the appropriateness of this change. This is particularly problematic with a fad, as many companies feel compelled to keep up with the "corporate Joneses." Obviously, this is not a good reason for implementing a work design program. Existing problems may be better solved through other means, such as fixing faulty equipment, improving supervision, or providing increased technical training. If the actual sources of problems lie in some of these areas, work design programs may merely create more problems than solutions.

2. **Will Employees Be Able to Adapt?** Even if a work design program appears appropriate, the organization must consider employees' readiness for change. Employees may not be ready for change for several reasons. First, employees may not have the competencies necessary to perform the new tasks. To deal with this issue, the organization must provide extensive training for employees. But not all employees will be able to learn the new skills. One organization, for example, found that 5 percent of the employees could not perform the newly designed jobs, even with the appropriate training. The organization must decide what to do with those employees.

   Not all employees desire work involving greater autonomy and control that characterizes many of the work redesign programs. Some employees actually prefer simple, routine work, and they will be unhappy having to make many of the decisions traditionally made by the supervisor. You will need to consider, then, whether the employees will be less satisfied and motivated in their newly designed jobs.

   Finally, it is important to consider whether middle-level managers and supervisors can adapt to the new system. In many cases, it is these employees who are most resistant to change, because in many cases they will lose their authority and control, if not their jobs. Many supervisors and managers have trouble adjusting to the new and quite different tasks and responsibilities that come with the work team, TQM, or the virtual organization.

3. **Are Organizational Practices, Policies, and Culture Compatible with the Program?** Even if employees have the requisite skills and interest, organizational

practices, policies, and culture may create barriers to work redesign. Existing technology may hamper or even preclude programs such as the work team. Particularly in a union environment, where such things as job descriptions are determined through contract negotiation, any work redesign program may create conflict and tension. Finally, various organizational control systems may be dramatically affected by work redesign. Consider, for example, the accounting system that existed in the purchasing department of one large organization. In order to maintain close financial controls, employees were greatly limited in their interactions with vendors. The purpose of these regulations was to reduce opportunities for theft and other dishonest behavior. Introduction of work redesign programs may have interfered with these controls. In short, it is important to think carefully before recommending a work redesign program. Although these techniques can improve productivity as well as employee satisfaction and morale, there is no guarantee they will work.

❖ Conclusion

We have discussed many different work design systems, ranging from the classical approach to the virtual organization. As you read, there is no one best approach to work design. Each of the approaches has both advantages and disadvantages. Some of the approaches involve few changes in existing norms, technology, and human resource practices, while other approaches require significant modifications in these areas. Before an organization embarks on a redesign program, it must consider whether this is the most appropriate improvement technique, whether employees can adapt, and whether the organizational practices, policies, and culture are compatible with the intended work redesign. If the answer is no to any of these issues, caution is recommended. Finally, while some of these work redesign programs may be fads, they have left their mark on workplace practices for many years to come.

❖ Applying Core Concepts

1. Think of a job you have had, or ask a friend to describe a job he or she has had. What type of work design did this job have?
2. Review the job and organization described in the opening case. How appropriate would each of the following work redesign approaches have been: job enlargement, job enrichment, quality circles, team concept, total quality management, reengineering, and a virtual organization? If you were the manager in charge, which work redesign program would you have chosen? Why?
3. Describe some of the responsibilities and tasks for the human resource function in the opening case if Myra's Mystery decides to implement a total quality management program.
4. Do you think a work redesign approach would have solved the problems described in the opening case? Why or why not?
5. How do you think a work team approach would affect your job if you were Fiona's supervisor at Myra's Mystery? What would you do as the supervisor to adjust to these changes?

6. Consider the company you work for now or one you hope to work for in the future. Would it be a virtual organization? Why or why not? What if the company decided to "go virtual?" How might that affect you and your career?

❖ Key Terms

Scientific management	Work team	Functional arrangement
Employee empowerment	Total quality management	Process arrangement
Job enlargement	(TQM)	Virtual organization
Job enrichment	Continuous improvement	
Quality circle	Reengineering	

❖ CHAPTER 12 *Experiential Exercise 1*

G. G. Games

G. G. Games (GGG) is a toy manufacturer that has been in business for 95 years. It is known for high-quality, innovative board games that are sold primarily for age groups 10 years and up, including adults. Some of the more popular games produced by GGG (of which you may not be familiar), include King Tut's Tomb, Squeeze Play, and Shuckle-Mania. GGG is composed of the traditional functional areas, including marketing, sales, manufacturing, human resources, and accounting, as well as product development. The issue that you are addressing is the product development group, which is responsible for design of new games. Product development is critical for GGG because consumers are always seeking new games to purchase. In fact, new products create almost one-fourth of GGG's sales in any given year.

The product development group at GGG has traditionally been quite different from the other areas in many ways. The product development group is composed of 25 employees, including a vice president, 2 managers, 2 administrative assistants, and 20 "creative types" (included in the creative types are 4 design artists). Unlike other professional employees, who typically come to work in business attire, the product development employees make a point of only working in casual clothing (typically, jeans and a T-shirt). Second, the product development group works with a minimal amount of interaction with other employees. In fact, their office is located quite some distance from the two GGG factories and the corporate office. Third, this group works in almost complete secrecy; only the CEO and president of GGG are allowed to attend its meetings. As a result of the secrecy, the product devel-

opment group has been nicknamed the PIA (product development intelligence agency), after the CIA. Fourth, the product development group members never attend company functions, including the annual picnic. Fifth, the product development group makes a point of ignoring any feedback or suggestions from other employees. In fact, this has recently led to problems with quality, because the design of one of the games was so intricate, that production made the pieces with numerous errors. As a result, most employees avoid the product development employees and consider them to be arrogant snobs. The president and CEO, however, have a strong background in product development and view this group as extremely important to the success of GGG. Of course, the product development employees recognize this special relationship and work hard to maintain the good will of the president and CEO.

The product development group operates in the following way. Group members are responsible for different types of games (for example, educational, specialized, adult). Using a variety of sources, members continuously research and investigate new ideas. Once a month, the entire group meets to discuss new ideas. Decisions are made about the most promising ideas, and small committees are formed to develop the ideas further. The committees' ideas are then reviewed, and further decisions are made. Ultimately, the project group develops a lengthy proposal, including sample pieces, which is approved by the vice president of product development. This vice president must then present the ideas to the CEO and other top executives of the company, who must ultimately approve a project. From there, the project is taken to marketing and production, who offer new suggestions, and sometimes require major modifications that consume considerable time. Before production, the CEO must make final approval.

Last week, the president of GGG suggested that changes must be made in how the product development group operates. One of the reasons for this change, she noted, is that other companies are significantly decreasing the lag time between design and production. GGG's lag time apparently is one of the longest in the business now. A second problem is that recent new products have created problems at the production stage. This in turn has led to further delays and in some cases, defective products.

You should take the role of the vice president of human resources, and discuss how you will restructure the product development group to address the two problems mentioned above. Be sure to indicate what problems your proposal may encounter and how you will address those problems. Be sure to incorporate issues and solutions from this chapter as well as other chapters in this book (for example, pay for performance, performance management).

❖ CHAPTER 12 *Experiential Exercise 2*

What's Up with the MN-12?!

As labor relations supervisor in the Detroit Frame Plant, you have been given a substantial amount of responsibility for establishing a team of employees that will produce a subframe for one your company's new products. The new product is referred to by its technical designation, MN-12. Employees will produce the subframe for the MN-12 using new production technology for which the company has spent a great deal of money to acquire.

The workforce in your plant is unionized, and you have been through many hours of negotiation with the union about how to implement the team concept in the MN-12 area without threatening the union. The employees who will produce the subframe have bid into the positions, meaning they self-selected for the MN-12 work team in accordance with the existing union contract, based on seniority and an acceptable performance record.

In preparation for their new role, employees selected to produce the subframe were given a great deal of training on subjects that included teamwork, the plant's organizational structure, and how to operate the new production technology. They also traveled to another plant to see how the MN-12 subframe fits into the final product and why it was essential that their output meets exacting standards. You feel that these employees have been given a great deal of attention and training and have a chance to be part of an exciting experiment with work teams in a unionized setting. The rest of the plant will continue to operate in the tradi-

tional fashion, with employees reporting to foremen who will direct their efforts. Therefore, you were both surprised and dismayed when you received a list today (shown below) of concerns and problems from the MN-12 employees. In two weeks the MN-12 line is scheduled to go into full production, and you aren't in the mood for any nonsense. To make things more complicated, any decisions that affect the "terms or conditions" of work on the MN-12 line, such as job rotation, *must* be approved by the union.

Perusing the list, your first reaction is that the MN-12 employees are acting like over-indulged children. As you continue to study the list, however, you see that many of the issues are legitimate and need to be addressed. Still, though, you are disappointed that the employees aren't acting with enough initiative to at least offer suggestions about how they want to handle issues such as how to replace each other for restroom breaks. And item 15 on the list makes you downright mad. Although employees working on the MN-12 won't have a traditional supervisor, they will have a resource person who will act as the team's facilitator, helping them succeed. The person selected by management for this role is Margie Bayne, the only female production supervisor in the plant. Although Margie's job performance among the plant's supervisors is middling, management wants to try her out in this new role because they believe she will be best able to adapt to the new role of resource person. You suspect that the team's objection to having Margie as their facilitator is based on prejudice against women (none of the MN-12 team members are women), but you have no way of knowing this only from reading the list of concerns and problems.

After reading the list you sit and think about what to do. First, you try to manage your emotions, which at the present are a mixture of disappointment, concern, and irritation. You're also beginning to wonder if the team concept is going to work in your plant. You decide to take a lunch break a little early today and come back to the list in—you hope—a better frame of mind.

Instructions

1. Organize the concerns and problems raised by the MN-12 team members into groupings of similar items. Create a descriptive label for each of these groupings.
2. For each grouping you arrived at, list general approaches you will use to begin to address that group of problems or concerns.
3. You want the team members to become more adept at solving their own problems and exercising initiative (within the bounds of the union contract, of course). What actions could be taken to achieve this aim?
4. Item 15 is a serious one. On one hand, in no way do you want the team members dictating who will be their resource person. On the other hand you want the team to succeed, and if they harbor ill feelings toward their resource person, this could cause problems. You also worry about potential effects on Margie Bayne. Pulling her off the MN-12 could damage her self-esteem, but if you leave her on the MN-12 you may be sending her into a hostile environment. What set actions would you take to deal with item 15?

MN-12 Team Members' Concerns and Problems

1. Why gauges are not the same when subassembly is completed?
2. How often will team members be allowed to hold problem-solving meetings?
3. How much time will be allowed for each meeting?
4. Will team members be utilized first for scheduling overtime?
5. Will team members be allowed to have personal time off if notified in advance with no problem?
6. Fans and mats for floor?
7. Location of water fountains?
8. Job rotation?
9. How will we replace each other for use of the restroom?
10. How will we make up group? In what way will this take place?
11. The work load of the leader? How will he be selected?
12. Will team members be able to utilize everything we were trained for?
13. How will our breaks be organized? Will team members be allowed to set up breaks? Will everyone break at same time?
14. Will there be a relief-man?
15. We don't want Margie Bayne for a resource person, not even for a little while.
16. Why are skilled trades not a part of the natural work team?
17. Will seniority play a role in job placement?
18. Other workers on MN-12 should have same team concept and training, to avoid conflict.

(Note: this case was developed and written by Brad Gilbreath.)

❖ Chapter 12 References

1. R. Griffin, *Task Design: An Integrative Approach* (Glenview, IL: Scott, Foresman, 1982).
2. M. Williams, "Back to the Past," *Wall Street Journal*, 24 October 1994, A1, A4.
3. Griffin, *Task Design*.
4. M. Campion and C. McClelland, "Follow-up and Extension of the Interdisciplinary Costs and Benefits of Enlarged Jobs," *Journal of Applied Psychology* 78 (1993): 339–51.
5. Griffin, *Task Design*.

6. J. Campbell and R. Pritchard, "Motivation Theory in Industrial and Organizational Psychology," in *Handbook of Industrial and Organizational Psychology*, ed. M. Dunnette (Chicago: Rand McNally, 1976).

7. Griffin, *Task Design*.

8. J. R. Hackman and G. R. Oldham, *Work Redesign* (Reading, MA: Addison-Wesley, 1980).

9. R. Guzzo, R. Jette, and R. Katzell. "Effects of Psychologically Based Intervention Programs on Worker Productivity: A Meta-analysis," *Personnel Psychology* 38 (1985): 275–91.

10. D. Katz and R. Kahn, *The Social Psychology of Organizations* (New York: Wiley, 1978).

11. W. Mohr and H. Mohr, *Quality Circles* (Reading, MA: Addison-Wesley, 1983).

12. B. Dumaine, "The Trouble with Teams," *Fortune*, 5 September 1994, 86–92.

13. Ibid.

14. R. Guzzo and G. Shea, "Group Performance and Intergroup Relations in Organizations," in *Handbook of Industrial and Organizational Psychology*, vol. 3, ed. M. Dunnette and L. Hough (Palo Alto, CA: Consulting Psychologists Press, 1992).

15. R. Griffin, "Consequences of Quality Circles in an Industrial Setting: A Longitudinal Assessment," *Academy of Management Journal* 31 (1988): 338–58.

16. J. Case, "When Teamwork Is Un-American," *Inc.* (November 1993): 29–30.

17. Dumaine, "The Trouble with Teams."

18. E. Aranda, L. Aranda, and K. Conlon, *Teams: Structure, Process, Culture, and Politics* (Upper Saddle River, NJ: Prentice-Hall, 1998).

19. Ibid.

20. Dumaine, "The Trouble with Teams."

21. F. Bleakley, "How an Outdated Plant Was Made New," *Wall Street Journal*, 21 October 1994, B1, B11.

22. Dumaine, "The Trouble with Teams."

23. B. Spencer, "Models of Organization and Total Quality Management: A Comparison and Critical Evaluation," *Academy of Management Review* 19 (1994): 446–71; and H. Costin, *Management Development and Training: A TQM Approach* (Fort Worth, TX: Dryden, 1996).

24. R. Schuler and D. Harris, "Deming Quality Improvement: Implications for Human Resource Management as Illustrated in a Small Company," *Human Resource Planning* 14 (1991): 191–207.

25. G. Dobbins, R. Cardy, and K. Carson, "Examining Fundamental Assumptions: A Contrast of Person and System Approaches to Human Resource Management," in *Research in Personnel/Human Resource Management*, ed. G. Ferris and K. Rowland (Greenwich, CT: JAI Press, 1991).

26. R. Krishnan, A. Shani, R. Grant, and R. Baer, "In Search of Quality Improvement: Problems of Design and Implementation," *Academy of Management Executive* 7 (1993): 7–20.

27. R. Hill, "When the Going Gets Rough: A Baldrige Award Winner on the Line," *Academy of Management Executive* 7 (1993), 75–79.

28. R. Chang, "TQM Goes Nowhere," *Training & Development* 47 (1993): 22–29; and J. Dean and D. Bowen, "Management Theory and Total Quality: Improving Research and Practice through Theory Development," *Academy of Management Review* 19 (1994): 392–418.

29. W. Lee, "Deming's Not for Us," *Wall Street Journal*, 31 January 1994, A12.

30. "The Promise of Reengineering," *Fortune*, 3 May 1994, 94–97.

31. D. Rigby, "What's Today's Special at the Consultants' Café?" *Fortune*, 7 September 1998, 162-163.

32. Greengard, "Reengineering: Out of the Rubble," *Personnel Journal* 72 (1993): 48A–48O.

33. M. Hammer and J. Champy, *Reengineering the Corporation: A Manifesto for Business Revolution* (New York: HarperCollins, 1993).

34. T. Steward, "Reengineering: The Hot New Managing Tool," *Fortune*, 23 August 1994, 41–48.

35. Hammer and Champy, *Reengineering the Corporation*.

36. Ibid.

37. Rigby, "What's Today's Special."

38. Hammer and Champy, *Reengineering the Corporation.*
39. D. Kirkpatrick, "The E-Ware War: Competition Comes to Enterprise Software," *Fortune,* 7 December 1998, 102–12.
40. S. Silverstein, "The Cutting Edge," *Los Angeles Times,* 16 June 1997, D1.
41. J. Coyle and N. Schnarr, "The Soft-Side Challenges of the "Virtual Corporation," *Human Resource Planning* 1 (1995): 41–42.
42. R. Barner, "The New Millennium Workplace: Seven Changes That Will Challenge Managers—and Workers," *Futurist* (March/April 1996): 14–18.
43. A. Townsend, S. DeMarie, and A. Hendrickson, "Virtual Teams: Technology and the Workplace of the Future," *Academy of Management Executive* (August 1998): 17–29.
44. Ibid.
45. Coyle and Schnarr "Soft-side Challenges."
46. J. D. Osburn, L. Morgan, and E. Musselwhite, with C. Perrin, *Self-Directed Work Teams: The New American Challenge* (Homewood, IL: Irwin, 1990); and Hackman and Oldham, *Work Redesign.*

Chapter 13

Safety and Health

After reading this chapter, you should be capable of:

1. Understanding the Occupational Safety and Health Act of 1970 and what it covers.
2. Explaining the four approaches companies have used to reduce workplace accidents.
3. Discussing current safety and health issues in the workplace.
4. Offering suggestions as to how organizations can improve safety and health in the workplace.

Opening Case

Poultry plants constitute one of the fastest-growing industries in the United States today, employing more than 200,000 workers nationwide. In some small towns, the poultry plant is one of the few employers offering full-time jobs that pay above minimum wage. Although these businesses offer many job opportunities, critics feel that poultry plants take advantage of workers and contain dangerous, demeaning work. The typical poultry plant hires workers to perform a variety of tasks, ranging from preparing the birds for slaughter to removing the feathers to packing the processed parts into cardboard containers for shipment. All of these tasks have their own unique dangers and difficulties. For example, after the birds are slaughtered and plucked, mostly by machines, workers must remove the poultry's limbs and organs. In many plants, however, the workers are closely grouped together and work with sharp knives and tools. The opportunity for accidental cuts is always present.

Packing the poultry presents different problems for workers. At one plant, workers must lift at least 12 five-pound boxes per minute and place them into a larger container. This means that each worker must lift 3,600 pounds per hour each workday. In a typical poultry plant all workers face conditions that include cold temperatures throughout most of the plant, slippery floors, poor sanitary conditions, and extremely fast-paced work.

Critics also charge that workers have little or no freedom in most poultry plants. A commonly cited problem is that workers are required to ask supervisors for permission to use the restroom. Without permission, a worker who leaves to use the bathroom can be dismissed. Industry spokespeople defend the conditions by acknowledging that the work is dirty and demanding. In light of the nature of the job, they maintain that they are doing everything they can do to ensure safety and health standards. Most of the workers who are employed at these plants have little formal education, and the plants have high turnover rates. A growing number of poultry plant workers are illegal immigrants and worry about being caught.[1]

Do you wonder whether any laws protect workers from safety hazards such as those that seem to exist in poultry plants? Might there be steps companies can take to decrease accidents?

This chapter addresses safety and health issues as they may affect workers' physical and mental well-being in the workplace. As you will learn, companies are legally required to protect workers from many safety and health hazards in the workplace. Some companies have gone beyond legal requirements and provide additional programs and practices to improve employee safety and health on the job. These, and related issues, are addressed in this chapter. First, you will read about the laws that govern safety and health in the workplace, followed by a discussion of organizational programs for reducing workplace accidents. The third section of this chapter addresses current issues in workplace safety and health, including violence, lower-back-pain ailments, drug and alcohol use, psychological stress, and indoor pollution.

The Law and Workplace Safety and Health

Occupational Safety and Health Act of 1970: An Introduction

Congress passed the **Occupational Safety and Health (OSH) Act of 1970** after a great deal of deliberation and discussion. The basic purpose of this law was to reduce the high rate of workplace accidents, injuries, and deaths in the United States. At the time the OSH Act passed, it was estimated that more than 2 million workers became disabled from workplace accidents in the United States annually, and almost 15,000

Occupational Safety and Health (OSH) Act of 1970
Passed by Congress in 1970, the purpose of this law was to reduce the high rate of workplace accidents, injuries, and deaths in the United States.

U.S. employees died from work-related accidents each year. In addition, it was estimated that workplace accidents and safety hazards resulted in billions of dollars lost in medical costs, time off from work, and related expenses.[2]

While the OSH Act is quite complex, it contains four basic provisions:

1. The duty to maintain a workplace that is safe and healthful for employees
2. The duty to comply with specific standards
3. Record-keeping and reporting obligations
4. A mandate for various regulatory agencies

Each of these provisions, along with their implications for you as an employee, is discussed next.

Maintaining a Safe and Healthful Workplace: Your Employer's Basic Obligation

The OSH Act basically requires your employer to do the following:[3]

1. Comply with basic safety regulations
2. Eliminate hazards to safety and health

The OSH Act covers most private-sector businesses in the United States, including all 50 states as well as the District of Columbia, Puerto Rico, and U.S. territories. Unlike many of the employment discrimination laws that you read about in other chapters, this act is not affected by the size of the company. Even a company with two employees is covered by the OSH Act.[4] Box 13.1 discusses your workplace rights as an employee.

The only organizations excluded from OSH Act coverage are as follows:[5]

1. Self-employed workers
2. Farms that employ only immediate members of the farmer's family
3. Businesses covered by other federal agencies' health and safety rules
4. Federal, state, and local government employees

Clearly, then, nearly all private-sector employees are covered by the OSH Act. Government employees are not covered.

Several entities were created to administer and oversee the OSH Act. The **Occupational Safety and Health Administration (OSHA),** a branch of the U.S. Department of Labor, is the major agency. OSHA has four main responsibilities:[6]

1. Establishing safety standards
2. Permitting variances, or exceptions, to those standards
3. Inspecting workplaces
4. Issuing citations, indicating a violation of OSH Act regulations

Two other relevant entities are the **Occupational Safety and Health Review Commission (OSHRC)** and the **National Institute for Occupational Safety and Health (NIOSH).** The purpose of the OSHRC is to review appeals from companies that have been issued a citation by OSHA. NIOSH provides research and training support for OSHA. The research performed by NIOSH focuses on developing new safety and health standards; the training is for OSHA inspectors and other staff involved with OSH Act enforcement.

Occupational Safety and Health Administration (OSHA)
The major agency created to administer and oversee the OSH Act, including establishing safety standards, permitting variances (exceptions) to those standards, conducting inspections of workplaces, and issuing citations to indicate a violation of OSH Act regulations.

Occupational Safety and Health Review Commission (OSHRC)
The purpose of the OSHRC is to review appeals from companies that have been issued a citation by OSHA.

National Institute for Occupational Safety and Health (NIOSH)
NIOSH provides research and training support for OSHA. The research focuses on developing new safety and health standards; the training is for OSHA inspectors and other staff involved with OSH Act enforcement.

YOUR TURN

Box 13.1
Workplace Facilities: Your Rights as an Employee

The OSH Act provides basic laws that apply to workplace facilities. Failure to follow these regulations may be a violation of the OSH Act. The following is only a partial list of an employer's obligations. Does your current employer provide all of these features?

1. **Cleanliness.** The workplace must be kept as clean and neat as permitted by the nature of the work (a poultry plant cannot be expected to be kept as clean as a clothing store). Restrooms and water fountains should be cleaned regularly. Does your company appear to meet this standard?
2. **Toilets.** The company must provide separate toilets for men and women, unless the toilet can be locked from inside and used only by one person at a time. A formula for calculating the number of toilets that must be provided depends on the number of employees. Both hot and cold water must be available in the restroom. Does your current employer provide these?
3. **Temperature.** Comfortable temperatures must be maintained in the facility, though the act does not define precisely what that temperature is. It is understood to be a temperature that would not adversely affect workers' health or safety. Recall in the opening case that poultry plants are generally cold environments; however, they appear to meet legal regulations in this regard.
4. **Noise.** Certain noise levels may not be exceeded. Employees must be provided with protective equipment and occasionally tested for hearing impairment when noise levels exceed 85 decibels for more than eight hours.
5. **First Aid.** At a minimum, first aid equipment must be available at the facility. Moreover, medical care must be available within a reasonable distance of the workplace, or someone trained in first aid must be at the facility, or a doctor must be available when needed.
6. **Fire Equipment.** In addition to having an emergency fire prevention plan, the company must have an evacuation plan, an alarm system, and appropriate types of fire extinguishers.
7. **Food Service.** Food service areas must be hygienic; food must be unspoiled and properly prepared and stored.

Source: Adapted from L. Joel, *Every Employee's Guide to the Law* (New York: Pantheon, 1993).

Depending on the nature of the business, your employer must follow either the guidelines that have been developed for the industry or the OSH Act's **General Duty Clause,** which requires compliance with basic standards and makes the employer responsible for providing a workplace that is free from recognized safety and health hazards.[7]

General Duty Clause
OSHA guidelines that require compliance with basic standards, as well as the responsibility of providing a workplace that is free from recognized safety and health hazards.

Complying with Specific Standards

Safe-use standards have been developed for some industries and for many types of materials. One industry for which there are specific standards is the construction industry. Many materials are also covered by standards for safe use issued by OSHA, including electrical systems, asbestos, lead, and blood-borne pathogens. Each of these standards is described in documents available from the Government Printing Office, located in Washington, D.C. These documents are lengthy and difficult to understand, yet knowing their contents is critical for avoiding OSHA citations. Organizations such as the National Safety Council offer workshops in understanding these laws.[8]

Recall the opening case involving a poultry plant. Do you think that OSHA has developed specific standards for this industry? If you answered no, you are right. Critics maintain that standards for the poultry industry should be developed. But poultry plants still have to obey rules specific to the equipment they use. For example, one plant was fined for having an exposed piece of equipment that caused serious injury to a worker's legs. Other plants have been fined for failure to provide proper fire safety, as well as other violations. Some critics maintain that poultry plants would be much safer if industry-specific standards were developed.[9] Box 13.2 examines the likelihood of injury in small and large workplaces.

A related regulation, the **Hazard Communication Standard of 1985,** covers all hazardous chemicals. As of 1987, companies covered by the OSH Act must meet the requirements of the Hazard Communication Standard. Specific details of this law are discussed in the next section.

Record-Keeping and Reporting Obligations

As with most laws, the OSH Act requires extensive record keeping and reporting. The basic record-keeping and reporting obligations are as follows:[10]

1. A listing of work-related injuries and illnesses **(OSHA form No. 200)**
2. Records of work-related injuries and illnesses **(OSHA form No. 101)**
3. Various right-to-know information
4. Other items

OSHA Form No. 200. This form, shown in Figure 13.1, must be used by most employers with more than ten workers (certain industries, such as retailers, are not required to keep these forms). The company must complete this form by recording information about workers who are injured or become ill as a result of the job and if the injury or illness resulted in death, days off from work, transfer, termination, medical treatment, unconsciousness, or work or motion restrictions. This information must be summarized and posted by February 1 of each year. Employees, former employees, and OSHA officials must also be allowed access to the form.

OSHA Form No. 101. Employers who use Form No. 200 must also complete this form. Form No. 101 requires detailed information about work-related injuries and illnesses, including the circumstances of the incident, a description of the injury or illness, and the name of the doctor and hospital that provided treatment.

Various Right-to-Know Information. Many other important laws and regulations give you, the employee, the right to be notified of possible safety and health issues. One of the most important of these, the Hazard Communication Standard of 1985, requires companies to provide their employees with information concerning hazardous chemicals. The law requires companies to provide this information through several means:

■ Material safety data sheets, which are developed by the manufacturers of the chemicals. These forms describe the properties of the chemicals, indicate the proper means of using them, and offer medical advice if workers are exposed to the chemicals;
■ Employee training on how to interpret the material safety sheets, how to identify when the chemical is being improperly stored or exposed, and related safety measures;
■ Proper labeling of the chemicals.

Hazard Communication Standard of 1985
A regulation that covers all hazardous chemicals. As of 1987, companies covered by the OSH Act must meet the requirements of the Hazard Communication Standard.

OSHA Form No. 200
This form must be used by most employers with more than ten workers. The form records information about workers who are injured or become ill as a result of the job and if the injury or illness resulted in death, days off from work, transfer, termination, medical treatment, unconsciousness, or work and motion restrictions.

OSHA Form No. 101
Employees who use Form No. 200 must also complete this form, which requires detailed information about work-related injuries and illnesses, including the circumstances of the incident, a description of the injury or illness, and the name of the doctor and hospital that provided treatment.

TALES FROM THE TRENCHES

Box 13.2
Are You More Likely to be Injured at a Small Company or a Big Company?

Obviously, a production factory is going to have more accidents than a securities firm. But what about small companies compared to large companies? Does the company's size affect the number of accidents that occur? The answer appears to be yes. Smaller companies appear to have a much higher accident rate than bigger companies. From 1988 to 1992, more than 4,000 workers died at companies with fewer than 20 employees. During the same period of time, only 127 employees died at companies with more than 2,500 workers. Taking into account the differential size of the workforce, there were 1.97 deaths per thousand workers at small companies and .004 deaths per thousand workers at large companies.

Why the great difference in the number of job-related deaths in small as compared to large companies? There are a number of explanations. First, small businesses generally have fewer resources to deal with safety issues. One person may be responsible for human resources, safety, and general administration issues in a small company. In a large firm, several staff members may specialize in the safety area. Small companies also face greater business competition. Renaissance Metals, for example, a small metal refinishing company, routinely violates OSHA rules by failing to remove elevator doors. But removing the doors would cost the company anywhere between $300 and $1,600, when the company only charges $500 for the entire job. As the owner explained, being required to remove the doors would mean other companies who did not remove the doors would simply get the business instead. Many small businesses only survive because they keep their costs down, which may include neglecting certain safety standards.

Another factor that accounts for the higher death rate at small companies is the limited attention OSHA gives to these businesses. Because certain small, low-hazard industries are exempt from some OSH Act regulations, and OSHA does not monitor smaller companies nearly as closely as it does larger ones, small companies are under less pressure to establish effective safety programs and practices. For example, after 56-year-old Ulysses Griffin died from severe silicosis (a disease of the lungs), it was found that the firm he worked for, Commercial Steel Treating Company, had failed to provide workers with proper information and equipment for working with silica dust.

The bottom line is that the risks of job-related accidents, illnesses, and death are higher at a small company than at a large company. The onus may be on you, the employee, to ensure that your company is complying with the relevant OSH Act laws.

Source: Adapted from B. Marsh, "Workers at Risk," *Wall Street Journal*, 3 February 1994, A1, A5.

This standard also requires that the employer develop a plan describing how these activities will be conducted.

In addition to the Hazard Communication Standard, your employer has other obligations to inform you of hazardous and toxic chemicals that are used or produced at the facility. For example, your employer must provide relevant information about health and safety hazards within a month after your employment starts or after you are transferred to a different job that involves exposure to additional substances. Your employer must also provide such information if you request it in writing.

Despite all of these obligations, many companies neglect to provide information. Poultry plants, like those described in the opening case, for example, have been accused of providing workers with little more than a brief lecture on hazardous chemicals and the problems they might cause.

Other Items. Your employer also is obligated to post copies of any citations issued by OSHA, as well as a copy of the OSHA Job Poster illustrated in Figure 13.2.

Figure 13.1 — OSHA 200 Log

Bureau of Labor Statistics
Log and Summary of Occupational
Injuries and Illnesses

| NOTE: | This form is required by Public Law 91-596 and must be kept in the establishment for 5 years. Failure to maintain and post can result in the issuance of citations and assessment of penalties. *(See posting requirements on the other side of form.)* | | | RECORDABLE CASES: You are required to record information about every occupational death; every nonfatal occupational illness; and those nonfatal occupational injuries which involve one or more of the following: loss of consciousness, restriction of work or motion, transfer to another job, or medical treatment (other than first aid). *(See definitions on the other side of form.)* |

Case or File Number	Date of Injury or Onset of Illness	Employee's Name	Occupation	Department	Description of injury or illness
Enter a nondupli-cating number which will facilitate comparisons with supple-mentary records.	Enter Mo./day.	Enter first name or initial, middle initial, last name.	Enter regular job title, not activity employee was performing when injured or at onset of illness. In the absence of a formal title, enter a brief description of the employee's duties.	Enter department in which the employee is regularly employed or a description of normal workplace to which employee is assigned, even though temporarily working in another department at the time of injury or illness.	Enter a brief description of the injury or illness and indicate the part or parts of body affected. Typical entries for this column might be Amputation of 1st joint right forefinger. Strain of lower back; Contact dermatitis on both hands. Electrocution—body
(A)	(B)	(C)	(D)	(E)	(F)

PREVIOUS PAGE TOTALS →

TOTALS (instructions on other side of form.) →

OSHA NO. 200

FOLD

Source: S. Kahn, B. Brown, and M. Lanzarone, *Legal Guide to Human Resources* (Boston: Warren, Gorham, and Lamont, 1995).

Figure 13.1 (continued)

U.S. Department of Labor

For Calendar Year 19 _____   Page ___ of___

Company Name	Form Approved O.M.B. No. 1220-0029
Establishment Name	
Establishment Address	

Extent of and Outcome of INJURY						Type, Extent of, and Outcome of ILLNESS													
Fatalities	Nonfatal injuries					Type of Illness								Fatalities	Nonfatal Illnesses				
Injury Related	Injuries With Lost Workdays				Injuries Without Lost Workdays	CHECK Only One Column for Each Illness (*See other side of form for terminations or permanent transfer.*)								Illness Related	Illnesses With Lost Workdays				Illnesses Without Lost Workdays
Enter DATE of death Mo./day/yr.	Enter a CHECK if injury involves days away from work, or days of restricted work activity, or both.	Enter a CHECK if injury involves days away from work.	Enter number of DAYS *away from work.*	Enter number of DAYS of *restricted work activity.*	Enter a CHECK if no entry was made in columns 1 or 2 but the injury is recordable as defined above.	Occupational skin diseases or disorders	Dust diseases of the lungs	Respiratory conditions due to toxic agents	Poisoning (systemic effects of toxic materials)	Disorders due to physical agents	Disorders associated with repeated trauma	All other occupational illnesses		Enter DATE of death. Mo./day/yr.	Enter a CHECK if Illness involves days away from work, or days of restricted work activity, or both.	Enter a CHECK if Illness involves days away from work.	Enter number of DAYS *away from work.*	Enter number of DAYS of *restricted work activity.*	Enter a CHECK if no entry was made in columns 8 or 9.
(1)	(2)	(3)	(4)	(5)	(6)	(a)	(b)	(c)	(d)	(e)	(f)	(g) (7)		(8)	(9)	(10)	(11)	(12)	(13)

Certification of Annual Summary Totals By _____ Title _____ Date _____

FOLD

OSHA NO. 200

POST ONLY THIS PORTION OF THE LAST PAGE NO LATER THAN FEBRUARY 1.

Figure 13.2 **OSHA Job Poster**
Job Safety and Health Protection

The Occupational Safety and Health Act of 1970 provides job safety and health protection for workers by promoting safe and healthful working conditions throughout the Nation. Provisions of the Act include the following:

Employers

All employers must furnish to employees employment and a place of employment free from recognized hazards that are causing or are likely to cause death or serious harm to employees. Employers must comply with occupational safety and health standards issues under the Act.

Employees

Employees must comply with all occupational safety and health standards, rules, regulations and orders issued under the Act that apply to their own actions and conduct on the job.

The Occupational Safety and Health Administration (OSHA) of the U.S. Department of Labor has the primary responsibility for administering the Act. OSHA issues occupational safety and health standards, and its Compliance Safety and Health Officers conduct jobsite inspections to help ensure compliance with the Act.

Inspection

The Act requires that a representative of the employer and a representative authorized by the employees be given an opportunity to accompany the OSHA Inspector for the purpose of aiding the inspection.

Where there is no authorized employee representative, the OSHA Compliance Officer must consult with a reasonable number of employees concerning safety and health conditions in the workplace.

Complaint

Employees or their representatives have the right to file a complaint with the nearest OSHA office requesting an inspection if they believe unsafe or unhealthful conditions exist in their workplace. OSHA will withhold, on request, names of employees complaining.

The Act provides that employees may not be discharged or discriminated against in any way for filing safety and health complaints or for otherwise exercising their rights under the Act.

Employees who believe they have been discriminated against may file a complaint with their nearest OSHA office within 30 days of the alleged discriminatory action.

Citation

If upon inspection OSHA believes an employer has violated the Act, a citation alleging such violations will be issued to the employer. Each citation will specify a time period within which the alleged violation must be corrected.

The OSHA citation must be prominently displayed at or near the place of alleged violation for three days, or until it is corrected, whichever is later, to warn employees of dangers that may exist there.

Proposed Penalty

The Act provides for mandatory civil penalties against employers of up to $7,000 for each serious violation and for optional penalties of up to $7,000 for each nonserious violation. Penalties of up to $7,000 per day may be proposed for failure to correct violations within the proposed time period and for each day the violation continues beyond the prescribed abatement date. Also, any employer who willfully or repeatedly violates the Act may be assessed penalties of up to $70,000 for each such violation. A minimum penalty of $5,000 may be imposed for each willful violation. A violation of posting requirements can bring a penalty of up to $7,000.

There are also provisions for criminal penalties. Any willful violation resulting in the death of any employee, upon conviction, is punishable by a fine of up to $250,000 (or $500,000 if the employer is a corporation), or by imprisonment for up to six months, or both. A second conviction of an employer doubles the possible term of imprisonment. Falsifying records, reports, or applications is punishable by a fine of $10,000 or up to six months in jail or both.

Voluntary Activity

While providing penalties for violations, the Act also encourages efforts by labor and management, before an OSHA Inspection, to reduce workplace hazards voluntarily and to develop and improve safety and health programs in all workplaces and industries. OSHA's Voluntary Protection Programs recognize outstanding efforts of this nature.

OSHA has published Safety and Health Program Management Guidelines to assist employers in establishing or perfecting programs to prevent or control employee exposure to workplace hazards. There are many public and private organizations that can provide information and assistance in this effort, if requested. Also, your local OSHA office can provide considerable help and advice on solving safety and health problems or can refer you to other sources for help such as training.

Consultation

Free assistance in identifying and correcting hazards and in improving safety and health management is available to employers, without citation or penalty, through OSHA-supported programs in each State. These programs are usually administered by the State Labor or Health department or a State University.

(continued)

Figure 13.2 (continued)

Posting Instructions

Employers in States operating OSHA approved State Plans should obtain and post the State's equivalent poster.

More Information

Additional information and copies of the Act, specific OSHA safety and health standards, and other applicable regulations may be obtained from your employer or from the nearest OSHA Regional Office in the following locations:	Atlanta, GA	(404) 347-3573
	Boston, MA	(617) 565-7164
	Chicago, IL	(312) 353-2220
	Dallas, TX	(214) 767-4731
	Denver, CO	(303) 844-3061
	Kansas City, MO	(816) 426-5861
	New York, NY	(212) 337-2378
	Philadelphia, PA	(215) 596-1201
	San Francisco, CA	(415) 744-6670
	Seattle, WA	(206) 442-5930

Under Provisions of Title 29, Code of Federal Regulations, Part 1903.2(a)(1) employers must post this notice (or facsimile) in a conspicuous place where notices to employees are customarily posted.

Washington, D.C.
1991 (Reprinted)
OSHA 2203

Lynn Martin

Lynn Martin, Secretary of Labor

U.S. Department of Labor
Occupational Safety and Health Administration

Mandate for Regulatory Agencies: OSHA's Activities

In addition to establishing safety standards, OSHA has two key enforcement responsibilities:[11]

1. Inspections.
2. Establishment of variances.

The Inspection. To enforce the OSH Act, OSHA relies heavily on the inspection of workplaces. An inspection is ordinarily not conducted unless it is chosen through random selection or an employee complaint. Unlike other agencies that must notify a business before they can inspect it, OSHA generally does not give any forewarning of an inspection. Rather, the OSHA inspector will simply arrive at the facility and request admission. After explaining why the facility was chosen, the purpose of the inspection, the standards likely to apply, and other relevant information, the inspector will conduct an initial exploration. Among the items the inspector will examine are OSHA Form No. 200, evidence regarding implementation of the Hazard Communication Standard program, and other safety and health practices. Generally, if the company's employee lost-workday rate appears below average and no employee complaints have been filed, a limited inspection will be conducted.

After the inspection, the area director of the OSHA office will determine what, if any, citations should be issued to the company. Any proposed citations must be provided to the company in writing. The company has a variety of opportunities to reduce or even eliminate the citations, through negotiation with OSHA, appeal to OSHRC, or ultimately suing through the federal court of appeals.

Variances. In certain cases, an employer may request either a temporary or permanent exception to an OSHA standard. For example, a company may wish to experiment with a new cover on a power machine, which would require them to deviate from the standards. Toward that end, the company would seek an **OSHA variance.** OSHA

OSHA variance
In certain cases, an employer may request either a temporary or permanent exception to an OSHA standard and must seek a variance. OSHA would inspect and possibly hold a hearing on the proposed deviation. If OSHA agrees to the modification, a variance would be granted, thus permitting this deviation.

would inspect and possibly hold a hearing on the proposed deviation. If OSHA agrees to the modification, a variance would be granted, thus permitting this deviation.

In sum, myriad laws promote safety and health in the workplace. In addition to the legal requirements, the financial costs associated with injury, illness, and deaths, as well as the moral and ethical implications, have led companies to develop a variety of programs and policies to lower the rate of workplace accidents. Some of these practices are discussed next.

Company Efforts to Reduce Workplace Accidents

Companies' efforts to reduce workplace accidents may be organized into four categories:

1. Empowering employees
2. Rewarding employees
3. Training employees
4. Testing employees

Empowering Employees

In keeping with current trends in employee empowerment (see Chapter 12), many companies are granting employees the authority to improve safety in the workplace. State Fair Foods, a division of Sara Lee Corporation, instituted employee safety teams in its burrito and corn dog manufacturing plant. The teams have permission to correct safety problems immediately, without obtaining approval from management. The teams found that the major contributors to workplace accidents were relatively minor items, such as slippery floors and poor lighting. Within two years of implementation, almost 70 percent of the employees had participated on a safety team. Norfolk Southern Railroad implemented a similar program. In addition, the company moved more than half of its corporate safety employees to the operating divisions so that they could work more closely with the safety teams. As a result of this as well as other changes, Norfolk reduced the number of injuries on the job from 6.06 injuries to 2.0 injuries per 200,000 person hours worked.[12] At Sonoco Products Paper Division, production employees have both the authority and obligation to stop a machine from operating if they determine work conditions are unsafe.[13]

Rewarding Employees

Companies use a variety of rewards to improve employee safety. Landstar Systems, a trucking firm based in Connecticut, began to reward for safety results throughout the company. At the highest levels, managers and executives are evaluated on safety during their yearly performance review. The drivers, who are independent owner-operators, are eligible for various rewards. First, an annual reward, the President's Safety Award, is given to safe drivers. Second, drivers who have excellent safety records (including no moving violations) and are top revenue producers are eligible for a major reward program that can lead to savings bonds and sea cruises. State Fair Foods also uses monetary compensation to reward employees who do not have accidents, and the company maintains a trophy room for displaying the safety awards the company wins.[14]

Another way to reward safety behavior is to use intrinsic approaches. One method is to graph safety behaviors and post the results in a visible spot. Workers can then help establish a goal for improvement following training or some other kind of intervention. Subsequent to the intervention, safety behavior can be graphed so that workers can see the improvements.[15]

The use of rewards is clearly one way to reduce accidents. But can you see any potential problems with rewarding employees? One problem is that employees and companies may neglect to report injuries and accidents. In turn, this can lead to penalties by OSHA or, from an employee perspective, greater safety and health problems.[16]

Training Employees

In addition to training requirements mandated by the OSH Act, many companies have developed and implemented additional safety training programs. Landstar Systems conducts employee safety training as part of its orientation program for new hires. This day-and-a-half session emphasizes the role that all workers have in safety, and the loss associated with even one accident. At Sonoco Products, new hires at the cylinder mill and corrugating department go through four days of classroom training in safety principles, followed by on-the-job training. Before beginning to work independently, each new hire must work for one week as an apprentice with a more experienced employee.[17]

Companies also train current employees. Sonoco employees participate in a safety program that emphasizes awareness of safety problems created by other workers. But, as described in Chapter 11, traditional training programs may fail to change on-the-job behavior. So Occidental Chemical adopted a different approach, called the Safety Congress. The purpose of the Safety Congress was to increase employee commitment to and involvement in safety programs. Toward that end, the Safety Congress comprised both management and production employees, who made presentations about safety and discussed the implications for the company. What both parties learned was that safety practices varied a great deal from plant to plant, and that employees often received mixed messages about the relative importance of safety and production goals. As a result of the Safety Congress, employees came away with much greater commitment and involvement in safety programs.[18]

Testing Employees

Various selection procedures have been used to screen out applicants who pose a safety risk. The two most common approaches are drug and personality tests. (Because drug testing was discussed in Chapter 5, we will only discuss personality tests here.) In terms of personality tests, some evidence suggests that certain measures can successfully predict accidents. The Safety Locus of Control Scale, for example, has been examined in several studies, using bus drivers, hotel employees, and grocery store workers. In each case, the Safety Locus of Control Scale was found to be a useful predictor of job-related accidents.[19] Other studies have shown that measures of distractibility and social maladjustment are useful predictors of accidents.[20]

In sum, a variety of programs and practices are available to help companies reduce accidents. By using combinations of these approaches, companies will be able to significantly reduce accidents. We turn now to a discussion of some current safety and health issues in the workplace and discuss programs and practices that companies are using to deal with them.

Current Safety and Health Issues in the Workplace

In this section, you will read about issues such as violence in the workplace, lower back pain, cumulative trauma disorders, drug and alcohol abuse, psychological stress, and indoor air pollution. Regardless of the nature of your job, you may be vulnerable to one or more of these problems. We begin first with a discussion of workplace violence. Box 13.3 discusses the characteristics that may typify a potentially violent employee.

Workplace Violence

Almost everyone has heard of incidents where a current or former employee went on a rampage, wounding or killing other workers. More than one thousand people were murdered at work in the United States during 1992, a 30 percent increase from the 1980s. Some of the best-known incidents involve post office workers, such as the postal carrier who shot 14 people in 1986. Homicide is now the second highest cause of death at work. Only transportation accidents are responsible for more deaths. These statistics have clearly frightened both employees and employers, and companies have initiated a variety of programs and policies to alleviate the problem.[21]

More Careful Preemployment Screening. Some companies ask applicants for information about prior criminal convictions. But applicants may lie, and not all violent people have prior convictions. Other companies have turned to paper-and-pencil tests to try to screen out potentially violent workers. This may work to some degree with new applicants, but for an organization like the U.S. Post Office, with more than 700,000 current employees, this is not a tenable solution.[22]

Conflict Resolution Programs. Given that many cases of violence are caused by prior disagreements between coworkers, some companies are developing conflict resolution programs to defuse the problem. The U.S. Post Office, for example, has established a team of workers whose responsibility will be to solve workplace conflicts. While this tactic may have some promise, violence-prone employees may be no more satisfied with this program's outcome than with the other events or decisions that upset them.

Anonymous Reporting Systems. Some companies are establishing anonymous reporting systems so that coworkers can provide information to the proper authorities

YOUR TURN

Box 13.3
Profile of a Workplace Killer

Wondering whether a coworker of yours may go on a shooting rampage? Experts have developed a list of characteristics that typifies many employees who commit violence in the workplace. Some of the key characteristics of a perpetrator of workplace violence include the following:

- Generally male, in his 30s or 40s.
- Expects to lose his job or has lost his job.
- Has a history of conflicts with other people at work.

- Tends to stay by himself.
- Has trouble accepting authority.
- Tends to blame problems on other people.
- Has threatened other people at work.
- Is extremely interested in guns.

Many people may fit this profile; it does not mean they are going to commit violence at work. Other experts say that certain work environments predispose employees to violence. Some of the characteristics of

violence-prone organizations include the following:

- There is much labor–management friction.
- Many grievances are filed by employees.
- Injury claims, particularly psychologically based, are common.
- Employees are overworked.
- Employees experience much stress.
- An authoritarian management style is used.

Source: Adapted from H. Bensimon, "Violence in the Workplace," *Training & Development* (January 1994): 26–32.

without their identity being revealed. The U.S. Postal Service, for example, instituted this kind of system, and received 10,000 phone calls. In response, postal inspectors spent 100,000 hours investigating tips. Of course, many of these calls will prove to be meaningless.

Increased Security Measures. One of the most important steps that a company can take to reduce workplace violence is to improve its security measures. One law firm, after an unhappy client shot eight workers, keeps its doors locked and provides an emergency alarm for the receptionist. You are probably familiar with the combination lock used by most airports on entrances to airplanes, which was implemented after similar incidents.

Despite concerns over workplace violence, some experts maintain the threat is greatly exaggerated. Statistics show that in 1993, only 59 employees were killed by current or former coworkers. Given that there are 120 million workers in the United States, the odds of being killed by a coworker are 1 in 2.1 million, so you are much more likely to be struck by lightning (where the odds are 1 in 600,000 of dying). Other studies have added to the confusion by reporting different statistics. A 1994 study conducted by the Justice Department, for example, reported that one million employees are victims to nonfatal workplace violence each year. This study has been criticized on two grounds, however. First, many of the violent acts occurred in areas other than the actual facility, including in garages and on public property. Second, the survey included attacks on police, security guards, and convenience-store workers, occupations which are prone to violence. Research reported by Northwestern National Life also indicated high levels of workplace violence—as many as 25 percent of workers were allegedly harassed, threatened, or physically attacked during a 12-month period. But the study had a relatively low response rate (perhaps as low as 29 percent), so it is quite possible that many of the nonrespondents had not been victims of such behavior.[23]

In sum, workplace violence is certainly a safety issue that should concern both companies and employees. Whether it is an epidemic, however, is not quite clear.

Lower Back Pain

Lower back pain and associated disabilities constitute one of the largest sources of days missed from work and are major contributors to an organization's workers' compensation costs. As shown in Box 13.4, "Some Common Causes of Lower Back Pain," certain physical features of jobs appear to increase the likelihood that an employee will experience lower back pain. The workers most likely to experience lower back pain are trash collectors, nurses and nurse's aides, truck drivers, heavy equipment operators, mechanics, maintenance workers, manual laborers, warehouse workers, protective service employees (such as police officers), and typists. Based on Box 13.4, can you explain why these jobs would be particularly susceptible to lower back pain? The answer is that all of these jobs involve either lifting (for instance, nurses), pushing or pulling (such as warehouse workers), carrying (manual laborers, for example), or body vibration (such as heavy equipment or truck drivers). Finally, if you are between the ages of 35 and 45, you are in the age group most likely to experience lower back pain because the effects of aging are most dramatic at this age. Workers younger than 35 who report lower back pain are most likely to develop the symptoms as a result of inexperience with the aggravating tasks.[24]

Company Programs to Reduce Lower Back Pain Problems. Companies have emphasized two basic strategies for reducing lower back pain problems: selection and placement, and training.[25]

Careful Selection. Many companies screen applicants for future or current lower back disability. Medical examinations are the most common approach; frequently, a spinal X-ray is part of the examination. While you might think an examination by a medical professional would effectively screen out employees with current or future lower back pain, research indicates that medical examinations and spinal X-rays are less than accurate predictors of such problems. A physical fitness or physical strength test is the second most common procedure to assess future or current lower back pain disability. Such tests appear far more promising than the medical examination, but more research is needed. Finally, a relatively new approach to selection and placement is the use of computerized movement analyzers, which record a person's movement and strength from a variety of positions. Use of these machines is far too recent to objectively analyze their effectiveness. In any case, based on the Americans with Disabilities Act of 1990, attempts to select workers on the basis of lower back pain disability may be considered discriminatory.

Training Programs. Many companies offer training as an approach for reducing lower back pain. Table 13.1 provides an outline of a typical lower-back-pain training program. As you can see, a typical training program addresses several basic areas shown to be helpful in reducing problems, including awareness of the causes of lower back pain, recommendations for proper lifting and sitting techniques, and suggestions for basic exercises and health care.

In sum, lower back pain and related disabilities are a problem both for the company and the employee who suffers from them. If you have a job that involves some or

YOUR TURN

Box 13.4
Some Common Causes of Lower Back Pain

1. **Lifting Objects That Weigh between 25 and 35 Pounds.** These are the objects that are most likely to cause lower back pain. Objects that are lighter are easier to lift and therefore cause less strain. Workers are more careful in lifting objects that are heavier than 35 pounds; objects that are much heavier than 35 pounds usually require a mechanical aid or assistance from a second person. How often do you lift objects that weigh between 25 and 35 pounds in your job?

2. **Pushing and Pulling Objects.** If you spend much time at work pushing and pulling heavy objects, you are more likely to experience lower back pain. How often do you perform such tasks in your job?

3. **Carrying Heavy Items.** This category poses similar risks as those caused by lifting, but with an added element of risk because carrying items may create sudden and severe strains to the back. Two activities are particularly prone to create lower back pain: shifts in weight as the object is moved and slips in the employee's hands or feet. How often do you carry heavy items in your job?

4. **Prolonged Periods of Sitting.** If you work in a sedentary office job, you may spend little or no time lifting, pushing, pulling, or carrying objects. You are, however, not immune from lower back pain as workers who sit for long periods of time, especially in cramped positions or at desks or tables that are not at proper heights, may experience occasional symptoms.

5. **Body Vibration.** Jobs that involve continuous vibration, such as heavy truck drivers and operators of heavy construction equipment, can lead to lower back pain. While standards for what constitutes unsafe amounts of vibration exist, they are not legally binding on companies, and many jobs exceed the standards. Does your job involve much body vibration?

Source: Adapted from J. Hollenbeck, D. Ilgen, and S. Crampton, "Lower Back Disability in Occupational Settings: A Review of the Literature from a Human Resource Management View," *Personnel Psychology* 45 (1992): 247–78.

all of the activities listed in Box 13.4, you should consult your physician for suggestions (for example, exercises) to avoid future problems.

Cumulative Trauma Disorders

Have you ever worked in a job where you experienced aches in your wrist, shoulder, or arms? In the 1980s, this was frequently identified as carpal tunnel syndrome. Repetitive stress injury was first identified in the 1990s. Together, these ailments are frequently referred to as **cumulative trauma disorders (CTDs).** First, let's discuss some popular myths about these ailments, then we will examine what the legal requirements are in this regard.[26]

Popular Myths about CTDs. There is a great deal of mistaken information about CTDs. What follows next is a list of some of the most common myths about this ailment, along with the facts about each. You will see that relatively little is known about these problems.

1. **Myth: Repetitive stress injury** is another name for carpal tunnel syndrome. **Fact:** These are quite different ailments. Repetitive stress is usually a form of muscle strain, generally not crippling. **Carpal tunnel syndrome** involves pressure on the

cumulative trauma disorders (CTDs)
Trauma to the wrist, shoulder, or arms, such as repetitive stress injury and carpal tunnel syndrome.

repetitive stress injury
First identified in the 1990s, this injury is a form of muscle strain, not usually crippling.

carpal tunnel syndrome
First identified in the 1980s, this injury involves pressure on the median nerve, which is located in the wrist, and often requires surgery.

Table 13.1 A Typical Lower-Back-Pain Training Program

Worksite Assessment

   I. Review your job for risk factors, lifting techniques, safety equipment, etc.
  II. Take slides of employees at work
 III. Review injury records

On-Site Education

    I. Introduction
      A. Present facts regarding back injury
      B. Overview of general causes of back injury
      C. Outline goals of the session
   II. Anatomy
      A. Overview of vertebrae, ligaments, muscles, discs, joints, and nerves
 III. Causes of Back Injuries
      A. Poor posture
      B. Forward bending
      C. Decreased flexibility
      D. Poor physical fitness
      E. Accidents
      F. Poor work habits: Proper/improper standing, sitting, lying, lifting
 IV. Basic Body Mechanics
      A. Principles of lifting
      B. Proper sitting, sleeping, standing, driving positions
   V. Health Education
      A. Aerobics
      B. Flexibility and exercises
      C. Strength and exercises
      D. Home program: Daily living and household activities (for example, getting out of bed, dressing, tooth brushing, vacuuming, dishes, shopping, cooking, etc.)
      E. Nutrition
      F. Weight control
      G. Stress management
      H. Relaxation techniques
 VI. First Aid
      A. What to do for a new injury
VII. Summary
      A. Summarize anatomy, posture, body mechanics, exercise program
      B. Provide written materials on all topics and exercises presented
      C. Life back care: Practical application of methods
      D. Peer pressure and team effort

On-Site Follow-up

   I. Monitor safety and injury records
  II. Review injured employees' records
 III. Make further recommendations if needed

Source: J. Hollenbeck, D. Ilgen, and S. Crampton, "Lower Back Pain Disability in Occupational Settings: A Review of the Literature from a Human Resource Management View," *Personnel Psychology* 45 (1992): 247–78.

median nerve, which is located in your wrist. It often requires surgery. While these are often lumped together as CTDs, they are different ailments.

2. **Myth:** Repetitive stress primarily affects workers who use keyboards (such as secretaries). **Fact:** Keyboard users account for only 12 percent of reported cases. As shown in Figure 13.3, the occupations most affected by repetitive stress injuries include meatpackers, automobile manufacturers, and poultry processors.

3. **Myth:** Preventing CTDs involves simple alterations of work tasks and work conditions (such as the position of one's chair). **Fact:** Relatively little is known about how to prevent CTDs. Some research indicates that remedies such as wrist rests on the keyboard exacerbate, rather than alleviate, the problem.

4. **Myth:** CTDs are by-products of the modern workplace. **Fact:** There is ample evidence that CTDs occurred several centuries prior to our time. Modern-day technology has not created this problem.

Figure 13.3   **Repetitive Stress Injuries by Year and Occupation**

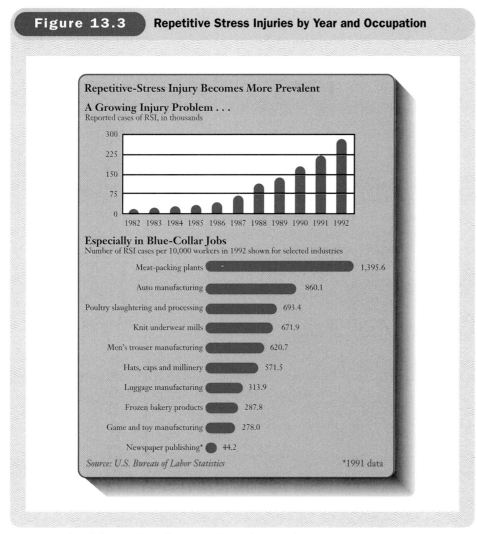

Source: E. Felsenthal, "Out of Hand," *The Wall Street Journal*, July 14, 1994, p. A4.

Now that you know something about the facts regarding CTDs, you may wonder why this ailment is causing so much commotion in the workplace. The answer is that both sufferers of the symptoms and OSHA have become involved in legal action.

Legal Action Regarding CTDs. CTDs present an important issue in the workplace because of lawsuits filed by workers who charge that improper equipment has caused them to suffer. The defendants, who include IBM, AT&T, and Eastman Kodak, make keyboards, cash registers, and grocery-store scanners. In fact, more than 3,000 lawsuits have been filed against such companies. Millions, if not billions, of dollars are at stake. One major problem is that practically no research exists regarding CTDs, so there is little scientific proof one way or the other regarding the causes of CTDs. The only significant court ruling to date took place in England, where a judge ruled against a plaintiff who worked on a computer to edit a newspaper. In dismissing the claim, the judge noted that cumulative trauma disorder was an unknown concept and did not have any medical status.[27]

In a carefully watched case that began in 1988, OSHA conducted an investigation of a Pepperidge Farm plant that produced the Milano cookie. OSHA found that 69 employees who worked on putting the tops on this cookie suffered from a variety of cumulative trauma disorder ailments and levied a $1.4 million fine against the plant.[28] Pepperidge Farm fought this judgment in court, and the judge reduced the penalty to less than $300,000. The major reason for reducing the fine was that OSHA did not prove that reasonable procedure existed for reducing the hazard. That is, the court decided that no known cure or procedure existed for reducing the problem.[29] As a result, OSHA recently released proposed standards for CTDs and related syndromes. The standards would require such things as the company paying for vision tests and corrective lenses for employees who spend more than four hours daily using video-display monitors. The standards also include a list of high-risk tasks, such as use of vibrating tools for more than two hours at a time and activities requiring the identical motion being repeated every few seconds for more than two hours.[30]

Cumulative trauma disorder is an important topic today, and changes will occur in the workplace as more becomes known about this problem. If you work in a job that involves a combination of the following—rapid and repetitive motion, awkward positions, powerful limb movements, strong vibrations, and little control over the pace of work—you may be susceptible to CTDs.[31]

Drug and Alcohol Use

Anywhere from 5 percent to 10 percent of employees report using drugs either at work or off the job. The cost to business and industry of drug and alcohol use is somewhere in the billions of dollars, due to decreased productivity, higher absenteeism, and increased medical bills. In addition, drug and alcohol use has been tied to many accidents, particularly in the transportation and construction industry. As a result, certain industries and many companies have adopted programs to alleviate drug and alcohol-related problems. Companies have emphasized two solutions: employee testing and **employee assistance programs (EAPs).**[32] Because employee testing was addressed in Chapter 5, however, only EAPs will be discussed next.

An EAP is an organization-sponsored program that helps identify workers in need of counseling, motivates them to obtain the needed counseling, and provides the proper counseling sources.[33] While many EAPs were initially established to help with drug- and alcohol-related problems, they are now used to help with any type of psy-

Employee Assistance Program (EAP)
An organization-sponsored program that helps identify workers in need of counseling, motivates them to obtain the needed counseling, and provides the proper counseling sources.

chological problem (for example, depression) that an employee is experiencing. Although most programs allow employees to self-refer, in many cases it is the supervisor who prompts the employee to seek treatment from the EAP. Toward that end, many companies train managers to use a procedure known as constructive confrontation. **Constructive confrontation** involves four basic steps:[34]

1. The supervisor confronts the employee with evidence of unsatisfactory performance.
2. The supervisor provides coaching to improve the employee's performance.
3. At the same time, the supervisor encourages the employee to contact the EAP.
4. The supervisor continues to inform the employee of the consequences of continued unsatisfactory performance.

While many companies use EAPs, some have questioned their effectiveness, as well as their basic features. Whether constructive confrontation, for example, is truly the best strategy has yet to be demonstrated. Nevertheless, many companies have found EAPs to be a cost-effective alternative to other treatment sources that employees might use. In addition, some companies believe that presence of an EAP promotes positive employee relations.[35]

Companies will continue to be concerned with employee drug and alcohol use. Although many organizations use drug testing and EAPs, the problems associated with these substances are unlikely to go away anytime soon.

Psychological Stress

Simply reading the word *stress* may cause your palms to get clammy, your heartbeat to increase, and your breathing to become more rapid. Whether you are only attending school, or attending school while working part time or full time, you will sometimes experience stress. Psychological stress has been linked to numerous problems, including greater susceptibility to the common cold, ulcers, colitis, and other ailments. Hospital employees' stress levels have been linked to higher rates of malpractice lawsuits and medication errors.[36] In some cases, work-related stress may result in workers' compensation payments to employees, amounting to hundreds and thousands of dollars in additional costs to the company. Psychological stress, then, can be a major expense for organizations. The remainder of this section addresses the causes of stress and what companies can do to reduce stress-related problems. Box 13.5 lists some interesting Web sites related to stress and other workplace health and safety issues.

What Causes Stress? Among the many explanations for what causes psychological stress at work, the demand–control model is one of the most popular.[37] According to the **demand–control model of stress,** two factors determine the amount of stress you, as an employee, will experience. One factor is *job demands*. Job demands include the degree to which you must work quickly with great concentration, have more to do than you are capable of completing in the allocated time (often referred to as role overload), or have conflicting requirements (such as two bosses with different standards). There are other sources of job demands as well, such as role ambiguity (being unsure of what the expectations or goals of your job are), the lack of feedback regarding your job performance, and the fear of job loss.[38] Job demands are the psychological perception that you have of the job; a physically demanding job, for example, is not perceived as demanding if you are physically fit.

constructive confrontation
Useful in helping supervisors prompt employees to seek treatment from the EAP, constructive confrontation involves four steps: (1) the supervisor confronts the employee with evidence of unsatisfactory performance; (2) the supervisor provides coaching to improve the employee's performance; (3) at the same time, the supervisor encourages the employee to contact the EAP; and (4) the supervisor continues to inform the employee of the consequences of continued unsatisfactory performance.

demand–control model of stress
The theory that states that an employee will experience the most stress when the job has high demands and little control.

The second factor is *control*, specifically the amount of control that you have in the job with regard to making decisions and using different skills. A worker in a traditional assembly line that is based on scientific-management principles engages in little or no decision making. In addition, because the worker performs one or two simple tasks over and over again, the worker has little or no skill variety. A worker in this type of position would have low control.

According to the demand–control theory, an employee will experience the most stress when the job has high demands and little control. As an analogy, how would you feel if you were driving a car at 80 miles per hour (high demand)? Your stress level would undoubtedly depend on how well you controlled the vehicle (for example, you had a firm grip on the steering wheel and the pavement was ice-free). You would probably not mind being in a speeding vehicle as long as you had control. But how would you feel if you did not have control over the car? What if the road was icy? In that case, you would probably experience a great deal of stress![39]

Based on the demand–control model, some jobs have been found to elicit far greater stress than other jobs. Figure 13.4 provides some average ratings for different jobs on the demand–control dimensions. The jobs that are rated highest on stress include telephone operator, waitress, and garment stitcher.

We have emphasized stressors that are created at work. In today's world, however, especially given the number of dual-career families, many employees experience stress emanating from conflicts between work and nonwork sources. Stress may arise, for instance, when an employee wants to attend his child's birthday party but is unable to because his supervisor requires him to work overtime. In addition, workers often suffer at work from stress emanating from their personal life, including financial difficulties, marital problems, and life changes.[40]

Now that you know what the causes of stress are, you will read about two kinds of programs companies use to reduce stress.

Stress Management Training. Several programs and practices are available to help organizations reduce stress in the workplace. One approach is to provide stress management workshops, in which employees receive training in how to deal with stress. Table 13.2 provides a sample program for this kind of workshop. As you can see, the emphasis in this stress management workshop is on strategies that an employee can use to reduce stress. The stress-management-workshop approach emphasizes the treatment of the demand aspect of stress.[41] Stress management programs differ from one another in terms of their focus—some emphasize relaxation techniques (such as

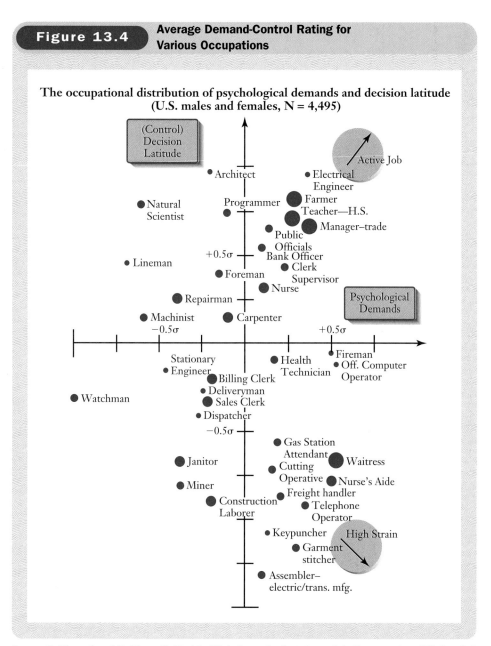

Figure 13.4 Average Demand-Control Rating for Various Occupations

The occupational distribution of psychological demands and decision latitude (U.S. males and females, N = 4,495)

Source: R. Karasek and T. Theorell, *Healthy Work: Stress, Productivity, and the Reconstruction of Working Life* (New York: Basic Books, 1990).

meditation), others focus on practical skills (such as time management) to reduce stress, while other workshops use a combination of these techniques.[42]

Other stress reduction efforts focus on changing the organization, particularly by increasing employee control. As you read in Chapter 12, many companies are empowering workers to make decisions while increasing skill variety. A side benefit of such programs is that they may lower stress levels in the workplace.[43]

Table 13.2	Sample Agenda for a One-Day Stress Management Workshop

1. What is stress?
2. How much stress do you experience?
3. How does stress affect you?
4. What causes stress?
5. Why do different people experience stress differently?
6. Coping with stress.
   - Learning to relax
   - Exercising
   - Eating right
   - Confronting stress
7. Designing a stress reduction program.

Source: Adapted from M. Matteson and J. Ivancevich, *Controlling Work Stress* (San Francisco: Jossey-Bass, 1987).

wellness programs
Some organizations have implemented worksite wellness programs to improve the overall physical and mental health of their workforce. They typically involve a series of educational and behavioral change courses designed to encourage smoking cessation, proper diet and nutrition, and improved physical fitness.

Wellness Programs. Although not designed solely to alleviate stress, many organizations have implemented worksite **wellness programs** to improve the overall physical and mental health of their workforce. Such programs are relatively new; however about 75 percent of large companies now offer some type of wellness program.[44]

Wellness programs typically involve a series of educational and behavioral change courses designed to encourage smoking cessation, proper diet and nutrition, and improved physical fitness. Northern Telecom, for example, recently implemented a wellness program that includes a low-cost fitness center, weight management classes, and a long list of physical education courses, including martial arts. Employees pay a nominal fee of $10 per month ($15 for the family) to attend programs. Seventy percent of the employees now participate. Nike, the sports equipment company, boasts one of the best fitness centers in the country. The fitness center includes weights and two aerobic studios, as well as tennis and basketball courts. In addition, there are volleyball courts, a five-mile running track, and a large lake on the premises.[45]

Despite the popularity of wellness programs, there has been little rigorous examination of their effectiveness. Many companies, however, report high employee enthusiasm and satisfaction with such programs. Northern Telecom, for example, found that 91 percent of the employees agreed that the program improved the quality of their worklife and reduced stress.[46] One of the most carefully conducted studies of wellness programs reported an average cost per employee of $17 to $39 annually. The cost of the programs, then, was relatively low. In terms of risk prevention (such as a reduction in high blood pressure), the nature of the wellness program had a major effect. Yet, programs that only provided courses or a fitness facility had a negligible effect on risk prevention. Significant improvements were reported only if the program featured an administrator who contacted employees at risk and provided encouragement to them. Thus, the mere presence of a fitness center appears not to be enough; someone must prompt the employees to participate.[47]

In sum, psychological stress is a common problem in the workplace. Although many companies have programs to alleviate stress, much of the responsibility is on the employee to learn how to cope. Although this is easier said than done, here's some sound advice:

1. Only worry about the important stuff.
2. Nothing at work is that important.
3. Find enjoyable things to do, such as reading and walking, that will enable you to relax.

Indoor Air Pollution

If you primarily work indoors, you may be exposed to airborne health hazards. We will discuss two of the more commonly considered ones: sick building syndrome and tobacco smoke.

Sick Building Syndrome. According to the World Health Organization, you have **sick building syndrome** if the following apply:

1. You have an abundance of skin and mucous membrane irritations.
2. You experience ailments such as headaches and fatigue.
3. You work in a modern office building.

sick building syndrome
Caused by either bacterial or fungal contamination of the heating and cooling ducts, or vehicle fumes from outside air, the symptoms include skin and mucous membrane irritations, headaches, and fatigue, which are thought to be caused by working in a modern office building.

Have you ever experienced such symptoms? It is generally assumed that sick building syndrome is caused by either bacteria or fungi contamination of the heating or cooling ducts or by vehicle fumes from outside air. However, two studies published in the early 1990s have cast doubt on the authenticity of sick building syndrome. In these two studies, ventilation levels were increased, yet no reduction in sick building syndrome was reported. On the basis of these studies, some experts have concluded that no evidence supports such a syndrome.[48] Whether scientists will find evidence for this ailment in the future is unclear. If you feel you are suffering from this syndrome, try to eliminate sources of fumes and obtain more fresh air, by opening any windows or simply going outside more frequently.

Tobacco Smoke. Smoke from cigarettes, cigars, and pipes may create health problems for both smokers and nonsmokers. The following facts are widely accepted.[49]

1. Tobacco causes more deaths than alcohol, drugs, car crashes, and AIDS combined.
2. Tobacco causes one out of every six deaths nationwide.
3. Almost 400,000 Americans die each year due to cigarette smoking.

While the risks to smokers have been known for quite some time, the effects of secondhand smoke on nonsmokers have only recently become known. Although some controversy remains as to the danger of secondhand smoke, most experts agree that the risk of lung cancer is increased by exposure, if only by a small amount.[50] In the past few years, many employers have begun to actively combat smoking. Organizations have several reasons to reduce or eliminate smoking among employees. First, smokers tend to have higher health insurance claims than nonsmokers. Second, smoking may be a safety hazard on the job. Third, in some states, employees can receive workers' compensation for smoke-related illnesses. Fourth, OSHA has proposed regulations to cover indoor air quality and smoke, and other regulations exist that prohibit smoking.[51] Organizations use a variety of policies to reduce smoking:

1. **Refusing to Hire Smokers.** A few companies, such as Lockheed Aeronautical and Turner Broadcasting System, officially refuse to hire applicants who smoke. Note

that in some states, such as Missouri, an employer cannot discriminate on the basis of an applicant's smoking habits. In these states, it is illegal to refuse to hire or terminate employees merely because of their tobacco use away from work.[52]

2. **Restricting Smoking at the Worksite.** The most common organizational strategy to reduce employee smoking is to restrict smoking at work. For example, Capital Blue Cross, located in Harrisburg, Pennsylvania, introduced restricted smoking areas in 1988 wherein employees were only permitted to smoke in certain areas of the employee lounge. By 1991, management decided to limit smoking only to a covered patio area. The policy was modified again in 1992 to permit smoking only in certain areas at certain times. Some companies have gone a step further and banned smoking altogether at the workplace. The Bank of Santa Clara in California is one such example. Despite the fact that the president of the bank is a smoker, this bank recently banned smoking in its building. Why? The city of Santa Clara recently passed a law outlawing smoking in the workplace—penalties may include fines and even imprisonment.[53]

3. **Imposing Penalties on Smokers.** Some companies penalize smokers by adding a surcharge to their health care costs. Texas Instruments charges an additional $10 per month to employees for each covered family member who smokes, up to $30 extra per month. According to company officials, this surcharge does not even come close to the extra costs of medical care for the company.[54]

   In short, companies are actively involved in reducing smoking. Given that many Americans favor smoking bans, such programs are likely to be accepted by most employees. Organizations concerned about negative reactions on the part of employees should thoroughly explain the reasons for the policies, focusing on concern for employees' health and well-being, rather than on the company's financial gain.[55] Finally, despite the many reasons to restrict smoking, 30 states have laws protecting smoking rights, and right-to-privacy laws may offer some protection to smokers as well.

❖ Conclusion

Safety and health in the workplace is an important concern for both companies and employees. Many laws govern safety and health in the workplace, and it is important for companies to know and follow these laws to avoid legal problems. Through the use of employee empowerment, training programs, reward systems, and the careful selection of employees, companies should be able to reduce their accident rates. Several current safety and health issues were also discussed in this chapter. Employees should encourage their employer to develop and implement safety and health programs to address such things as workplace violence, lower back pain, and alcohol and drug use. By providing effective programs to address these issues, an employer will reduce expenses and have a more productive workforce. Employees, in turn, will experience improved health and safety.

❖ Applying Core Concepts

1. Does the Occupational Safety and Health Act apply to your current job? Why or why not? If the act does not cover your job, do you think it should? What tools, pieces of equipment, machinery, or equipment are affected by this law?
2. As noted in the chapter, OSH standards specific to poultry plants do not exist. Should specific standards be developed? Why or why not?
3. If poultry processors wanted to improve safety in the plants, which of the four approaches described in this chapter do you think would work best? Why?
4. Which of the current safety and health issues in the workplace concern you most in your current job or future career plans? What has your company done to address these concerns? What would you expect your company to do in the future to address these issues?

❖ Key Terms

Occupational Safety and Health (OSH) Act of 1970

Occupational Safety and Health Administration (OSHA)

Occupational Safety and Health Review Commission (OSHRC)

National Institute for Occupational Safety and

Health (NIOSH)

General Duty Clause

Hazard Communication Standard of 1985

OSHA form No. 200

OSHA form No. 101

OSHA variance

Cumulative trauma disorder (CTD)

Repetitive stress injury

Carpal tunnel syndrome

Employee assistance program

Constructive confrontation

Demand–control model of stress

Wellness programs

Sick building syndrome

❖ CHAPTER 13 *Experiential Exercise*

Trouble Waiting to Happen

Jane Hoops works for Carter Cardboard. Her job involves operating a large cutting machine. Carter Cardboard produces custom-ordered cardboard pieces, that are purchased by other companies for use in a wide variety of products, including suitcases, briefcases, and purses. Carter Cardboard purchases the raw material from paper companies and cuts the cardboard to the desired shape and size. Carter Cardboard is a small company, employing about thirty workers. Most of the workers are immigrants to the United States, have been with the company for 10 to 15 years, and would have a

difficult time finding jobs elsewhere. Jane is one of the newer employees. Although the wages are low, she manages to pay all of her bills (though she has practically no money in savings). Perhaps the best feature of the job is that it offers a good pension plan and excellent medical coverage. These aspects are particularly important because Jane is a single mother, who is rearing two young children.

Since she has begun working at the company, Jane has observed the company becoming increasingly unconcerned about work conditions. In particular, the cleanliness and safety of the facility have worsened substantially since Jane began working at Carter Cardboard. It is quite common to find scraps of material on the floor. This is particularly problematic at the beginning of the month, when a large order of vinyl-coated material is usually cut, because these materials are particularly slippery. Although she has never fallen at work, Jane has slipped several times.

In addition to finding scraps on the floor, Jane feels several of the cutting machines lack required safety features (such as covers). When she complained to Ronnie, the supervisor, about this hazard, he answered: "These machines may not have the federally required covers—but you know that many government rules are ridiculous. Don't you usually drive over the posted speed limits on the highways? Besides, no one has ever gotten hurt on our machines." The second time she asked him what he was going to do about the problem, he snapped back: "If you don't like the work conditions, why don't you just quit? There are plenty of people who would be happy to get your job."

Most recently, Jane has found instances where the electrical wiring seemed loose or thinly worn. When she mentioned this fact to the owner (who occasionally walks through the manufacturing area), he said: "Well, I'd like to rewire this entire building but I'm afraid we just don't make enough money in this business to pay for rewiring. In fact, we actually lost money last year, and I worry that a major expense like this could close the business down."

One week ago, Jane's best friend at work, Nashina, received a mild electrical shock when she accidentally brushed against some electrical wiring. Jane cannot take this any longer. She knows that the company violates many OSHA rules, but she doesn't want to lose her job either. Although she has applied for other jobs in the past year, she has not received any job offers. What do you recommend that she do?

❖ Chapter 13 References

1. T. Horwitz, "9 to Nowhere," *Wall Street Journal*, December 1, 1994, A1, A8.
2. B. Mintz, *OSHA: History, Law, and Policy* (Washington: Bureau of National Affairs, 1984).
3. J. Ledvinka and V. Scarpello, *Federal Regulation of Personnel and Human Resource Management* (Boston: PWS-Kent, 1991).
4. M. Rothstein, C. Craver, E. Schroeder, E. Shoben, and L. Vander Velde, *Employment Law* (St. Paul, MN: West, 1994).
5. N. Tompkins, *A Manager's Guide to OSHA* (Menlo Park, CA: Crisp Publications, 1993).
6. Ledvinka and Scarpello, *Federal Regulation.*
7. Tompkins, *A Manager's Guide to OSHA.*
8. P. Sunstrom, "Become the Company's OSHA Oracle," *Security Management* (March 1994): 24–32.
9. Horwitz, "9 to Nowhere."
10. L. Joel, III, *Every Employee's Guide to the Law* (New York: Pantheon Books, 1993).
11. Tompkins, *A Manager's Guide to OSHA.*
12. M. Verespej, "Better Safety Through Empowerment," *Industry Week*, 15 November 1993, 56–68.
13. J. Lee, "Sonoco Stresses Employee Involvement to Alter Company's Safety Performance," *Pulp & Paper* (March 1992): 198–200.
14. Verespej, "Better Safety."
15. T. Krause, "A Behavior-Based Safety Management Process," in *Applying Psychology in Business*, ed. J. Jones, B. Steffy, and D. Bray (Lexington, MA: Lexington Books, 1991).
16. Horwitz, "9 to Nowhere."
17. Lee, "Sonoco Stresses Employee Involvement."
18. S. Smith, "Occidental Chemical: Making Changes for the Better," *Occupational Hazards* (May 1992): 65–68.
19. J. Jones and L. Wuebker, "Accident Prevention through Personnel Selection," *Journal of Business and Psychology* 3 (1988): 187–98.

20. C. Hansen, "A Causal Model of the Relationship among Accidents, Biodata, Personality, and Cognitive Factors," *Journal of Applied Psychology* 74 (1989): 81–90.

21. J. Rigdon, "Companies See More Workplace Violence," *Wall Street Journal*, 12 April 1994, B1, B6.

22. H. Bensimon, "Violence in the Workplace," *Training and Development* (January 1994): 26–32.

23. E. Larson, "Trigger Happy," *Wall Street Journal*, 13 October 1994, A1, A11.

24. J. Hollenbeck, D. Ilgen, and S. Crampton, "Lower Back Pain Disability in Occupational Settings: A Review of the Literature from a Human Resource Management View," *Personnel Psychology* 45 (1992): 247–78.

25. Ibid.

26. E. Felsenthal, "Out of Hand," *Wall Street Journal*, 14 July 1994, A1, A7.

27. N. Taslitz, "OSHA, ADA, and the Litigation of CTDs," *Managing Office Technology* (March 1994): 39–46.

28. Felsenthal, "Out of Hand."

29. Taslitz, "OSHA, ADA."

30. E. Felsenthal, "Guide on Repetitive Stress Injuries Fails to Provide Specific Solutions," *Wall Street Journal*, 19 July 1994, B8.

31. Horwitz, "9 to Nowhere."

32. M. Harris and L. Heft, "Alcohol and Drug Use in the Workplace: Issues, Controversies and Directions for Future Research," *Journal of Management* 18 (1992): 239–66.

33. W. Sonnenstuhl and H. Trice, *Strategies for Employee Assistance Programs: The Crucial Balance* (Ithaca, NY: ILR Press, 1986).

34. Ibid.

35. F. Luthans and R. Waldersee, "What Do We Really Know about EAPs?" *Human Resource Management* 28 (1989): 385–401.

36. J. Jones, B. Barge, B. Steffy, L. Fay, L. Kunz, and L. Wuebker, "Stress and Medical Malpractice: Organizational Risk Assessment and Intervention," *Journal of Applied Psychology* 73 (1988): 727–35.

37. R. Karasek, "Job Demands, Job Decision, Latitude, and Mental Strain: Implications for Job Redesign," *Administrative Science Quarterly* 24 (1979): 285–306.

38. M. Matteson and J. Ivancevich, *Controlling Work Stress* (San Francisco: Jossey-Bass, 1987).

39. R. Karasek and T. Theorell, *Healthy Work: Stress, Productivity, and the Reconstruction of Working Life* (New York: Basic Books, 1990).

40. M. Frone, M. Russell, and M. L. Cooper, "Antecedents and Outcomes of Work-Family Conflict: Testing a Model of the Work-Family Interface," *Journal of Applied Psychology* 77 (1992): 65–78.

41. Matteson and Ivancevich, *Controlling Work Stress.*

42. R. Kahn and P. Byosiere, "Stress in Organizations," in *Handbook of Industrial and Organizational Psychology*, vol. 3, ed. M. Dunnette and L. Hough (Palo Alto, CA: Consulting Psychologists Press, 1992).

43. L. Levi, *Preventing Work Stress* (Reading, MA: Addison-Wesley, 1981).

44. J. Mason, "The Cost of Wellness," *Management Review* (July 1994): 29–32.

45. J. Bers, "Rising Health Costs Put FM & Wellness in the Spotlight," *Facilities Design and Management* (May 1994): 68–71.

46. Mason, "The Cost of Wellness."

47. J. Erfurt, A. Foote, and M. Heirich, "The Cost-Effectiveness of Worksite Wellness Programs for Hypertension Control, Weight Loss, Smoking Cessation, and Exercise," *Personnel Psychology* 45 (1992): 5–27.

48. S. Hughes and B. Holt, "Is Sick Building Syndrome for Real?" *Journal of Property Management* (July/August 1994): 32–34.

49. R. Ramsey, "It's Time to Settle the Smoking Issue Once and for All," *Supervision* (November 1994): 14–23.

50. "Secondhand Smoke: Is It a Hazard?" *Consumer Reports* (January 1995): 27–33.

51. R. Yandrick, "More Employers Prohibit Smoking," *HRMagazine* (July 1994): 68–71.
52. Ibid.
53. S. Cocheo, "Smokers: Step Outside to Read This," *ABA Banking Journal* (October 1994): 127, 128.
54. Yandrick, "More Employers Prohibit Smoking."
55. J. Greenberg, "Using Socially Fair Treatment to Promote Acceptance of a Work Site Smoking Ban," *Journal of Applied Psychology* 79 (1994): 288–97.

Part 5

Maintaining Effective Employee-Employer Relationships

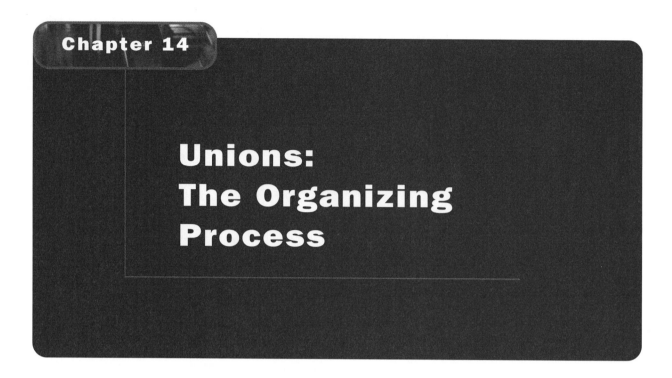

Chapter 14

Unions:
The Organizing
Process

Core Concepts   After reading this chapter, you should be capable of:

1. Applying the basic laws governing the relationship between unions, employees, and management.
2. Explaining why workers might wish to have a union represent them.
3. Understanding the basic steps in a union campaign.
4. Discussing the issues and laws that apply in a union campaign.

Opening Case

Rachel has worked for several years at EZ-Rest, a company that manufactures office chairs. Tomorrow a critical vote will take place. At issue is whether the workers at EZ-Rest will be represented by a union. As she thinks about how to vote, Rachel knows it will not be an easy decision. A great deal has happened within the company in the last year and a half, and both the union and management have campaigned hard. No matter how the election goes tomorrow, things are going to be quite different.

As Rachel thinks back to the first day she worked at the company, changes have already been quite dramatic. The firm was then owned and managed by the grandson and granddaughter of the founder, who started the company in 1903. In fact, it was the grandson and granddaughter who had interviewed and subsequently offered her the job. The business was rather small, with only about 200 full-time workers. Work hours were not rigidly set: employees sometimes came in an hour early and then left an hour early, and they could take lunch whenever they wanted. People stopped to chat with one another occasionally, and sometimes the owners even joined in. Dress was casual, and laughter could often be heard in the office area. Once a month, there was a company picnic, and the owners contributed all of the drinks, hot dogs, buns, and potato chips. During the entire first six months Rachel worked there, not a single person was fired. But at the end of her first six months at EZ-Rest, the grandson and granddaughter sold the business to someone else, and the atmosphere changed almost overnight.

The new owner, Mr. Payne, had a completely different view of business. First, he fired the two top managers, who had worked for the company for 20 years, and replaced them with his own son and daughter. Neither the son nor daughter had ever managed other employees. Both had recently graduated from college (although nobody knew what their majors were). Next, the new owner hired a consultant to review the business and make recommendations for changes. Based on the consultant's report, the business was moved to an older building in a different location, which didn't even have a

lunchroom or lounge area. The new location was also much more difficult to get to, as no public transportation was nearby. Another change that the consultant brought about was a new employee handbook, which, among other things, contained a dress code (no more jeans, T-shirts, or casual footwear allowed) and included a provision stating that employment could be terminated at any time for any reason at all.

But the two final blows came when the new owner announced that every employee's pay would be reduced by 10 percent, and then terminated 15 people as part of a "cost-cutting program." The next day, Joe and Mary, the two most senior employees, went around the office asking people to stay after work for a meeting at Xanadu's (the local eatery). At that meeting, for which nearly everyone showed up, Joe and Mary explained that they had been in contact with a union for the purposes of becoming organized. They went on to explain the advantages of being unionized, as well as the stages in a union campaign.

Little did Rachel know how stressful the workplace would become. One year after the meeting at Xanadu's, a union election was scheduled. Management hired a consultant to help fight the union. Both the union and management held meetings, and management passed around flyers detailing stories of union corruption. In the meetings, the owner talked about the number of businesses that were closed when they became unionized. When asked if the same would happen to this business, he simply smiled and said, "Who knows? I certainly wouldn't exclude it from the realm of possibilities."

As she thinks about these matters, Rachel really wonders whether she should vote for the union or not. As the union representatives tell it, only under the union will she have job security, reasonable wages and benefits, and a secure future. Yet according to management, having a union will create nothing but problems, and a good chance of having no job. How should she vote in the election tomorrow?

As you will see in this chapter as well as the next, unions play an important role in human resources. Regardless of whether the company you work for is unionized, or is trying to avoid becoming unionized, a union is an important force to reckon with. In this chapter, you will learn why employees might wish to unionize and how union campaigns work. You will also read a brief history of unions and learn about the various laws that govern the relationship between unions, management, and employees. We begin, however, with a discussion of what exactly a union is and what role it performs for the employees it represents.

What Is a Union?

union
An organization of workers whose purpose is to represent the employees in their dealings with management.

According to the dictionary definition, a **union** is simply an organization of workers. (Chapter 15 will describe the structure of a union, as well as some of the important positions within a union, in greater detail.) The primary purpose of a union is to represent the employees in their dealings with management. A union fulfills this function through three mechanisms:

1. The union is responsible for negotiating a contract with management that covers the terms and conditions of employment, including pay, benefits, work hours, and job assignments.
2. The union is responsible for overseeing the provisions and rules of the contract.
3. The union is responsible for representing employees in grievances or complaints filed against the company.

We will discuss each of these mechanisms in greater detail in Chapter 15. For now, it should be clear that through these mechanisms, the union has a significant influence on human resources within an organization. Let us turn next to a brief history of unions in the United States, which will give you a greater understanding of the relationship between management and unions. Because of the important role laws played in the history of unions, they will be discussed in this section as well.

Unions in the United States: A Brief History[1]

In the Beginning

If there is one word to summarize the history of unions in the United States, the word would be "conflict." Organized unions in the United States did not appear until the early 1800s. Prior to this time, the labor market was such that no real need for a union existed. A shortage of people in early colonial America, as well as a surplus of cheap land in the country, provided many opportunities for employees who were dissatisfied with their jobs. But as business conditions began to change in the 19th century, unions representing skilled trades, such as carpenters and tailors, appeared. Management used two tactics to fight these early unions. One tactic was to form employer organizations, which pooled their resources to resist such demands as wage increases. A second approach was to fight unions through the courts, by arguing that labor unions comprised an illegal conspiracy to restrain trade. To management's delight, the courts largely accepted this argument, and beginning in 1806, numerous courts ruled that union activities, such as strikes, were illegal. Not until 1842 did the courts begin to recognize that a union strike could, under some circumstances, be legal.

For the most part, though, U.S. unions enjoyed a feast-or-famine kind of existence during the 19th century. When the economy was doing well and the unemployment rate was low, unions fared well. In periods when the economy worsened and the unemployment rate increased (such as during the 1840s, when large numbers of immigrants arrived from Europe), union strength declined. For example, in 1836, 300,000 workers belonged to a union, representing more than 6 percent of the workforce. By the mid-1870s, on the other hand, only 50,000 employees were union members.

The late 1800s marked the earliest attempts to form a large, national union. The first such attempt, the Noble and Holy Order of the Knights of Labor, was founded by tailors who sought to organize a wide range of workers. The Knights' membership grew rapidly, from 9,000 in 1878 to 700,000 in 1886, following a highly successful strike against Wabash Railroad in 1885. But rapid growth in membership created numerous problems, resulting in the subsequent decline and extinction of the Knights by 1900. As the Knights' strength began to decline, however, a new union took its place: the American Federation of Labor, better known by its acronym, the AFL.

The Rise of the AFL

The American Federation of Labor (AFL), founded in 1881, was highly influenced by one of its earliest presidents, Samuel Gompers. A highly pragmatic and skilled leader, Gompers adopted several principles that ensured the success of the new organization. One major principle was that individual unions within the AFL umbrella would remain autonomous; essentially, the AFL practiced organizational decentralization. Another key principle was that the AFL, unlike many predecessors, espoused no particular political or ideological position. Rather, the AFL emphasized job-related goals, such as wage increases, that virtually everyone could accept. These and other principles ensured much greater internal cohesiveness than earlier labor organizations, such as the Knights of Labor, had experienced. As a result of the success of the AFL, the number of unionized employees grew from about 500,000 in 1897 to more than 2 million by 1904, an unparalleled growth rate in the history of unions. For a comparison of U.S. union history to that in other countries, see Box 14.1.

The fast rise in U.S. unionization did not go unchallenged. Management fought back using a variety of tactics, including discharging workers with union sympathies and using military forces to end strikes. Such tactics often ended in violence. In one of the most publicized events, eleven children and two women died when their tent site was burned to the ground by the militia. Businesses also successfully sought support from the court system, which frequently ruled against union activities and in favor of management.

World War I and Its Aftermath

The growth of the AFL continued through World War I. Its success was aided by support from the president of the United States in exchange for Gompers' promise not to strike and interfere with the war effort. But once again, union growth reached a halt during the 1920s. Among the reasons were Samuel Gompers' death, the courts' continued antagonism toward unions, and a major campaign by management to defeat unions. By 1929, fewer than 3 million workers were unionized.

INTERCULTURAL ISSUES IN HUMAN RESOURCES

Box 14.1
The History of Unions: An International Perspective

While the history of unions in the United States is characterized by conflict with management, that is by no means a typical pattern in the rest of the world. As an example, if you visited West Germany, you would find that the term *codetermination* is used to describe union–management relations in some of the largest industries. The concept of codetermination is, in fact, required by various laws, such as the Codetermination Law of 1951, which requires coal, iron, and steel companies to fill half of the seats on the supervisory board (contrary to the name, this board is comparable to a board of directors in the United States) with employee representatives. Work councils also have the right to participate in certain major management decisions. Another feature of co-

determination is the position of labor director, who is chosen by the supervisory board from a slate of union leaders. The labor director is actively involved in general management activities, and this individual must be a member of the executive committee. New laws passed since the Codetermination Law of 1951 have extended codetermination to other industries in West Germany as well.

Japan has also experienced a much more cooperative relationship between unions and management than the United States has. Perhaps in keeping with the cultural emphasis on cooperation and group harmony, post–World War II union growth was strongly encouraged by Japanese corporate leaders. In contrast to the United States, where management

typically resisted unions, unions in Japan enjoyed positive relations with management. In fact, management often openly directed pro-company employees to join in union activities, if only to help moderate the unions. Despite strong management support, unions at various times have taken strong stands against the company. Initially, management responded by forming a second union in hopes of destroying the original union. When that strategy failed to work, management turned to a more participatory model and actively sought suggestions from the union to avoid problems. In fact, company executives and union leaders typically maintain cordial relations, often socializing together.

Source: Adapted from C. Kerr and P. Staudohar, *Industrial Relations in a New Age* (San Francisco: Jossey-Bass, 1986).

Wagner Act (National Labor Relations Act, NLRA)
Passed in 1935, this law gives workers the right to organize and participate in union activities, prohibits various management tactics that would discourage unions, outlaws company-sponsored unions, and forbids the company from discriminating against employees for participating in union activities.
National Labor Relations Board (NLRB)
Established by the Wagner Act, this board is responsible for administering and interpreting the act and related laws.

The Depression Years and the Wagner Act

While the Depression years led to major job losses in the United States, President Franklin Roosevelt and his New Deal policies marked the beginning of a major shift in public policy toward unions. In 1935, Congress passed a law known as the **Wagner Act** (named after the senator who drafted it), or, more formally, the **National Labor Relations Act (NLRA).** As you can see from Table 14.1, the Wagner Act is much a pro-union law. Among other provisions, this law gives workers the right to organize and participate in union activities, prohibits various management tactics that would discourage unions, outlaws company-sponsored unions, and forbids the company from discriminating against employees for participating in union activities. The NLRA also established the union election process, as well as the **National Labor Relations Board (NLRB),** which is responsible for administering and interpreting the act.[2]

World War II and the Taft-Hartley Act

The years following passage of the NLRA were generally good ones for the union movement. Despite internal bickering and formation of a new union federation called the Committee for Industrial Organization (CIO), which competed with the AFL, the number of unionized employees swelled. By the end of 1941, more than 10 million employees were union members, an increase of more than 7 million in just three years. During World War II, unions continued to grow in terms of membership. As a result, unions became more active in politics, and after World War II they increasingly turned to strikes and work stoppages to achieve their goals. But this turn of events led to public sentiment for curbing union power. In 1947, the **Taft-Hartley Act** (named after the congressmen who sponsored the bill) or, more formally, the **Labor-Management Relations Act,** was passed. This act was a pro-management law designed to protect employers from unfair union practices. As you can see from Table 14.2, the Taft-Hartley Act gives companies basic rights in their dealings with the union.[3]

Taft-Hartley Act (Labor-Management Relations Act) Passed in 1947, this act was a pro-management law designed to protect employers from unfair union practices.

Post World War II and the Landrum-Griffin Act

The percentage of the private-sector workforce that was unionized peaked in the mid-1950s, when approximately one out of every three workers belonged to a union.

Table 14.1   **The National Labor Relations Act: A Pro-Union Law**

The NLRA protects you, as a union member, union organizer, or employee in the following ways:

1. It prohibits the company from firing you because you engage in union activities or are a member of the union.
2. It prohibits the company from refusing to hire you because you belong to a union.
3. It prohibits the company from denying you the opportunity to form a union.
4. It prohibits company-sponsored unions.
5. It prohibits the company from threatening you with regard to union activities or union representation.
6. It prohibits the company from banning you from discussing the union during work breaks.
7. It prohibits the company from discriminating against the union with regard to room usage and similar privileges.
8. It provides for numerous other requirements, such as good-faith bargaining by both management and the union in establishing a contract.

Table 14.2   **The Taft-Hartley Act: A Pro-Management Law**

The Taft-Hartley Act protects companies from a variety of union practices. Included among the provisions are the following:

1. It prohibits the union from requiring employees to be a member of the union in order to be hired (in other words, a *closed shop* is illegal).
2. It bans *featherbedding*, in which companies pay employees who are not actually working.
3. It allows management to discuss the ramifications of unionization with employees.
4. It prohibits unions from refusing to bargain with the company.
5. It prohibits unions from charging excessive dues.
6. It permits the president of the United States to halt a strike if public health or safety are threatened.

Although the 1950s in many ways was a good time for unions (for instance, the AFL and CIO merged to form the AFL-CIO, which increased their strength), several events occurred that proved detrimental to unions. First, unions received a great deal of negative publicity during this time regarding possible corruption. Second, internal conflicts among unions continued, leading to, among other events, the expulsion of the International Brotherhood of Teamsters from the AFL-CIO. Third, Congress passed legislation that further restricted unions. In particular, the **Landrum-Griffin Act** (or, more formally, the **Labor-Management Reporting and Disclosure Act**) was passed by Congress in 1959.

Whereas the first two major laws (the Wagner Act and the Taft-Hartley Act) protected unions and companies, respectively, the major purpose of the Landrum-Griffin Act was to protect employees from unions. The Landrum-Griffin Act provides the following rights for employees.[4]

Landrum-Griffin Act (Labor-Management Reporting and Disclosure Act)
Passed in 1959, this act's major purpose was to protect employees from unions.

1. The right to equal treatment by the union.
2. The right to free speech and assembly.
3. The right to fair discipline hearings.
4. The right to fair union elections.
5. The right to fair representation.
6. The right to sue the union.

Some of the specific details of your rights as an employee under this act are provided in Table 14.3.[5]

Recent Union Trends

The mid-1950s marked the beginning of a decline that continues even today both in the number of unionized private-sector employees, as well as in the influence of unions in the workplace and on the political scene. As shown in Figure 14.1, there has been a fairly steady decline in the percentage of unionized employees in the private sector. Al-

---

Table 14.3   **Landrum-Griffin Act: A Pro-Employee Law**

The Landrum-Griffin Act mandates various employee rights in terms of the way the union deals with them. These include the following:

1. As part of the right to free speech and assembly, you have the right to speak out during meetings, as well as the right to publicly criticize a union leader.
2. You have the right to vote for local union representatives, and a secret ballot must be used.
3. Even if you refuse to join the union that represents your work group, the union must treat you equally.
4. The union has an obligation to do its best to represent you in such matters as arbitration hearings; if it fails to do so, you may sue the union, for a kind of malpractice.
5. While the union has the right to discipline you under certain circumstances, you have the right to a fair hearing, including sufficient time to prepare for the hearing, a written copy of the charges, and access to a lawyer if the union is using one.

| Figure 14.1 | Percentage of Unionized Employees |

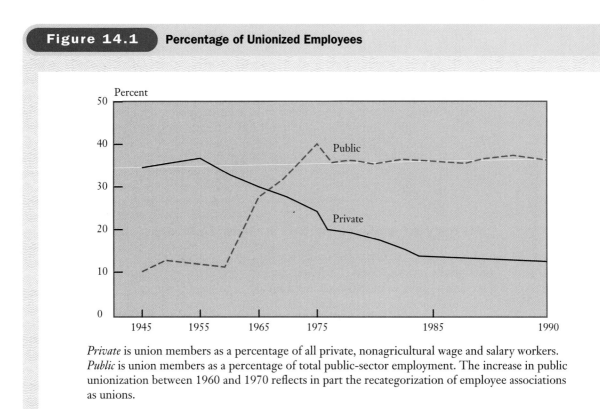

Private is union members as a percentage of all private, nonagricultural wage and salary workers. *Public* is union members as a percentage of total public-sector employment. The increase in public unionization between 1960 and 1970 reflects in part the recategorization of employee associations as unions.

Source: R. Edwards, *Rights At Work* (Washington, D.C.: The Brookings Institute, 1993): 85.

though many reasons have been offered as to why union strength has declined, four reasons stand out:

1. Unions appear to have put fewer resources into attracting new members in the last few decades; this may be changing, however.
2. Recent legal decisions have generally sided with management and, in turn, have weakened union power.
3. Companies have stepped up their campaigns to keep out unions.
4. Workers are increasingly critical of unions and less likely to see unions as helpful, especially in light of new civil rights and privacy laws.[6]

At present it seems that the number of unionized workers is continuing to decline. In 1998, only 9.8 percent of private-sector employees were unionized, and some estimate that only 7 percent of private-sector employees will be union members by the year 2001. But more than one-third (37.5%) of public-sector workers were unionized in 1998. In comparison, recall that about 33 percent of private-sector employees were union members in the mid-1950s. Whether unions will ever flourish again remains a major question.[7]

In sum, unions in the United States have had a history of resurgence, followed by decline, only to revive again. Over the years Congress has passed three major laws affecting unions. An easy way to remember the order of these laws is to keep in mind that they occur in the reverse alphabetical order: the oldest law is the Wagner Act, followed by the Taft-Hartley Act, and then the most recent one, the Landrum-Griffin Act. If you think about it for a while, the focus of each of these laws makes a great deal of sense. The Wagner Act is pro-union, which is understandable because, before its passage, union activity was often deemed illegal. The Taft-Hartley Act, on the other hand, attempted to rectify a perceived imbalance that favored unions. This law, then, limits or prohibits certain union activities and practices. Finally, the Landrum-Griffin Act recognizes the rights of the individual employees, which may have gotten lost in the contest between union and management. If you wish to visit some Web sites pertaining to unions, see Box 14.2. Next, you will read a brief history of unions in the public sector or government.

History of Unions in the Public Sector[8]

The union experience in the public sector, or government, differs in several ways from that in the private sector. The laws represent one major difference. Public-sector employees wishing to form unions faced a major legal barrier for many years because they were exempt from coverage under the NLRA, which provided only private-sector employees with the right to unionize. Not only did public-sector employees not have the right to unionize, but under certain amendments to the NLRA, federal employees who went on strike could be discharged and barred from reemployment for three years. Similar laws and judicial decisions in other states, such as the Condon-Wadlin Act in New York (which required discharge for strikes by state employees and a ban on salary increases for that unit for three years), maintained this restriction for other public-sector employees. Only among postal workers were unions popular, as various laws passed in the early part of the twentieth century provided limited support for unions in this arena.

In 1962, President John F. Kennedy wrote Executive Order 10988, laying the groundwork for a series of laws that greatly increased the rights of public-sector employees to unionize. In 1970, the Postal Reorganization Act mandated that postal workers be covered by the private-sector union laws. Other federal employees were granted extensive unionization rights through the Civil Service Reform Act of 1978. Table 14.4 summarizes some of the key points regarding unionization rights mandated by these two laws.

Legislation granting unionization rights for state and local government employees began in the 1960s. Because these laws are decided by each state, however, they vary greatly. Thus, while 28 states have incorporated comprehensive laws similar to private-sector regulations, other states have either no laws (as is the case in Louisiana and South Carolina, for example) or have laws covering only some public employees. For example, Indiana permits collective bargaining only for teachers. Missouri permits collective bargaining for all public employees *except* certain law enforcement employees, civilian National Guard employees, and teachers. Moreover, Missouri's law permits only limited negotiation rights.

As a result of favorable laws passed in the early 1960s, public-sector unions grew rapidly during this time. In the years between 1962 and 1982, for example, the number of unionized workers in the public sector more than doubled. The most dramatic growth occurred for state and local employees. The percentage of these workers who belonged to a union increased by almost 300 percent, far exceeding the union growth for federal employees, which increased by 60 percent.

Webbing Around

Box 14.2

http://www.labor.org.au/ about_unions/why_join/ This Web site provides information, from a union's perspective, on why you should join a union.

http://www.unions.org/ This Web site will give you access to many unions' Web pages, as well as other valuable resource information.

http://www.nlrb.gov/assist. html#15 Here you can find out a great deal more about the union election process.

Table 14.4	Federal Employees' Unionization Rights under the Civil Service Reform Act and the Postal Reorganization Act	
Topic	**Civil Service Reform Act (1978)**	**Postal Reorganization Act (1970)**
Overall administration	Federal Labor Relations Authority	National Labor Relations Board
Basic employee rights	Form, join, and assist unions (or refrain) free from interference, restraint, or coercion	Same (Labor Management Relations Act)
Unfair labor practices	Several; the most important concerned with organizing and good-faith bargaining	Similar
Collective bargaining	Good-faith bargaining required on personnel policy, practices, and working conditions, with many provisions and exceptions	Good-faith bargaining on wages, hours, and terms and conditions of employment; few topics unlawful
Resolution of contract disputes	Mediation, fact-finding, and whatever action deemed necessary by the Federal Service Impasses Panel to settle the dispute	Mediation, fact-finding, and binding arbitration

Source: C. J. Coleman, *Managing Labor Relations in the Public Sector* (San Francisco: Jossey-Bass, 1991).

Now that you have read about the history of unions, you may wonder why an employee or group of employees would want a union to represent them. We will discuss that topic next.

Why Workers Join Unions

Workers' interest in and willingness to vote for union representation is a function of three key factors:

1. Job dissatisfaction.
2. Lack of control.
3. Positive attitudes toward and perceptions of unions.

A good way to remember these factors is to use the acronym SLAP, which stands for (dis)*Satisfaction*, *Lack* of control, *Attitudes* toward and *Perceptions* of unions. Each of these factors is described in greater detail next.[9]

Job Dissatisfaction

Job dissatisfaction is the basic factor that encourages employees to consider unionization. Although many issues may contribute to job dissatisfaction, several stand out in explaining why employees may join a union:

1. Wages and benefits
2. Job security
3. Safety
4. Promotions
5. Supervisors

The first four issues probably will not surprise you. Unions generally negotiate higher wages and benefits for employees. Historically, unions have helped employees to maintain job security by specifying the terms and conditions under which layoffs can occur. In many cases, the union also provides substantial financial aid to workers who have lost their jobs. Unions also help to improve unsafe conditions in the plant. In terms of promotions, if you have ever been passed by for advancement, you likely questioned the fairness of the decision. Unions offer procedures to make promotion decisions more objective; typically, promotions in a unionized facility will be heavily based on seniority. But what about satisfaction with supervisors? Ineffective supervisors are often a major source of problems, because they may show favoritism, make arbitrary pay decisions, and engage in other such behaviors. The union offers to reduce the power of the supervisor and restore the balance of control to the workers by requiring the supervisor to make personnel decisions on the basis of much more objective criteria, such as seniority. The union also provides a mechanism for the employees to challenge supervisory decisions (such as a formal grievance procedure). Hence, wages, benefits, job security, safety, promotions, and poor supervision are areas that the union usually addresses. On the other hand, dissatisfaction with the kind of work that you do is *unlikely* to influence your interest in joining a union. Can you think of why this might be? One answer is that the union will have little or no effect on the kind of work that you do. If anything, in fact, unions may prefer that workers do simple, routine work. If you like much more variety in your work, you may find a union problematic.[10]

Returning to the opening case, the employees of EZ-Rest were considering voting for union representation. Do you recall some of the factors that seemed to lead up to this situation? Two major factors seemed most pertinent: the pay cut and the terminations of several employees. If you were an employee, how would you feel about your pay and job security at EZ-Rest? Given these considerations, it is not surprising that the employees sought union representation.

Lack of Control

If the expression "the grass is always greener on the other side" is at all true, few workers are satisfied. It is not surprising, then, that only 25 percent of workers today consider themselves extremely satisfied (compared with 40 percent in 1973).[11] So, why aren't unions much more popular? The answer lies, in part, with the control issue. Have you, for example, ever been dissatisfied with your pay, benefits, and other aspects of a job? Did you think about joining a union? If you said no, why didn't you think of joining a union? Was it because you chose to change jobs instead? Or did you try to improve matters by complaining or threatening to sue the company for discrimination?[12] Several alternatives exist to eliminate employee dissatisfaction besides forming a union.[12] But some workers lack the control to change jobs, complain, or threaten to sue. The job market for their occupation may be limited, and they may lack the resources to pursue a lawsuit. They may have tried complaining to management, only to have been ignored or perhaps told to leave if they were unhappy. Employees who lack control over the situation are more likely to seek union representation as a means of improving their job satisfaction than are employees who have control and can find another job or change the situation.[13]

What about EZ-Rest, the company in the opening case of this chapter that was in the midst of a union campaign? Do you think the employees had much control over matters there? It would appear that the new owner made major changes without the input of the employees. That is probably one reason employees felt little or no control in the situation. Recall also that the two most senior employees, Joe and Mary, contacted the union. Because they were the most senior employees, they were probably also the oldest and would likely face the most difficult time obtaining a new job. If the employees at EZ-Rest did indeed feel they had little control over the situation, they would probably be interested in having a union represent them.

Positive Attitudes Toward and Perceptions of Unions

This factor has two separate components, both of which are important. To illustrate the attitude part, play the word-association game for a moment. When you think of the word *union*, what is the first thought that comes to mind? Some people will immediately think of words such as *helpful, fair*, and other positive adjectives. Other people will respond with words such as *corrupt, strikes*, and *unfair*. The words you associate with unions often depend on your background and experience. In general, some people have favorable attitudes toward unions and will be more likely to vote for union representation, others have negative attitudes toward unions and would be less likely to vote for union representation. Box 14.3 describes the success union activity has had in the health care industry. Table 14.5 contains a set of items that measure your attitudes about unions in general. As you can see, this attitude is affected by such issues as your perceptions of union corruption, the degree to which you believe unions are helpful, and the amount of power you think they have.[14]

The second component, perceptions, refers to specific beliefs regarding the ability of the union at issue to help the employees. If workers believe that the union in question can improve the workplace features that employees are dissatisfied with, such as pay, job security, and treatment by supervisors, they will be more likely to vote in favor of and join the union. Research shows that when it comes to voting in an actual election, the perceptions or specific beliefs about the union are the most important.[15]

At EZ-Rest, the union probably had a distinct advantage in that the new owner of the company had made several significant changes that adversely affected the employees. As such, the workers' perceptions of the union were probably much more positive than if the new owner had made none of those changes.

In sum, employees will be more likely to vote for a union when they are dissatisfied with such factors as pay, benefits, and job security; when they believe they lack control

TALES FROM THE TRENCHES

Box 14.3
Health Care Industry: A Hot Bed of Union Activity

While unions seem stymied in many industries, union campaigns have been fairly successful in the health care industry, particularly in hospitals and nursing homes. In the last five years, the number of union elections in this industry has risen dramatically. And compared to most other industries, unions have been fairly successful in elections here, winning 53 to 58 percent of the time, depending on the specific year being examined.

Why have unions been targeting, and winning, elections in this industry? Experts point to the dramatic cost-cutting going on in the health care field, which has led to salary reductions, closures, layoffs, and the use of lower-skilled workers to do tasks traditionally performed by higher-paid employees. A good example is Crouse Irving Memorial Hospital, located in Syracuse, New York. In the first election, the union lost by a wide margin. After nurses were given a 6 percent pay cut, the union conducted a new campaign, and this time it won.

Another reason for the increased success of unions here is a small, but significant, change in the law. The change involves a 1991 Supreme Court decision that hospital workers may be divided into eight categories (registered nurses, clerical employees, and so on). Previously these workers were lumped into fewer categories, which made elections more difficult for unions to win. Finally, while many traditional unionized industries have had declining numbers of workers to unionize, the health care industry has added many workers over the last few years. This industry, therefore, has been a rich source for union organizers.

Sources: Adapted from R. Tomsho, "Mounting Sense of Job Malaise Prompts More Health-Care Workers to Join Unions," *Wall Street Journal*, 9 June 1994, B1; and S. Deshpande and D. Flanagan, "Determinants of Union Victory in the Health Care Sector," *Health Care Management Review* (Summer 1994): 64–69.

| **Table 14.5** | **Assessing Your Attitudes Toward Unions** |

For each of the statements below, mark a "1" if you agree and a "0" if you disagree.

1. Unions are often corrupt.   _____
2. Unions cause more trouble than they are worth.   _____
3. Unions are unnecessary in today's world.   _____
4. Unions have far too much power.   _____
5. Unions are more concerned about their own agenda than about the
   workers they represent.   _____

Add up the scores on the questions. If your total score is 1 or less, you are relatively likely to support unionization. If your total score is 2 or 3 you are relatively unlikely to support unionization. If your total score is 4 or 5, you are likely to oppose a union no matter how dissatisfied you are.

---

and therefore have no other means of dealing with the dissatisfying situation, and when they have favorable attitudes toward unions and believe the union in question will improve things. Now that you have read about why workers may wish to have a union, you will read about why managers generally dislike unions, followed by a discussion of the process that companies go through in becoming unionized.

Managers' Attitudes Toward Unions

Besides historical factors, there are other reasons why an adversarial relationship exists between management and unions. A primary reason why managers resist unions is because of the restrictions the unions place on managerial discretion and decision making. In essence, the presence of a union means that management can no longer choose to do merely what is in its best interests. The existence of a written contract, which specifies how promotions will be made, how layoffs will be decided, and so forth, largely ties management's hands. Relatedly, if an employee feels his or her treatment has violated the terms of the contract, the employee will have an opportunity to overturn the decision. Many managers therefore believe unions endanger the profitability of the firm. Because this is a widespread perception, a great deal of research has been conducted to examine the effect of unions on various important business and human resource outcomes.

A summary of these findings indicates the following:

1. Employees who work at unionized companies on average are paid 10 percent more than employees who work at nonunionized companies.[16]
2. Unionized firms tend to be somewhat less profitable than nonunionized firms.[17]
3. Unionized firms are no more likely to have layoffs, closures, or bankruptcy than are nonunionized firms.[18]

In sum, while presence of a union will certainly reduce managerial discretion and control, and often raise wages while lowering profits, unions do not seem to increase the likelihood of job loss or bankruptcy. However, the negative effects of unionization are sufficient reason for most companies to fight to keep unions out. You will have noticed that discussions of labor, management, and unions often use specialized terms. Definitions of some of those terms are in Box 14.4.

How Companies Become Unionized: The Union Election

In many ways, a **union election** is similar to a political election. The union in the EZ-Rest case would have followed specific steps before reaching election day.[19]

Step 1: Initiation of Contact

The union election begins with contact between the workers and the union. The contact may be initiated by either party; the union may contact the employees or the employees may contact the union. In the opening case, Joe and Mary contacted the union first.

Step 2: Authorization Cards

Regardless of how the contact is initiated, the second step of the process requires that at least 30 percent of the relevant employees sign **authorization cards.** If you examine Figure 14.3, you will see what an authorization card looks like. This step may be compared to the process of obtaining sufficient numbers of signatures of eligible voters for a political candidate to appear on the ballot. In the present case, at least 30 percent of the eligible "voters," or employees, must sign the authorizations cards for the campaigns to proceed to Step 3. Failure to obtain signatures from at least 30 percent

union election
The process used to establish a union within an organization. The union election begins by contact between the workers and the union. At least 30 percent of the relevant employees must sign authorization cards, after which the group may petition the NLRB for permission to hold an election.

authorization cards
The equivalent of obtaining sufficient numbers of signatures of eligible voters for a political candidate to appear on the ballot. At least 30 percent of the relevant employees must sign these cards.

YOUR TURN

Box 14.4
What Type of Shop Do You Work In?

If you have ever worked in a unionized company, you probably have heard the term *union shop* or *agency shop*. You may even have heard an older union member discussing the term *closed shop*. What do these terms mean? These terms refer to various conditions that an employee must meet in order to be hired and remain employed if his or her job is represented by a union.

A *closed shop* is a union–management agreement that only union members will be hired. If you applied for a job in a closed shop, you would have to be a union member *before* you could be hired. This type of arrangement was permitted under the law until 1947, when the closed shop was prohibited under the Taft-Hartley Act.

Although the Taft-Hartley Act prohibits the closed shop, the union shop is permitted under this law. In a *union shop*, applicants who are hired are required to join the union within a certain period of time. A Supreme Court decision, however, ruled that no law can force an individual to join an organization against his or her will. According to the Supreme Court, Congress intended to allow an agreement requiring covered individuals to pay dues. This is called an agency shop. Thus, while an agency shop is permitted by law, employees can only be required to pay union dues—they cannot be required to join the union. Now, you may wonder what the difference between paying union dues and joining the union means in prac-

tical terms. The primary difference is that some portion of union dues goes toward supporting various political causes, so if you are not a member of the union, you are eligible for a refund of that portion of the dues.

Finally, you may have heard the expression "right-to-work state." In a *right-to-work state*, such as Georgia, even an agency shop is prohibited by the law. The Taft-Hartley Act permits states to decide whether they will be a right-to-work state. To date, 21 states have right-to-work laws. In these states, it is not possible to force employees of a unionized company to pay dues, let alone join the union. As you can see from Figure 14.2, most of these states are in the southern or western part of the United States.

of the eligible employees means that the campaign is over. Once the union believes it has at least 30 percent of the necessary signatures, it may petition the National Labor Relations Board (NLRB) for permission to hold an election. Although this step was not mentioned in the EZ-Rest case, it is necessary in order to hold the actual election.

While signing an authorization card does not require that the employee vote in favor of the union in the actual election, you should be aware that the company may consent to recognize the union even without an election if more than 50 percent of the employees signed the authorization cards. Signing an authorization card, then, is vital for the union campaign to continue.

Step 3: Petitioning the NLRB

bargaining unit
Refers to the employees who will be voting in the election; if the union wins, these are the employees the union will represent.

Once the NLRB receives the petition, it must determine what the appropriate bargaining unit should be. The **bargaining unit** refers to the employees who will be voting in the election. If the union wins, these are the employees who will be represented by the union. The NLRB determines the bargaining unit on the basis of such factors as the similarity of employees with regard to their pay, benefits, type of work performed, physical proximity, organization structure, and so forth. The aim is to establish a bargaining unit in which covered employees share common interests and goals. In addition to determining the appropriate bargaining unit, the NLRB must decide whether an election can be held. Several factors may prohibit an election from being held. These include the following:[20]

1. A union election was held within the last 12 months.
2. The employees of the bargaining unit are already covered by another union.
3. The union has engaged in unfair practices, such as coercing employees to sign authorization cards.

Figure 14.2   **"Right-to-Work" States**

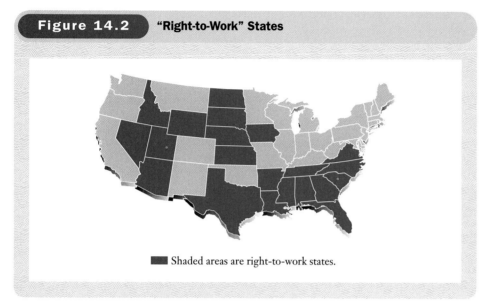

◼ Shaded areas are right-to-work states.

Source: D. McWhirter, *Your Rights at Work* (New York: Wiley, 1993).

Figure 14.3   **Authorization Card**

UNITED GLASS AND CERAMIC WORKERS OF NORTH AMERICA, AFL-CIO, CLC

OFFICIAL MEMBERSHIP APPLICATION AND AUTHORIZATION

I hereby apply for membership in the United Glass and Ceramic Workers of North America, AFL-CIO, CLC. I hereby designate and authorize the United Glass and Ceramic Workers of North America, AFL-CIO, CLC, as my collective bargaining representative in all matters pertaining to wages, rates of pay and other conditions of employment. I also authorize the United Glass and Ceramic Workers of North America, AFL-CIO, CLC, to request recognition from my employer as my bargaining agent.

SIGNATURE OF APPLICANT _____

EMPLOYED BY _____

APPLICATION RECEIVED BY_____

DATE _____

Source: G. Dessler, *Personnel/Human Resource Management* (Englewood Cliffs, NJ: Prentice-Hall, 1991).

Step 4: The Campaign

Assuming the NLRB authorizes an election, the next step is for both the union and management to present their arguments to the workers. Because of the company's easy access to employees, legal requirements stipulate that management must refrain from certain activities. An easy way to remember the forbidden activities is to think of them as a **"no SPITting" rule.** Specifically, management may not do any of the following: [21]

1. *S*py on union activities
2. *P*romise changes in personnel practices
3. *I*nterrogate employees
4. *T*hreaten employees

Examples of each of these categories are provided in Table 14.6, along with alternative actions that are allowed by the law. As you might guess, there are many ambiguous situations related to these laws. For example, consider the issues of threats. Do you see the distinction between saying "this facility *will* close if the union wins" and saying "some facilities close when a union wins?" According to labor laws, the first statement is an illegal threat; the second is permissible because it is only a statement of fact. From an employee's perspective, however, the implications of these two statements may be the same.

To return to the opening case, you may remember that the new owner talked about companies that closed when they became unionized. That would probably be legal, because he did not say that the same would happen to this company. And when he was asked if that would happen to EZ-Rest, he answered, "Who knows?" So, it is likely that his comments would be considered facts, rather than threats. Do you think his comments sounded threatening? Even though you may interpret them that way, as long as he sticks to the facts (for example, it is true that some companies close after becoming unionized), his comments are permissible under the law.

The ultimate punishment that can be leveled against the company for violation of campaign laws is automatic recognition of the union. A company that violates too many of these regulations runs the risk of losing by default.

Table 14.6	No SPITting: Dos and Don'ts for Management During the Representation Campaign

Don't	Do
1. Spy on employees by attending union meetings; listen to phone conversations about unions.	1. Allow employees to tell you what happened in meetings.
2. Interrogate employees; have private meetings with individual employees, where you ask about the union; ask in face-to-face meetings with employees about their feelings for the union.	2. Meet with employees in groups to discuss issues; have anonymous surveys publicly completed by employees.
3. Promise specific changes; add new benefits; promotions, and such.	3. Ask employees to give the company a chance to make changes.
4. Threaten employees, say that the facility will close, jobs will be eliminated, or the union will go on strike.	4. Say the facility might close, unions sometimes strike, jobs might be lost.

Because the union campaign is similar to a political campaign between two or more rival candidates, it should not surprise you that union campaigns have certain common themes. Some of the most common themes or campaign issues that management uses include the following:[22]

1. Things are not so bad.
2. Management provides certain rewards, which might disappear with unionization.
3. A union cannot guarantee anything.
4. A strike may occur; if so, everyone will lose.
5. Union representatives are outsiders; they don't really care about employees.
6. Give management a chance to improve things.

Thus, most of the issues raised by management revolve around two broad factors:

1. Things currently are not so bad.
2. The union will only make matters worse.

Four common union themes are the following:

1. Things may improve, but only because management feels challenged by the union.
2. Management is trying to frighten employees by threatening them.
3. The union is the employees; employees decide whether to strike.
4. Unions are good (unions may use quotes from appropriate respected public figures to support this assertion).[23]

Because management is in a defensive position in many union campaigns, the union often has the opportunity to go on the offensive and criticize many management actions.

In addition to these basic themes, both the union and management use a variety of specific tactics and techniques during the campaign. Some of the more common management tactics are to do the following:

1. Hire a labor lawyer
2. Hire a consultant
3. Fire employees who actively support the union
4. Spread rumors about job loss or the facility closing
5. Delay the election date
6. Give new benefits[24]

Do any of these tactics surprise you? You might wonder whether some of them, such as firing union supporters, are legal given what you read earlier in this chapter. In fact, several of these tactics, such as firing union supporters, are illegal under the National Labor Relations Act, which bans discrimination on the basis of union affiliation or activity. So why do companies often engage in such behaviors? Many companies believe that this is a useful way to intimidate workers so that they will vote against union representation. Careful research shows, however, that illegal tactics do not always benefit the company. While spreading rumors about possible plant closure, for example, does appear to discourage workers from voting for the union, delaying the election may actually backfire and appears generally to encourage workers to vote in favor of the union. Some frequently used tactics, then, appear to arouse more, rather than less, sympathy for the union.[25]

On the other hand, there is evidence that consultants and supervisors play a positive role in defeating the union. Consultants specializing in union campaigns, used in nearly 50 percent of union campaigns, appear to be a significant factor in defeating the union. Supervisors, perhaps because of their close relationship with the "voters," also appear to have a major effect on whether the union wins. If supervisors argue against the union, the union is likely to lose the election.[26]

Some of the most popular union tactics are the following:[27]

1. Mailing letters to employees describing the union and its benefits.
2. Holding meetings with employees.
3. Confronting the company.
4. Coordinating resources with other unions.
5. Working with community leaders to support unionization.

Compared with management tactics, which union tactics are most effective remains somewhat unclear. Much more depends on how the union communicates with the employees and the content of the communication, rather than the particular tactics used by the union. Most importantly, the union must develop a close, personal relationship with the employees. As an analogy to the political process, voters are often swayed by that intangible factor referred to as "charisma" as much as they are affected by the specific issues, such as crime and taxes.[28]

Step 5: Election Results

In order to win the election, the union must receive a simple majority (50 percent, plus 1) of the votes cast. It is also possible that the election will involve several unions wishing to represent the employees. If there is no simple majority, a run-off election is held between the two choices receiving the highest number of votes (this may include the "no union" option).

How have unions fared in elections over the years? If you remember the history of unions described earlier, it will not surprise you that unions have experienced more election losses than victories over the last few decades. In terms of the overall vote, while about 75 percent of workers would vote for a union in 1950, this number shrank to only 49 percent by 1989. Not surprisingly, then, the number of campaigns won by unions has declined from about 76 percent in the early 1950s to fewer than 50 percent by 1993. Thus, unions have experienced increasing difficulty in expanding their base of employees.[29] The only area in which unions have significantly increased in size is in the public sector or government offices, but even that trend has slowed during the past two decades.

❖ Conclusion

The history of unions in the United States is a long, often bitter story of two competing interest groups. In the last 40 years, however, management has increasingly held the upper hand over unions. The major exception has been the growth of unions in the public sector, but even that trend has slowed lately. Many laws now govern the relationship between unions, management, and employees, such as the Wagner Act, the Taft-Hartley Act, and the Landrum-Griffin Act. Workers may wish to have union representation for several basic reasons. As you also read, the union campaign has several distinct steps. The union campaign also has numerous laws governing what can be said and done, particularly by management. As you will see in the next chapter, once a union wins the election, the order of business becomes that of negotiating a contract and making sure that it is properly followed.

❖ Applying Core Concepts

1. Imagine the following situation: Chris Matthews, the owner of a manufacturing business, finds out that a local union has contacted the employees at the plant. In response, Chris posts the following memo: "I recently learned that a union has contacted you regarding possible representation. I can tell you now that I oppose any union, and if somehow the union won an election, I would refuse to negotiate a contract. I will immediately shut down the facility as well. Moreover, if I find out that any of you participate in any way with the union, I will immediately fire you." Is this memo legal? What laws have been violated?
2. Given what you read about EZ-Rest in the opening case, what might the new owner have done differently so that the workers did not become interested in unionization? What actions could he have taken during the campaign that were legal?
3. Explain how a union campaign is similar to a political campaign.
4. Considering laws you read about in earlier chapters, such as various civil rights acts, explain why workers may see unions as less helpful today than they were in the past.
5. How do you feel about unions? What factors (such as your work experience) do you think explain your feelings toward unions?

❖ Key Terms

Union	Taft-Hartley Act (Labor-Management Relations Act)	Union election
Wagner Act (National Labor Relations Act)		Authorization cards
	Landrum-Griffin Act (Labor-Management Reporting and Disclosure Act)	Bargaining unit
National Labor Relations Board (NLRB)		No SPITting rule

❖ CHAPTER 14 *Experiential Exercise*

Union Organizing at SGA Industries[30]

Introduction. President White sat in his office at SGA Industries thinking about the union election taking place down at the plant auditorium. He felt that the company had waged a successful campaign to persuade workers that their best interests would be served only if the company remained union free. As he awaited the election results, his mind began to wander back to the events leading up to today's election.

Background. SGA Industries is best known as the world's largest producer of women's hosiery and employs approximately 6,500 people in 10 plants in 5 communities in Georgia and South Carolina. The company's headquarters is located in Anderson, Georgia. The company's sales subsidiary, SGA, Inc., has 12 offices in major market areas throughout the United States and sells its products directly to distributors around the world. The company's strategy of strong identification with the customer has made the SGA name one of the most recognized in the entire hosiery industry.

SGA was founded in 1907 by Sam Gerome Anderson. Anderson built the company and the community was named after him in 1910. Ever since, the fortunes of Anderson residents have been interwoven with those of SGA. Over the years the company supported the community; donating land and money for churches, schools, and hospitals and providing jobs for nearly a third of the town's residents. As the years passed, further expansion and product diversification occurred, and the company gained a reputation as an industry leader in the design, production, and marketing of women's and men's hose and undergarments.

After the death of the last family member, Alexandra Anderson, SGA was managed by four chief executive officers in less than a dozen years before the company was purchased for $250 million by Jack Phillips. The new owner was a well-known Atlanta entrepreneur and business leader. Soon after the purchase, Phillips appointed Ted White as president of SGA.

Labor–Management Relations. Over the years SGA enjoyed a reputation as a steady job provider in an unstable industry. The company provided for its workers and treated them like family members. Many believe that the company's generosity to its employees and the town of Anderson helped to defeat an earlier union organizing drive by the Textile Workers of America by a vote of 3,937 to 1,782. At the time of the vote, the chairman called it "an expression of confidence by employees." The SGA vote was viewed as a severe blow to union organizing efforts in the South.

When Phillips purchased SGA, he announced that his major goals would be to improve the community and to improve the quality of life for SGA employees and their families. Phillips invested over $100 million to reach these goals. The total included funds for pay increases, new job benefits, capital improvements, in-cluding the use of robots, community improvements, and other contributions. These improvements were also accompanied by a shift in management philosophy. The theme of the new management approach was self-sufficiency, and it signaled an end to the benevolent paternalism that had so long characterized employee relations at SGA. Greater emphasis was placed on employee performance and productivity.

During the mid-80s, the entire hosiery industry experienced major problems. Growing foreign competition and imports had a negative impact on domestic hosiery manufacturers. Many manufacturers attempted to reverse the impact by intensive capital investments in new technology, reorganization and downsizing of plants, and by instituting programs to improve employee productivity and efficiency. SGA was not spared from this competition. Its international sales fell dramatically from $26 million to $10 million. Faced with increasing imports and weak consumer sales, the company was forced to lay off 1,500 employees, reduce pay scales, and to rescind many of the perks that the workers had enjoyed under the Anderson family. Many of these changes drew worker protests and created a good deal of tension between workers and management.

Wages in the industry had been rising steadily but were still lower than wages in the manufacturing sector in general. On a regional basis, the differential was still quite wide, with a study showing that wages ranged from $5.56 per hour in South Carolina to $8.90 in Michigan. In addition, as technology advanced, more skilled operatives were required, thus increasing the cost of turnover to companies. Employers in the industry also were becoming increasingly more dependent on women and minorities for employees. At SGA 40 percent of the employees were women and 35 percent of the total work force were minorities. Minorities and women made up less than 2 percent of the management staff.

The Election Campaign. Despite its earlier defeat, the Amalgamated Clothing and Textile Workers Union (ACTWU) was back in Anderson, armed and ready for an organizing effort that would divert the attention of SGA management for several long and tense months.

While many employers learn of union organizing efforts by their employees only after the National Labor Relations Board informs them, the ACTWU's efforts to organize SGA employees were clearly out in the open a full nine months before the election. With a union office in downtown Anderson and a healthy budget, the ACTWU, led by Chris Balog, engaged in one of the most sophisticated union organizing efforts ever seen in the area. Using computerized direct mailing to stay in touch with workers and extensive radio and television advertising, the union effort at SGA attracted wide attention. Many observers felt that the outcome of ACTWU's drive would have significant implications for the ability of labor unions to make inroads into traditionally nonunion regions of the country.

Union's Campaign. The campaign issues developed and communicated to workers were for the most part predictable. Job security was brought to the front early and was easily introduced to the campaign in the wake of selective plant closings and over 1,500 layoffs by SGA management. In addition, in attempting to become more competitive in the face of increasing foreign competition, increased workloads and reduced wage rates were key issues raised by the union. The union repeatedly accused Phillips of engaging in unfair labor practices by threatening to sell or close the company if the union were to win bargaining rights for SGA workers. To a certain extent, the union did expand on the traditional wages, hours, and working conditions issues typically raised in organizing efforts. As the campaign progressed, Phillips became a focal point of union rhetoric, and the union attempted to portray Phillips as a greedy and ruthless city slicker from Atlanta who was not interested in the long-term survival of SGA and its employees.

Management's Campaign. While Phillips became a focal point of union criticism as the campaign wore on, his role in management's response to the organizing effort was critical throughout the months preceding the election. With President White leading the anti-union campaign, backed by a sophisticated strategy developed by an Atlanta law firm, specializing in anti-union campaigns, SGA was able to quickly respond to every issue raised by the union.

The SGA strategy to defeat the union organizing effort included extensive meetings with community, business, and religious leaders in an attempt to influence workers' views about the union. Extensive use of anti-union films were required viewing for workers on company time. Letters sent to workers' homes by President White and Phillips emphasized the need for team spirit, not only to keep the union out, but to overcome the threat created by hosiery imports. President White put it this way: "We intend to do everything that is proper and legal in this campaign to defeat the union. This is essential if we are to remain competitive in the hosiery business. Every day we are facing more and more foreign competition. Not only do our workers understand this, but I think the public does also. We have been able to communicate with our workers in the past, and we don't need a third-party voice. We all must work together as a team. The only way SGA can beat the encroaching foreign competition is to streamline and consolidate our operations."

White and Phillips made repeated visits to plants to shake hands and listen to workers' concerns. The weekly employee newsletter was filled with anti-union letters written by workers and community members. Late in the campaign a letter went out to SGA workers from Jack Phillips explaining why they should vote against the union (see Exhibit A). In response to the union claim that Phillips was attempting to sell the company, Phillips also told the workers that "SGA is not for sale, but if I determine that the company cannot operate competitively, I can and I will cease to operate SGA. This is entirely up to me, and nobody can stop me—including this union."

Employees' Views. The employees were divided over the union organizing campaign. Several employees formed an Anti-Union Committee which organized an SGA Loyalty Day. A statement by Terry Floyd, a shift leader, summed up the view expressed by some employees: "We, as employees of SGA, do not feel that it is in the best interest of our company and its employees to be represented by ACTWU. Many generations of the same families have worked at this plant; part of our strength is family heritage. I'm afraid a union will destroy that strength. We feel that a union is not needed and that we can work with management as a team." At one rally sponsored by the Anti-Union Committee, "No Union" badges, "Be Wise–Don't Unionize" T-shirts, and "Vote No" hats were worn by several hundred employees.

Other workers expressed support for the union. One worker stated, "We need a union for protection. At least it would give us a voice. Supervisors can be too arbitrary." Others pointed to pay increases and bonuses for top management in the wake of wage cuts and layoffs for plant workers. Many older employees, who remembered the generosity of the Anderson family, also

TO ALL SGA EMPLOYEES:

It is only fair for you to know SGA's policy on unions. Our policy is quite simple. We are absolutely opposed to a union at any of our plants. We intend to use every legal and proper means to stay non-union.

As you know, the hosiery industry has been under great pressure and competition from foreign firms. Sales in the industry have dwindled over the past few years and we are in a poor profit position. Our government has done little to protect your jobs and stop the imports from eroding our sales. Only you and I can save this company and your jobs.

Our whole industry has been forced to modernize our production process to make it more efficient. In fact you know that many firms have merged together to strengthen their market position. Our company, too, will have to explore the possible advantages of pooling resources and products. In the long run such strategy can only benefit employees and management alike. I know bringing in the ACTWU at this time will only drive up our operating expenses and jeopardize our chances of making such arrangements. Only management has the right to decide how to operate this company. If we find we cannot operate this company profitably, we may be forced to consider other options.

We are convinced that unions have the tendency to create an adversarial relationship between employees and management. Cooperation and teamwork cannot exist in such a hostile environment. It is only through cooperation and teamwork that we will get through the crisis.

No SGA employee is ever going to need a union to keep her job. We know that ACTWU cannot help this company or you and will probably cause us to lose even more of our market and threaten your job security. I urge you—do not vote for the union. Let's all pull together and remember the goodwill of the Anderson family and how it has stood behind you all of these years.

Sincerely,

Jack Phillips

Jack Phillips
Chief Executive Officer

---

expressed bitterness toward SGA and worried about their pensions.

Questions

1. What was the impetus for the union organizing effort at SGA Industries?

2. Discuss SGA's strategy in managing the representation campaign.

3. Discuss any potential unfair labor practice charges SGA management might face as a result of their campaign strategy.

❖ Chapter 14 References

1. A. Sloane and F. Witney, *Labor Relations* (Englewood Cliffs, NJ: Prentice-Hall: 1977).
2. D. Leslie, *Labor Law in a Nutshell* (St. Paul, MN: West, 1986).
3. D. McWhirter, *Your Rights at Work* (New York: Wiley, 1993).
4. Ibid.
5. Ibid.
6. R. Edwards, *Rights at Work* (Washington: The Brookings Institute, 1993).
7. Labor Letter, *Wall Street Journal*, 30 August 1994, A1.
8. C. J. Coleman, *Managing Labor Relations in the Public Sector* (San Francisco: Jossey-Bass, 1990).
9. J. Brett, "Why Employees Want Unions," *Organizational Dynamics* (Spring 1980): 47–59.
10. R. Dunham and F. Smith, *Organizational Surveys* (Glenview, IL: Scott, Foresman, 1979).
11. "Work Week," *Wall Street Journal*, 29 November 1994, A1.
12. C. Rusbult, D. Farrell, G. Rogers, and A. Mainous, "Impact of Exchange Variables on Exit, Voice, Loyalty, and Neglect: An Integrating Model of Responses to Declining Job Satisfaction," *Academy of Management Journal* 31 (1988): 599–627.
13. S. Youngblood, A. DeNisi, J. Molleston, and W. Mobley, "The Impact of Work Environment, Instrumentality Beliefs, Perceived Labor Union Image, and Subjective Norms on Union Voting Intentions," *Academy of Management Journal* 27 (1984): 576–90.
14. M. Zalesny, "Comparison of Economic and Noneconomic Factors in Predicting Faculty Vote Preference in a Union Representation Election," *Journal of Applied Psychology* 70 (1985): 243–56.
15. S. Deshpande and J. Fiorito, "Specific and General Beliefs in Union Voting Models," *Academy of Management Journal* 32 (1989): 883–97.
16. S. Jarrell and T. Stanley, "A Meta-Analysis of the Union–Nonunion Wage Gap," *Industrial and Labor Relations Review* 44 (1990): 54–67.
17. Labor Letter, *Wall Street Journal*, 23 August 1994, A1.
18. Ibid.
19. H. Cheeseman, *Business Law: The Legal, Ethical, and International Environment* (Englewood Cliffs, NJ: Prentice-Hall, 1992).
20. S. Kahn, B. Brown, and M. Lanzarone, *Legal Guide to Human Resources* (Boston: Warren, Gorham, & Lamont, 1995).
21. Ibid.
22. J. Getman, "Ruminations on Union Organizing in the Private Sector," in *Human Resources Management: Readings*, ed. F. Foulkes (Englewood Cliffs, NJ: Prentice-Hall, 1989).
23. Ibid.
24. R. Peterson, T. Lee, and B. Finnegan, "Strategies and Tactics in Union Organizing Campaigns," *Industrial Relations* 31 (1992): 370–81.
25. R. Freeman and M. Kleiner, "Employer Behavior in the Face of Union Organizing Drives," *Industrial and Labor Relations Review* 43 (1990): 351–65.
26. Ibid.
27. Peterson, Lee, and Finnegan, "Strategies and Tactics."
28. Getman, "Ruminations on Union Organizing."
29. Edwards, *Rights at Work.*
30. Source: S. Nkomo, M. Fottler, R. Mcafee (1996). *Applications in Human Resource Management.* Cincinnati, OH: South-Western. Contributed by Gerald E. Calvasina, The University of North Carolina at Charlotte.

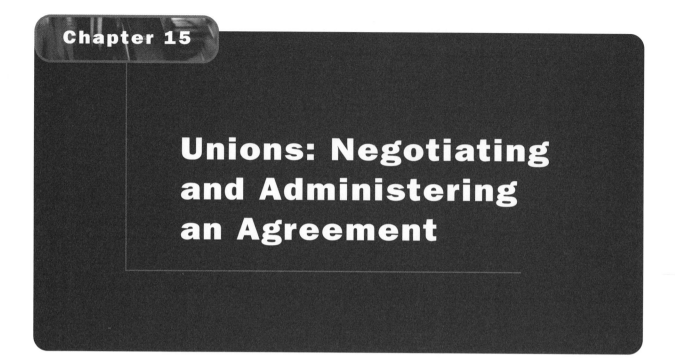

Unions: Negotiating and Administering an Agreement

After reading this chapter, you should be capable of:

1. Explaining the structure of a union.
2. Discussing the steps in contract negotiations.
3. Describing the steps in a typical grievance procedure.
4. Defining a union decertification election.
5. Providing suggestions for improving management–union relationships.

Opening Case

Phyliss Martin, a maintenance worker at Wilson Ship Builders, was recently terminated by the company. A brief history of her case is as follows. About one year ago, a random drug test revealed that Phyliss recently had used marijuana. For this, she was suspended without pay for one week. About one month later, Phyliss was arrested near her home and indicted for drug possession with the intent to distribute illegal substances. Because Wilson Ship Builders is the major employer located in a small town, her arrest was reported on the front page of the newspaper as well as on the 10 o'clock news. The company terminated her on the grounds that she violated its policy prohibiting employees from using illegal drugs while on company grounds or on company business, and that illegal drugs are cause for dismissal even if used off the company grounds if they have a negative effect on performance or the safety of the employee or other employees. In addition, conviction for a felony crime was cause for immediate dismissal. Because Phyliss is a union worker, however, she is covered by a contract that gives her the right to file a grievance, or to seek reconsideration of this decision. In fact, she may be able to seek reconsideration through an impartial third party, typically referred to as an arbitrator. The arbitrator, if her grievance goes that far, will attempt to determine whether in fact the company's decision has been fair, in light of the terms and conditions of the bargaining agreement.

Given what you have read about Phyliss Martin's case, do you think that the decision to terminate her was fair in light of the bargaining agreement?

What would you have ruled if you were the arbitrator? In an actual case similar to the one described here, the arbitrator decided that the company had indeed been wrong in discharging Phyliss. His reasoning was that the company had no proof that she was under the influence of drugs when she was arrested. Moreover, the contract only permitted termination when the employee is convicted of a felony crime. At the time of the termination, Phyliss had been arrested and indicted, but had not yet been found guilty.

Regardless of whether you agree or disagree with the arbitrator's decision, it should be clear to you through this example that employees covered by a union contract may have considerable protection from management decisions. Indeed, as identified in the previous chapter, a major function of the union is to administer the contract and represent the employees in disputing management decisions. As in the situation experienced by Phyliss Martin, the protection afforded by the union can be considerable.

This chapter discusses in greater detail the key functions performed by a union in a covered facility. As you will see, the union must first negotiate a collective bargaining agreement (or, in the case of a facility in which the contract will expire, the union must renegotiate a new contract). Once a contract is negotiated and approved by the relevant parties, the union's task is to administer the contract and represent the employees in the grievance process. In addition, you will read about some suggestions that might help management to maintain effective relationships with the union.

Union Structure: Who's Who in the Union

Labor unions have three major levels in their organizational structure.[1] As shown in Figure 15.1, the local unions form the first layer in the **union structure.** Each local union represents a group of employees working in one area for the company. The local union is responsible for negotiating the contract, administering the contract, and organizing nonunionized workers. As a member of a union, you are likely to interact most often with two people in the local union: the business representative and the

union structure
Labor unions have three major levels in their structure: the local unions form the first layer; national and international unions form the next level; and federations represent the top of the union structure.

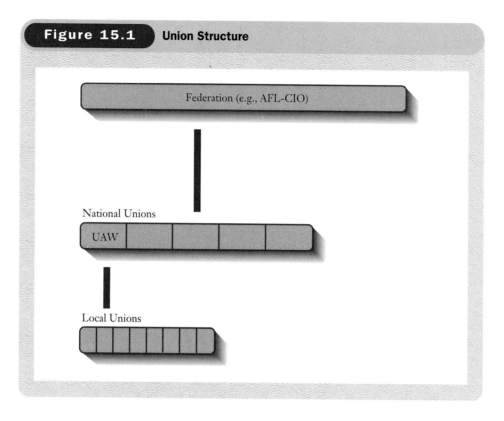

Figure 15.1   **Union Structure**

Federation (e.g., AFL-CIO)

National Unions

UAW

Local Unions

business representative
The business representative's primary responsibility is to represent the union in contract negotiations, and also is responsible for collecting union dues, paying union bills, and communicating with the national union.

union steward
The union steward plays a key role in day-to-day relationships with management, usually performing the union-related work on a part-time basis.

union steward. As suggested by the term, the **business representative** plays a key role in the success of the local union. Usually a full-time job, the business representative has the primary responsibility for representing the union in contract negotiations. He or she will also represent the union at certain stages in the grievance process and has a major responsibility for collecting union dues, paying union bills, and interacting with the national union. The **union steward** plays a key role in day-to-day relationships with management. Typically, the union steward holds a regular job within the company and performs the union-related work on a part-time basis. Most grievances begin with the union steward. Both the business representative and the union steward, then, play an important role in the local union.

National and international unions form the next level in the structure. As shown in Figure 15.1, they are composed of local unions. Presently, there are nearly 200 national unions in the United States. Their rules and regulations stipulate the conditions under which the local unions operate. The national union generally has extensive power over the local union, including the right to approve any contracts, strike decisions, and so forth. The national union also plays a major role in formulating policies, such as collective bargaining goals. The local union pays dues to the national union. In return, the national union provides a variety of support activities to the local unions, including legal assistance, financial assistance during strikes, and various educational services. The national unions are operated by officers who are elected by delegates from the local unions.

Federations represent the top of the union structure. As discussed in Chapter 14, the American Federation of Labor and Congress of Industrial Organizations (AFL-CIO) is an example of a large, powerful federation. More than 100 national unions belong to the AFL-CIO. This federation is governed by an executive council and delegates from the national unions. The federation provides numerous services to the national unions that belong to it, and it frequently engages in political activities.

Now that you understand the structure of a union, you will read about the two primary tasks performed by the union for its bargaining unit employees: negotiating and administering the union contract.

Negotiating the Union Contract

The purpose of the union contract is to establish rules and regulations, agreed to by both union and management, that will govern human resources practices (promotions, pay, benefits, job assignments, and so forth) for the bargaining unit employees. As you can see in Figure 15.2, negotiation of a union contract generally involves four steps: preparation, initial stages, middle stages, and final stages. We will consider each step in greater detail.[2]

Preparation for Negotiations

Unlike earlier years, when contract negotiations were often characterized by shouting, threatening, and other aggressive behaviors, contract negotiations today are far more frequently the product of thorough preparation. This is because most union contracts must be negotiated every few years, so treachery or overt manipulation on the part of one side is likely to backfire the next time around. Preparation for the negotiation requires that both parties determine their basic objectives and obtain and analyze information on each of the bargaining issues. For example, in preparing for its 1994 through 1997 collective bargaining objectives, the United Rubber Workers union decided on four basic goals:

1. Increasing wages and obtaining cost-of-living adjustments
2. Improving job security
3. Providing further training and career development programs
4. Improving pension programs[3]

Let us consider one bargaining issue in greater detail and see what kinds of information will be collected in preparing for the negotiations. Specifically, we will consider the kind of information that will be obtained for determining the appropriate wage.

Determining Appropriate Wage. Three factors are generally considered in determining the appropriate wage:

1. The wage paid by other comparable companies
2. The company's ability to pay
3. The cost of living

The first factor, often referred to as the comparative norm, is the wage paid by other companies. While this may sound fairly simple in principle, in practice, the comparative norm is much more complex. For example, what are "other comparable companies"? Are they all companies in the same industry (such as all automobile manufacturing firms), regardless of size and profitability? Second, the company negotiating the contract may actually be part of several industries, not just one industry. Third, the job itself may be treated differently in different companies, or the pay package may differ from company to company. Union and management negotiators may, therefore, arrive at widely varied figures, based on which information they think is most relevant.

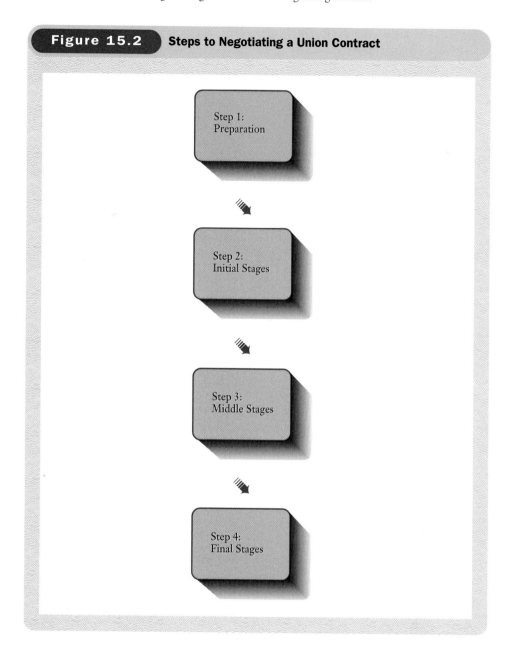

Figure 15.2   Steps to Negotiating a Union Contract

Step 1:
Preparation

Step 2:
Initial Stages

Step 3:
Middle Stages

Step 4:
Final Stages

The second factor, the ability to pay, concerns the ability of the company to pay a particular wage. A major determinant of ability to pay is the company's profitability. As simple as this sounds, in practice, it too is far more complex. One reason for the complexity is that current profitability does not necessarily indicate future profitability. A company may, for example, be prospering currently, but indicators may suggest a downturn in the near future. Second, profits may be used for various capital improvements, which in turn provide less money for wages. Whether this in fact is a better use of profits may be debatable. Finally, even if a company is quite profitable, a wage increase may drive up the cost of the product or service, which in turn may result in business loss. For example, in the major league baseball strike of 1993–94, the owners claimed that the high average salary earned by players was driving some teams out of business and proposed a salary cap. In turn, the players' union argued that the more profitable owners should simply subsidize the less profitable owners. Even with the same information, union and management negotiators may arrive at different conclusions as to the company's ability to pay.[4]

The final factor used to determine the appropriate wage is the cost of living. Unions, in particular, believe that a fair wage is one that enables the workers to live in a reasonably comfortable fashion. Various governmental agencies, such as the Bureau of Labor Statistics, provide information as to how much it costs to live at a reasonable standard in different parts of the country. In addition, because the cost of living can be expected to rise over the term of the contract, both sides will attempt to estimate the future inflation rate. Again, different sources of information on which to base estimates can lead to different conclusions. Of course, in industries that are experiencing serious economic problems, cost-of-living increases may be impossible. In 1994, for example, union workers at United Airlines agreed to wage cuts over a six-year period; in exchange, however, workers would obtain partial ownership of the company.[5]

Aside from negotiating the basic wage, rules for modifying the basic wage may be adopted in the contract. For example, some union contracts may include an automatic adjustment, referred to as an **escalator clause,** that adjusts wages (both up and down), depending on the cost of living. Another type of rule, the wage reopener, permits renegotiation of the contract if requested by either the union or management. Clearly, much preparation is required by both sides in order to arrive at a contract that will be acceptable to all relevant parties.

escalator clause
A clause included in some union contracts that adjusts wages (both up and down), depending on the cost of living.

Besides obtaining relevant information for each issue, management should obtain information from supervisors and managers as to what specific problems have arisen with previous contracts. From the union's perspective, it is important to communicate with members to determine what issues and concerns they have, so that a contract can be negotiated that they will endorse. Once preparation has been concluded by both sides, they are ready to move to the actual bargaining process. During the bargaining process, chances of a positive outcome may depend on knowing the likelihood of a strike. Box 15.1 offers some indicators of strike probability.

Initial Negotiation Stages

Frequently, an initial meeting between union and management focuses on exchanging information on each party's position. In most cases, the union provides a list of its positions on such issues as pay increase, benefits, and so forth. These positions may be highly unrealistic, the main goal from the union's perspective being to satisfy members that the union is doing its best. Both parties often invite guests, who attend in a ceremonial role. Unions, for example, may have members of other unions attend their initial meetings.

Middle Stages of the Bargaining Process

At this intermediate stage, both union and management should have a fairly good idea as to the key objectives of the other side. Each side secretly determines what it will concede on each issue, as well as its key objectives. Based on this information, serious negotiations begin. In 1994, for example, unions at General Electric (GE) began the negotiation process with high expectations because GE had had excellent profits. The company, however, was reluctant to give in to the union demands. The high expectations of the union, coupled with GE management's resistance, led to diminished progress as the expiration date of the contract drew near.[6]

YOUR TURN

Box 15.1
Some Important Clues for Predicting Which Plants Will Strike

A comparison of plants that have gone on strike with plants that did not go on strike suggests certain clues useful in predicting the strike decision. One major difference between the striking and nonstriking plants was the number of grievances filed and the number of days it took to settle a grievance. On average, striking plants had about 50 grievances over a three-month period, while nonstriking plants had around 10. Moreover, it took roughly three times longer to resolve a grievance at the striking plants. A second major difference was the number of complaints filed by the third shift. At striking plants, the third shift typically had many more complaints than at the nonstriking plants. Why should complaints by the third shift be an important clue? The third shift may be a critical indicator of problems because being at work at night (generally from 11 p.m. to 7 a.m.), these employees generally have the least contact with management (top management rarely is around at night), the least experienced supervisors (the most senior supervisors will prefer day work), and the most equipment-related problems (support services are usually the most limited at this time). The third shift therefore is often the best indicator of union–management friction. Another important clue was the amount of overtime. Among the striking plants, overtime was generally required by the union contract, with penalties for workers who refused the request. By contrast, in the nonstriking plants, provisions for easing the burden of overtime work were provided, such as rotation among departments and extra rewards (such as tickets to local sports events) for those working overtime. Striking plants also gave much more power to supervisors, including the right to terminate, while nonstriking plants gave much less power to supervisors. Finally, plants differed with regard to organizational structure. Striking plants tended to be one of many plants in the company or division, while nonstriking plants tended to be the only plant in the division or company. While the precise reason for this finding is unclear, the multi-plant arrangement means that top management has much less awareness of employee relations problems. Furthermore, many human resource practices may be established at the company and division level, which may not be appropriate for all of the plants. It may be that lack of specific attention to each plant results in more labor strife.

Plants interested in reducing the likelihood of a strike should carefully monitor these indicators and, where problems appear, take steps to address them.

Source: Adapted from W. Imberman, "Who Strikes—and Why?" *Harvard Business Review* (November/December 1983): 18–28.

Two strategies often used are the trading point procedure and the counterproposal approach. Each of these is explained in greater detail next.

Trading Point Procedure. This technique is a form of "horse-trading" approach. Essentially, the **trading point procedure** involves one side saying to the other, "We'll concede on this issue (such as wage increases), if you concede on this other issue (for example, overtime pay).

trading point procedure
The trading point procedures involve one side saying to the other: "We'll concede on this issue (for example, wage increases), if you concede on this other issue (for example, overtime pay)."

counterproposal
This technique involves making an offer in response to the other side's offer.

Counterproposal. This technique involves making an offer in response to the other side's offer. For example, the union may ask for a $1.00-per-hour raise. Management may then make a **counterproposal** of a $.50 raise, along with double overtime. Counterproposals are actually used by the National Labor Relations Board as evidence of good faith bargaining, which is required under the National Labor Relations Act (see Chapter 14).

In sum, the middle stages of contract negotiation involve serious discussion and activity. The final stages of the negotiation process are often the most important ones, though.

Final Stages of Contract Negotiations

In many cases, the contract negotiations will go down to the wire as both sides wait until the old contract runs out or a strike is about to occur. An imminent strike deadline may, in fact, force both parties to reconsider their priorities. In the 1994 GE example, the contract negotiations were concluded shortly before a strike deadline. In the final agreement, the union received the highest wage increase and best improvement in pension funds in years, but it received few gains in other areas, such as job security. In fact, the union contract even required employees to pay more for health benefits than in previous years.[7]

In order to avoid a strike, two mechanisms are often used: joint study groups and mediation.

Joint Study Groups. As suggested by the term, a **joint study group** is a task force, composed of both management and union representatives (and often third parties as well) for the purpose of examining issues of particular concern in a nonadversarial setting. The group is often established immediately after a contract is negotiated, so that both sides are able to discuss controversial issues well before a new contract is negotiated. With sufficient time, many problem areas may be worked out before the next set of negotiations takes place.

joint study group
A joint study group is a task force, composed of both management and union representatives, and often third parties as well, for the purpose of examining issues of particular concern in a nonadversarial setting.

Mediation. In **mediation,** a neutral party meets with the union and management to work out an agreement. It is important to note that the mediator's suggestions are not binding on either party. That is, either side may choose to reject the mediator's proposals. The purpose of mediation, then, is to involve an independent, neutral party who can generate new solutions for a negotiation impasse. In many cases, a mediator has indeed been helpful in resolving an impasse. The United States government operates the Federal Mediation and Conciliation Service, which provides mediators for businesses that are experiencing difficulty in contract negotiations. Many states also provide similar services. During the major league baseball strike of 1993–94, President Clinton appointed William Usery to serve as a mediator.

mediation
In mediation, a neutral party meets with the union and management to work out an agreement (the mediator's suggestions are not binding on either party).

Research has shown that the most effective mediators are highly experienced in the mediation process and work hard to generate new, creative solutions. As one effective mediator stated it, "Mediation doesn't start until both of the parties have told the mediator there's no more room for compromise."[8]

When No Contract Can Be Negotiated

When a contract cannot be successfully negotiated, workers may choose to go on **strike,** or refuse to go to work. Although relatively rare, a strike can be quite disruptive to an organization. This is particularly true for a large organization, where a strike at one plant may force other plants and facilities to slow down or even close as a result. For example, if an automobile manufacturer experiences a strike at the brake production facility, it may not be possible to continue to build cars at other facilities because no brakes are available. The strike, or the threat of one, is the union's ultimate weapon against the company. That is one reason why, in recent times, as businesses increasingly hire **replacement workers** (often referred to as "scabs") to replace striking workers, union power has diminished significantly. Recent attempts to pass congressional laws limiting a company's right to hire replacement workers have failed, much to the chagrin of unions.

strike
When workers refuse to go to work.

replacement workers
Often called "scabs," replacement workers are hired to replace striking personnel.

Another reason why the threat of a strike has diminished in value to the union is that companies have developed extensive backup plans. For example, in coping with the 1994 strike by the United Automobile Workers (UAW), Caterpillar used a variety of strategies, such as utilizing replacement, temporary, and management workers to operate its manufacturing facilities; shifting work to nonunion production sites; and making extensive use of automation.[9]

Despite the broad publicity when a strike occurs, such events are relatively rare in the United States. During 1993, there were only 32 work stoppages. In 1997, there were 29 work stoppages.[10] Box 15.2 lists some Web sites relevant to union topics.

Should Public-Sector Employees Be Allowed to Strike?

One of the most controversial issues regarding public-sector employees concerns the right to strike. Currently, only about 10 states legally permit public-sector employees to strike, and even these states apply restrictions (police and firefighters are typically prohibited from striking, for example). Nevertheless, public-sector employees do sometimes go on strike, even when illegal. In 1988, for example, 9 major strikes by public-sector employees involved some 16,000 workers. Over the years, the vast majority of the strikes have occurred in education settings (in fact, you may have had additional vacation from school as a result), with the next largest number occurring in the mass transit area.[11]

Should public-sector employees have the right to strike? What do you think? Here are some of the basic reasons for permitting them to strike.[12]

1. **Few Public-Sector Jobs Are Really Essential.** Aside from police and firefighters, one could argue that few public-sector jobs are critical for proper functioning. For example, many jobs could be subcontracted with private firms, such as trash removal and bus driving. With few exceptions (perhaps police and firefighters), the public could function effectively without these workers.

2. **Preventing Strikes Leads to Other Forms of Protest.** Even if the employees are prohibited from striking, they can usually use other means to express their discontent. For example, police can refuse to issue tickets, firefighters can refuse to carry out certain routine work (such as conduct inspections), and so forth. According to this argument, prohibiting strikes simply means the workers will use other approaches to express their displeasure with the terms and conditions of work.

3. **Penalties for Striking Create Other Problems.** As just noted, public-sector employees often strike, even if prohibited. The penalties for such illegal actions, however, may create more problems. For example, an illegal New York prison-guard strike resulted in 8,000 employees having their pay cut. The guards then appealed the penalties on an individual basis, which required more than 2,500 hearings. The hearings required the state to spend substantial amounts of time and money. This argument suggests that the costs of prohibiting strikes outweigh any gains.

Here are some of the arguments against permitting public-sector workers to strike:

1. **Public Employees Have Unfair Control.** Compared to their private-sector counterparts, the "employer" in the public sector has relatively little power to respond to a strike. The employer in the public sector cannot lock out the employees

WEBBING AROUND

Box 15.2

http://www.nwu.org/grv/ grvdiv.htm#grvhow This Web site shows how union members file a grievance against the company. Do you think the procedure described there is fair?

http://lotto-mail.com/ download.htm This Web site provides a copy of one union contract.

http://nabet57.com/ Visit the Web site of this union. Do you like it?

http://www.aflcio.org/home. htm This union Web site has an extensive amount of interesting information.

and cannot lose customers or revenue. Because most public-sector organizations have a monopoly on their product or service (for example, public transportation, public schools), the customers have little or no choice but to encourage management to settle. Under this argument, there is an essential difference between the public and private sectors, and therefore strikes should not be permitted in the public sector.

2. **Penalties for Strikes Must Be Enforced in Order to Work.** In response to the third reason given in favor of allowing public-sector employees to strike, some argue that enforcement of penalties for striking has simply been too lax to be meaningful. According to this argument, then, consistently applied penalties for striking would definitely inhibit illegal strikes.

Clearly, there are important points on both sides of the argument regarding the right of public-sector employees to strike. Whether laws change in the future remains to be seen.

Current Trends in Contract Negotiations

In recent years, contract negotiations have produced relatively small increases in workers' pay. In 1994, despite a growing economy, wages on average increased only 2 percent for the first year covered by the contract, representing one of the smallest increases on record. More than 20 percent of the contracts provided no raise for workers during the first year covered. Over the life of the contract, bargaining agreements covering 1,000 or more workers in the private sector averaged annual pay increases of 2.3 percent, compared to 2.1 percent, 3 percent, and 3.2 percent, in 1993, 1992, and 1991, respectively.

At the same time, some contract negotiations have focused on areas besides wage increases. In the health service industry, for example, the National Health and Human Care Employees Union negotiated a contract that guaranteed jobs of all covered workers with at least two years of service. Layoffs created by financial emergency would be decided by a four-person committee, composed of two union members and two management personnel. Terminated employees would be given as much as 80 percent of their salaries and family health insurance for one year. Management also agreed to give the union 30 days' notice of any proposed job changes, thus providing an opportunity for the union to respond.[13] In today's world, where job security is relatively low, contract provisions providing protection from layoffs may be more valuable to union members than are large pay increases.

INTERCULTURAL ISSUES IN HUMAN RESOURCES

Box 15.3
Union Changes: An International Perspective

Unions are undergoing many changes, not only in the United States, but in the world. In some countries, unions are experiencing the same loss of workers as in the United States. Great Britain, for example, has experienced a decline in the number of trade employees represented by a union, as a result of workforce reductions and plant shutdowns. In other areas of the world, changes in unions have been much more profound. The Republic of Korea, for example, has experienced myriad changes in the last ten years. Major labor law reforms in 1987 resulted in a large increase in the number of union members in just two years, followed by a small decline in the next two years. A variety of bills to provide further labor reforms, including allowing public-sector employees

to unionize, were vetoed by the president in the early 1990s. In 1992, the government attempted to pass legislation weakening the unions, whom it blamed for economic problems. Concerted opposition from Korean unions, as well as from the International Labour Organization, which Korea joined in 1991, prevented passage of this legislation. Union activists hope that additional laws more favorable toward unions can be passed in the coming years.

The situation for unions is quite different in mainland China. Recent changes in standards of living have led to much greater awareness of workplace problems. Large numbers of workers are employed in low-paying, dangerous factory settings. Fires often break out, leading to many deaths. For

example, explosions in mines during the first three months of 1994 resulted in the deaths of more than 750 workers. Some human rights groups and international unions are clamoring for sanctions against China until workplace conditions are improved. There is only one legal union in China, the All-China Federation of Trade Unions, which does little to prevent these problems. Some dissidents have considered establishing a new union, called the League for the Protection of Workers' Rights. Another response has been an increase in strikes. Although illegal, the number of strikes increased to more than 8,000 in 1993. How Chinese unions will fare in the future is unknown.

Sources: Adapted from P. B. Beaumont, and R. I. D. Harris. "Trade Union Recognition and Employment Contraction. Britain, 1980–1984," *British Journal of Industrial Relations* 29 (1991): 49–58; Y. Park, "Industrial Relations and Labour Law Developments in the Republic of Korea," *International Labor Review* 132 (1993): 581–82; and M. W. Brauchli and J. Kahn, "Toil and Trouble," *Wall Street Journal*, 19 May 1994, A1, A4.

In sum, successfully negotiating a union contract is a complicated, potentially lengthy task. Although many contracts are negotiated with little conflict, other contracts are only resolved after considerable negotiation or even a strike. Union changes are occurring all around the world, as discussed in Box 15.3.

Administering the Union Contract

Once a contract has been successfully negotiated, the major task becomes administration of the contract. While negotiating the contract may seem difficult and time-consuming, administering the contract can be far more difficult and time-consuming. The reason for this is twofold: first, the contract cannot anticipate every possible situation or issue that will arise, second, many situations will be less than clear-cut as to how they fit within the language of the contract. In many cases, questions will arise as to whether management has violated the contract. Virtually all union contracts, therefore, include a grievance procedure. As described in the opening case, a **grievance procedure** provides a mechanism for the employee or union to dispute a decision that is believed to be in violation of the contract. Because of the importance of the grievance procedure, it will be discussed in greater detail next.

grievance procedure
A grievance procedure provides a mechanism for the employee or union to dispute a decision that is believed to be in violation of the contract.

The Grievance Procedure

Although no one grievance procedure is used by all companies, most grievance procedures have the following steps: [14]

1. The employee, with assistance from the union steward, files the necessary forms to initiate a grievance. At this stage, the employee and the shop steward meet with the first-line supervisor to resolve the dispute. About 20 percent of grievances are resolved at this step.[15]
2. If the employee is not satisfied with the solution proposed by the first-line supervisor, he or she can go to the next level of supervision (such as the shift supervisor) to resolve the conflict. At this stage, the union's business representative may represent the grievant. Approximately 34 percent of grievances are resolved at this step.[16]
3. If the employee is not satisfied with the decision in Step 2, he or she may seek resolution at the next level of management, which may involve the plant manager. At this step, the employee would probably be represented by a higher-level union representative, such as the local union's vice president. Nearly one-third of grievances are resolved in Step 4.[17]
4. If the employee still is not satisfied with the outcome, he or she has the right to request an arbitration hearing. An arbitration hearing involves a neutral third party or arbitrator, who will listen to the arguments of both sides and make a ruling. Unlike decisions made by a mediator, which either party may reject, both parties must accept the arbitration decision. Just over 10 percent of grievances proceed all the way to arbitration.[18]

Employee's Perspective on the Grievance Procedure

Why would the union encourage you to file a grievance? Three reasons may be offered. First, the union may feel that the terms of the contract have been violated. For example, the union may believe that your supervisor disciplined you without just cause. Second, the union may be fulfilling its obligation to represent you in a fair manner, having you file a grievance will serve as evidence that the union is fulfilling this legal obligation. Third, the union may encourage you to file a grievance for political reasons, such as a need to seem tough with management and stand up for its members.[19]

You may be wondering what the chances are that you will be victorious if your grievance proceeds all the way to the arbitration stage. Research indicates that the nature of the grievance is a decisive factor. If you are involved in a discharge, you have a 50 percent chance of losing the case and approximately a 33 percent chance of having a compromise being awarded (for example, you might be suspended for one week without pay). If you are filing a grievance for a lesser discipline action (such as a one-day suspension), you have slightly more than one in three chances of completely winning your case, a similar probability of completely losing, and slightly less than a one-in-three chance of obtaining a compromise. In most cases, then, it is in your best interests as an employee to file a grievance if you are in a unionized facility and feel mistreated.[20]

We turn now to a more detailed examination of the arbitration stage of the grievance process, which plays an important role in management–union relations.

Arbitration Process

The **arbitration process** is referred to as a "quasi-legal" proceeding because it resembles a courtroom hearing, but the rules are not as formalized. For example, a

arbitration process
Resembles a courtroom hearing, but the rules are not as formalized. An arbitrator is selected, and that person is responsible for making a final ruling after considering all of the relevant evidence and testimony, and providing a decision and explanation in a written report.

contract may state that only one person will serve as an arbitrator or that a mutually agreed-upon arbitrator will be used. No one standard procedure determines how the hearing will proceed. Although there are no specific rules for the arbitration process, some common features exist. We will discuss two areas in greater detail: the selection and the role of the arbitrator and the arbitration hearing.[21]

Selection and Role of the Arbitrator. There are three basic procedures for choosing an arbitrator:

1. One person is chosen to serve on all arbitration hearings.
2. A panel of arbitrators serves on a rotating basis.
3. The parties obtain a list of possible arbitrators from the American Arbitration Association or Federal Mediation and Conciliation Service and ultimately choose one.

The role of the arbitrator is twofold. First, the arbitrator must conduct the hearing in an appropriate fashion. He or she must provide a fair opportunity for both sides to present their case, ensure proper procedures are followed, and make decisions about what evidence may be presented. Second, the arbitrator is responsible for making the final ruling. In this capacity, the arbitrator must consider all of the relevant evidence and testimony, and provide a decision and explanation in a written report.

Arbitration Hearing. The arbitrator serves as the judge during the hearing. Both sides make an opening statement, followed by the introduction of relevant evidence. Either party may show exhibits, which may contain information such as the relevant contractual statements (recall in the opening case that the arbitrator paid close attention to the exact wording of the union contract). Following the exhibits, both sides will call witnesses to testify. The witnesses generally testify under oath. After testifying on behalf of one side (for example, management), the witnesses may be cross-examined by the other side (the union). The arbitrator may also ask questions of the witnesses. At times, union, management, or arbitrator may request an actual visit to the location where the incident occurred. Following testimony by witnesses, both parties provide their closing arguments, which may be delivered either orally, in writing, or both.

Although the arbitration process is lengthy and time-consuming, it is a highly regarded and relatively efficient means of resolving disagreements. Perhaps that is one reason why arbitration is being used in many more areas today, including settlement of consumer complaints and employment discrimination charges. As demonstrated in the opening case, the precise wording in a bargaining agreement is extremely important. Failure by the organization to have an appropriate contract can lead to many subsequent grievances and, ultimately, important management decisions may be overturned. If, upon reflection, you think labor arbitration might be an interesting line of work, Box 15.4 offers further insights into that career.

Eliminating the Union

Once a union is elected to represent the employees, is it a permanent fixture? The answer is no. Just as the workers may decide to vote in a union to represent them, the workers may choose to vote out the union. This latter process is referred to as a

YOUR TURN

Box 15.4
So You Want to Be a Labor Arbitrator?

Did reading about arbitration stimulate your interest in becoming a labor arbitrator? If so, here is some information that will help you decide whether this is a viable career option. First, you should know that many arbitrators are members of the National Academy of Arbitrators (NAA), which requires either substantial experience as a labor arbitrator or more limited experience in labor arbitration coupled with other activities such as writing in the area of labor–management relations. If you have had experience working on behalf of unions or management dealing with union issues, you may not be able to join the NAA. Given this information, you should not be surprised that few people begin their careers as arbitrators. Rather, most current arbitrators started in a law, teaching, or industrial relations career, and then began doing arbitration on a part-time basis.

In terms of the arbitrator's career stages, initial entry appears to be the most difficult. Because no licensing or certification is needed to be a labor arbitrator, and given the way in which they are selected, major emphasis is on age and experience. Most labor arbitrators are in their late 40s when they work on their first case. As one labor arbitrator put it, there are two ways to deal with one's early career stage: having a full-time job to pay one's bills or having a great deal of patience. Moreover, most arbitrators work in this capacity only on a part-time basis. Not surprisingly, then, a large percentage of part-time arbitrators are lawyers or teachers, careers that allow them to conduct arbitration while maintaining a full-time job.

As indicated above, many arbitrators are members of the NAA. In fact, some management–union contracts require that only NAA members be

used as arbitrators. It will not surprise you, then, that NAA arbitrators average more than three times as many cases annually (57 on average) than non-NAA arbitrators (17 on average).

By now you are probably wondering whether it is financially worthwhile becoming a labor arbitrator. In 1986, the average fee per case was slightly over $1,000. The average NAA member reported earnings of about $65,000, while the average non-NAA member (who is probably doing this activity on a part-time basis) earned roughly $15,000 annually.

With all of these facts in mind, it is clearly difficult to become a labor arbitrator, and few people make a great deal of money doing arbitration. Clearly, this is not a career most people should plan on having.

Source: Adapted from M. Bognanno, C. Coleman, eds., *Labor Arbitration in America* (New York: Praeger, 1992).

decertification campaign. In the political context, this is similar to impeachment. The process of decertification is much like the representation campaign. At least 30 percent of the employees in the bargaining unit must indicate an interest in an election before the actual election will be held. After the National Labor Relations Board approves the petition, an election will be held to determine the status of the union. As in the representation campaign, a simple majority of the employees (50 percent plus 1) voting against the union will eliminate union representation.[22]

Just as restrictions limit what management can do during the representation campaign, restrictions limit what management can do during the decertification campaign. These restrictions are quite similar to the ones described in Table 14.6.[23]

Given the continuing decline of unionized workers in the United States, it should not surprise you that decertification elections have increased over the years, from about 100 annually in the 1950s to 490 in 1994. Moreover, the union is losing roughly 75 percent of the time and rarely is able to be reinstated.[24] Box 15.5 offers a case study in union decertification.

We conclude this chapter with some suggestions that may help organizations to maintain effective labor–management relationships.

decertification campaign
Just as the workers may decide to vote in a union to represent them, the workers may choose to vote out the union.

Box 15.5
Why One Company Decertified the Union

Northeast Color Research, Inc., a custom photography lab located in Massachusetts, became unionized when it grew from 2 to 25 employees. Like many small companies, lack of clear human resource policies and a shortage of skilled supervisors led to discontent among the employees. Of the 12 employees who were eligible to vote for representation by the United Food and Commercial Workers Union, 9 voted yes.

From the start, Joanne Frederick, CEO of Northeast, resented the interference of a union. At the same time, she admitted that the union was helpful to her in certain ways. For example, union rules enabled the company to more easily enforce discipline procedures. Nonetheless, Frederick consulted with a labor attorney for advice on how to legally counter the union. As a result of the attorney's suggestions, Frederick took several actions. First, she began to improve

certain aspects of the workplace, such as the employee lounge, that were not covered by the union contract (what advantage do you think this provided?). Second, she began to replace supervisors who had poor management skills with more effective supervisors. Third, she accepted union provisions in the contract that she knew employees would not like, such as narrow job descriptions (which the employees would find too restrictive because they wanted to gain as much experience as possible).

Many of the employees began to dislike the union rules. For example, the highly skilled employees resented the union's emphasis on seniority rather than qualifications. Ten months after the contract was signed, the employees met with Frederick to discuss various company issues. When the employees asked why a broken machine had yet to be replaced, she replied that the costs associated with the

union had prevented it from being fixed. The employees became upset and realized that there were certain drawbacks to the union. She then mentioned that employees could contact the National Labor Relations Board regarding decertification. Within hours, the employees called to tell her they had initiated a decertification effort. Based on a straw vote indicating little support for keeping the union, the union withdrew, thereby avoiding a humiliating election.

Although decertification is still relatively rare, it is most common in small businesses. In the case of Northeast Color, the union faced several disadvantages, particularly a lack of understanding of the nature of this type of business, which led to the union's removal shortly after being voted in.

Source: Adapted from R. C. Wood, "The Decline and Fall of a Union," *Inc.* (October 1982): 134.

Developing Harmonious Labor-Management Relations: Suggestions for Employers

Management can take several steps to improve its relationships with the union.

1. **Reconsider the Nature of Labor–Management Relationships.** As described in the previous chapter, although union–management relationships have generally been acrimonious in the United States, some unions and companies have attempted to form a completely different relationship. The implications of this new relationship for the union, and how it compares with the traditional role unions play, are provided in Table 15.1. As you can see, the role of unions in the future may be to serve as a partner with, rather than adversary to, management.[25]

The 1992 contract negotiated between AT&T and the Communications Workers of America (CWA) exemplifies this new relationship. Described as the "Workplace of the Future," the contract creates a multilevel partnership between the union and man-

Table 15.1	The Traditional Role versus the New Role Unions May Play	
Topic	**Traditional Role**	**New Role**
1. Corporate policy	No role	Represents workforce
2. Organizational effectiveness	No role	Facilitates and inputs
3. Work design	Bargaining issue	Participates
4. Rewards	Bargaining issue	Bargains for and helps administer and design
5. Quality of work life	Bargaining, grievances	Facilitates, monitors

Source: Adapted from E. E. Lawler and S. A. Mohrman, "Unions and the New Management," *Academy of Management Executive* 1 (1987): 293–300.

Table 15.2	Components of a Recent CWA and AT&T Contract

1. **Local Level:** CWA and AT&T managers agree on various mechanisms to be implemented (information sharing, self-managed teams, and so on).
2. **Business Division Planning Councils:** CWA and AT&T representatives establish and monitor new technologies and work structures, and jointly engage in human resource planning.
3. **Constructive Relationship Council:** Addresses corporation-level issues and resolves issues brought by local-level and business-division planning councils.
4. **Human Resources Board:** Composed of three top executives, two union officers, and two outside human resource experts, this component is responsible for human resource issues from a long-term perspective.

Source: Adapted from M. Bahr, "Communications Workers of America," *Quality Progress* 26 (1993): 59–60.

agement. As shown in Table 15.2, this contract establishes task forces and committees, with union and management representatives, that will enable both sides to work together on important issues that face the organization. What is particularly interesting about this contract is that the union has a far greater role in long-term human resource planning, as well as in general business issues, than unions have had in the past. Other companies that have developed such innovative relationships with unions include a Shell Oil plant in Ontario, Canada, and the United Auto Workers and General Motors in the Toyota plant in Fremont, California. In these latter instances, which were new or radically redesigned plants, the union played an active role with management in planning and implementing new management approaches.[26] Whether such contracts become commonplace remains to be seen.[27]

2. Implement Programs to Improve Labor–Management Relations. As described in Chapter 12, many companies have implemented programs to increase employee empowerment while improving productivity and quality. These programs, as well as information meetings between union officials, employees, and plant managers, have been found to reduce grievances and the need for disciplinary actions. Managers must be educated as to the importance of harmonious labor–management relationships in ensuring high labor efficiency and outstanding product quality. Indeed, research shows that positive labor relationships do improve the bottom line.[28]

3. **Improve the Grievance Process.** Maintaining an effective, fair grievance procedure is an important aspect of the labor–management relationship. Companies are therefore encouraged to examine the efficacy of the grievance procedure on an ongoing basis. Some organizations, for example, have introduced an additional, half step in the traditional four-step system that involves an informal meeting between the affected parties in an attempt to avoid arbitration. Other organizations have established special boards for the purpose of reducing case backlogs. Some organizations also have found that supervisors are poorly trained in handling and responding to grievances, and that supervisors often have only limited understanding of the collective bargaining agreement. To address these shortcomings, companies have developed training programs for supervisors, thereby leading to fewer grievances and more effective responses.[29]

❖ Conclusion

In conclusion, unions play a major role in the human resource area. By requiring that virtually all terms and conditions of employment are determined with its input, the union has established itself as a major factor in the human resource function of the company. Once a union is elected, a contract governing all aspects of the employment relationship between workers and management will be written, and a great deal of managerial decision making and discretion over such matters as pay increases, terminations, and job assignments is eliminated. A grievance procedure is included, enabling workers to appeal management decisions. Failure on the part of management to deal effectively with the union ultimately increases conflict and reduces organizational productivity and quality.

❖ Applying Core Concepts

1. Do you work in a union facility? If not, ask a friend or relative who does to answer these questions. What is the name of your business steward? Your business representative? What is the name of the local union? What national or international union does it belong to? Does it belong to any federation? You may wish to obtain more information from a federation office. The AFL-CIO, for example, maintains a Web page on the World Wide Web (www.aflcio.org).

2. Find information about a recent situation in which the union accepted a contract after a strike (for example, the major league baseball strike of 1993–1994). What were some of the factors that produced an acceptable contract? In your opinion, which party (management or union) gave in?

3. Explain why you think the typical grievance procedure works well. Why would a union want to have a grievance system?

4. What are the barriers to a widespread, radical change in the way union-management relationships operate in the United States? Can you think of any outside

forces (for example, the changing business environment) that might alter the traditional relationship between unions and management?

5. Given what you read in Chapters 14 and 15, what are your ideas about the relevance and value of unions? If you are covered in your current job or were covered in a previous job by a union contract, do you think things would have been better for you without the union? What about for the company? If you were not covered by a union contract, would you have preferred to have one? Why or why not?

❖ Key Terms

Union structure	**Counterproposal**	**Grievance procedure**
Business representative	**Joint study groups**	**Arbitration process**
Union steward	**Mediation**	**Decertification campaign**
Escalator clause	**Strike**	
Trading point procedure	**Replacement workers**	

❖ CHAPTER 15 *Experiential Exercise*

Labor Arbitration [30]

I. Objectives:
  1. To familiarize you with the arbitration process.
  2. To give you practice in presenting a case before others.
  3. To examine issues relating to contract administration.
II. Out-of-Class Preparation Time: 40 to 50 minutes
III. Procedures: Either at the beginning of or before class each student should read the exercise. To start the exercise, the instructor will divide the class into the following three groups:
  1. Union representatives (approximately five individuals)
  2. Company representatives (approximately five individuals)
  3. Arbitrators (all remaining participants, divided into groups of three to five members)

The union representatives should meet and carefully examine the following section, "The Union Position," and prepare to argue and defend this position. The company representatives should do the same with reference to "The Company Position." Meanwhile the arbitrators should read both the union position and the company position and discuss among themselves the arguments for and against each position.

After both the union and company representatives have prepared their position statements, each should present their case to the arbitrators. Each group will be allowed five minutes for their presentation and an additional five minutes to counter the other group's position.

After all presentations are complete, each group of arbitrators will have 10 minutes to discuss the case and reach a decision. These decisions should be presented, along with the reasoning behind them, to all participants.

Finally, the instructor may (optionally) present the arbitrator's actual decision in this case.

The Issue

Was the grievant discharged for just cause? The company claimed the employee's negligence of duty resulted in the discharge and the union claimed poor performance was the issue. If the union is right, what should be the remedy?

Pertinent Provisions of the Union Agreement

Article I. Purpose of the Agreement. The management of the company and the direction of the working force, including the right to plan, direct, and control operations, the right to hire, suspend, transfer, or discharge for just and sufficient cause, to relieve employees from duties because of lack of work or for other legitimate business reasons and the right to introduce new or improved methods or facilities of production is vested exclusively in the company; provided, however, that such rights shall not be exercised for the purpose of discriminating against any employee, and such rights shall not conflict with the provisions of this agreement.

Article 33. Discipline and Discharge. 33.1. In cases of poor job performance, the following procedure dealing with discipline will be accomplished with written notification to the Union:

a. Formal written warning in the first instance with copy to the employee.
b. In subsequent instances, formal written warning and/or suspension without pay for a period not to exceed five working days.
c. In the event three or more instances occur, one of which results in a suspension, within any two-year period, discharge for just cause will be accomplished.

33.1.1. For purposes of this article, job performance shall include consideration of the following factors:

1. Attendance record, including absenteeism, tardiness, and proven abuse of sick leave
2. Adherence to industrial safety rules
3. Adherence to Company house rules
4. Ability to perform assigned tasks satisfactorily

33.2. In cases of personal misconduct, the disciplinary action taken, including discharge, will be consistent with the gravity of the offense.

Background

The grievant was employed as a service technician for the ABC Petroleum/Gas Company from August 1990 to April 1999. On January 26, 1999, grievant was dispatched to a customer who reported a strong odor. Grievant's service report showed that he spent 26 minutes on the call, that no leaks were found, and that no repairs were made. The grievant did not take a pressure/manometer test.

Later that same day, in response to a second call, another technician was sent to the customer's home. The second technician checked the gas tank and gauge readings, added some gas, used the track, and did the pressure/manometer test. He tested the lines and isolated the source of the gas odor at a leak in the heater connector after the shutoff valve on the heater. The leak was located less than two feet from the pilot light on the water heater, which was lit. The technician replaced the heater connector and put the old one in the back of his truck. Subsequently, the grievant's immediate supervisor talked with the second technician and examined the damaged heater connector. On January 28, 1999, the supervisor met with the grievant and informed him that he was being suspended, pending an investigation. The reason for the suspension was "Negligent in responding to report of gas odor on January 26, failure to perform leak investigation according to company procedures/leaving party with hazardous condition." By letter on April 16, 1999, grievant was notified that he was being terminated based on the company's findings indicating that "the incident was of such serious nature that we would be remiss in continuing your employment as a technician."

The Company's Position

The company contends that the grievant failed to follow normal procedures necessary to determine whether there was a gas leak, and that leaving the customer in a hazardous condition constituted just cause for discharge. The grievant's failure to find or repair the gas leak was not poor performance but negligence of duty. The company defined poor performance as involving a lack of skills or intelligence and that the grievant's behavior was not caused by a lack of skills or innate inability. The company specifically refers to Article 1.3, which permits the company to discharge an employee for "just cause" and that under Article 1.3, no prior warnings are required. The company also noted in its presentation that the employee was previously suspended for 5 days in 1996, and that he has been reprimanded on numerous occasions for various infractions.

The Union's Position

The union contends that the grievant should have been disciplined under section 33.1 for poor job performance. The union contends that grievant performed three of the four tests usually performed and that at worst used poor judgment in not pressure testing the system. Further, the union contends that the company failed to give grievant adequate notice of the rule or the consequences of his action. The grievant did not have knowledge that he could be discharged for negligence in performance of his duties. Further, the union claimed that the company did not conduct a proper investigation and relied solely on the report of the second technician sent to the customer's home. The company made no attempt to visit the job site to determine firsthand if grievant had followed company rules.

❖ Chapter 15 References

1. A. Sloane and F. Witney, *Labor Relations* (Englewood Cliffs, NJ: Prentice-Hall, 1977).
2. Ibid.
3. M. Cimini and C. Muhl, "Labor-Management Bargaining in 1994," *Monthly Labor Review* (January 1994): 23–39.
4. Ibid.
5. Ibid.
6. Ibid.
7. Ibid.
8. S. Briggs and D. Koys, "What Makes Labor Mediators Effective?" *Labor Law Journal* 40 (1989): 517–20.
9. Cimini and Muhl, "Labor-Management and Current Labor Statistics," *Monthly Labor Review*, July 1998: 69–123.
10. Ibid.
11. C. J. Coleman, *Managing Labor Relations in the Public Sector* (San Francisco: Jossey-Bass, 1990).
12. Ibid.
13. L. Williamson and P. Brown, "Collective Bargaining in Private Industry, 1994," *Monthly Labor Review* (June 1995): 3–12.
14. A. Zack, *Grievance Arbitration* (Lexington, MA: Lexington Books, 1989).
15. J. Davy and G. Bohlander, "Recent Findings and Practices in Grievance-Arbitration Procedures," *Labor Law Journal* (March 1992): 184–90.
16. Ibid.
17. Ibid.
18. Ibid.
19. Ibid.
20. P. Breslin and P. Zirkel, "Arbitrator Impartiality and the Burden of Proof," *Labor Law Journal* (June 1993): 381–84.
21. Zack, *Grievance Arbitration*.
22. D. Savino and N. Bruning, "Decertification Strategies and Tactics: Management and Union Perspectives," *Labor Law Journal* (April 1992): 201–10.
23. A. Bethke, R. Mondy, and S. Premeaux, "Decertification: The Role of the First-Line Supervisor," *Supervisory Management* (February 1986): 21–23.
24. Savino and Bruning, "Decertification Strategies," and G. Jelf and J. Dworkin, "Union Decertification Research: Review and Theoretical Integration," *International Journal of Conflict Management*, 8 (1997): 306–337.
25. E. Lawler and S. Mohrman, "Unions and the New Management," *Academy of Management Executive* 1 (1987): 293–300.
26. Lawler and Mohrman, "Unions and the New Management."
27. I. Lobel, "Labor-Management Cooperation: A Critical View," *Labor Law Journal*, May 1992, 281–89.
28. H. Katz, T. Kochan, and M. Weber, "Assessing the Effects of Industrial Relations Systems and Efforts to Improve the Quality of Working Life on Organizational Effectiveness," *Academy of Management Journal* 28 (1985): 509–26.
29. M. Gordon and S. Miller, "Grievances: A Review of Research and Practice," *Personnel Psychology* 37 (1984): 117–46.
30. Source: S. Nkomo, M. Fottler, R. McAfee, *Applications in Human Resource Management* (Cincinnati, OH: South-Western, 1996). Contributed by Gerald E. Calvasina, The University of North Carolina at Charlotte.

Employee Rights

Core Concepts — After reading this chapter, you should be capable of:

1. Understanding the conditions under which you may be protected from a termination.
2. Explaining when you can examine your personnel file.
3. Determining whether or not your company can search your desk, briefcase, or other work areas.
4. Recognizing the problems associated with a workplace romance.
5. Understanding how to use disciplinary procedures.
6. Discussing different types of work schedules.

Opening Case

Yesterday, you found yourself in a rather interesting discussion with several of your coworkers during lunch time regarding the company, On-Line Books, Inc. The discussion began when Linda mentioned that last month she noticed that her desk seemed to have been searched over the weekend. Although nothing was taken, several items in the drawers had been moved and the papers on her desk had been scattered. Because she locks her desk every night, she wondered who might have opened the drawers. When she mentioned it to her supervisor, he acted somewhat embarrassed and mumbled something about security having a copy of everyone's desk keys.

"Now, why would they search my desk?" asked Linda during the lunch time discussion. Jim replied, "I don't know why your desk would be searched, but someone in my office (whose name will go unmentioned) feels he has been turned down for promotions because eight years ago he was charged with sexual harassment. Although the charges were investigated and proven false, he worries that the allegations are still listed in his personnel file and have left a permanent stain on his career." Jean then spoke up and said, "Do any of you remember Bill Norris? Do you know why he left?" Someone in the group mumbled, "Because of a personality clash with top management?" Jean shook her head and whispered, "I heard that Bill had an extramarital affair with one of the secretaries in the executive suite. Our CEO believes that such affairs are immoral, and so he fired Bill." After looking around to make sure no one else was in earshot, Philip replied in a hushed tone, "If you think that's bad, an employee in my department was fired suddenly without any forewarning. No one had any idea why, because his performance appraisals had been excellent during his four years with On-Line Books. The only possibility he could think of was that he had been interviewed on TV about his views on abortion two days before the termination. And we all know how the executive vice president of operations feels about abortion issues! So, the only explanation for his being fired seemed to be his views on abortion."

As you reflect on some of the comments made yesterday, you wonder whether these stories are true, and if they are true, can a company really take these actions? You are especially concerned about the employee who was allegedly fired for his views on abortion, because the implication is that anyone could be fired simply on the grounds that one's supervisor holds a different opinion on some matter. As you consider your own experience both in this company and at previous jobs, you can recall certain management actions that seemed wrong to you at the time. At one company, you found your supervisor reading e-mail that you had left on your computer screen. The e-mail revealed some private matters in your life, and you noticed that your boss was much more uncomfortable with you after that and never asked you to go to lunch again. When you worked for a different company, you found out that one of the vice presidents had been listening in on certain employees' phone calls, even though some of these calls were of a personal nature.

You are probably wondering by now whether companies actually have the legal right to engage in activities like the ones described. Can you, for example, be terminated for expressing your opinion regarding abortion? Can an employer search your desk or locker without permission? What about access to your personnel files to make sure they are accurate? Does your employer have the right to restrict your romantic relationships? Can your boss read your e-mail and listen to your phone conversations? These and other related issues will be discussed in much greater detail in this chapter. Employee rights, as you will see, comprise an evolving and changing area of law. You will also see that, in many instances, what is legal depends on the state where you work.

The remainder of this chapter is divided into several sections. First, you will read about your legal rights if you are terminated, followed by a discussion of your rights to examine your personnel records. Third, we will discuss rights to privacy. Fourth, you will read about current organizational approaches to workplace romances, followed by an overview of disciplinary procedures. Finally, you will read about your rights regarding hours of work and various organizational programs to increase work schedule flexibility. We begin with a discussion of your legal rights if you are terminated.

Terminations: For Good Cause, Bad Cause, or No Cause at All

employment-at-will
When employees are employed "at will," or at the will or discretion of the company. This means that if an employee can leave the work relationship at any time he or she desires, an employer has the same right.

Recall in the opening case of this chapter that Philip talked about an employee who was terminated, perhaps because of his televised statements about abortion. Can you be fired for a reason like that? It may come as a surprise to you that many employees are employed "at will," that is, at the will or discretion of the company. The **employment-at-will (EAW)** concept in the United States goes back more than 100 years ago to a court case in New York. In that case, the court ruled that an employee could be fired for any reason at all, regardless of whether the reason was a good one (say, the employee stole company equipment), a bad one (the supervisor did not like the color of the employee's tie), or there was no reason at all (maybe the supervisor just felt like firing someone).

If employment-at-will seems completely unfair to you, consider the matter from a completely different perspective—that of the company. In other words, how would you feel if you were a manager in the following situation. In the middle of the busiest season of the year (for instance, you work for a tax accounting firm and it is two days before April 15), one of your three employees announces that she is quitting. Would you have the legal right to force her to continue working? Of course not. Well, according to the courts in the 19th century, it seemed quite logical that if an employee could leave the work relationship at any time he or she desired, an employer should have the right to terminate an employee at any time. The principle that you could be terminated at any time is generally referred to as employment-at-will.[1]

During the 1970s and the 1980s, however, the employment-at-will principle was challenged in many state courts. In these cases, the plaintiffs argued that a wrongful discharge had occurred. Such cases received much attention in the popular media. One widely publicized study, for example, found that employees in California won nearly 70 percent of the wrongful discharge cases, and average awards to plaintiffs were well over $500,000![2] As you will see next, the likelihood that you will win a wrongful discharge suit depends much on the state in which you are employed. You will read first about exceptions to employment-at-will, followed by suggestions for what companies can do to reduce the chances they will be successfully sued for wrongful discharge.

Exceptions to Employment-at-Will

What does it take for an employee to win a wrongful discharge lawsuit? Let us begin by discussing the various legal considerations that are used to show the employee was wrongfully discharged. These may be sorted into six categories:

1. Civil rights and labor laws
2. Written contracts
3. Implied contracts
4. Covenant of good faith and fair dealing
5. Public policy
6. Statutory law

It is important to note that the third, fourth, and fifth categories are not based on specific, written laws. Rather, they are legal principles that have been applied to the employment-at-will area. Therefore, they are subject to change from time to time. Furthermore, their applicability varies from state to state. As you can see from Table 16.1, California courts have accepted all three of these exceptions; employees in the state of California therefore have considerable protection from wrongful discharge. At the other extreme, Utah courts have not accepted any of the exceptions. In that state, employers have the upper hand. Each of these six categories will now be discussed in greater detail.[3]

Table 16.1	States That Recognize Exceptions to Employment-at-Will		
State	**Implied Contract ***	**Whistleblower/ Public Policy**	**Good Faith**
Alabama	✓	N	X
Alaska	✓	N	✓
Arizona	✓	✓	N
Arkansas	✓	✓	N
California	✓	✓	✓
Colorado	✓	N	N
Connecticut	✓	✓	✓
Delaware	X	N	N
Dist. of Columbia	✓	✓	N
Florida	N	X	N
Georgia	N	X	N
Hawaii	N	✓	X
Idaho	✓	✓	N
Illinois	✓	✓	X
Indiana	X	✓	X
Iowa	N	✓	✓
Kansas	✓	✓	X
Kentucky	N	✓	N
Louisiana	N	N	N
Maine	✓	N	X
Maryland	N	✓	X
Massachusetts	N	✓	✓
Michigan	✓	✓	N
Minnesota	✓	N	X
Mississippi	✓	N	N
Missouri	N	✓	N
Montana	N	✓	✓
Nebraska	N	✓	N
Nevada	N	✓	✓
New Hampshire	✓	✓	✓
New Jersey	✓	✓	N
New Mexico	✓	✓	X
New York	✓	N	X
North Carolina	X	✓	N
North Dakota	N	N	✓
Ohio	✓	N	N
Oklahoma	✓	N	X
Oregon	✓	✓	X
Pennsylvania	✓	✓	X

(continued)

	Table 16.1	(continued)	

State	Implied Contract*	Whistleblower/ Public Policy	Good Faith
Rhode Island	N	√	N
South Carolina	√	√	N
South Dakota	√	√	N
Tennessee	X	√	N
Texas	N	√	N
Utah	N	N	N
Vermont	N	N	N
Virginia	N	√	N
Washington	√	√	N
West Virginia	√	√	X
Wisconsin	N	√	X
Wyoming	√	N	N

*An "implied contract" is one formed by oral statements, employee handbooks, or conduct of the parties.

√ Courts in this jurisdiction have generally recognized this exception to the doctrine of employment-at-will (where either party may terminate the relationship at any time and for any reason).

X Courts in this jurisdiction have generally not recognized this exception to employment-at-will.

N Courts in this jurisdiction, though they may or may not have heard cases on this issue, have failed to reach a definitive conclusion or establish a clear precedent regarding this exception to employment-at-will.

Source: L. G. Joel, *Every Employee's Guide to the Law* (New York: Pantheon Books, pp. 61–62, 1993).

Civil Rights and Labor Laws. As you have read in previous chapters, many laws—the Civil Rights Act of 1964 and the Age Discrimination in Employment Act, to name but two—protect employees from discrimination on the basis of their sex, race, religion, age, and other characteristics. If an employee can show that he or she was fired on this basis, the employee can win the job back, back wages, and possibly other forms of relief (such as attorney's fees). Because these are federal laws, they apply in all states.[4]

Written Contracts. Some workers have written contracts or agreements that specify the terms and conditions under which a termination may take place. Can you think of any occupations where a written contract might be commonly used? Many professional sports, for example, provide players with a written contract. Most tenured faculty have a written contract that specifies the terms and conditions of a termination. Also, as described in Chapters 14 and 15, unionized employees usually have written contracts that specify in great detail the causes for termination, as well as the procedures for disputing a termination. Nevertheless, the vast majority of employees do not have written contracts. As with the first category, written contract laws apply in all states.[5] Box 16.1 discusses written contracts from the employee's perspective.

implied contract
An implied agreement between employer and employee regarding an aspect of the job, such as the statement "Once you pass the probationary period, your job is guaranteed for life." Employee handbooks can also be considered implied contracts.

Implied Contract. Even if you were not given a written contract, you may be able to demonstrate that the company made an **implied contract** with you. There are many ways in which a company may have made an implied contract. As one example, an interviewer may say to you, "Once you pass the probationary period, your job is guaranteed for life." In some court cases, this statement or similar statements have been taken as implied contracts and are grounds for victory by the plaintiff. Another

Your Turn

Box 16.1
Written Contracts: An Employee Perspective

Knowing that a written contract can provide you some protection from being terminated, you may want to know more about securing one. In fact, a written contract or a similar agreement is much more common for middle-level managers than in the past. It is estimated that about 25 percent of mid-level managers are getting some type of written agreement, up from only 5 percent just a few years ago. Aside from the protection from being terminated, there are other reasons for trying to get a contract. Take, for example, Arnold Margolis. In the summer of 1992, Sweet Life Foods hired Margolis as director of health and beauty aids at an annual salary of $72,000. Although he received a letter stipulating this agreement, the company withdrew the offer without explanation several days before he would have begun. In the meantime, not only had he resigned from his previous job, but he had already moved from New York to Connecticut. Over a year later, Margolis still had not yet found a suitable job. If he had insisted on a written contract, he would have fared better.

In general, the greater the demand for your skills and expertise, the more likely you are to obtain a written agreement. One financial executive was able to negotiate a written agreement stipulating that if he left the company, he would be provided continued medical benefits until he found employment at a company offering the same level of benefits. Why was he able to negotiate this kind of agreement? "They wanted the guy a lot," explains a headhunter. Aside from that general principle, if you are moving from another part of the country to accept the new job, you should be in a better position to get a written agreement. For example, a senior manager living in Chicago accepted a job in a town in Iowa with fewer than 20,000 residents. One condition for accepting the job was a written agreement stating that he would be reimbursed for moving back to Chicago if he stopped working for the company. Most top managers joining a financially troubled business insist on a written agreement providing a guaranteed income if the company fails.

Some companies require the employee to give something in return for the written agreement. Often-times, this is an advance warning of quitting. In certain industries, the employee must agree to a no-compete clause, with which the employee agrees not to work for a competing firm for a certain period of time, even after he or she has left the company.

Should you get a written contract, be sure the document states that the agreement is binding. You may also wish to consult with an attorney.

Source: Adapted from J. Lublin, "Before You Take That Great Job, Get It in Writing," *Wall Street Journal*, 9 February 1994, B1.

example of an implied contract involves the employee handbook. Many employee handbooks, for example, describe a progressive disciplinary procedure wherein an employee would be warned of any performance problems, followed by counseling. Only if the problem was still not resolved would the employee be terminated. But in some cases the company failed to follow its handbook procedures; the employee often was terminated without warning or opportunity to improve. In certain states, the courts have ruled that the company had, on those grounds, violated an implied contract.[6]

Some implied contract arguments that may sound rather weak to you were successful in court. Consider the following actual court cases:

1. An employee terminated before one year of employment had a letter stating the salary as an annual sum; the court recognized this as an implied contract lasting one year.
2. An employee who worked for one company for many years moved to another state to work for another employer. He was terminated after a short period of time. Given that he left a secure position he had held for many years to work for this new firm, the court held this to be an implied contract.[7]

Covenant of Good Faith and Fair Dealing. This exception to employment-at-will may be used when the reason for the termination was clearly inappropriate or the conditions under which the firing was made were extremely inconsiderate of the employee. With regard to the first situation, an employee with 25 years of seniority was terminated just before a customer placed a $25 million-order. The court decided that the real reason for the termination was so that the company would not have to give the employee the large commission he would have earned. As an example of the second situation, the classic case concerns a restaurant owner who lined up the waitresses and terminated them one at a time when they did not indicate who was stealing.[8]

Public Policy. This exception to employment-at-will may surprise you because it seems obvious that an employee would win; in turn, this should indicate to you how pervasive the notion of employment-at-will was until about 20 years ago. In a **public policy** exception to employment-at-will, the employee has either committed an action or refused to commit an action that is in the interest of the common public good. Some examples include participating in jury duty, reporting the company's violation of some rule or regulation (often referred to as *whistleblowing*), or refusing to commit a violation of the law (such as refusing to dump toxic waste). Does it surprise you that in years past the company had a legal right to terminate you for those actions? The fact that in many cases your company had such a right indicates how well-entrenched employment-at-will was in the United States.[9]

Statutory Law. Recall that the three exceptions you just read about are not written, or statutory laws. Rather, they are legal principles that have been applied to the employment-at-will area. Only one state, Montana, has a formal, written law regarding wrongful discharge. Passed in 1987, the Wrongful Discharge From Employment Act was designed to strike a balance between workers' rights and companies' rights. This law specifies that a wrongful discharge has occurred in any of the following instances:[10]

1. The termination was connected to a public policy issue (for example, the employee refused to do an illegal act).
2. The termination was not for good cause and the employee had passed probation.
3. The company violated its written human resource policies.

While there have been attempts to pass similar legislation in other states, such as California and Wisconsin, as well as on the federal level, so far these attempts have been unsuccessful. Some states do, however, have much more limited statutes, protecting whistleblowing or other public policy exceptions.[11]

Recommendations for Organizations

Companies are encouraged to take the following precautions to limit their liability in wrongful discharge cases:[12]

1. **Review the Employee Handbook and Modify as Needed.** Companies should review their employee handbooks for any language suggestive of promises or guarantees of employment. Expressions such as "permanent·employee" and "you will be fired only for just cause" should be eliminated. On the other hand, the handbook should include a statement like the following: "This handbook is intended only as

a source of information, not as a binding employment contract, and the provisions contained herein are subject to change without notice."

2. **Train Supervisors and Hiring Managers.** All personnel that are responsible for hiring and firing should receive information about the nature of implied contracts and other exceptions to employment at will.

3. **Consider Including a Statement in the Application Blank to Clarify the Company's Liability.** Most application blanks contain a statement like, "I understand that my employment is at the will of the company, and that I may be terminated at any time for any reason."

4. **Examine Any Other Policies That Might Be Interpreted as an Implied Contract.** Some companies initially hire employees on a probationary status. At the end of this period, some companies refer to successful employees as being "permanent." In some courts, this designation has been accepted as an implied contract. This and similar policies should be carefully examined and changed if necessary. In general, any proposed termination should be carefully reviewed by the human resource manager or company attorney before action is taken.

Personnel Files

In the opening case of this chapter, one of the employees mentioned that a coworker may have been denied promotions because of earlier sexual harassment charges. Although the charges had proven false, the concern was that the charges had created a permanent mark on the worker's personnel file. Do you think employees should have the right to examine their records or files? Do you think employees should have the right to correct their records or files? Most employees believe they should have both of these rights. Legally, however, your right to examine and correct your personnel file depends on where you work. If you are a federal government employee, you will have more rights than do most other employees. We will begin, then, with the rights of federal government employees, and then move on to other workers.

Federal Government Employees and Access to Personnel Files

If you are a federal employee, you have a right to your personnel files under the **Privacy Act of 1974** (for more information see http://www.tncrimlaw.com/foia_indx.html). This law covers only federal administrative agencies (for instance, the Food and Drug Administration), and it allows individuals who work at these agencies the right to examine their records and to correct any mistakes in the records. If you are not an employee covered by the Privacy Act of 1974 (for example, if you work for the private sector), other laws may grant you the right to review your file. These are discussed next.[13]

Privacy Act of 1974
The law that gives federal employees a right to their personnel files (this law covers federal administrative agencies and allows individuals who work at these agencies the right to examine their records and the right to correct any mistakes in the records).

Private-Sector and State and Local Government Employees

While no comprehensive national laws cover employees' rights to their personnel files, many states have enacted such laws. Table 16.2 contains a summary of these laws for each state. As you can see, 27 states have laws that grant employees the right to review

| Table 16.2 | States Providing Access to Personnel Records | | |

State	Personnel Files	Medical Records	Remove/Explain
Alaska	√	—	—
Arizona	public employees	—	—
Arkansas	√	√	—
California	√	—	—
Connecticut	√	√	√
Delaware	√	√	√
District of Columbia	District Employees	—	√
Illinois	√	—	√
Iowa	√	—	—
Kentucky	public employees	—	—
Louisiana	—	√	—
Maine	√	—	—
Massachusetts	√	—	√
Michigan	√	—	√
Minnesota	√	—	√
Nebraska	public employees	—	—
Nevada	√	—	employer's option
New Hampshire	√	—	√
North Dakota	public employees	—	—
Ohio	—	√	—
Oklahoma	—	√	—
Oregon	√	—	—
Pennsylvania	√	—	√
Rhode Island	√	—	—
South Dakota	public employees	—	—
Tennessee	public employees	—	—
Texas	public safety personel	—	—
Utah	public employees	—	—
Washington	√	—	—
Wisconsin	√	—	√

Personnel Files: √ indicates that, in general, both public and private employees are covered by the law requiring access to personnel files. "Public employees" means only public employees must be given access to their files and that private employers are not expressly covered.

Medical Records: √ indicates that medical records are expressly included among the records to which employees must be given access. (A √ under Medical Records only indicates that the law refers to medical records specifically and not to personnel records in general.)

Remove/Explain: √ indicates that employees are allowed to request that their employer remove erroneous or dated material with which the employee does not agree; or in the alternative, the employee has a right to insert an explanation, which must remain a permanent part of the file.

Note: States not listed do not have specific laws regarding access to personnel files.

Source: L. Joel, *Every Employee's Guide to the Law* (New York: Pantheon Books, p. 164, 1993).

their personnel records, and some states have laws that provide access to company medical records. Your legal right to see your personnel files, then, depends on where you work. If you work in Mississippi, for instance, you have no legal right to examine your personnel records.[14]

Because these laws are written by each state, they differ from one another in many ways. We will discuss these laws in greater detail, with attention to how they differ from state to state.[15]

Are All Organizations Covered? The state laws differ widely in terms of which organizations are covered and which are exempt. If, for example, you work in Minnesota and your organization employs only 15 workers, you would have no legal right to your personnel files. That is because the law only covers organizations with 20 or more employees. If you worked in Illinois, however, you would have the legal right to see your files, because the law in this state covers organizations with 5 or more employees.

Which Employees Can View Their Files? Some states, such as Washington, permit only current employees to view their personnel files. Other states, such as Pennsylvania, also permit employees on leave and employees on layoff (as long as they are eligible for recall) to review their files. Several states, including Connecticut, Illinois, and Nevada, permit former employees to review their records, but only up to a certain time (for example, Nevada allows an employee to review records only up to 60 days after leaving the company).

What May Be Seen as Part of a Personnel File? The state laws differ in terms of what is considered part of the personnel file. A handful of states, such as Michigan, ban certain information from appearing in the file, such as political affiliations, publications, and other nonwork-related items. The Americans with Disabilities Act specifically requires that medical information be kept separate from the personnel file. Aside from this, states differ in terms of what information in the personnel file may legally be concealed from the employee. In most states, you, as an employee, have no right to see documents that involve a third party. Can you think of such a document that you might have a keen interest in seeing? The best example might be a letter of reference, written by a professor or former employer. Most states do not give you the right to examine those documents. Generally, employees also have no right to examine information that will be used in criminal investigations. Some of these laws even permit the company to conceal documents regarding investigations of alleged violations of employment laws. To return to the opening case, depending on the state in which On-Line Books was located, the anonymous employee may or may not have had the legal right to review the materials about alleged sexual harassment.

How Do Employees Initiate a Request to Review Their Files? By now you may be wondering just what you need to do to obtain a copy of your personnel file. The answer depends somewhat on where you are. In some states (such as Maine and Michigan), your request must be in writing, that is, you would need to draft a letter stating your interest in reviewing your personnel file. In some states, you would also need to indicate which documents you wish to see (as is the case in Michigan) or the purpose of the inspection (as in Delaware) or both.

What Can You Do If You Discover an Error in Your File? Now that you have reviewed your personnel file, you may believe that it contains a mistake. Perhaps a previous performance rating is lower than it was supposed to be, or the number of absences from work is wrong. Most state laws require that you, as an employee, first inform the company of the error. If the organization disagrees with you, you will be required to submit a written statement explaining your assessment. A few states, such as Illinois, Michigan, and Minnesota, provide the employee with a legal recourse for removing false information.

What If Your Company Denies You the Right to Review Your Files? Your company may deny you access to your personnel file for two reasons. First, your company may simply be unaware of your rights. Second, your company may not wish to share information with you. In either case, the penalty and the law to enforce your rights differ from state to state. In states such as Wisconsin, employers that deny you access to your file may be fined up to $100 each day. Other states (such as Illinois and Michigan) allow you, as an employee, to sue the company. In some cases, you may even be able to collect damages and court costs. Again, the exact procedures and penalties will differ from state to state.

So far, we have been discussing your *legal* rights with regard to personnel files. Some companies have established internal regulations, beyond legal requirements, that provide access to personnel files if an employee requests a review. Why do you think an organization would open itself up to that kind of scrutiny, as well as to extra time and expense? There probably are two answers to that question. First, from a self-preservation standpoint, some companies decide they are best off developing internal regulations. They believe that failure to impose their own regulations will lead to government-imposed requirements, which will create greater problems. Second, some companies believe that internal regulations promote a greater sense of fairness on the part of employees, which in turn will improve employee satisfaction and commitment to the organization.

Whether the federal government will impose future regulations covering access to personnel files of private-sector organizations remains to be seen. In sum, depending on your employer and the state where you work, you may have a legal right to examine and correct your personnel files. In many cases, however, you will gain access to this information only as part of a successful civil rights lawsuit or charge under the Occupational Safety and Health Act.[16] For more information about employee rights, investigate the Web sites listed in Box 16.2.

Do you think an organization should have the right to search your purse, clothing, car, or other areas? What about the right to read your e-mail? As you will see, the U.S. Constitution may provide some protection from unfair searches and seizures. In many cases, however, your only protection will be what is referred to as "common law privacy," or perhaps a law covering communications. These sources of protection from your company in connection with searches and seizures are described in greater detail next.

Privacy Rights in the Workplace

In the opening case of this chapter, Linda mentioned that her desk may have been searched over the weekend by the company. Do you think the organization should have a right to search your purse, locker, desk, or other areas? What about the right to read your e-mail? Or the right to listen to your phone conversations? All of these issues involve your right to privacy in the workplace. In this section, you will read about the various laws and legal guidelines that cover your right to privacy in the workplace.

WEBBING AROUND

Box 16.2

Here are some useful Web sites in the area of employee rights:

http://www.charred.com/ This company sells equipment that will enable your organization to monitor the sites employees are surfing.

http://www.erols.com/rwobo/ employeerights/index.html This Web site will provide you with more information on employee rights, as well as referral information for finding a qualified lawyer to help you with a problem.

http://www.employerhelp. org/freereports/ handbookselfevaluator.htm Take this quiz to see if your employment handbook could create legal problems.

http://www.aclu.org/issues/ worker/legkit6.html Review ACLU's materials on wrongful discharge and proposed policy to address this issue. Do you agree with their approach?

http://www.faceintel.com/ This Web site was created by a person to discredit Intel, the large computer products firm. What do you think of this approach? Should a company be allowed to restrict such Web sites?

Specifically, we will review Constitutional rights, state laws, common law right to privacy, and the Electronic Communications Protection Act.[17]

U.S. Constitution

Although the term "privacy" is not explicitly mentioned in the U.S. Constitution, the Supreme Court of the United States has recognized that the right to privacy in the workplace is covered by the Fourth Amendment, which provides that it is "The right of the people to be secure in their persons, houses, papers, and effects, against unreasonable searches and seizures, shall not be violated." In a famous case involving an employee search issue, the Supreme Court ruled that "Some government offices may be so open to fellow employees or to the public that no expectation of privacy is reasonable." Thus, the Supreme Court ruling opened the door to a "reasonableness" standard—where the purpose of the search seemed reasonable in light of a good reason to search, or where the employee should have had a clear expectation that his or her office, desk, or other area, might be searched, the employee's right to privacy would be diminished. For example, U.S. Customs might reasonably search an employee's jacket when there was reason to believe that a missing package of jewels might be there. However, for the most part, the U.S. Constitution covers only public-sector workers and not private-sector workers.[18]

Ten states provide some constitutional right to privacy. Only California, however, covers private-sector workers. In California court cases, the courts have also applied the "reasonableness" standard in determining whether an employee's privacy has been violated or not.

Common Law Privacy

Common law privacy goes back to the late 19th century, when Samuel Warren and Louis Brandeis introduced this legal concept in a *Harvard Law Review* article. This legal protection provides for four activities that might constitute an invasion of privacy:

1. Intrusion upon seclusion
2. Misappropriation of someone's name or likeness

common law privacy
A general principle that protects an employee from searches and seizures in a nongovernmental organization.

3. Unreasonable publicity
4. Putting someone in a false light

In terms of invasion of privacy by reading an employee's e-mail or searching the person's desk, it is the first activity, intrusion upon seclusion, that is most likely to be violated. Although some states do not recognize common law privacy, others do. The basic determination of whether a business has violated the intrusion upon seclusion principle is based on four considerations:

1. Was the intrusion intentional?
2. Was the company's action highly offensive?
3. Was the employee's activity highly offensive?
4. Did the company have a legitimate purpose in its action?

In deciding whether the search of a desk or the reading of an employee's mail violated common law privacy, a court would consider such factors as whether the company had a policy that was communicated to employees that desks might be searched or that e-mail might be examined. In fact, it has been estimated that company investigation of employee e-mail is increasing rapidly. Before you send inappropriate e-mail, you should carefully consider the consequences if your boss were to read the e-mail. Another factor companies must consider is their intentions in reading employee e-mail. If, for example, the company is investigating a possible sexual harassment charge, that might be a "legitimate purpose." In general, it is safe to say that employees have a difficult time winning a common-law privacy lawsuit.

The Electronics Communication Privacy Act of 1986

Electronics Communication Privacy Act of 1986
This act prohibits the interception of oral, wire, and electronic communications, except during the course of business or when one party has consented.

The **Electronics Communication Privacy Act (ECPA) of 1986** covers a variety of communications, including oral, wire, and electronic forms. Essentially, a person who intentionally intercepts or attempts to intercept such forms of communication, or exceeds authorization access to electronic storage of such communication, may be liable under this law. Although not explicitly covered, the courts have ruled that e-mail is considered under this law as a form of communication. There are several exceptions to this law by which communication might be monitored, including (1) monitoring during the course of business and (2) when one party has consented to having a third party monitor the communication.

There are three practical implications of this law:

1. An employer who makes it clear to employees that communications such as e-mails, telephone calls, and other forms of communication may be monitored is generally safe from liability under the ECPA.
2. An employer can intercept communications and determine whether the communication is business-related or personal. If the communication is business-related, the company has a right to continue to read or monitor the communication. If the communication is personal, the company should stop and not continue to monitor the communication.
3. The company has the right to prohibit personal communication in the workplace.[19]

In sum, several different laws cover employee privacy in the workplace. Organizations have the right to maintain appropriate discipline and to enforce legitimate policies in the workplace. Explaining to employees that their desks and other belongings may be searched and that their conversations and e-mail may be monitored is advisable. The two key questions all companies should ask themselves are: (1) are these efforts reasonable or not? (2) have employees been effectively notified that their desks, lockers, or other areas may be searched and that e-mail, telephone calls, and other forms of communication may be monitored or checked?

Returning to the opening case of this chapter, then, Linda may have had grounds for a lawsuit, particularly if she could show that employees did not expect to have their desks searched and depending on the particular state in which she works.

Workplace Romance

Compared to years past, romantic relationships at work are much more common today. When President Bill Clinton had a romance in the White House with Monica Lewinsky, many people felt that it was not relevant to the job and that it was his personal business. In the opening case of this chapter, one employee commented that Bill Norris was fired because of an extramarital affair he had with a secretary in the company. Does that sound fair to you? In light of the public reaction to Bill Clinton's relationship with Monica Lewinsky, attitudes toward workplace romance appear to be far more lenient than in years past. Have you ever had a romantic relationship with someone at work? How would you feel if you were terminated for such a relationship? In this section we first examine why companies are concerned about these relationships, then we look at employees' rights in workplace romances. We conclude with a description of current organizational policies regarding workplace romance. You can gauge your own attitude toward romances in the workplace by answering the questions in Box 16.3.

Romantic Relationships: Why Companies Are Concerned

You may remember from Chapter 2 that sexual harassment could occur in two ways. One way is a *quid pro quo* situation, in which a supervisor requests sexual favors from another employee in exchange for pay increases, promotions, and similar personnel actions. Alternatively, sexual harassment charges could be brought if the employee can prove that the workplace is stressful owing to the sexual behavior that occurs *(hostile environment)*. Under the quid pro quo approach, a workplace romance may end with the subordinate claiming that she (or he) was forced into this relationship in order to receive pay raises or promotions. Under the hostile environment approach, one employee actually won a lawsuit when she demonstrated that she was treated poorly because other coworkers were having romantic relationships with their supervisors, while she refused to engage in such behavior. In short, one major concern organizations have with romantic relationships on the job is the possibility they will turn into sexual harassment lawsuits.[20]

A second concern on the part of organizations is that romantic relationships are disruptive. First, romantic relationships may create tension in the workplace, as the couple exchanges whispers, glances, and so forth. Matters may become even worse when the relationship ends and the two employees begin avoiding one another. Second, it is often feared that favoritism will occur or perhaps will be suspected of occurring. During the early 1980s, for example, William Agee, then CEO of Bendix Corporation, became romantically involved with Mary Cunningham. In a much

YOUR TURN

Box 16.3

Your Attitude toward Workplace Romances

To examine your attitude toward romance in the workplace, indicate whether you agree (A) or disagree (D) with each of the following statements. When you finish filling in your answers, compare your answers with the responses of 200 CEOs.

1. Office romances increase the possibility of favoritism or the appearance of favoritism. _____
2. Office romances can create an unbusinesslike appearance. _____
3. Office romances expose the company to sexual harassment suits. _____

4. Given the number of hours managers spend in the office nowadays, office romances are inevitable. _____
5. The incidence of office romance has increased in the past 10 years. _____
6. In the long run, office romances inevitably result in problems for the company. _____
7. When an office romance develops, one of the parties should leave the company voluntarily. _____

Now, compare your answers with the results of a survey of 200 CEOs.

Item Number	% Agree	% Disagree	% Not Sure
1	86	13	1
2	78	21	1
3	77	20	3
4	51	46	3
5	35	39	6
6	21	75	4
7	17	78	5

Do the percentages from the survey of CEOs surprise you? How do your answers compare?

Adapted from A. B. Fisher, "Getting Comfortable with Couples in the Workplace," *Fortune*, 10 October 1994, 138–42, 144.

publicized story, Mary Cunningham rose quickly to upper management ranks, and the two spent many hours together. According to Agee and Cunningham, their time was spent working on business-related matters; but various parties, including the board of directors, became outraged, and eventually Mary Cunningham was forced to leave.[21]

Despite concern about the disruptive nature of romantic relationships, there is anecdotal evidence to the contrary. Consider Pam and Lou Shuckman, both recruiters for Accountants on Call, a temp service for accountants. Now married, they met at a company-sponsored junket. They believe that being married makes them much more productive, as they are able to share their knowledge and ideas with one another. The company seems to agree. A recent company newsletter announced, "The couple that bills together, thrills together." And there is no scientific evidence indicating that work romances reduce productivity.[22]

Aside from these reasons, many companies are simply conservative. They may especially frown upon extramarital affairs, if only out of religious or moral convictions. Romances between unmarried employees may be discouraged if there is any public display of affection.

Workplace Romances: Your Legal Rights

Now that you have read about companies' concerns, you may wonder whether employees have any rights regarding workplace romances. Recall that while private-sector employees do not enjoy a right-to-privacy law, there are some common-law right-to-privacy principles. One such concept, referred to as "intrusion upon seclusion," might provide a right for employees to engage in workplace romances.

Some states also prohibit discrimination on the basis of marital status. It is possible that such a law could be used to prove discrimination against unmarried persons engaged in a workplace romance. Finally, recall that in the Agee-Cunningham story, the woman was forced to leave the organization. Indeed, in past years, some organizations had a written policy requiring that the employee in the romantic relationship with less status leave the organization. But this often resulted in sex discrimination, as a woman typically holds the lower-level job. If your company's policy discriminates against you on the basis of marital status or gender, you may have grounds for a lawsuit.[23]

Organizational Policies Regarding Workplace Romances

In the last few years, most companies have chosen to implement limited policies regarding workplace romances. Yet some companies retain what may seem rather broad restrictions. For example, Wal-Mart Stores decided several years ago to terminate two employees who had a sexual relationship. This decision was based on Wal-Mart's official policy to terminate any employee who commits adultery. As it turns out, the woman, who was legally separated from her husband, had sex with a single male employee. Sound extreme? Technically, adultery is illegal in every state. But New York state law guarantees employees the right to privacy outside of the workplace, as long as the activity is not illegal. Since adultery is illegal, Wal-Mart might have gotten away with this action, except for one catch: someone who is legally separated is not committing adultery. The attorney general of New York was therefore able to sue Wal-Mart Stores for a violation of state laws.

Relatively few companies have policies that are as restrictive as the one at Wal-Mart. In fact, a recent survey showed that 70 percent of companies permit workplace romances, while 28 percent permit, but discourage it. Only 2 percent of companies surveyed banned workplace romances. Many companies do have a policy that people romantically involved with each other cannot have a supervisor–subordinate relationship. Apple Computer, for example, specifically states in its handbook that no direct reporting or contractual relationship can be formed with a member of your immediate family, relative, or individual with whom you have a "significant personal relationship." Other companies have tried to educate employees with regard to the potential problems associated with workplace romances. DuPont, for example, addresses the issue as part of sexual harassment training. DuPont has an official policy that if an employee has a personal relationship that could negatively affect the company, the employee has an obligation to inform management and pursue ways to prevent any negative consequences.[24]

If a company is considering adopting or reviewing a workplace romance policy, the following guidelines should be considered.[25]

1. Rather than having a blanket statement restricting or banning workplace romances, restrictions should only apply to cases in which the relationship might interfere with the work activity, such as when a supervisory–subordinate romance exists or when one of the parties has influence over the other party with regard to pay, promotions, and so forth.
2. The policy should not be restricted to workplace romances alone; it should cover any type of personal relationship, including parent–child relationships and relationships between spouses.

Box 16.4

What You Say *Can* Hurt You

Do you enjoy talking with your peers at work? Ever talk with your co-workers after work about the job, your family, or personal problems? Have you ever attended your company's employee assistance program (EAP) for counseling? If you have done any of these things, or thought about it, be careful what you say. It can hurt you.

Consider the story of Lewis Hubble, who worked at Kmart's distribution center for nearly 30 years. When Hubble met Al, a new employee at the center, they became instant friends. They ate lunch together, and even went drinking occasionally after work. But Al was really an undercover investigator, working with several others posing as new employees. They allegedly wrote reports about what employees said and did. According to a lawsuit filed by the employees claiming a violation of their rights, the report included information about their drinking habits, sexual preferences, personal problems, as well as other non-job-related information. A Kmart spokesperson will only say that the undercover agents were looking for a crime ring suspected of operating through the distribution center.

But it's not just undercover agents who may tell the company what you have said. A legal assistant in Oregon filed a workers' compensation claim for wrist pain she claimed was caused by her job. At an administrative hearing to contest her claim, lawyers for the company claimed her injury wasn't caused by the job at all. Rather, they argued that her pain was caused by emotional stress and hormonal problems induced by an abortion. How did the lawyers learn about her abortion? They had interviewed her coworkers, several of whom she had talked with about the abortion.

Some companies are trying to make it even easier for coworkers to provide such information. Merck & Co., Northern Telecom, and Boise Cascade are among the companies that have a 24-hour confidential, toll-free number for employees to call when they have information on such illegal activities as stealing and drug use.

Such practices, not surprisingly, have led to countersuits by employees. Pamela Black, for example, was suspected of on-the-job drug use by her employer, Freedom Newspapers Inc. According to Black, she was suspected of drug use because she was taking drops for an eye inflammation problem. Based on telephone calls from employees, the company launched a surveillance operation, which culminated in a 7-hour interrogation of Black. In her lawsuit, Black maintains the company asked her a variety of personal questions, including such subjects as relationships with her children and men. She was then fired, allegedly for poor performance.

So whom can you trust? Many people think that company counselors, frequently working for the employee assistance program (EAP), are safe. In fact, your company may even tell you that the content of your discussions with your counselor is confidential. The reality may be quite different. For instance, Donnie Burgess, a computer specialist at a greeting-card company, used his company's EAP in 1988.

In 1992, when he was suing the company for breach of contract, the company's lawyers used his EAP file to bring evidence that Burgess had certain personality problems. Well, you might think, don't EAP counselors have any personal ethics? Garth Elliott, director of an EAP program, had personal ethics and refused to hand over files for his organization to use against employees. The result? The company seized the files anyhow, and demoted him.

Not all companies are disingenuous about the uses of EAP information. Morgan Stanley, known as having one of the most ethical and well-run EAPs, tells employees that information they provide to the EAP may be made available to management if the employee sues the company. The bottom line is you should be cautious in talking with coworkers and company representatives.

Sources: E. Schultz, "Employee Beware: The Boss May Be Listening," *The Wall Street Journal*, July 29, 1994, C1, C16; and E. Schultz, "If You Use Firm's Counselors, Remember Your Secrets Could Be Used against You," *The Wall Street Journal*, May 26, 1994, C1, C20.

3. If there is a chance that one of the covered situations might materialize, the parties involved should be given a sufficient time period (perhaps a week) to resolve the problem.
4. Employees should be given advance notice of the policy before it is implemented in order for them to prepare for any changes that will be necessary.

In short, current thinking is that companies can have only limited control over workplace romances. Above all, companies are advised to ensure that the policy is reasonable, job related, and does not unfairly discriminate against one type of relationship over others. Going back to the opening case of this chapter, then, firing Bill Norris because he had allegedly had an extramarital affair could be quite difficult to defend in court.

Finally, in addition to the areas already addressed, many states grant additional protection to employees with regard to legal behavior off the job (such as smoking) and, in some cases, even your political activities (for example, expressing your support for a particular political candidate). Many states have a law protecting employees from employment discrimination based on their use of tobacco and alcohol products after work hours. Finally, the common law privacy rights that you read about may apply to situations where an employee is disciplined or terminated for a variety of non-job-related activities. Stay tuned to more changes and additional laws in this area.[26] The information in Box 16.4 serves as a reminder that employees should always use caution in their discussions at the workplace.

Now that you have read about some major areas of employee rights, we will discuss employee disciplinary procedures. As you will see, managers and supervisors should determine and communicate disciplinary actions in a suitable manner.

Employee Disciplinary Procedures

Although disciplinary procedures are relatively infrequently used, the way in which they are made and communicated may affect employees' perceptions of their supervisor. Among the most common reasons for disciplining employees are absenteeism and tardiness problems, performance deficiencies, drug use on the job, negligence, misconduct (such as fighting at work or playing pranks), and insubordination. Most organizations today use two key concepts in meting out disciplinary action: progressive discipline and due process. Each of these terms is explained in greater detail next.[27]

Progressive Discipline

Recall from Chapter 7 that both professional and legal standards encourage companies to give employees sufficient warning and opportunity to correct performance problems. The same notions underlie **progressive discipline.** In a progressive discipline system, the employee is given ample warning of performance or other work-related problems. Failure to change his or her behavior is accompanied by increasingly harsher disciplinary action. Thus, a typical progressive disciplinary system will have four basic steps:[28]

1. The employee is notified of the problem and warned that disciplinary action will be taken if the problem is not solved.

progressive discipline
In a progressive discipline system, the employee is given ample warning of performance or other work-related problems. Failure to change his or her behavior is accompanied by increasingly harsher disciplinary action.

2. If the problem is not solved, the employee is reminded that the problem remains, and a written warning is placed into his or her file.
3. If the problem is still not solved, the employee is suspended (temporarily barred from working) without pay for a short period of time.
4. Finally, if the problem is not solved, the employee is terminated.

While harsher disciplinary action is generally appropriate, in some instances more immediate action is needed. For example, an employee who walks through the workplace carrying a firearm may need to receive more than just a verbal warning; in that case, immediate suspension without pay may be the most appropriate action while a thorough investigation is undertaken to determine whether a termination is in order.

Due Process

due process
The notion that employees have the right to be treated fairly, particularly when being disciplined.

Due process is based on the notion that employees have the right to be treated fairly, particularly when being disciplined. Generally, due process involves these four features:

1. Employees are aware of the company's expectations and the consequences of not meeting those expectations (for instance, employees are aware of the conditions under which termination will occur).
2. Consequences are predictable and consistent.
3. Disciplinary actions are based on facts that are obtained from an investigation.
4. Employees have an opportunity to hear the facts and explain the situation from their perspective.[29]

Organizations that incorporate these features in their disciplinary procedures will experience better employee relations and reduce legal liability.

Taking Disciplinary Action

For most managers and supervisors, communicating the need for disciplinary action is one of the least pleasant aspects of their job. If you review Chapter 7, you will see that it describes a set of steps for giving informal feedback and indicates the appropriate place for a mention of disciplinary action. In addition to the steps outlined in Chapter 7, the following suggestions are offered:[30]

1. **Explain to the Employee Precisely What the Action Is, Why It Is Necessary, and When the Action Will Take Place.** Employees need to know that actions will be taken in order to believe the subsequent action is fair.
2. **Complete a Thorough, Careful, and Neutral Investigation of the Facts before Deciding to Discipline.** Document your investigation and be sure to have witnesses sign their names to statements.
3. **Check Company Policies.** Many companies have written policies about disciplinary actions. For some situations (such as fighting on the job), immediate termination may be required. Failure to follow company policies may have negative consequences for managers and supervisors.

Although taking disciplinary action is not a pleasant task, it is critical for maintaining motivation in the workplace and ensuring that rules and regulations are fol-

lowed. If the organization is sued or a union grievance is filed, adherence to these suggestions will be critical for defending the company's disciplinary actions. Next, you
will read about the termination process.

Terminating an Employee: The Termination Meeting

Terminating an employee can be uncomfortable. Most managers find firing an extremely stressful experience and may go out of their way to procrastinate from it.
Nevertheless, delaying this task can make matters even worse as the employee's performance continues to worsen and to demoralize others. A great deal of planning
should occur before a company terminates an employee. The next sections address
who should conduct the meeting, when it should be conducted, where it should be
conducted, how it should be conducted, and what happens afterward.[31]

Who Should Conduct the Meeting? Generally, two people should be present at
the termination meeting: the immediate supervisor and an HR staff person. Two advantages to having more than one person are that, first, a witness can confirm what occurred in the meeting, and, second, if the meeting begins to drag out, the other person
can help keep on task.

When Should the Meeting Take Place? Traditionally, the termination meeting
takes place at the end of the workweek, usually Friday. However, most experts agree
that this is a poor time for the employee, because he or she can do little on the weekend to address this often traumatic experience. Thus, it is generally recommended that
the termination meeting take place early in the week, and that holidays, birthdays, and
other special times be avoided.

Where Should the Meeting Take Place? The termination meeting should take
place in a private, neutral location, such as a meeting room or other office. Meeting in
a public area, in front of other employees, is a poor idea, as the employee might later
sue, charging public humiliation. Meeting in the supervisor's office could be problematic if the employee refuses to leave.

How Should the Meeting Be Conducted? There are many recommendations
as to what should be said to the employee, what should not be said to the employee,
and how these points should be said. The main points are as follows:

1. Get to the point about what this meeting is about.
2. Communicate that the decision is final.
3. Briefly explain why the decision was made.
4. Listen to the employee, do not get into an argument.
5. Treat the employee with dignity.

The entire meeting should take no more than 10 to 15 minutes.

What Should Happen After the Meeting? Given the potential for violence or
destruction of company property, the organization must be extremely careful. Many
companies today have the fired employee escorted by security staff to his or her desk
or locker for clean up, after which the employee is escorted out of the facility. Other

companies have the employee escorted out of the facility first, and the employee's property is then mailed to him or her. In any case, it is generally advised that a responsible party ensure that the terminated employee is escorted properly to ensure that no violence or destruction occurs.

In sum, terminating an employee is a major HR responsibility. These kinds of decisions must be handled carefully to avoid problems and lawsuits down the road.

Next, you will read about hours of work and what employees' rights are in that regard. You will also learn about some of the programs companies have used to increase work schedule flexibility.

Employee Rights and Work Hours

Did you ever have a job where you worked more than 40 hours per week? Did you wonder whether you had a legal right to refuse to work more than 40 hours per week? Following a discussion of that issue, you will learn more about several work schedule programs that companies have implemented to give employees greater flexibility and control over their work hours, such as flextime, compressed workweeks, and job sharing. First, we address the issue of the number of hours an organization can require you to work.

Working More Than 40 Hours per Week: Your Rights

Few laws restrict the number of hours your company can require you to work. Aside from the Fair Labor Standards Act (FLSA), which requires companies to pay nonexempt workers an overtime wage, there is little regulation of the hours worked by adults in the United States. The major exception to this general rule occurs at the state level, wherein some states have limits on the number of consecutive hours or days that workers in certain occupations (primarily transportation-related jobs) can work. About two dozen states also have certain break requirements, such as a required 30-minute meal period for every 5 hours of a 6-hour workday. Interestingly, certain other countries, such as Sweden, do have national laws that affect the hours of work. The Working Hours Act in Sweden, for example, specifies that the workweek must not average more than 40 hours for a 4-week period. Moreover, work between midnight and 5 A.M. is restricted, and there are limitations on overtime.[32]

If you live in the United States, you have little legal control over your hours of work. As you will see next, some companies require employees to work shiftwork. Other companies, however, have implemented programs that provide employees with some control over their work schedule. Do you think you work too many hours? Too few? Compare your work hours to employees in other countries in Box 16.5.

Shiftwork

shiftwork
Any type of schedule in which the majority of the work hours occur between 4 P.M. and 7 A.M.

Shiftwork is any type of schedule in which the majority of the work hours occur between 4 P.M. and 7 A.M. Workers who work the third shift (usually from 11 P.M. to 7 A.M.), for example, would be considered shiftworkers.[33] Some employees work on a rotating shift schedule: they work the morning shift (perhaps 7 A.M. to 3 P.M.) during the first week, the second shift (3 P.M. to 11 P.M.) during the next week, and the night shift (11 P.M. to 7 A.M.) during the third week. Shiftwork has a negative connotation;

INTERCULTURAL ISSUES IN HUMAN RESOURCES

Box 16.5
Do You Work Enough Hours?

Do you think you work enough hours? One way to determine whether you are putting in enough hours at your job is to examine the number of hours people work in other parts of the world. Consider the work hours in two of the world's greatest industrial nations: Germany and Japan. While the hours worked by manufacturing workers has actually declined over the last 35 years in these two countries, it has increased in the United States. In fact, West German production workers average only about 1,500 hours of work annually, while U.S. workers average nearly 2,000 hours of work annually (Japanese workers average more than 2,100 hours of work each year). Part of the reason for the relatively fewer hours worked by German workers is a law that requires West German companies to give at least five weeks' paid vacation annually. Another reason German workers work fewer hours is their attitude toward work. As one German supervisor stated it, "Work hard when you're on the job and get out as fast as you can." And, unlike many U.S. workers who work overtime on a regular basis or who work a second job, German workers tend to avoid working overtime or second jobs. In fact, German law prohibits workers from working during their paid vacations. Does Germany sound like a better place to work? As an employee it might be. But you should also know that on average, U.S. workers have bigger homes and more cars than both German and Japanese workers. From a manager's perspective, neither Germany nor Japan may sound quite so good either—U.S. workers are more productive than either German or Japanese workers.

But even in the United States, some companies are becoming increasingly considerate about the hours their employees work. Consider Mary McCarthy-Coyle, a fast-track employee at Deloitte & Touche, the accounting firm. When McCarthy-Coyle recently met with her mentor, Denise Buonopane, she was given one major message: reduce your work hours. McCarthy-Coyle routinely works 100 hours each week. So why has Deloitte & Touche told her to slack off? Primarily because turnover at Deloitte & Touche had reached epidemic levels, as high as 25 percent annually among female employees. Partners at the company are also being encouraged to set an example. Buonopane, herself a mother of three young children, occasionally works a 7-day week. But she sets her limits in other ways. For example, she will not travel over the weekend.

Not all firms encourage their workers to reduce work hours. Consider a suit brought against the law firm Cleary, Gottlieb, Steen & Hamilton, filed after a new attorney committed suicide. The lawsuit, filed by the employee's father, charges the company forced the employee to work long hours (often 20-hour days) with impossible deadlines. Law firms are notorious for their long hours—some New York law firms allegedly require up to 3,000 billable hours each year. Because not all work hours are billable, an attorney may need to work 4,000 hours to reach that goal, or an average of about 80 hours per week!

Sources: Adapted from A. Stevens, "Suit over Suicide Raises Issue: Do Associates Work Too Hard?" *Wall Street Journal*, 15 April 1994, B1; S. Shellenbarger, "A Crucible in Balancing Job and Family," *Wall Street Journal*, 14 December 1994, B1; D. Benjamin and T. Horwitz, "German View: 'You Americans work too hard—and for what?'" *Wall Street Journal*, 14 July 1994, B1, B5; and M. Magnet, "The Truth about the American Worker," *Fortune*, 4 May 1992, 48–65.

most workers dislike it because it interferes with leisure activities and conflicts with our natural biological sleeping cycles or circadian patterns.[34]

Organizations that use shiftwork generally do so because of economic or business necessity. Can you think of some types of organizations that might use shiftwork? Hospitals, law enforcement agencies, and all-night convenience stores are a few of the organizations that must use shiftwork. Many production facilities also use shiftwork; the cost of shutting down and starting up again or leaving the plant idle is simply too high.

Research on the effects of shiftwork has supported the concerns many employees have with this schedule. Studies have indicated that employees who have shiftwork tend to experience less sleep, suffer from more sleep interruptions, and feel more weariness than other workers. In terms of general health, shiftworkers have been found to have more appetite problems, greater levels of tension, higher blood pressure, and decreased physical fitness. Shiftwork schedules are often cited as the reason for high turnover, decreased job performance, and higher divorce rates. On the other hand, some studies also report beneficial advantages of shiftwork. To some extent, the effects depend on individual characteristics. "Night owls," people who like late hours, may actually prefer shiftwork over the standard workday schedule.[35]

Flextime

flextime
Deciding which hours of the day you will work. The basic purpose of flextime is to decrease employees' conflicts between work and personal schedules.

Do you have the right to decide which hours of the day you work? If so, you are probably the beneficiary of a **flextime** program. The earliest flexible work hours program was introduced in France in the mid-1950s. The concept spread to many other European cities in the 1960s, and it was rapidly adopted by companies in Germany, Switzerland, and France. Flextime caught on later in the United States. The first major company to implement flextime in the United States was Control Data Corporation, which began its program in 1972. Although currently only about 10 percent of workers in the United States participate in a flextime program, many more companies are beginning to recognize the value of flexible work hours.[36] Harris Bank of Chicago, for example, recently implemented a flextime program that provides much greater flexibility to employees. One result of the program is that the evening hours, traditionally disliked by all employees, are covered much better now that staff members have more flexibility to set their own schedules.[37]

There are several different versions of flextime.[38] They differ in terms of whether the schedule can change on a daily basis, whether a working day can vary in terms of hours worked, and whether the employees must be present for core time every working day. Figure 16.1 illustrates different types of flextime programs.

Figure 16.1   **Types of Flextime Programs**

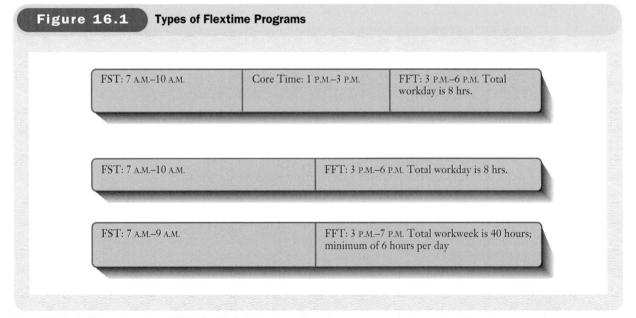

Note: FST is flexible starting time; FFT is flexible finishing time. Core time represents the hours that all employees must be present.

The basic purpose of a flextime schedule is to decrease conflicts between an employee's work and personal schedules. Some workers, for example, may be responsible for taking their children to school and therefore may be unable to arrive at work before 9 A.M. Other workers may simply prefer to finish work at 4 P.M. rather than 5 P.M. every day. Yet other workers may prefer to sleep later, arrive at work at 10 A.M., and finish work at 6 P.M.

In general, anecdotal evidence indicates that most employees and supervisors strongly favor flextime programs. But do flextime programs really make a difference from the organization's perspective? In terms of job attitudes, research shows that flextime programs have a consistently positive effect. Moreover, once employees begin a flextime program, they rarely wish to return to a standard work schedule. Tardiness also tends to drop dramatically; some companies report that tardiness virtually disappears. However, flextime has much less of an effect on productivity and performance, which are unlikely to decline—some studies show no change in productivity and performance. One explanation is that productivity only increases when work groups previously had to share equipment, a practice that flexible hours can help to eliminate. Otherwise, flextime has no effect on productivity.[39]

Despite the positive effects of flextime, two problems often arise:

1. **Supervisor Resistance.** About 20 percent of supervisors express displeasure with flextime. Their dissatisfaction usually stems from the need to expend more time and effort to schedule workers and greater difficulty in communicating with employees, who may not always be present at the same time.
2. **Increased Overhead Costs.** Because the total workday may be longer (some workers arrive as early as 7 A.M. while others work as late as 7 P.M.), utility and other overhead costs may rise slightly.[40]

Despite these difficulties, flextime appears to offer many advantages. You will read next about a different type of work schedule that attempts to provide more flexibility to employees: the compressed workweek.

Compressed Workweek

How many days should there be in the workweek? Many people assume that a workweek should be five days long. But some organizations use a **compressed workweek,** in which employees work a full week in less than five days. Mobil and Gulf Oil, the first reported company to use a compressed workweek in the United States, adopted a 4-day 40-hour workweek in 1940. It was not until 1960, however, that another U.S. company adopted this program. Approximately 25 percent of large companies in the United States currently either offer or require certain employees to work on a compressed work schedule.[41]

compressed workweek
A workweek in which the work hours are reallocated so that they are completed in less than 5 days, for example, a 4-day, 40-hour workweek.

Although there are many different types of compressed workweek schedules, the four most common appear to be the following:[42]

1. **4/40.** Employees work 10 hours each day for 4 days; employees are off work for 3 days, usually over the weekend.
2. **Floating 4/40.** Employees work four 10-hour days, with 4 days off, in a cycle.
3. **4.5/40.** Employees work four 9-hour days and one 4-hour day, with two and a half days off.

4. **5/45–4/36.** Employees work 9-hour days, alternating between 5-day and 4-day weeks.

The key feature of the compressed workweek, then, is that the work hours are reallocated so that they are completed in fewer than five days. Unlike flextime, employees do not have a choice in the times they work.

The purpose of the compressed workweek is to provide a schedule better suited to either the workers' or the organization's schedule. Under what circumstances do you think that workers might desire a compressed work schedule? Consider employees who must commute long distances to arrive at work (for example, in California some workers may spend two hours commuting each way). In other cases, a compressed work schedule will meet the needs of both the employees and the organization. Consider the following situation in which all of a police department's patrol officers wished to take their vacations during the summer. Administration, however, was concerned about understaffing during peak vacation times. The solution was to implement a compressed workweek, in which each police officer worked a 12-hour, 4-day schedule followed by 4 days off from work.[43]

The effects of the compressed workweek show somewhat mixed results. While many employees favor the opportunity to have more leisure time, the workers who are most favorably predisposed are those who are least satisfied with their jobs. The likely explanation is that if you don't like your job, a schedule that reduces the days you must come to work is quite appealing. While a compressed workweek may reduce tardiness, some research also indicates the opposite effect; perhaps some workers have difficulty adjusting to earlier starting times on workdays. Of greatest concern, though, is that the effects of the compressed workweek on productivity are quite mixed. Those organizations that reported no change in productivity have attributed this effect to worker fatigue (in one study, as many as 45 percent of the workers reported being tired) or workers taking on a second job during their off days. Finally, a compressed workweek can lead to greater scheduling problems, overtime payment problems, and conflict with personal schedules.[44]

❖ Conclusion

You have read about different aspects of employee rights. As you can see, employees are slowly gaining more rights with regard to terminations, access to personnel files, searches, workplace romances, and legal behaviors outside of work. Much depends, however, on the state where the employee works. With regard to work schedules, employees have relatively fewer rights. Many companies, however, have begun to introduce their own flexible work schedule programs to give employees greater choice and control. Compared with the workplace even 30 years ago, employees have many more rights today than in the past.

❖ Applying Core Concepts

1. You show up to work tomorrow and your boss says, "I hate your hairstyle; you're fired." Can he or she do this to you? Under what circumstances might you be able to sue successfully?
2. You would like to see your personnel file. When you ask your boss, he or she says, "No way!" What can you do?
3. Can your company search your desk? Explain your answer.
4. What policies does your company or university have in place regarding use of the Internet? Do you know if your use of the Internet is being monitored? Do you think employees' use of the Internet should be monitored?
5. What do you think of President Bill Clinton's affair with Monica Lewinsky? Do you think it affected his job? Explain.
6. Given your current or anticipated job, what type of work schedule would you like most? Why?

❖ Key Terms

Employment-at-will (EAW)

Implied contract

Covenant of Good Faith and Fair Dealing

Public policy

Privacy Act of 1974

Common law privacy

Electronics Communication Privacy Act of 1986

Progressive discipline

Due process

Shiftwork

Flextime

Compressed workweek

◆ CHAPTER 16 *Experiential Exercise 1*

Employee Rights Case

Presented below are four situations involving employees' potential misconduct. Your task is to decide for each case what to do with the employee. Your decision can be doing nothing at all, immediate termination, suspension until further investigation, or anything else you think is appropriate.

In each case, you should consider the rights of all relevant parties including the employee, the supervisor, the company, coworkers, and customers. Among your considerations should be: (a) ethics, (b) employee rights, (c) company image, (d) employer rights. If you are discussing this in groups, have one person in the group represent the employee, one person the supervisor, one person the coworker, customer, or whomever the complaining party is, and one person represent top management.

Finally, you should consider each situation in terms of (1) what should be done without consideration of the law and (2) what should be done given the laws that pertain. Be sure to identify the laws that might pertain in each situation.

Situation 1. One Saturday night, a vice chancellor of a private, prestigious university sees the manager of external relations leaving a bar that is well known for drugs and prostitution. The manager is walking with several people dressed in leather jackets and torn-up jeans. From the way the manager is walking, she seems to be intoxicated. She is saying crude obscenities as she walks.

Situation 2. One Friday evening, two mid-level managers of a large computer products firm are seen posting signs announcing an upcoming meeting of the American Nazi Party on telephone poles (this is being done on their own time). The evidence is provided in a videotape taken by a customer of this firm, who is threatening to provide the videotape to television stations.

Situation 3. One of your employees accidentally left an invitation on his desk that he wrote for an orgy he is holding at his house for homosexual men only. The coworker says he found the invitation on the employee's desk. The coworker noticed the content of this invitation, which included sexually explicit statements, as well as pictures. The coworker is demanding that the employee be terminated, given the offensive nature of the invitation.

Situation 4. A manager of information systems at a grocery store chain was recently arrested and charged with making and selling pornographic pictures and movies of children. He is out on bail, and would like to continue working at your company. He has always performed well on the job and has never had any kind of problem at work. However, a well-known ultraconservative citizens' group that operates in the small town where the store is located has written a letter to the store manager demanding he be fired immediately or they will boycott the chain.

◆ CHAPTER 16 *Experiential Exercise 2*

What Should I Do? [45]

Spencer, the employee relations manager at a company that owns a chain of assisted-living facilities, reminisced about when he first met Viola Rodriguez. At that time Viola had been a promising 24-year-old completing her bachelor of business administration. Spencer had interviewed Viola on campus and, after the usual on-site interviews and reference checks, offered her a job as an administrator in training, an offer she accepted. People hired into this job usually completed a one-year training program, rotating through different departments to learn various federal and state guidelines. Three months after Viola was hired, however, the administrator of one of the company's facilities left, leaving a vacancy Spencer and others thought Viola was the logical choice to fill. When Spencer offered Viola the new position, he told her that they had planned for her to head the facility, just not so soon, and he assured her that she would have support from him and others in the company. He also assured her that the facility she was to head was in good shape and had no problems. Viola accepted the position. She now was charged with responsibility for a facility with 70 employees and annual revenues of $500,000.

Three months after Viola assumed her new position, one of her key employees, Nancy, director of nursing, came due for a performance review. Nancy had worked in the facility for 16 years and had been director of nursing for 10 years. Viola, however, felt that Nancy was not performing her job well; much of her high-priority work was not being completed. On several occasions Viola discussed items of concern and asked Nancy how she planned to handle them. Later, after not hearing back from Nancy about the items, Viola asked what progress had been made. When little or no progress had been made, Viola discussed potential solutions with Nancy. Nancy's typical response was, "I'm working on it." Although Nancy was due for a performance review, Viola decided to postpone it to see if Nancy's performance improved. Unfortunately Viola did not inform Spencer about the performance discrepancies she had noticed or about her decision to delay Nancy's performance appraisal. Nevertheless, Viola gave Nancy satisfactory ratings, on the hope that Nancy would be motivated to improve.

Over the next few months Nancy's performance did not change appreciably and, seven months later Viola decided it was time to go ahead with the performance review. Instead of rating below average on problem areas, Viola chose to make no ratings of those areas. She told Nancy that she would not rate those areas until her performance improved. Although Nancy did not say much during the performance review session, she did acknowledge the ratings by saying "okay." Near the end of the performance-review session Viola asked Nancy if she had any questions or comments, to which Nancy replied "no," ending the session.

After the performance review session Viola prepared a list of Nancy's duties and responsibilities as a way to provide more role clarity for Nancy. About an hour after the session Viola gave Nancy the list, saying "This might be a good foundation, a starting point for improvement if you would like to use it." She discussed the list with Nancy, who seemed fine. Viola hoped that Nancy would be able to make the needed improvements and she believed that, if Nancy wanted to, she could.

In the following weeks Nancy continued to show up for work, but she behaved a bit standoffishly around Viola and she told some other staff members that "I'm

only going to work 8:00 to 5:00 from now on—no extra hours for me!" She also said she was upset because this was the first time in 10 years she hadn't received a raise. She was overheard saying to one staff member, "this company will never fire me. I know more dirt about this facility than anyone would believe, and I will tell the world if they try to fire me!"

It wasn't long until Viola began receiving complaints about Nancy's job performance. Some of Nancy's peers said that, when they asked Nancy for something they needed, she would reply, "I don't have time; I'm doing other things." This caused problems because Nancy's work affected the performance of others and, ultimately, the quality of care provided to residents. Nancy was also affecting the facility's finances because she was not completing some of the paperwork that allowed the organization to receive the highest reimbursement. When other departments expressed their frustrations about Nancy to Viola, she spoke with Nancy about the problems. Unfortunately the discussions had no effect on Nancy's work performance. At this point, exasperated at the lack of improvement, Viola called Spencer to inform him about the problem and seek advice.

As Spencer began to gather background on what had been transpiring, the situation became more problematic. Nancy had never used all her paid time off, but this year she decided she should, and in mid-October she requested to have every other week off from then until Christmas. However, because Nancy did not clearly designate and train someone to take care of her department during her absences, all this time off made matters worse.

During Nancy's first week off, the person left in charge was unaware of the additional responsibilities that had fallen on her. She experienced a great deal of stress because she had her own job responsibilities to perform along with Nancy's, and Nancy had not given her all the information she needed to handle the job. To make matters worse, though, Nancy and the president's wife are good friends, and who knows what would happen if Nancy were fired.

Spencer decided that he'd better travel to Viola's facility to deal with the situation more effectively. As he was en route, the following thoughts were running through Viola's mind:

- Nancy must not be concerned about her job.
- Doesn't she see the nursing department is in turmoil?
- Does she realize she's not doing her job?
- Do I need to replace her or live with it?

■ How would I begin the steps to terminate someone who's been here for 16 years?

Instructions

1. Assume the role of Spencer. What should Viola do? Come up with a package of suggestions for her.

2. Now give Viola some tips on how to implement your suggestions. For instance, if you advise Viola

to take disciplinary action, what should she do and what should she say to Nancy?

3. How should Viola *and* Spencer follow up after implementing your suggestions? In other words, what medium- and long-term actions should each of them take?

4. Would you fire Nancy at this point? Why or why not?

❖ Chapter 16 References

1. K. Sovereign, *Personnel Law* (Reston, VA: Reston Publishing, 1984).
2. S. Youngblood and L. Bierman, "Employment-at-Will: New Developments and Research Implications," in *Research in Personnel and Human Resource Management*, vol. 12, ed. G. Ferris (Greenwich, CT: JAI Press, 1994).
3. L. G. Joel III, *Every Employee's Guide to the Law* (New York: Pantheon Books, 1993).
4. M. Rothstein, C. Craver, E. Schroeder, E. Shoben, and L. Vander Velde, *Employment Law* (St. Paul, MN: West, 1994).
5. Joel, *Every Employee's Guide.*
6. Ibid.
7. Sovereign, *Personnel Law.*
8. Ibid.
9. Rothstein et al., *Employment Law.*
10. Youngblood and Bierman, "Employment-at-Will."
11. D. Koys, S. Briggs, and J. Grenig, "State Court Disparity on Employment-at-Will," *Personnel Psychology* 40 (1987): 565–77.
12. Joel, *Every Employee's Guide.*
13. D. Bennett-Alexander and L. Pincus, *Employment Law for Business* (Chicago: Irwin, 1995).
14. Joel, *Every Employee's Guide.*
15. J. Coil and C. Rice, "Determining Whether Employees Have a Right to Review Personnel Records," *Employment Relations Today* 19 (Autumn 1992): 335–46.
16. Sovereign, *Personnel Law.*
17. A. Rodriguez, "Comment: All Bark, No Byte: Employee E-mail Privacy Rights in the Private Sector Workplace," *Emory Law Journal* (Fall 1998): 1439–73.
18. D. McWhirter, *Your Rights at Work* (New York: Wiley, 1993).
19. G. Webster, "Respecting Employee Privacy," *Association Management* (January 1994): 142–43, 146.
20. Joel, *Every Employee's Guide.*
21. L. Jenner, "Office Dating Policies: Is There a Workable Way?" *HR Focus* (November 1993): 5.
22. A. B. Fisher, "Getting Comfortable with Couples in the Workplace," *Fortune*, 3 October 144, 138–42.
23. Ibid.
24. J. Segal, "Love: What's Work Got to Do with It?" *HR Magazine* (June 1993): 36–41.
25. Jenner, "Office Dating Policies."
26. Ibid.
27. Rothstein et al., *Employment Law;* Joel, *Every Employee's Guide.*
28. R. Arvey, G. Davis, and S. Nelson, "Use of Discipline in an Organization: A Field Study," *Journal of Applied Psychology* 69 (1984): 448–60.

29. J. Redeken, *Employee Discipline: Policies and Practices* (Washington: Bureau of National Affairs, 1989).

30. G. Latham and K. Wexley, *Increasing Productivity through Performance Appraisal* (Reading, MA: Addison-Wesley, 1981).

31. K. Karl, and C. Sutton, "A Review of Expert Advice on Employment Termination Practices: The Experts Don't Always Agree," In R. Griffin, A. O'Leary-Kelly, and J. Collins (Eds.), *Dysfunctional Behavior in Organizations* (Stanford, CT: JAI Press, 1998).

32. U. Weigelt, "On the Road to a Society of Free Choice: The Politics of Working Time in Sweden," in *Working Time in Transition*, ed. K. Hinrichs, W. Roche, and C. Sirianni (Philadelphia: Temple University Press, 1991).

33. S. Nollen, *New Work Schedules in Practice* (New York: Van Nostrand Reinhold, 1982).

34. T. Akerstedt, "Adjustment of Physiological Circadian Rhythms and the Sleep-Wake Cycle to Shiftwork," in *Hours of Work: Temporal Factors in Work-Scheduling*, ed. S. Folkard and T. Monk (Chichester, England: Wiley, 1985).

35. M. Frese and K. Okonek, "Reasons to Leave Shiftwork and Psychological and Psychosomatic Complaints of Former Shiftworkers," *Journal of Applied Psychology* 69 (1984): 509–14.

36. J. Pierce, J. Newstrom, R. Dunham, and A. Barber, *Alternative Work Schedules* (Boston: Allyn & Bacon, 1989).

37. S. Shellenbarger, "More Companies Experiment with Workers' Schedules," *Wall Street Journal*, 13 January 1994, B1, B6.

38. Nollen, *New Work Schedules in Practice.*

39. D. Ralston, W. Anthony, and D. Gustafson, "Employees May Love Flextime, but What Does It Do to the Organization's Productivity?" *Journal of Applied Psychology* 70 (1985): 272–79; and C. Orpen, "Effect of Flexible Working Hours on Employee Satisfaction and Performance," *Journal of Applied Psychology* 66 (981): 113–15.

40. Pierce et al., *Alternative Work Schedules.*

41. Ibid.

42. Nollen, *New Work Schedules in Practice.*

43. J. Pierce and R. Dunham, "The 12-Hour Work Day: A 48-Hour, Eight-Day Work Week," *Academy of Management Journal* 35 (1992): 1086–98.

44. Nollen, *New Work Schedules in Practice.*

45. This case was prepared by Brad Gilbreath and Christina Schwindt.

Prior to the late 18th century, aside from agricultural work, most goods were produced through a system of master craftsmen and apprentices. Due to the close relationship between the two (for example, apprentices often lived in the master craftsman's house or shop), the apprentice was cared for by the master craftsman or his family. The Industrial Revolution, however, led to development of the assembly line, which in turn led to the hiring of many low-skilled employees. Because assembly line employees were considered interchangeable and more or less equally capable, factory owners spent more time and attention on the technological improvements, rather than on the employees. But by the late 1800s, focus intensified, from a variety of quarters, on the workers. As people became more aware of hazardous working conditions, heavy dependence on child labor, and low wages, unions began to form and demand the right to organize and negotiate for higher wages. In return, some managers began to recognize the need to pay closer attention to workers. Historians generally agree that National Cash Register (NCR) was the first business to have a human resource department, which was created by the company president as a response to a major strike by the union.

As employers entered the 20th century, recognition of the importance of human resource practices grew. In 1913, for example, Ford Motor Company doubled its wages (from $2.50 per day to $5.00 per day) in order to decrease its turnover rate. This same year, Congress created a new agency, the U.S. Department of Labor, for the purpose of improving the work life.

The early part of the 20th century witnessed the development of two approaches to managing human resources. One approach, scientific management, or Taylorism, sought to design jobs to maximize efficiency. Under this approach, the company would identify the appropriate number of employees needed, determine the most effective way to perform each task, and provide training to the workers where necessary. The second approach that emerged in the beginning of the 20th century was personnel psychology, which emphasized the testing of people's ability for the purpose of identifying the best candidates for each job. The Bureau of Salesmanship Research, for example, was established in 1915. Among its major projects was the development of a test battery for selection of salespeople. Compared with scientific management, then, personnel psychology focused on choosing the appropriate employees to fit the demands of the job.

Within a few years, interest in HR grew rapidly. As World War I began, the Labor Department established a variety of laws and policies to make sure that the military effort was not hindered by employee-employer problems. Columbia University offered the first HR course in 1920. The next major event in the HR field was a series of workplace studies that was completed in the 1930s. Generally referred to as the Hawthorne studies (after Western Electric's Hawthorne plant, where some of this research was performed), these workplace research projects examined the effects of illumination, pay incentives, and rest breaks on work productivity. Much to their surprise, investigators found that social relations, including team development, informal work group norms, and supervision, had a far greater impact on productivity. This research, along with a series of studies examining job attitudes, marked the beginning of the human relations era.

During the 1930s, pro-union sentiment also grew, leading to passage of the National Labor Relations Act, which gave employees great leeway in organizing a union and restricted employers from various unfair practices that would prevent unionization.

The demand for HR programs heightened during World War II as a result of mass drafting by the armed forces and employment of women in manufacturing jobs previously occupied by men. Tests were developed for the armed forces to place draftees in the most appropriate positions. Extensive use was made of training technologies to enable women to succeed at jobs in which they had not previously worked.

After World War II, unions rapidly built strength, and increased to a point at which they represented nearly 25 percent of the workforce in 1947. However, muscle-flexing by unions led to passage of the Taft-Hartley Act, which reduced the power of unions. Perhaps in part a reaction to the strength of unions, quality of work life (QWL) became a major concern for business and industry during the 1950s and continuing through the 1960s. Studies by Dr. Herzberg and Drs. Hackman and Oldham indicating the importance of intrinsic rewards, led to programs that modified jobs to increase workers' responsibility, recognition, and enjoyment of the work itself. In subsequent years, the QWL movement spawned HR practices such as quality circles, employee involvement, and the team concept.

Although many significant events took place in the United States during the 1960s, HR was most dramatically affected by passage of the Civil Rights Act of 1964. Up until this time, relatively few laws governed HR, particularly in the private sector, and those that did exist were relatively simple or levied limited penalties. The Civil Rights Act of 1964, however, banned discrimination in the employment context on the basis of race, sex, religion, or national origin. As a result, every manager was now responsible for a whole new set of concerns and issues. Since the passage of this law, many more laws have been passed that affect employment decisions and their complexity continues to grow.

By the mid-1970s, global competition had become a serious issue for businesses in the United States. Partly as a response to this trend and partly due to growing awareness of the need to utilize all possible resources, HR became an increasingly important function in many organizations. The development of various formulas and algorithms to quantify both the costs and gains of any HR program or practice enabled organizations to hold HR staff increasingly accountable for results. By the late 1980s, the HR function was increasingly viewed as a key player in business decisions in most large companies.

The 1990s shaped up as an era of challenges for the HR function. The last decade of the 20th century began with a major recession in the United States, which resulted in a period of limited demand for employees. Coupled with the fact that large organizations continued to face serious competition both at home and abroad, many organizations chose to cut their workforce. Small businesses, on the other hand, continued to grow in number and became a major source of new jobs. As the 1990s ended, however, companies began to prosper once again, with almost all companies in the United States experiencing a shortage of qualified applicants in many positions. By contrast, Asian countries, once heralded as the economic giants of the 21st century, experienced major financial crises and many employees were losing their jobs in these countries. These rapid changes in supply and demand for employees and goods and services have led to increased interest in human resource management processes.

Another trend during the 1990s was an increased cynicism regarding various management and HR programs. Consider, for example, the popularity of Scott Adams'

Dilbert cartoon and the various books, such as the Dilbert Principle (and especially one of the cartoon characters, the evil HR director, CatBert), that were written. Many experts speak of the broken "psychological contract" between workers and companies, leading to a variety of changes in the way employees view careers, rewards, and other work conditions.

A third trend in the 1990s has been the increasing globalization of business, with an increasing number of companies doing business in other parts of the world besides the United States. The presence of the Internet, e-mail, and other methods of communication has enabled companies to overcome geographic barriers and has created new ways of conducting business transactions. Companies can now conduct business across borders with little or no start-up cost; employees can "work" for an organization even if they never step foot in the organization's facility or meet face-to-face with their supervisor. Increasing numbers of companies now operate as "virtual organizations," without a physical location. Time will tell just how these changes will affect business and industry, as well as careers.

Finally, the late 1990s witnessed increasing emphasis on quality of life. Increasingly, employees emphasize their nonwork interests and goals, with work playing a less central role than in the past. Fewer employees are interested in moving into managerial careers in large organizations; more individuals are seeking to go into business for themselves. The large population of dual-career families means that neither partner is quite as willing as in the past to relocate or accept a job offer if opportunities are not available to their spouse. As we enter the 21st century, then, human resource management will continue to face a variety of ever changing challenges.

❖ Reference

1. This material was adapted from M. Losey, "HR Comes of Age," *HRMagazine* 43 (SHRM 50th Anniversary Issue Supplement, 1998): 40–53; and M. Minehan, "SHRM: Futurist Task Force," *HRMagazine* 43 (SHRM 50th Anniversary Issue Supplement, 1998): 77–84+.

Add-On Plan A cafeteria plan in which all existing benefits are maintained and new ones added.

Adverse Impact The selection process or procedure has a disproportionate effect on a protected group (for example, women).

Affirmative Action Emphasis on recruitment of traditionally underrepresented groups; altering managerial and supervisory attitudes to eliminate prejudice; removing discriminatory barriers in hiring and promotions; and using a quota, or giving preferential treatment in hiring and promotion, to groups that have been underrepresented in the organization's workforce.

Age Discrimination in Employment Act of 1967 Prohibits age discrimination. When first passed, it applied only to individuals between the ages of forty and sixty-five. In 1978, it was changed to include individuals under seventy years of age. In subsequent years, Congress abolished the age cap for almost all jobs.

Ambiguity The rating scales are vague or unclear.

Americans with Disabilities Act of 1990 Prohibits most other employers from discriminating against the disabled. Also addresses the definition of disability. Also requires that employers offer reasonable accommodations.

Amount of Learning Refers to the competencies that trainees acquired from the program; the amount of learning is measured in the context of the training program, not on the job.

Applicant Flow A method of assessing whether the plaintiff's group was adversely affected by the selection procedure that involves comparison of the hiring rate of the plaintiff's group to the hiring rate of the majority group.

Applicant-Initiated Recruitment Applying for a job by either walking in and completing an application, or by mailing in a resume in the hope that a position is available.

Apprenticeship A formal program involving a combination of classroom instruction and hands-on practice and training, primarily in skilled crafts such as carpentry.

Arbitration Process Resembles a courtroom hearing, but the rules are not as formalized. An arbitrator is selected, and that person is responsible for making a final ruling after considering all of the relevant evidence and testimony, and providing a decision and explanation in a written report.

Assessment Center An extended work sample.

Authorization Cards The equivalent of obtaining sufficient numbers of signatures of eligible voters for a political candidate to appear on the ballot. At least 30 percent of the relevant employees must sign these cards.

Bargaining Unit Refers to the employees who will be voting in the election; if the union wins, these are the employees the union will represent.

Behavior Observation Scales A behaviorally based approach that has the rater evaluate the frequency with which the employee engages in various behaviors.

Behavioral Change This aspect of program success refers to the degree to which the trainees' behavior on the job has been affected by the training program.

Behaviorally Anchored Rating Scales A rating system that defines the dimension in terms of behavior and where the points on the scale are defined, or anchored, in behavioral terms.

Behaviorally Based Scales Developed as a response to the shortcomings of the graphic scale approach, the behaviorally based scale provides a set of scales that are defined in a precise, behavioral fashion.

Benchmark Jobs Jobs that are similar or comparable in content across firms.

Benchmarking Involves comparing an organization's human resource practices and programs to other organizations.

Biographical Information Blank (BIB) Utilizes a broader range of questions on an application form, particularly those pertaining to past achievements and personal goals and aspirations, which are scored with a standardized key.

Bona Fide Occupational Qualification (BFOQ) Suitable defense against a discrimination charge only where age, religion, sex or national origin is an actual qualification for performing the job.

Bottom-Up Forecast When department managers make estimates of future human resource demands based on issues such as new positions needed, positions to be eliminated, expected overtime, hours worked by temporary, part-time, or independent contractors, and expected changes in workload by department.

Broadbanding A pay structure that contains relatively few grades, with much greater range in each as compared to the traditional pay structure.

Business Representative The business representative's primary responsibility is to represent the union in contract negotiations, and also is responsible for collecting union dues, paying union bills, and communicating with the national union.

Business Strategy Refers to the approach that companies take in conducting business.

Cafeteria Benefits A benefits plan that provides a choice between taxable (usually cash) and nontaxable elements of compensation (such as health insurance).

Carpal Tunnel Syndrome First identified in the 1980s, this injury involves pressure on the median nerve, which is located in the wrist, and often requires surgery.

Cases Written descriptions of organizational situations.

Central Tendency An alternative to the leniency effect where raters rate practically all employees about average.

Chrono-functional Resume The type of resume that combines the chronological and functional resume.

Chronological Resume The type of resume that lists each of your jobs, beginning with the most recent and ending with the first job you held.

Civil Rights Act of 1866 The first of many laws banning race discrimination in private companies, unions, and employment agencies, passed in 1866.

Civil Rights Act of 1964 A comprehensive law banning workplace discrimination (which covers race, color, religion, sex, and national origin) passed in 1964.

Civil Rights Act of 1991 A further delineation of civil rights, resulting from several controversial Supreme Court decisions during the late 1980s. Some key changes include making it easier for employees and job applicants to win lawsuits; prohibiting the use of different norms, based on race or sex, for scoring tests; permitting use of jury trials; expanding coverage of discrimination laws to U.S. citizens working for U.S. companies based in other countries; and allowing employees and job applicants to win punitive damages.

Classroom Training An instructor addresses and presents material to a group of trainees.

Closed Internal Recruitment System Employees are unaware of job openings and therefore do not have the opportunity to formally apply.

Coaching Informal, unplanned training and development activities provided by supervisors and peers.

COBRA The Consolidated Omnibus Budget Reconciliation Act (COBRA) of 1985 requires companies with 20 or more employees to offer continued coverage of health insurance to participants who would otherwise no longer be eligible to participate in the health insurance plan.

Cognitive Ability Test Intelligence test given to applicants.

College Campus Recruitment A method of recruiting by visiting and participating in college campuses and their placement centers. Advantages: the placement center helps locate applicants and provides resumes to organizations, applicants can be prescreened, applicants will not have to be enticed away from a current job, and applicants have lower salary expectations.

The college campus placement center is one method of finding a job in your career field. The center provides applicants' resumes to organizations seeking workers and sets up prescreening interviews for the organizations. Resource material is also available to help students find information about the different careers available.

Common Law Privacy A general principle that protects an employee from searches and seizures in a nongovernmental organization.

Comparable Worth The concept that jobs of equal worth or value should be paid the same, even if the jobs are completely different.

Comparative Approaches Rating forms that require the rater to compare each employee to the other employees, also known as the bell-shaped curve that is particularly common in freshman and sophomore college courses.

Compensable Factors The determinants of job worth.

Competency-Based Pay A system where managerial and professional employees are paid for their level on key competencies.

Competency Modeling A recent approach to job analysis that focuses on the mission and vision statement to generate broadly defined knowledge and abilities to create an integrated HR system.

Compressed Workweek A workweek in which the work hours are reallocated so that they are completed in less than 5 days, for example, a 4-day, 40-hour workweek.

Concrete Results Training-program success is rated in terms of the bottom-line outcomes, such as increased productivity, reduced accident rate, or whatever the objectives of the training program were.

Constructive Confrontation Useful in helping supervisors prompt employees to seek treatment from the EAP, constructive confrontation involves four steps: (1) the supervisor confronts the employee with evidence of unsatisfactory performance; (2) the supervisor provides coaching to improve the employee's performance; (3) at the same time, the supervisor encourages the employee to contact the EAP; and (4) the supervisor continues to inform the employee of the consequences of continued unsatisfactory performance.

Contamination When a rating form has additional, irrelevant performance dimensions that may contaminate the performance appraisal.

Content Validity Another method of demonstrating job relatedness, where the selection procedure should (1) comprise a simulation of the job, (2) have scores based on concrete and observable behavior by the test taker, (3) represent important aspects of the job, and (4) assess activities for which the person will not receive training if hired.

Continuous Improvement Emphasizes ongoing efforts to improve productivity and quality.

Copayment The amount of money an employee must pay for a specific health service.

Correlation Coefficient A statistic that summarizes the relationship between two variables or measures.

Counterproposal This technique involves making an offer in response to the other side's offer.

Covenant of Good Faith and Fair Dealing An exception to employment-at-will that may be used when the reason for the termination was clearly inappropriate or the conditions under which the firing was made were extremely inconsiderate of the employee.

Criterion-Related Validity Study One method of demonstrating that a procedure is job related. The organization would use the selection method, or predictor, with a large number of applicants or current employees to obtain measures of job behavior, then use statistics to calculate the relationship between the predictor and the criteria.

Cumulative Trauma Disorders (CTDs) Trauma to the wrist, shoulder, or arms, such as repetitive stress injury and carpal tunnel syndrome.

Decertification Campaign Just as the workers may decide to vote in a union to represent them, the workers may choose to vote out the union.

Defamation Slander or libel that can result in a lawsuit.

Deferred Profit Sharing The retirement fund contributions are usually made only by the employer and are determined by the profitability of the company.

Deficiency When a performance appraisal form is missing key aspects of job performance.

Defined Benefit Pension Program Described in terms of what the employee will receive upon retirement, the plan relies on a formula that determines exactly what the employee will receive upon retirement.

Defined Contribution Pension Program In this program, each participating employee has an individual fund into which contributions may be made by the company, the employee, or both, depending on the specific type of plan.

Demand–Control Model of Stress The theory that states that an employee will experience the most stress when the job has high demands and little control.

Disability Income If an employee were to become completely disabled and unable to work, Social Security would provide monthly payments.

Disparate Treatment When an employer treats people differently or evaluates them by different standards, depending on their age, sex, race, or other protected categories.

Distributed Training A training program conducted in short sessions over a longer period of time, such as one hour per week for 16 weeks.

Due Process The notion that employees have the right to be treated fairly, particularly when being disciplined.

Elder-Care Insurance An insurance program that pays for medical care at home or in a nursing home.

Electronics Communication Privacy Act of 1986 This act prohibits the interception of oral, wire, and electronic communications, except during the course of business or when one party has consented.

Employee Assistance Program (EAP) An organization-sponsored program that helps identify workers in need of counseling, motivates them to obtain the needed counseling, and provides the proper counseling sources.

Employee Empowerment Refers to how much decision-making power and authority employees at the lowest level of the organization acquire as a result of the work design available to organizations.

Employee Polygraph Protection Act of 1988 Prohibits most private-sector organizations from requiring a polygraph test as a condition of employment. Polygraph tests can be given only when there are specific, legitimate circumstances, such as if a theft has occurred.

Employee Referrals An excellent source of job applicants, employee referral means using personal contacts to locate job opportunities.

Employee Retirement Income Security Act (ERISA) An act instituted in 1974 to eliminate pension mismanagement and abuse.

Employee Stock Ownership Plan (ESOP) The ESOP provides employees with company stock while at the same time allowing the company to borrow money from a bank at a reduced tax rate.

Employment Agencies Organizations that serve as a third party, matching applicants to jobs.

Employment-At-Will When employees are employed "at will," or at the will or discretion of the company. This means that if an employee can leave the work relationship at any time he or she desires, an employer has the same right.

Entry Stage The point at which the individual begins a new job.

Equal Employment Opportunity Commission (EEOC) Created by Title VII of the Civil Rights Act of 1964, the agency that processes discrimination charges and writes regulations pertinent to congressional laws.

Equal Pay Act of 1963 An amendment to the Fair Labor Standards Act of 1938 that attempts to eliminate sex discrimination in pay.

Equipment Simulators Used for jobs or tasks where improper use of actual equipment would pose a danger to the trainee (or others) or where risk of substantial financial loss exists.

Escalator Clause A clause included in some union contracts that adjusts wages (both up and down), depending on the cost of living.

Executive Order 11246 A law passed by President Johnson in 1965 that applied to government contractors and prohibits discrimination.

Exempt Employees Employees who are not covered by the law's provision that requires companies to pay time and a half for overtime; often applies to executive, administrative, and professional employees.

External Issues Events or trends outside of the organization, such as workforce demographics and technology.

External Recruitment Sources Tap applicants from outside of the organization. Advantages include new perspectives gained by bringing in new employees and a large pool of applicants. May be necessary for increasing minority and female representation in the workforce.

Fair Credit Reporting Act A modified act that allows an employer to collect third-party information about an employee or applicant within certain specific guidelines of consent and disclosure.

Fair Labor Standards Act of 1938 A congressional law passed with the intent of improving working conditions and living standards.

False Positive Occurs when a drug test mistakenly identifies the subject as a drug user.

Family and Medical Leave Act (FMLA) Passed in 1993, this act requires companies that have at least 50 employees to grant an unpaid leave to employees who meet any of the following conditions: the employee has become responsible for a child; the employee is providing care for a child, parent, or spouse with a serious health condition; or the employee is experiencing a serious health condition that leaves him or her unable to perform the job.

Fee-For-Service Program The traditional health-insurance program in which the employee or the employer or both pay for each medical service provided.

Fiduciary A person to whom property or power is entrusted for the benefit of another, such as a person who has authority over pension plan management, assets, or administration.

Flexible Spending Account (FSA) FSAs allow an employee to pay for health-care expenses or dependent-care assistance expenses on a before-tax basis.

Flextime Deciding which hours of the day you will work. The basic purpose of flextime is to decrease employees' conflicts between work and personal schedules.

"For Cause" If good reason exists to believe en employee may have been under the influence of drugs during work, the company may require the employee to take a drug test.

401(k) A type of savings program that has become quite popular since its introduction in 1981. The 401(k) program permits employees to place $10,000 each year into a retirement fund tax-free until it is withdrawn.

Functional Arrangement The traditional arrangement of organizational structure that is organized by departments and work is organized by task and job similarity.

Functional Resume The type of resume that lists skills and experiences.

Funding Rules Requires the pension plan to have sufficient funds so that promised benefits will be available to employees when they retire.

Gain-Sharing Plan Provides a payout when productivity improvements occur.

General Duty Clause OSHA guidelines that require compliance with basic standards, as well as the responsibility of providing a workplace that is free from recognized safety and health hazards.

Glass Ceiling Refers to an invisible barrier that prevents women from advancing to higher levels within the organization.

Grade Overlap The amount of overlap that exists between grades.

Graphic Scales A type of performance evaluation form that uses broad, relatively ambiguous work dimensions, such as quality, leadership, and reliability.

Graphology Handwriting analysis.

Green Circle Rates Apply to employees whose salaries are below the minimum of their respective grade.

Grievance Procedure A grievance procedure provides a mechanism for the employee or union to dispute a decision that is believed to be in violation of the contract.

Guaranteed Investment Contract (GIC) A type of fund offered by most companies that is similar to bank-sponsored accounts, guaranteed investment contracts have one major difference: GICs are usually held by insurance companies.

Halo This error occurs when one aspect of the subordinate's performance affects the rater's evaluation of other performance dimensions.

Hay Plan A preestablished job evaluation plan that is widely used for evaluating executive, managerial, and professional positions.

Hazard Communication Standard of 1985 A regulation that covers all hazardous chemicals. As of 1987, companies covered by the OSH Act must meet the requirements of the Hazard Communication Standard.

Health Maintenance Organization (HMO) A network of medical professionals and hospitals that provides health care for participants.

Honesty Test Two types of honest tests: overt and personality-based. The overt test asks questions that directly address test takers' perceptions and feelings about honesty. Personality-based tests tend to be somewhat less obvious as to what they are assessing and focus on personality traits associated with dishonesty.

Hostile Environment Sexual Harassment An environment created by unwelcome sexual advances, requests for sexual favors, and other verbal or physical conduct of a sexual nature.

Human Resource Demand The procedure for predicting the number of employees that will be needed in the future, usually by using quantitative and qualitative methods.

Human Resource Planning The process of examining an organization's or individual's future human resource needs compared to future human resource capabilities, and developing human resource policies and practices to address potential problems.

Human Resource Supply The number of employees the company is likely to have in the future.

Immigration Reform and Control Act Provides additional protection against discrimination on the basis of national origin, and even protects certain noncitizens of the United States such as individuals who are permanent residents of the United States or who have declared an intention to gain citizenship in the United States.

Implied Contract An implied agreement between employer and employee regarding an aspect of the job, such as the statement "Once you pass the probationary period, your job is guaranteed for life." Employee handbooks can also be considered implied contracts.

Improshare Stands for "improved productivity through sharing," and focuses on the number of hours of work. Improshare also involves a formula that compares input to output, where input is the number of hours that it should take to complete the work compared with the number of hours it actually took to do the work.

In-Network A list of medical professionals that are associated with the plan (POS, HMO, or PPO).

Individual Assessment Conducted by a psychologist, this assessment lasts four to eight hours and involves a ninety-minute interview as well as personality and cognitive ability tests.

Individual Incentive The payout is based on the individual employee's performance, and performance is evaluated using an objective standard.

Intentional Discrimination A practice where employers refuse to hire applicants of a particular race, religion, or gender simply out of prejudice; earlier referred as to *evil intent*.

Internal Issues Events or trends within the organization, such as business strategy, organizational structure, and company profitability.

Internal Recruitment Sources Provide applicants who already are employed by the organization. Advantages include less expense, greater speed in completing the recruitment process, less orientation time for new employees, and an effective motivator for employees.

Internet/Intranet Training A computer is used to present material to trainees either on a need-to-know basis, at their own pace, or in their own offices.

Internship A program providing work experience to students prior to their graduation from an academic program.

Job Analysis The process of collecting information about two basic issues: What the job entails, and the knowledge, skills, abilities and other requirements needed to perform the work.

Job Burnout A sense of emotional exhaustion, lack of energy, feeling of depersonalization toward coworkers or clients. A sense of personal failure and limited progress at work are all characteristics of burnout. One cause lies within the individual employee, whereas a second cause lies within the nature of the work.

Job Classification Categories or classes are defined in terms of responsibility for subordinates, contact with other departments, amount of education required, and technical skills involved.

Job Description A list of the tasks and functions performed by each employee.

Job Enlargement Involves increasing the number of tasks performed by each employee and having jobs that are somewhat less specialized.

Job Enrichment Increasing job satisfaction by using such intrinsic factors as achievement, recognition, and the work itself of enforcing extrinsic factors such as company policy and supervision.

Job Evaluation A systematic, objective procedure for determining the value of a group of jobs for the organization.

Job Grades A manager may choose to sort jobs into a smaller number of grades or classes, usually into ten to twenty different grades.

Job Knowledge Test Measures comprehension of basic facts.

Job Posting When an organization publicizes job openings on bulletin boards, electronic media, and similar outlets.

Job Relatedness Refers to whether the selection procedure is related to job requirements or job outcomes.

Job Rotation A formal, planned program involving the assignment of trainees to varying jobs in different parts of the organization.

Job Specification A list of competencies needed to successfully perform the job.

Joint Study Group A joint study group is a task force, composed of both management and union representatives, and often third parties as well, for the purpose of examining issues of particular concern in a nonadversarial setting.

Judgment Errors Errors made due to poor judgment, poor decision making, and biases.

Labor Market Survey Provides information as to what other organizations that compete for employees are paying; used to determine what other companies are paying employees so that an organization can effectively recruit and retain its workers.

Landrum-Griffin Act (Labor-Management Reporting and Disclosure Act) Passed in 1959, this act's major purpose was to protect employees from unions.

Leniency Many raters give higher performance evaluations than deserved, a practice often created by organizational policies and practices.

Long-Term Disability (LTD) Insurance Insurance that covers long-term disabilities, usually for periods of time greater than six months.

Management-by-Objectives An evaluation system that uses clearly defined objectives or goals, with a specified time frame in which they will be reached.

Market Pricing An approach to developing a pay structure that essentially downplays internal value and relies almost exclusively on external value to determine pay.

Markov Analysis A quantitative procedure of determining supply that uses historical rates of promotion, transfer, and turnover to estimate future availabilities in the workforce.

Massed Training A training program conducted in long sessions and a compacted timetable, such as a two-day program that includes four four-hour sessions.

Mastery Stage The next stage after entry when employees seek to attain a high degree of success in their work.

Maximum Out-of-Pocket Annual Payment The most that an employee would have to pay for medical expenses in a single year.

McDonnell-Douglas v. Green A 1973 case that outlined a more elaborate three-step process for examining hiring or promotion discrimination under the disparate treatment concept.

Mediation In mediation, a neutral party meets with the union and management to work out an agreement (the mediator's suggestions are not binding on either party).

Mentor A person who is higher up the organization and who can provide career advice and support to a less senior employee.

Merit Pay The payout is based on the individual employee's performance, performance is evaluated in a subjective fashion, and the payout is added to the employee's base salary.

Meta-Analysis Developed by Frank Schmidt and John Hunter, this statistical procedure for summarizing past research has indicated that cognitive ability tests have adequate validity across virtually all jobs.

Modular Plan A cafeteria plan in which the employee is offered a choice of several benefit "packages" or modules.

Multiple Regression Analysis Relies on factors or predictors that determine the demand for employees, such as revenues, degree of automation, and so forth.

National Institute for Occupational Safety and Health (NIOSH) NIOSH provides research and training support for OSHA. The research focuses on developing new safety and health standards; the training is for OSHA inspectors and other staff involved with OSH Act enforcement.

National Labor Relations Board (NLRB) Established by the Wagner Act, this board is responsible for administering and interpreting the act and related laws.

Negligent Hiring A finding that an employer is responsible for using poor selection procedures after an employee inflicts harm on the customer or other third party.

Newspaper Advertisements A method of

job recruitment by advertising in newspapers. Advantages include quick placement of ads, flexibility in terms of information, and the ads can target a specific geographic area.

No SPITting Rule The legal requirements that stipulate what management cannot do to employees who are unionizing: spy on union activities, promise changes in personnel practices, interrogate employees, or threaten employees.

Nonexempt Employees Employees who are covered by the law's provision that requires companies to pay time and a half for each hour that an employee works more than 40 hours per week.

Occupational Safety and Health (OSH) Act of 1970 Passed by Congress in 1970, the purpose of this law was to reduce the high rate of workplace accidents, injuries, and deaths in the United States.

Occupational Safety and Health Administration (OSHA) The major agency created to administer and oversee the OSH Act, including establishing safety standards, permitting variances (exceptions) to those standards, conducting inspections of workplaces, and issuing citations to indicate a violation of OSH Act regulations.

Occupational Safety and Health Review Commission (OSHRC) The purpose of the OSHRC is to review appeals from companies that have been issued a citation by OSHA.

Off-the-Job Training Training conducted away from the worksite.

Office of Federal Contract Compliance Programs (OFCCP) Government agency that wrote and enforces a document referred to as "Revised Order No. 4," which contains the guidelines for affirmative action to remedy the underutilization of women and minorities in firms that have government contracts.

On-the-Job Training Training provided at the worksite.

One-On-One Instruction A person who serves as a trainer for the organization meets with and instructs a trainee at the workplace.

Open Internal Recruitment System Employees are made aware of potential openings and have the opportunity to formally apply.

Organization-Wide Incentive The payout is based on the performance of the plant, division, or organization; performance is evaluated using an objective standard.

Organizational Analysis The purpose of this analysis is to examine the organization, unit, or department and determine its basic business strategy, objectives, and goals.

Organizational Structure Refers to how work tasks are assigned, who reports to whom, and how decisions are made.

OSHA Form No. 101 Employees who use Form No. 200 must also complete this form, which requires detailed information about work-related injuries and illnesses, including the circumstances of the incident, a description of the injury or illness, and the name of the doctor and hospital that provided treatment.

OSHA Form No. 200 This form must be used by most employers with more than ten workers. The form records information about workers who are injured or become ill as a result of the job and if the injury or illness resulted in death, days off from work, transfer, termination, medical treatment, unconsciousness, or work and motion restrictions.

OSHA Variance In certain cases, an employer may request either a temporary or permanent exception to an OSHA standard and must seek a variance. OSHA would inspect and possibly hold a hearing on the proposed deviation. If OSHA agrees to the modification, a variance would be granted, thus permitting this deviation.

Out-of-Network Any medical professional not associated with the plan (POS, HMO, or PPO). If an employee chooses a doctor that is out-of-network, the cost will be higher than using an in-network professional.

Outsourcing When companies contract their work to other companies and individuals to save money.

Paid Time Off Includes vacation, holidays, and personal absences.

Panel Interview A group of interviewers interview a candidate at the same time. This type of interview reduces the effects of personal biases any individual interviewer may have.

PAQ A standardized job analysis questionnaire that may be used for nearly any job.

Passage Stage Refers to the point during which the employee prepares to change jobs or employers.

Pay-for-Performance Plan A program where some pay is based on the individual, the team, or the organization's performance.

Pay Range The range of pay a manager chooses for each grade.

Pay Structure Designates the base pay for each job.

Pension Benefit Guaranty Corporation Serves as an insurance program whereby pension plan participants are guaranteed at least some benefits even if the fund is depleted.

Person Analysis Addresses the question of whether employees are deficient in important tasks and competencies and whether training would address these deficiencies.

Personal Absences Allowed on certain days in which the employee is unable to come to work for reasons beyond his or her control, such as jury duty, family death, military duty, divorce hearings, and doctor visits.

Personality Test A test given to an applicant that will supposedly predict the type of personality a candidate has and how that personality will affect job performance.

Point Method Job Evaluation One of the most commonly used job evaluation procedures that involves forming a committee, selecting and defining compensable factors, establishing and defining levels for each compensable factor, determining the total number of points for the system, dividing total points among compensable factors, distributing points to each level on every factor, and evaluating the jobs.

Point-Of-Service (POS) Plan A plan that attempts to combine the advantages of the HMO with the advantages of the PPO.

Position Allocation and Control Procedure A more traditional approach to estimating the demand for employees, position allocation and control procedure uses rules determined by top management in estimating future needs.

Preexisting Condition An illness, injury, or pregnancy that an individual has prior to becoming covered by the health insurance plan.

Preferred-Provider Organization (PPO) A network of medical professionals and hospitals that have agreed to give discounted services. Unlike the HMO, participants may go to any medical professional or hospital they wish.

Pregnancy Discrimination Act of 1978 An amendment to the Civil Rights Act of 1964, which states that an employer cannot require maternity leave of a particular length; must provide the same terms and conditions for a leave of absence for childbirth as is provided for other medical conditions; and must offer those returning from medical leave the same or an equivalent job and employment conditions.

Prevailing Wage Laws Require companies with certain government contracts to pay workers the standard wage for the area, either the wage paid to a majority of workers in the area or a wage based on a weighted formula, which may be used if there is no single wage for the area.

Primary-Care Physician The physician chosen through an HMO that decides what kind of treatment is needed and provides referrals to the appropriate specialists within the HMO.

Privacy Act of 1974 The law that gives federal employees a right to their personnel files (this law covers federal administrative agencies and allows individuals who work at these agencies the right to examine their records and the right to correct any mistakes in the records).

Process Arrangement The arrangement of an organization that is organized by activities that provide value to the customer.

Product Market Survey Provides information as to what other organizations providing the same product or service are paying their employees; used to make sure that the organization's payroll costs are not higher than its business competitors.

Profit-Sharing Plan Pay is linked to some index of profitability.

Progressive Discipline In a progressive discipline system, the employee is given ample warning of performance or other work-related problems. Failure to change his or her behavior is accompanied by increasingly harsher disciplinary action.

Public Policy An exception to employment-at-will in which the employee has either committed an action, or refused to commit an action, that is in the interest of the common public good.

Quality Circle Originating in Japan in the early 1960s, the quality circle usually has between three and fifteen members who meet on a regular basis. Their purpose is to identify, discuss, and solve production or business-related problems within the members' work area.

Quid-Pro-Quo Sexual Harassment A Latin phrase meaning something in exchange for something else, such as a supervisor offering an employee a promotion or raise or other personnel action in exchange for sexual favors.

Race Norming A method used to eliminate adverse impact by separating norms for different racial and gender groups.

Ranking Method of Job Evaluation Involves a committee ranking jobs from most valued to least valued by the organization.

Ratio Analysis Involves comparison of the number of employees to some index of workload.

Realistic Job Preview (RJP) A systematic method for providing information to job applicants about the more challenging aspects of a job.

Reasonable Accommodation A modification or adjustment to a job, the work environment, or the way things usually are done that enables a qualified individual with a disability to enjoy an equal employment opportunity.

Reasonable Cause Based on its initial investigation, the EEOC may decide that a case has merit, or reasonable cause, to pursue a settlement or a suit.

Red Circle Rates Apply to employees whose salaries exceed the maximum of their respective grades.

Reengineering A radical process of redesigning business procedures and structures.

Rehabilitation Act of 1973 Prohibits discrimination against disabled individuals; applies only to government employees or businesses having contracts with the federal government.

Repetitive Stress Injury First identified in the 1990s, this injury is a form of muscle strain, not usually crippling.

Replacement Planning A method of forecasting human resource supply, which involves an assessment of potential candidates to replace existing executives and other high-level managers as they retire or leave for other organizations.

Replacement Workers Often called "scabs," replacement workers are hired to replace striking personnel.

Right-to-Sue Notice A notice issued from the EEOC that gives you the right to have a lawyer take your case in a discrimination suit.

Role Plays A technique whereby trainees act out an assigned role in a hypothetical situation.

Rucker Plan A variant to the Scanlon plan, this plan replaces sales as the measure of output with "value added," which is the sales value of production after subtracting nonlabor costs.

SAWNOF Approach The "Sit And Watch

Nellie Or Fred" method of training, in which the employee is instructed to sit and watch "Nellie" or "Fred" (usually an experienced worker).

Scanlon Plan Relies on a formula that contains two factors: a monetary index of output, reflecting how much was produced, and a measure of input or what it might cost the company to produce this output. The goal of the plan is to lower the input relative to output.

Scientific Management The classical approach to job design, which concentrates on such principles as specialization and simplification, repetitiveness, mechanical pacing, limited interpersonal interaction, and predetermined work techniques.

Search Firm A private employment agency that works for the employer and maintains lists of qualified candidates.

Severity A bias in the opposite direction, in which a supervisor has a tendency to rate too harshly.

Shiftwork Any type of schedule in which the majority of the work hours occur between 4 P.M. and 7 A.M.

Short-Term Disability (STD) Insurance Insurance that covers short-term disabilities, usually for a period of six months or less.

Sick Building Syndrome Caused by either bacterial or fungal contamination of the heating and cooling ducts, or vehicle fumes from outside air, the symptoms include skin and mucous membrane irritations, headaches, and fatigue, which are thought to be caused by working in a modern office building.

Skill-Based Pay An approach that represents a significant departure from the traditional pay structure, this procedure rewards workers for the skills or knowledge they have mastered.

Social Loafing The phenomenon in which one or two team members fail to do their fair share, leaving other team members to compensate for their lack of performance.

Social Security/Medicare Two government programs that receive funding from employees and their companies, which are used for retirement, disability, survivor benefits, and health-care expenses.

Stock Analysis An alternative approach for showing that the selection procedure had an adverse effect is to compare the percentage of the protected group members in the organization's workforce to the percentage of the protected group members in the labor market.

Stress Interview An interview technique that is an attempt by the interviewer to see how a candidate fares under duress.

Strike When workers refuse to go to work.

Structured Interview Uses a predetermined set of questions that are clearly job-related, such as the behavior description interview and situational interview.

Succession Planning Similar to replacement planning, except that it is more long term and developmentally oriented and is likely to involve input from several managers and the recommendation of various developmental activities for the candidates to ensure the ability to fill positions as they open.

Summary Plan Description A certain type of report that details the fiscal health and outlines the company's pension plan and that must be available to all new participants.

Survivor Benefits Depending on the age and status of an employee's spouse and children, they may be eligible for monthly Social Security benefits if the employee dies.

Taft-Hartley Act (Labor-Management Relations Act) Passed in 1947, this act was a pro-management law designed to protect employers from unfair union practices.

Task/Competency Analysis Involves obtaining information from the organizational analysis to examine the tasks performed in each job and determine the competencies needed to perform these tasks effectively.

Task/Competency Inventory A job analysis technique that focuses on both the tasks performed in the job and the competencies needed to perform them.

Team Incentive The payout is based on the team's level of performance, and performance is evaluated using an objective standard.

Television and Radio Ads Methods of job recruitment by advertising open positions using television and radio spots. Advantages: These ads are more likely to reach individuals who are not actively seeking employment, ads are more likely to stand out, and they enable the organization to target the audience more carefully. A considerable amount of creativity can be used in designing the ad.

Temporary Employees Employees hired for short-term projects or to fill a position created by personnel who are on leave, and so on. Temporary employees often are less expensive for businesses and can be added or dropped without having to terminate them. The task of recruiting, hiring, disciplining, and so forth is the responsibility of the placement agency, not the company.

360-Degree Feedback Information is gathered from a variety of sources, including subordinates who complete performance appraisals, then the results are summarized for the employee and areas needing improvement are discussed.

Total Quality Management TQM emphasizes a business objective (quality) and articulates various policies, practices, and management philosophies to support that objective and to enhance product or service quality.

Trading Point Procedure The trading point procedures involve one side saying to the other: "We'll concede on this issue (for example, wage increases), if you concede on this other issue (for example, overtime pay)."

Traditional Interview The most common type of interview, which allows the interviewer a great deal of discretion in terms of which questions are asked and in what order.

Trainee Reactions An important index of program success, trainees are asked to record their reactions by means of a survey or questionnaire at the end of the training session.

Training and Development Planned efforts by organizations to increase employees' competencies.

Training Needs Analysis An assessment by the organization of its employees training needs.

Transfer of Training The principle that employees transfer the competencies learned in the training period onto their jobs.

Tuition Reimbursement Tuition reimbursement programs vary in terms of the amount of reimbursement they provide, but they usually provide 75 to 100 percent reimbursement contingent on a passing grade.

Undue Hardship Exists if the accommodation to enable a qualified individual with a disability to enjoy an equal employment opportunity would involve considerable expense or difficulty to the company.

Unemployment Compensation Provides payments to an employee who is terminated by such means as a layoff (not for being fired or quitting).

Union Election The process used to establish a union within an organization. The union election begins by contact between the workers and the union. At least 30 percent of the relevant employees must sign authorization cards, after which the group may petition the NLRB for permission to hold an election.

Union Steward The union steward plays a key role in day-to-day relationships with management, usually performing the union-related work on a part-time basis.

Union Structure Labor unions have three major levels in their structure: the local unions form the first layer; national and international unions form the next level; and federations represent the top of the union structure.

Union An organization of workers whose purpose is to represent the employees in their dealings with management.

Urinalysis A urine sample test for drugs.

Utility Refers to the benefits versus costs of using a particular selection procedure.

Utility Analysis A relatively recent approach to choosing which, if any, human resource programs should be implemented, utility analysis considers the financial benefits versus the costs of any human resource program and attempts to base the choice of program on its dollar value to the organization.

Utilization Analysis A method of affirmative action planning where the employer must compare the race, sex, and ethnic composition of the workforce to the race, sex, and ethnic composition of the labor market.

Utilization Review A process by which medical services are analyzed and reviewed.

Vacancy Analysis Similar to the Markov analysis, except that it is based on managerial judgments of the probabilities of promotion, transfer, and turnover rates.

Validation Study A method of demonstrating that a test is valid by statistically examining its relationship with job performance.

Vertical Career Advancement System Characterized by job advancement up a clearly delineated path within a specific functional area.

Vesting Refers to the rights an employee has to the pension benefits if employment is terminated prior to retirement.

Videotape Training A videotape is used to present material to a group of trainees.

Virtual Organization A network of companies or employees connected by computers.

Wagner Act (National Labor Relations Act, NLRA) Passed in 1935, this law gives workers the right to organize and participate in union activities, prohibits various management tactics that would discourage unions, outlaws company-sponsored unions, and forbids the company from discriminating against employees for participating in union activities.

Weighted Application Blank (WAB) An objectively scored application form.

Wellness Programs Some organizations have implemented worksite wellness programs to improve the overall physical and mental health of their workforce. They typically involve a series of educational and behavioral change courses designed to encourage smoking cessation, proper diet and nutrition, and improved physical fitness.

Work Samples A brief simulation of major job activities.

Work Team The typical work team consists of between 3 and 30 employees, with one person assigned as the team leader; the team may have anywhere from some control to complete control over the project or problem.

Worker Adjustment and Retraining Notification Act Requires certain companies to give notice to employees of closure or layoff.

Workers' Compensation A benefit that provides income and payments for workers or survivors of workers injured, disabled, or killed on the job.

Index

Page numbers appearing in italics refer to tables and figures.